D1605746

New York University Studies in Near Eastern Civilization
Number XVIII

Peter Chelkowski and Jill N. Claster, General Editors

New York University Studies in Near Eastern Civilization

The participation of the New York University Press in the University's commitment to Near Eastern Studies provides the American and international public with a greater diversity of exposure to professional perceptions of the Near East. Focusing on those various peoples, religions, arts, and cultures of the Near East who throughout the centuries have profoundly influenced and given form to mankind's most fundamental concepts and whose economic and political spheres have been wide reaching, this series, New York University Studies in Near Eastern Civilization, seeks, solicits, and publishes significant research in this ever vital area. The concept embraces many facets of the Near East, welcomes varied and even disparate interpretations as well as concentration on specific historical periods, including the whole spectrum of social scientific approaches. It is, moreover, particularly sensitive to work in two aspects of the area as a whole that reflect the University's expertise and concern, and that have perhaps received less attention than their excellence merits. These are literature and art. Again with the intention of widening the impact of New York University Press publications, the series welcomes translations of significant Near Eastern literature, as an integral part of its attempt to deepen and enrich the experience of Near Eastern thought, prose, and poetry, for an audience unacquainted with the original languages.

Peter Chelkowski
Jill N. Claster
General Editors

Christians and Muslims in Ottoman Cyprus and the Mediterranean World, 1571–1640

Ronald C. Jennings

NEW YORK UNIVERSITY PRESS
New York and London

NEW YORK UNIVERSITY PRESS
New York and London

Library of Congress Cataloging-in-Publication Data
Jennings, Ronald C., 1941–
Christians and Muslims in Ottoman Cyprus and the Mediterranean
World, 1571–1640 / Ronald C. Jennings.
p. cm. — (New York University studies in Near Eastern
civilization ; no. 18)
Includes bibliographical references and index.
ISBN 0-8147-4181-9 (alk. paper)
1. Cyprus—History—Turkish rule, 1571–1878. I. Title.
II. Series.
DS54.7.J46 1992
956.45'02—dc20   92-3108
                          CIP

c 10 9 8 7 6 5 4 3 2 1

To All the People of Cyprus, Past and Present,
Particularly Those Now in Turkish Cyprus

Contents

Acknowledgments

Cevdet Çağdaş, who founded the Ethnography Museum out of a former Mevlevi Tekke in Lefkoşa, permitted me to work there even as an unknown visitor during wartime. His wife, Jale, then the administrator in charge, allowed me there, of her own volition. Soon she introduced me to her husband, and to life in Turkish Cyprus. Although its facilities were quite limited, the Çağdaş family, and every single person on the staff helped me in anyway that they could, anytime I asked.

Mustafa Haşim Altan introduced me to his archive in Girne and encouraged me to design a research plan which would utilize it. Whatever facilities the archive had were generously made available to me, insofar as the impoverished state could afford. The archive practically became a home for me and my family, as the gardens surrounding the archive provided us with fresh grapes, grapefruits, oranges, lemons, pomegranates, and figs, as the seasons changed. The staff of the archive rivaled that of the Ethnography Museum in friendliness. Altan also spent hours helping me understand local personal and place names. I was allowed to browse wherever I wanted.

I wish to thank the late Elaine W. Harris, an "Old Brit" whose love and life inspired me and my family, with her loyal cook, Tiafana, along with other "Old Brits," the stoic and friendly Col. Ronald and Betty Holden.

I wish to thank my "Old American" friends from Girne, with whom I share many memories, John and Trinette Horner.

I want to thank my "mixovaroi" friends, from New York and Girne,

Ayhan and Mary Kaymak, along with their children, who had one of the sandiest beaches in Girne, with whom I shared many pleasant swims and Saturday evening meals, until they finally moved to Magosa.

I salute the people of Turkish Girne (with its beautiful sea), nearly every single one an immigrant from elsewhere on the island, who had to abandon their own houses and find ways to operate those of other people, no easy task.

Also I salute the people of Turkish Lefkoşa, who live totally isolated, still protected by their ancient city walls.

The Turkish National (or Communal) Library in Lefkoşa made itself easily accessible, and has a useful collection of materials about Cyprus.

The Magosa Public Library has a pretty useful collection of travelers to Cyrpus.

The Evkaf Dairesi of Lefkoşa controls all of the traditional Islamic institutions, and their revenues, in all of Cyprus. It also controls most of the judicial registers, unfortunately, for it is not a comfortable place to work. It is an extremely powerful institution.

I wish to thank the two men who are in my opinion the most eminent people in Ottoman Studies in the world, Prof. Andreas Tietze, Director of the Oriental Institute in the University of Vienna, and Prof. Halil Inalcik, University Professor in the History Department of the University of Chicago, now both reluctantly retired, who took time from their busy lives and, at different stages, carefully read through this entire manuscript, providing new insights, and helped eliminate many errors.

I wish to thank my former UCLA teachers, Prof. Stanford J. Shaw, of the History Department, Prof. Tietze, and Prof. Speros Vryonis, Jr., who now holds the Alexander S. Onassis Chair for Hellenic Studies at New York University, who have supported my career to the fullest in their different ways.

Prof. Suraiya Faroqhi, now at the University of Munich, and Dr. Marcella T. Grendler, now in North Carolina, both provided helpful encouragement and valuable suggestions.

I wish to thank two former research assistants at the University of Illinois, Bonnie Mangan, now with the Library of Congress, and Dr. Virginia Danielson, who worked faithfully, independently, and imaginatively to help organize my research notes, sometimes a tedious task.

About one quarter of a National Endowment for the Humanities Fellowship for Independent Study and Research was spent in Cyprus as well as the full tenure of a Research Grant from the Joint Committee on the Near and Middle East of the American Council of Learned Societies and the Social Science Research Council.

I am very grateful to the University of Illinois Research Board, which provided money for both research trips and research assistants.

I am grateful to the University of Illinois Library, for its excellent collection, and for the service of interlibrary loan.

The office staff of the History Department did an excellent job typing this manuscript, as they have other manuscripts through the years. I also want to thank Despina Papazoglou Gimbel for her patience with a very difficult manuscript.

I spent three weeks in London working at the British Library.

I wish to thank my children, Ronald and Christina, who accompanied me to Cyprus, and helped share some of the beauties and pleasures of that island.

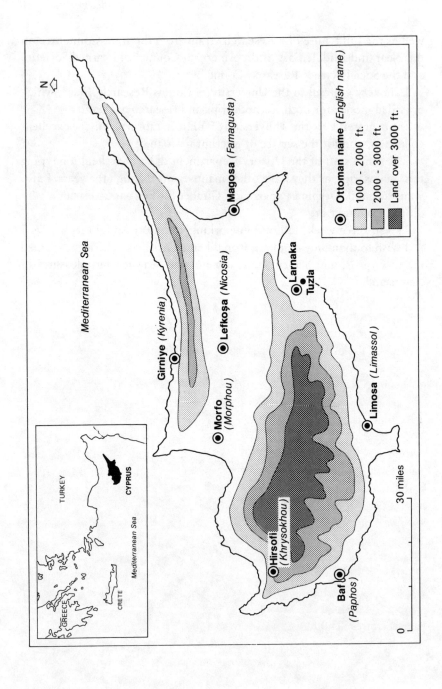

Introduction

Cyprus is located in the extreme easternmost part of the Mediterranean sea, about 65 kilometers south of Anatolia (Asia Minor) and less than 110 km from Syria. The island is marked by two important mountain ranges extending east-west, which make much of the land uncultivable. The thin northern, or Kyrenia, range has very steep slopes, and leaves only quite a narrow littoral in most places, though well watered and extremely fertile; that range nearly reaches a height or around 1000 meters. The Trodoos mountains of the south are broader, thicker, and very much taller, reaching as high as 1950 m. Because of the steep slopes, little cultivation is done in the northern range, while the Trodoos has extensive cultivated areas, where grapevines grow. Although mountain villages are quite uncommon in the north, they proliferate in the south, particularly for grapes, but small plots of grains, fruits, and vegetables are not unusual.[1]

The flat central plateau stretching some 100 km between Morfo (Morphou) bay to the west and Magosa (Famagusta, or Salamis) bay to the east already by Venetian times had become the granary of the island. There the combined wheat and barley (occasionally supplemented by vetch or oats) might constitute 60% to 75% of the value of village crops; the alluvial soil there is rich, having worn off the mountains over the centuries. The foothills also may be used for intensive grain production but they are as likely to produce a rich variety of fruits and vegetables or commercial crops; cotton was particularly prevalent, although sugar cane, flax, hemp, and silk cocoons were all common. Cyprus was famous for its fertility. In many areas very intensive agriculture had developed, where streams, wells, and water mills supplied abundant water. Cyprus stood as a crossroads between East and West from 1192 until 1571, when it was finally reconquered by another native eastern empire, the Ottoman one.

Cyprus seems to have been a rather thickly settled and prosperous place at least since the bronze age, when its abundant copper and tin deposits helped make it a center of long distance trade in the eastern Mediterranean. Rich cedar, cypress, and pine forests which apparently once covered most of the island were central to the development of important local smelting and shipbuilding industries. Iron ore enabled an early transition of Cyprus into the iron age. By the time it was added to the Roman empire in 58 B.C. it apparently had thriving mercantile and commercial centers as well as copious grain production, although with deforestation shipbuilding had become a thing of the past, and forests were thereafter increasingly restricted to hills and mountains. Partly because of its close proximity to the earliest centers of Christianity in Palestine, it became one of the earliest centers of Christianity. But the rise of Islam and its early spread to Syria made Cyprus a frontier.

Cyprus remained in the Orthodox church with the rest of the Greek-speaking world. As part of the Eastern Roman, or Byzantine, empire it had its own autonomous church with an archbishop. It was visited by great numbers of Christian pilgrims who were traveling to Jerusalem and the other Christian holy places of Palestine.[2]

A remarkable agreement was reached between the Umayyad caliphate of Damascus and the Eastern Roman, or Byzantine, empire to administer the island jointly, bringing an end to the bitter fighting and destructiveness which had marked the recent history of the two powerful empires which contended for that strategic frontier province, with its many ports.[3] From 688 until 965 Cyprus was so administered, and probably spared much destruction. That agreement benefitted both sides. The joint rule was brought to an abrupt end by the brilliant Byzantine conquerer Nicephorus Phocas who took also Cilicia and later Antioch from Muslim control. So Cyprus fell under the direct rule of a renascent Byzantium.[4] In 1185 a Byzantine rebel named Issac Comnenus seized control of the island, but he was partly responsible for its fall to crusaders when he dealt rather arrogantly with Richard the Lion-hearted of

England and lost his throne, the last Greek Orthodox ruler of the island for almost 800 years.

The Greek Orthodox island of Cyprus became part of the Latin world during the crusades, and it remained under Latin rule centuries after the fall of Acre, the last crusader outpost on the mainland. Seized by Richard the Lion-hearted of England on his way to the Holy Land for the Third Crusade, Cyprus quickly passed into the custody of a French crusading family named Lusignan. Cyprus played a focal role in the crusades; its strategic location and useful ports enabled crusaders to pass safely to the Holy Land and to concentrate military forces there before and after campaigns. Its agricultural wealth easily produced surpluses which might be turned over to soldiers. While the Levant mainland was gradually falling to Muslim forces, the Lusignan family held tightly on to Cyprus, where they were practically invulnerable because of the absence of good Muslim navies.[5] Even when the Lusignans had to submit themselves as tributary to the powerful Islamic Mamluk empire of Egypt and Syria, they continued to exercise great autonomy. When the Venetians managed to take over the island from the Lusignans, their tributary obligations remained very much in effect. That obligation to pay a large annual tribute to the Mamluks passed to the Ottoman empire in 1516–17, after the Ottomans had conquered first Syria and then Egypt, thus ending the Mamluk empire. The excellent fortifications of Cyprus, and its vast agricultural surpluses made the island a genuine treasure house for its rulers.[6]

The Mamluk empire of slave soldiers centered in Egypt and Syria had, by the end of the 14th century become the most powerful state in the Muslim world.[7] In 1426, with 150 to 180 vessels, taking a great amount of booty, they invaded Cyprus. At least on one other occasion, in 1460, they were able to intervene directly in Cypriot affairs. Normally, however, they were little involved in naval matters, and piracy thrived in the person of some unscrupulous people protected by their rulers, for the Mamluks never had a naval expertise which paralleled their excellence as land soldiers (namely heavy cavalry). The kingdom of Cyprus was in the early years a fervent participant in the crusades, and crusaders moving to and from the Holy Land found supplies and safe garrisons. Much irregular warfare broke out between Muslims and Christians whom the Mamluks could not control and Cyprus did not want to control. Eventually when Venice ruled Cyprus the policy was more directed toward establishing good trading relations between the two empires. One special factor in the relations of Cyprus and the Mamluk empire was the annual tribute that had been paid since 1426. In that year the king of Cyprus had the misfortune of being captured with part of the army with which he had invaded Egypt. In return for his release, the king was forced to pay a huge one-time ransom and then promise to pay an annual tribute of 5000 ducats to the sultan. At least by 1460, the tribute had been raised to 8000 ducats per annum. When Venice intrigued to take over Cyprus, promises were made to continue that tribute, even when very close commercial relationships developed between the two states. When the Ottoman empire brought an end to the Mamluk empire in 1517, the Venetians had to agree to transfer their payment of the tribute to the Ottoman sultans with whom they also had vital trading connections.

Centuries of Crusader rule left a legacy of outstanding fortifications in Cyprus just as it did along the coastline of the Levant. Because of the sometimes exploitative nature of Lusignan rule, as well as the widespread antipathy between Latin and Greek Orthodox Christians, they needed such fortifications nearly as much for internal security as for external. The Lusignans built massive fortifications around their capital Lefkoşa and their great port of Magosa. In the interval when Venice ruled the island, important developments in cannon during the 16th century forced the new rulers to undertake the expense of changing the system of fortifications from one in which height was the primary consideration to a quite different system where thickness of the fortifications was primary. The Venetian empire expended great amounts of money and labor to change both fortresses into massive thick-walled buildings; with Lefkoşa that also included greatly reducing the dimensions of the fortifications, although their circuit remained extremely large. A second coastal fortress, at Girniye, received some improvements, but that was a very small place. The Lusignans lived in their capital, in certain nearby villages, or in the northern range. During the summers they preferred to live in the northern mountains, where mostly for their own personal security they erected large fortifications at St. Hilarion, Buffavento, and Kantara, all important passages in that range. With their construction, the Lusignans had personal safety from internal surprises. Claiming penury, the Venetians chose to destroy those fortifications rather than trying to rebuild them when an Ottoman attack became imminent. They did, however, make Lefkoşa and Magosa practically invulnerable.[8]

How can one of the greatest Ottoman military feats ever, the brilliantly organized invasion and conquest of Cyprus between July 1570 and August 1571 by combined land and naval forces occur at the very same time as the battle of Lepanto in 1571, the greatest Ottoman defeat since Timur beat Ottoman sultan Bayezid I at the battle of Ankara in 1402? The Ottomans hardly lost even a single major battle in the century before that. Probably the Ottoman commander at Lepanto lacked decisiveness and resolution, for which he was dismissed, but remembering the long, uninterrupted succession of military and naval victories which had been achieved in the previous century, the success in Cyprus at that very time, and the successes which would occur for the next decade or more, it is hard to adjudge the defeat at Lepanto as decisive in any way, even as a portent of misfortune which might follow later. It seems obvious that the conquest of Cyprus was much more important than the battle of Lepanto. None of the victorious allies of Lepanto occupied any territories, won any strategic advantages, or were able to follow up that single isolated success. The Ottomans stripped Venice of its richest and wealthiest possession anywhere and its most important overseas naval bases, at the same time depriving Latin Christian pirates of their most important base, and Venice was forced to pay huge reparations to the Ottoman empire.

Originally I hoped to study the period from 1580 to 1640, beginning well after the conquest, when Ottoman rule was completely established, so that I would not have to focus at all on Venetian rule there or the military aspects of the Ottoman conquest. However, since many of the sources begin with the process of conquest there was not nearly enough information to approach it that way. Moreover, the radically different understanding that Andrew Hess has brought to the battle of Lepanto and the publication by the Turkish Ministry of War of lots of Ottoman documents about those two campaigns probably will necessitate a thorough new study, so I did not want to be guessing in that area too much. Anyway, 1571 marks the completion of the Ottoman conquest of Cyprus. The year 1640 marks the death of the reforming sultan Murad IV, the only first-rate ruler since the death of sultan Suleyman in 1566, whose reign was a great boon to the empire, but whose death left the empire once again in weak hands. (A second reason for trying to study that time period is that a detailed Ottoman tax and population survey of the urban and rural wealth of the island was prepared in 1572, immediately after the conquest, and it was widely but erroneously believed that a second such complete register had been compiled in 1641.)

I strive to give the history of a small, largely Greek-speaking and mostly Greek Orthodox island in the easternmost Mediterranean from the time that an ascending Islamic state, the Ottoman empire takes over in 1570–1571 from a series of Latin Christian outsiders who starting in 1192 as a direct consequence of the Third Crusade in the Holy Land perpetuated themselves as an ethnicly, linguistically, and religiously distinctive ruling class. The feudal system of western Europe was carried almost intact into Cyprus. Latin Lusignans and their largely French and Italian helpers formed a local aristocracy which, though small, became the predominant social and economic force on the island. Their role as aristocracy continued almost unchallenged even after Venetians won Cyprus for their own empire in 1489.

The Ottoman conquest in certain, but not all, ways abruptly ended many aspects of nearly three centuries of Latin rule. A new state with many different goals and purposes took over from the Latin ruling class by in part bestowing on the Greek Orthodox majority a very different form of government. In general the position of the old ruling aristocracy was quickly transformed. Certain buildings of the Latins were handed over to Orthodox or to Armenians. Some of the aristocracy naturally fled to Venice or other places, and so did some of the class of Orthodox Christians who had profited most from Latin rule. Undoubtedly some of the most enterprising of the aristocracy found ways to perpetuate themselves by becoming Muslim or Orthodox. Much, however, of the power of the old aristocracy was ended.

Cyprus is often cited as an early model in the development of plantation agriculture, where monocultural agriculture imposed by the feudal aristocracy created a highly sophisticated system through the skillful management of wells, irrigation channels, and water mills, and developed highly efficient sugar cultivation and manufacturing. That system made immense profits, but supposedly created an overdependence on international markets. Then the more efficient plantation system of the Atlantic supposedly required changes in Cyprus, and thereafter monocultural cotton was created by the Venetians. The detailed population and taxation survey of 1572 challenges that notion, however, for of the

174 villages paying more than 10,000 akce per annum in agricultural taxes, only one produced cotton worth as much as 40% of its total agricultural produce. That was Pano Veli (?) village in Limosa district, which produced 59%. Next came Kefale in Mazoto district with 36%, Poli in Hirsofi district with 34%, and Suriyane Hori village in Pendaye with 33%. So of the 174 villages paying the most taxes, only four (a mere 2%) paid taxes on cotton worth a third of their entire produce; three more villages produced between a quarter and a third (4%); and five more produced between a fifth and a quarter, meaning a mere 7% (12) paid as much as 20% of their agricultural taxes on cotton (which had almost completely replaced sugar as the international market collapsed on levantine sugar). If the village cultivators of Cyprus had reasons to complain, then, it was not because they had become so vulnerable to vicissitudes of international markets but because the aristocratic ruling class had little sympathy for the cultivating class and displayed feelings of religious and perhaps cultural superiority.

Cyprus was a place that slaves were most likely to be sold or transported to, because they were very much in demand, particularly in sugar fields and in sugar factories, where very laborious tasks had to be carried out. The northern Pontic regions were especially important; Venetians used Tana as a source for much plantation labor in Cyprus which required great numbers of workers. Cane sugar was very important in places like Morfo (Morphou), Lefka, Aheliye (Akhelia), Kukla (Kouklia), Baf (Paphos), Lapta (Lapithos), and especially Piskopi (Episkopi) and Kolos (Kolossi).

This manuscript results from the convergence of three different interests of mine: 1) the interrelationships of religious, linguistic, and ethnic groups; 2) provincial social and economic organization; and 3) the development of the Mediterranean world in the 16th and early 17th centuries.

Judicial records are one of the best sources for information about religious, linguistic, and ethnic groups, although often it is impossible to be more precise than Muslim and non-Muslim (or Christian in Cyprus). Distinguishing different groups of Muslims is often excruciatingly difficult, when possible, because the personal names used are so very similar and no need is ever felt to differentiate among Muslims. Occasionally differentiations are made among non-Muslims in Cyprus. Probably all of the Jewish and Armenian Christian Cypriots are explicitly identified as such, and they usually even have distinctive personal names. Often Greek Orthodox Cypriots can be distinguished by their personal names, although many Armenians and Maronites have "Greek" personal names because they as small minorities have been culturally and linguistically assimilated into the majority. Certain kinds of population and taxation records also distinguish between Muslims and non-Muslims; and sometimes even Jews, Armenians, or other Christians may be differentiated there.

Judicial records are also very important sources for provincial organization. Because of my long-standing desire to understand how the local societies and economies functioned, I have been fascinated from my first hesitant attempts to read them by the candid looks at human lives which come only from judicial registers. Other sources like imperial orders or law codes give more static vantages points, concealing the dynamism which marks human life. Ottoman judicial records, at least from the times and places that I have investigated, provide detailed summaries of each legal case, as well as verbatim copies of all official orders sent to the local government.

My old interest in the development of the Mediterranean world in the 16th and early 17th centuries was inspired in many, but by no means all, ways by F. Braudel's seminal study of the Mediterranean in the age of the Habsburg emperor Philip II. As far as the Mediterranean world goes, it is well known that massive studies of a very sophisticated and provocative nature, have been made of the northwestern, or Latin Christian, parts, but only a few pioneering studies have dared to treat the Islamic parts, which occupy all of the remainder of the shores. Studies of the Orthodox Christian northeastern parts of the Mediterranean have been dealt with only a little more seriously than the Islamic parts.

NOTES

1. The distinguished ancient historian M. Rostovtzeff gives important details about the political, social, and economic role of Cyprus in antiquity, with its extensive grain cultivation, its important forests which were often used for ship timbers and smelting, olives, grapes, animals, bees, forests, and mining (some silver, but predominantly copper, which through time took so much of the forests for smelting metals). *The Social and Economic History of The Hellenistic World.* 3 v. (2nd ed.) Oxford, 1953. pp. 37, 65, 75, 85, 89, 93,

111, 127, 169f, 172, 202, 339, 360, 381–384, 1071, 1168–1170, 1354, 1387, 1612f, 1644. A really first-rate work of scholarship covering the whole period from the stone age to 1948, in four impressive, only infrequently ponderous, and usually very cautious volumes, British classicist George Hill, *A History of Cyprus*. v. 1 covers the period from the Stone Age to the conquest by Richard Lion Heart, really an admirable introduction to the island; v. 2 covers the Frankish period, 1192–1432; v. 3 covers the Frankish period, 1432–1571; v. 4 covers the Ottoman province, the British colony, 1571–1948, ed. Harry Luke, after the death of Hill. Cambridge, 1940, 1948, 1952.

2. The basic study of the church of Cyprus is still, J. Hackett, *A History of the Orthodox Church of Cyprus from the Coming of the Apostles Paul and Barnabas to the Commencement of the British Occupation (A.D 45–A.D 1878), together with some account of the Latin and other churches existing on the island*. London, 1901. Since the establishment of the Lusignan dynasty after 1192, the overwhemingly Orthodox majority had to endure subordination to the Latin church until the Ottomans took over. See Hill's important chapter entitled "The Two Churches, 1220–1571," v. 3, chapter 16, pp. 1041–1104. "The tendency to fusion which we have noticed in Cyprus was due to the weakening of Latins who wandered into the Greek fold, rather than to any approach from the Greek side," p. 1104. See also H. T. F. Duckworth. *The Church of Cyprus*. London, 1900.

3. R. J. H. Jenkins, "Cyprus between Byzantium and Islam, A.D. 688–965," v. 2, pp. 1006–1014 in G. E. Mylonas and D. Raymond, eds., *Studies Presented to David Moore Robinson*. St. Louis, 1953. See also Hill, v. 1, chapter 12,"Byzantium and Islam," pp. 257–329 for important information.

4. Cyprus during the crusades and under the Lusignans and Venetians has been given a very solid traditional study by G. Hill, v. 2 and 3. Not very much was added by Harry Luke, "The Kingdom of Cyprus, 1291–1369," pp. 340–360, and "The Kingdom of Cyprus, 1369–1489," pp. 361–395 in K. M. Setton, series ed. *A History of the Crusades*, v. 3, Harry W. Hazard, section ed., *The Fourteenth and Fifteenth Centuries*. Madison, 1975. See also Freddy Thiriet, *La Romanie Vénitienne au Moyen Âge. Le développement et l' exploitation du domaine colonial vénitien (XIIe–XVe siècles)*. Paris, 1959.

5. The changes made by the Venetians in the older walls are described in great detail by Hill, v. 3, pp. 842–864. For an excellent technical discussion, see John F. Guilmartin, Jr., *Gunpowder and Galleys. Changing Technology and Mediterranean Warfare at Sea in the Sixteenth Century*. Oxford, 1974. Note page 4, "If there was any single technological development which caused the decline of the Mediterranean world and brought about the rise of northern commercial dominance it was the development and spread of the use of effective heavy cannon." See also, pp. 67f, 157f, 257, and *passim*.

6. Frederic C. Lane was one of the earliest and best scholars who dealt with the great wealth of the island of Cyprus and its vital role in the Venetian trade. See, for example, "The Mediterranean Spice Trade: Its Revival in the Six-

teenth Century," in Brian Pullan, ed. *Crisis and Change in the Venetian Economy in the Sixteenth and Seventeenth Centuries*. London, 1968. pp. 22–46, esp. 37f. See also "Venetian Shipping during the Commercial Revolution," pp. 3–24 in *The Collected Papers of Frederic C. Lane*. Baltimore, 1966. Also *Venice. A Maritime Republic*. Baltimore, 1973. pp. 297–300.

Fernand Braudel places great importance on the role which Cyprus had for Venice. *The Mediterranean and the Mediterranean World in the Age of Phillip II*. tr. S. Reynolds. New York, 1976, especially pp. 15f, 148ff. See also, F. Thiriet, *La Romanie Vénitienne . . .*, p. 435f. Apostolos E. Vacalopoulos, *The Greek Nation, 1453–1669. The Cultural and Economic Background of Modern Greek Society*. New Brunswick, 1976. See also William H. McNeill, *Venice. The Hinge of Europe 1081–1798*, who concludes a full-blown plantation economy, Chicago, 1974, pp. 54 and 76, and also Sydney Nettleton Fisher, *The Foreign Relations of Turkey, 1481–1512*. Urbana, 1948. pp. 39f, 54, and 92.

7. On the Mamluk dynasty, which conquered Cyprus in 1370 and demanded tribute from the Lusignans, and then Venice, until Ottoman Sultan Selim I ended that empire in 1516, see Hill, v. 2 and 3, pp. 370, 467ff, and 832. See also: Halil Inalcik, *The Ottoman Empire, the Classical Age 1300–1600*. tr. N. Itzkowitz and C. Imber. New York, 1973. pp. 31, 33f, 56, 96f, 137, 195f, 201. Stanford J. Shaw, *The History of the Ottoman Empire and Modern Turkey*. v. 1, *Empire of the Gazis*. Cambridge, 1976. pp. 34f, 79, 83–85, 153.

8. Hill's is one of the most detailed and reliable accounts of the conquest of Cyprus in 1570–1571, and the immediately ensuing battle of Lepanto of 1571, involving the Ottoman navy, on the one hand, and a Christian alliance of Venice, the Spanish Habsburgs, and the Papacy, on the other. Hill received some excellent advice about Ottoman sources from Paul Wittek. v. 3, pp. 878–1040, 1161f. Hill also discusses the 300,000 ducats which Venice agreed to pay as a war indemnity in March 1573. v. 4, p. 37. Since then a major collection of documents has been published by Emin Aysan, *Kıbrıs Seferi (1570–1571). Türk Silahli Küvvetleri Tarihi*, IIIncü cilt. Ankara, 1971.

According to Andrew C. Hess, "The Battle of Lepanto and Its Place in Mediterranean History," *Past and Present* 57. 1972. 53–73, "With extraordinary speed, the Ottoman state demonstrated both the sufficiency of its naval resources and the effectiveness of its bureaucracy through the reconstruction of its fleet within two years of the battle of Lepanto." pp. 62, 63–73. Ottoman sources give no indication of a major blow to Ottoman power or prestige, nor to a loss of self-confidence; Selim II acknowledged his personal negligence. The Ottoman empire recovered immediately, still unchallenged at sea, and continuing expansion in North Africa by eliminating the remaining Habsburg fortresses there, so that they had the upper hand at least until a truce of 1580. Hess found that Ottoman sources show absolutely no adverse effects of Lepanto because of their vast resources and excellent military and bureaucratic organization. Compare two other authoritative articles by Hess, "The Evolution of the Ottoman Seaborne Empire in the Age of Oceanic Discoveries, 1453–1525," *American Historical Review* 75. 1970. 1892–1919, and "The Ottoman Conquest of Egypt (1517) and the Beginning of the Sixteenth Century World War," *International Journal of Middle East Studies* 4. 1973. 55–76.

Guilmartin has challenged Hess's views, saying that there is evidence that the Ottomans "never quite recovered from Lepanto. Certainly they never again displayed the same tactical agressiveness at sea." *Gunpowder and Galleys* . . ., p. 156. He claims that the Ottomans never recovered from their loss of skilled manpower after Lepanto, although he has no evidence. p. 272. He believes that the war of Cyprus and Lepanto begin a change in the systems of Mediterranean conflict. pp. 272f.

According to a footnote in Hill based on a letter from Wittek the most important Ottoman chronicler treating the conquest of Cyprus is Mustafa ʿAli, because he personally attended that campaign, but unfortunately that is available only in manuscript. Hill, v. 3, pp. 1149ff. Other chroniclers, except for Ibrahim Peçevi and Muneccimbaşi seem to support Hess's view. The contemporary Selaniki, who died in 1599 gives an authentic account of the conquest of Cyprus in 1570 and the battle of Lepanto. He says that while Sultan Selim II was still a prince, a ship coming from Egypt, and belonging to him, had taken refuge from a storm on Cyprus, and gifts which were intended for him had been seized. Soon after he became sultan, he sent a fleet of 84 vessels to brings soldiers and conquer the island. Then in 1571, he had 184 vessels who had believed that they would win at Lepanto, but lost because it was late in the season, and many vessels were not ready for battle. Of his fleet, only 42 returned from Lepanto. It was resolved to rebuild exactly the number of vessels which had been destroyed. Special taxes (ʿavariz akce and kurekci) were levied on the people. The new commander Kilic ʿAli did not waste a moment; within 120 days the new, completely refurbished fleet of 134 sailed out. The enemy had dealt them a serious blow, but they recovered. *Tarih-i Selaniki*. Istanbul, 1281. pp. 100–104.

Another important account is that of Ibrahim Peçevi (1574–1649). According to him the sultan felt forced to act against Cyprus in 1570 because Venice had been allowing brigands *(eşkiya)* to attack ships, travelers, merchants, and pilgrims going to Egypt. Also, since Cyprus had formerly been under Muslim rule, it was especially important to restore it. According to Peçevi, after the defeat at Lepanto, 250 vessels were readied for the following year; with a new commander, but because of the disaster the previous year, Ottomans were very wary of attacking, and withdrew to Istanbul. *Tarih-i Peçevi*. (2 v.) Istanbul, 1283. v. 1, pp. 486–491.

According to the great scholar and naval historian Katib Çelebi (1609–1658), the Ottomans had attacked Cyprus in 1570 because of the interference of brigands *(eşkiya)* from the island with Muslim merchants and pilgrims on ships; Venice would not accept responsibility. Then after the defeat at Lepanto eight arsenals built the exact number of new vessels which had been destroyed, namely 150, under the supervision of (Sokollu) Mehmed Paşa, who sailed with no opposition. *Tuhfet ul-Kibar fi esfar el-bahar*. Istanbul, 1329. pp. 95ff. See also *The History of the Maritime Wars of the Turks*. tr. James Mitchell. London, 1831. pp. 72–79. Another important account is that of Muneccimbaşi, (d. 1702), who asserts that Cyprus was conquered because the people violated an agreement with Sultan Suleyman, when they had attacked and plundered Ottoman vessels. He asserts that both sides avoided each other after Lepanto. Muneccim Başi Derviş Ahmed Efendi, *Sahaif ul-akhbar*. tr. Şa ʿir Nedim Efendi. Istanbul, 1285. v. 3, pp. 523–529. Another important Ottoman historian Demetrius Cantemir calls the Ottoman defeat at Lepanto, coming right after the great victory at Cyprus, the worst Ottoman defeat since the defeat of Sultan Yildirim Bayezid; it occurred because the Ottomans were thoroughly unprepared. Selim grieved about it, and prayed, then appointed a new commander who returned boldly with 250 ships and vigorously attacked, which frightened the Christian fleet into withdrawing. When the loss was more than amply avenged, Selim in gratitude adorned certain sacred buildings. *The History of the Growth and Decay of the Ottoman Empire*. tr. N. Tindal. London, 1734. pp. 222–226.

Braudel, in his revised English translation, points to pirates in and around Cyprus almost necessitating the Ottoman attack to attain security. By that time he had become aware of the important subsequent Ottoman naval advances after 1571 like La Goleta and Tunis, but still maintains that although definitely not the only cause of Ottoman decline, it was quite important. *The Mediterranean* ..., pp. 312, 1080ff, 1088. Christian privateers began to make great advances. Venice betrayed the "holy" Alliance, partly because of the enormous expenses of its fleet. Venice gave back all the territory it had recently conquered in Albania, returned all Ottoman prisoners without ransom, limited her fleet to 60 galleys, and paid 300,000 sequins in reparations. The demise of the Ottoman fleet was hastened by the inactivity which followed the Ottoman-Spanish Habsburg treaty of 1580. pp. 1127 and 1141f. Hess, on the other hand, insists that it was only the Portuguese and Spanish Habsburgs who needed that truce of 1580, for the Ottoman empire had vast resources and vigor at that time. "The Battle of Lepanto ...," pp. 66f.

The Greek Cypriot scholar Costas P. Kyrris has made a number of important, often seminal, studies concerning the Christians of the island under Ottoman rule. Especially provocative is "Symbiotic Elements in the History of the Two Communities of Cyprus," *Kypriakos Logos* 8. 1976. 243–282. "L'importance sociale de la conversion à l'Islam (volontaire ou non) d'une section des classes dirigeantes de Chypre pendant les premiers siècles de l'occupation turque (1570–fin du XVIIe siècle)" pp. 437–462 in *Actes du premier congrès international des études balkaniques et sud-est européennes*. v. 3, *Histoire*. Sofia, 1969. "Cypriote Scholars in Venice in the 16th and 17th Centuries," pp. 183–272, in J. Irmscher and M. Mineemi, eds., *Über Beziehungen des Griechentums zum Ausland in der Neueren Zeit*. Berlin, 1968.

And others listed. According to Theodore Papadopoullos, despite possibly abundant Ottoman archival materials from other parts of the empire, such records ". . . should be rather scanty as concerns Cyprus," because of its late conquest of 1570 and was "one of the most neglected and maladministered" of provinces. *Social and Historical Data on Population (1570–1881)*. Nicosia, 1965. pp. 4f.

R. Jennings, "The Population, Taxation, and Wealth in the Cities and Villages of Cyprus, According to the Detailed Population Survey *(Defter-i Mufassal)* of 1572," *Journal of Turkish Studies, Raiyyet Rusumu Essays Presented to Halil Inalcik* 10. 1986. 175–189. From that register of 1572 great variety was found, rather than monopoly or overconcentration. This parallels a situation described by Jean Richard, "Une économie coloniale? Chypre et ses resources agricoles au Moyen-Âge," *Byzantinische Forschungen, Internationale Zeitschrift für Byzantinistik* 5. 1977. 331–352.

Richard mentions grains like wheat and barley, legumes like carobs, lentils, chick-peas, green beans, peas, and vetch, as well as grapes, raisins, wine, olives, sesame, fruits, and vegetables being produced. Such products, not just sugar and cotton, were widely cultivated. He also suggests skillful use was made of water and other imaginative agricultural innovations rather than slave labor. Cyprus agriculture offered the people the possibility of leading a good life, not colonialism. Braudel is wrong to believe that idea of colonial life with monocroping. There was quite a mixed agriculture. pp. 337–343, 346, 349f.

ONE

The Women of the Island

The Ottoman conquest and the ensuing implementation of Islamic law undoubtedly had profound effects on the legal position of women and on family life. The impact of a century of Venetian rule over the Greek Orthodox majority is difficult to conjecture, particularly in this aspect most removed from public scrutiny. Even to get an impression of the position of women in family and public life in the traditional Orthodox Byzantine society and economy is difficult. The Latin and Venetian ruling classes of Cyprus were not noted for their high morality, while the reputations of the later Lusignan family and the Latin aristocracy were unsavory. Certain 16th-century travelers noted the ease with which seamen and merchants made liaisons with women of some Aegean islands, but Cyprus is as far from some of those islands as is Venice itself. If the functioning of the local popular society is difficult to perceive, still the degree of public dissipation practiced in the late Lusignan court would not likely have occurred in the Ottoman province, although indeed the machinations in the imperial Ottoman harem during the period of the "sultanate of women" perhaps are in some ways comparable. An aura of dissoluteness adhered popularly to the women of the island where Aphrodite/Venus was born, and for centuries after the establishment of Latin crusader states in the Levant, many less sophisticated western Europeans looked askance at morality there. Whether they believed upright Christians corrupted and debilitated by long (or even brief) interrelationship with less moral, effeminate Greeks and godless Muslims, or whether they believed immorality was the inevitable effect of the hot climate, many of the unsophisticated felt moral contempt for their Levantine cousins.[1]

In their writings, western European travelers, pilgrims, and merchants largely ignore the women of Cyprus. Much of what they imagine is based on romantic presuppositions about the island of Venus. So the imagination of the priest Ludolf of Suchen was provoked when he passed Baf (Paphos) early in the 14th century: "For the soil of Cyprus, and especially where the castle is, if a man sleep thereon, of its own self will all night through provoke a man to lust."[2] Compare the Venetian patrician Francesco Suriano, who made his pilgrimage in 1484: "The women are lewd. The country and climate of themselves incline to fleshly lust and nearly everyone lives in concubinage. In the days of king Jacques the women went about attired in a seductive manner like nymphs. Now they go decently dressed."[3] The society of 16th-century Cyprus separated men from women in public and required a modest dress of women, as had the Orthodoxy of Byzantine Cyprus. In 1553 the pilgrim John Locke observed: "Their women are always separated from the men, and generally they are in the lower ende of the church."[4] The merchant Elias of Pesaro noticed this separation, which he attributed to immorality: "They do not allow their women to show themselves in the town by day; only by night can they visit their friends and go to church." That was in order to prevent "the frequent adulteries."[5] The Italian pilgrim Nicolas de Martoni, who visited Cyprus in 1394, reported that Magosa (Famagusta) was famous for its courtesans. Nevertheless, he acknowledged that all the women of the island "wear black mantles on their head so that their faces can hardly be seen."[6] Of more substance is Martoni's testimony to the integration of women into the vigorous camlet industry of Magosa: No woman was allowed to leave the city without the permission of the commander, and had to post bail at the court for her return, if she was allowed to leave, but permission was rarely given. "The reason alleged is that men cannot live in that city but for the women who spin and prepare wool for the camlet, for they have hardly any other means of living."[7]

In 1683 the Dutch Orientalist Cornelius van Bruyn found that the women of Cyprus dressed much like in "Turkey," with a handkerchief around the head as a headdress.[8] Two 18th-century contemporaries, Richard Pococke and Van der Nyenburg, described the Cypriot women as not so covered. The latter compared their dress to the women of

Rhodes, except wearing no veils.[9] According to Pococke the women
". . . go unveiled, so they expose themselves in a manner that in these
parts is looked on as very indecent."[10]

Islam places great emphasis on personal and family morality, and
long before the 16th century its legists had worked out in elaborate
detail those portions of the Sharia which relate to women and family
life. With noteworthy exceptions, 16th-century Islam seems to have
profoundly affected the social and economic ethos of its believers. Islamic legists strove to make that law permeate the lives of all Muslims,
but non-Muslims were left a great deal of autonomy in their life styles,
particularly in regard to their personal and communal morality, and so
the effects of Islam as a state religion on the society are unpredictable.
After the Ottoman conquest, for the first time in centuries, Muslim
women and families, both immigrants and converts, appeared in Cyprus.
The protection of Islamic law, particularly through their traditional
protectors, the kadis and their courts, was made available to all women,
even the Greek Orthodox majority for whom it probably was not oblig-
atory. One may wonder what experiences these immigrant Muslim
women or local converts had which made them aware of the existence
of this protection and made them seek out its protection for themselves.
By 1595, within 25 years of the Ottoman conquest, a large number of
women from Lefkoşa (Nicosia), the nearby villages, and perhaps all over
Cyprus were active participants in the court system; indeed, that probably was the case in 1580 or even earlier. At least some of the credit for
the rapid institutionalization of the system must go to the kadis.

The protections offered women by the Sharia court of Lefkoşa are
basically the same offered by similar courts elsewhere in the Ottoman
empire, although no doubt local traditions and political developments
had some impact. Women were entitled to many of the same legal rights
as men and they had equal opportunity to use the court to ensure those
rights. Of course, women in the Greek Orthodox majority had the
alternative of solving their problems within their own religious community; but in any dispute a Sharia court deigned to hear, the judgment
was made in terms of the Sharia itself. The Sharia court of Lefkoşa had
behind it the full sanction of the Ottoman state, for it was the obligation
of all Ottoman officials to obey and implement its decisions. Women
particularly used the court to settle matters of marriage and divorce, to
secure the support or maintenance necessary for their livelihoods, to

secure or otherwise to use their personal property, and to complain of physical violence of one kind or another. In fact, however, cases involving women covered a whole gamut of problems, profound or trivial, which concerned them.

An important indicator of the relevance of the court to their lives is the frequency with which they used it. Of 958 cases surviving from 1593–1595 (1002–1003), 230, or 24%, involved at least one woman. Of 130 cases from a fragment of 1580 (988), 23% involved at least one woman. The figure for the 175 cases of 1607–1610 (1016–1018) was only 11%, but that volume is exceptional. More typically, 21% (248) of 1184 cases in 1609–1611 (1018–1019) involved at least one woman, and for the 1630s the figure is 35% (183 of 528). (See table 1.1.) Almost a quarter of all the judicial cases heard before the court of Lefkoşa involved at least one woman. Almost three-quarters (73%) of those women were Muslims, although more than one woman in four who had business before this Islamic court was a Christian.[11]

Traditionally Sharia courts encourage individuals to testify in person, and legal agents *(vekil)* may only be used in the absence of a litigant, not as advisers. Although women were permitted in almost all cases to use an agent, and so remain in the privacy of their homes, only about 35% of the women did so, either to avoid attending in person or because really not at hand. The proportion of Christian women attending the court in person was noticeably greater than that of Muslim women. While only 23% of Christian women had recourse to a legal agent, over 39% of the Muslim women did so.[12] In 1633–1637 Christian women used the court with a slightly greater frequency compared to Muslim women than Christian men did compared to Muslim men. The proportion of women using the court who were Christians increased by over half between 1610 and 1633, from 24% to 38%. Presumably the growing proportion of women using the court reflects the adjustment of the local people to the new Islamic legal order.

Of course, the court was primarily a man's place. While women came there with special problems, all of the kadis and police officials were men, and so were all the local people who collected around the court long hours overseeing its operations, perhaps even gossiping. No woman would have stayed there long. Even virtually all the witnesses were men, for although women's eyes were presumed to be as good as those of men, their minds were not; besides, encouraging women to appear in

Table 1.1
Women and the Court of Lefkoşa

years	total cases	total with a woman	% with women	total with Muslim women	% with Muslim women	total with zimmi women	% with zimmi women	total with Muslim women with vekil	% with Muslim women with vekil	total with zimmi women with vekil	% with zimmi women with vekil	total for all women with vekil	% with women with vekil
988 (1580) 1002–1003 (1593–1595)	130 958	30 230	23% 24%	15	71%	6	29%	5	33%	3	50%	8	38%
#1A 988 (1580) 1002–1003 (1593–1595)	1088	260	24%	196	76%	61	24%	78	40%	15	25%	93	36%
#2 1016–1018 (1607–1610)	175	19	11%	13	76%	4	24%						
#3 1018–1019 (1609–1611)	1184	248	21%	203	77%	59	23%	74	36%	15	25%	89	34%
#4 1043–1046 (1633–1637)	528	183	35%	113	62%	69	38%	54	48%	15	22%	69	38%
total	2975	710	24%	525	73%	193	27%	206	39%	45	23%	251	35%

Note: Figures for cases with Muslim women plus those for zimmi women do not necessarily equal the figures for the total number of cases with women. Sometimes cases involved more than one woman. Occasionally a case had both Muslim and zimmi women, only one of whom had a vekil. Scrupulous efforts were made to make tables as precise as possible; the level of accuracy is satisfactory for my claims.

public regularly even in the service of justice was apparently not desired. Women rarely served as witnesses in Ottoman Sharia courts. Usually when they did so the matter was uncontested, and their testimony counted only half that of a man. Perhaps they accepted those disabilities themselves and so did not shirk to bring problems before the kadis.

In a few instances women did serve as witnesses at the Sharia court of Lefkoşa. For example, ʿAyni bint ʿAbdullah and Dost bint ʿAbdullah made known that ʿAyşe bint ʿAbdullah was four or five months pregnant, a matter of modesty concerning women alone.[13] Mehmed bn Ahmed, ʿAbdur-Rahman bn ʿAbdullah, and from women Asya bint ʿAbdullah and Cemile bint ʿAbdullah confirmed the testimony of Hadice bint ʿAbdullah of Lefkoşa that Sakina bint Mustafa owed her 13,711 akce from a loan *(karz)*.[14] Muslime Hoca bint Pir ʿAli and Raziye bint Resul, women, and Caʿfer beg bn ʿAbdullah testified that the late Hasan kethuda by Ilyas was owed 3000 akce ... [15] ʿUdul-i Muslimin Mehmed bn Hasan, Meyhan bint Halil, and Fatma bint Ridvan testified confirming the claim of the Armenian woman Altun that her husband still owed her the 3000 akce loan *(karz)* she had given him.[16] Only in matters considered peculiarly female does the testimony of women alone ever suffice.

In any case, women did make serious claims at the court of Lefkoşa with some regularity. For example, a Greek Orthodox woman of Harcodiye (?) village of Mesariye kaza had ʿOmer çavuş bn ʿAbdullah and Musliheddin halife summoned to court in the presence of the provincial governor *(mir miran)* Mehmed Paşa for entering her house, beating her, and seizing her property because they claimed her husband owed money to the treasury *(miri)*.[17] Another zimmi woman made a similar claim against Memi çavuş bn ʿAbdullah of the divan-i Kibris çavuşes.[18] Still another Greek Orthodox woman, ltesat (?) bint Andreye of Kazumina (?) quarter of Lefkoşa made a claim that long ago ʿAli reʾ is bn Bedr had seized her and taken her for a slave and wife.[19] ʿAyşe bint ʿAli of Haydar Paşa quarter of Lefkoşa, through her agent *(vekil)* Mehmed bn Ahmed, claimed that Huseyn bn ʿAbdullah still owed 200 akce that he had borrowed *(karz-i hasen)* from her late husband.[20] Fahrul-muhadderat Fatma hatun bint Hasan aga of Lefkoşa had for her vekil Hasan aga bn ʿAbdulllah who claimed before musellem Mustafa çavuş representing provincial governor *(mir miran)* Mustafa Paşa that her late brother Musli efendi was owed 20,000 akce for certain goods he had given.[21]

Aluce (?) bint Şeyhi, wife (*ʿavret*) of celali leader (*başbug*) Şaʿban of the mainland (Ote Yaka) sets forth a claim (*t.d.*) against Huseyn bn Mehmed: My husband (*zevcum*) Şaʿban gave some of my goods to Huseyn to pay his debt (*deyn*). I did not want to give them, and I did not give my permission. I want my right (*hakkum*). Let Huseyn be asked about the matter. Huseyn acknowledges receiving the goods in payment for Şaʿban's debt, but he asserts he had no knowledge that they belonged to the wife. She has no proof. When he is asked to take an oath, he does so.[22]

Mariye bint Hiristofi, wife, and Ancola, daughter of the late Christian Nikola v. Papa Todori of Menagri village of Gilan kaza in Cyprus acknowledge (*ik./iʿt.*) before Ramazan beg bn ʿAbdullah: The accused has illegally (*fuzulen*) taken possession of the entire property and goods we inherited from the deceased. We want them. A settlement was reached amicably with the intervention of upright people (*muslihun*).[23]

Women, in turn, were obligated to answer serious legal claims made against them in court. They had to respond to all charges and to produce evidence just as men did, although such claims were not frequent. Mahmud beg, spahi of Balicu (?) village of Lefkoşa, summoned to court a non-Muslim woman named Pereşkonu bint Benaki (?) of that village, accusing her of illicitly having sexual intercourse with another villager. When the woman called upon the people of the village to attest to her reputation for good behavior, they did.[24] Perviz beg bn ʿAbdullah claimed the property of Christian (*zimmiye*) Anzola bint Laristiyo, widow of the late Pavlo, who went to Venice.[25] Zaʿim Perviz beg claimed that a slave girl named Rahime absconded with 15,000 altun and Mustafa kethuda.[26]

It was even possible for a woman to make claims against her husband, father, or other male relatives, although such claims obviously were infrequent. Contrariwise, a man might have to make serious charges against his own wife or female relatives.

Husna bint Murad claimed that her husband Mergeri v. Kuluk, Armenian, always treats her cruelly (*cefa ve eza*) . . .[27]

Muslime bint Bedr (?) demands 3000 akce delayed dowry (*mehr-i mueʾ ccel*) from her husband Mustafa ʿAli bn Ramazan. He acknowledges only 1000 akce debt. Divorce (*hulʿ*) is made.[28]

Already by 1593–1595 (1002–1003) women had secured an important role as property holders in Lefkoşa and elsewhere in Cyprus. Thirteen percent of all property transfers (i.e., house and other major structures, with or without surrounding land) and 15% of all land transfers involved women. Women were involved in 14% (23 of 166) of the total number of land and property transfers mentioned at that time. While the small number of land sales and purchases were in equal proportions, women sold more than four pieces of property for every one they bought, which of course means that women proportionately were accumulating property. By 1609–1611 (1018–1019) not only were women still involved in 15% of land transfers but in addition they were involved in 31% of all property transfers. Overall that meant women were involved in 26% (22 of 84) of the total land and property transfers. Land transfers were few, but sales exceeded purchases; property sales exceeded purchases by more than fivefold. Despite the clear trend of disposing of their land and property, women had come to control a considerable and steadily increasing proportion of land and property. There was the basis for at least a limited economic impact on the community.

Quite a large number of land and property transfers were recorded in 1633–1637 (1043–1047), and the proportion of those, particularly the former, involving women increased significantly, as if the long-term effects of the application of Islamic inheritance laws were being felt. At least one woman was a party to 31% of all land transfers, double the proportion of earlier times; at the same time women were buyers or sellers in 30% of property transfers. At that time they were more than three times as likely to sell land as to buy it, and almost three times as likely to sell property. Nevertheless, women were involved in 30% (39 of 128) of all transfers in 1633–1637.

The proportion of property held by women increased steadily over half a century. The proportion of all land and property held by women in 1595 was already substantial, and by the 1630s that proportion had doubled. Of course the tendency of women to sell also remained a long-term trend; they either spent or saved the cash they received in payment. Evidently women did not invest their capital in land and property as actively as some men did, but they acquired it nonetheless. Indeed, land and property may not even have been considered as investments, for the principles of Islamic law ordained that the price of property should not be increased unless its real value also was increased somehow. As the society and economy of Cyprus developed under the influence of Ottoman institutions, the position of women was at least in some ways enhanced.

In matters of accumulating, managing, and claiming property women showed real vigor. A large proportion of those using the court were looking after their own property. They accumulated land, houses, and money through inheritance, through dowries, gift, or by purchase. Since the Islamic law applied by the court required that female as well as male relatives share in estates of close relatives, theoretically there should have been as many women property holders as men.While in fact that was not the case, many women did accumulate property. Although they tended to sell inheritance shares to male relatives, thus reducing the extent of their own holdings, they must have acquired money then. If that did not bring them economic independence, it certainly must have brought them some security. Frequently women had to seek the support of the kadi to protect their property from men, but the court seems to have provided firm support then. Again, a man occasionally found a woman so firmly in control of contested property that he had to make recourse to the court. Whatever economic influence women had outside of their homes on the local community was certainly closely related to their ownership of property.

Inheritance was the most common way women accumulated property, and men too. The court followed regular procedures in the implementation of inheritance laws; although the judicial records of Lefkoşa do not explicitly itemize estates or record their assignment to particular heirs, many cases involved rival claimants who had settled their disagreements and others involved heirs who had divided an estate amicably and wanted a public record that they had done so. From before 1595, and probably even before 1580, an authority was firmly in control which was able to ensure the regular transfer of inheritance to women, albeit at one-half the rate received by male relatives of the same degree. Even non-Muslim women frequently availed themselves of this right. The experience of owning and managing personal property of even a limited size provided elementary economic responsibility and worldly experience, and even when advice from husbands and male family members was readily available. That is a step toward economic independence.

Special provisions were made in Cyprus for women who were capable of cultivating land to inherit that from their fathers in the absence of sons. Spahis were required to allow such women the right to cultivate the land; they could not transfer it to another, charging the "registration fee" *(resm-i tapu)* as they did when there were no heirs who could cultivate it properly.

Huseyn çavuş of Lefkoşa and Ridvan beg bn ʿAbdul-Mennan as vekils state *(t.k.):* Fields called Manastiryeri near Girniye gate belonging to the late Mehmed, çelebi, with water-wheel well *(dolab kuyusi),* are suitable for title registration *(tapu).* Perviz beg, steward of the tax-farm charged with inheritance, registered it for ʿAyşe for 2000 akce. The right of possession *(hakk-i tasarruf)* is given to the woman . . .[29]

To governor *(sancagi begi),* know that Christian *(zimmiye)* Belime (?) sent a man to my Porte. It was said that her father died without male children *(evlad-i zukur),* so lands in her possession were given to the spahis, interfering with her rights. She should be given her fathers' lands. I wrote that you should give her her father's lands. If anyone dies without a son or brother, his land goes to *tapu* for another. If he has a son or brother, it goes to him. And daughters who have the ability to perform agriculture may request their father's lands. It is my order. Registration fee *(resm-i tapu)* of 300 akce may be taken for the best lands, 200 akce for average land, and 100 akce for the worst land.[30]

Altun bint Sinan of Kaysariye inherited 7000 ʿosmani akce from her late father of Aya Sofya quarter.[31] Janissary Yusuf bn Hasan inherited an estate *(menzil)* from his late mother Emine bint Ahmed.[32] Two wives of the late Ibrahim çavuş inherited 1957½ akce, and two daughters Emine and Rahime inherited 4567½ akce apiece; a son Ilyas inherited 9135 akce.[33] The late Fatma bint ʿAbdullah died without heirs *(varis),* so her effects *(muhallefat)* belong to the treasury *(miri).*[34] The estate of the late Meryem bint ʿAbdullah amounted to 14,655 akce.[35] A son and daughter of the late Ayla hatun inherited 32,000 akce and 16,000 akce respectively. The mother herself inherited 12,000 akce.[36]

ʿAbdul-Kerim çavuş, called Kara Baş, stated *(t.k.):* I give my garden *(bagce)* of known boundaries as a gift to my daughter Fatma, and my houses *(evler)* of known boundaries at Kizil kule quarter in Lefkoşa as a gift *(hibe)* for my daughter ʿAyşe. If I die, let my son ʿAbdul-Halim not interfere.[37]

Cemile bint Şaʿban kethuda and her brother Receb compromise on terms of settlement of their late father's estate.[38] Rabi ʿa bint Mehmed of Incirlu village of Lefkoşa sells her estate *(menzil)* at the village to her husband ʿAli bn ʿAdbullah for 5000 akce.[39] Mehmed çavuş bn Ibrahim of Seray quarter in Lefkoşa sells three houses *(menzil)* in the quarter to Meryem bint Mahmud for 5000 akce.[40]

A few women became lenders or borrowers, not rare phenomenon in the Middle East. Sometimes the money owed women was simply unpaid dowry and maintenance, as in the cases of 545 akce owed Cemile bint Yener by her husband Mehmed bn ʿAbdi and the 300 akce owed by Pir Dede bn Maksud to his wife Teslime bint Behine (?).[41]

Sakina bint Mustafa of Lefkoşa made a claim *(daʿva)* against Hadice bint ʿAbdullah who has her agent *(vekil)* Yusuf çavuş bn ʿAbdullah: Formerly she gave me 3000 akce as a loan *(karz-i hasen)*. I have paid part. Hadice denies this; a male and two female witnesses confirmed Sakina's testimony and it was accepted.[42] Hadice claimed that the original debt was 13,711 akce but she had compromised *(sulh)* for 10,711 akce.[43]

Barsun v. Mercan, Armenian, acknowledges still owing Fatma hatun, who has ʿOmer aga as agent *(vekil)*, 2160 of the 6160 akce from the purchase of two mules.[44]

Mahmud beg bn ʿAbdullah says *(b.k.)* before his wife Christian *(zimmiye)* Covani: Two years ago I sold her a cloak *(ferace)* for 2000 akce to be paid in 160 days. In payment she was to give olive oil *(revgan-i zeyt)* and other goods, but she has not. Let her be questioned; I want to be paid as I should. Acknowledged by Covani.[45]

Muʾmine bint Sefer of Lefkoşa says before Rabi ʿa hatun: I gave her a cloak *(ferace)* for 15 guruş. She acknowledges that.[46]

Armenian Altun formerly lent her husband Murad 3000 akce *(karz)* which he has not yet repaid. . . .[47]

Women were allowed to take oaths on the same principles as men, to substantiate their own testimony when better evidence was lacking. At that time, however, oath-taking was not very common in the court of Lefkoşa.

Although Hano (?) bint Yarcute (?), guardian *(vasi)* for the minor sons of the late Christian Duka of Aya Mariye village of Lefkoşa, had no proof for her claim that the 15 donum land *(yer)* and 2 houses *(ev)* at the village had been given by Marko, she was asked to take an oath and did so.[48] Although Raziye bint Halil of Lefkoşa had no proof that her husband Nurullah and her uncle Gazi had sold her house *(menzil)* to haci ʿAli beg bn ʿAbdullah, an oath was proposed to her and she swore that the sale had been made without her consent. On the basis of her oath, the sale was cancelled *(fesh)*.[49] Muʾmine bint ʿAdbul-Gani was able to take an oath that she had not received her proper share of inheritance from her late husband Baba Nazar, which was being administered by another wife, Raziye bint Yusuf.[50]

Mustafa beg bn ʿAbdullah says *(b.m.)* that his wife ʿAyşe, whom he has divorced, had Pervane beg as agent *(vekil)*: The dowry *(mehr)* of Pervane beg's daughter ʿAyşe, who was my wife, was 4000 akce. She gave it to me as a gift *(hibe)*. Pervane denies the claim. When an oath is proposed to ʿAyşe, she declines to take it *(nukul)*.[51]

Sometimes women were guarantors for payments of the debts of others *(kefil bil-mal)*. Should the debtor default in payment, the guarantor pledged to pay the debt with her own money. Christian Mariya bint Yovan was guarantor for 10 altun debts owed by Ridvan and ʿAli.[52] Zimmiye Hiristine of Behine (?) village of Evdim nahiye was guarantor *(kefil bil-mal)* for 166 goats *(keçi)* and 438 akce which her husband Birişko v. Hiristofi owed ʿAbdur-Rahman kethuda bn Ismaʿil; and in turn Mehmed reʾis bn Mustafa was guarantor for her, to ensure doubly the payment of the debt.[53]

More frequently than men women served as guardians *(vasi)* for minor children. (Islamic law conceives a child who has lost one parent as an orphan *(yetim, yetime)*. The duties of the guardian include protecting any property of the orphan; Islamic law of inheritance made it quite likely that an orphan would have at least a modicum of property. While the father of an orphan would be expected to raise the child with his own resources unless he were impoverished, the mother or other relatives would probably seek the authorization of the court to draw a fixed amount per day from the orphan's estate to pay for his maintenance. Sometimes remarriage, old age, or change of residence led to changes in guardian, and of course when the child came of age no guardian was necessary at all. Being the guardian of a minor required a sense of responsibility, and the office was not to be taken lightly. Among the kadi's special responsibilities were to oversee the activities of guardians and to protect orphans. Sometimes another person, usually also a relative, might be established as overseer *(nazir)* of the estate of a particular child.

Lalezar bint ʿAbdullah, guardian (fem. *vasiye*) before the Sharia of Mustafa and Rahime, minor son and daughter of the late Suleyman su başi of Lefkoşa, has as legal agent Huseyn bn ʿAbdullah, who says *(t.m.)*:

Previously my *muvekkile* (who appointed one vekil) accepted the office and requested that the money for maintenance *(nafaka ve kisve)* be fixed by the court. When experts *(ehl-i vukuf)* were asked, they said that 8 akce per day apiece, a total of 16 akce/day, should be allotted, so that amount was fixed.[54]

When a guardian was needed for the minor son Ismaʿil of the late Mahmud of Lefkoşa, his mother Ummi was appointed, and his uncle Nasrullah çavuş was made overseer *(nazir)*. 5 akce/day was alloted.[55]

Rodosli Suleyman bn Seydi stated *(t.m.)* before his daughter Ayla: I was guardian for her orphans, the minor boy *(sagir ogli)* Mehmed and the minor girl *(sagire kiz)* Belkis. I have resigned. Let the guardianship *(vasiyet)* go to my daughter. She accepts.[56]

It is registered at the request of the aforementioned Ayla that her minor son's share of inheritance was 32,000 akce, her daughter's share 16,000 akce.[57]

Hacer (?) bint Yani, guardian and mother *(valide)* of the minor Musa Seydi bn Mehmed, for herself and as legal agent states *(b.k.)* before Cyprus mutesellim Hasan kethuda who has Piyale beg as agent. She may sell some of the orphan's property if it is most useful *(enfiʿa)* to do so . . .[58]

When the late Mustafa beşe of Orta koy of Lefkoşa died, his mother Safiye bint ʿAbdullah was appointed to take custody of the inherited property of the minor girl *(sagire)*. Now she is marrying, so she is dismissed *(ʿazl)* as guardian. She is replaced by the uncle *(ʿamm)* of the girl, ʿAli bn Seydi Han. He accepts.[59]

Evidence of women with regular occupations outside the family system and traditional agriculture is almost entirely lacking. The socioeconomic system severely restricted their fields of activities, so that they did not serve as shopkeepers, merchants, or artisans; a notable exception is the weaving of cotton and wool cloth.[60] If a few women can be shown to have participated in money lending, that was only as slight aberration from the traditional roles and a small part of their lives. ʿAyşe bint ʿAbdullah was a servant *(hidmetkar)* in the house of ʿOsman çavuş bn ʿAdbullah until she died.[61] The mother of Mehmed bn Kasim aga of Girniye (Kyrenia), as administrator *(mutevelli)* of a small foundation, managed revenues of 1000 akce/year due the important Medineʾ-i Munevvere foundation.[62] Two Christian women are identified as brokers *(dellale):* Loize was charged with owing Mehmed bn Ibrahim 10 guruş from the purchase of muslin *(tulbend),* and broker Maro sold provincial governor *(mir miran)* Ahmed Paşa 11,150 akce's worth of silk shirts, sugar, and handkerchief on credit.[63]

On the other hand, the traditional system was oriented to providing women with a reasonable level of maintenance or support, whether married, divorced, or widowed. At least when adequate resources were available, the court could ensure that. When women married, dowries *(mehr)* were set which were legally the property of the wife only. Part was paid in advance *(mehr-i mu'accel,* prior to the consummation of the marriage), and the remainder *(mehr-i mu'eccel)* was payable if the woman was divorced or widowed. In addition, her husband was legally obligated to pay for her support and maintenance so long as she continued to live with him and refrained from any immoral behavior.[64]

Dowries varied considerably, affected by many factors; perhaps the higher ones would be over-represented in the court records. The dowry Fatma bint Hasan received from 'Ali bn Musa was 1200 akce.[65] Apparently when spahi Mehmed of Kutumize (?) village of Lefka kaza married twelve-year-old Fatma bint 'Abdullah of that village he gave her a dowry of 2000 akce, half *mehr-i mu'accel* and half *mehr-i mu'eccel.* The money had come to him from her as a gift, although the sum was possibly only part of a larger dowry.[66] 'Ayşe bint Pervane beg had given her 4000 akce dowry as a gift *(hibe)* to her husband Mustafa beg bn 'Abdullah.[67] Safiye bint haci Bayram of Lefkoşa had received a dowry of over 4200 akce from Ahmed beg bn Ilyas.[68] A few days after their divorce Zeyni (?) bn haci Hamze of Lefkoşa and his former wife 'Ayna bint 'Abdullah remarried. She received a mere 400 akce then.[69]

Seyyide Hadice bint seyyid Receb of Lefkoşa, according to the testimony of two witnesses, has as agent her brother es-seyyid 'Ali çelebi, who stated *(ik/tk)* in the presence of her husband fahr ul-a'yan Mustafa su başi bn Yusuf: My *muvekkile* (who appointed me vekil) married Mustafa with 24,000 akce *mehr-i mu'eccel.* Now he is paying it from his property.[70]

Typically marriages were arranged by the woman's father or other close male relative, but the Cyprus *sicils* provide no evidence about how consulting was done, and what input, if any, the bride and groom made.[71]

Little mention of marriage is found in the judicial records of Lefkoşa, for marriage, as a private contract, did not require any official state or religious sanction. If official lists of amounts of dowries were kept, a different place of registry must have been used. Divorces and incumbent settlements frequently were recorded. The *hulᶜ* divorce, technically made at the request of the wife or by mutual agreement, carried less social stigma against the man; the wife's formal acquiesence had to be registered. There is no basis for conjecturing the number of other divorces, although divorce certainly was not uncommon. Except in the case of some *hulᶜ* divorces when the wife specifically renounced claim to part or all of her dowry, divorce and remarriage could be a costly procedure for a husband.[72]

Divorce was usually a simple procedure. Unless the woman was in some way culpable, she received the payment of her delayed dowry *(mehr-i muʾeccel)* and she received a per diem maintenance allowance long enough to make certain that she was not pregnant. After that she was free to re-marry and probably would do so almost immediately.

Halil bn Musa of Lefkoşa states *(tm)* before his wife Fatma bint Hasan: If she renounces delayed dowry *(mehr-i muʾeccel),* maintenance allowance *(nafakaʾ-i ʿiddet),* and other dues *(hukuk),* we are divorced *(muhalaᶜa).* Fatma accepts *hulᶜ.* A certificate of divorce *(huccet-i hulᶜ)* is ordered.[73]

Mehmed bn ʿAbdullah, janissary, of Lefkoşa before Loize bint Ciryako who has, according to the testimony of two witnesses, her father Ciryako as agent *(vekil):* She is my wife. If she renounces delayed dowry *(mehr-i muʾeccel),* I divorce her. She accepts.[74]

Ibrahim bn ʿAbdur-Rahim states (tm) in the presence of his wife Sultan bint Mustafa: Sultan renounces delayed dowry *(mehr-i muʾeccel)* and her claim for money. I divorce her *(bayin talak).* She accepts.[75]

Fatma bint Suleyman of ʿArab Ahmed quarter makes a claim *(daᶜva/tk)* against Ahmed bn Musa: I was Ahmed's wife. We were incompatible at night (?) in bed (?) *(semerde ʿadem-i imtizac olmagla);* we have separated *(mufarakat iktiza).* We made *hulᶜ* and I renounced my delayed dowry *(mehr-i muʾeccel)* and maintenance *(nafakaʾ-i ʿiddet).* Now Ahmed claims that we still are married. When proof is asked of Fatma, from upright Muslims Muharrem boluk başi bn Mehmed and ʿAbdun-Nasr bn ʿAbdul-Celil confirm her.[76]

Rabiʿa bint Hasan of Terbiyodi quarter of Lefkoşa has as legal agent Mustafa bn Huseyn for acknowledging *(ik/tk)* in the presence of ʿAli bn ʿAbdullah: Rabi ʿa is ʿAli's wife, but they are incompatible *(ʿadem-i imtizac).* She gave him *(hibe)* a house *(menzil)* at the quarter; now he renounces claim to it. Rabi ʿa renounces claim to 5000 akce *mehr-i muʾeccel* and to maintenance allowance *(nafakaʾ-i ʿiddet)* and they make *hulᶜ.* Neither has any further claims against the other.[77]

Very little evidence of polygamy is found; probably it was uncommon. Lalezar bint ʿAbdullah and Yasemin bint ʿAbdullah were widows of the late Suleyman su başi.[78] Among the heirs of the late haci Huseyn bn Hasan of Karni village of Girniye, who died on a pilgrimage *(hac)*, were four wives *(zevcat varisesi)*, Fatma bint ʿAbdullah, Umm Gulsum bint haci Ilyas, ʿAyşe bint Yusuf, and another ʿAyşe. He also left two daughters, Umm Hanum and Selime . . .[79] Elsewhere in an estate settlement the late Baba Nazar's widow *(zevceʾ-i metrukasi)* was executrix. Raziye bint Yusuf, as guardian for her minor son Mehmed, makes a statement *(bm)* before Muʾmine bint ʿAbdul-Gani, other wife *(zevceʾ-i uhrasi)* of the deceased: All effects of the deceased were sold and everyone got his share. Muʾmine claims a house in Ahmed Paşa quarter. Muʾmine says that she did not get her share. She has no proof, but when an oath is proposed to her, she takes it.[80] Among the heirs of the late Ibrahim çavuş of the provincial council *(divan-i Kibris) muteferrikas* (a special service group) were two wives.[81]

Mixed marriages of Muslim men and Greek Orthodox women certainly were not uncommon. That was the verdict of a number of western visitors to Cyprus, and it is evident from the judicial registers as well.[82] For example, ʿAli bn Halil and Petro bint Ledike (?) were married,[83] as were Huseyn and Kutlu bint ʿAbdullah, (?)[84] janissary Mehmed bn ʿAbdullah and Loiz bint Ciryako,[85] and Mehmed beg bn ʿAbdullah and Covani.[86] Mariye married Bayram bn ʿAbdullah with the permission of her father Papa Toma of Aye Yolofi of Lefkoşa.[87] However, the marriage of a Christian man with a Muslim woman was impossible.

Fatma bint ʿAbdullah of Poli village of Hirsofi in Leftoşa: I have converted to Islam. After it was registered, my husband Yanno v. Manolya was invited to submit to Islam but he did not become a Muslim. He acknowledges that he has no claim against Fatma.[88]

Karçire v. Filipo of Cados (?) village of Mesariye kaza makes a claim *(t.d.)* against Musa beşe bn Ahmed: Four months ago he took my wife Çako bint Manuel (?) by force *(cebren)* and he has kept possession *(tasarruf)* of her until now. Let him be asked. I want my rights *(ihkak-i hakk)*. Musa beşe replies that Çako was honored with Islam in the presence of Muslims, at that time, and she took the name Fatma. Her husband was offered a chance to go to Islam but he declined. A man named Şenlik Hoca arranged Fatma's marriage *(ʿakd-i nikah)* to me. The claimant asserts that Çako has not become a Muslim nor has he been invited to. When she was summoned to court, she said, in truth I entered Islam at that time and my name is Fatma; my husband was invited to Islam.[89]

Much more common were women converted to Islam, as evidenced by an Arabic personal name and substitution of the impersonal name ʿAbdullah for the Christian names of their fathers. Born Muslims and converts to Islam, male and female, seem to have intermarried without any distinctions.

Summary

Many of the travelers and pilgrims who passed through Cyprus over the years believed that the island's people might still bear at least some of the pernicious effects of having been the site of a temple, and indeed reputed birthplace of Aphrodite (Venus), for Cyprus remained popularly known as the island of Venus. By the time of the crusades no small proportion of the contemporary writers looked askance at popular morality there. Partly this was derived from the growing Latin Orthodox rivalries and hostilities. Other people attributed it to the corrupting influence of a hot climate. Still others blamed the pernicious influence of living near Islam.

It is extremely difficult to have any perception of what life in Byzantine Cyprus may have been like. It is just as difficult under the Lusignans or Venetians, except for occasional references to corrupt people of the Latin aristocracy. It is a subject even less known than during the Ottoman empire. All that really can be said with any kind of confidence is what sorts of things were happening after the Ottomans added Cyprus to their territories, because of the judicial records which survive today.

Under the rule of the Latin Lusignans, and under the Venetians, too, there is a lot of evidence, much of it chronicled by George Hill in great detail, for the harsh discrimination against the Greek Orthodox majority, but also including the small Armenian community as well, in social, economic, and legal ways; it is hard to believe that such treatment would have been much less burdensome on women than on men. Ottoman rule brought with it conditions where Orthodox women could use the court whenever they needed. Moreover, absolutely no official regulations were made which restricted any occupations, or even city quarters, for Muslims. I find it very hard to imagine that would not improve the lot of those women.

There is good reason to believe women sat in the back parts of churches, away from men. Under Islam, that surely would have remained unchanged, and women in mosques, anyway, would have been less numerous. Women often wore black mantles, or black handkerchiefs, or perhaps both.

Women had a very important role in the active camlet industry, or at least that was the case in Magosa where spinning and preparing wool for the camlet industry was vital to the prosperity of that city. Camlet was less important elsewhere, but still of consequence for local economies. If women were involved in other industries, we do not know. Almost nothing is known even about the camlet workers; they are not mentioned in judicial records, nor in other Ottoman archival records. Either it was not very common for women to be involved in factories or doing artisanal work away from their homes, or it was very poorly documented.

Some reports suggest that the women of Cyprus were less secluded and covered than normal, but a few reports say the opposite. Islam places great importance on personal and family morality. The Sharia profoundly affected the social and economic ethos of believers. Legists strove to make that law permeate the lives of not only all believers but also all others who were subject to the state. After the conquest of 1570–1571, a steadily growing number of women used the court of Lefkoşa, local Christians, recent converts to Islam, and older Muslims, too. One of the special duties of kadis was to look after the interests of all women. In response to this opportunity, women especially from Lefkoşa, but also from other towns, and even a number of villages took advantage. (We have absolutely no evidence about the existence of Orthodox Christian or other non-Muslim courts at any time.)

The protections offered by the Sharia courts of Cyprus were quite similar to those of Sharia courts throughout the Ottoman empire at that time, although local conditions and politics doubtless had at least some impact. At any rate, whenever any party to a dispute, Muslim, Christian, or Jewish wanted to use the court, all others had to accede to following the Sharia. Likewise it was the obligation of all officials to carry out the Sharia insofar as possible. Women particularly used the court to settle problems of marriage or divorce, to secure the support and maintenance for their livelihoods, to get their inheritance rights, or to complain about physical violence. In fact, however, their cases concerned a whole gamut of matters profound and trivial. Nearly a quarter of all of the 2975 cases discovered remaining between 1580 (988) and 1640 (1046) involve at least one woman. Nearly three-quarters (73%) of those cases involved at least one Muslim. (Unfortunately it has been almost impossible to find any evidence about the actual numbers, or proportions, of Muslims and Zimmis.) During certain kinds of cases (excluding criminal ones) women were granted a privilege not so readily granted men, of having a legal agent represent them. Thirty-nine percent of the Muslim women chose that option, while only 23% of the Christian women did so. Traditionally the Sharia court urges people to represent themselves at court. The steadily growing proportion of women using the court undoubtedly is a clear indicator of growing trust on the part of the women who used it.

Of course, the court was primarily a man's place. All of the kadis and court officials were men, as were nearly all of the local people who collected around the court long hours overseeing its operations. Nearly all of the witnesses were men, for women's eyes were presumed as good as men's but their minds were not. Perhaps encouraging women to appear in public all the time was considered undesirable. When they did testify as witnesses in court, it was usually a personal matter of some sort; also the testimony of women counted only half that of men at court. Two reliable witnesses were needed to be equivalent to a man.

On the other hand women did make serious claims at the court with some regularity. They made claims against janissaries, against police from the governor's office, and against spahis. They made complaints against husbands, father, sons, and other relatives without any difficulties. Women also had to answer serious legal charges made against them, almost always in person, for using a legal agent *(vekil)* at such a time was not permissable.

One of the most important rights which women had concerned buying, selling, and inheriting land and property. Between 1580 and 1637 the judicial records reveal a steadily increasing proportion of women in both land and property transfers. In 1593–1595 (1002–1003) 15% of land transfers and 13% of the property transfers involved at least one woman. By 1609–1611 (1018–1019) the proportion of land transfers remained 15%, but the proportion of property transfers had increased to 31%. In 1633–1637 (1043–1046), the proportion of land transfers involving women had increased to 31%, while the proportion of property transfers held steady at 30%. The total proportion of all transfers had increased from 14% to 26% to 30% during those periods. Perhaps influenced by the inheritance practices, one finds that women were selling much more than they were buying. Of a total of 19 land transfers involving women, women sold more than twice as much as they bought (13 sold, 6 bought). In the cases of property the proportion of women selling is even greater (of 65 total, 50 sale and 15 buying). In the realm of both land and property women seem to have been selling much more than buying. Obviously, women did not very often accumulate land or property as was the case of many men. However, some women did show great vigor in accumulating, managing, and claiming property.

Much of their wealth must have come from inheritance. The rules of the Sharia made women as inheritors at half the rate of men of similar relationships. Property might also be acquired by women through dowries, through gift, or purchase. Many women, including not a few Christian women, availed themselves of this right by going right to the kadi. The experience of owning and managing their own property provided at least elementary economic responsibility and world experience, even if advice from husbands and male family members may have been readily available.

In the absence of sons, special provisions were made in Cyprus for daughters who were capable of cultivating the land of their own deceased fathers if there were no sons, and if they paid a relatively small registration fee to the timar spahi.

A few women became lenders or borrowers, not a rare phenomenon in the Middle East. The fact that women occasionally give loans to husbands or relatives is another argument supporting the assertion that women actually took possession of inheritance or dowries, and that they had their own property separate from males around them. The number of loans involving women in Cyprus was small. Probably women gave credit to relatives, or to other females most commonly. But lending to or borrowing from unrelated men was certainly not unknown. Selling inherited land or property was one source of capital, and dowries were then another.

Sometimes women were guarantors for the debts of others *(kefil bil-mal)*. In that case, should the debtor default, then the woman would become liable. Any Muslim or Christian with resources could do that for anyone else. That was not uncommon. Women served as guardians *(vasi)* of minor children even more frequently than men did. That meant protecting any property of the child, usually inheritance, until he came of age. Women were never obligated to pay anything either for their own maintenance or for their children, however wealthy they may have been; because according to the Sharia the husbands had to pay the entire expenses for all wives and children. Being the guardian of the child required a sense of responsibility, and was not to be taken lightly. Among the most important duties of kadis was to make sure that guardians acted fairly, to protect the well-being and property of minors.

Almost no evidence was found in any of the records about women working outside the traditional agricultural system or family life. We can mention women giving credit. We can mention the camlet industry of Magosa. We can mention a few women who served as administrators *(mutevelli)* of small foundations. Two Christians are mentioned as brokers *(dellale)*. A Muslim convert was mentioned as a household servant *(hidmetkar)*.

Fortunately, the traditional system was very much oriented towards providing all women with a reasonable level of maintenance. When adequate resources were available, the court could assure that. When men married, they were obligated to provide wives with at least the level of support to which they were accustomed. Dowries, which were to be the personal property of the wife, were to protect a woman who was divorced or widowed. The full burden of maintenance of wife and children was the responsibility of the husband. Dowries varied considerably. Those mentioned in the judicial records of the court at Lefkoşa widely varied in amounts, but unfortunately evidence is sparse. One must use them with caution because it is often not completely certain that other factors mentioned in the marriage contracts might have included other forms of remuneration, and it is likely that higher ones would be mentioned more than the lower ones. Typically marriages were arranged by the woman's father or close male relatives; however the judicial records of Cyprus give no indication of what role bride and groom paid. Marriage was strictly a private contract which did not require any official state or religious sanction. If lists of dowries were kept, a separate registry must have been used.

Divorces and incumbent settlements were frequently recorded. Divorce was a simple procedure, considered undoing of the marriage contract. Divorce was normally done unilaterally by the husband, who had to pay a maintenance allowance to make sure that the wife was not pregnant. After completing that waiting period, the divorced woman would marry anyone she wanted. The *hulʿ* divorce, technically made at

Table 1.2
Land and Property Transfers

years	Land Transfers			Property Transfers			Total Transfers			women buy land	women buy property	women sell land	women sell property
	total	total with women	% with women	total	total with women	% with women	total number	total with women	% with women				
#1A	40	6	15%	126	17	13%	166	23	14%	3	3	3	14
#2	none			none			none						
#3	20	3	15%	64	19	31%	84	22	26%	0	3	2	17
#4	42	13	31%	86	26	30%	128	39	30%	3	7	10	19
total	102	22	22%	276	62	22%	378	84	22%	6	13	15	50
										women buy 19		women sell 65	

the request of the wife, or by mutual agreement, carried less social stigma on the man; the wife's formal acquiesence therefore had to be recorded. There is no basis for guessing the frequency of divorce. Except in the case of *hulᶜ* it could be a costly procedure for a husband.

Very little evidence of polygamy was found in Cyprus, or elsewhere, for that matter. The few instances discovered involve people who may have been janissaries or police officers.

Mixed marriage between Christian women and Muslim men were not uncommon according to both the judicial registers and western sources. The judicial registers suggest that such people followed the Sharia, too.

NOTES

1. See R. Jennings, "Pilgrims View the Women of the Island of Venus," *Balkan Studies* 30.1989.213-220. Cf. P. Canaye for Naxos in 1573. *Voyage du Levant* . . . (1573). Paris, 1897. pp. 171f. On the sultanate of women, see S. J. Shaw, *History of the Ottoman Empire and Modern Turkey*. Cambridge, 1976. p. 179. H. Inalcik, *The Ottoman Empire: The Classical Age 1300–1600*. London, 1973. pp. 60f, 86f. Ahmed Refik, *Kadinlar Saltanati*. 3 v. Istanbul, 1923.

2. C. D. Cobham, *Excerpta Cypria. Materials for a History of Cyprus*. Cambridge, 1908. p. 19; Ludolf von Suchen, *De Itinere Terra Sanctae*. ed. F. Deycks. Stuttgart, 1851. p. 30.

3. Cobham, p. 49; Frate Francesco Suriano, *Il Trattato di Terra Santa e dell'Oriente*. ed. P. G. Golubovich. Milano, 1900. p. 243n.

4. Cobham, p. 69; R. Hakluyt, *The Principal Navigations* . . ., Glasgow, 1903. v. 5, p. 86.

5. Cobham, p. 75; Elias of Pesaro, "Voyage éthnographique de Venise à Chypre," *Revue de Géographie* 4.1879.225. In 1335 Jacobus de Verona reported that the women showed only their eyes in public and wore black; Martoni gave an identical report in 1394. The credulous Cotovicus, briefly a visitor in 1598, called the women lascivious. Cobham, p. 199. Cf. R. J. H. Jenkins, who held that "harlotry was certainly encouraged by the rigorous seclusion of women in polite society," a rather capricious and polemical indictment of all Byzantine society. *Cambridge Medieval History*, Cambridge, 1967 (hereafter referred to as *C. M. H.*). v. 4, pt. 2, pp. 88f. That certainly is not the impression given by Georgina Buckler, however, in "Women in Byzantine Law about 1100 A.D." *Byzantion* 11. 1936. 391–416.

6. He said that they attributed the practice to their sorrow on the loss of Acre, but that can hardly be true for many of the Greek Orthodox, unless it was

sorrow that the Latins had come to their island. Cobham, p. 24; Nicolas Martoni, *Relation du Pèlerinage à Jerusalem . . . (1394–1395)*, in *Revue de l'Orient Latin* 3. 1895. 631. ed. L. Legrand.

7. Cobham, p. 22; Martoni, *Relation . . .*, pp. 628f.

8. Cobham, p. 243; Cornelis de Bruyn, *Reizen . . .* Delft, 1698. pp. 377f.

9. Cobham, p. 246.

10. Cobham, p. 268; John Pinkerton, *A General Collection of the Best and Most Interesting Voyages and Travels in all parts of the world.* London, 1811. v. 10, p. 591. Richard Pococke adds that most treat their wives as servants, they never sat and talked with them, and had them wait on their tables and then eat afterwards. According to R. J. H. Jenkins this has Byzantine antecedents. *C. M. H.*, v. 4, pt. 2, pp. 88f.

11. That figure had reached 1 in 3 in the 1630s.

12. One does not know if Christian women went out more freely or if the upper class Muslim were particularly encouraged to stay at home; regardless, that phenomenon occurred also in contemporary Kayseri and Trabzon. R. Jennings, "Women in Early 17th Century Ottoman Judicial Records—The Sharia Court of Anatolian Kayseri," *Journal of the Economic and Social History of the Orient* (hereafter referred to as *JESHO*) 18. 1975. 60.

13. Lefkoşa sicil, #3 10–2; 12 Şevval 1018.

14. I 157–1; II Rebiᶜ II 1003.

15. 3 84–2; III Sefer 1019.

16. 4 34–2; I Rebiᶜ II 1044. See also 4 134–2.

17. I 10–2; II Ramazan 988.

18. I 18–1, 2; II Ramazan 988.

19. I 147–1; II Rebiᶜ I 1003.

20. I 168–2; selh Rebiᶜ II 1003.

21. 2 37–2; II Muharrem 1018.

22. 2 74–2; III Muharrem 1018.

23. 2 117–1; II Muharrem 1018.

24. 4 137–1; I Şaban 1045.

25. I 83–2; Sefer 1003.

26. I 38–7; Şaban 1002.

27. 3 25–3; 9 Zil-Kade 1018. Ibn (or bn) was used in those records to indicate sons of Muslims; veled (v.) indicates sons of non-Muslims.

28. 3 55–7; III Cumadi II 1019.

29. I 26–4; I Receb 1002. Cf. 26–3.

30. I 100–2; 1 Rebiᶜ I 1002.

31. I 117–5; 1002.

32. I 166–3; selh Rebiᶜ II 1003.

33. I 172–1; II Cumadi I 1002.

34. 2 70–2; II Receb 1016.

35. 2 112–1; Muharrem 1017.

36. 3 4–6, 7; III Zil-Hicce 1018.

37. I 29–5; 28 Receb 1002.

38. 1 93–3; I Rebiᶜ I 1003.

39. 3 61–1; after III Cumadi II 1019.

40. 4 2–3; I Şaban 1043.

41. 1 14–3.5; 19 Ramazan 988. For Kayseri, Jennings, "Women . . .," pp. 102ff, "Loans and Credit in Early 17th Century Ottoman Judicial Records —The Sharia Court of Anatolian Kayseri," *JESHO* 16. 1973. 194ff and *passim.* S. D. Goitein, *A Mediterranean Society.* Berkeley, 1967. v. 1, p. 256.

42. 1 159–2; 19 Rebiᶜ II 1002.

43. 1 163–1; III Rebiᶜ II 1003.

44. 3 1–3; III Zil-Hicce 1018.

45. 3 17–3; 27 Şevval 1018.

46. 3 126–6; before I Ramazan 1019.

47. 4 34–2; I Rebiᶜ II 1044.

48. 1 63–3; II Muharrem 1003.

49. 1 117–2; II Muharrem 1018.

50. 3 67–2; II Receb 1019.

51. 3 119–3; before II Şevval 1019. For other examples, see 4 64–2; 144–1.

52. 1 25–3, 4; Cumadi II 1002.

53. 4 4–3; III Şaban 1043.

54. 1 57–2; 1 Ramazan 1002. 57–3 involves a different widow and her orphaned children with the same problem.

55. 1 149–4; Rebiᶜ II 1003.

56. 3 4–3; III Zil-Hicce 1018.

57. 3 4–6.

58. 3 52–4; II Cumadi II 1019.

59. 4 15–2; I Şevval 1043.

60. This is known in the Lusignan period from N. de Martoni (Cobham, pp. 22ff; *R. O. L.,* pp. 627f, 637f) and in the Venetian one from Elias of Pesaro (Cobham, pp. 73ff; *R. de G.,* pp. 251ff), from Corancez early in the 19th century (Cobham, p. 240), and from official reports early in the period of the British protectorate (*Cyprus Blue Book, 1889–1890.* Also *1892–1893*). A bazaar of women in Lefkoşa is known from the mid-19th century, but its origin is unknown. Archduke Louis Salvator, *Lefkosia the Capital . . .* London, 1881. pp. 46, 50f. See also "Lefkosha," *EI².*

61. 1 196–4; II Cumadi II 1003.

62. 3 1–8; III Zil-Hicce 1018.

63. 3 144–1; III Cumadi I 1019.

64. On dowry, see al-Marginani, *The Hedaya or Guide. A Commentary on the Mussulman Laws,* tr. Charles Hamilton. Lahore, 1963 pp. 44–58. Yvon Linant de Bellefonds, *Traité de droit musulman comparé.* Paris, 1967. v. 2, pp. 199–255. Ö. N. Bilmen, *Hukuki Islamiyye ve Istilahati Fikhiyye Kamusu.* Istanbul, 1968 v. 2, pp. 368ff, 446–480. I. M. d'Ohsson, *Tableau général de l'Empire Othoman.* Paris, 1787–1824. v. 5, pp. 171–174. On

maintenance, see Marginani, pp. 140–149; Linant de Bellefonds, v. 2, pp. 256–286; Bilmen, v. 2, pp. 368ff, 446–480; d'Ohsson, v. 5, pp. 178–183.

65. 1 94–3; II Rebiᶜ I 1019.
66. 1 107–2; 3 Cumadi I 1003.
67. 3 119–3; before II Şevval 1019.
68. 1 195–2; I Cumadi II 1003.
69. 1 33–2, 5; I Şaban 1002.
70. 4 3–1; I Şaban, 1043. Some nine references to dowry have been found in the period 1635–1640. They illustrate the great diversity in amounts: 200 akce, 500 akce, 1500 akce, 2000 akce, 5000 akce, two at 12,000 akce, 24,000 akce, and 40,000 akce. Obviously the larger ones are disproportionately represented. 4 3–1, 96–3, 115–1, 144–1, 148–3, 152–1, 197–2, 232–1, 248–1.
71. 1 82–1; Sefer 1003. 3 8–6; before 3 Şevval 1018.
72. R. Jennings, "Divorce in the Ottoman Sharia Court of Cyprus," *Studia Islamica* (forthcoming).
73. 1 68–5; Muharrem 1003.
74. 1 225–3; I Şevval 1002.
75. 1 278–2; II Zil-Kade 1002.
76. 4 20–2; III Sefer 1044.
77. 4 148–3; I Şevval 1045.
78. 1 57–2, 3; 1 Ramazan 1002.
79. 3 32–1; after II Zil-Kade 1018.
80. 3 67–2; II Receb 1019.
81. 1 172–1; II Cumadi I 1003. See also 4 110–1; 1 Muharrem 1045.
82. Cf. R. Pococke, in Cobham, p. 269; Pinkerton, v. 10, pp. 592f. W. Turner, in Cobham, p. 449. C. Kyrris, "Symbiotic Elements in the History of the Two Communities of Cyprus." *Kypriakos Logos* (hereafter referred to as *K. L.*) 8. 1976. 246f, 260.
83. 1 5–5, 6–2; 9, 10 Ramazan 988.
84. 1 18–1, 2; II Ramazan 988.
85. 1 225–3; I Şevval 1002.
86. 3 16–3; 27 Şevval 1018.
87. 1 77–5; Sefer 1003. See also 1 31–2, 77–5, 240–1; 3 47–7, 48–1, 137–4. 197–1.
88. 1 240–1; I Şevval 1002. According to the Sharia, the wife's conversion to Islam made them divorced.
89. 3 9–7; before 12 Şevval 1018.

TWO

Islamic Pious Foundations *(Evkaf)* and Public Welfare

Byzantine Cyprus certainly had a well-established system of charitable foundations, most of which were of private establishment, although the imperial families were also expected to be charitable and merciful. Hospitals, orphanages, and hostels for the aged and the poor all were normally founded. It is very difficult to get any grasp what happened to those old Christian institutions because only a tiny fraction were mentioned in the records studied. Of course, a number of the new founders were local Cypriots who converted to Islam, but no evidence exists of acceptable Christian foundations established after 1571. Nor is there any evidence of preexisting foundations ever being taken over in toto. Ottoman practice, from the Sharia, provided great security and stability for donations. It was required that they be given forever, directly supervised by the mutevellis, and under the general direction of local kadis.

The *vakf* traditionally involved the irrevocable donation of personal possessions in perpetuity in order to provide revenues to support activities broadly construed as charitable. Pious foundations *(evkaf)* might pay the salary of an imam, construct a mosque, or repair a public well. In earliest times land was preferred for donation because of its immutability, but the Ottomans permitted movable property and even cash lent for interest.

Some Islamic forms became established almost immediately on Cyprus, such as mosques, the muezzin's call to prayer, and Sharia courts replete with kadis. The Islamic institution of vakf grew much more slowly. Evkaf are one of the chief ways by which Muslim communities look after public welfare and benefit the common good.[1] Created in perpetuity, their impact is cumulative. Most of Anatolia had already by that time been under Turkish Islamic rule for over half a millennium. Wealthy and middle class citizens had embellished their cities with mosques, medreses, baths, market places, fountains, and water channels since the time of the Anatolian Seljuks. Residential quarters and villages sometimes had evkaf to support their communal needs. Such institutions evolve only gradually. In Cyprus between 1571 and 1640 the institution of vakf was less developed than in many older Islamic areas. As a newly conquered territory its lands were vulnerable to appropriation for imperial or dynastic benefits rather than local ones.

Before the conquest in 1571 Cyprus had no residential Muslim communities. Frequently evkaf are established by Muslims proud of their cities who want to beautify them, by devout Muslims wishing to serve God or to be generous with their fellow Muslims.[2] For a time Cyprus had no wealthy native Muslims, no wealthy merchants from old families, and no native 'ulema. All except some local converts were outsiders whose ties of home and family initially were outside the island. Not surprisingly, then, many of the early founders of *evkaf* were from the military class.

The Military and *Evkaf*

In the early period of Ottoman rule in Cyprus the military officer class predominated over pious foundations *(evkaf)*. Most of the early founders or donors *(vākif)* and their administrators *(mutevelli)* derived their wealth from holding military office. Of 32 foundations mentioned in the judicial registers up until 1611 at least 16 had military origins. Of the remainder, three were of imperial foundation (Sultan Selim Han, Haremeyn-i Şerif, and Medine-i Munevvere),[3] one attached to a village, another two to churches, and only two (Mevlana Musliheddin efendi and mufti Sa'deddin efendi bn Muharrem) can be identified as from the religious class ('ulema). Of the military founders, two bore the title *beg,* two *çavuş,* and three *aga,* while six had been high-salaried imperial provincial governors *(mir miran* or *begler begi)* of Cyprus (Lala Mustafa Paşa, 'Arab Ahmed Paşa, [Hadim?] Ca'fer Paşa, Okci zade Mehmed Paşa, Sefer Paşa, and [Frenk?] Ca'fer Paşa). In all likelihood they had acquired that property while in office.

In newly conquered Cyprus the establishment of a wealthy military class could be expected to precede that of a wealthy religious class, so the preponderance of military founders is no surprise. However, the administration of foundations has traditionally belonged to the religious class. As masters of both reading and writing the way of Islam, they controlled the administration of foundations while deriving much of their income (and no doubt influence as well) from that service. Of 30 Cyprus mutevellis (administrators) named prior to 1611, 15 were military officers. Of the military-officer administrators, two were su başi, three each were aga and çavuş, and five were beg. Of the remainder, two were women,[4] two others Christians, while only four can be identified with the religious class. One of the latter was a dervish, another a mufti (or *şeyh ul-Islam*), one a descendent of the Prophet Muhammad *(seyyid)*, and one a prayer leader and preacher *(imam* and *hatib)*. Either the military controlled such affairs carefully and squeezed out the religious class or Cyprus's Muslims had not yet been able to develop an energetic educated class of their own. Initially, at least, those foundations with military founders, particularly those founded by governors, were both wealthier than the others and more likely to be administered by military officers.

By 1633 (1043) a trend toward civilian predominance had been established. Of the 14 evkaf mentioned after that year only two were founded by members of the military class, and only five of the 16 mutevellis mentioned can be associated with that class. Although up to 1611 (1019) the origins of half the evkaf were military, as were those of half of the mutevellis, after 1633 (1043) only 14% of the evkaf and 21% of the mutevellis had such ties. Obviously the military-officer class lost their earlier predominance, even allowing for the likelihood that later generations of some of those families may have separated from the military class while retaining economic and social prestige first acquired there. (See table 2.1.)

The absence of information about individual mutevellis has made it impossible to detect predominance of particular families over particular evkaf, but one may presume that to have happened at least with the family *(evladiye)* evkaf. Probably Seyyid Mehmed bn Seyyid Kasim and Kasim çavuş bn Mehmed, mutevellis of the ʿArab Ahmed Paşa evkaf, were father and son (or son and father). If the Huseyn aga who was mutevelli of the evkaf of the late Sultan Selim Han was the same Huseyn

Table 2.1
Evkaf Mentioned in Cyprus Judicial Records

Evkaf	prior to 1611 (1019)	1633–1637 (1043–1046)		before 1611	1633–1637
number	32	14			
origin			military		
military	16	2	paşa	6	1
ulema	2	2	aga	3	
imperial	3	3	çavuş	2	
quarter &			beg	2	
village	1	1	beşe	1	
		(+3 village churches)			
zimmi	2	3	kethuda	2	
no information	8	3	su başi	0	1

Mutevellis mentioned in Cyprus judicial records

number	30	16
origin		
military	15	5
ulema	4	2
zimmi	2	5
women	2	0
no information	7	4
military mutevellis		
beg	5	3
çavuş	3	0
su başi	2	0
aga	3	1
beşe	0	1

	military evkaf	total evkaf		military evkaf mutevellis	total evkaf mutevellis
to 1611	16	32 = 50%	to 1611	15	30 = 50%
1633–1637	2	14 = 14%	1633–1637	5	16 = 21%

aga who administrated the Haremeyn-i Şerif evkaf, he must have been a powerful figure as local head of those two important imperial evkaf (4 146–2; I Şevval 1045. 79–1; III Receb 1044). Of the five military mutevellis three were beg and one was aga; Derviş ʿAli, Şeyh Musa, mufti Saʿdeddin efendi bn Muharrem, and hafiz haci Mehmed çelebi bn Hoca (and here the monk Yorgi might be included) belonged to the religious class. Imperial evkaf tended to be controlled by military mutevellis,[5] while notables often controlled those of urban quarters and villages.

Of the identifiable foundations *(evkaf)* mentioned in 1633–1637 (1043–1046) two were military in their foundation (Haydar Paşa, Suleyman su başi), four were imperial (Sultan Selim Han, Valide Sultan, Medine-i Munevvere, and Haremeyn-i Şerif), one was religious (Seyyid ʿOmer efendi), and three were established by non-Muslim (i.e., zimmi) villagers.[6] At least two others were centered in villages and two more in urban quarters, a pattern which more closely resembles the contemporary situation in Anatolia.[7] Oddly, only five foundations mentioned in the early period are also mentioned in the 1630s: those of Sultan Selim II, Medine-i Munevvere, Haremeyn-i Şerif, Mevlevi Tekke, and Suleyman beg/su başi. Probably most of the evkaf were of so small a scale that within a quarter of a century of their foundation they had fallen to little consequence. Debased coinage and excessive inflation after 1580 must have shortened their useful lifespans, for example, making inadequate specific stipends allotted to charitable purposes such as subsistence wages for mosque functionaries.

The Sources of Revenues of Cyprus Foundations

Ottoman pious foundations of the 16th and 17th centuries traditionally provided credit to their communities as lending institutions.[8] In Lefkoşa they did so to some extent. Although most credit offered by the foundations was in relatively small amounts, some had substantial resources to lend out. Yusuf bn Idris borrowed 100 akce from the foundation of ʿArab Ahmed Paşa, ʿOmer beg bn Veli 1040 akce, and Mustafa bn Huseyn 660 akce (1 85–5, 6; Sefer 1003.208–1; II Ramazan 1002). The foundation of Sefer Paşa made a loan *(karz)* for 3000 akce (1 146–2; II Rebiʿl 1003. 3 85–4; after III Sefer 1019). The vakf of Ibrahim aga was owed 4000 akce by vaʿiz Musli efendi, imam of Aya Sofya camiʿi, 1000 akce by Mustafa bn ʿAbdullah, and 2000 akce by Musa, a total of 7000 akce (1 284–3; 27 Zil-Kade 1002).

The Mevlevi Tekke lent 7000 akce to a villager named Mehmed bn Cerid (4 102–3; III Ramazan 1044). Suleyman su başi evkaf had lent 2000 akce to Hasan boluk başi who died in Egypt (4 115–3; II Muharrem 1045). The late Armenian Ilyas owed 2000 akce to the evkaf of the church of Terbiyodi quarter *(mahalle)* in Lefkoşa (4 129–3, 130–1; III Receb 1045). The evkaf of the main mosque *(camiᶜ-i şerif)* in the town of Lefka was owed 880 akce by a non-Muslim *(zimmi)* villager named Çakoleki v. Zorzi (4 182–2; I Receb 1046). Ayşe bint ʿAbdullah took 3000 akce at 20% interest from the evkaf of Merdibanli çeşme quarter, agreeing to pay 3600 akce at the end of the year (4 234–2; 18 Ramazan 1045). The mutevelli of a vakf for repairing roads and bridges in Lefkoşa was accused of lending money to the poor at 20% or 30% interest, thereby violating the condition of the donor that only 10% interest be charged (#78/34 (20) #564; undated) 61,595 akce in assets of the evkaf of Haci Seydi mescid were turned over to racil Muharrem beşe bn ʿAbdul-Vehhab when he replaced Hasan beg bn ʿAbdullah as mutevelli (4 153–3; I Şevval 1045). Not only did the evkaf of Hazret-i ʿOmer camiᶜ (also called ʿOmeriye) charge 20% interest on loans, a *fetva* permitted the evkaf to charge that rate on rents which were not paid properly in advance for the year (4 130–3; III Receb 1045). Suleyman beg, the new mutevelli of the Camiᶜ-i Cedid (Yeni Camiᶜ), received assets of 128,000 akce belonging to the evkaf, including 90,000 akce from former mutevelli Şeyh Musa, 2000 akce from the heirs of the late former mutevelli Hasan efendi, 3000 akce from the late Ibrahim Paşa, 5000 akce from the rent of a mill, and 1000 akce from the rent of a garden *(bagce)* (4 237–5; III Zil-Hicce 1046). The few instances noted of credit given by evkaf suggest either that evkaf in Cyprus were not highly affluent or that they simply were not highly sophisticated credit-giving institutions. Nevertheless, many evkaf supported themselves by their income from money lending, and they provided an important source of capital for an economy eagerly seeking credit.[9]

The evkaf of Lefkoşa controlled an array of urban buildings which they rented to the highest bidders, sometimes for long periods *(icare-i tavile)*, to acquire the incomes which they devoted to pious purposes.[10] Legally their property was inalienable in perpetuity and they had a privileged tax status. Rents and length of their tenure fluctuated, sometimes sharply, because of external factors such as inflation or debasement of coinage and local factors such as short-term price fluctuations, shortage and abundance, and degree of political stability. In bad times, or worsening ones, mutevellis would eagerly rent for longer times at lower prices, while prosperity and stability encouraged mutevellis to raise rents and to reduce rental periods.

Several Cyprus foundations provided commercial shops in Lefkoşa which they rented at the highest rent they could.[11] For example, that of ʿArab Ahmed Paşa rented a bread bakery *(ekmek dukkani)* for three akce/day (1 84–4; Muharrem 1003. Cf. 24–5). The foundation of Emir efendi rented six shoemaker shops *(babucci dukkani)* for 114 akce/month (1 73–4; Muharrem 1003). Hamamci haci Mehmed, racil, had rented the Buyuk Hamam in Lefkoşa from the foundation of the late Mustafa Paşa to the end of the year for 16,000 akce until kethuday-i boluk-i yeniçeriyan ʿAbdur-Rahman and Bali çavuş offered to pay an additional 1000 akce per year (1 287–6; III Zil-Kade 1002. 292–2; I Zil-Hicce 1002). The new hamam *(hamam-i cedid)* of ʿOmeriye camiʿ evkaf was rented for three years for 4000 akce until haci Bayram agreed to pay 500 akce/year more (2 21–2; III Şaban 1016). A shop of Sultan Selim Han evkaf could only be rented for five years for 270 akce/month, and five others in ruined condition were rented for nine years *(icare-i tavil)* for the total of a mere 2400 akce (4 79–1; III Receb 1044. 192–2; II Cumadi II 1046).

A Christian priest of Degirmenlik village of Lefkoşa tried to rent one of the water mills *(degirmen)* of the evkaf of Sultan Selim Han (1 210–1; I Ramazan 1002). That foundation also possessed a new *han* in Lefkoşa called Yeni Han (later Buyuk Han)[12] which, besides eight rooms, had 12 shoe stores in front of it, a coffee house *(kahve hane)*, and a bakery *(borekci furuni)* which rented for three years for 28,200 akce/year (2300 akce/month) starting I Zil-Kade 1002; soon a man named Ibrahim offered to pay a higher rent (1 280–4; III Zil-Kade 1002. 282–3; 24 Zil-Kade 1002). That same foundation had a butcher shop *(kassab dukkani)* which it rented to deaf ʿAli the butcher (sagir ʿAli kassab) for 10 years at one akce/day to be paid monthly (1 323–1; III Cumadi II 995. Cf. 325–1; I Zil-Hicce 1002). (Hadim) Caʿfer Paşa foundation had a shop which it rented for four akce/month, while the foundation of Okci zade Mehmed Paşa rented another for two akce/day (1 23–2; Receb 1002. 61–1; II Muharrem 1003. 236–1; II Ramazan 1002). Two shops in the covered market *(suk)* of the Sultan Selim foundation were rented for 25 akce/month by semerci haci Ridvan, who died without heirs *(evlad-i zukur);* Mahmud efendi not only agreed to raise the rent to 40 akce/month, he also made a cash payment of 3000 akce for the expenses of the cami^c (2 9–1; I Sefer 1016). (Frenk) Ca^{c}fer Paşa foundation rented a new *han* with a shop and a coffee house for 21,000 akce/year, to be paid monthly (2 20–3; I Ramazan 1016). A coffee house in the market *(çarşu)* was rented to kahveci Derviş ^{c}Ali bn Mehmed for 15 akce/day, a weaver's shop *(cullah)* of the foundation of Mahmud Çelebi rented for 25 akce/month, and a borekci shop and a waterwheel *(tolab)* of Sa^{c}deddin efendi's vakf each rented for one akce/day (3 47–5; I Cumadi II 1019. 3 155–6; II Rebi^c II 1019. 3 85–6; after III Sefer 1019).

Several foundations possessed houses, other residential buildings, fields, and gardens which they rented. (Hadim) Ca^{c}fer Paşa foundation had a house it rented for five akce/month, while that of Mustafa Paşa had five two-storied *(fevkani)* and four single-storied *(tahtani)* houses which it rented for 80 akce/month (1 23–2; Receb 1002. 2 11–1; II Ramazan 1002). Holdings in agricultural lands might range from a single field to a very large estate *(çiftlik).* Half an estate belonging to Aya Sofya evkaf, the gift of Mustafa Paşa, was rented for 19,000 akce/year (3 63–2; I Receb 1019. Cf. 2 7–1; I Muharrem 1017). The vakf of Mustafa Paşa included several large estates *(çiftlik)* with 600 *donum* irrigable *(su basar)* land; yet another estate had 5000 donum fields *(tarla)* (2 22–1; I Receb 1016). In 1630 (1040) the evkaf of Haydar Paşa, Seyyid ^{c}Omer efendi, and Merika village church had houses for rent. The evkaf of Haydar Paşa at Lapta village of Girniye kaza included five estates (4 57–1; I Sefer 1044. 77–1; III Receb 1044. 132–2; III Receb 1045). Aye Hurte village church and Merika village church evkaf had fields and vineyards (three donum of the former, six of the latter) which they rented for income, while the Valide Sultan evkaf rented at least an estate. (4 132–2; III Receb 1045. 146–2; I Şevval 1045. 4 171–3; II Cumadi II 1046).

Immediately after the conquest of Cyprus former Latin ecclesiastical property which fell into the possession of the Ottoman state became available to local Muslim communities to create and to support needed religious institutions. For example, all the houses and shops that had been held in trust for pious use *(mevkuf)* in Lefkoşa were sold for 90,000 filori, and vineyards, gardens, olive orchards, sugar fields, lands, and movable and immovable property were sold with some conditions to tax collectors *(ʿummal)* for 310,000 filori. They were supposed to be sold for a just price *(hakk karari)*, namely their price during the time of the infidels *(kefere)*, and if that was not known they were only to be rented (118/59 [23] #310; 23 Zil-Hicce 979). According to a fetva, evkaf of those churches *(keniselerun evkafi)* were not valid *(sahih)*. In Magosa the former church of 'Aya Nikola, which was turned into a mosque, had 10 houses *(hane)*, 2 underground storage places *(mahzen)*, and 8 shops *(dukkan)* in its vakf; when they were rented for 22½ akce/day, or 675 akce/month, that was not adequate for the expenses of the mosque. The daily salaries alone of all the servants *(huddam)* of the mosque were 87 akce, or 31,320 akce/year. When all the evkaf were looked at, 178 houses, 73 rooms *(oda)*, 15 underground storage places, 72 shops, 20 gardens *(bostan)*, 3 pastures *(çayir)*, and so on were found, with a monthly rent of 5313 akce, or 177 akce/day, and 3756 akce/year was received from rents. Moreover, a *ziʿamet* of 20,000 akce/year was given to Ahmed, mutevelli of the mosque, for carrying out his office (118/58 (18) #304; 18 Zil-Hicce 979). The evkaf of the church called San Sasko in Magosa, which was needed as a mosque, was to be bought by the treasury *(miri)* at a fair price *(hakk karari)* and the revenues made available to the Muslims of Magosa for that mosque (148/45 KPG 6/5–247 #229; 23 Zil–Hicce 979).

In all matters regarding pious foundations, the kadi represented the authority of the state. He alone decided whether or not any proposed donation was legitimate in accordance with the Sharia and the traditions of the Ottoman state. He also determined whether or not any particular action lay within the terms set forth in writing by the founder.

Imperial order *(emr-i şerif)* for the vakf of the late Mustafa Paşa. To kadi, know that muteferrika Mehmed, son of the late Mustafa Paşa who died while a vezir, came to my Porte: Suleyman, one of his freed slaves and mutevelli who oversees the evkaf, had not given an accounting *(muhasebe)* for two years. The vakf had 120,000 akce when Suleyman died. I order that when my order arrives, correct the matter if there is a problem. (1 102–1; III Receb 1002, Kostantiniye)

The kadi ordered that a berat be given to zimmis Piyero v. Loize of Lefkoşa and Hiristifani v. Podi (?) to certify that they should dredge the water flowing in 2400 pipes *(kunk)* on the road of Taht-i Kalʿe (1 83–1; Sefer 1003).

The Administration of Cyprus *Evkaf*

The pious purposes of evkaf donors in Cyprus were often intimately mixed with self-interest. It was common practice for the donor to designate his own children *(evlad)* or other relatives and their descendants *(evlad-i evlad)* in perpetuity as administrators *(mutevellis)*, thus continuing at least a limited degree of family control over the property, in theory for as long as the line endured. Indeed the office of mutevelli of at least major evkaf usually included a generous salary in remuneration for the relatively modest duties. Doubtless overseeing large estates *(çiftlik)* such as the very wealthy ones made vakf by high ranking officials not only enhanced the economic status of the administrator but also assured his social status in the community.

Lala Mustafa Paşa, the conqueror of Cyprus, later rose to *vezir*.[13] His son muteferrika Mehmed was the mutevelli of his evkaf, the annual revenues of which then amounted to 120,000 akce just on the island. The affairs of that evkaf in Cyprus were supervised by a freed slave *('itk)* of the Pasha, Suleyman, who received a salary of 30 akce/day. After Suleyman su başi died, another freed slave of the Pasha, Sarikci Ca'fer beg, approached the court and, claiming to be in every way suitable and competent for the office, was appointed (1 102–1; III Receb, Konstantiniye. 133–1; 28 Ramazan 1002, Konstantiniye. 225–1; III Ramazan 1002). More than a decade later the supervision of the evkaf of the late Lala Mustafa Paşa remained in the hands of his freed slave bevvab Hamze aga, for example, and then former Cyprus timar defterdari Piyale efendi (2 48–1; I Şevval 1016).[14]

The mutevelli of 40,000 akce in revenues made vakf for Medine-i Munevvere by the late Cyprus mir miran Ca'fer Paşa was his freed slave *('itk)* 'Ali beg (1 197–3; III Cumadi II 1003). Likewise Murad bn 'Abdullah was a freed slave of the late 'Arab Ahmed Paşa (1 27–3; gurre Cumadi II 1002). Cyprus janissary aga Yusuf aga bn Perviz beg chose himself as mutevelli of the large estates *(çiftlik)* which he made vakf; he instructed that, after his death, his descendants *(evlad)* and his descendants' descendants *(evlad-i evlad)* should serve as mutevellis, and if they perished supervision should pass to the dervish lodge *(zaviye)* (2 22–1; 1 Receb 1016). When the Jew Refayel v. Lazari of Lefkoşa made vakf a large house for the poor of the local Jewish community, he chose himself as mutevelli, further designating that his descendants and other Jews of the community should continue as mutevellis so long as there were any; then supervision would pass to the dervish lodge (2 50–2; I Receb 1016). When haci Keyvan bn ʿAbdul-Mennan of Lefkoşa made vakf all his fields and property at Incirlu village, he was to be mutevelli for the rest of his life and then the office was to pass to his descendants, his descendants' descendants, then to his freed slaves *(ʿutaka)* and the descendants of his freed slaves *(evlad-i ʿutaka)*, and finally, were those lines to die out, half to Haremeyn-i Şerif and half to Mevlevi Hane (2 65–1; I Cumadi II 1016). According to the conditions set forth by Mehmed with property inherited from his late father Kasim aga of Girniye, his mother ʿAlem Imroz (?) became mutevelli (3 1–8; III Zil-Hicce 1018). The late ʿAli beşe bn ʿAbdullah of Koçak village designated his daughter Selime hatun to be mutevelli of the 100 olive trees *(zeytun agaci)* and 100 guruş he made vakf (3 35–2; before 7 Zil-Hicce 1018). Mevlana Ahmed efendi bn Saʿdeddin efendi of Lefkoşa kaza made vakf an estate *(çiftlik)* he inherited at Degirmenlik village with the condition that the mutevellis should be his descendants *(evlad)* (4 235–1; 12 Rebiʿ II 1043, Uskudar).[15]

Nevertheless, mutevellis had to meet local standards of education, learning, and morality. Local kadis oversaw their activities. Appointments of administrators for the large evkaf of the imperial family and high officials came from the imperial palace, although kadis were the agents for overseeing them as well. Aspirants to the office of mutevelli might report misdeeds or inadequacies of the current office holder and try to get themselves appointed instead.

Official receipt *(tezkere)* of mir miran ʿAli regarding the mosque *(camiʿ-i şerif)* built and made vakf by the late ʿArab Ahmed Paşa of Lefkoşa castle. Mutevelli Kasim is removed from his position at 10 akce/day on account of his treachery. Also among the freed slaves of Ahmed Paşa is this Murad bn ʿAbdullah, who has raised this matter. He is suitable *(yarar)*, honest *(mustakim)*, upright *(salih)*, and pious *(mutedeyyin)*, so he is appointed at 10 akce/day. (1 27–3; gurre Cumadi II 1002)

Official receipt *(tezkere)* to kadis of Lefkoşa and Magosa. Veli, mutevelli at 40 akce/day of the evkaf for the camiʿ-i şerif called Aya Sofya of the late Sultan Selim Han in Lefkoşa and Magosa, has died. It is necessary to fill this office. Hafiz haci Mehmed çelebi who presently is muʾezzin and *naʿt hvan* (reader of a eulogy to the Prophet) at Aya Sofya camiʿ in Lefkoşa, is upright, pious, and learned *(ehl-i vukuf)* and in every way suitable. He is appointed starting 14

November 1594 (1 Rebiᶜ I 1003). Carry out the duties as they have been done in the past. . . . Defterdar Bali efendi. (1 141–1)

Also in the self-interest of the donors was the practice of having the Koran read in their names—usually for their souls—at regular intervals.[16] Of course a fee or allowance had to be tied to the Koran readers, who many times were relatives of the donor. The Koran was read in Arabic; the court required proof that the would-be reader in fact had that skill.

Haci Hasan bn Yusuf who for 1½ akce/day recited *(tilavet) cuz-i şerif* (a thirtieth part of the Koran) for the soul of the late (Hadim) Caᶜfer Paşa at Aya Sofya camiᶜ in Lefkoşa of his own free will renounces it. The present imam of that mosque ᶜAbdut-Tevvab bn Mehmed is a man of learning and knowledge *(ehl-i ᶜilm)* and a man of the Koran *(ehl-i Koran)*. He is appointed. (1 285–2; 29 Zil-Kade 1002)

Haci Mehmed (?) bn Hoca Key (?), presently preacher *(hatib)* of Aya Sofya in Lefkoşa, acknowledges *(ikrar)* in the presence of Musliheddin efendi, dismissed *(maᶜzul)* from the kaza of Lefka: The 2400 akce made vakf by the late Ibrahim aga for reciting *ᶜamme-i şerif* (the short verses from the 78th sura on) and *tebareke* (67th sura) in the camiᶜ is owed me by Musliheddin. Now I have received that aforementioned 2400 akce in full from him. (1 83–3; Muharrem 1003)

The same preacher *(hatib)* was also mutevelli of 7000 akce made vakf by that Ibrahim aga for the recitation of *yeis-i şerife* and *tebareke-i şerife* (1 284–3; III Zil-Kade 1002). ᶜAbdi çavuş was appointed to recite one *cuz-i şerif* for the late Gazi (Lala) Mustafa Paşa. (1 142–3; II Rebiᶜ I 1003) 4000 akce/year of the money made vakf by janissary aga Yusuf aga was to go to someone who prayed *(duᶜa)* for him. (2 22–1; 1 Receb 1016) Caᶜfer Paşa bn ᶜAbdul-Mennan tied four akce/day to the imams and one akce/day each for the muezzins and for candles for the mescids of two villages on condition that every day after morning prayer *(sabah nemaz)* they should perform *(tilavet sure-i yeis* and after evening prayer *(salat ul-ᶜisa)* they should perform *sure-i tebareke*. An additional two akce/day was assigned to each of 10 men at Aya Sofya for performing *sure-i ana fetiha,* for reading one *cuz-i şerif,* and for reading the whole Koran *(hatim-i şerif)* every three days (2 14–1; III Muharrem 1016). Not only was Selime hatun, daughter of the late ᶜAli beşe bn ᶜAbdullah of Koçak village, the mutevelli of her father's vakf, she also read *cuz-i şerif* for him (3 35–2; before Zil-Hicce 1018).

Ibrahim efendi bn Mustafa, present imam of the mosque *(mescid)* of Debbag Hane quarter acknowledges *(ikrar, iʿtiraf)* in the presence of Hizir çelebi bn Hasan beg: The late çeri başi Husrev beg allotted 200 akce for the imam of the mosque to perform *(tilavet) sure-i şerif* every morning. I have received money for this. (3 169–1; II Şaban 1019)

The office of mutevelli of large evkaf was often remunerative. Administering several at once or supplementing an already-good salary with the revenues as mutevelli of a single vakf might make a man quite prosperous. The mutevelli of ʿArab Ahmed Paşa vakf received 10 akce/ day (or 3600 akce/year), as much as the revenue of a small timar (1 27– 3; gurre Cumadi II 1002). The acting *(kaym makam)* mutevelli on the island for the Lala Mustafa Paşa evkaf received 30 akce/day (or 10,800 akce/year), a lucrative sum (1 133–1; 28 Ramazan 1002, Konstantiniye). Kapuci Mehmed, who replaced the late kapuci Veli as mutevelli of evkaf of the late Sultan Selim Han, received 40 akce/day (14,400 akce/ year) for his services (1 189–1; 29 Rebiʿ I 1003, Konstantiniye). The vakf for Aya Sofya founded by mir miran Okci zade Mehmed Paşa paid two akce/day to its mutevelli; later that vakf paid mutevelli Mehmed 40 akce/day but then the evkaf could no longer afford that because it had become extremely weak (1 236–1; II Ramazan 1002. 158/99 (12); undated). Four decades later an overseer *(nazir)* of the evkaf of Sultan Selim Han was paid six akce/day from the income *(mahsul)* of the evkaf (4 240–2; 26 Rebiʿ I 1044, Konstantiniye).

Order to Cyprus begler begi: You sent a letter making known that Mehmed, who was mutevelli of the evkaf of Aya Sofya camiʿ in Lefkoşa castle *(kalʿesi)* on the island of Cyprus, has died. That evkaf has become extremely weak; it cannot be registered for 40 akce. When a new person was needed, you made known that haci Kasim çavuş with a 15,245 akce timar tied to Ic Il sancagi is suitable *(yarar)* and you made a petition that the office of mutevelli be given to him with a ziʿamet. Now it is forbidden for the administration of a vakf to be given with a timar *(timar ile tevliyet virulmek memnuʿdur)*. That order was written formerly . . . (158/99 (12) #284; undated)

A few donors *(vākif)* of family *(evladiye)* evkaf specifically enumerated the pious expenditures to be made from annual revenues and then stipulated that all remaining revenues should go to their administrators. Those positions undoubtedly were the most lucrative of all. After directing the payment of certain fixed sums to Haremeyn-i Şerif evkaf and to various functionaries of the Mevlevi Tekke in Lefkoşa, haci Keyvan bn ᶜAbdul-Mennan then specified that all the remaining revenues should go for the expenses of administration and overseeing (i.e., *tevliyet* and *nazaret*). Haci Keyvan and his descendants were, of course, the administrators (2 65–1; 1 Cumadi II 1016). That vakf was judged not to be necessary *(lazim)* in accordance with the opinion of Imam-i aᶜzam Ebu Hanife and all property was ordered returned to the donor; however, it was determined valid and necessary in accordance with the opinions of the Imameyn, Ebu Yusuf and Mehmed bn Hasan eş-Şeybani.[17] One vakf of Caᶜfer Paşa bn ᶜAbdul-Mennan was organized in quite a similar way, with certain specific sums allotted for Haremeyn-i Şerif and for various functionaries of the Mevlevi Tekke and all remaining revenues, whatever they may be, assigned to the mutevelli and the overseer *(nazir);* at least the former had to be a descendant of the donor. Caᶜfer Paşa's vakf, too, was at first judged not to be necessary *(lazim)* in accordance with Imam-i aᶜzam and all its property was ordered returned. When the mutevelli challenged the kadi's decision, it was found valid in accordance with the opinions of the Imameyn (2 22–1; 1 Receb 1016).

It was the duty of kadis to oversee and supervise the proper adherence to the terms of evkaf.

Piyero v. Loize and Hiristifani v. Podi (?) of Lefkoşa stated *(tm)* in the presence of ᶜAbdi çavuş, mutevelli of the evkaf of the late Mustafa Paşa: Formerly governor *(mir miran)* Ahmed Paşa made vakf 3000 akce for repairing the water flowing on the road of Taht-i Kalᶜe, which had 2400 pipes *(kunk)*. Formerly Suleyman su başi, who was mutevelli of the evkaf, had spent that money repairing the water of Hazret-i ᶜOmer, which is on the road of Taht-i Kalᶜe. ᶜAbdi denied that. When proof was requested from the zimmis, Zeyneb bn ᶜAli reis, architect *(miᶜmar)*, and Huseyn bn ᶜAbdullah confirmed them. . . . (1 83–1; Sefer 1003)

The Favorite Charities of Cyprus Donors

Within Cyprus the two institutions most esteemed by donors *(vākif)* were first the Aya Sofya camiᶜ and then the Mevlevi Tekke (dervish convent) in Lefkoşa. The former was the Lusignan and Venetian cathedral located at the very center of the round walls, which from 1571 became the principal mosque of the city. The latter, just inside Girniye gate, was built before 1600. The ᶜOmeriye camiᶜ is noteworthy because Lala Mustafa Paşa dedicated it to ᶜOmer, the second caliph of Islam, in gratitude for his miraculous appearance during the siege of Lefkoşa.

1. **Aya Sofya Mosque**[18]. The evkaf of Sultan Selim Han paid 6 akce/day to the imam of Aya Sofya cami[c], 4 akce/day to a muezzin, and 40 akce/day to its mutevelli. The mosque had its own mutevelli to look after contributions from other evkaf (1 84–1; Muharrem 1003. 285–4; Zil-Hicce 1002. 141–1; I Rebi[c] I 1003). Mir miran Okci zade Mehmed Paşa made vakf at least a shop (*dukkan*) for Aya Sofya, and others had donated a butcher shop, other shops, and large estates (*çiftlik*) (1 236–1; II Ramazan 1002. Cf. 1 325–1; I Zil-Hicce 1002. 2 42–4; 1 Receb 1011. 3 63–2; I Receb 1019). A vakf established by Ibrahim aga paid Koran readers for reading in Aya Sofya, as did the Sultan Selim evkaf (1 83–3; Muharrem 1003. 284–3; III Zil-Kade 1002. 151–1,2; Rebi[c] II 1003). The Aya Sofya mutevelli was apparently in charge of arranging the transfer of Cyprus evkaf funds worth 40,000 akce annually to Medine-i Munevvere (1 197–3; III Cumadi II 1003). Estates made vakf by Ca[c]fer Paşa bn [c]Abdul-Mennan paid Koran readers at Aya Sofya; in particular 10 men there were each to be paid two akce/day (2 14–1; III Muharrem 1016). Even a Jewish vakf paid 120 akce/year for candle wax (*revgan-i şem[c]*) for the mosque (2 50–2; I Receb 1016).

2. **Mevlevi Tekke (Convent)**[19]. The deed of foundation (*vakf name*) of Ca[c]fer Paşa bn [c]Abdul-Mennan from 1607 (1016) provides 1800 akce/year for dervish cloaks (*hirka*) for the şeyh, imam, muezzin, *tarikatci* (order members), and other spiritual teachers (*pir*) of the Mevlevi Hane near Girniye gate (2 14–1; III Muharrem 1016). According to the deed of foundation of the late Lala Mustafa Paşa, whoever recites *Mesneviy-i Şerif* in the Mevlevi Hane near Girniye gate in Lefkoşa castle should be paid two akce/day, while the imam, muezzin, prayers (*du[c]aci*), and (?) should each be paid one akce/day. In addition, he provided that on the 15th of every Şaban and on every Aşure (10 Muharrem), 920 akce should be provided for the poor (*fukara*) of the house (*hane*). Another 4000 akce/year was allotted for those who prayed (*du[c]a*) for the donor. Finally, should the line of the donor die out, the administration of the evkaf would fall to the Mevlevi Hane (2 22–1; I Receb 1016). The deed of foundation (*vakf name*) of haci Keyvan bn [c]Abdul-Mennan provides three akce/day for the salary (*vazife*) of the şeyh (şheykh) of Mevlevi Hane near Girniye gate in Lefkoşa castle for reciting the Mevleviy-i Şerif, two akce/day for ine imam of the tekke, and one akce apiece for its muezzin, prayers (*du[c]aci*), order members (*tarikatci*), and cook (*aşci*);

another eight akce/day was to be divided among the poor *(fukara)* of the houses, making a total income of 17 akce/day, to be paid monthly. Keyvan also provided that if his line should die out the administration of half the evkaf should pass to the tekke (2 65–1; 1 Cumadi II 1016). A vakf to provide inexpensive housing for the Jewish poor of Lefkoşa designated the Mevlevi Tekke to take over the administration of the vakf in the absence of Jews; more important, any income beyond 120 akce/ year annual expenditure and what was necessary to keep the house in repair was to go to the tekke (2 50–2; I Receb 1016).

In June, 1608 (Rebiᶜ I 1017) the income of the tekke (Tekye-i Şerif) of Mevlana at Girniye gate was: 2 akce/day each for the reader of the *Mesnevi* and for the duties of *duᶜaci dede*, plus an additional 15 akce/ month, from the vakf of Caᶜfer Paşa; 20 akce/day (600 akce/month) from the vakf of Saᶜdeddin for the reader of the *Mesnevi*; 2 akce/day for readers of *Mesneviy-i Şerif*, and 1 akce/day each for imam, muezzin, prayer *(duᶜaci)*, and the community *(taife)*, plus 5 akce/day (150 akce/ month) for dervishes *(dervişan)* and their kitchen, or, in total, 330 akce/ month from the vakf of Yusuf aga-i yeniçeriyan sabika (former janissary aga); 510 akce/month from the vakf of haci Keyvan, 3 akce for a *Mesnevi* reader and 1 akce each for an imam, muezzin, prayer *(duᶜaci)*, and cook *(aşci)*; 10 akce/day (300 akce/month) from the vakf of haci Keyvan; 900 akce/month from the vakf of Saᶜdi çavuş; 1 akce/day (30 akce/month) from the coffee house *(kahve hane)* of the vakf of Suleyman beg; and 5 akce/day (150 akce/month) for poor dervishes from the vakf of the late Kat Ibrahim çelebi. They were collected by Derviş Yusuf (2 76–1).

3. ᶜOmeriye Mosque.* Another patronized by Ottoman donors of evkaf was the great Companion of the Prophet and second rightly guided caliph ᶜOmer (ᶜUmar ibn al-Khattab). The Augustinian church of Lefkoşa was converted to a mosque and dedicated to him.[20]

To Cyprus begler begi and to Lefkoşa kadi: My vezir [Lala] Mustafa [Paşa] made a petition (ᶜarz) to my Porte. When Lefkoşa castle *(kalᶜesi)* was conquered *(feth)* with the help of God, he made a petition to my Porte that a camiᶜ with the patronymic *(kunye)* ᶜOmer bn ᶜAvs be made where Mustafa made his first prayer *(nemaz)*. He built *(bina)* a hamam for the imam, preacher *(hatib)*, and other

* also called Hazreti-ᶜOmer

functionaries *(murtezikalar)* there. Now they have made known that they do not want the hamam to be built. If they build a hamam, every loss *(zarar)* will occur to the vakf. I order that when my order arrives, you should look and see if there is a need for a hamam like that. If so, let it be built by vakf again. Let the hamam be built by someone from outside *(haricdan)*. (1 204–2; III Rebiʿ II 988)

The late Gazi Mustafa Paşa made an evkaf *(taʿyin)* from his own property *(mal)* for the beautiful place of worship *(maʿbed-i latife)* called Hazret-i ʿOmer camiʿ-i şerif in Lefkoşa castle on the island of Cyprus. Now it is right and necessary to perform *(tilavet)* in that camiʿ: after morning prayer *sure-i yeis,* after mid-afternoon prayer *(salat-iʿasr), sure-i necm* (53rd sura), and after nightfall *(ʿişa), suret ul-melek,* for each of which two akce/day salary *(vazife)* is assigned *(taʿyin).* Mevlana uş-şerif şeyh ʿAli is upright and religious *(salih ve mutedeyyin).* (1 205–3; 7 Cumadi II 1003)

4. The Holy Cities of Mecca and Medina. The favorite charities of Cyprus donors *(vākif)* beyond the island itself were the Holy Cities of Mecca and Medina in Arabia.[21] Usually the purpose of such evkaf was to support the poor of the Holy Cities. Forty thousand akce/year was made vakf for the evkaf of Medine-i Munevvere by the late Caʿfer Paşa bn ʿAbdul-Mennan; later several estates *(çiftlik)* with unspecified revenues at other villages were donated. Clearly Caʿfer Paşa was a devotee of Medina (1 197–3; III Cumadi II 1003. 2 14–1; III Muharrem 1016). Mehmed bn Kasim aga tied houses and gardens at Girniye kaza and lands *(arazi)* at Temploz village to an extent that the mutevelli, his mother, would be able to send 1000 akce every year to Medine-i Munevvere (3 1–8; III Zil-Hicce 1018). Haci Keyvan bn ʿAbdul-Mennan donated an estate at Incirlu village of Lefkoşa which, among other charitable institutions, was to provide 2000 akce/year for Haremeyn-i Şerif evkaf (2 65–2; 1 Cumadi II 1016). Likewise an estate *(çiftlik)* at Iliya village of Girniye kaza with 13 two-storied *(fevkani)* and single-storied *(tahtani)* houses *(menzil),* two underground storage depots *(mahzen),* two olive oil presses *(zeytun degirmen),* and over 290 olive trees, was to pay 2000 akce/year to Medine-i Muneverre; when the line died out, the entire property was to pass to the vakf (4 146–2; I Şevval 1045). Present janissary aga of the island of Cyprus Yusuf aga bn Perviz beg made vakf estates *(çiftlik)* at Piskobi and Morfo with the condition that 16,000 akce in revenues be given annually to Haremeyn-i Şerif and other evkaf for readings for the soul *(ruh)* of the *server-i enbiya* and *habib-i huda* Muhammed Mustafa; one vakf of Caʿfer Paşa requires a similar annual expenditure of 3000 akce for the souls of Muhammed, ʿAli, and the Companions *(Eshab)* (2 22–1; 1 Receb 1016. 2 14–1; III Muharrem 1016). At one period a total of 422,000 akce/year was being collected from the treasury *(hazine)* of Cyprus for the poor *(fukara)* of Haremeyn-i Şerif (#160/89 [42] #24).

5. **Local Communities.** Urban quarters and villages were frequently designated beneficiaries of pious donations. Indeed those two units prob-ably represented primary focuses of personal loyalties. Şamakli village mosque *(mescid)*, for example, had a vakf which supported it (3 85–4; after III Sefer 1019). So did the church *(kenise)* of Aye Hurte (?) village of Lefkoşa kaza (4 112–1; II Muharrem 1045). Merdibanli Huseyn quarter of Lefkoşa had a vakf for its mosque *(mescid)* which gave ʿAyni bint ʿAbdullah a 3000 akce loan at 20% interest (4 234–2; 18 Ramazan 1045). The church of Terbiyodu quarter had its foundation, too (4 130–1; III Receb 1045). For the vakf of the church of Merika (?) village mutevelli Veliyatdi (?) v. Kistintin purchased six donum of vineyards and a house *(hane)* at another village (4 132–2; III Receb 1045). In Cyprus nearly all the foundations organized that way explicitly served communal houses of worship, although elsewhere that was not always the case.

6. **Non-Muslims (Zimmis).** Although it is not clear what difficulties Zimmis faced in establishing evkaf, they did succeed in establishing them, both for their places of worship and for their own communities. Although three donum of lands *(arazi)* in Aye Hurte (?) village in Lef-koşa kaza had belonged to the evkaf of the church *(kenise)* for more than 40 years, the late Bavlo v. Zorzi of that village and his descendants had usurped that property when rahib Yorgi was mutevelli; the present mutevelli, Mihayel v. Kistintin, successfully proved the evkaf's owner-ship (4 112–1; II Muharrem 1045). The vakf for the church of Merika (?) village acquired vineyards and a house from Istave (?) bint Paka (?) three years ago for 1680 akce (4 132–2; III Receb 1045). Zimmi Murad v. Eymur beşe, mutevelli of the church of Terbiyodi quarter, asserted that the vakf was owed 2000 akce by the late Ilyas, whose orphans have as guardian *(vasi)* their mother the Armenian Mogal bint Haristo (4 129–3, 130–1; III Receb 1045).

Rafayel v. Lazari of Kal'e-i Lefkoşa acknowledges before Hamze aga, whom he appointed mutevelli: The 50 two-stories houses and six one-storied houses at Zeyn ul-Abidin quarter in the castle, of known boundaries, which I bought from the Jew *(Yahudi)* Iliya, I make a valid vakf *(sahih)*, with its water, well *(kuyu)*, threshing floor *(harman)*, and all its dependencies *(cemi' tevabi'ile)*, with this condition *(şart):* During his lifetime let him be mutevelli, and let that house *(dar)* be rented to poor Jews *(Yahuda fukarasina)*. Every year let 120 akce from the rent *(icare)* be given for candlewax *(revgan-i şem')* for the mosque *(cami'-i şerif)* called Aya Sofya in Kal'e-i Lefkoşa. Let them repair *(ta'mir)* the house with the money that remains from the rent. Let it be possessed *(mutasarrif)* for dervish lodges. After him let the mutevellis be the descendants of the descendants of his descendants *(evlad-i evlad-i evlad)*. After the share for the vakf is given every year, let the rest be possessed for the dervish lodges. After the descendants of the donor possess it, let the mutevelli be appointed *(nasb)* from the Jewish community *(Yahudi taifesinden)*. Let poor Jews live in that house. After 120 akce is given every year for the rent of that mosque for candlewax, let the house *(dar)* be repaired with the remaining money. After that I handed over *(teslim)* that house to the aforementioned mutevelli. After the mutevelli confirmed *(tasdik)* the donor in his presence . . . , the vakf was found necessary. (2 50–2; I Receb 1016)

A "Slave Family" of Wealthy Donors

Conspicuous among the founders and administrators of evkaf was the slave family of "'Abdul-Mennan," Ca'fer, Keyvan, Mehmed, and Dilaver, all important men in Cyprus between 1590 and 1610.[22] The most powerful of the family, and undoubtedly the wealthiest, was (Frenk) Ca'fer Paşa who served as governor *(mir miran)* of the province and later as kapudan of the fleet. Ca'fer was a generous patron of the Holy Cities of Mecca and Medina, Aya Sofya cami'i in Lefkoşa and the Mevlevi Tekke. The administration of his evkaf was restricted to his men, among whom were Mehmed efendi bn 'Abdul-Mennan and 'azablar agasi Dilaver aga bn 'Abdul-Mennan, and then to his descendants (2 14–1; 20–3; 22–1; 76–1). Haci Keyvan bn 'Abdul-Mennan of Lefkoşa castle also was a patron of the Mevlevi Tekke and Haremeyn-i Şerif, although on a much more modest scale than Ca'fer Paşa. He had endowed the former with 2000 akce/year, the latter with over 800 akce/month. Like Ca'fer, Keyvan required that the administration of the vakf be confined to his descendants *(evlad)* (2 65–1; 76–1).

Besides being an administrator of evkaf of Ca'fer Paşa, former defter kethudasi Mehmed efendi bn 'Abdul-Mennan made vakf a single olive tree at Eglence village of Lefkoşa kaza, capable of producing about three kile per year, with the stipulation that the income be used to repair a fountain *(çeşme)* and water channel *(su yoli)* which he had created with an earlier vakf (2 13–1; II Muharrem 1017). Another freed slave of Ca‘fer Paşa was ‘Ali beg, mutevelli of his evkaf, who supervised the annual transfer of 40,000 akce to Medine-i Muneverre (1 197–3; III Cumadi II 1003).

A vakfiye of present Cyprus begler begi, mir miran Ca‘fer Paşa bn ‘Abdul-Mennan dated 21–30 June 1599 (I Muharrem 1008) gives in detail huge holdings being made vakf: six separate estates, *(çiftlik)*, each one vast enough to contain land in several villages. They are enumerated by mutevelli ‘Osman beg bn ‘Abdul-Mennan in the presence of Haremeyn-i Şerif mutevelli Ahmed bn Mehmed. Lands are included in Lefkoşa, Limosa, and Tuzla nahiyes, all his private property *(mulk)*. One estate contained 5 two-storied *(tahtani)* and single-storied *(fevkani)* houses, 4 houses with fruit trees, 4 gardens, 1000 donum of fields *(tarla)*, 2 more houses, 4 vineyards, 10 yoke of oxen, 600 head of sheep and goats, and 150 keyl each of wheat and barley for seed *(tohum)*. Another estate included lands and pastures at several villages, 11 houses with courtyards *(havli)*, 10 yoke of oxen, 800 sheep and goats, along with 200 keyl each of wheat and barley for seed. Still another included 20 two-storied and single-storied houses, 7 irrigable gardens with fruit trees and olive trees, a new vineyard, an oil mill *(zeytun degirmani)*, a wind mill *(yel degirmani)*, and a water mill *(su degirmani)*, 2500 donum of irrigable fields, 200 head of sheep and goats, and 100 keyl each of wheat and barley for seed.

From the revenues, 40,000 akce/year is to be delivered to the Tomb of the Prophet plus another 20,000 akce/year for the preachers, imams, and muezzins at the Tomb to divide equally among themselves. Another 5000 akce should be used for the purchase of olive oil *(revgan-i zeyt)* from the island. Six thousand akce cash should go to the mutevelli and the şeyh of the evkaf of kutb ul-‘arifin Mevlana Hudavendigar (Celaleddin Rumi) in Konya, to buy their distinctive garb. The mutevelli ought to receive 15 akce/day, and whoever is şeyh ul-Islam in Istanbul ought to receive 5 akce/day as overseer *(nazir)* of the vakf; a scribe *(katib)* should receive 8 akce/day and a collector of the revenues *(cabi)* 5 akce/day. The remaining income of the estates should remain the property of his descendants and his freed slaves and their descendants, finally to be joined to the evkaf of Haremeyn-i Şerif. (19/80, p. 207–208 #151; 16/116, p. 210 #151)

Two years later Ca‘fer Paşa seemed intent on using up what holdings he might have forgotten in 1598 (1008), or perhaps had recently acquired: for example, 280 olive trees and nine carob trees along with houses at a village of Tuzla kaza. In Magosa, five two-storied and single-storied houses, fruit trees, gardens with irrigation channels, eight shops in various places, a coffee house, two grist mills *(tahuni),* a well, and more were set aside and made a valid vakf to support those in Aya Sofya cami^c in Magosa, particularly those who pray for his soul *(ruh-i şerif)* on Friday, but also for the expenses of a water channel *(su yoli)* which brings water to Magosa. As in his other foundations Ca^cfer required that the mutevellis be his descendants (16/116, p. 310–311 #152).

In 1607 (1016), promoted to commander *(kapudan)* of the imperial fleet, Ca^cfer Paşa founded yet another vakf. That vakf constituted still another estate *(çiftlik);* the mutevellis were again supposed to be his descendants, and extra revenues again were to accrue to them. From the revenues, 3000 akce/year was assigned to the servants of the Tomb of Muhammed. A sum of 640 akce/year was assigned for beeswax *(revgan-i şem^c)* for Aya Sofya cami^c in Lefkoşa and 1800 akce for whoever related the *Mesnevi* and whoever was şeyh of the Mevlevi Hane, as well as for the dervishes, their imam, and muezzin. More money went to Ca^cfer Paşa mosque *(mescid),* near Baf gate. Regular prayers and Koran-readings were to be made for him (16/116, p. 211–212 #153).

Flexibility and Pragmatism of Administrators and Kadis

Under certain strictly controlled circumstances it was possible to circumvent explicit stipulations of the donor *(vākif).* Vakf property might even be sold if the testimony of experts showed that it was most advantageous to the vakf to do so. Authority to act lay with the kadi in his role as overseer of evkaf.

^cAbdi çavuş bn Yusuf, mutevelli of the evkaf of the late Mustafa Paşa in Lefkoşa, set forth a claim in the presence of Turak çavuş bn ^cOmer, zi^camet-holder *(ez-za^cim):* The Pasha's evkaf is in ruins *(harab).* Imperial permission was granted to sell landed property *(^cakar)* which is not beneficial *(muntefi^c),* namely seven single-storied *(tahtani)* and three two-storied *(fevkani)* uninhabitable ruined houses *(harabe evler)* in the city. To do so is in every way beneficial to the evkaf. They should be sold to Turak in accordance with the imperial order *(firman)* for 7000 akce. Experts *(ehl-i vukuf)* confirm that the estate *(menzil)* is in ruins *(harabe),* not beneficial to the vakf, and should be sold at the imperial market *(suk-i sultaniye).* (1 203–1; 1 Receb 1003)

To Cyprus begler begi, to Lefkoşa kadi, and to Magosa kadi: You, Lefkoşa kadi, sent a letter *(mektub)* to my Porte. Some houses *(evler)* and shops *(dukkan-*

lar) of the vakf of the late Mustafa Paşa, who died while vezir, in Lefkoşa castle and Magosa castle belonging to the mosque *(camiᶜ-i şerif)* called Hazret-i ᶜOmeriye in Lefkoşa castle are in ruins *(harabe)*. They are not able to be occupied or to be rented for the vakf. When that was attested to *(muşahede)*, and when it was petitioned *(ᶜarz)* to exchange that for something useful for the vakf, in accordance with the Sharia, an order was made. I order that you investigate the matter in accordance with justice *(hakk ve ᶜadl)* and see what should be done in accordance with the Sharia. You should do what is most useful *(enfaᶜ)* for the vakf. Now some people, exceeding their authority *(fuzulen)*, issued an order *(emr-i şerif)* and made known that they did not want the hamam to be built. If they build the hamam, every loss will occur to the vakf. (1 204–1; II Şaban 999)

A garden called Dizdar Bagce outside Baf gate, with a water wheel *(tolab)* and trees *(escar)*, was made vakf for a school *(mekteb)* of the conqueror of Cyprus the late Mustafa Paşa, and formerly was rented every year. Now it is in ruins *(harabe)*, its walls destroyed and stones falling down. It no longer is of any use to the vakf. It is rented for nine years *(icare-i tavile)* for 400 akce in advance *(muᶜaccelen)* to Mustafa beşe on the condition *(şart)* that he make it flourish, pay 1200 akce/year for the school, and repair *(taᶜmir)* the water wheel and garden walls. Let that 1200 akce be paid month by month. (2 63–1; 1 Muharrem 1016)

Helva usta ᶜAli of Lefkoşa bought five shops of the evkaf of the late Sultan Selim Han from present mutevelli Huseyn aga's substitute *(kaym makam)* mevlana Mehmed efendi for 2400 akce for nine years (i.e., for 150 akce/year) because they are in ruins *(harabe)*. (4 79–1; III Receb 1044)

The estate *(çiftlik)* of Lakine (?)/Lakite (?) village of Lefkoşa kaza, made vakf for ᶜOmeriye mosque by the late Mustafa Paşa, conqueror of the island of Cyprus, should be taken from those who do not pay rent and given immediately for 12 years for 38,000 akce/year to zimmis (Christians) Filibo v. Bernardi, Papa Kargi (?) v. Papa Yani, Loizi v. Andreye, and Bernardi (?) v. Covani. They have agreed to expend 20,000 akce/year for the renewal of some rooms and a stable and to provide 200 loads of fertilizer *(gubre)* every year for the fields of the foundation. (2 7–1; I Muharrem 1017)

If the court could be convinced that selling the property or using it in some other irregular way would enhance its value, that could be done. In particular, emergency methods might be taken where through neglect, war, or natural hazards vakf property was destroyed.[23]

Conclusion

The predominance of members of the military class among both donors and administrators of foundations up to the period 1610 is to be expected. Among the local Muslims, the military would have been the first to have had salaries and other income in quantities large enough to permit such generosity or indeed to have need to fear imperial confiscation. Not only were they the most frequent donors, their foundations were also the wealthiest (except for the imperial evkaf, a different category because their founders never went to Cyprus). Military administrators maintained military influence over the evkaf. Nevertheless, until an educated local ʿulema (religious class) could be trained, the military were the best-educated group in the community; they were the only group capable of providing administrators who could read, write, and keep accurate records. (It would be interesting to learn whether or not the sharp decline in the influence of military over evkaf is connected with a corresponding decline in their socioeconomic position.)

The sources of income of the foundations of Cyprus were agriculture, urban commercial rent, and interest from lending. Agricultural holdings ranging from small fields, orchards, gardens, or vineyards to huge estates provided by far the greatest proportion of all evkaf revenues. Next in importance were the many shops, houses, hamams, hans, and covered markets of Lefkoşa, and to some extent Magosa. Finally, a few evkaf supported themselves all or in part by lending out money granted to them for that purpose at interest rates of from 10% to 20%. The urban commercial evkaf provided an array of buildings to meet the needs of the merchant community, while the money-lending evkaf provided the community with much-needed capital at a fair interest rate.

Among the pious purposes served by local evkaf were payment of all or part of the salaries of mosque functionaries and the provision of water for the citizens of Lefkoşa and Magosa. The favorite concerns of Cyprus donors during the period c. 1580–1640 were the mosque of Aya Sofya and the Mevlevi Tekke in Lefkoşa and the great foundations connected with the Holy Cities of Arabia. Favorite stipulations included the recitation of Koranic passages, or sometimes prayers, for the donor after his death by the administrators or by other mosque and tekke functionaries. Only a few foundations were centered in urban quarters or villages, devoted to the interests of those communities, as was common in Anatolia, but those that had begun to appear in the 1630s may perhaps be considered harbingers of the future. Some of those evkaf belonging to Christian communities no doubt antedated the Ottoman conquest; but perhaps among the Muslims the disparate individuals and families, whether as immigrants from scattered communities in Anatolia or as local converts, had finally lived together long enough to find common interests, to develop mutual trust, and to give for the benefit of their neighbors.

Latin ecclesiastical property seized at the time of the conquest provided a windfall for the new Muslim communities in Lefkoşa and particularly in Magosa where the Latin church establishment had been large and there were few Muslims (or Greek Orthodox) to claim it. When local Muslims petitioned that they needed another mosque, fine abandoned churches were available; if they lacked adequate revenues to support their mosques, much captured property was available to be so dedicated.

Many donors, particularly wealthier ones, required that the administrators always be their descendants; sometimes not just the descendants of the donor but indeed descendants of his freed slaves were to be administrators in perpetuity. The absence of surnames prevents judging how that was practiced except in a few cases where claims to establish such relationships were made before the court; likewise it is not possible to discover whether certain families may have been especially active as vakf administrators. Such evkaf were designed at least in part to secure the self-interest of the family of the donor, and administrators of the larger evkaf received handsome salaries. Perhaps the most lucrative of all were the few evkaf which stipulated that all revenues not specifically assigned should go to the administrators. However, the administrators had to meet minimal qualifications set by the court, depending on the requirements of the donors. Sometimes, either in piety or out of concern that the vakf might not be judged necessary, donors stipulated that particular revenues should go to the local kadi, or mufti, or the şeyh ul-Islam in Istanbul.

The court of Lefkoşa was responsible for ensuring that the terms of the donors were adhered to. However, the court supervised with a flexibility which permitted or even encouraged the evkaf to pursue their own economic self-interest. Foundations with urban commercial property rented to the highest bidder to maximize revenues in good times, for the rents could be raised whenever a qualified person bid more; in order to attract renters during times of economic or political instability or disorder a vakf could lower rents and extend terms. The key question was for the court, or court-appointed experts, to agree that a particular

action was most useful for the vakf. The court and the experts understood something about economic and social utility; they allowed the
evkaf to meet new problems with a bit of pragmatism rather than
clinging to the letter of texts of deeds of pious foundations *(vakf name)*.
So foundations in Lefkoşa were aided in dealing with problems brought
on by inflation, natural disasters, new competition, or other emergencies.

NOTES

1. A comprehensive list of buildings, services, and miscellaneous other benef-
    ices connected with various evkaf has been published by Halim Baki Kunter
    in "Türk Vakıfları ve Vakfiyeleri üzerine mücmel bir etüd," *Vakıflar Dergisi*
    1. 1938. 103–129. Also included is a list of titles of officials obligated to
    carry out those duties, who in many cases must also be considered among
    the "services" supported by evkaf. pp. 111ff.
2. Cf. Haim Gerber, who finds a "rudimentary 'public spiritedness' " in Bursa.
    See his paper "The Waqf Institution in 17th century Anatolian Bursa,"
    submitted to the *International Seminar on the Social and Economic Aspects
    of the Muslim Waqf,* Jerusalem, 24–28 June 1979. One might say the same
    about Kayseri.
3. On the importance of sultanic evkaf to the urban economy, see Ö. L.
    Barkan, "Social and Economic Aspects of Vakifs in the Ottoman Empire in
    the 15th and 16th Centuries," *International Seminar.* . . . H. Gerber gives a
    detailed account of the functioning of such evkaf for the 17th century in the
    important city of Bursa. *International Seminar* . . .
4. Women do not seem to have played a conspicuous role as founders of evkaf
    in that period in Cyprus. However, 36% (913 of 2517) of evkaf recorded in
    the Istanbul defter of 1546 were founded by women. Ömer Lütfi Barkan
    and E. H. Ayverdi, *İstanbul Vakıfları Tahrir Defteri 953 (1546) Tarihi.*
    Istanbul, 1970. p. vii. Likewise 39 of 151 total evkaf listed in Ankara by
    Ongan were founded by women. Halit Ongan, "Ankara Şer'iye Mahkemesi
    Sicillerinde Kayıtlı Vakfiyeler," *Vakıflar Dergisi* 5.1962.213–222. Roded
    and Marcus estimated, respectively, that women founded 41% and 36% of
    17th–19th century evkaf in Aleppo. Ruth Roded, "The Waqf in Ottoman
    Aleppo," *International Seminar* . . . Abraham Marcus, "Piety and Profit:
    The Waqf in the Society and Economy of 18th Century Aleppo," *Interna-
    tional Seminar* . . .
5. According to Akdağ they were *ayan* and *eşraf*, i.e., notables. Mustafa Ak-
    dağ, *Türkiye'nin İktisadi ve İçtimai Tarihi.* v. II, 1453–1559. Ankara, 1971.
    p. 26. Those in Bursa, according to Gerber, were men of state with military
    titles who had to keep careful records. *International Seminar* . . .
6. Five out of the 42 evkaf identified in the sicils of Lefkoşa were founded by

non-Muslims. For zimmi evkaf in Kayseri, see R. Jennings, "Zimmis (Non-Muslims) in Early 17th Century Ottoman Judicial Records—The Sharia Court of Anatolian Kayseri," *JESHO* 21.1978.276ff. See also "Loans and Credit in Early 17th Century Ottoman Judicial Records—The Sharia Court of Anatolian Kayseri," *JESHO* 16.1973.204, 207, 209. M. E. Düzdağ has published over a hundred fetvas from Ebus Suud concerning zimmis. *Şeyhülislam Ebussuud Efendi Fetvaları Işığında 16. Asır Türk Hayatı.* Istanbul, 1972. pp. 89–107. Zimmi evkaf were relatively uncommon; for example, none are listed in the 1546 evkaf defter for Istanbul published by Barkan and Ayverdi and only one of 106 Ankara evkaf listed by Ongan for the 16th, 17th, or 18th century was founded by a zimmi. H. Ongan, "Ankara Şer'iye Mahkemesi...," *Vakıflar Dergisi* (hereafter referred to as *VD*) 5.1962.217 (#87). Akdağ, however, reports the existence of numerous Christian and Jewish evkaf in Istanbul on the basis of research in Istanbul judicial records. *Türkiye'nin...*, v. 2, p. 40. Roded found 10% of Aleppo evkaf non-Muslim, mostly from the 19th century, while Marcus calculated only 4.5%. "The Waqf...," and "Piety and Profit...," in *International Seminar...*

7. That was true of contemporary Kayseri. According to Roded, 70% of Aleppo evkaf over a later period were identified with town quarters. p. 12. Marcus found all but 15 dedicated to causes within Aleppo. p. 10. For other examples, see Kunter, "Türk Vakıfları...," p. 122, #34; p. 123, #9. Barkan indicates that such evkaf usually were centered around mosques. Barkan and Ayverdi, *İstanbul Vakıfları...*, p. xxvii.

8. Numerous instances of credit offered in Kayseri by evkaf are cited in Jennings, "Loans and Credit...," pp. 178f, 203ff. Forty-six percent of the evkaf (1161 of 2517) listed in the 1546 Istanbul defter lent money at interest. Barkan and Ayverdi, *İstanbul Vakıfları...*, p. xxxi. According to Yediyıldız, 32% of the 18th-century Anatolian evkaf he studied lent money at interest. B. Yediyıldız, "La Portée Économique des Vaqfs Turcs au XVIIIe siècle," *International Seminar...* According to Marcus, the normal rate in 18th-century Aleppo was 10% although rates as high as 18% occurred. "Piety and Profit..." Cf. Halil Inalcik, "Capital Formation in the Ottoman Empire," *The Journal of Economic History* 29.1969. 100ff, 132ff. Akdağ also has evidence on money-lending evkaf. *Türkiye'nin...* v. II, pp. 211f. Mutafčieva considers evkaf to have been the main institution of credit in the Ottoman empire. "Problèmes fondamentaux de l'étude du Vakf en tant que partie de la structure sociale et économique des Balkans sous la domination Ottomane (XVe–XIXe siècles)," *International Seminar...* For a perspective discussion of the origin and development of the institution see Jon E. Mandaville, "Usurious Piety: The Cash Waqf Controversy in the Ottoman Empire," *IJMES* 10.1979.289–308.

9. On the basis of 16th-century Istanbul judicial records Akdağ has traced a pattern of rising interest rates, finally reaching 20% legally. *Türki-*

ye'nin . . . , v. II, pp. 206–214. A similar pattern can be traced in Kayseri and Trabzon. Cf. Inalcik, "Capital Formation . . . ," p. 132ff. Barkan and Ayverdi give detailed information on the use of interest. *İstanbul Vakıfları* . . . , p. xxxi. According to Akdağ, Barkan and Ayverdi (pp. xxxi, xxxviiff), and Mutafčieva ("Problèmes fondamentaux . . .") interest rates became excessive and usury a severe problem in the latter part of the 16th century. For further evidence consult M. Akdağ, *Celali İsyanları (1550– 1603)*. Ankara, 1963. pp. 37ff, 55. The 18th-century evkaf studied by Yediyıldız lent money for 15% interest. "La Portée . . ."

10. According to Marcus 14% of vakf property in Aleppo was houses and they provided 19% of vakf revenues. "Piety and Profit . . ." In 18th–19th-century Aleppo the vast majority of evkaf were small endowments of buildings. Roded, "The Waqf . . ." Six percent of the total revenues of the 18th-century evkaf studied by Yediyıldız were from houses. "La Portée . . ." Gerber calculated that 24% of the houses in late 17th-century Bursa were vakf. "The Waqf Institution . . ." Cf. Suraiya Faroqhi, "The Tekke of Haci Bektaş: Social Position and Economic Activities," *IJMES* 7.1976.183–208 and "Vakif Administration in 16th Century Konya. The Zaviye of Sadreddin-i Konevi," *JESHO* 17.1974.145–172.

11. Thirty percent of the total revenues of the 18th-century Anatolian evkaf studied by Yediyıldız came from commercial buildings, especially small shops. "La Portée . . ." In Aleppo Marcus found that 33% of vakf property and 54% of revenues came from that source. "Piety and Profit . . ."

12. Cf. Gönül Öney, "Büyük Han (The Great Inn) and Kumarcilar Hani (The Gambler's Inn) at Nicosia," pp. 277–282, with detailed ground plans and photographs, in the *Proceedings of The First International Congress of Cypriot Studies*. Ankara, 1971. Cf. Fikret Çuhadaroğlu and Filiz Oğuz, "Kıbrıs'ta Türk Eserleri/Turkish Historical Monuments," pp. 12f, in *Rölöve ve Restorasyon Dergisi* 2.1975.1–76. Also Cevdet Çağdaş, *Kıbrısta Türk Devri Eserleri*. Lefkoşa, 1965.p. 11.

13. A Bosnian educated in the imperial palace, Lala (or Kara, or Gazi) Mustafa Paşa (d. 1580) had reached the rank of Şam begler begi when he was made commander of the Cyprus expedition. Later he was commander in the east and distinguished himself by conquests in Georgia and Shirvan, finally attaining the rank of vezir. Bekir Kütükoğlu, "Mustafa Paşa," *İslam Ansiklopedisi* (hereafter referred to as *İA*); J. H. Kramers, "Mustafa Pasha Lala," *EI*.[1]

14. In Ottoman society freed military slaves were often treated as family members. Indeed, that was frequently the case with other slaves too.

15. See 2 48–1, 50–2; 3 19–2; and 4 146–2 for other examples of *evladiye* evkaf.

16. Several examples of this practice may be found in Barkan and Ayverdi, *İstanbul Vakıfları* . . . , pp. xxviif. Cf. Kunter, "Türk Vakıfları," #29, p. 125.

17. The criteria for the establishment of a valid vakf put forth by Ebu Hanife were notoriously onerous. Ebu Yusuf, on the other hand, seems to have considered a vakf valid almost from the moment the words are expressed. For Mehmed Şeybani the vakf became established only when the property was handed to the administrator. Unless the vakf is necessary in the opinion of the Imameyn, it is unnecessary in the opinion of the Imam-i ʿAzam. Ali Himmet Berki, "Hukuki ve İçtimaî Bakımdan Vakıf," *VD* 5.1962.12f. Fuad Köprülü, "Vakıf müessessesinin hukukî mahiyeti ve tarih tekamülü," *VD* 1.1938.1–6. Cf. Düzdağ, *Şeyhülislam . . .* , p. 299. Cf. Barkan and Ayverdi, *İstanbul Vakıfları . . .* , pp. xxiif.

18. For a complete description and history of the church see chapter 4, "Église métropolitaine Sainte-Sophie de Nicosie", pp. 78–141, 713–715, in C. Enlart, *L'Art Gothique et la Renaissance en Chypre.* 2 v. Paris, 1899. See also George Jeffery, *A Description of the Historic Monuments of Cyprus.* Nicosia, 1918.

19. The Mevlevi Tekke was a convent of the so-called order of Whirling Dervishes, with its central headquarters in Konya, where the tomb of the founder Mevlana Celal ed-din Rumi is located. Barkan has systematically revealed the role of dervishes in the spread of Islam in the Ottoman empire. "Osmanlı İmparatorluğunda bir İskân ve Kolonizasyon Metodu olarak Vakıflar ve Temlikler I, İstilâ devirlerinin Kolonizatör Türk Dervişleri ve Zaviyeler," *VD* 2.1942.278–353. Speros Vryonis has stressed the key role played by evkaf in the competition in Anatolia between Islam and the Orthodox church. *Decline of Medieval Hellenism in Asia Minor and the Process of Islamization . . .* Berkeley and Los Angeles, 1971. p. 352. Mutafčieva has emphasized the importance of evkaf in supporting the presence of dervishes in the Balkans. "Problèmes fondamentaux . . ." R. O'Fahey has stressed the importance of zaviyes and tekkes in the process of conversion on the frontier in the Sudan. "Endowment, Privilege and Estate in the Central and Eastern Sudan," *International Seminar . . .*

   The Mevlevi were one of the most prestigious orders in the Ottoman empire; their role in the islamization of Anatolia was considerable, although it would be very difficult to document a similar role in Cyprus. Abdülbaki Gölpınarlı, "Mevlevilik," *İA;* Vryonis, *Decline . . .* , pp. 381–396. T. Yazici, D. S. Margoliouth, and F. de Jong, "Mawlawiyya," *EI².* The Mevlevi Tekke in Lefkoşa is mentioned by C. Çağdaş, who made the tekke into an ethnographic museum organized on a dervish theme. *Kıbrısta Türk Devri . . .* , pp. 21f. Cf. F. Çuhadaroğlu and F. Oğuz, "Kıbrıs'ta Türk Eserleri . . . ," pp. 12f. Oktay Aslanapa, *Kıbrısda Türk Eserleri.* Lefkoşa, 1978.

20. The church is described by C. Enlart, *L'Art Gothique . . .* , v. 1, pp. 162–167.

21. A summary of an order *(telhis)* of vezir-i ʿazam Yemişçi Hasan Paşa mentions 640,000 akce or 36 *yük* akce (3,600,000) from Cyprus belonging to Haremeyn-i Şerif. In 1601 (1010) the total revenue of Haremeyn-i Şerif was

37,144 altun, which was dispersed as follows: 8806 altun to Ka'be-i Mu'azzama in Mecca, 25,685 altun to Medine-i Munevvere, and 1622 altun to Jerusalem (Kuds-i Şerif). Cengiz Orhonlu, *Telhisler (1597–1607)*. Istanbul, 1970. pp. 28f, 133. Lala Mustafa Paşa had established a vakf for Haremeyn-i Şerif in Jerusalem when he was Şam begler begi. See Uriel Heyd, *Ottoman Documents on Palestine, 1552–1615*. Oxford, 1960. p. 145. For a detailed study of Harameyn-i Şerif in a more distant Ottoman province at a later time see M. Hoexter's study of Algiers. "Waqf al-Haramayn and the Turkish Government in Algiers," *International Seminar . . .*

22. Ca'fer Paşa was either a palace slave or the slave of some high officials, and a convert to Islam. At the same time he seems to have had a slave household of his own. On the subject of slaves' slaves see I. M. Kunt, "Kulların Kulları," *Boğaziçi Üniversitesi Dergisi* 3.1975.27–42. The usual patronymic taken by converts to Islam was 'Abd Allah, slave of God, but as V. L. Ménage has shown, high Ottoman dignitaries frequently used one of the beautiful names of God instead. "Seven Ottoman Documents from the Reign of Mehemmed II," in S. M. Stern, *Documents from Islamic Chanceries*. Cambridge, 1965. pp. 112–118. Ca'fer Paşa bn 'Abdul-Mennan, called Frenk, is one such official. Possibly some of the "sons" of 'Abdul-Mennan are relatives of Ca'fer, but most likely they are members of his slave household. "'Abdul-Mennan" does not occur in the records, either as a personal name or as a patronymic, except in regard to the household of Ca'fer Paşa. That Ca'fer Paşa served as kapudan-i derya briefly (1606–1608) under Ahmed I after having been begler begi of Cyprus. J. von Hammer, *Geschichte des Osmanischen Reiches*, Wien, 1809. v. 4, p. 386. İ. H. Danişmend, *İzahlı Osmanlı Tarihi Kronolojisi*, Istanbul, 1950. v. 3, pp. 545.

23. According to Gerber the system functioned efficiently in 17th-century Bursa, particularly because of the "far-reaching" control and administration of the kadis and the high 'ulema. "The Waqf Institution . . ." Marcus reached similar conclusions about the court as "highly pragmatic and responsive to daily demands," as "a realistic body," and as dynamic and flexible. "Piety and Profit . . ." Certainly that conclusion could be drawn for 17th-century Kayseri.

THREE

Kadi, Court, and Legal System

The law imposed by Ottoman law courts, including that of the province of Cyprus, was the Sharia *(şer^c-i şerif)*, the sacred law of Islam. The court itself was called the place of assembly of the Sharia *(meclis-i şer^c* or *mahfil-i şer^c)*, or colloquially just "Sharia" *(şer^c)*. In Cyprus during the period 1571–1640, as in many other places in the empire at that time, that court served all the people, not just Muslims. Although the masses of the island's Greek Orthodox Christians may have had the legal right to apply to their own clergy in certain internal matters of a communal nature involving fellow believers, no records of any such courts survive, and indeed few references even suggest their very existence. Greek Orthodox and other Christians used the Sharia court of Cyprus very frequently, not just in "mixed" cases but in cases involving other members of the same faith.

Technically speaking, three kinds of law were applied at the Sharia court of Lefkoşa: Sharia, *kanun,* and *^cadet* or *resim. Kanun* is imperial law, which derives its authority from the command of the sultan. *^cAdet* (or *resim*) is customary law, which existed at the sufferance of the sultan, but really derived its authority from its alleged antiquity. At other times or in other places circumstances may have differed, but in the province of Cyprus during the period of this study the role of both imperial law and customary law was extremely marginal. I did not find even five cases at the court of Lefkoşa where local people made claims on the basis of kanun, although in a few instances the Porte did explicitly base imperial orders on such law. References to customary law in either court cases or correspondence received by the kadi are even fewer. (Omitted in this discussion are the mass of documents found in sources other than the court registers.) Moreover, even in law cases where references are made to imperial or customary law the method of using such laws is explicitly stated as being in accordance with the Sharia *(şerᶜe gore, şerᶜ mucibince, şerᶜ-i şerif mucibince)*.

People went to court to insist that the Sharia be carried out. When Hasan çelebi bn Ebu Bekr of Hirsofi made a claim that Ahmed beşe bn ᶜAbdullah had struck his head with a stone and injured it, Hasan asked that Ahmed be questioned about the matter and that the Sharia be carried out *(icra-i şerᶜ)* (4 10–2; I Ramazan 1043). After ᶜAbdul-Baki çelebi bn ᶜAli of Lefkoşa claimed that Filori v. Hiristofi of Peristerone village of Morfo kaza blocked his way and struck him while coming from the village to the city, he asked that the Sharia (that is, the law) be carried out *(icra-i şerᶜ)* (4 15–1; I Şevval 1043). Pano bint Zako of Kado Kopiya village of Morfo kaza asked that the Sharia be carried out because kassab Huseyn beşe bn ᶜAbdullah had struck and injured her at the village (4 171–1; II Cumadi II 1046). The female broker Maro of Lefkoşa asked that the Sharia be carried out against Luka v. Nikolo of that city for wrongly saying that he saw her lying on a mattress with her son-in-law *(damadi)* (4 198–2; II Şaban 1046).

ᶜAli beg, administrator of the foundation of Caᶜfer Paşa in Lefkoşa, its overseer Mehmed beg, and others asserted that a certain house and shop of known boundaries near the bazaar had been dedicated to a pious foundation in accordance with the Sharia (1 23–2; I Receb 1002). Janissary Piyale bn ᶜAbdullah, guardian of the orphan Ibrahim, after due judicial consideration *(maᶜrifet-i Şerᶜ-i şerif ile),* had preacher *(hatib)* Mehmed çelebi of Girniye appointed to educate the boy (1 80–1; Sefer 1003). Hiristine of Pahna village of Evdim nahiye was ordered in accordance with the Sharia to pay the debt of her husband Peraşkoge v. Hiristofi to ᶜAbdur-Rahman kethuda bn Ismaᶜil (4 4–3; III Şaban 1043).

Ibrahim oda başi bn Emrullah of Lefkoşa made a claim *(daᶜva/tk)* against Yusuf beg bn ᶜAbdullah of Girniye: Eight years ago I sold Yusuf 3000 vakiye of coffee, linen *(bez)* . . . , and a musket *(tufenk)*, which was sold by consent of the Sharia *(ᶜilm-i şerᶜi ile)* . . . Now he prevaricates about paying. Let him be forced to pay in accordance with the Sharia *(icray-i şerᶜ)*. (4 5–1; II Şaban 1043)

In legal disputes one party may brand the behavior of another party as contrary to the Sharia, in order to stigmatize that action as reprehensible. Komi v. Agosti of Kato Deftere village of Lefkoşa kaza claimed that, contrary to the Sharia, Hasan çavuş bn Kasim had seized possession of his vineyard on the outskirts of the village because he owed him some money; he made oppression and injustice (4 187–1; II Receb 1046). When Spahi Mehmed oda başi claimed the fee for leaving farmland uncultivated from Meraʿin v. Çąkuri and (?) of ʿArefi village of Mesariye kaza, the villagers asserted that to demand that tax from them is contrary to the Sharia (4 67–1; III Sefer 1044).

When formal complaints were made at court, they were almost always made in the form: I want my complaint to be considered in accordance with the Sharia.

Hasan çavuş bn Ahmed, in the presence of Mehmed Paşa, made a claim against janissary Mustafa bn ʿAbdullah: This Mustafa cursed my mouth and wife (or private parts? ʿavret) and he treated me with contempt. I demand that he be punished in accordance with the Sharia. Next Hasan çavuş made a similar complaint against Huseyn bn Çoban, also a janissary: While sitting in my presence he cursed my mouth and my wife (or private parts? ʿavret). Twice he blocked my way with a knife. Let him be punished in accordance with the Sharia. (1 4–1, 2; I Ramazan 988)

Cemile bint ʿAbdullah claimed that her husband Mustafa bn ʿAbdullah had done her a great evil by not giving her dowry and maintenance allowance after he divorced her: I want the Sharia carried out. (1 14–6; 17 Ramazan 988)

ʿAbd ul-Gani bn haci Salih of Lefkoşa claimed that present beyt ul-mal hassa emin Suleyman had not given him inheritance rights to the property of his late father at Hazret-i ʿOmer quarter: I want my inheritance in accordance with the Sharia. (1 16–3; 21 Ramazan 988)

Under the supervision *(mubaşiret)* of ʿOmer aga acting for governor ʿAli Paşa, Andreye v. Papa of Aya Nisani (?) village of Lefka kaza claimed that spahi Ahmed beg bn ʿAli had taken his three altun by force to an illegal place. I want it in accordance with the Sharia, asserted Andreye. (1 86–4; Sefer 1003)

ʿAli bn Veli and Mustafa of Kaymakli village made claims against two brothers of Poliyosimo village of Girniye kaza, Piyero and Ferencesko, sons of Anzilo: They came upon us and injured us. We want that to be considered in accordance with the Sharia. (3 8–1; I Zil-Kade 1043)

The city *su başi* brought Luyi v. Hiristodiye to court with Mariye bint Hiristofi, claiming that Luyi had that woman living in his house and she was not his wife, relative, or in-law *(na-mahrem)*. Let it be investigated in accordance with the

Sharia. Luyi said: Her brothers gave her to me as a servant *(hidmetkar)*, but I did not get permission from the Sharia (i.e., the court, *izn-i şer*ᶜ).

ᶜAbdul-Kadir boluk başi and Keyvan boluk başi state *(ihzar/bm)* before Luyi v. Hiristodiye, reᶜaya of Aya Heme (?) place *(mevzi*ᶜ*)* of Aya Demre village: In his house a *na-mahren* named Mariye bint Hiristofi serves him. Let him be asked. Is this permissible in accordance with the Sharia? Luyi says: I did not get permission from the court *(izn-i şer*ᶜ*)* for Mariye but her brothers Ciryako and Kosdindi sent her to me to serve me. Ciryako and Kosdindi confirm that. (3 34–1;2; II Zil-Kade 1018)

ᶜAbdullah v. ᶜAbdullah, an Armenian of Lefkoşa, asserted that he wanted the Sharia carried out against Bayram bn Ridvan who had blocked his way and struck and injured him with a rock (3 156–1; Rebiᶜ II 1019). Hasan bn ᶜAbdullah of Aya Demre village was the object of widespread criticism from within his village, for drinking wine all the time, and for being annoying and oppressive to the people, contrary to the Sharia. Haci Keyvan, ᶜAbdul-Kadir boluk başi bn Ahmed, Yusuf bn Mehmed, and Huseyn bn ᶜAli, all spahis, and villagers Piyale bn ᶜAbdullah, ᶜAli beşe bn ᶜAbdullah, Marko v. Kistinti, Yorgi v. Yakimo, Lare (?) bint Çilepo, Hiristine bint Yakimo, and Vero bint Zanuc testified that they did not want him in their village (3 146–10; III Cumadi II 1019).

An official transcript of a law case from the judicial registers was called a canonical document *(huccet-i şer*ᶜ*i)*. Hasan efendi bn ᶜAli of Gilan used such a document to prove that he and Viryoni v. Nikolo of that place had settled their mutual debt claims years earlier (4 9–1; I Ramazan 1043). Such a document was used by Hacedor v. Sari Hizir to prove that his late father had repaid part of his former debt to the late kadi Habib of Lefka (1 295–3; Zil-Hicce 1002). With such a document Huseyn çelebi showed that he had given certain property at Aya Demre village of Lefkoşa kaza to his grown sons Hasan and Huseyn çelebi (1 144–1; 1 Receb 1003).

Guardians *(vasi)* were usually referred to as guardians before the Sharia. Ahmed bn ᶜAbdullah was guardian before the Sharia for the orphans of the late Ahmed çavuş of Lefkoşa (1 70–4; Muharrem 1003). Halil bn Ahmed was guardian before the Sharia for Ahmed, Hanim, ᶜAyşe, and another ᶜAyşe, minor children *(evlad-i sigar)* of the late Hasan beşe (2 33–1; I Rebiᶜ II 1044). Gaine (?) bint Gazel (?), an Armenian, was guardian before the Sharia and mother *(valide)* of a minor son *(sigar ogli)* of the late Armenian Mosis (4 9–2; I Ramazan 1043). ᶜAyşe hatun, mother of the orphans of the late Mehmed efendi of Lefkoşa, was appointed before the Sharia for the orphans; then, when she died, Nu-rullah çelebi bn Hasan kethuda was appointed (4 14–1; I Şevval 1043).

Very frequently imperial orders sent to the Cyprus court contained an injunction not to do anything contrary to the Sharia. Such an order to the Cyprus governor, the chief financial officer, and the kadis of the island summarizes complaints made by non-Muslims on the island about local abuses and concludes: "When my exalted decree *(hukm-i şerif)* arrives, see that it is carried out in regard to this matter. It is my order that the tax *(harac)* be taken only from those who are present. Do not do anything that is contrary to the Sharia or the fetva. It is oppression to take from those who are not alive and present *(mevcud)* (2 36–1; Konstantiniye, 4 Zil-Hicce 1016).

Even the official fixed prices on consumer goods were noted before the court. Nuʿman bn ʿAbdullah, the local muhtesib in Lefkoşa, made a claim against Ibrahim of the grocers guild for selling roasted chick-peas *(leblebi)* for 15 akce/vakiye when the official fixed price *(narh)* before the Sharia was only eight akce (4 109–3; 1 Muharrem 1045).

Rahib (monk) Yanaci, canonical legal agent *(vekil-i şerʿi)* of rahib abbot *(gumenos)* Filosefu of Belikano (?) monastery in Hirsofi nahiye, testified that because the abbot is a monk and does not earn money, his head tax *(cizye)* should be canceled. The agent asserted that it is not permissible in accordance with the Sharia to demand head tax and an agricultural tax *(ispence)* from him. (4 192–1; II Receb 1046).

When death or accident occurred without witnesses, and sometimes under other circumstances, an investigative committee was immediately dispatched from the court. An old woman fell and injured her head in Komini (?) quarter of Lefkoşa. Behine v. Zako, Yakimo v. Manuyel, Nikolo v. Zikar (?), and another Yakimo v. Manuyel came from that quarter and reported that the woman had fallen and injured her head. They asked that someone from the Sharia go and investigate. From the Sharia Ibrahim halife bn Ahmed efendi, from the governor's office Pekçe çavuş in supervision *(mubaşiret)* for deputy *(musellim)* Ahmed aga, along with the Muslims whose names were listed below went and investigated. When the woman confirmed the assertions of the men who had come from the quarter, she affirmed that if she perished, no claim should be made against the people of the quarter for blood money *(dem* and *diyet)* (4 189–1; II Receb 1046).

Other Duties of Kadis

Besides their strictly judicial functions, the kadis in Cyprus seem to have overseen virtually every group and institution which existed.

Even military officers, for example, used the court the same way that other people did. When Ahmed bn Hasan and Hasan bn ʿAbdullah disagreed in their claims to the command *(agalik)* of the armorers *(cebeci)*, the kadi of Lefkoşa scrutinized the berats, the imperial orders, and other documents in order to determine that Ahmed had the valid claim (1 31–3; I Şaban 1002). Spahi Hasan beg bn Veli of Ayri (?) village of Pendaye kaza made a claim at court for money owed him by villagers of his timar (1 254–3; III Şevval 1002). On the other hand, when zimmi Ergiro of Morfo village complained to the Porte about injustices on the part of his spahi, a letter was sent to the Lefkoşa kadi ordering him to consider the complaint and make sure that justice was done (1 134–2; II Cumadi I 999). Kadis also were notified of the assignment of timars in their districts, as when the kadi of Lefkoşa was notified of the assignment of an 8999 akce timar in a village in his kaza to Hasan (2 43–2; Lefkoşa. Receb 1016).

Disputes involving janissaries also fell within the scope of the kadi. By using the court Ahmed bn ʿAli was able to force former janissary aga Ahmed to return of some of his property (1 89–1; Rebi ʿII 1003). Zimmi Şimas of Lefkoşa was able to win a similar claim against janissary haci Mehmed bn Yusuf (1 44–1; III Şaban 1002). In 1016 the kadis in Cyprus province *(eyalet)* received orders to carry out a detailed inspection of the local janissaries, in order to find out how many janissaries lived in their spheres of jurisdiction and yet did not train or attend campaigns ... (2 32–1; Haleb, III Şevval 1016). Even janissary boluk başi Memi bn Himmet satisfactorily settled his claim against janissary Hizir, when Hizir paid 6000 ʿosmani akce. (1 37–1; 16 Şaban 1002).

Police officers also brought certain matters concerning their duties to the attention of the court. City muhtesib haci Huseyn brought bazarci Seydi ʿAli to court for selling sweet pomegranates short weight (1 316–3; 1 Muharrem 1003). Muhtesib ʿAli brought three breadbakers, all brothers, to court for drinking and not being able to speak calmly: haci ʿAli bn ʿOmer, ʿOmer, and Mehmed (1 252–3, 4, 5; Şevval 1002). Other police, the su başis, who were the governor's men, also relied on the kadi and his authority. City su başi Mustafa beg had to report to the court that Hasan bn Ahmed had taken Mehmed beşe bn ʿAli from his custody the previous night while he was bringing him to court (3 75–6; III Receb 1019). ʿAli su başi of Lefkoşa and chief nightwatchman *(ʿases başi)* Mustafa su başi came to court in the middle of the night to report that Emine, Rahime, and Fatma, wives of Maʿcunci Mehmed, Yusuf bn ʿAbdullah, and katib Mehmed çelebi of Aya Sofya quarter, had complained that their husbands were drinking wine together in their presence; people from the court *(şerʿ)* had gone to investigate and found it that way, so they asked about the reputations *(hal)* of those people (4 30–1; III Rebiʿ I 1044). Another police official, the chief court summoner *(muhzir başi)* Husrev beg bn ʿAbdullah, at court renounced his office in favor of present chief summoner ʿOmer beg bn Turmuş (3 105–4; II Ramazan 1019). Finally, when the imperial government wished to ban all cultivation, use, or sale of tobacco everywhere, orders were sent to local kadis, who were urged to punish offenders severely and show no pity on them (4 228–1; Konstantiniye, I Rebiʿ II 1044).

Along with the governor and the chief financial officer kadis were responsible for general supervision of tax collecting. An order from Aleppo in 1607–1608 (1016) addressed to the governor, the chief financial officer, and the kadis of Lefkoşa, Girniye, Mesariye, Magosa, Karpas, Tuzla, Morfo, and Pendaye concerns the allocation of the required levy of grain for that year's campaign *(sursat)* from each province, which was supposed to be collected from all reʿaya and delivered to piers *(iskele)* from where it might be handed over to the army (2 34–1; Haleb, 10 Şevval 1016). Those same officials were exhorted to make certain that taxes were only collected from the actual number of people living in each place, so that a current list of all those with such tax obligation had to be compiled (2 36–1; Konstantiniye, 8 Rebiʿ I 1016). An order from the governor of Cyprus to all the kadis reiterates in detail the problems of keeping an accurate assessment and orders them to énsure the accuracy of the list (2 26– I Şaban 1016). At the local level that responsibility fell to kadis.

Kadis had a special obligation to protect the weak and vulnerable. Much of the relatively secure position of women may be attributed to the concern of various kadis in Lefkoşa and elsewhere on the island of Cyprus who staunchly maintained their legal rights in the face of oppression. Similarly kadis protected the rights of non-Muslims so that they were able to function effectivley in Cyprus during the period studied. As has been demonstrated previously, non-Muslims relied on the courts frequently even for matters involving their co-religionists.

All re'aya looked to the kadis for protection and defense of their rights. When experiencing the oppression of the tax farmers, the wage-laborers *(irgad taifesi)* of Piskobi and Kulaş made a petition to Piskobi kadi 'Ali efendi because although they worked diligently through the year they were not provided with any grain for maintenance; the tax farmers did not pay them enough for their services to provide the necessities of life, so all are hungry (1 226–1; I Şevval 1002). When people complained to Lefkoşa kadi Bali efendi of the stewards *(umena)* of the tax farms of the candle factory *(şem'hane)* and the office of the archbishop *(piskoposluk)* extorting excessive duties from them, they anticipated that he would intervene on their behalf (1 134–1; Lefkoşa, II Muharrem 1003).

Yet another traditional function of the kadi was as overseer of pious foundations. In Lefkoşa that was combined with overseeing the affairs of members of the religious class *('ulema)*. One son of Mustafa Paşa complained to the Porte that the current administrator *(mutevelli)* of the foundation of his late father, Suleyman, who had just died, had not provided an accounting for the past two years, so the kadi was ordered to correct the problem immediately (1 102–1; Konstantiniye, III Receb 1002). Mihayel v. Kistintin, mutevelli of the church *(kenise)* in Aye Hurte village of Lefkoşa kaza, made a claim at court against Milo (?) bint Pavlo of the village who supposedly had usurped property of the foundation (4 112–1; II Muharrem 1045). Mevlana 'Abdur-Rahman halife bn 'Abdul-Kerim, imam of the mosque *(mescid)* in Top hane quarter in Lefkoşa, announced at court in the presence of Ekmel hoca bn Mahmud that he hoped to make a pilgrimage to the Ka'be that year and would leave Ekmel as acting imam (3 135–1; 28 Rebi' II 1019). When the office of muezzin of the mosque of Seray (?) oni quarter was vacant, from that quarter Yedekçi Isma'il, haci Mehmed bn Yusuf, Mehmed bn Cullah, and others of the people came to court and announced that haci Isma'il bn Huseyn was upright and religious and so they wanted him to be their muezzin (3 140–3; 28 Rebi' II 1019. He was to be paid 4 akce/day).

Haci Isma'il bn haci Huseyn states: While I was muezzin of Sinan Paşa mosque *(mescid)* in Seray oni, Mehmed bn Yusuf pronounced me reprobate *(tefcir)*. Let him be asked. Mehmed says that the community of the mosque *(cema'et)* and the imam do not want Isma'il. Imam 'Abdur-Rahman, menla Bekr bn 'Abdul-Gani (?), Ahmed bn 'Abdul-Kerim, and Mehmed kethuda bn 'Abdullah say: In truth, Isma'il is lazy and negligent of his duties. We do not want him; we want the aforementioned Mehmed. Registered. (3 142–2; III Cumadi I 1019)

Kadis themselves were liable to the judgments of courts and might be summoned there in the same ways that other people were.[1]

Present Magosa kadi mevlana seyyid Ahmed efendi and Mesariye kadi mevlana Musliheddin efendi have a dispute over jurisdiction in eight villages. Ahmed claims that they have always been part of Magosa but now Musliheddin tries to usurp them. From the upright men *('udul)* Mehmed bn Ca'fer, Huseyn bn Ahmed, and others en masse *(cemi'-i kesir)* confirm seyyid Ahmed efendi and Musliheddin is restrained from interfering. (1 274–3; II Zil-Kade 1002)

Mehmed çelebi bn Huseyn and Huseyn beg, spahis of Akaçe village of Morfo kaza state before Veli efendi, Morfo kadi: Veli went around the district *(nahiye)* five times in the last 10 months, claiming provisions and maintenance from the re'aya. He took five akce from every adult male *(nefer)* for head tax and four akce for tax *(vergi)*. We gave it to him personally. When Veli was asked, he said: I took four akce apiece for head tax in that village; I did not take it for maintenance *(nuzul)*. I went to the re'aya twice for business. I did not take other things. (2 69–3; 14 Rebi' I 1017)

Zimmi Ferencesko of Akakçe village of Morfo kaza states: We gave the afore-mentioned Veli Efendi a total of 12 akce apiece, including eight akce apiece for head tax. They used to give only five akce to those who came. . . . (2 69–4; 14 Rebi' I 1017)

Besides the array of civil and criminal cases that a judge dealt with, the kadi of Lefkoşa also handled other matters related to his role as the highest ranking Ottoman official in the city.

Although the kadi did not personally keep local records, he was responsible for seeing that records were kept accurately. That included in particular the note books of detailed population records for the province of Cyprus which provided the basis for much of the taxation. For even if no censuses were taken during the period 1572–1641, local registers listing all the tax-paying populace by name had to be kept up, or at least the names of non-Muslims who paid the head tax. Otherwise the system of tax collection would disintegrate, and there would be no way to identify city dwellers who had illegally migrated from their villages.

In all disputes the kadi determined the correct interpretations of written documents. Was a certain man a legal resident of that village? Did he pay a certain tax? Is he obligated to pay that tax? How much should he pay? How much did he pay? Whose timar is that? What are the precise boundaries of that timar? Whose tax farm is that, and what precisely are the obligations of the tax farmer? The kadi did not have the authority to give his own orders regarding such problems, but he did make decisions on the basis of the existing documents.

The judicial records provide almost no personal information about the kadis, although sometimes current or out-of-office kadis used the court as private citizens. They participated in business and owned land, as might be expected from relatively high-salaried and well-educated members of the Ottoman elite. Mevlana haci Ahmed efendi bn haci ʿOsman, kadi of Tuzla, was involved in a long standing dispute over trade with the abbot *(igumenos)* of an Orthodox monastery (4 92–2; I Ramazan 1044). The following year that same mevlana haci Ahmed efendi bought two large estates at ʿOmeriye quarter of Lefkoşa from Emine bint haci Idris, one for 20,000 akce, the other for 32,000 akce (4 155–1; 17 Zil-Hicce 1045). At almost the same time Ahmed efendi bought a very large estate at Zohiye (?) village in Morfo nahiye from Mustafa çelebi bn ʿAli for 20,000 akce and paid Mustafa çelebi an additional 18,000 akce for a half share of 500 donum of arable fields on the outskirts of the village (4 155–2; I Zil-Hicce 1045). Within less than a year mevlana haci Ahmed efendi bought a very large estate including gardens and water mills at Lapta village in Girniye nahiye from racil haci Ibrahim beşe bn Hizir of Lefkoşa for 22,000 akce (4 187–2; II Receb 1046).

Other kadis may also have been wealthy. A large estate of literally hundreds of donums of large estates *(çiftliks)* at various villages was designated as private property for mevlana Ahmed efendi, son of the late Saʿd ed-din efendi, of Lefkoşa so that he could make it into a foundation *(vakf)* (4 235–1; 12 Rebiʿ II 1043, Uskudar). Mustafa çavuş of Cebni (? or Çimi?) village of Alaiye kaza owed 80 riyali guruş to former Mesariye kadi mevlana Mustafa efendi bn Mahmud efendi (4 238–2; III Zil-Hicce 1046). Present Magosa kadi ʿAli efendi, however, owed 328 riyali guruş to Musa beşe bn Mehmed beg of Belgrad(e), which he paid through Musa's legal agent *(vekil)* present Mesariye kadi mevlana Mustafa efendi bn Mahmud efendi (4 215–3; I Ramazan 1045). Such wealth in the possession of kadis was not obvious at earlier times. Perhaps the passage of several decades of Ottoman rule was necessary before well-to-do local families produced wealthy sons who had the education and other qualifications to serve as local kadis.

On at least one occasion several kadis of Cyprus may have been guilty of extortion and oppression, although neither the origin of the complaint nor the identity of the offenders was revealed in the imperial order sent to the governor and kadis of the island. The kadis were accused of forcing re'aya to sell honey *(bal)*, olive oil (? *zeyt*), chickens *(tavuk)*, carobs *(harbot)*, barley *(arpa)*, and wheat *(saman)* to them for less than half the official fixed price *(narh carinun nisfi)*. When the people *(ahali)* wanted certain leaders *(kethuda)* appointed, the kadis appointed others whom the people did not want. The kadis went to villages where they extorted money to support their visits. . . . "I order that you, governor, and you, kadis, . . . should do what is necessary in this matter. You should not do anything contrary to the Sharia to the re'aya. I do not want to hear any more complaints about this matter" (162/60 (9) p. 266, #598KB).

In an order from the Porte directed to the governor of Cyprus, the misbehavior of former Baf (Paphos) kadi mevlana 'Abdullah for all sorts of sins and abominations *(enva-i kabahat u şen 'ati)*, which led the poor of that district *(nahiye)* to come and demand justice from this oppression *(zulm)*, was revealed. That kadi had been attempting to flee to the main land.

It was ordered that all who have claims to make against him *(da'vay-i hak idenlerile)* should come to court. If he has not been judged in accordance with the Sharia *(Şeri'e fasl)*, and if fifteen years have not passed, you should investigate in accordance with justice *(Şer 'ile hakk)*. You should note whether or not he has left any debts. You should register any transgressions of his. (164/75 (12) 57KE)

In a very few instances documents preserved in the court registers reveal information about salaries of kadis. Mevlana 'Alaeddin efendi was appointed to the kaza of Tuzla for 80 akce/day in 1593–1594 (1002) (1 101–1; undated). Piskobi kaza was assigned to mevlana Ahmed for five months at 80 akce/day starting 11 September 1607 (19 Cumadi I 1016) (2 86–2; III Şaban 1016, Haleb).

Present Magosa kadi mevlana seyyid Ahmed efendi and present Mesariye kadi mevlana Musliheddin efendi had a jurisdictional dispute over eight villages which Ahmed claimed had always been part of Magosa district but Musliheddin had usurped. Witnesses confirmed Ahmed's claim (1 274–3; II Zil-Kade 1002).

Even complaints against kadis were brought to the kadi to solve.

Mehmed çelebi bn Huseyn and Huseyn beg, spahis of Akaçe village of Morfo kaza say before Veli efendi, Morfo kadi: Veli went to the district *(nahiye)* five times in 10 months, claiming provisions and maintenance from the re'aya. He took five akce from every adult male *(nefer)* for head tax *(cizye)* and four akce as tax *(vergi)*. We gave it to him personally. When Veli was asked, he said: I took four akce apiece for head tax *(cizye)* in the aforementioned village. I did not take grain for military supplies *(nuzul)*. I went to the re'aya twice for business. I did not take other things. (2 69–3; 14 Rebi' I 1017)

More common than complaints about kadis, however, were complaints about other officials. Frequently the kadi was exhorted to prevent the abuses of various usurping officials. One order repeats the complaints that the tax farmers of the candle factory *(şem'hane)* and the office of the episcopate *(piskoposluk)* illegally collect food and money from the local people (1 134–1; II Muharrem 1003, Lefkoşa). Another details local complaints against spahis (1 134–2; II Cumadi I 999). A third brings complaints of abuses of several ruthless messengers *(çavuşes)* (1 137–1; III Şevval 1002, Konstantiniye). Yet another reports of the oppression of tax farmers (1 226–1; undated, 1002).

Legal Agents *(Vekil)*

The traditions of the Sharia court system encouraged litigants to come to the court in person with their own problems. Neither ignorance nor inexperience were held against those who came, since their only responsibility was to describe their knowledge of, or concern with, the matter. The Sharia, and the court of Lefkoşa between 1580 and 1640, discouraged the use of legal agents, although permitting them when a litigant was ill, absent, or even just busy under some circumstances. Women in particular might be excused from attending court if they wished.

Legal agents *(vekil)* could be appointed either by informing the court in person or by designating the agent in front of at least two witnesses who could attest to the appointment. A legal agent never accompanied a litigant to court but acted only in his absence. Anyone appointing such an agent had to give him full power of attorney, or at least power of attorney for the matter concerned. For those reasons, and because the

Table 3.1
Use of Vekil (Legal Agents)

sicil number	year	total cases	cases with vekil	%	cases with 2 vekils	total vekil
1A	1580, 1593–1595	1088	164	15%	12	176
2	1607–1609	175	7	4%	5	12
3	1609–1611	1184	138	12%	5	143
4	1633–1637	528	89	17%	8	97
total		2975	398	13%	30	428

Relatives of Vekils (Legal Agents)

	1A	2	3	4	total	%
wife	18	0	45	32	95	70%
sister	0	1	2	8	11	8%
daughter	2	0	8	1	11	8%
brother	2	0	2	2	6	4%
son	2	0	1	1	4	3%
mother	1	0	0	2	3	2%
father	0	0	2	0	2	1%
other	1	0	1	1	3	2%
total	26	1	61	47	135	

(N.B. 123 (91%) involve female relatives)

Women and Vekils (Legal Agents)

sicil number	total Muslim women	Muslim women with vekil	%	total zimmi women	zimmi women with vekil	%	total women	women with vekil	%
1A	196	78	40%	61	15	25%	257	93	36%
3	203	74	36%	59	15	25%	262	89	34%
4	113	54	48%	69	15	22%	182	69	38%
	512	206	40%	189	45	24%	701	251	36%

29% of vekils are for related women— 123   13% of vekils are zimmis—54
27% of vekils are for unrelated women—114   87% of vekils are Muslims—374
55%   237

courts discouraged it, legal agents were not usually used in contested litigation; in such cases it was almost essential that the claimant himself appear there. (See table 3.1).

Of almost 3000 legal cases studied only 13% involved one or more legal agents *(vekil)*. In each record book *(sicil)*, with the exception of the atypical #2, the proportion ranged between 12% and 17%. Since all cases have at least two litigants, it is a safe guess that only about 7% of almost 6000 litigants used legal agents. (Several cases involved more than one agent, but probably about an equal number of cases involved more than two litigants only one of whom had an agent. Those two categories more or less cancel each other out.)

Explanations are never given about why a particular person is appointed legal agent by another person. Thirty-six percent of all women using the court (40% of Muslim women and 24% of zimmi women) chose legal agents to represent them. Twenty-nine percent of all the legal agents were the husbands or male relatives of women who had business with the court, and another 27% were unrelated men whom for other reasons women had chosen to represent them. Although 34% of all the cases involved non-Muslims they used only 13% of legal agents, so clearly they attended court much more frequently than Muslims. Probably men, and women not represented by relatives, at least slightly preferred as legal agents men who were of minor local significance, whether in the military or religious classes. Local notables like 'ulema and military officers almost always had other notables represent them in their absence. Possibly other people asked friends from their quarter or village, or even more likely, communal leaders from those places who might have no status beyond that community but were of gravity and moderation.

Certainly no small clique monopolized the office of legal agent. Hardly ever does the name of one occur more than once in an identifiable fashion in any one record book *(sicil)*. From time to time the performance of his duties as a legal agent necessitated that his name appear more than once, in settling inheritance claims, for example, or in transferring property. Otherwise, that was rare. Clearly there was no class of "professional" legal agents (as sometimes may have gathered around other Islamic courts at other times).

The legal agents were not court officers. Every adult was eligible for the office. Anyone could appoint a legal agent whenever he wanted.

Instances occur, for example, of women serving as agents for men, including husbands. Not only could Muslims serve as agents for non-Muslims but the latter could serve for Muslims. The agent had exactly the same legal duties in court as the person he represented, to give the kadi all the information relative to ascertaining the truth. His duty was to represent, but not to advocate, the interests of the person who appointed him *(muvekkil)*. Moreover, the legal agent might have both judicial and nonjudicial duties, the latter of which were completely unrelated to the court.

Of 135 legal agents serving spouses and relatives, 123 (91%) represented women. Of that 135 70% represented wives, 8% each sisters and daughters, 4% brothers, 3% sons, 2% mothers, 1% fathers, and 2% others. Apparently women were much more closely linked to their husbands than to their fathers and brothers, although women who married at an early age may have had little need for the court when they were still living under their fathers' rooves.

Compromise *(Sulh)*

One of the more common ways of settling disputes in 16th and 17th century Ottoman legal procedure was by "compromise" or "reconciliation" *(sulh)*. The term compromise *(sulh)* actually included two categories of actions. The first involved the formal settlement of a standing disagreement which had previously been brought to court but had not been settled there either because all the evidence had not yet been submitted or because the evidence did not decisively favor one party. It was hoped that some formal or informal mediation might finally produce a more satisfactory result. The second kind of compromise *(sulh)* involved disagreements not previously brought to court for settlement but finally introduced there so that a formal record of the solution can be preserved. In neither case did the court make the settlement. The court simply heard and noted the solution, whatever it was. Thereafter, however, any party to the compromise might complain to the court about another party's failure to carry out the terms of the compromise. Such a dispute was heard by the same rules as all other disputes.

Generally compromise *(sulh)* is formally noted as having taken place through the mediation *(tevassut)* of upright people *(muslihun)*. The upright people do not belong, of course, to any specific group. Their identity varied from case to case. Settlement of one case might be by the mediation of distinguished men attending the court that day, in another case by friends, relatives, or neighbors. Indeed one can imagine mediation by people who are not especially "upright" yet who nevertheless might be so designated in the legal formulary because they are useful in helping the disputants reach a settlement.

With the mediation of upright people Hizir çelebi bn Hasan (?) and ʿAli bn ʿAbdullah compromised in their dispute over gardens at Aya Sozemeno village (3 32–2; II Zil-Kade 1018). With the mediation of upright people ʿAli beşe bn Yusuf and Beşer beg bn ʿAbdullah compromised in their dispute over whether or not he had sold him something on the mainland (Ote Yaka) (3 77–1; III Receb 1019). Upright persons mediated a compromise in the property dispute between racil Mehmed beşe bn Nasuh of Kaymakli village of Lefkoşa kaza and Mehmed çavuş bn Ibrahim, agent *(vekil)* and stepfather of Selimiye bint Budak of Lefkoşa (4 5–3; III Şaban 1043).

The process of compromise often involved the payment of specified sums of money in settlement. Mehmed beşe claimed that ʿAli boluk başi bn ʿAbdullah had owed his late father janissary ʿAli beşe bn ʿAbdullah 34 goats, but with the mediation of upright people Mehmed beşe compromised for 1440 akce (3 33–2; II Zil-Kade 1018). Receb claimed that Musa's late mother Fatma bint Himmet of Catoz village of Lefkoşa kaza owed his late father 5000 akce, but after the mediation of upright people a compromise was made for 2000 akce (4 134–1; III Receb 1045). Compromising in her claim to a house at ʿArab Ahmed quarter in Lefkoşa, Rahime hatun bint Mehmed accepted 3800 akce in settlement from racil Derviş beşe bn Mustafa (4 149–1; I Şevval 1045). After Kerime bint Caʿfer specifically claimed dowry, maintenance allowance, and one-eighth of the estate of her late husband Veli reis of Hazret-i ʿOmer quarter in Lefkoşa, the widow compromised for 2000 akce (2 35–3; uncertain).

Sometimes compromise followed a criminal charge. Ahmed bn ʿAli asserted that Mustafa beşe bn ʿAbdullah had struck him, but then with the mediation of upright people (which perhaps saved Mustafa a fine and corporal punishment) a compromise was reached (3 98–6; I Şevval 1019).

Under the supervision of Huseyn aga, from Aya Marina (?) village Mehmed Paşa, another Mehmed Paşa, Bostanci Mehmed beg, zimmi Piyero, Poli, and others state *(tm)* before Hamze beg bn ʿAbdullah: Of his own volition he set fire to his grain *(harman)*. It burned and destroyed our property *(mulk)* and grain. Hamze denied that. Then with the mediation of upright people *(muslihun tevassut)*, reconciliation *(sulh)* was made for 5000 akce. (1 79–3; Sefer 1003)

Under the supervision of ʿOmer aga for the governor *(mir miran)* ʿAli Paşa, Andreye v. Papa of Aya Nisani village of Lefka kaza says: This spahi Ahmed beg bn ʿAli took my three altun illegally by force. I want it in accordance with the Sharia. Ahmed denies that. Then, with the mediation of upright people, reconciliation is made for two altun. (1 86–4; Sefer 1003)

The Mufti

A mufti gives theoretical legal opinions in answer to abstract questions put to him in impersonal terms. The mufti considers only impersonal questions of law; he has no investigative authority of his own. He cannot seek out litigants, and he must give his answers only within the context provided by the one who seeks his legal opinion (the *fetva*). Moreover, he has no role in judicial procedure, for the local kadi is the only official who can judge whether or not a mufti's legal opinion *(fetva)* fits in the circumstances of a real legal case. In a province like Cyprus a mufti apparently had no duties other than to try to provide the best legal answers to the questions posed him. Never was the mufti of Cyprus consulted by a kadi to explain the applicability, or for that matter even the real meaning, of his legal opinions. Unlike the ubiquitous kadi, the local mufti performed no services to the province that were not of a strictly legal nature.

In the period studied the province of Cyprus apparently had a single mufti, who served in Lefkoşa. In legal cases references were made not infrequently to the existence of a legal opinion of a mufti *(fetva)* in the hands of one litigant or another, but only rarely was the complete text of a fetva given. Even more rare was to identify the name of the mufti involved. Nevertheless, the mufti of Cyprus was appointed by, or through, the Rumili kadi ʿasker, who resided in Istanbul, and was ultimately under the şeyh ul-Islam, the highest official of the Muslim millet. While the kadi ʿaskers and the şeyh ul-Islam had an array of other duties that they performed, and so were among the most powerful officials in the Ottoman empire, they also issued legal opinions. Some of their legal opinions reached Cyprus.

Most often fetvas were used like other written documents, to settle disputes. Sometimes they were used by high-ranking officials or other officers of state to substantiate their claims, but other times they were used by townspeople or villagers against such people. Very often a fetva was only one kind of evidence that a litigant would try to present to the court, along with the evidence of witnesses, or other kinds of written evidence. Again, a decision was made by the kadi, who had to determine what "evidence" was relevant in a particular case.

Before the governor's council a fetva was used by military officer Nasuh beg bn Yusuf to substantiate his complaint of oppression against Magosa district governor 'Ali beg, who unjustly took a horse worth 12,000 akce from the claimant to settle a debt which only amounted to 3000 akce (1 49–2; III Şaban 1002). At court the tax-farm superintendent *(iltizam emini)* of the tax-farms *(mukata'a)* of Mesariye kaza, Ibrahim çelebi bn Ramazan, used a fetva to help prove his claim that in the year 1591–1592 (1000) then-governor of the island Nuh Paşa had collected 500 kile of wheat and 300 (not 3000) kile of barley when documents show that he should have collected only 100 kile of barley along with that 500 of wheat (1 25–5; I Cumadi I 1002).

Spahi Musa of Vezace village of Lefkoşa says before Ergiro v. Ciryako: Ergiro left the village for another one. I want the fee for leaving a farm uncultivated *(çift boazan)*. Ergiro replies: I have lived in another village for 18 years. I have an imperial order *(emr-i şerif)* and also a fetva. Ergiro's fetva was examined and read. If zimmi claimant Zeyd left his village and went to another 18 or 20 years ago and settled there permanently, and if spahi 'Amr seized Zeyd and took money from him calling it the fee for leaving a farm uncultivated, is that oppression, or can he take that fee? The answer: No. So the spahi Musa is restrained. A document of the court decision *(huccet)* is given to Ergiro in accordance with the fetva and imperial order in his possession. (1 64–2; Muharrem 1003)

If Zeyd (i.e., John Doe) (non-Muslim subject, that is) leaves the place where he was born and lives in another village for 18 or 20 years and has settled there, and if spahi 'Amr (Richard Roe) takes money from him which he calls a fee for leaving a farm uncultivated, and if after that 'Amr oppresses Zeyd, can 'Amr demand that fee for every year? The Answer: No. It is oppression. It is necessary to restrain 'Amr. (1 135–1)

Spahi Mahmud bn Menteş of Karni village of Girniye kaza states before Ahmed bn Seyfi of that village: Ahmed's brother 'Omer died without male offspring *(evlad-i zukur)*. His land at the village is suitable for being assigned to another *(tapu)*, but Ahmed prevents my taking it. Mahmud presents a fetva. In accordance with the fetva, 'Omer's field is suitable for assigning to another *(tapu)*. (3 137–6; Cumadi I 1019)

Mehmed oda başi of spahis of Magosa castle tried illegally to demand the fee for leaving a farm uncultivated from Merai'ri (?) v. Çakuri of Lefkoşa. According to Merai'ri (?)'s fetva, if Zeyd does not have lands *(çift)* and fields *(tarla)* and has lived in another village for 35 years, the spahi cannot demand the fees paid by land-owning villagers (4 67–1; III Sefer 1044).

A fetva of 'Abdur-Rahman attested that once the legitimate taxes had been taken from a villager, it was forbidden to claim any other illegal taxes (4 238–1). An imperial order was sent to the governor and to the chief financial officer and to the kadis of the island of Cyprus in response to a petition presented to the Porte about the illegality of taking taxes from anyone who was not present and alive *(mevcud)*. The order contained a fetva from şeyh ul-Islam Sunullah attesting that it is illegal to try to take taxes, specifically the head tax *(harac)*, for those who have died or departed or converted (2 36–1; Konstantiniye, 8 Rebi' I 1016).

The mufti of Cyprus during at least parts of 1607–1608 (1016) and 1608–1609 (1017) was mevlana Sa'deddin efendi, who at least in one instance served as legal agent for şeyh ul-Islam Mehmed efendi (2 55–1; I Zil-Hicce 1017. 60–1; Magosa, II Rebi' I 1016). A fetva issued in 1593–1594 (1002) came from mufti Mehmed (1 199–2. Also 193–4).

The Armenian woman Mogal bint Haristo, mother and guardian of the orphans of Ilyas of Terbiyodi quarter, presented a fetva showing that certain property which the administrator of the church of that quarter claimed as vakf could never be legally made into a vakf because she owned it (4 129–3; III Receb 1045). A fetva of mutfti Mehmed revealed that it was not permissible to turn imperial land *(arazi miri)* in the form of fields owned *(tassaruf)* by anyone into vakf land (1 193–4; 1002).

Other fetvas presented to the court of Cyprus dealt with problems concerning rental property, relationships and inheritance, debts, remarriage, assault, and blood money (1 195–3; 1002. 199–2; 1002. 299–1; Zil-Hicce 1002. 328–1; Muharrem 1003. 94–2; Rebi' I 1003. 4 5–1; II Şaban 1043. 10–2; I Ramazan 1043).

Written Records

Written documents were widely used in Cyprus in the period 1580–1640. Officials used them for their own special purposes, and the people got theirs, from the court, the imperial government, and other sources, in order to preserve their own property or to protect their rights. The court had the authority to review and evaluate documents, to determine their meaning, and to decide which of conflicting documents had priority in different circumstances. People of all levels of society, including villagers, at least sometimes needed written records, not just the educated classes and businessmen.

The names and residences of all adult males were preserved in official record books *(defter)* kept in the provinces, along with their fathers' names. That record was extremely important for the imperial government, since it provided the basis for taxation. Mustafa çelebi, agent *(mubaşir)* for governor *(mir miran)* Ahmed Paşa's administrative officer *(musellim)* Mustafa kethuda, heard a claim of Mehmed beg bn ʿAbdullah, spahi of Aya Mame village, against Nikola, son of Kalace v. Kortes (?) of that village. Nikola was not registered in the official record books *(haric ez defter)*, although his father is a reʿaya from that village. Nikola then acknowledged that he was the son of a reʿaya and himself a reʿaya (1 210–2; II Ramazan 1002).

Indeed, in Cyprus where most villages were part of the timar system, the status of all cultivable lands had to be known and registered. Caʿfer beg bn Yusuf, superintendent *(emin)* of the tax farm *(iltizam)* of Bali ketri village of Lefkoşa, made a claim *(bm)* against the spahi of that village, Ibrahim beg bn Yusuf, claiming tithe *(ʿuşr)* for a field *(tarla)* of known boundaries in the possession *(tasarruf)* of Yakimo v. Çiryako of that village. Ibrahim countered, however, that the place *(yer)* in dispute had been a garden *(bagçe)* for a long time:

In the copy of the record book *(defter sureti)* that I possess it is a garden *(bagçe)*. When Ibrahim's copy of the record book was examined, garden *(bagçe)* was found registered there. Caʿfer beg confirmed that. (1 25–1; Cumadi II 1002)

Written records were also routinely given to people newly assigned to offices. Officials prepared at least two documents, one of which, the *berat*, was addressed to and handed over to the new office holder himself. Another copy (or copies) might be addressed to a kadi or to local officials.

Ahmed aga bn Hasan aga of the armorers *(cebeci)* of Lefkoşa made a claim *(tm)* against former armorer *(cebeci)* aga Hasan bn ʿAbdullah: The command of the armorers *(agalik)* was granted to me. I have an imperial berat and an imperial order *(emr-i Padişah)*. When in accordance with the berat and the order, I took possession of that office, Hasan rejected the orders. Let the letters of change, the berat, and the imperial order be examined and read in accordance with the Sharia. When the berat and the order in Ahmed's possession were examined and read, it was seen that the office had been granted to him and it was ordered that its revenues go to Ahmed aga. (1 31–3; II Şaban 1002)

Among the most important written records were those of the courts, which provided a detailed summary of each case heard. Those records are called religious law judicial registers *(şerʿi mahkeme sicilleri)*. Their contents had, of course, immense importance in the successful functioning of the legal system. Copies of individual entries in the judicial registers given to private individuals for their own use are usually called *huccet*. Such records were used especially to settle disputes over land and property holdings, debts, and inheritance. Those records had to be signed and sealed by the kadi of the time, yet still the testimony of eye witnesses might sometimes be required to ensure their acceptance.

Huseyn kethuda bn Hamze of Lefkoşa states before zimmis Yakimo v. Pereş-coge, Mihali v. Andon, and Piyero v. Bafid of Karpas kaza: At that place a priest *(papaz)* named Papa Filipo claimed 190 keyl of wheat *(bugday)* and 462 keyl of barley *(arpa)* from me, but he has dropped that claim. After that happened, the above-mentioned Zimmis have made the charge again. They said, we make that claim. However, Huseyn kethuda presented an official copy of the judicial register *(huccet-i şerʿiye)*. When it was examined, it revealed that the claim of the priest had been settled. It may not be heard again. (1 33–1; I Şaban 1002)

Mustafa çelebi, son of the late kadi Habib of Lefka, made a claim *(daʿva)* against Hacedor v. Sari Hizir: My late father gave Hacedor's father 72,150 akce. Let him pay now. Let Hacedor be asked. Hacedor acknowledges the debt, but he says that part of it had been paid before his father's death and the rest at the time of his death. I have a copy of the judicial register *(suret-i şerʿiye)*. When his *huccet* was examined, it was accepted. (1 295–3; Zil-Hicce 1002)

Yaʿkub bn Huda virdi of Lefkoşa states before Halil bn ʿAli, who is legal agent *(vekil)* for his wife Inan Paşa bint ʿAli: Inan Paşa is my wife. If she renounces dowry *(mehr)* and maintenance allowance given until she is legally determined not to be pregnant *(nafakaʾ-i ʿiddet)*, I will make divorce at her request *(hulʿ)*. She accepts that, so the issuance of a *huccet* for the divorce *(huccet-i hulʿ)* is ordered. (1 325–2; I Zil-Hicce 1002)

A dispute over property brought to court on I Cumadi II 1045 by Sosite (?), grown daughter of the late Pavla of Aya Peraşkoge quarter of Lefkoşa and racil ʿAli beşe bn Ahmed was settled by a *huccet* of Lefkoşa kadi Mehmed efendi dated 8 September 1606 (5 Cumadi I 1015) (4

119–2). Likewise a dispute over a vineyard *(bag)* in Kato Deftere village of Lefkoşa kaza between Komi v. Agosti and Hasan çavuş bn Kasim was settled by Hasan's *huccet* dated late September 1618 (I Şevval 1027), signed by former Lefkoşa kadi Haci efendi (4 187–1; II Receb 1046). When Miliye (?), daughter of the late Mustafa of Aya Yorgi Yeros village of Lefkoşa nahiye, was given possession by title deed *(tapu)* of the field *(tarla)* of her late father, a *huccet* was given to her (4 227–3; Cumadi I 1035).

Christian Hiristine, mother and guardian *(vasi)* of the minor children *(evlad-i sigar)* of the late Yasef v. Ilyas of Labta village of Girniye nahiye, makes a claim *(daʿva/tk)* against janissary Ibrahim beşe bn Hizir: A garden *(bağçe)* and other property at the village was disputed. Ibrahim has a *huccet* dated late March 1635 (I Şevval 1044) signed by former Lefkoşa kadi mevlana seyyid Yaʿkub efendi. Hiristine challenges the *huccet*, but ʿudul-i muslimin Ahmed beg bn ʿAli and Mustafa oda başi bn ʿAbdullah confirm Ibrahim. (4 143–2; III Ramazan 1045)

Fatma bint Bayram, widow and executrix *(zevceʾ-i metrukasi)* of the late ʿAli beşe bn Mehmed of Lefkoşa, makes a claim *(daʿva/tk)* against Mustafa beşe bn haci Eymur and Mustafa bn Hasan of Belabeşe village of Girniye nahiye: A house, garden, and other property at the village . . . are disputed by the litigants. Fatma claims the property had belonged to her husband and son. Fatma has a *huccet* dated late October 1627 (II Sefer 1037) signed by Girniye kadi mevlana Mustafa efendi. When the Mustafas question the *huccet*, ʿudul-i muslimin ʿAli bn ʿAli, Receb bn Veli, Şaʿban bn Veli, and Mustafa bn Mehmed confirmed it. (4 121–1; I Rebiʿ II 1045)

A *huccet* of mevlana Hamdi efendi, present deputy judge *(naʿib ş-şer)* at the court of Mahmud Paşa quarter in Istanbul dated 25 October 1634 (3 Cumadi I 1044) shows that ʿOmer çavuş bn Himmet of Lefkoşa owes 140 riyali guruş to Mustafa çelebi bn Ismaʿil (4 126–2; I Receb 1045). According to a *huccet* held by racil Receb beşe of Lefkoşa, Çakoleki v. Zorzi of Koremeno (?) village of Lefka nahiye owed him 11,400 akce (4 182–2; I Receb 1046). A *huccet* in the possession of Istefano v. Piro was challenged by Zorzo v. Yorolimo, legal agent *(vekil)* for and husband of Ruşhu, but the contents of that *huccet* were confirmed by Baba Kostintin, Baba Yorgi v. Polyo (?), and Piro (4 28–1; II Rebiʿ I 1044).

A *huccet* dated mid-March 1636 (I Şevval 1045) signed by former Hirsofi kadi mevlana seyyid Mehmed efendi settled an inheritance dispute between Yusuf bn Mustafa of Poli village of Hirsofi nahiye and

Mustafa beşe bn Ridvan of Androliko (?) village of that kaza (4 151–1; II Şevval 1045). Zivani used a *huccet* to confirm his guardianship in a property dispute with Mihail (4 7–1; I Ramazan 1043).

A *huccet* was issued by the court certifying that present Cyprus treasurer *(defterdar)* Bali efendi was legal agent *(vekil)* for the sultan's teacher *(hoca)* Mevlana Sa'deddin bn Hasan Çan, in accordance with the testimony of Mustafa çelebi bn Mehmed and Mustafa çavuş bn 'Ali. Next a dispute between Sa'deddin and Mehmed çavuş over Kucuk Hammam in Lefkoşa was settled because the former's *huccet* proved that it was his property. Finally, the agent Bali efendi sold that hammam, which was the property *(mulk)* of Sa'deddin, to Korkud efendi, present timar defterdar, for 60,000 akce (1 302–2, 3; III Zil-Hicce 1002).

When Inan Paşa bint 'Ali renounced through her legal agent *(vekil)* Halil bn 'Ali all claim to any payments from her husband Ya'kub bn Huda Virdi of Lefkoşa, both parties agreed to divorce by her request and a *huccet* of *hul'* was issued (1 325–2; I Zil-Hicce 1002).

Present Baf sancagi begi Ahmed and former Baf kadi mevlana Ahmed sent a letter and a copy of a court decision (called *suret-i sicil* and *huccet* in different places) to the Porte to complain of the general oppression *(zulm ve te'addi)* of Bali çavuş. Earlier there had been insufficient evidence against Bali to convict him and a compromise *(sulh)* had been made, but many Christians *(zimmis)* were fleeing to the land of the Franks (Firengistan). An imperial order is sent, then, to the Cyprus governor and the new Baf kadi that the matter should be re-investigated if it has not already been settled . . . (1 137–1; III Şevval 1002, Konstantiniye).

Other important documents included title deeds or certificates *(temessuk)*, imperial orders, and money transfers *(havale)*.

Title deeds were not used too frequently at the court in Lefkoşa, and it may be presumed that their possession in Cyprus was far from universal. However, Rahime hatun, widow and executrix of the late Hasan beg of Limosa, presented a title deed *(temessuk)* in her possession in order to secure possession of her late husband's 30 donum of arable fields *(tarla)* (4 78–2; III Receb 1044).

When Mustafa çelebi tried to collect from the steward of the imperial treasury 100,000 akce that the late Baf begi Mehmed beg owed him from a loan, Mustafa çelebi was unable to substantiate his claim because he lacked a *temessuk* (1 30–1; Receb 1002). Kordovan, baylos of the island of Cyprus, presented a *fetva*, a *temessuk*, a *huccet*, and an *emr* to the court in support of his claim before the island's chief financial officer defterdar Bali efendi (1 72–3; Muharrem 1003).

Imperial orders of two kinds might be useful to local litigants of Cyprus. First, a claimant might assert before the court that a particular general order is relevant to his own individual business. Second, a claimant might directly or through agents secure an imperial order which concerned only his own litigation.

Receb bn Şa'ban kethuda attested that his late father had made vakf fields and gardens at Kitriya village by means of an imperial order (1 46–2; III Rebi' II 1002). Musa, spahi of Vezace village of Lefkoşa, unsuccessfully attempted to secure back taxes of Ergiri v. Ciryako who had left that village for another one 18 years earlier because Ergiri showed that he had departed in accordance with an imperial order *(emr-i şerif)* (1 64–2; Muharrem 1003). Spahi Muhib bn Mer'i of Hirsofi dependent on Yuli (?) village tried to force the return of Ziya v. Istali (?) of that village, but Ziya had left over 20 years earlier, and an imperial order required that if he had been absent more than three years he could live in whichever place he chose (1 258–67, I Zil-Kade 1002).

Mehmed oda başi of the spahis of Magosa castle made a claim against two non-Muslims of Lefkoşa who, according to him, had illegally left his village in Mesariye kaza a few years before. Mehmed claimed that, according to his imperial order *(emr-i şerif)*, if 10 years have not passed, the villagers should be returned to their village or they should pay the tax for leaving lands uncultivated *(çift bozan resmi)* (4 67–1; III Sefer 1044).

When the abbot *(igumenos)* of Aya Mama monastery in Morfo na-hiye, the monk *(rahib)* Baba Eksendri, went to the Porte to complain about a long-standing dispute he had with the present kadi of Tuzla mevlana haci Ahmed efendi, he was given not only an imperial order *(emr-i şerif)* but also a letter *(mektub)* from the Rumeli kadi'asker about the problem (4 92–2; I Ramazan 1044).

Money transfers or letters of credit *(havale)* sometimes passed through the hands of the court in the routine process of settling disputes over debts. The people *(mahallesi ahalisi 'ammet)* of Mestotori (?) quarter received 4000 akce owed them by etmekci Mehmed bn Ahmed when the latter provided muhzir başi Ilyas aga with a money transfer *(havale)* (3 161–7; III Rebi' II 1019).

Kasim çavuş bn Haydar wanted a money transfer *(havale)* for the annual stipend *(saliyane)* from ʿAli bn Seydi (3 96–1; I Şevval 1019). Solimo v. Harito acknowledged having received a *havale* for three of the five guruş owed him by Loizo v. Kistintin through the hands of Selim bn Suleyman (3 31–5; II Zil-Kade 1018).

ʿAli bn Yusuf states before *(ihzar)* Yusuf bn Musa: Yusuf has my *havaleʾ-i şerʿ* worth 760 akce. He gave 60 akce but still owes 700 akce, which I want. Yusuf denies that. ʿIsa bn Ramazan and Hamze bn Suleyman testify that there was a *havaleʾ-i şerʿ*, of which Yusuf had paid 60 akce and still held the rest. (3 41–4; III Cumadi I 1019)

When an imperial order announced the appointment of a person to an office, at the same time a letter stipulating the nature, term (if any), and salary of the office was presented to the new appointee. That letter, a berat, remained his property for as long as he held office. As with other documents, only the kadi had the authority to judge whether or not a berat was valid. Sometimes new appointees were assigned even before the normal term expired. Sometimes two people were appointed to the same office, either in error or because of confusion about who in the imperial government should appoint people to a particular office. In either case, the local kadi had to examine the conflicting documents and determine who the legitimate officeholder was.

Ahmed aga bn Hasan, commander *(aga)* of the armorers *(cebeci)* of Lefkoşa, states *(tm)* before armorer commander Hasan bn ʿAbdullah: The command *(agalik)* was granted to me. I have an imperial berat and an imperial order *(emr)*. When, in accordance with the berat and *emr*, I took possession of the office, Hasan refused to obey the orders. Let the letters of change, the berat, and the imperial order be examined in accordance with the Sharia. When the berat and the imperial order in Ahmed's possession were examined and read, it was seen that the command of the armorers of Lefkoşa had been granted to Ahmed aga. The office and its revenues were ordered to him. (1 31–3; II Şaban 1002)

Spahi Mehmed oda başi possessed a berat confirming his right to collect certain taxes from residents of a village in Mesariye kaza; he was able to claim the fee for leaving land uncultivated from two villagers who had absented themselves (4 67–1; III Sefer 1044). A berat was issued for the castle warden *(dizdar)* of Lefkoşa (4 209–1; Konstantiniye, II Muharrem 1046). A berat was given for a ziʿamet in Lefkoşa nahiye, worth 50,360 akce, and vacant from the time of Mustafa bn Ahmed, was granted to Şahin starting 9 April 1635 (22 Şevval 1044) on condition of his living in the district *(sancak)* and going on campaign (4 219–1, 220–1; I Zil-Kade 1044). Idris aga, overseer *(nazir)* of the foundation of the late Sultan Selim han in Istanbul is dismissed, and Mustafa is appointed in his place starting 30 August 1634 (6 Rebi‘ I 1044) at a salary of six akce/day, to be paid from the revenues of the foundation (240–2; 26 Rebi‘ I 1044, Konstantiniye).

Hiristofi v. Luka was given a berat confirming that he lives in the city and is excused from paying the customary tax due for not cultivating his land (1 259–3; I Zil-Kade 1002).

A Greek Orthodox *(Rum l-asl)* zimmi slave named Petro v. Hiristofi had an official receipt *(tezkire)* that he had been emancipated for serving well (1 265–2; II Zil-Kade 1002). Margarita bint Yano had an official receipt *(tezkire)* that, as guardian *(vasi)* for the orphans of the late Yorolimo v. Piyero of Terhone village of Lefkoşa, she had sold two houses *(ev)* at the village belonging to the children (1 304–5; 1 Muharrem 1003). When Marikka paid his 5000 akce debt to Vehhab çavuş of Lefkoşa through Vehhab's legal agent *(vekil)* Bali efendi, he was given an official receipt *(tezkire)* which he brought to the court to register the matter in order to get an official document from the court *huccet* (1 318–4; 1 Muharrem 1003).

Proper documentation was particularly important in dealing with pious foundations. By presenting to the court the official document concerning the foundation *(vakf name)* of the foundation of the late ‘Arab Ahmed Paşa, its administrator *(mutevelli)* seyyid Mehmed bn seyyid Kasim proved despite the contrary claim by Huseyn çavuş that a certain bread baker's shop belonged to the foundation (1 24–5; Cumadi II 1002). After the document concerning the terms *(vakfiye)* of another foundation had been observed for 19 years, zimmi Hiristofi v. Petre encroached on its property and had to be restrained (1 46–2; III Rebi‘ II 1002). The document concerning the foundation *(vakf name)* of the foundation of the late Mustafa Paşa was in the trust of *(emanet)* ‘azablar agasi Hamze aga in Lefkoşa until Suleyman came to examine it (1 238–3; II Ramazan 1002).

Oaths

Oaths were used at the court of Lefkoşa only in the absence of more highly esteemed forms of proof like confessions, the testimony of two eye-witnesses, and certain written evidence. If the plaintiff lacked such proof, and if no compromise could be reached, the defendant might be asked to take an oath to support his denial. That was not common, for over all only about 4% of cases involved oath taking.[2]

The Hanefi law school required that oaths had to be sworn in the name of God at court in the presence of the kadi. That included Christians and Jews as well as Muslims. Sometimes the latter would be noted as having sworn by God who sent down the Koran to Muhammed, while Christians would be noted as having sworn by God who sent down the Gospel *(Incil)* to Jesus *('Isa)*.

Oaths at the court of Lefkoşa were given in quite an egalitarian way. The kadis administered oaths to men and women, Muslims and non-Muslims in exactly the same way. The oath of every male and female, Muslim and Christian, counted precisely the same as that of everyone else.

Rare instances of oaths taken at the request of police occurred, but then the police were just acting as any kadi, and indeed any adult, could. For example, when Ilyas bn 'Ala' eddin of Kunye village died there, Huseyn beg, agent *(mubaşir)* for governor Ramazan Paşa's administrative officer *(musellim)* Mustafa kethuda asked everyone in the village to take an oath of innocence (1 40–4; II Şaban 1002).

Usually oaths were reserved for defendants. However, in circumstances where the defendant not only denied the charge but added a positive assertion of his own, then in regard to the proof of that particular statement he became the "plaintiff" with the subsequent possibility that, lacking proof, he might demand an oath from the original plaintiff. That was uncommon, however. Neither was it common for anyone to decline the opportunity to take an oath.

Blood Money *(Dem Diyeti)*

In Ottoman legal practice communal responsibility is intimately connected with the payment of blood money *(dem diyeti)* in certain cases of homicide. Police officials, whose salaries were supplemented by a fraction of the blood money payments, were no doubt eager to establish responsibility in cases of injury or death. Those really or potentially liable for payments tried to provide proof of why they should not be held responsible.

Beyt ul-mal hassa ve ʿamme superviser *(emin)* of the city and officer *(mulazim)* Suleyman beg had as agent *(vekil)* Musli bn ʿAbdullah who acknowledged *(ik)* before Ahmed *(bn)* Turak and Musa bn Mustafa of Taht-i Kalʿe quarter in Lefkoşa castle: An old Christian woman *(zimmi)* fell into a well near the houses where they live. She was old; she fell by herself and perished. Blood money *(dem diyeti)* of 10 altun was received, and there is no further claim. (1 10–5; II Ramazan 988)

Halil bn Halil of Perestiyo (?) village of Lefkoşa, his wife Cennet, and his mother Suret are present in the court *(meclis-i şerʿ-i şerife)* and say in the presence of the people of the village *(ehl-i karye):* Our daughter Teslime bint Halil disappeared while she was sleeping among us in the night. We requested an investigation. ʿAli aga and Caʿfer beg, who were appointed agents *(mubaşir)* by ʿAli Paşa and superviser *(emin)* Perviz aga, respectively, were assigned. When they reached that village, the aforementioned Halil of his own volition confessed *(ikrar).* Halil said: Satan led me astray. I took my own daughter Teslime from her mother with the intention of making blood flow for the people of the village. I drowned her and left her in a ruined well *(kuyu).* Let us take the body out. Then ʿAbdul-Kerim çavuş, one of the Muslims present, pulled out the body with a hook *(çengal).* In truth the evidence is certain. Then the aforementioned Cennet, Suret, and Halil renounced claim against the people of the village. That was registered in the court record book *(sicil).* A copy was written at the request of the people of the village. (1 23–1; Receb 1002)

Mustafa ota başi bn Mehmed, guardian *(vasi)* before the Sharia for Mustafa, ʿAli, and Fatma, orphans of the late Emir ʿAli beşe of the Cyprus janissaries, who was killed *(maktul)* while living in Kakopetriye village of Lefka kaza, states *(tk/tm)* before Mihayel v. Tomazo and Baba Vasil v. Baba Viryoni of Galata village of that kaza: The blood money of the deceased is wanted at the governor's council *(divan-i Kibris)* and council of the Sharia *(meclis-i şerʿ).* Also maintenance *(nafaka, kisve)* is necessary for the orphans. I received 14,000 akce from Mihayel and Vasil as guardian. (4 70–1; I Receb 1044)

When a man named Hasan in Lefkoşa began to show signs of madness, a number of men summoned his son Ahmed to court to request that they either leave the quarter or take the man to a hospital *(timar).* Ahmed, however, acknowledged the madness of his father, saying: If my father perishes alone or falls in a well or gets lost, I have no claim for blood money against the people of the quarter (1 34–1; I Şaban 1002).

In some instances doctors required that patients in their care, or the closest relatives of their patients, swear not to make any claims against the doctor should he be unsuccessful. That was the case with a villager from Eskelon (?) village in Lefkoşa kaza who acted for his father Tomas (1 147–2; I Rebi 'I 1003).

Maintenance and Clothing Allowances *(Nafaka ve Kisve)*

The court had the authority, and the responsibility, to ensure that women were adequately supported by their husbands, and children by their fathers. Even after being divorced, women were entitled to that for a fixed time period. Children who inherited property from deceased fathers often were supported by that property, although first the mother or another guardian had to secure the kadi's permission. Fathers, on the other hand, unless impoverished, were expected to support their children from their own wealth without using the children's inheritances from their mothers. Other guardians, of course, could not be expected to expend their own resources on an orphan if he had inherited property, although to do so was honorable. The maintenance allowance *(nafaka)* and clothing allowance *(kisve)* were awarded as per diem allotments, which incidentally are accurate indicators of the minimal cost of living.

Cemile hatun bint 'Abdullah, divorced wife of janissary Mustafa, has two akce/day allotted for her maintenance. (1A 5–3; 9 Ramazan 988)

Siyuze (?) bint Bekr of Aya Sofya quarter states *(tk/tm)* at court: I do not have enough money to support the boy Derviş, son of my late daughter. I want maintenance allowance from his property. Three akce/day is allotted. (2 5–2; III Zil-Hicce 1016)

Yusuf çavuş of Lefkoşa states *(tk)* at court: The orphan son of the late Şa'ban bn Ibrahim needs maintenance and clothing allowance. Eight akce/day is allotted. (2 9–3; I Rebi' II 1016)

Arslan kethuda, guardian *(vasi)* for Mehmed, minor son *(sagir ogli)* of the late Ahmed Paşa who died while governor *(mir miran)*, who now is Tuzla sancagi begi, states *(bk/tm)* at court: 500 akce per day *(fi kul yevm)* for maintenance and clothing allowance is sufficient *(kifayet)* for Mehmed beg. That much is allotted for his servants and dependents. (4 61–3; I Sefer 1044)

Mehmed beşe bn Yusuf, guardian *(vasi)* of the minor daughter of the late Mustafa of Kaymakli village, states *(bk/tm)* at court: Now I have become guardian. Maintenance and clothing allowance are necessary from her inherited property *(mal)*. Four akce/day is allotted. (4 73–2; II Receb 1044)

Mehmed of Aya Sofya quarter of Lefkoşa states *(bk)* at court: When maintenance allowance is necessary for the minor Isma'il, four akce/month (?) is allotted. (4 77–2; III Receb 1044)

Halil boluk başi bn 'Ali, father of 'Ali, minor son of the late Narin bint 'Abdullah of Yanik (?) bagce quarter of Lefkoşa, acknowledges *(ik/i't)* before Hasan beşe bn Mehmed, for himself and as a guardian: A house *(menzil)* in that quarter is sold to Hasan for 5000 akce in order to get maintenance allowance for the child 'Ali. (4 91–1, 2; I Ramazan 1044)

Mehmed bn Suleyman, guardian *(vasi)* for the minor son Ahmed of the late Ahmed çavuş of Lefkoşa, states *(bk)* at court: Since I am guardian, the boy needs maintenance and clothing allowance from the property *(mal)* he inherited from his late father. Six akce/day is allotted. (4 139–4; III Şaban 1045)

'Ayşe bint Tuvana (?), mother and guardian of the minor children of the late Nebi beşe of Lefkoşa, acknowledges and states *(ik/tk)* before Ferencesko of Laçe village of Lefkoşa kaza: A house *(menzil)* at the village is sold to Ferencesko for 800 akce in order to pay a debt for maintenance allowance *(zaruret-i deyn-i nafakalari için)* . . . (4 141–3; I Ramazan 1045)

Receb bn Mustafa oda başi, brother of the minor son of the late Mustafa of Tirahon village of Lefkoşa kaza, says: I am guardian for my brother, a minor. He needs maintenance and clothing allowance. Four akce/day is allotted. (4 183–1; I Receb 1046)

Bedros v. Bolak (?), an Armenian of Lefkoşa, makes a claim *(da 'va/tk)* against Manuk, grown son of Bedros' late uncle *('ammisi)* Toma of Lefkoşa: When Toma died, his property was remitted canceling the debt *(itlak)*. He had no money or possessions left. His son Manuk was under my care *(hucr ve terbiye)*. For 13 years Manuk was supported by loans *(karz)* for five akce/day for his maintenance and clothing allowance. Former Lefkoşa kadi mevlana Mustafa efendi presented a signed official record of the case *(huccet)* dated I Rebi' I 1033 (late December 1623). Manuk replies: Bedros allotted me maintenance and clothing allowance. When I was small I did work *(hidmet)* for him. However, Manuk has no proof. When an oath is proposed to Bedros, he takes an oath by God who sent down the Gospel *(Incil)* to Jesus ('Isa) that nothing remains of the inheritance (muhallefat) of Manuk's father; all was allotted for maintenance and clothing. Of the 13 years, he was a minor for six years, and after that he was able to work. (4 174–1; III Cumadi II 1046)

Preemption *(Şuf ʿa)*

It is an established principle of the Sharia that all land owners have the right to buy any land immediately contiguous to their property when it is offered for sale, or even after it has been sold to another person, if they make known their desire immediately upon learning of the sale. That same right holds for co-owners of property offered for sale. The price must be a fair market price.

Ridvan bn ʿAbdullah states *(tk)* before Nikola v. Yakimo: I bought the estate *(çiftlik)* and house *(ev)* of Papa Androniko. Now Nikola wants to preempt [the sale] *şufʿa)*. (1 5–8; III Ramazan 988)

Bali çavuş bn Niyet (?) of Aya Hor (?) village of Lefkoşa makes a claim *(td)* against Ordek hatun: I bought three houses *(evler)* from her son *(sadri ogli)* for 20 altun. The sale was completed, payment was made, and I took possession. Then she began to seek preemption *(şufʿa)*, but it was too late. Ordek says that she did not give up her right of preemption. However, ʿudul-i muslimin Yusuf bn Ibrahim and Mehmed bn Mustafa confirm Bali. (1 254–2; III Şevval 1002)

Although the people of newly conquered Cyprus might be expected to have used preemption very frequently in order to preserve religious and ethnic separation, in fact no other instances were discovered besides the two mentioned above. Clearly even in 1580 the courts knew and understood preemption. The court records suggest, however, that people rarely claimed the right.

Cursing

Cursing *(şetm)* people is a distinct and fairly serious offense in Anatolian and early Ottoman law codes. In the old Dulkadir criminal code, the penalty was corporal punishment or a fine of 30 akce. In early Ottoman codes the penalty for cursing *(na meşruʿ kelimat)* was subjection to the bastinado *(taʿzir)*, plus an additional fine of one akce for every two strokes applied, the number of which was at the discretion of the kadi.[3]

Cursing was a social offense in the criminal law. People usually cursed others in ways designed to provoke or to antagonize them. Although sometimes curses may be uttered with quiet derision, cursing usually developed out of virulent antipathy, often perhaps spontaneously out of inflamed arguments. Probably cursing often grew out of or led to violence. Bringing the matter immediately to the attention of the court was a way to minimize conflict.

Cursing was not usually done in isolation. Probably police did not go out of their way to ferret it out but cared about cursing only when complaints were made. Not surprisingly police and military officers themselves appear to have been cursed relatively frequently. Sometimes that occurred in the line of duty. To the extent that they summoned to court people who cursed them, rather than resorting to violence or counter-taunts, that may be a positive sign. Anyway, cursing does not seem to have been a serious social problem in Cyprus.

Seyyid Mustafa su başi makes a claim *(da'va)* against racil Yusuf bn Ibrahim: On the night of 27 June 1594 (8 Şevval 1002) Yusuf cursed me *(şetm)* and called me a pimp *(pazenk)*. Let Yusuf be asked. When proof was needed, seven witnesses and others confirmed Mustafa. (1 248–1; II Şevval 1002)

Sa'di çavuş bn Hamze of Lefkoşa makes a claim *(da'va)* against Yusuf bn Kasim of the defenders of the castle of Lefkoşa: Yusuf cursed my faith *(iman)* and my mouth *(agiz)*. Yusuf denies that. 'Udul Ishak çavuş, 'Abdi bn 'Abdullah, Veli bn 'Ali, and Cihan çavuş confirm Sa'di. (1 269–1; II Zil-Kade 1002)

Halil bn Yusuf says before his son Yusuf: Yusuf cursed me. Yusuf denies that. Mehmed bn 'Abdullah and Ilyas bn Piri confirm Halil. (1 235–7; II Ramazan 1002)

Rahime bint Kalayci of Citane (?) village says before Maksud: He entered my house, struck me and hit my teeth. Maksud denied that; then he replied: Her son 'Abdul-Gaffar cursed my wife *('avret)*. Then I struck her (Rahime). (1 241–10; I Şevval 1002)

Veli says *(ihzar)* before Yani v. Marko: While I was buying figs *(incir)* in a grocer's shop *(bakkal dukkani)* Yani cursed my mouth and my faith. Yani denies that. Ibrahim bn Begi (?) and Mahmud bn Mehmed confirm Veli: In truth he cursed Veli in the way described. (3 38–5; III Cumadi I 1019)

Mustafa bn Hasan of Lefkoşa states *(bm)* before Murad v. Migirdic (?), an Armenian: He cursed my mouth and my faith. I want justice *(ihkak-i hakk)*. Murad denies that. (3 158–5; III Rebi' II 1019)

Nasuh, beardless boy *(emredd)*, says *(ihzar)* before Ahmed bn Haydar: He struck me. Ahmed acknowledges that but says that he did so after he had been cursed obscenely *(şetm galiz)*. (3 64–8; I Receb 1019)

Receb beg of Lefkoşa states *(bm)* before haci Vehhab: Vehhab came to my house and cursed *(şetm)* my wife and son. Let him be asked. Vehhab denies that. Derviş Mehmed bn haci Yusuf and Derviş Mustafa bn Ahmed confirm Receb. (3 125–9; II Şevval 1019)

Papa Baçisodi v. Loizo, Papa Maniko (?), and other priests *(papazlar)* say: Panederfo cursed us. Let him be asked. He denies that. Piyalu v. Zaniko (?) and Bernarto (?) v. Nikilo confirm the priests. (3 146–7; III Cumadi II 1019)

Mustafa bn Mehmed of Lefkoşa states *(bm)* before ʿAbdi çavuş bn Pir Ahmed: God forbid, ʿAbdi called me infidel, son of an infidel, *(kafir ogli kafir)*. I do not accept that. I want him asked in accordance with the Sharia, and I want justice done. ʿAbdi says: Mustafa said let them shit on the governor's head *(begler begi hazretlerinun başina yestehlesunlar)*. Then in reply *(mukabelesinde)* I said: You are not a Muslim. You are an infidel. That is registered. (3 159–2; III Rebʿ II 1019)

Receb beşe of Lefkoşa makes a claim *(td)* in the presence of Mehmed beg: Mehmed called me Jew *(cuhud)* Receb. Mehmed denies that. Huseyn bn Memi and Mehmed beşe confirm Receb. (3 177–4; 28 Şaban 1019)

Mehmed beg of Kaymakli village of Lefkoşa kaza makes a claim *(daʿva/tk)* against Yaro (?) v. Andreye of the village: The night of this writing he attempted the evil act *(fiʿl-i şeniʿ)*. I was being vigilant *(agah)*. I screamed. He struck me and cursed me *(galiz ile bana şetm eylemuşdur)*. I want justice done. When Yaro denies that, Maniço v. Istavriye and Fesenco v. Tomazo confirm Mehmed: Tonight screaming was heard from his house *(menzil)*. I was watching. Yaro struck *(darb)* the house *(hane)* and female slave (?) of Mehmed and he cursed. (4 104–1; III Ramazan 1044)

Racil Ahmed beşe of Pirastiyo village of Mesariye nahiye makes a claim *(iddiʿa/ tk)* against zimmi Savu of Mekuma (?) village: He killed my horse *(at)* and he cursed me *(şutum-i galiz)*. When Savu denies that, Ahmed is given a three-day delay to bring back proof. Now 30 days have passed. (4 106–2; I Şevval 1044)

Salaries of Kadis, and Kadis in Economic Life

Not much information is provided about the wages of kadis. Mevlana ʿAlaeddin efendi was assigned the kaza of Tuzla starting 21 May 1594 (1 Ramazan 1002) at a salary of 80 akce/day (1 101–1; from kadi ʿasker of Rum ili, Sunullah, III Şaban 1002). A decade and a half later the Rum ili kadi ʿasker assigned that office to former kadi mevlana Musa for 130 akce/day (2 17–2; 1 Zil-Kade 1016). Almost simultaneously Mesariye kaza, which was assigned for 80 akce/day to mevlana seyyid Mehmed and Mesariye kadi mevlana Resul, after one and a half years holding that office, was transferred to Hirsofi kaza for a salary of 70 akce/day. Both assignments began on 2 November 1606 (1 Receb 1015). (2 18–1; Konstantiniye, 7 Receb 1015). A year and a half later mevlana Ahmed was assigned to Piskopi kaza, then at a wage of 80 akce/day (2 86–2; Haleb, III Şaban 1016).

Tuzla kadi mevlana Ahmed efendi was involved in a trade agreement with abbot baba Eksendri of Aya Mama monastery in Morfo district (4 92–2; I Ramazan 1044). Present Magosa kadi ʿAli efendi was involved in long-distance trade, from which he had a debt of 328 riyali guruş to Musa beşe bn Mehmed beg of Belgrad (4 215–3; I Ramazan 1045). Mevlana Ahmed efendi bn Saʿdeddin efendi of Lefkoşa owned hundreds of estates (*çiftliks*) in various villages which he chose to make into a pious foundation (4 235–1; Uskudar, 12 Rebiʿ II 1043. 236–1; Konstantiniye, 1 Cumadi II 1043). Former Tuzla kadi haci Ahmed efendi bn haci ʿOsman purchased three large estates within a year: one in ʿOmeriye quarter of Lefkoşa worth 32,000 akce, a second at Ruhe (?) village in Morfo district worth 38,000 akce, and the third at Lapta village in Girniye district worth 22,000 akce (4 155–1; 17 Zil-Hicce 1045. 155–2; I Zil-Hicce. 187–2; II Receb 1046). Some kadis were rich.

Summary

Exactly the same law was applied all over the vast Ottoman empire, the sacred law of Islam, the Sharia, which equally applied over the rest of the contemporary Muslim world and which had been applied in its Hanefi form under the Abbasid caliphate starting in the middle of the 8th century. It was the official law for all of the people of Cyprus immediately starting with the conquest of 1570–1571. That was the only known court of that time, and was intended to handle all the problems and concerns of every Cypriot. The procedure is always described as "in accordance with the Sharia." During the very few times when other kinds of law were mentioned, such imperial law (*kanun*), or customary law (*ʿadet, resim*), they were judged as being within the scope of the Sharia.

Having the Sharia implemented is always considered the exact equivalent of doing justice. Saying that people have acted contrary to the

Sharia is to stigmatize their action as reprehensible. Almost all complaints can be reduced to, He violated the Sharia, and I want the Sharia enforced. Theoretically, at least, everyone has the same obligation to carry out the Sharia, including women and non-Muslims. It exempts children, however, because they by definition do not have sufficient intelligence or understanding to obey the Sharia. Part of growing up involves developing such intellectual and moral awareness that one is an adult, and can fully understand (and hence obey) the Sharia.

All adults are considered, by definition, fully able to comprehend and obey the law, and are responsible for doing it. People who were not adults often had a guardian *(vasi)* to represent their interest, especially in inheritance or property settlements, although even without such help, it was the duty of the kadi to ensure that all of the rights of the minor, and especially an orphan, were fully protected. Kadis were also especially charged to make sure that accurate weights and measures and the fair fixed prices of the market place were obeyed, as well as making sure that women were protected, and non-Muslims, too.

The official responsibilities of the kadis of Cyprus went far beyond merely making legal decisions. Disputes between members of different military corps were handled by kadis, who also were responsible for determining whose orders were valid, if there were conflicts or disagreements. If police officers of any sorts had disagreements with people, the court would determine who was right. All disputes regarding the timar system, who should control what timar, or what taxes should be paid, and to whom were also the province of the kadi. All other elements of the entire taxation system were under the supervision of the kadi; he was the final authority in every matter. Also people could make complaints of any nature about any people involved in the provincial government. He was also to help and protect the weak and the poor.

Kadis were in charge of making sure that the people who wished to establish pious foundations were acting within the scope of the Sharia, and hence were valid. Also they were responsible for making sure that terms and conditions of the donors were actually properly carried out. Even complaints against other kadis were occasionally made; they could be made at courts, or people could appeal to the Porte. Many kadis had other positions which helped supplement their salaries. Some were involved in various aspects of trade and commerce; others received stipends for carrying out local educational or administrative functions.

The court always strongly urged people to come to court in person, make known their complaints directly, and have them be settled immediately. If a person was ill, or out of town, or very busy, he might appoint someone with full power of attorney. The court encouraged people to come in person, and so in only 13% of the total cases were agents actually used. Women could more easily be excused in these matters, and so 36% of the women chose to use legal agents. It was almost mandatory for all parties in cases involving criminal disputes to come in person, unless they were aged, injured, or disabled. Any adult could act as a legal agent for anyone else.

The court was very strongly devoted to settling all disputes. Not infrequently people were willing to compromise in their disputes with different parties, making concessions to the extent that both parties agree formally to become reconciled in their dispute. There seem to have frequently been such people in the local town quarters or villages who formally got involved in helping people solve disputes. That seems to have been an active force within the communities. Compromise was admired.

The mufti of Cyprus had a quite limited scope of authority. He was a legal expert who should be qualified to give a theoretically accurate answer to any legal question posed. He had to confine his answer to the terms that were posed him, and he had no authority to question the accuracy of the petitioner. People armed with their fetvas (legal opinion) presented them to the kadis, who then judged their relevance to the claim, making their decisions on the basis of all the other evidence presented, too.

Great importance was given to having accurate written records. The court had its own official record book, where all of the deliberations were entered in detail, along with verbatim copies of all official correspondence reaching the court. The names and residences of all adult males were supposed to be preserved in a special register. Careful records were kept to reflect the operations of the timar system. Copies of cases heard at the court were frequently used by local people. Large numbers of written records concerned inheritance settlements. The Court register was also the official land register, and so land and property transfers were entered. Berats also were normally presented in writing. Documents reflecting the operation of pious foundations were frequently in use, as were the original vakfiye or vakf name, where the full text is written.

Oaths at the court of Lefkoşa were only used in the absence of more highly respected forms of proof, such as confessions, two eyewitnesses, or written evidence. If a plaintiff lacked proof, and no compromise was reached, the defendant might be able to take an oath of innocence.

Communal responsibility required the payment of blood money *(dem diyeti)* when it was impossible to determine who was responsible for a homicide, on the behalf of town quarters, or villages.

If a woman or child were unable to support herself, a per diem allowance might be established by the court drawing on resources of husband or father. The allowance was set at a level to enable the person to have not only adequate food but adequate clothing. Sometimes in emergencies, people who were not even related might be called upon. If people were capable of doing some sort of remunerative work, they might be taught; in the absence of family they might incur debt, which might be paid by becoming an apprentice or household servant. It was an established principle of the Sharia that co-owners, and owners of contiguous property had the right to buy the land, if they announced that as soon as they learned of an impending sale. Preemption, which was not too common, provided a way to fight the fragmentary tendencies of private property which is aggravated by the Islamic inheritance system.

Cursing was an offense in the criminal law. People usually cursed others to provoke or antagonize them, probably it often grew out of or led to violence. Bringing it to court immediately could help minimize conflict. Not surprisingly a significant number of cases brought to court and recorded involved police officers of various sorts who lodged complaints.

Almost nothing is known about the salaries of the kadis in Cyprus.

NOTES

1. For imperial efforts to control the evil actions of kadis, see pp. 75–79 in Halil Inalcik, "Adaletnameler," *Belgeler, Türk Tarih Belgeleri Dergisi* 2.1965.49–145. That study reveals systematic efforts by the central government to

eliminate abuses in the imperial administration, with the particular concern of bringing just rule throughout the empire.

2. They changed in frequency from 1% to 5% to 7%.
3. Uriel Heyd, *Studies in Old Ottoman Criminal Law*. ed. V. L. Ménage. Oxford, 1973. P. 71, 110 #53, 142 #39. 271f. Another Ottoman code required a fine of 40 akce with no strokes.

FOUR

The Military Corps (Janissaries and Spahis) and the Police

Very soon after the conquest of the island, the Porte assigned garrisons to castles located in strategic places. All of the castles except Lefkoşa were on the coast. Of course, the presence of fortifications was the main consideration in deciding where to establish new defensive positions, for it was far cheaper to repair and restore existing fortifications than to build new ones. The existing fortifications had been constructed on sites the strategic significance of which was already manifest. An analysis of the allocation of soldiers and money for these places in 1571–1572 (979–980) reveals much about how the Ottoman government regarded them. Surprisingly the funds allocated for the fortresses and defenses of Tuzla, Lefkoşa, and Magosa were at the same level. A sum of 2,671,280 akce was budgeted for the defense of Tuzla. Several classes of soldiers, 1045 in all, including 102 canoneers, were assigned there. Among the 1130 soldiers assigned to Lefkoşa were 152 canoneers; 2,562,502 akce was allocated for the castle. Although a breakdown of kinds and numbers of soldiers was not provided for Magosa, 2,618,222 akce was allocated for its defense. The defense of Baf, which received only about 30% of the funds assigned to Tuzla, Lefkoşa, and Magosa, was the responsibility of 310 soldiers with various specialties. The 774,658 akce allocated for Baf was more than twice the 353,110 akce provided for the castle of Girniye, and that was almost twice the 180,738 akce allocated for the defense of Limosa. The allocation of resources for the defense of those six places tells much about what the Ottomans hoped for them.

The most important commercial harbor on the island was Larnaka, or Tuzla, as the Ottomans referred to it. Most foreign ambassadors resided there. The castle *(kal'e)* officially had a garrison of 30 or 40 soldiers *(merdan)* and 10 or 15 canoneers *(topciyan)* to protect the harbor. Between 17,000 and 20,000 akce was officially allocated annually for the soldiers and between 7500 and 8500 akce for the canoneers.

The Janissary Corps

Originally the janissary corps was an elite Ottoman infantry composed entirely of slaves whose only loyalty was to the sultan. Conscripted for life as children from Christian villages, constantly drilled, converted to Islam, and garrisoned near the royal palace, they constituted one of the two great Ottoman military corps. With the weakening of the central government, their discipline broke down, free men were admitted, and their numbers increased. They spread to the provinces, where they participated in local economies.[1]

Starting in the 16th century admission to the janissary corps was first opened to freeborn Muslims. Soon the practice became widespread. The changes in recruitment patterns were profound. In 1593–1595 only 46% of janissaries whose full names are cited as legal agents *(vekil)*, witnesses *(şuhud)*, creditors, and lenders were of slave (non-Muslim) origin. In 1609–1611, that proportion had fallen to 25%, and by 1633–1637 it had reached 16%.[2]

Among the military creditors and debtors whose full names are given (that is, the name and father's name, with 'Abdullah used where the man is a convert), 29% (26 of 91) were converts to Islam, the other 71% were born Muslims. A breakdown of the number of converts by time period gives a striking indication of the new origins of janissaries after 1620. In both 1593–1595 and 1609–1611 36% of the military creditors and debtors whose full names are cited (10 of 28 and 12 of 33, respectively) are converts, 64% being native Muslims. However, in 1633–1637 that proportion had fallen by one-third to 12%, versus 88% native Muslims. Obviously recruitment patterns of Ottoman soldiers on Cyprus had changed drastically.

In the traditional Ottoman system the janissary corps was paid salaries directly by the Porte, while the spahis were supported by stipends from the revenues of agricultural taxes (the timar system). Those taxes were arranged in units of revenue reflecting the rank of the cavalryman and were paid locally rather than through the imperial government. However, in Cyprus on at least a few occasions janissaries actually held timars. A timar worth 6,299 akce in Lefkoşa nahiye was awarded to janissary Sefer beşe bn ʿAbdullah (2 19–3; 1016). Christian Şimas made a claim against haci Mehmed bn Yusuf of the janissaries, who had a timar (1 44–1; III Şaban 1002). Caʿfer Paşa had awarded a timar to the late Suleyman su başi, who was commander *(yaya başi)* of the janissaries of Cyprus (1 50–3; I Ramazan 1002). Such practice probably was unusual.

Janissaries, except in so far as they sometimes were su başis, almost never got involved in the apprehension of wrong-doers. Possibly the only exception was when ʿAbdul-Kadir boluk başi and Keyvan boluk başi testified that zimmi Luyi v. Hiristodiye of Aya Demre village improperly had an unrelated woman named Mariya living in his house (3 34–2; II Zil-Kade 1018). The reason for their involvement then is not clear from the case, although possibly an earlier case, not preserved, could provide an explanation.

Throughout the period under study janissary discipline was breaking down. Both the officers and the soldiers themselves were exhorted to obey their orders, not always to any avail. Janissaries all over the empire skipped campaigns. The necessity of attending those campaigns was stressed, for example, in an undated order to present Cyprus janissary commander *(serdar)* Veli çelebi (4 223–1). A charge was made against Huseyn çorbaci that, when a janissary in his unit *(ota)* had gone to Anatolia without permission *(bila izn)* to engage in trade *(ticaret)*, Huseyn had concealed the absence, and contrary to imperial law *(kanun)* had taken the salary *(ʿulufe)* of the missing man for himself. The Cyprus provincial council and Sharia court had already ordered that the names of any missing corpsmen were to be registered in two places and sent to the Porte, while at the same time immediately assigning the salary to other qualified people (4 45–1; II Muharrem). At that very time leaders of six janissary divisions *(boluks)* were accused in person before governor Caʿfer Paşa of having incited their subordinates to revolt against the governor (45–2; II Muharrem 1044).

Although legally slaves of the sultan, whose private property would normally pass to the Porte after they died, janissaries at least in some cases did pass property by inheritance. When janissary Iltimas (?) bn

'Abdullan of Tarhone (?) village of Lefkoşa died, 52,000 akce's worth of his property was sold to Ibrahim çavuş bn 'Abdul-Kadir by janissary Davud beşe bn 'Abdullah, who had been appointed guardian of the minor children of the deceased (1 156–3; II Rebi' II 1003). Presumably that sale would provide maintenance for the orphans.

When Musa beşe bn Isma'il died in Kaymakli village of Lefkoşa, his brother 'Abdur-Rahim bn Isma'il of Aşagi Koy (?) (village) of Kilis kaza on the mainland (Ote Yaka) stated *(bm)* before janissary Behram su başi bn 'Abdullah: Behram seized the effects of the deceased for the treasury *(miri)*. Let him be asked about my brother's effects in accordance with the Sharia. Behram denies that. 'Udul-i muslimin 'Abdi çavuş bn Pir Ahmed aga and 'Abdur-Rahim bn 'Abdur-Rahman confirm that. 'Abdur-Rahim is Musa's brother from the mainland. (3 94–2; Şevval 1019)

When Sefer beşe of the Cyprus janissaries, from Pahna village of Evdim kaza, died without male children *(evlad-i zukur)*, the fields *(tarla)* in his possession were suitable for assigning title *(tapu)*, in accordance with imperial law *(kanun)*. However, they were given to his daughters Hanim and Yasemin for 6000 akce (2 25–1; III Şaban 1013). Although women were not permitted to inherit landed property in some provinces, daughters there who were deemed capable of operating it were given first option to buy such land at a modest price *(resm-i tapu)*. In any case, whether Sefer's fields passed to his daughters or to some new holder, they were not being turned over to the imperial treasury.

Nevertheless, at least in a technical sense the Porte continued to treat the property of the janissaries as though they held it only for their lifetimes, as was the case with property of other slaves. A letter to the kadi of Cyprus from Mehmed, aga of the janissary corps, reminded him that the effects of deceased janissaries, conscript boys *('acemi oglan)*, cannoneers *(topci)*, and armorers *(cebeci)* belonged to the imperial treasury *(beyt ul-mal)* (4 242–1; II Rebi' I 1044). The evidence is too sparse to permit any conjecture about janissaries' inheritance in Cyprus.

Popular conceptions of the janissaries in the late 16th and early 17th centuries involve two particular activities: (1) as men of violence, and (2) as artisans and merchants. The court records of Lefkoşa reveal much detail about each of those two aspects.

(1) Some janissaries seem always to have been involved in violence. In the presence of Cyprus governor Mehmed Paşa, Hasan çavuş bn Ahmed of his messengers *(çavuşes)* brought to court and made separate charges

against janissaries Mustafa bn ʿAbdullah and Huseyn bn Şaʿban. Mustafa had cursed his mouth and his wife and treated him with contempt, as had been proven by the testimony of two eyewitnesses. Besides cursing Hasan çavuş's mouth and wife, Huseyn had blocked his way twice with a knife, as was attested by the same two eyewitnesses (1 4–1, 2; I Ramazan 988). Only after Ahmed bn ʿAli had sought the help of the court against former janissary aga Ahmed aga had Ahmed aga returned certain movable possessions of Ahmed's that he had taken (1 89–1; Rebiʿ II 1003).

Mehmed bn haci Resul of Aya Sofya quarter of Lefkoşa states *(tm):* At the market *(çarsu)* of the city this afternoon, in front of Mustafa's shop, janissary Mustedam wounded my father Hasan çelebi in two places with a knife. My father is not able to move; up until now he has lain wounded in his house. Let a man be sent from the court. I want his wounds to be investigated. From the court mevlana Mustafa efendi was sent, with the people *(cemm-i gafir)* whose names are listed below. They found Mustafa çelebi wounded by a knife on his left arm and on the top of his right shoulder. When he was asked who wounded him, he answered: Janissary Mustedam. If I die from these blows, my adversary is Mustedam. I have no claim against anyone else in this matter. Mevlana Mustafa efendi came to court and gave that information and it was registered. (1 162–3; 7 Cumadi I 1003)

Janissaries Ahmed bn Mehmed and Mustafa bn Ilyas came upon janissary ʿAbdun-Nasr bn Yusuf at the home of Ramazan bn Ishak and struck him with their knives and wounded him (1 240–7; I Şevval 1002).

Janissary (racil) Bayram beşe of Lefkoşa states *(tm)* before janissary scribe Şaʿban efendi: While playing with a jereed *(cirit)* I threw one at Şaʿban, but I do not know where it hit him. (1 303–2; Zil-Hicce 1002)

Huseyn beg of the imperial *(dergah-i ali)* spahis makes a claim *(daʿva/tk)* against racil Receb beşe bn Yusuf of the Cyprus janissaries: Yesterday Receb pulled my beard and struck my left arm with a knife, wounding me. Receb denies that. When Huseyn is asked for proof, upright Muslims *(ʿudul-i muslimin)* Mustafa beg bn Ramazan and ʿOmer beg bn Mustafa confirm him. (4 49–2; III Muharrem 1044)

Caʿfer Paşa, present governor of the island of Cyprus, holds a meeting at the Sharia court and the Cyprus council *(divan)*. With the aforementioned governor the janissary aga, kethuda, and all of the officers *(şorbaciler, çavuş, and zabitlar)* state *(bk/tm)* before haci Mehmed ota başi from the 8th aga division *(boluk)*, haci Emrullah ota başi from the 4th *boluk*, Suleyman ota başi from the 2nd boluk, ʿAli ota başi from the 7th *boluk,* Sadi çavuş from the 3rd *boluk,* Haci Veli ota başi from the 3rd *boluk,* and haci Derviş: It was heard that three days ago on Friday when the assembly *(cemʿiyet)* was wanted, they led people astray (or tempted them to sin?) *(igva ve izlal)* in front of Aya Sofya mosque. They said: Caʿfer Paşa oppresses us *(teʿarruz).* When the officers *(zevabit)* were asked, they said: In truth on Friday while we were performing ritual worship at the mosque, the aforementioned unit heads *(ota başis)* came in our presence. Some did what was heard. (4 45–2; II Muharrem 1044)

Janissaries certainly had no monopoly on local violence, however, and indeed janissaries sometimes had to go to court to seek protection from the abuses of others.

Janissary Resul of Mamoniye village of Kukla kaza makes a claim *(td)* against Serki (?) v. Linarda (?): He seized my two lambs from my dairy farm in the village. I want them. Serki (?) denies that. When Resul was asked for proof, Ancoli v. Nikola and Nikola v. Covan (?) confirmed him. (1 191–2; I Cumadi II 1002)

Christians Istefan v. Yakub, Hiristofi v. Filori, and Yakimo v. Luka of Vadele village killed janissary Kara ʿAli when he came upon them drunk and carousing with a woman (1 5–4; I Ramazan 988). Emir ʿAli beşe of the Cyprus janissaries was killed while living in Kakopetriye village of Lefka kaza. When Mustafa ota başi bn Mehmed, guardian of the orphans of the deceased, sought blood money *(dem diyeti)* from Mihayel v. Tomazo and Baba Vasil v. Baba Viryoni of Galata village, he was given 14,000 akce (4 70–1; I Receb 1044).

(2) Janissaries, although members of the military elite, frequently used the court of Lefkoşa, where in most matters they were subject to the same procedures as other users of the court. A dispute between Iskender çavuş bn Isfendiyar and janissary Yusuf bn Mehmed over a field *(tarla)* between Boli and Milo (?) villages of Hirisofi kaza was settled at the Sharia court (1 16–2; 21 Ramazan 988). When the administrator *(mutevelli)* of Caʿfer Paşa foundation in Lefkoşa contested the claims of janissary kethuda Pervane kethuda, haci Mehmed, and Hasan efendi to a house and shop near the market *(çarşu),* the dispute was settled by the local kadi (1 23–2; Receb 1002). Likewise the court records preserve evidence of janissaries buying and selling land and property, giving and receiving loans, and otherwise engaging in business of the market place.

Almost one-sixth of all instances of credit involved people identifiable as janissaries: 16% (about 96 of 591). It has elsewhere been noted that janissaries gave twice as much credit as they received.

Janissary Hizir paid a debt of 6000 ʿosmani akce to present janissary boluk başi Memi bn Himmet (1 37–1; 16 Şaban 1002). Zimmi Lefteri v. Covan was imprisoned for more than six months before he paid the 1000 akce he owed janissary Mehmed bn ʿAbdullah of Lefkoşa (1 192–3; I Cumadi II 1003). Former Lefkoşa kadi mevlana Musliheddin efendi died leaving a debt of 384 (akce?) to janissary Huseyn (1 222–2; II Şaban 1001). ʿAli boluk başi bn ʿAbdullah owed the late janissary ʿAli beşe bn ʿAbdullah 34 head of goats *(keçi)* (3 33–2; II Zil-Kade 1018). Racil Huseyn çelebi of the Cyprus janissaries made a compromise *(sulh)* with Filozide, widow of the late Filori of Istefani village of Baf nahiye, for 3000 akce her late husband owed him from a loan *(mudaraba)* (4 145–1; III Ramazan 1045). ʿOmer çavuş bn Himmet of Lefkoşa still owed 50 gurus, of a former 140 riyal guruş debt to Mustafa çelebi bn Ismaʿil of Istanbul (4 126–2; I Receb 1045).

The Buyuk Hamam of the foundation of the late Mustafa Paşa in Lefkoşa was rented for 16 years to janissary haci Mehmed racil, but janissary kethuda ʿAbdur-Rahman and Bali çavuş wanted to raise that rent to outbid Mehmed (1 287–6; III Zil-Kade 1002. 292–1; I Zil-Hicce 1002. 307–3; III Zil-Hicce 1002). Janissary Yusuf beşe bn Mehmed of Mesariye kaza sold 13 donem of sown cotton to Piro v. Gasparo for 200 guruş (3 12–4; 10 Şevval 1018). Janissary Haci was caught selling barley *(arpa)* in excess of the official fixed price; that matter too was brought to the Sharia court (3 73–3; III Receb 1018). On the other hand, a dispute between racil Kara Mehmed beşe of Degirmenlik village of Lefkoşa kaza, of the Cyprus janissaries, and janissary racil Ibrahim beşe over the selling price of European satin *(Firenci atlas)* was twice heard in the presence of present Cyprus governor *(mir miran)* ʿAli Paşa at the governor's council *(divan)* and the Sharia court; possibly the reason was that foreigners *(mustemin)* were involved in other aspects of the dispute (4 142–3; III Ramazan 1045).

In the earlier periods some janissaries served as administrators *(mutevelli)* of foundations, including janissary kethuda Pervane, janissary aga of Cyprus Yusuf aga bn Perviz beg, and Lefkoşa ʿazablari agasi Dilaver aga bn ʿAbdul-Mennan (1 23–2; Receb 1002. 2 22; 1 Receb 1016). After about 1610 that practice declined. A foundation established by someone identified only as Yusuf, aga of the janissaries, provided a small income for the convent of the Mevlevi dervishes in Lefkoşa (2 76–1; 1 Rebi' I 1017).

In several instances cases involving janissaries are noted as having been heard at the Cyprus provincial council *(divan-i Kibris) and* at the Sharia court *(mahfil-i şer', meclis-i şer')*. From that context it is impossible to tell whether such cases were heard like other cases at the Sharia court, except with representatives of the provincial governor or even the governor himself present, or whether those cases were heard at some special meeting place of the governor's council with the kadi also present. Since those cases are registered in the court records chronologically, like all other cases, it seems likely that the Sharia court was the meeting place. However, it is not impossible that the scribe who recorded the cases could have attended a session of the governor's council outside the Sharia court and then immediately thereafter entered the details in the court record book.

It is easy to understand why governor Ca'fer Paşa would have summoned the Cyprus council *(divan)* and the Sharia court to hear testimony about several corps leaders fomenting rebellion against him, even if there is no indication of any differences in the procedure of that court (4 45–2; II Muharrem 1044). Neither is it surprising to find the provincial council the site of janissary çorbaci haci Hizir su başi bn Karaman hoca's claim against Ibrahim bn Yakub of Kuri koy (village). Ibrahim had blocked the way of a zimmi, who had sought the assistance of Hizir's slave *('abd-i memluki)* Dilaver bn 'Abdullah; then Ibrahim had struck Dilaver on the head with a rock *(taş)*, and only the intervention of the people of the village had saved Dilaver. Janissary Mehmed beşe bn 'Omer and 'Abdi bn 'Abdi had also been involved in that dispute, for which they too were convicted by the testimony of the same witnesses (4 49–1, 50–1, 2; III Muharrem 1044). A dispute over the death of janissary Emir 'Ali beşe while living in Kakopetriye village of Lefka kaza and the payment of blood money *(dem diyeti)* was heard before the provincial council and the Sharia court (4 70–1; I Receb 1044). Surely the dispute between janissary racil Kara Mehmed beşe of Degirmenlik village of Lefkoşa kaza and janissary racil Ibrahim beşe did not need to be heard at the Cyprus council and the Sharia court in the presence of governor 'Ali Paşa except for the fact that other aspects of the dispute involved non-Muslim foreigners *(mustemin)* (4 142–3; III Ramazan 1045).

Fiscal records with references to the size of the janissary garrison in Cyprus exist from at least 1593 (1002). Especially because of the internal confusion engulfing the empire at that time, their credibility is moot. Presumably the rolls of janissaries in Cyprus were sometimes inflated, with men who would not or could not fight. Presumably, too, salaries were collected by officers and other officials in the name of the deceased or missing. In many places in the empire janissaries came to dominate the guild of butchers.

The oldest survey found indicates a total of 937 janissaries, but another fiscal record book from that same year notes only 897. Of five other notations found between 1594 (1003) and 1602 (1011), all but one were well below 900; that was in 1596 (1005). A total of 878 janissaries were recorded for 1594 (1003), 879 for 1598 (1007), and a mere 838 for 1596 (1005). The greatest number of janissaries recorded at any time were 963, both in 1602 (1011) and in 1607 (1016), and 1003 in 1608 (1017).

Operating the janissary corps was expensive. The lowest levels reached for their expenses *('ulufe)* during the decade and a half between 1593 (1002) and 1608 (1017) was 417,233 akce in 1594 (1003), 434,128 akce in 1593 (1002), and 434,934 akce in 1601 (1010). The highest expenditures were 452,832 akce in 1602 (1011), 459,913 akce in 1607 (1016), and 462,209 akce in 1608 (1017).

According to fiscal records, the number of janissaries assigned to Cyprus between 1617 (1026) and 1632 (1042) was usually slightly in excess of 900 and the total annual expenses incurred by the corps ranged between 400,000 and 500,000 akce. The greatest number of janissaries during that period was 963 in 1620 (1030), and 956 in 1627 (1037). The smallest number of janissaries on the payroll was 890 in 1626 (1036) and 877 in 1632 (1042). The greatest total expenses allocated for the Cyprus janissaries was 461,647 akce in 1620 (1030), and 485,345 akce in 1627 (1037). The smallest allocations discovered were 440,882 in 1617 (1026), and 418,162 akce in 1632 (1042).[3]

Spahis

The term spahi describes a large group of cavalrymen stationed in provinces and paid through the timar system, whereby agricultural revenues due the Porte from villages were paid directly to them, as their entire income. They were made up almost completely of free Muslims who were required to reside in the provinces where their timars were located, to serve on military campaigns when summoned, and to aid provincial governors in local law enforcement.[4]

Suits and claims were made against spahis just as against janissaries. In particular villages had broad rights and were able to summon them to court to make complaints against them. Under the supervision of ʿOmer aga acting for ʿAli Paşa, Andreye v. Papa of Aya Nisani (?) village of Lefka kaza claimed that spahi Ahmed beg bn ʿAli had illegally taken his three altun by force (1 86–4; Sefer 1003).

Mehmed bn ʿAli of Incirli village acknowledged *(ik)* before Mehmed, spahi of the village, and topcular boluk başi Mahmud: They gave Yusuf 15 donem fields *(tarla)* at the village to cultivate, but they are mine. (1 269–3; II Zil-Kade 1002)

ʿOsman bn Yusuf, an adolescent of Lefkoşa, claimed that Lefkoşa spahi Bayram cundi bn ʿAbdullah had collected excessive money from his father's estate, but ʿOsman had no proof (1 334–2; Receb 1003). A fetva of ʿAbdur-Rahman mentions a forbidden levy called "su başilik" wrongly being collected by spahis (4 238–1). A case initiated by spahi Uveys kethuda doubtless stems from his concern with rumors which may have been spread about his behavior towards the villagers.

Haci Uveys kethuda of the spahis of Ori (?) village of Lefkoşa kaza, presently ʿazablar kethudasi, states *(bm/tk)* before Hirsofi, Ciryako v. Ciryako, and Andon v. Simiyo of the re ʿaya of the village: We heard that they claimed that we took fines *(cerime)* unjustly and that we struck *(darb)* and cursed *(şetm)* them. They deny that, saying: Uveys is our spahi. He did not take any fines or goods from us. Neither did his companions. He did not strike us nor curse our families. (4 186–1; I Receb 1046)

Spahis also had a role keeping law and order in the villages of their timars, although the court records show surprisingly little about such activities. Probably primary responsibility for making complaints lay with the villagers, so maybe only exceptional cases reached the spahi.

Spahi Çakir beg bn ʿAbdullah, on behalf of Mustafa kethuda who held *(zabt)* the village for the Cyprus treasurer *(defterdar)*, made a claim against Zeyno v. Loiz of Voni village in Lefka kaza for striking Saguri v. Kostintin with a knife. A deputy judge *(naib)* and other people went in person to investigate with Çakir beg and then returned to the court to make their report (1 185–2; selh Cumadi I 1003). Village spahis haci

Keyvan, ʿAbdul-Kadir boluk başi bn Ahmed, Yusuf bn Mehmed, and Huseyn bn ʿAli, as well as several other men and women from the village, testified that a certain Hasan bn ʿAbdullah always drank wine, tormented *(rencide)* people, and oppressed them *(zulm ve teʿaddi),* so that he should be expelled from the village (3 146–10; III Cumadi II 1019). Spahi Mahmud beg of Elihod (?) village of Lefkoşa testified that he had heard *(mesmuʿum)* that Pereşkogu of that village had had sexual relations *(fiʿl-i şeni)* with Yani v. Baba Hiristotoli of that village (4 137–1; I Şaban 1045).

Whether in the interests of local villagers or in their own self-interest, Mehmed çelebi bn Huseyn and Huseyn beg, spahis of Akaçe village of Morfo kaza, charged that Morfo kadi Veli efendi had gone out to the villages five times in the past ten months, wrongfully claiming provisions and maintenance each time, as well as collecting excessive taxes (2 69–3; 14 Rebiʿ I 1017).

After Maro bint Yakimo of Eglence (?) village of Lefkoşa kaza had failed to prove her claim that Filori v. Istaliyano of the village had struck her and cursed her and he had taken an oath to the contrary, Filori asked that the woman's reputation *(keyfiyet-i ahvali)* be asked of the spahis of the village. Then haci Hizir oda başi and Yusuf boluk başi testified that Maro is malicious *(şirre)* (4 170–1; II Cumadi II 1046).

Another function of Cyprus spahis was seizing and looking after stray animals, for which the owners had to pay a per diem fee in reclaiming them. For example, Aya Demre village spahi haci Keyvan bn ʿAbdullah held a stray cow *(inek)* of Pavlo v. Dimitri of Eliyo (?) village of Mesariye kaza (3 166–4; II Şaban 1019). Oda başi Mehmed, spahi of Limbiye and Kakoteri(?) villages of Lefkoşa, claimed that allowance *(yave)* when he found a cow *(inek)* (3 5–4; 1 Zil-Hicce 1018). So too Mehmed beg bn Sefer, spahi of Litronde village of Lefkoşa, made a claim for *yave* (1A 279–6; II Zil-Kade 1002).

Spahis in Cyprus, unlike janissaries, were inactive in business and trade. Perhaps their "higher" socioeconomic status prevented their participation. They were involved in important credit transactions, although about half as frequently as janissaries. Spahis gave credit much more frequently than they borrowed, one and a half times as frequently (22 to 15), but that too is less than the janissaries.

The proportion of converts among people identified as spahis whose full names are given and who appeared as legal agents *(vekil),* witnesses (şuhud), creditors, or debtors is virtually the same as the proportion of janissaries. For spahis the figure is 47%, while for janissaries it is 46%. What a strange phenomenon that equal proportions of janissaries and spahis were converts. Indeed, the cycle for spahis remarkably parallels that for janissaries, particularly if one discounts the middle period. For spahis the proportion rises from 46% in 1593–1595 to 64% in 1609–1611 before falling to 20% in 1633–1637. Comparable figures for janissaries are 46%, 25%, and 16%.[5] Of course the spahi sample is very small, and may be distorted by not automatically having counted all those with the title *aga* as spahis.

The condition that provincial spahis must live in the province where their timars were is expressed, for example, in a warrant *(berat)* for a 50,360 akce zi'amet (a "timar" paying more than 20,000 akce/year) assigned to Mustafa bn Ahmed (4 219–1; I Zil-Kade 1044). For failing to do that, or for failing to go on campaigns when required, a spahi might be reassigned a timar of a lower value or even face outright dismissal (4 219–1; I Zil-Kade 1044. 2 58–1; II Ramazan 1013). Spahi 'Omer was almost dismissed from his 7500 akce timar when he was suspected of having gone to the mainland but when that proved untrue, the timar was confirmed in his name (1 98–2; I Cumadi I 1002, Lef-koşa).

Traditional laws required that timars be assigned, removed, and transferred only under the authority of the Porte or, sometimes, the provincial governor.[6] Several instances occurred in Cyprus, however, where timar-holders bought, sold, or traded timars, publicly registering that change at the Sharia court. 'Ali bn Ibrahim, for example, renounced ownership of his 6,666 akce timar, which he gave to Mehmed bn 'Abdullah for 25,000 akce (1 154–3; I Rebi' II 1002). Mustafa beg bn 'Abdullah paid 35,000 akce for a timar (which could not have been worth more than 20,000 akce!) to Huseyn çelebi (3 37–1, 2; I Zil-Hicce 1018. A kilic timar, yet).

Hizir beg by Zeynel (?) states *(bm)* before Mahmud hoca bn 'Abdur-Rahman: Two and a half years ago at Limiyad (?) village of Gilan nahiye I bought a timar worth 6,666 akce from Mahmud for 35,000 akce; but the timar was not as described in the record book *(defter)*. It was worth only 5000 akce, so I returned it *(muraca'at)*. Mahmud replies: I bought that timar as a 6,666 akce timar from kassab Mustafa bn 'Abdullah, who is here. Mahmud acknowledges Hizir's claim, and the sale is found void *(noksan)*. (3 23–9; 7 Zil-Kade 1018)

Village land the revenues of which were assigned to timars in Cyprus passed by inheritance to adult male descendents, or sometimes other relatives, of a deceased timar holder. Such heirs lacking, cultivated fields *(tarla)* accrued to the state and were redistributed by the spahi to other would-be cultivators in return for the payment of a one-time fixed fee called *resm-i tapu,* which is not to be considered a sale price nor a rental fee. The court records are silent about how a would-be cultivator located a timar holder with uncultivated land assigned to his timar, and vice versa. However, formal legal agreements had to be concluded.

A very unusual circumstance occurred when an architect *(mi⁽mar)* named Andon v. Petre, a non-Muslim, became a spahi:

Andon v. Petre, architect, who is spahi of Kilohdere village of Lefkoşa, acknowledges *(ik/it)* in the presence of Hiristofi v. Petra: When Mehmed beg died without male heirs *(evlad-i zukur),* fields *(tarla)* in the village were suitable for title registration *(tapu),* in accordance with imperial law *(kanun).* Hiristofi took them for 4000 akce *resm-i tapu.* I confirm his right of possession. (1 39–3; II Şaban 1002)

Mehmed bn Iskender, canoneer *(topciler)* commander *(oda başi)* of Lefkoşa, Mehmed bn ʿAbdi, and Halil bn ʿAbdullah acknowledge *(ik)* before Loizo v. Petriyo: 16 donem of fields *(tarla)* at Morfo village are suitable for title registration *(tapu)* because there are no male heirs. They are assigned to Loizo for 1020 akce. (1 276–1; II Şevval 1002)

Hizir bn Mehmed, spahi of Monastir village, assigned lands and houses to zimmis Covan v. Luyi, Pavlo, Petro, and Tomazo for 500 akce *resm-i tapu* (1 105–3; Rebiʿ II 1003). Spahi Behram bn ʿAbdullah of Lefkoşa made a claim against Bernardi v. Zozi for not paying *resm-i tapu* (3 32–3, 5; II Zil-Kade 1018). Spahi Mahmud bn Menteş of Karni village of Girniye kaza made claim against Ahmed bn Seyfi of the village for refusing to pay *resm-i tapu* when his brother ʿOmer died without male heirs *(evlad-i zukur)* (3 137–6; after II Şevval 1019).

Mehmed oda başi of the spahis of Magosa castle *(kalʿe)* states *(tk/tm)* before Dimitri v. Çakuri and Eliyondi of Lefkoşa: They are my reʿaya, people *(ahali)* of ʿAdemi (?) village of Mesariye kaza which I possess with a warrant *(berat)* of the sultan *(padişah).* A few years ago they fled from there *(terk-i vatan)* . . . They are reʿaya elsewhere and cause me loss *(gadr).* Either let them be returned . . . or let them pay me the tax for leaving their land uncultivated *(çift bozan resmi)* . . . (4 67–1; III Sefer 1044)

Practically the only way timar lands could be altered or alienated from a spahi was by making them part of a pious foundation, as when mevlana Ahmed efendi bn Saʿd ed-din efendi of Lefkoşa was permitted to make some large estates *(çiftliks)* a foundation. Even then the intermediary step of making them private property *(mulk)* was required (4 235–1; 12 Rebiʿ II 1043, Uskudar.berat).

When a villager left uncultivated lands which were part of a timar and moved to a town or another village, he was obligated to pay annually a fixed sum of money, called *çift bozan resmi*. If, however, his absence was unnoticed for 15 years, or if he evaded the spahi for that long, thereafter no *çift bozan resmi* was necessary and he became a legal and legitimate resident of the new place. In Cyprus, however, that penalty was applied only to those who abandoned their fields *(tarla)*, not to those who only left orchards and gardens, which comprise a different category of land.

Musa spahi of Vizace village of Lefkoşa claimed *çift bozan resmi* from Ergiri v. Ciryako. However Ergiri replied that he had lived in another village for 18 years and produced satisfactory evidence that his assertion was true, so Musa was enjoined from seizing him and taking his money (1 64–2; Muharrem 1003). Su başi ʿAli Yar bn Suleyman of Pendaya village of Lefkoşa claimed *çift bozan resmi* from Yakimo v. Yano, but when Yakimo demonstrated that he had no fields *(tarla)* in the village, but only vineyards, it was determined that ʿAli could not claim the money (1 73–1; Muharrem 1003). Ergiro of Morfo village may have gone all the way to Istanbul to complain about a spahi who wanted to require him to pay *çift bozan resmi* after he had been absent 18 years in another village; a letter expressing the injustice of such behavior then was sent to the Lefkoşa kadi, who was ordered to do nothing contrary to the Sharia and imperial law *(kanun)* (1 134–2; II Cumadi I 999). Also a fetva was presented as proof (135–1).

Mihail v. Gaspari of Lefkoşa makes a claim *(daʿva)* against Piri bn ʿOsman of the Lefkoşa kapuciler: He unjustly claims 60 akce *çift bozan resmi* from me. Piri says: Mihail's father was my reʿaya and so is he. Mihail asserts that he has lived in Lefkoşa for almost 20 years. (1 165–2; II Cumadi I 1003)

Occasionally a timar was assigned to someone not of the free cavalry class. The case of the Greek Orthodox architect Andon v. Petre has already been cited. When spahi Derviş of the castle volunteers *(gonullu-*

leri) of Magosa died, his 6666 akce timar at Togni village of Mazoto nahiye was given to Mehmed çelebi, muezzin of the Cami ʿi-i şerif in Lefkoşa (1 139–1; Sefer 1003). Janissary ʿOsman bn Emin was assigned a timar and became a spahi (1 24–3; I Receb 1002). Janissary haci Mehmed bn Yusuf also had a timar (1 44–1; III Şaban 1002).

Police

Although police are stigmatized by important observers of Ottoman society like Mustafa ʿAli and Evliya çelebi, the Ottoman court system, modeled on the Sharia, seems to de-emphasize police power.[7] However cruel police may have been, and on this Evliya çelebi is very colorful, their legitimate sphere of authority was rigidly limited. In almost all criminal cases the initiative came from the victim or his family, who personally approached the kadi and complained to him. Every Muslim, as well as every other Ottoman subject, had the right either directly or through an agent to summon to court anyone else. Since those summoned to court were obligated to go there on their own as soon as possible, the police needed to use force only infrequently.

In Cyprus occasionally someone refused a summons, but the response of the court then was simply to send an official summoner *(muhzir)* with a written summons. Occasionally, too, police, encountering a crime in progress, intervened of their own volition. Police, it seems, dealt only with matters of public crime unless someone brought to their attention violations taking place in secret. Moreover, when they did investigate crimes, they frequently acted in the company of an explicitly delegated representative of the court, along with other "Muslims" who happened to be available. Force was to be used only as a last resort.

The *su başi, ʿasses başi, muhzir,* and *muhtesib* were typical Ottoman police officers. The first two were in the service of the provincial governor, who was charged generally with maintenance of law and order on the island but who almost invariably did so in Cyprus through the chiefs of police *(su başi)* and night watchmen *(ʿasses başi)*. In the governor's name they might even initiate legal cases against presumed criminals. They operated virtually autonomously in his absence, for the judicial registers indicate that the governors had scant personal interest in the details of maintaining law and order.

The office of muhzir (court summoners, and muhzir başi, chief court summoner) was dependent on the court and independent of the provincial governor. Besides keeping order in the court, muhzirs orally summoned people to court on behalf of litigants who were themselves unwilling or unable to do so. In Cyprus, the muhzir başis were appointed by local kadis, although formal confirmation by the Lefkoşa kadi and the provincial governor also seem to have been necessary. So kadi ʿAli of Magosa notified those two officials that he had appointed a man named Husrev to the office (2 21–1; III Cumadi II 1016). That muhzir başi, Husrev beg bn ʿAbdullah, voluntarily renounced the office of chief summoner, along with 6000 akce in salary, in favor of ʿOmer beg bn Turmuş (3 105–4; II Ramazan 1019). The summoners did not initiate legal cases against criminals; probably they lacked the authority to use force to carry out their duties, that belonging to the governor's men only.

Another special police office in the Ottoman province of Cyprus was that of muhtesib. Although among the most ancient and powerful in Islam, that office must have already been introduced to Cyprus centuries before the Ottoman conquest. In the Lusignan period the "mathesep" ". . . was inspector of weights and measures, streets and bazaars, all kinds of trades and professions. He could punish with the lash, with the wand, and with the strapado, and fine up to one ducat."[8] The office had been assimilated into the Latin Crusader states, whence it passed to Cyprus. As patrollers of bazaars, muhtesibs played an important role in ensuring that businessmen met standards of honesty in their weights and measures and obeyed the official fixed prices.

Yusuf sold cotton at a deficient weight. Written at the request of muhtesib Şaʿban. (3 6–5; 1 Zil-Hicce 1018)

Haci ʿOmer bn haci Cumʿa said: I bought Tirablos soap at the bazaar for 28 akce/vakiye. I found some dirt in it. Written at the request of the muhtesib. (3 24–6; I Zil-Kade 1018)

Huseyn bn Hasan sold watermelon for more than the official fixed price. Written at the request of muhtesib Şaʿban. (3 61–5; III Cumadi II 1019)

A grocer brought to court by Lefkoşa muhtesib Nuʿman bn ʿAbdullah claimed that the muhtesib had treated him unfairly by separating out some of the chick-peas he had for sale, thus making them appear underweight (4 109–3; 1 Muharrem 1045).

Muhtesib ʿAli says: This bread baker haci ʿAli bn ʿOmer is a habitual drinker *(içici)* who is not able to be calm *(vekare)* and understanding *(anlama)*. Written at the request of the muhtesib. (1 252–3; II Şevval 1002)

Şehir muhtesibi haci Huseyn states *(tm)* before bazarci Seydi Kadi: When sweet pomegranate was 1 akce for 500 dirhems, he sold an akce's worth 75 dirhems underweight *(eksik)*. When it was weighed at court, that was found to be so. Registered. (1 316–3; 1 Muharrem 1003)

Among the income of the Lefkoşa muhtesib in 1003 was 10,000 akce/year for the candle wax factory *(mum hane)*, which muhtesib haci Huseyn sold for three years for a total of 30,000 akce to Andreye v. Pernardi (1 304–3; Muharrem 1003).

Muhtesibs traditionally had the authority to punish on the spot anyone who acknowledged his guilt; others had to be brought to the kadi, where the same standard of proof was demanded as in other litigation. The muhtesib functioned independently of the kadi. Like the police chief and night watchman, but probably unlike the muhzirs (summoners), the muhtesibs had the authority to arrest and forcibly bring to court people against whom they themselves had no personal claims.

The use of firearms was strictly controlled and restricted to members of the military class, which would exclude muhzirs and muhtesibs. A musket, for example, was among the effects of the late Hasan su başi (4 37–1; III Rebiʿ II 1044). When a messenger from the acting governor *(kaym makam)* had his musket out in public, that was considered an action necessary to register in the court records.

It was registered that when the messenger *(çavuş)* from the acting governor *(kaym makam)* came at the request of the reʿaya, he took out his musket *(tufenk)* in public. (3 146–6; III Cumadi II 1019)

Ottoman law forbade carrying in public not just firearms but all other weapons of war as well, including swords, knives, bows and arrows.

In Cyprus when police investigated charges of wine drinking and other immorality representatives of the court sometimes joined them in their investigation. Usually the grounds for arrest involved "public" drunkenness. The private home was sacrosanct.

ʿAli bn Hamze of Lefkoşa and his black *(ʿarab)* slave were apprehended drunk in the middle of the night. (3 8–4; I Muharrem 1019)

Mustafa bn Ahmed and ʿIsa, su başis of Lefkoşa, say *(ihzar)* before haci Mehmed and Vehhab: They drank wine *(şurb-i hamr)* in public *(ʿala melaʾ in-nas)*. The smell of wine *(raiha)* was present on their breath. It was recorded. (3 57–3; III Cumadi II 1019)

Za ʿim ul-vakt Mustafa su başi and night watchman *(ʿasses başi)* ʿAli su başi say: We apprehended Armenian Anderik v. Keşiş of Terebiyoti (?) quarter drinking wine *(şurb-i hamr)* at night in the market place *(suk)* of that quarter. (3 149–3; III Cumadi II 1019)

Public uproar over individual patterns of drunkenness might involve summoning police to the quarter or village to complain about an objectionable individual whom the police by chance had not encountered. Complaints such as the two which follow could also be carried directly to the court.

Haci Keyvan, ʿAbdul-Kadir boluk başi bn Ahmed, Yusuf bn Mehmed, and Huseyn bn ʿAli, spahis of Aya Demre village, and from the village Piyale bn ʿAbdullah, ʿAli beşe bn ʿAbdullah, Marko v. Kistinti, Yorgi v. Yakimo, Lare (?) bint Çaliyo (?), Hiristine bint Yakimo, Vero bint Zanuca (?), and other people of the village state *(bm)* before Hasan bn ʿAbdullah: Hasan always drinks wine in our village; he torments us *(rencide)* without cause, and he oppresses *(zulm ve teʿaddi)* contrary to the Sharia. We do not want him in our village. Registered. (3 146–10; III Cumadi II 1019)

Haydar beg, present city su başi, and night watchman *(ʿasses basi)* ʿAli su başi state *(bm)* before ʿAbdul-Kerim bn Suleyman of Aya Sofya quarter: ʿAbdul-Kerim drinks wine in the quarter. He is not free of debauchery. I want the people of the quarter to be asked about his reputation *(keyfiyet-i hal)* and for that to be registered. Haci Yusuf bn ʿAbdullah, Ahmed oda başi bn ʿAbdul-Celil, Piyale bn ʿAbdullah, Derviş, Haydar bn ʿAbdullah, and the people of the quarter *(ehl-i mahalle-i ʿamme)* come to court: In truth, we cannot say he is good. He always drinks wine in the quarter. He is constantly involved in debauchery *(fisk ve fucur)*. We do not want him in our quarter. (3 162–5; III Rebiʿ II 1019)

In two instances wives came to report their husbands drinking in their own houses in the company of other men. Such was the sanctity of the private home that probably police would not otherwise have entered there even if they had good evidence that drinking was taking place. The husbands must have so infuriated their wives by their drinking that at least in one case the woman left her house at night.

ʿAli su başi of Lefkoşa and Mustafa su başi, night watchman *(ʿasses başi)* of Lefkoşa, come to court *(mahkeme)* in the middle of the night and state *(bk)*: Maʿcunci Mehmed and Yusuf bn ʿAbdullah of Aya Sofya quarter brought Katib Mehmed çelebi to their house *(menzil)*. Their wives Emine, Rahmine, and Fatma complained that the men were drinking wine. Let people from the Sharia go and investigate. Let their reputation *(hal)* be investigated and registered. Katib-i mahkeme Ibrahim halife bn Ahmed efendi and the Muslims whose names are listed below went to that house and observed. The aforementioned Mehmed, Yusuf, and katib Mehmed çelebi testify that wine was being drunk when the women who came to court *(meclis)* were there. It is recorded. (4 30–1; III Rebiᶜ I 1044)

ᶜAli beg and Mehmed bn ᶜOsman, who are su başi and night watchman *(ᶜasses başi)* of Lefkoşa, state *(bk):* A man entered the house *(menzil)* of Hasan bn Salih of Terebiyoti (?) quarter of Lefkoşa, where he was living. His wife Fatma hatun came to court *(meclis)* to report that the men were drinking wine. Let it be investigated. Servants *(huddam)* from the court *(mahkeme)* of Kadi zade ᶜAbdullah beg bn Fazlullah were sent with the Muslims whose names are listed below to the house of Hasan. Although his wife the aforementioned Fatma was present, Hasan was drinking wine with Derviş ᶜAli, Yusuf, and another ᶜAli. When they witnessed this, ᶜAbdullah had it registered at the court *(meclis)*. (4 110–2; 1 Muharrem 1045)

Once a complaint against a su başi was made by a woman who succeeded in proving before the court her own good reputation.

Benefşe bint ᶜAbdullah of Lefkoşa says: On Ramazan night when I was visiting with the wife of my neighbor *(hem civar)* Gavrail at his house, ᶜAbdul-Kadir, who is city su başi, accused me of something bad *(tohmet)*. Let experts *(ehl-i vukuf)* be asked about my reputation *(ahvali)*. Mehmed bn Hasan, Suleyman bn Nebi, and others say that she is upright *(salah)*, religious *(diyanet)*, and of good behavior *(husn-i istikam)*. Their testimony is accepted and she is acquitted *(beraʾ et)*. (1 257–2; I Zil-Kade 1002)

The police supervised other matters of public morality. It was forbidden, for example, for a man to have in his house an unrelated woman without first gaining permission of the court. Yusuf bn Kasim and Luyi v. Hiristodiye were summoned for court for having neglected to do that.

Saᶜdi çavuş of Lefkoşa states *(tm)* before Yusuf bn Kasim: Yusuf brought an unrelated *(na mahrem)* woman to his house. Let him be asked. Yusuf denies that. ᶜAbdi bn Mehmed and ᶜAbdi bn ᶜAbdullah confirm Saᶜdi's statement. (1 273–1 I Zil-Kade 1002)

Luyi v. Hiristodiye was brought before Mariya bint Hiristofi by the city police chief, who said: Luyi has an unrelated *(na mahrem)* woman in his house. Let it be investigated in accordance with the Sharia. Luyi says: Her brothers gave her to me as a servant *(hidmetkar)*, but I did not get permission of the court *(izn-i şerᶜ)*. (3 34–1; II Zil-Kade 1018)

ʿAbdul-Kadir boluk başi and Keyvan boluk başi state *(ihzar/bm)* before Luyi v. Hiristodiye, reʿaya of Aya Tane (?) *(mevziʿ)* of Aya Demre village: In his house an unrelated *(na mahrem)* woman Mariya bint Hiristofi serves him. Let that be investigated. Does he have permission of the court *(izn-i şerʿ)?* Is that permissible in accordance with the Sharia? Luyi says: I did not ask permission of the court for Mariya but her brothers Ciryako and Kosdindi sent her to serve *(hidmet)* me. The two brothers confirm that. (3 34–2; II Zil-Kade 1018)

From Lefkoşa the su başi and Hasan kethuda state *(tm)* before haci Hasan bn Yusuf: Previously he stopped families coming from the hamam. He stopped a group of women with impudence. Hasan replies: In truth I stopped them on the way and talked to them when they came on horseback. Registered. (1 305–1; Zil-Kade 1002)

Although the Sharia permitted requiring different styles and colors of dress by members of different religious groups and even by classes of Muslims, late 16th and early 17th century court records give scant evidence of legal cases on such subjects. In one instance a Muslim repeatedly wore green on his head (presumably a green turban) although that color was legally restricted to a class who claim direct descent from the Prophet Muhammed. As usual no punishment is mentioned, but the court may be presumed to have exercised patience in dealing with the culprit.

Ahmed bn Ibrahim of Lefkoşa makes a claim *(t.d.)* against Ahmed bn Muharrem of that city: Ahmed took green for his head. Although he was ordered not to do so, he wore green on his head again. So Ahmed is warned not to wear green again. (3 8–7; I Muharrem 1019)

Conversion to Islam was a very serious act, and any reneging on conversion was of the utmost concern.

ʿOmer beşe bn Sefer, lieutenant *(yasakci)* from the city su başi, states *(ihzar/bm)* in the presence of Loizo v. Zako: The above Zako formerly acknowledged in the presence of Muslims that he was a Muslim. Now he says in public that he is an infidel *(kafir)*. Let the court be asked. Zako denies that. When proof was asked of ʿOmer, from the upright Muslims *(ʿudul-i muslimin)* Hamze boluk başi bn Mustafa and ʿAbdi beşe confirm ʿOmer beşe's statement that Zako had claimed to be a Muslim. Their testimony is accepted and registered. (3 57–4; III Cumadi II 1019)

Sometimes police were involved with private individuals in arranging the settlement of criminal cases. Lefkoşa police chief *(su başi)* Yusuf beg and haci Mansur bn haci Ahmed jointly made a formal statement at court that seven men, all recognized, had entered Mansur's shop in the middle of the night and stolen some things (3 86–4; III Sefer 1019). When Bagdad bint ʿAbdi stated at court that beardless *(emredd)* Mahmud had tried to rape her *(tasarruf)*, that was registered in the court records at the request of the city su başi (3 116–2; after II Ramazan 1019)

Su başis also took possession of lost property and enumerated the estates of the deceased. For example, city su başi Haydar beg and nightwatchman Carullah made a complete inventory of the estate of the late Armenian Murad who died without heirs (3 135–6; 28 Rebiʿ II 1019). When the galleon of zimmi Kara Solak was broken up off Cape Arnavud in Hirsofi kaza, the people there wanted help and Mehmed su başi was sent to assist in the enumeration of the goods (2 6–1; 1016?).

Sometimes debts and other legal obligations were settled through the intermediaries of police. For example, zimmi Panederfo asserted in court that he had given the 1000 akce he owed Baki çavuş to the muhzir başi (3 121–2; after II Ramazan 1019).

Another duty of police was to participate in investigations of certain violent crimes, particularly when a body was found. An investigative group — constituting one person from the court, one person from the provincial governor's office (usually a su başi), and whatever Muslims happened to be present at court and could undertake the immediate movement to another quarter or even to a distant village — might be commissioned. (The investigators then are usually the instrumental witnesses *(şuhud ul-hal)* for the case.)

Seydi Mustafa bn Veli, appointed overseer *(mubaşir)* for the matter for the council *(divan)* of Cyprus, states *(bk)* in the presence of ʿAyni bint ʿAbdullah of Aya Demre village of Lefkoşa: Her six-year-old son fell in a well *(kuyu)* and drowned. Let people investigate and see what happened. ʿAyni replies: My son fell in the well three months ago. I have no claim against anyone in the village. (3 47–1; I Cumadi II 1019)

Present city su başi Huseyn says before *(ihzar)* the zimmis of Aya Kuşani quarter: At the quarter this bread baker Yakimo v. Zovan was found wounded *(mecruh)* on his head. I want the marks *(eser)* of the wound to be investigated *(keşf)*. In truth the zimmi does have a wound on his head. (3 162–1; III Rebiʿ II 1019)

Sometimes the people of a quarter or of a village had claims to make against residents of their own communities. In Cyprus such complaints were apparently made through the city su başi and the night watchman. The court had the authority to grant their requests for the expulsion of such people from their communities.

Mustafa beg, city su başi, and night watchman (*ˁasses başi*) ˁAli su başi state before Ismaˁil bn haci Mustafa: Last night Ismaˁil, drunk inside Aya Soyfa mosque (*camˁ-i şerif haremi*), grabbed hold of the beardless boy (*emredd*) ˁAbdul-Mennan and attempted the wicked act (*fiˁ-i şeniˁ*). Muslims rescued the boy from him. I want Ismaˁil to be asked in accordance with the Sharia; I want justice done. Ismaˁil denies that. When Mustafa and ˁAli are asked for proof concerning the correctness (*sidk*) of their claim, from the upright Muslims (*ˁudul-i muslimin*) haci Sinan bn ˁAbdullah, Ilyas bn Mursel, Hizir bn haci Emirce (?), and Veli bn ˁAbdullah confirm Mustafa and ˁAli in detail. (3 155–5; II Rebiˁ II 1019)

Mustafa beşe, city su başi, and night watchman ˁAli su başi state (*bm*) in the presence of Kahtan beşe bint Mehmed of Aya Sofya quarter: The people say she does many things contrary to the Sharia. I want the people of the quarter to be asked about her reputation (*keyfiyet-i hali*). Hasan beşe bn ˁAbdul-Halim, Yusuf bn ˁAbdullah, ˁAbdi bn Huda Virdi, ˁAbdi çavuş bn Yusuf, ˁAli çavuş bn Ahmed, and others came to court. They said: In truth we cannot say anything good concerning her. It is necessary that she be sent away from our quarter. If she is sent out, good. If not, all of us will continue to move out. (3 156–5; Rebiˁ II 1019)

Summary

One of the first actions after the Ottoman conquest was to restore fortifications which had been destroyed during the assaults, especially vulnerable ones on the coast. That meant especially Magosa, which had been taken after such a heavy cost in men and supplies. Tuzla (Larnaka), Baf, Girniye, and Limosa all had to be provided with garrisons for their strengthened fortifications. Perhaps Lefkoşa had received the most damage, although because of its location inland, the danger perceived there was less.

Traditionally the Ottoman army had been divided into two key units, the janissary corps and the spahis. Originally the janissaries had been an elite infantry, recruited largely through the devşirme levy as Christian slaves, converts to Islam, who were garrisoned near the royal palace, always ready to help the ruler, and constantly drilled, to counter the much larger mostly Muslim cavalry, the spahis, who were required to live in the provinces, and were paid through the timar system, and who were supposed to stay away from the capital, but were allowed to marry had have families, and were only a little less awesome than janissaries.

With the weakening of the central government the discipline of the janissaries began to break down. They were allowed to marry and have families, and freeborn Muslims were allowed to enroll. Their numbers increased greatly, and many were stationed away from the capital, like in Cyprus. By 1593–1595, according to the judicial registers only 46% of the janissaries mentioned were still of slave origin, and by 1633–1637, that proportion had fallen to 16%. Recruitment patterns of the janissaries in Cyprus had changed drastically.

Discipline apparently was breaking down, for many janissaries skipped campaigns to which they were ordered. Although still technically slaves of the Porte, cases occurred of the estates of janissaries' being inherited. Other cases reveal them as landowners. Popular conceptions of janissaries as men of violence and as artisans and merchants, particularly butchers, are reflected in the judicial registers. Much more attention is given to their role in the business and commerce of the community, especially in the matter of credit, where one finds them much more prominent as lenders than borrowers. (One percent of all instances of credit involved janissaries, although they were part of the military elite.) Immediately after the conquest a number acted as directors *(mutevelli)* of pious foundations, but with the passage of time that became less common. Their numbers ranged between 878 and 1003.

Spahis were the calvary men stationed in the provinces and paid through the timar system and normally recruited from free Muslims only. Suits by and against spahis were made just as by and against janissaries. Spahis had only a very minor role in keeping order in the villages connected with their timars. Another function of spahis involved dealing with stray animals. They were hardly at all involved with business or trade. Some gave credit, but much less frequently than janissaries. Suprisingly, the proportion of spahis who were converts to Islam were almost exactly the same as janissaries.

Special taxes had to be paid by villagers who left uncultivated timar lands assigned to them. One zimmi, an architect, had a timar assigned him.

Many scholars have reported that from early in the 16th century important changes happened within the janissary corps. Free Muslims were increasingly allowed to participate. Marrying, having children, and living outside the barracks were widely practiced; the corps shifted from being a small group confined to the capital to being stationed in a number of provinces, including Cyprus. They became fully part of the local economy. Whether they actually became corrupt is harder to tell, for in the judicial system they seem to have been acting normally.

One of the most fundamental rights given to every adult by the Sharia was to summon anyone else, however important, to court. Moreover, such a summons ideally was to be accepted immediately. It is the obligation of anyone summoned to court to go there as quickly as possible, whether innocent or guilty. If ignored, a court official, the muhzir, was authorized to intervene, and get him there as quickly as possible.

One finds three kinds of police in Cyprus. (1) First muhzirs, who work for the court and have the responsibility of getting people there, although everyone was supposed to go automatically (2) The muhtesib worked to maintain law and order in the market places, especially for accurate weights and measures, and fair prices, apprehending people who broke laws publicly. (3) Police from the governor's office, the su başi, and the nightwatchmen (*'asses başi*). All were normally concerned with public immorality, unless a personal appeal was made as in the case of drunkenness in a home. They took custody of lost or stolen property.

Firearms and other "weapons of war" were forbidden to all but the military class in Cyprus, and were normally kept away even from them, usually in the custody of some sort of castle warden, except when needed, for military campaigns, or local emergencies.

Collective complaints might be made by town quarters, or by villages, against people who drank excessively, committed rape, acted lasciviously, or behaved in a rowdy way. It was not rare for people of a quarter or village to make a collective request that a person, or persons, be required to leave the community permanently. However, people so accused still had the right to prove their innocence, or their general good reputation.

NOTES

1. H. Inalcik, *Ottoman Empire* . . . , pp. 48, 51, 118, 161. Many acted as "artisans and traders." They "invested their money in trading ventures and usury." p. 98.

2. #1A, 17 of 37; #3, 13 of 53; #4, 10 of 62. Lefkoşa sicil no.
3. MMD #2437, 2475, 2229, 324, 2361, 3020, 914, 1425, 934, 958, 1189, 1801. Tapu defter #708. Girniye archival nos.
4. H. Inalcik, Ottoman Empire . . . , pp. 11–181.
5. #1, 13 of 28; #3, 21 of 33; #4, 4 of 20.
6. In some instances sancak begis and kadis had that authority, at least with smaller timars, but even in those cases the timars were still transferred by the authority of the state.
7. On the tense relations of the people and the police, see Mustafa Akdağ, Celali İsyanları (1550–1603), Ankara, 1963. "Ehl-i Örfe Karş' Sancaklarda Ayaklanmalar," pp. 109ff; "Kadılar ile Reayanın Birleşmesine Karşı Ehl-i Örf'ün Tutumu," pp. 117ff; "Ehl-i Örf'e Karşı Halkın Kendini Koruma Hakk'. (Birinci Adalet Fermanı)," pp. 150ff, and passim. On Palestine at that time, see U. Heyd, Ottoman Documents on Palestine 1552–1615. Oxford, 1960. pp. 47, 59ff. See Heyd, . . . Criminal Law, "muhzir," p. 236f, "muhtesib," pp. 1, 229–234; for "su başi", see index, "authority to execute sentences," "restraint of, malpractices of," "as investigator, prosecutor." Braudel, too, is convinced of the general "rapaciousness" of Ottoman authorities. p. 693.

   Cf. Evliya Çelebi on the muhtesib ". . . by whom all defaulters in buying and selling were punished, according to their offences, with imprisonment and torture; such as covering their heads with the entrails of beasts, or nailing their ears and noses to a plank." Likewise the ʿasses başi and su başi, ". . . two police-officers attended by executioners, provided with whips and scourges, but not with rods and stocks (falaka)." p. 53. In Istanbul the su başis had 600 men who "with sticks in their hands, are an unmerciful set of people; they arrest, execute, strike, and hand." Evliya Çelebi, Narrative of Travels in Europe, Asia, and Africa, tr. by J. von Hammer. London, 1834. Seyahatnamesi. 10 vol. Istanbul, 1896–1938.

   According to Mustafa ʿAli, the continual crimes and oppression of the su başis provide an embarrasment to the provincial governor. A. Tietze, "The Poet as Critique of Society . . . ," Turcica 9.1977.120–160, esp. 123, 150. Cf. Mustafa ʿAli's Counsel for Sultans of 1581. ed. A. Tietze. pp. 36, 79.
8. Hill, v. 2, p. 54. v. 3, p. 1160. Although Hill believes that the function of the muhtesib in an Islamic state was even broader, that does not seem to have been the case in Ottoman times, especially in Cyprus. v. 4, p. 5.

FIVE

The Zimmis: Greek Orthodox Christians and Other Non-Muslims

Zimmis, the Law, and the Court

In accordance with Islamic law, Ottoman subjects were divided into two broad classes: Muslims and zimmis (Arabic *dhimmi*, protected people). The law knows no Turk, Arab, or Kurd, only those who have come to God and are true believers, i.e., Muslims; likewise it knows no distinctions between old believers and new converts.[1] All non-Muslims who had submitted themselves to the authority of the Ottoman state and paid taxes were as a consequence entitled to protection of their lives and property and the right to practice their own religion. In the court of Lefkoşa the name Greek Orthodox *(Rum)* was never used; that group were always called zimmis. Although other zimmis — the minorities — were often identified as Armenian *(Ermeni)*, Maronite *(Suryani)*, or Jew *(Yahudi)*, those distinctions had no significance in regard to legal rights, only for administrative organization. Popularly, and even in official communications, zimmis may have sometimes been referred to as infidels *(kafir, pl. kefere)*, deniers of God, but in legal records almost without exception they were simply zimmis. Protecting their interests was one traditional charge to kadis.

Ottoman kadis were obligated to apply the same standard of justice for both zimmi and Muslim. True, the law did not suppose the same level of honesty and integrity of zimmis as of Muslims; so the testimony of zimmis against Muslims is suspect. However, each zimmi should be entitled to the same protection of life and property as each Muslim, and the court should strive diligently to secure that equality. In Lefkoşa zimmis used the court frequently, and they made the same kinds of complaints as Muslims. There any zimmi could make a complaint against any Muslim, including government officials; he could summon to court, or have summoned there, anyone he wished. He could produce witnesses (who had to be Muslim if testifying against another Muslim), present written evidence, or take an oath by God who sent down the Gospel *(Incil)* by means of Jesus *('ala 'Isa)*. Every Muslim had the same obligation to answer the summons of and to reply to the charges of a zimmi as those of another Muslim. Of course, no system functions perfectly.

Zimmis used the Sharia court of Lefkoşa with a considerable frequency. Of 2800 cases in sicils of 1580 (988) and 1593–1595 (1002–1003), 1609–1611 (1018–1019), and 1633–1637 (1043–1046) more than one-third involved at least one zimmi. Moreover, 15% involved only zimmis (and no references to zimmi communal courts were found). Another 19% of all the cases were intercommunal, indicating considerable economic and social interaction. Although a superficial attempt has been made to further subdivide the intercommunal cases into those initiated by Muslims (60%) and those initiated by zimmis (40%), such classifications fail to distinguish among hotly contested cases, innocuous ones, and notary registrations; sometimes it is impossible to determine with whom a case really originated. Anyway, the table shows the levels of participation for the three time periods to be relatively constant. The table does indicate a small but steady increase in zimmi participation in the court between 1593 and 1637, although surprisingly the highest level of participation (43%) was in 1580. Perhaps the proportion of cases involving only zimmis also increased significantly between 1580 and 1609.

Zimmis used the court for all the same reasons Muslims did.

Marko v. Mihal of Lefkoşa acknowledges *(ik)* before Nikola v. Marko: While my brother-in-law Yano v. Istefan was living in Nikola's house *(ev)*, he disappeared. When I made an inquiry about him, a ten-day delay *(mehl)* was given and Nikola found Yano well and brought him to court. I renounce all claim against Nikola. (1 84–2; Muh. 1003)

Selimo v. Pavla and his mother Horineli (?) bint Filori of Aya Kuşa quarter of Lefkoşa acknowledge *(ik)* before Paskali v. Bernarto, Zano v. Karçire, and others: My father Pavla took 12 altun in capital *(sermaye)* from the people of the village for a bread bakery *(ekmekcilik)*. I will be guarantor for the property *(kefil bil-mal)*. The people of the quarter accept that. (1 246–4; II Şevval 1002)

Zazo v. Zorzi of Fitre (?) village of Lefkoşa sets forth a claim *(td)* before his son Loizo: I sold my son a cow *(inek)*. I want the money. He stalls. I want it in accordance with the Sharia. Yorgi says, I paid the money to my father. I owe him nothing. When proof is sought, from the village Teryako v. Simiyo and Vasil testify that Zazo did receive the money from his son. (3 6–3; 1 Muh. 1019)

Yagob v. ᶜIsa (?) of Degirmenlik village of Lefkoşa acknowledges *(ik/iᶜt)* before zimmiye Andreye bint Yakimo of the village: Garden *(bagçe)* at village sold to her for 4660 akce. (4 48–1; III Receb 1044)

Loizo v. Yorgi of Lefkoşa sets forth a claim *(daᶜva/tk)* before Yasif: Yasif owes me 500 akce from a loan *(karz-i şerᶜ)*. Now he delays *(teᶜallul)*. Yasif says: Three years ago he offered me 500 akce if I would marry Kozinli ... (?), unmarried girl *(bakir zimmiye)* of Seniyo (?) village in Lefkoşa. I sent my mother Firancesko to the village to arrange the marriage. Loizo gave me the 500 akce as a gift *(hibe)*. (4 49–3; III Muh. 1044)

Istavri v. Andreye, zimmi of Lefkoşa, sets forth a claim *(td)* before Ismaᶜil bn Perviz beg, steward *(emin)* of inheritance *(beyt ul-mal-i hassa ve ᶜamme):* The late Zozicuni (?) v. Makri (?) of Marego (?) village who died without heirs owed me 67 kirmizi altun from a loan *(karz)*. I want it. When the emin asked for proof, upright Muslims *(ᶜudul-i muslimin)* haci Huseyn bn Belal and Behram bn ᶜAbdullah confirm him. After examining the antecedents of the witnesses *(tez-kiye, taᶜdil)*, their testimony is accepted. (1 171–2; II Cumadi I 1003)

Papa Yano v. Dimitre of Ayos (?) village of Lefkoşa acknowledges *(ik)* before Hasan beg bn Kasim: four one-story houses *(tahtani evler)* at the village were sold to Hasan for 1000 akce. (1 277–1; II Zil-Kade 1002)

Ahturi (?) v. Yorgi of Lefkoşa came to court and complained of oppression *(tazallum):* Huseyn bn ᶜAbdullah and Suleyman bn Mehmed struck me. (3 152–6; II Rebiᶜ II 1019)

Mariye bint Hiristofi, wife, and Ancola, daughter, of the late zimmi Nikola v. Papa Todori of (?) village of Gilan kaza acknowledge *(ik/iᶜt)* before Ramazan beg bn ᶜAbdullah: He has unjustly *(fuzulen)* taken possession of *(tasarruf)* the entire property and goods we inherited from the deceased. We want them. With the mediation of upright people, settlement *(sulh)* is made. (2 117–1; Muh. 1018)

Land and Property

Evidently the ratio of Muslim land and property holdings to zimmi holdings was quite constant. Here "land" refers strictly to fields, gardens, vineyards, orchards, and pastures, while "property" refers to all land with any house, shop, mill, or ancillary structures regardless of how much land also was involved. Zimmi land sales to Muslims were slightly in excess of their land purchases from Muslims. So 33% of the land which came up for sale (34 of 102) belonged to zimmis, but only 26% of that land (27 of 102) belonged to them after all the intercommunal transfers had been completed. For the zimmis that was an overall loss of 21%, while representing a 10% gain for the Muslims. Property transfers were extremely stable. While zimmi sellers held 32% of property put up for sale (87 of 276), they still held 31% (86 of 276) after the sales had been completed. Presumably in the half-century between 1593 (1002) and 1637 (1046) the proportion of land and property held by zimmis was stable or perhaps declined very slightly.

More problematic is what proportion of land and property Muslims and zimmis really held. It is inconceivable that Muslims held 70% of the land and property on the island, or even in the Lefkoşa area. Although the court records were the official registry of land and property transfers, possibly some transfers may have been recorded at local courts by local judges *(naibs)*. The transfers in the sicils include every kaza and nahiye in Cyprus, but in fact those from remote districts are only a smattering compared to the large number from Lefkoşa and its surrounding villages. Perhaps Muslims were more mobile than zimmis and came to the Lefkoşa court more frequently, or perhaps their settlements clustered nearer the capital and those of zimmis were in more distant areas. Maybe a considerable proportion of zimmis lived in more isolated and conservative environments where property was only passed by inheritance or marriage, not by sale. In any case, the eccentric variations in land and property transfers between Muslims and zimmis in the different sicils suggest caution. Moreover, the sicils record transfers, not holdings, and surely total zimmi holdings far exceeded those of Muslims. The only solid evidence is that 20% of the land and property transfers involved just zimmis, while another 23% were mixed. So zimmis were involved in 43% of all land and property transfers found, Muslims in 81%. Whatever the proportions in which they owned land, it is safe to say that between 1593 and 1640 those proportions were quite stable.

The frequency of intercommunal land and property transfers points to the close proximity in which Muslims and Christians lived in Lefkoşa and indeed over much of the island. Of all transfers 23% were intercommunal: 25% of the land transfers and 22% of the property transfers. Thus, even if there had been wholly Christian or wholly Muslim areas before 1593 (1002), almost a quarter of land and property eventually would have been in mixed or integrated areas. Generally speaking, selling land and property to adherents of another faith did not cause any social stigma. A man wishing to sell land or property doubtless sold it to whomever would pay the most, or, if demand were slow, to anyone who would buy it. Twenty-five of the 102 sales of fields, vineyards, gardens, and orchards were intercommunal, so the new owners, often indeed the new neighbors, were of a different faith. Often the neighborhood already was integrated. Sixty-one of 276 sales of land with fixed buildings on it were intercommunal. Much or most of that property included houses, making Muslim families and Christian families increasingly intermixed. Indeed, they successively occupied the same houses, which means either that the Christian houses were also built to provide special privacy for women or that the practice was unimportant to some of both communities. Listings of the names of the owners of land or property contiguous to that for sale reveal that some neighborhoods already were mixed even prior to the transfer. More and more Muslims and Christians would become neighbors. Although the sample is modest, it shows a similar pattern continuing over four decades: in 1593–1595 (1002–1003) 23% (39 of 166) of transfers were mixed, in 1609–1611 (1018–1019) the proportion was 21% (18 of 84), and in 1633–1637 (1043–1046) 23% (29 of 128). If that sample is representative of the whole period, and if that practice reflects the situation on the island of Cyprus as a whole, then the Christian and Muslim people of Cyprus in that period lived by their own preference in the greatest of intimacy — as neighbors.

Islamic law permits preemption (*şuf'a*) whereby a land or property holder had the right to purchase land or property contiguous to his own at a fair market price if the owner should decide to sell it. A co-owner of land or property also had that right. The neighbor had merely to appear in court as soon as he learned of the sale. Thus it was easily possible for a single individual, several neighbors, or even a whole quarter to preserve the religious, ethnic, or economic characteristics of their neighborhood if they wished. In fact, however, *şufʿa* was rare in Cyprus between 1580 and 1640. Only the two cases below were found.

When Ridvan bn ʿAbdullah wanted to buy the estate *(çiftlik)* and house *(ev)* of Papa Andreniko, Nikolo v. Yakimo claimed *şufʿa*. (1 5–8; III Ramazan 988)

Bali çavuş bn Niyet (?) of Aya Hor village of Lefkoşa sets forth a claim *(td)* before Ordek hatun: I bought three houses *(evler)* from her son for 20 altun. The transaction was completed; I had paid and taken possession. Now she claims *şufʿa*, but it is too late. Ordek hatun claims that she did not give up the right of *şufʿa*, but upright Muslims *(ʿudul-i Muslimin)* Yusuf bn Ibrahim and Mehmed bn Mustafa confirm Bali's claim that she did. (1 254–2; III Şevval 1002)

Conversion to Islam

In the decades following the Ottoman conquest of Cyprus many of the island's Christians converted to Islam. Contemporary observers and modern scholars have usually attributed that conversion to official compulsion, but no contemporary local sources substantiate that view except a few travellers embarrassed at the circumstances (as Venetians, or as Christians) who had no way of guessing how the new converts really felt. Although the level of conversion cannot be measured precisely, there are several indicators of its extent. In 1593–1595 (1002–1003) 31% (32 of 102) of the adult male Muslims whose names and fathers' names were cited as legal agents *(vekil)* were converts, as were 28% (34 of 123) of those names as witnesses *(şuhud,* or *ʿudul-i Muslimin)* to legal cases and 41% (58 of 143) of those named as instrumental witnesses *(şuhud ul-hal)*. More than a third of such Muslims appearing at court at that time were converts. What the highest proportion ever reached was or when it was reached can only be conjectured, but obviously the intensity was temporary. In 1580 (988) only 24% (46 of 190) of instrumental witnesses were converts, in 1609–1611 (1018–1019) the still-substantial proportion of 23% of legal agents *(vekils)* (17 of 75), 17% of witnesses (31 of 179), and 30% (59 of 195) of instrumental witnesses were converts — almost a quarter in all. By 1633–1637 (1043–1046) the proportion of convert vekils was down to 18% (11 of 61), while that of witnesses had fallen all the way to 6% (7 of 112) and that of instrumental witnesses to 14% (17 of 130). In the earlier decades the numbers of converts must have been very large, for there really is no reason why a convert would be more likely to carry out those offices at court than a born Muslim. Even the presence in the 1630s of 12% converts among the aforementioned Muslim groups was far from insignificant.[2]

Only a few cases of conversion to Islam are recorded in the surviving sicils, although in fact converts did have to register their change of religion at court if only to adjust their tax status. The minimal information needed was the name, place of residence, statement of faith, and new Muslim name adopted. No instances of massive conversion or indeed anything but individual conversion have been found.

Dimitri v. Yakimo of Aya Yorgi village in Lefkoşa kaza says: I come to the true faith. I leave the infidel religion (*kefere dini*). After he said, 'There is no God but God; Muhammad is the messenger of God' (la illa lahu Muhammad resul ullah), the name Mehmed was registered for him. (1 6–7; I Ramazan 988)

A woman whose name in the world of ignorance (*'alem-i cahiliye*) was Horsi became a convert. When she became a Muslim, the woman, called Fatma, named Suleyman bn 'Abdullah as legal agent (*vekil*) for her acknowledgement that she came to Islam. Hasan bn 'Abdullah and Kayman bn 'Abdullah confirmed the agency (*vekalet*). Suleyman came to court and acknowledged (*ik/i'*t): Fatma, who made me legal agent (vekil) for this matter, came to Islam on 3 October 1594 (17 Muharrem 1003). She confirms God (Allah) and unity (*tevhid*) and hazret-i Muhammed Mustafa and Islam. After this she is a Muslime like any of the people of Islam (*ehl-i Islam*). It is ordered (*hukum*) and recorded. (1 67–3; Muh. 1003)

Mustafa bn 'Abdullah of Poyin (?) village of Hirsofi in Lefkoşa says: While formerly called Toydi (?) v. Zanoci, God made a day for confession (*iman ruzi*) of faith. God made Islam my lot. No one forced me (*tahrik*) or compelled (*cebr*) me. I did so of my own free will (*husn-i ihtiyar*). Registered in sicil. (1 230–1; I Şevval 1002)

Fatima bint 'Abdullah of above village says: While formerly called Andreye bint Piyero, God made a day a confession of faith. God made my lot Islam. No one forced or compelled me. I did so of my own free will. Registered in sicil. (1 230–2; I Şevval 1002)

Ridvan bn 'Abdullah says: While I was Loize v. Yakimo I came to Islam. Mehmed bn Mustecab and Muharrem bn 'Abdullah confirm this. Their testimony is accepted. (1 283–5; III Zil-Kade 1002)

Ca'fer bn 'Abdullah is legal agent for acknowledgement of the former Mariya of the world of ignorance *('alem-i cahiliye)* of Perestiyo (?) village of Lefkoşa that she has become a convert to the true faith *(muhtediye)*, that she has come to Islam and taken the name Emine *(ik/i't):* The above-mentioned Emine, who made me agent, came to Islam on 25 October 1594 (10 Muharrem 1003). She acknowledges the unity of God *(tevhid)* and Muhammad. After that day she is a Muslim like all people of Islam. She is given a copy *(suret)* of this document. (1 319–1; I Muh. 1003)

Nikolo v. Yorgi of Hirsofi kasaba says *(bm/tm):* Up until now I have been an infidel in error *(zalal)*. I became a Muslim *(şeref-i Islamile muşerref olub)*. When I said the words of faith *(kelime'-i şehadet):* 'There is no God but God; Muhammed is his messenger,' I confessed *(ikrar)* clearly and eloquently. I turned from false religion *(batile din)*. It is ordered that he has entered Islam. When he turned from the tax obligations of the infidels *(tekalif-i kefere)*, this document *(vesika)* was written. (4 65–1; II Sefer 1044)

Zimmi Totodori, youth *(emredd)* of about 10 years old, from Orta Koy village of Lefkoşa kaza: Now I have left false religion *(din-i batili terk idub)* and have been honored with Islam. He takes the name Mustafa. (4 178–2; III Cumadi II 1046)

Not only adult men but also women and children were among the converts. Obviously they were proselytized carefully. Anyone of age could convert, even a wife or child, but it was the duty of the court to make certain that the conversion was voluntary. A woman whose new modesty from her conversion to Islam prevented her from coming in person might designate a vekil to bring her statement of faith to the court. In these contexts the use of the word infidel *(kafir)* obviously springs from the convert, although in fact the statements seem formulaic. Strictly speaking conversion to Islam simply requires a statement of faith with no legal registration, but the Ottoman bureaucracy needed accurate records of Muslims and zimmis for tax purposes, and in any case it may have pleased the Muslim community to proclaim their successes in public places. Sometimes economic incentives were offered as well, although they are not completely explicable from their contexts; what appeal that may have had to youths cannot be said.[3]

A girl who was named Filori came to court of her own free will from the hands of Usta Mehmed and entered Islam and took the name Raziye. The aforementioned Mehmed gave three kirmizi altun to present Lefkoşa kadi Perviz efendi, who gave it to her. (1 293–2; I Zil-Hicce 1002)

Mariya bint Yakimo of Ayos (?) village of Lefkoşa acknowledges *(ik/i^t)* before Kosta v. Petro: I gave my daughter to work for him *(hidmet)*. She fled from him. She came to court and of her own wish she became a Muslim. After she became a Muslim she took two kirmizi filori from present Lefkoşa kadisi Mevlana Perviz efendi. My daughter was handed over to be in honorable service . . . (1 317–2; I Muh. 1003)

Several instances occurred where only one spouse converted. Usually divorce followed. In fact, that may have been a way for zimmiye women to find relief from an unbearable marriage. At any rate, the converted women, whether previously married or not, easily found husbands. A few cases suggest that sometimes a zimmiye woman might have converted in order to be able to marry a Muslim she already had her heart set on.

After Fatma bint 'Abdullah of Yoni (?) village of Hirsofi in Lefkoşa converted, her husband Yano v. Matoliya (?) was invited to submit to Islam, but he did not do so. He says he has no claim against Fatma. (1 240–1; I Şevval 1002)

Yunus çavuş bn Ahmed, present Evdim emin in Lefkoşa says *(tm)* before Mariya bint Araste (?): Mariya came here from Baf kaza with her husband Loize. While they were living at the house of Bali beg, God made Islam her lot. No one forced her or compelled her. After she did so, her husband Loize was invited to submit to Islam, but he did not. Then she married Mustafa. Mariya has become a convert to the true faith. Let this be investigated and written in the sicil. When Yunus is asked for proof, seyyid 'Osman çavuş bn Arslan and Suleyman çavuş bn Aydogmuş confirm Yunus. Registered. (1 247–3; II Şevval 1002)

Karçire v. Filipo of Cados village of Mesariye kaza sets forth a claim *(td)* before Musa beşe bn Ahmed: Four months ago Musa beşe took my wife Çako bint (?) by force *(cebren)* and he has kept possession *(tasarruf)* of her until now. Let him be asked. I want my rights to be established *(ihkak-i hakk)*. Musa beşe replies that Çako was honored with Islam before the Muslims at that time; she took the name Fatma. Karçire was offered the chance to come to Islam but he declined. A man named Şenlik Hoca arranged Fatma's marriage to me *('akd-i nikah)*. Karçire claims that Çako had not become a Muslim nor had he been invited to. When she was summoned to court, she said, in truth, I came to Islam at that time and my name is Fatma; my husband Karçire was invited to Islam. (3 9–7; 13 Şevval 1018)

Musa beşe says: When Çako, wife of Karçire v. Filipo, became a Muslim, he was asked the question, Will you come to Islam? but he refused *(iba)*. (3 10–6; 14 Şevval 1018. Registered the following day)

Husna/Husniye (?) bint Murad, Armenian wife, says *(bm)* before her husband Mergeri (?) v. Kuluk (?), Armenian: He always treats me cruelly *(cefa ve eza)*. I do not want him. He denies that *(munkir)*. Then Husna becomes honored with Islam. After she takes the name 'Ayşe, her husband is invited *('arz)* to Islam but he does not accept, so 'Ayşe's separation *(tefrik)* is ordered. (3 25–3; I Zil-Kade 1018).

Mustafa bn 'Abdullah says *(ihzar/bm)* before his zimmiye wife *(zevce' -ı kafiresi)* Lena bint Vasil: Three months ago when I became honored with Islam *(Islama müşerref ollub)*, I proposed Islam to her but she did not accept. I am a Muslim and I want to divorce her as soon as possible. She admits not accepting Islam. (3 66–3; II Receb 1019)

His daughter Mariye and his son Yorgi, who are 10 years old *(on yaşinda)*, become Muslims. They take the names of 'Ayni and Ridvan. (3 66–4; II Receb 1019).

Yusuf bn Mehmed of Lefkoşa [not even a convert] says *(tk)* before his wife Meryem bint Ilyas, zimmiye: My wife Meryem is an infidel *(kafire)*. When I invited her to Islam, she did not agree *(raziye olmadugi)*, so I divorced her three times. I am divorced. She is a divorcée *(mutallaka)*. (3 137–4; 28 Rebi' II 1019)

Muslim "missionaries," perhaps dervişes, must have worked hard to win such converts.[4] The conversions of the married women are particularly striking, even if one was out of personal animosity towards a husband. Zimmiye women certainly had the right to convert on their own volition, and some Muslims must have worked particularly to convert them. Economic incentives might have appealed less to women converts, who did not have to pay *cizye/harac*. Perhaps youths were particularly susceptible, and the court supervised the guardianship of all orphans and their estates; usually zimmis acted as guardians *(vasis)* in such cases, however.

Reversion from Islam to their former faith by converts was absolutely forbidden. Such was the momentum of Islam at that time however that apostasy from it must have been virtually nonexistent. In one instance a city police official did make a charge against a man named Zako.

'Omer beşe bn Sefer, yasakci from şehir su başi, stated *(ihzar/bm)* before Zako v. Loizo [the text says Loizo v. Zako, but that must be a mistake]: Formerly

Zako acknowledged in the presence of Muslims that he was a Muslim. Now he says in public that he is an infidel *(kafir)*. Let the court be asked. Zako denies that *(munkir)*. When proof is asked of ᶜOmer, from ᶜudul-i muslimin Hamze boluk başi bn Mustafa and ᶜAbdi beşe confirm his claim. Accepted by the court. Registered. (3 57–4; II Cumadi II 1019)

Presumably Zako was given the choice of being honored with Islam again or execution, but court records do not explicitly reveal punishments.

Some times it must have been hard to keep informed about who had converted. A zimmi neighbor or acquaintance might appear one day wearing the turban ostensibly reserved to Muslims.

Ibrahim bn Ramazan before this Hiristofi v. Andon: I saw Andon at night wearing a turban *(dulbend)*. After questioning, he denied *(inkar)* that. The latter replied, I am a Muslim, I serve in the castle garrison *(hisar eri)*. When proof was asked, ᶜAli bn Mustafa, Hizir bn Bali, Ridvan bn ᶜAbdullah, and Piyale bn ᶜAbdullah confirmed Hiristofi. (1 223–3; III Ramazan 1002)

There is some evidence that late in this period the Orthodox church began to act more forcefully, if still surreptitiously, with followers who were on intimate terms with Muslims, particularly in the case of intermarriage.

Milu bint Andoni of Çeliye (?) village of Tuzla nahiye says *(bk/tm):* Up until now like my ancestors I have belonged to the Christian millet *(millet-i Nasara)*. I have not become a Muslim. I am an infidel *(kafire)*. When I wished to perform our false rites *(ayin-i batilimuz)* at the church *(kenise)*, the monks *(rahibler)* who were our priests *(papaslar)* prevented me from entering saying, 'You married a Muslim *(Musliman zevci etmuş idin)*.' It is probable *(muhtemel)* that when I perish they will not bury me in accordance with infidel rites *(ayin-i kefere)*. I want a memorandum *(tezkere)* showing that I am an infidel *(kefere)*. (4 197–1; I Şaban 1046)

Zimmi Ciryako of . . . gro (?) vil. of Limosa nahiye says *(bk/tm):* Up until now I have been a Christian *(millet-i Nasara)*. I was an infidel *(kafir)*, I went to church in my village and practiced false *(batil)* religion. When I wanted to enter the church in the village, the priest *(babas)* said, 'You are a Muslim.' Now they want to keep me from entering the church. Let it be registered to show that I am one who admits *(muᶜterif)* to being a Christian. (4 85–3; I Şaban 1044. Compare that with a case of Sefer 1003 when a village priest gave his daughter permission to marry a Muslim, 1 77–5.)

When Fr. Jerom Dandini passed through Cyprus en route to the Levant, he reported the presence of thousands of converts. Dandini, a philosophy instructor in Perugia, was sent by the general of the Franciscan order in 1596 to the patriarch of the Maronites. He spent over three months incognito in Cyprus, where he reconnoitered the condition of the local Maronites, and other Roman Catholics as well. Dandini believed that most of the Muslims were renegades "who turn Mahometans, to render their lives more easy and supportable; so that it seems an easy task to recover this isle . . . for the renegadoes could no sooner see the Christian soldiers, but they would throw off their turbans, and put on hats instead, and turn their arms against the Turks."[5] That theme is a common one not just of foreign visitors to Cyprus but all over the Ottoman empire, although for centuries it remained a naive and self-deluding idea, dangerously ethnocentric and religiocentric. Thus Cotovicus (1598–1599) reported that the Ottoman governor Jafer pasha was hostile to local Christians. Lithgow (1610) believed the people of Cyprus needed rescue, while des Hayes claimed that the people were so impoverished and oppressed that they hardly had anything but carobs to eat. Louis des Hayes, a French ambassador who briefly visited Cyprus in 1621, reported that the governor of Cyprus did not want the local Christians to convert to Islam because of the attendant losses of tax revenues. In 1670 the French pilgrim N. Hurtel met three Greeks in Lefkoşa who gave him a similar story: "Very many of them, unable to bear any longer this cruel tyranny, wish to turn Turk; but many are rejected, because (say their lords) in receiving them into the Moslem faith their tribute would be so much diminished."[6]

The Jews

Although travellers and pilgrims frequently commented on the absence of Jews from Cyprus, in the early Ottoman period a small community lived in Lefkoşa. Occasionally a zimmi is identified as a Jew *(Yahudi* or *Yahuda taifesi);* if all Jews are identified that way, and probably most were, then both their numbers and their impact on the court were small. However, one Jew does stand out, an important tax farmer *(multezim)* named Isak or Ishak.

As tax farmer *(multezim)* of Istaliye (?) village of Kukla kaza with his partner *(şerik)* zimmi Loizo, for 3000 akce he gave Mustafa çavuş title deed *(tapu)* to fields *(tarla)* whose owner had died without male offspring *(evlad-i zukur).* That was a right generally limited to spahis on their timars (1 22–2; Receb 1002). Isak and the people around him were involved in questionable activities. Once he sent Lazari v. Andon to go to his house near the harbor *(limon)* to bring back eight kile of rice *(pirinc)*. When Lazari returned to Lefkoşa he was summoned to court to account for what he had done; he took an oath that he had sold the rice as he had been instructed (1 54–2; I Ramazan 1002. cf. 54–3, 5).

Ishak, a Jew, *'amil*, of Lefkoşa acknowledges *(ik)* before Lazar v. Andon: While Andon was in my service *(hidmetumde)* I sent him to my wife Polazha (?) at the harbor *(limon)* to get eight *keyl* rice *(pirinc)*. He went and took the rice but I do not know to whom he gave it. Lazar acknowledges that he took the rice; but when Isak was imprisoned *(habs)*, I gave it to his other wife *(diger zevci)* (?) Lazar was asked to take an oath; after he took it, he was given a berat. (1 209–3; I Ramazan 1002)

Behram bn 'Abdullah states *(tm)* before above Isak: Isak has my cloth folded around his waist like an apron *(hibak)*. I want it. Denied. Isak takes an oath. (1 54–4; I Ramazan 1002)

Porta Papaz, Vasil v. Lariyo, Ziyareska (?) v. Simiyoni, and many others of Kulaş village of Piskobi kaza complained that Isak had exceeded his tax farm *(mukata 'a)* collecting dues from them, and indeed an order from the deputy of the provincial governor *(kethuda' -i mir miran)* to the kadis of Piskopi and Kukla draws to their attention claims that over the past three years zimmis Silostre and Isak had taken 230 kantar of cotton *(penbe)* extra from that tax farm *(mukata 'a)*. Finally it was established by former emin Loize that the total amount in error was 260 kantar (1 58–4; same. 1 97–3; 29 Receb 1002. Further complaints followed in II Ramazan 1002. 1 220–4).

Isak's position obviously did not suffer, however, for in an entry of early August 1594 (II Zil-Kade 1002) Magosa begi 'Ali beg acknowledged that he had received in full the 50,000 akce due for ship supplies *(kadirga muhimmati)* in 1592–1593 (1001) from Isak, tax farmer *(multezim)* and agent for the tax farms *(mukata 'at)* of Limosa (1 274–4. cf. 274–5).

Vasil v. Iliya of Ayo Kostinti village of Limosa says before Kaprice (?) v. Yorgi: He was a servant *(hidmetkar)* of the Jew Isak. he stole Liyandi's 19 altun. Then we took it from him. Denied. Mahmud beg, spahi, Tomazi v. Petre, and Vasil v. Andon attest to the truth of Vasil's statement. (1 249–2; II Şevval 1002)

A man named Bayram v. Ishak of the Jewish people *(Yahudi zumresi)* of Lefkoşa, almost certainly the son of Isak the Jew, was involved in international trade. He had sent Yasef v. Ibrahim with money to Venice *(Venedik)* to make trade *(ticaret)*. Bayram's capital *(sermaye)* was used to buy 120 vakiye of tin *(kalay)*, one barrel *(varil)* of tin plate *(teneke)*, one barrel of brass *(sari teneke)*, and 420 knives *(çift bicak)*, which were delivered to Kuçuk Han in Lefkoşa at the cost of 1500 akce for his service *(hidmet)* (1 293–3; I Zil-Hicce 1002). Possibly another son (Or is it Ishak himself? The reading is very dubious). Ishak (?), the Jew, owed 200 akce to Şeyh ʿAbdullah of Lefkoşa from his purchase of a donkey *(eşek)* (3 60–3; III Cumadi II 1019).

The name Jew could be used with disapprobrium.

Receb beşe of Lefkoşa makes a claim *(td)* before Mehmed beg: He called me 'Jew' Receb *(cuhud)*. Mehmed denies that. Huseyn bn Memi and Mehmed beşe confirm Receb's claim. (3 177–4; III Şaban 1019)

Perhaps linking the Jews and Gypsies *(Kibtan ve Yahuda taifesi)* in later documents regarding the collection of *cizye/harac* was also an indication of disapprobrium (4 229–2; I Muh. 1044. 4 237–1; III Şaban 1045).

The Jewish community resided within the walls of Lefkoşa. A document of I Rebiʿ II 1044 refers to a Jew named Yasef v. ʿImran, recently deceased, an inhabitant of Han-i ʿatik; his wife (?) became guardian for his minor daughters (4 32–2, 3). A large estate with 50 two-storied *(fevkani)* and six single-storied houses *(tahtani)* within the castle *(kalʿe)* at Zeyn ul- ʿAbidin efendi quarter was bought by Refayel v. Lazari from the Jew Iliya. With its water, well, and threshing area *(harman)*, he dedicated the house as a foundation to be rented at a low rate to poor Jews who lived there. The donor himself was to be administrator *(mu-tevelli)* during his own lifetime, and thereafter control would pass to his descendants. Every year 200 akce of the rent was assigned to purchase candle wax for the camiʿ -i şerif called Aya Sofya in the castle of Lefkoşa (2 50–1; I Receb 1016).

Besides Lefkoşa Isak also had a house at the harbor. Another Jew, Desilno (co?) v. Yahya (?) of Lefkoşa, had a house, gardens, and 120 donum arable fields *(tarla)* at Genose (?) village of Hirsofi nahiye which he sold to ʿAli bn ʿAbdullah, janissary, for 840 akce (1 277–5; II Zil-Kade: 1002). In addition, two villages of Lefka (Aya Yorgi and Aya Nikola) and two villages of Girniye (Koromandi (?) and Mamili (?)) are identified as having Jews (2 108–1; 1 Rebiʿ I 1017). Prior to the Ottoman conquest the only Jews on the island were about 25 families of Levantine, Sicilian, and Portuguese Jews who all lived in Magosa, according to Elias of Pesaro who was there during the autumn of 1563. All lived "comfortably without exertion" by money lending. "As soon as the Christians see a fresh Jew arrive to stay here they ask him if he wants to lend money." If he says yes, both they and the other Jews are pleased.[7]

The Armenians

The Armenian community of Cyprus also was relatively inconspicuous during the early years of Ottoman rule. If, as seems to be the case, they may be associated almost exclusively with the name Armenian *(Ermeni)* or with their quarter *(Ermeni mahallesi)* in Lefkoşa, their impact on the community was small. Although a few lived elsewhere, that is hard to verify because many had personal names which cannot easily be distinguished from Greek or Turkish ones. Some came originally from Anatolia and maintained connections there. The cases involving Armenians reveal surprisingly little interaction with the other communities of the city. Perhaps they lived in relative isolation during the period 1580–1640.[8]

Among the Turkish names encountered are Murat v. Çoban, Murad v. ʿAvs, Kara Biyik, Tanri virdi, Allah virdi, Yunus v. Kara Goz, and feminine Altun and Husna. They do not make up very large a proportion of the Armenian personal names which occur, and probably most of them had come to Cyprus from nearby parts of Anatolia. When they came, or how, as *surgun* for example, is unknown but some maintained connections there. The guardian *(vasi)* of the late Armenian Abraham v. Tetiyos produced witnesses to attest to the fact that the deceased had a sister in Nigde sancagi, and the Armenian Temame (?) bint Gazel/Guzel, as guardian *(vasi)* for and mother of the minor children of the late Armenian Mosis, sold his house *(menzil)* in Sozi Hisar to Armenian Kablan v. Serkis (1 313–3; 8 Muh. 1003. 4 9–2; I Ramazan 1043). Armenian (?) v. Erekil sold his house in Hizir Ilyas quarter of Atana kasaba to Armenian Yunus (?) v. Kara Goz (3 26–2; 10 Zil-Kade 1018). An imperial order of 26 September 1634 (3 Rebiʿ I 1044) from Kostantiniye to the Cyprus begler begisi, to the Cyprus cabi defterdari, and to the kadis in Cyprus concerns collecting the cizye of the Armenian community *(Ermeni taifesi)* from Anatolia scattered *(perakende)* on the island (4 240–1).

The only instances of credit given by Armenians were intracommunal: Armenian Yavet v. Kara Biyik claimed Armenian Murad v. Yasef owed him three and a half guruş and Armenian Altun claimed that her husband Armenian Murad owed her 3000 akce (3 33–8; II Zil-Kade 1018. 4 34–2; I Rebiᶜ II 1044). Armenian Paresun (?) v. Mircan owed 6160 akce to Fatma hatun for two mules and also nine guruş to zimmi Behine v. Petro, while the Armenian Allah Virdi owed four guruş to the Muslim woman Zeyneb bint Nebi and 50 akce to Mehmed bn ᶜAbdullah. Armenians Ohan v. Emircan (?) and Yasef b. Tanri Vir(di) owed 40,000 akce to Ganber bn ᶜAbdullah of Lefkoşa from a loan *(muᶜamele² -i şerᶜiye)* (3 1–3; III Zil-Hicce 1018. 3 17–4; 27 Şevval 1018. 3 87–3; III Sefer 1019. 3 137–3; 28 Rebiᶜ II 1019. 3 137–2; same). The Armenian Bali owed one filori to ᶜAli, (3 131–1, 2, 3; same) and Irer (?) v. Selman owed Ishak bn Salih 420 akce for leather *(gon)* (3 153–9; II Rebiᶜ II 1019). Zimmi Murad v. Eymur beşe, mutevelli of the church *(kenise)* of Terbiyodi quarter, claimed that the late Armenian Ilyas of that quarter owed its vakf 2000 akce (4 129–3; 130–1; III Receb 1045). Murad v. ᶜAvs, Armenian, disappeared leaving a debt of 34 guruş to Mehmed beşe bn Imam Kuli (3 23–6; I Zil-Kade 1018). Thus it can be seen that, while few instances of credit involved Armenians at all, none had given credit to anyone outside their own community. A few Armenians were in debt to outsiders, however.

Of six instances of land and property transfers involving Armenians which survive, five involve only Armenians. Two instances cited above involved transfers of properties outside of Cyprus. Two more involved the sale of houses *(menzil)* in the Armenian quarter, one by Hiristofi v. Tomazo to Hiristofi … (?) v. Piyero for 720 akce and the other by Merik/Kazik (?) v. Ciryako to Yorgi v. Davit for 2460 akce (1 106–2; Rebiᶜ II 1003. 1 265–5; II Zil-Kade 1002). The fifth was Habbaz Mansur's sale of his house *(menzil)* at Terbiyodi (?) quarter to Baba Filibo v. Yakimo for 7760 akce (3 106–3; 4 Ramazan 1019). In the one instance of purchase from outside the Armenian community, Kara Goz, having bought a house at a place unspecified from Mehmed beşe bn Imam Kuli for 34 guruş, disappeared without paying his debt (3 23–6; I Zil-Kade 1018. Cf. 29–3; II Zil-Kade). That also suggests relative self-containment among the Armenian community in Lefkoşa.

Otherwise the Armenians were relatively inconspicuous. An Armenian woman Husna bint Murad apparently converted to Islam to escape her husband Mergeri (?) v. Kuluk (?) (3 25–3; 9 Zil-Kade 1018). Armenian Anderik v. Keşiş of Terbiyodi quarter was arrested by za'im ul-vakt Mustafa su başi and 'asses başi 'Ali su başi for drinking wine (*şurb-i hamr*) at night in the market (*suk*) in the quarter, and Armenian Murad v. Migirdic was charged with cursing Mustafa bn Hasan (3 149–3; III Cumadi II 1019. 3 158–5; III Rebi' II 1019).

Mustafa bn Hasan of Lefkoşa says (*bm*) before Murad v. Migirdic, Armenian: Murad cursed my mouth (*agz*) and faith (*iman*). I want justice done (*ihkak-i hakk*). Denied. Registered. (3 158-1; III Rebi' II 1019)

'Abdi bn Mustafa says (*bm*) before Murad v. Murad, Armenian: He struck me, and imprisoned (*habs*) me. Denied. (3 138–7; after 28 Rebi' II 1019)

'Abdi bn Mustafa of Lefkoşa says (*bm*) before above Murad, Armenian: He struck me and imprisoned me. Let him be asked and let justice be done. Denied. When 'Abdi has no proof, an oath is proposed (*teklif*) to Murad that he did not do as 'Abdi charged. Murad takes the oath and it is registered. (3 138-8; same)

A Muslim, on the other hand, was convicted of assaulting a local Armenian.

'Abdullah (?) v. 'Abdullah (?) Armenian, of Lefkoşa says (*bm*) before Bayram bn Ridvan: He blocked my way and struck me with a rock (*taş*) and injured (*mecruh*) my head. I want the Sharia enforced. I want justice done (*ihkak-i hakk*). Denied. 'Udul-i Muslimin Mustafa beşe bn Mehmed and 'Ali bn Ibrahim confirm the Armenian. (3 156-1; same)

In 1636–1637 (1046) at least one Armenian, Yageb, lived in Koyunli village of Lefkoşa kaza (4 191–1; II Receb 1046). No other references to Armenians living outside of Lefkoşa were found.

The Maronites (Suryani)

Jerom Dandini, officially dispatched to the Maronite patriarch in 1596 by the general of the Franciscan order, must be considered an expert on the Maronite church in Cyprus. Maronites were there "in great numbers," and indeed one of only three Maronite bishops outside Mount Lebanon was found there. From Dandini's perspective the Maronites seem to have been a clearly defined community. Although the Maronite church in Lefkoşa was "in poor condition," he lists 19 Maronite villages by name, each having at least one parish.[9]

People identified as Suryani (Maronite) used the court quite infrequently, although in successive cases Meryem bint Iliyas, divorced wife of Yusuf bn Mehmed of Lefkoşa, was identified as first "zimmiye" and then "Suryani taifesi," so important evidence about them may well be lost (3 137–4, 5; after 28 Rebi' II 1019).

None of the Suryani are identified with towns. Indeed the only two villages they are identified with in the court registers are in Lefkoşa district: Hitriya (Kythrea = Degirmenlik) village and Banu Hurşuh (?) of Degirmenlik. In the former Suryani Mariya bint Yasef, as mother and guardian of her daughter Heta (?), helped settle the estate of her late husband Luka v. Semail (?) (3 18–8; 28 Şevval 1018). In the latter Istefano and Erlegiro (?), sons of Yakimo of Banu Hurşuh (?) sold a flourishing house *(hane)* and a ruined one *(harabe)*, trees, and a garden, along with water rights, to Yasef v. Hate (?) Suriyani for 9000 akce (4 26–1; I Rebi' I 1044).

Other Suryani mentioned include Ziya (3 137–5; after II Ramazan 1019), Ibraşim (?) v. 'Abdullah, Suryani, Ziya v. Yorgi, Suryani, Serkiz, and Musa v. Andoni, Suryani (3 25–4; 10 Zil-Kade 1018. 3 32–4; II Zil-Kade 1018).

Latin Christians (Nasara)

The few people indentified as Nasara probably are Latins (Roman Catholics). Behine v. Ya' kub was one of the Latin (Nasara) witnesses *('udul-i Nasara)* in the settlement of a matter of guardianship involving an Armenian Gregorian from Nigde (1 313–4; 8 Muharrem 1003). Another was zimmi Ciryako of Dagiro (?) village of Limosa district *(nahiye),* who had always been a Latin Christian *(millet-i Nasara)* and remained one but was excluded from his village church by the priest *(babas),* who accused him of being a Muslim (4 85–3; I Şaban 1044). Milu (?Milo?) bint Andoni of Celiye village of Tuzla nahiye was excluded from her village church after marrying a Muslim (4 197–1; I Şaban 1046). Nasraniye Sidilu (?Cendilu?) bint Hiristofi of Aya Lome quarter of Lapta village of Giriniye district *(nahiye)* bought a substantial estate *(menzil)* there from Raziye bint 'Abdullah, including two two-storied and four one-storied houses, with one and a half donum of gardens *(bagçe)* and four hours of water every market day *(Bazar gun)* (4 100–2; II Ramazan 1044). A Croatian *(Hirvadi l-asl)* slave of the Nasara taifesi, who presumably would have been of the Latin church, fell into disputes over his emancipation (1 279–3; II Zil-Kade 1002).

Latins might easily pass themselves as Maronites, and vice versa, if circumstances mandated it. One might conjecture that immediately after the Ottoman conquest would have been a wise time for Latins to try to remain inconspicuous, for they were the enemy, both to the new rulers and to the Orthodox Christian majority on Cyprus, but Ottoman sources are silent on that subject. What little evidence has been found on that subject, regarding foreigners *(harbis)*, Latins, and Maronites, suggests that the situation of the Latins was not so very precarious as some scholars have conjectured.[10]

Priests and Monks

Among the groups of zimmis which can be identified in the judicial records, one of the most conspicuous is the clergy, that is, priests and monks of towns, villages, and monasteries. Despite the obvious sacramental differences between Christian clergy and Muslim ulema, and despite the absence of monasticism in Islam, the two groups played very similar roles in the socioeconomic system. Most of the Christian clergy were no less exempt from having to earn their living than Muslim religious functionaries. They shared the same tax-exempt status. Like the ulema, the clergy owned land, or rented it, they engaged in trade and commerce, they lent and borrowed money. Christian clergy seem to have had no more aversion to dealing with Muslims than other zimmis did.

Papa (priest) Yani v. Vasil and another zimmi from Miliya village of Hirsofi kaza sold two and a half kantar of cotton *(penbe)* to ʿOmer bn Ibrahim of the Lefkoşa "volunteers" *(gonulleri)*, with six years credit (1 15–5; II Ramazan 988). Baba (priest) Petro v. Feranci of Dali village of Lefkoşa kaza sold 50 carded cotton *(mahluc penbe)* to janissary Mehmed beşe (4 200–2; II Şaban 1046). Rahib (monk) Baba Eleksendri went all the way to the Sublime Porte to get an imperial order and a letter from the kadi ʿasker in order to settle his claim against his former business partner, a kadi.

Rahib Baba Eleksendri, abbot *(gumonas = igumenos)* of Aya Mama monastery in Morfo nahiye acknowledges *(ik/iʿt)* before present Tuzla kadisi mevlana haci

Ahmed efendi: Formerly Ahmed and I had a dispute *(niza')* over business and trade *(mu'amelat ve ahz ve i 'ta)*. A compromise *(sulh)* was made for 18,000 akce, but when I was not given the money for the settlement *(bedel-i sulh)*, I went to the Porte *(asitane' -i se'adete)*, and when I brought up the aforementioned matter, I was given an imperial order *(emr-i şerif)* and received a letter *(mektub)* from the Rumili kadi 'asker when I went. When I presented the letter and order and again made claim *(da'va)*, a compromise was made for 30 keyl of barley *(arpa)* and 20 keyl of whet *(bugday)*. I have no further claim. (4 92–2; I Ramazan 1044)

Papa Filipo v. Papa Toma of Aya Luka quarter was owed 120 akce by Yorgi v. Manuel (3 34–7; II Zil-Kde 1018). Nikolo v. Kirago and Yerlovati (?) v. Mestotori (?) of Terbiyodi (?) quarter and others owed a total of 900 akce to Baba Kistintin v. Piro of that quarter (4 247–1; undated). Papa Nikola owed 1200 *(dirhem)* to janissary Mehmed beşe (1 58–1; I Ramazan 1002). Baba Petro owed zimmi Istavriye 5040 *(dirhem)* (3 104–4, 5; 4 Ramazan 1019). Papa Klito v. Petro owed 20 sikke to Laverço v. Nikola (3 167–6; II Şaban 1019). Baba Luka owed 80 guruş to Mustafa oda başi (4 244–2; c. II Receb 1044). Baba Leta (?) v. Andoni of Degirmenlik village owed 4000 akce to Huseyn çavuş (4 244–4; III Receb 1044).

Suleyman, janissary, says: I want two Venedik guruş from Papa Fote (?), zimmi. Denied. Suleyman has no proof. When an oath is proposed to the priest, he takes it. (1 291–3; 9 Zil-Hicce 1002)

Clearly the clergy were more often borrowers than lenders. Perhaps that reflects a certain precariousness in their economic status.

Papa Lefteri v. Kiryako and Papa Andon v. Kiryako owned vineyards at Paliçoz (?) village of Pendaye kaza (1 184–2; 26 Cumadi I 1003). Papa Nikola v. Filibo, priest *(papaz)* of Musa çelebi village of Lefkoşa was able to sell his three one-story houses *(tahtani evler)* at the village to racil Mehmed bn 'Abdullah for 1800 akce, and Papa Yano v. Dimitre of Ayos (?) village of Lefkoşa was able to sell his four one-story houses *(tahtani evler)* at the village to Hasan beg bn Kasim for 1000 akce (1 210–1; I Ramazan 1002. 277–1; II Zil-Kadr 1002). Papa Nikola v. Filipo bought four one-story houses *(tahtani evler)* at Aya Pereşcoga quarter in Lefkoşa from Huseyn bn Yusuf for 2760 akce (1 301–1; Zil-Hicce 1002). The monks *(rahibler)* who lived in Aya Yani Mesologo monastery bought some places around the monastery from Polyo v. Kostindin of Lefkoşa for 12,000 akce (1 330–3; II Şaban 1002). Hiristofi v. Yakimo, rahib of Elvidose (?) quarter, owned houses *(evler)* there which he had earlier bought from zimmiye Lena bint Kosarivi (?) for 6000 akce (3 51–3; II Cumadi II 1019). Baba Andoni v. Lefteri of Kalamit (?) village of Pendaye nahiye sold his 24 donum vineyards *(bag)* at the village to Mehmed bn ʿAbdun-Nebi of Lefkoşa for 10,000 akce (4 31–2; II Rebiʿ I 1044). Baba Simiyo bought a garden *(bagçe)* at Degirmenlik village of Lefkoşa from zimmiye (?) bint Ergiro for 2000 akce (4 57–2; I Sefer 1044). Rahib Argiro (?) v. Peraşkoge of Eskalari village of Lefkoşa nahiye sold his garden (bagçe) with one- and two-story houses at Gerbi (?) village of Morfo nahiye to several zimmis for 10,000 akce (4 102–1; III Ramazan 1044). Baba Ciryako v. Savu bought a house, courtyard *(hane, havlu)* etc. at Temlos/Temblos village of Girniye kaza from Manesko v. Madyo of the village for 640 akce (4 190–1; II Receb 1046).

Several clergy were involved in disputes over possession of certain property such as donkeys, oxen, water rights, and other land and property, usually with other zimmis (1 17–6; 21 Ramazan 988. 3 148–4, 5; III Cumadi II 1019. 3 148–2; III Cumadi II 1019. 4 16–1; II Şevval 1043. 4 141–1; I Şaban 1045). One priest was struck by another, and several priests were cursed by a zimmi.

Papa Çatiyo (?), zimmi of evlad-i Sineg (?) says *(tm)* before Perato Papa v. Sefletiyo (?): He entered my house in the night me and struck me *(darb-i şedid)* on the arm. (1 32–4; 3 Şaban 1002)

Papa Bahtyodi v. Loizo, Papa Maniku (?), and other priests *(papazlar)*: Panedorfo v. (omitted) cursed *(şetm)* us. Let him be asked. Denied. Piyalu v. Zanko and Zano (?) v. Nikolo confirm the claimants. (3 146–7; III Cumadi II 1019)

Several clergy were accused of theft, one of rape, and one of murder. In addition popular complaints were raised against two others. Nearly all the complaints originated among zimmis.

Şilviya bint Yani, zimmiye of Lakatamiye village says *(bm)* before Baba Yorgi v. Baba Yani of village: One month ago Baba Yorgi came upon me *(uzerime gelub)* in the middle of the night. I was alone. He made fornication *(zina)*. Let him be asked. Denied. (3 66–5; II Receb 1019)

Loizo v. Andreye of Lakatamiye village of Lefkoşa, as agent *(vekil)* sets forth a claim *(td)* before Baba Yorgi v. Baba Yani of the village: Previously in the middle of the night Baba Yani entered the house of my son's wife Şilviya and took her by force *(cebren tasarruf)*. Let him be asked. Denied. When Loizo is asked for proof, Vinsas (?) v. Misten (?) and Zorzi (?) v. Loico (?) came to court and confirmed that Baba Yorgi came out of her house in the night, although they did not see anything concerning *(mute ʿallik)* fornication *(zina)*. It is registered. (3 71–2; II Receb 1019)

Above Baba Yorgi acknowledges that he borrowed some money from Halici zade, musellim of Mustafa Paşa . . . (3 71–3; same)

Huseyn bn Mustafa of Kurikoy village says *(bm)* before Artimo v. Tomasi, rahib of Urmani (?) village: He mounted my donkey *(merkeb)* and without my knowledge he took it and went. I found my donkey in front of his house. I want him asked in accordance with the Sharia. Artimo replies: In truth, I mounted his donkey, but he cut its tongue. (3 153–2; II Rebʿ II 1019)

Above rahib says: I took the donkey and brought it to my house (3 153–3; same) *Huccet*. Huseyn bn Mustafa of Kuri village says *(bm)* before Papa Arsimo v. Tomaz, rahib of Lefkoşa: Formerly he cut out the tongue *(dil)* of my donkey, I want justice done *(ihkak-i hakk)*. Denied. Huseyn has no proof. When an oath is proposed that he did not do as Huseyn claimed, the zimmi took it on the Incil. (3 158–6; same)

Above Huseyn acknowledges *(ik)* before above Papa: I claimed *(daʿva)* that he cut the tongue of my donkey. I was not able to substantiate *(isbat)* the claim. (3 158–7; same)

Papa Paçi says *(bm)* before Anzelo v. Yorgi: Starting 15 years ago I worked three years for him and he has not paid me. The claim is not heard. (3 148–3; III Cumadi II 1019)

Papa Paçi v. Hiristofi of Dikimo village of Girniye says *(bm)* before Anzelo v. Yorgi: I sold him an ox *(okuz)* for 840 akce. He delays paying. Denied. Then he acknowledges it. (3 148–4; same)

Above Anzelo sold above Papa a donkey *(merkeb)*. (3 148–5; same)

Above Anzelo says *(bm)* before above Papa: He stole my small rug *(kaliçe)*. Let him be imprisoned *(habs)*. He has my money also. Denied. (3 148–6; same)

Mustafa ota başi guardian *(vasi)*, before the Sharia for the orphans *(eytam)* Mustafa, ʿAli, and Fatma of the late Emir ʿAli beşe of Cyprus janissaries who was killed *(maktul)* while living in Kamosine (?) of Lefka kaza says *(bk/tm)* before from the village zimmis Luyi v. Zorzi, Baba Luka v. Luyi, Loizo v. Tomazo, Andon v. Baba Filori, and others: Baba Vasil and Mihayel killed Emir

ʿAli beşe and that was proved at court *(divan-i Kibris mahfil-i şerᶜ)*. I have no claim against the people of the village. (4 71–1; I Receb 1044)

Baba Kostindin v. Piro, rahib of Terbiyoti quarter of Lefkoşa, says *(ihzar/tk/tm)* before from the quarter Piro v. Andon (?), Vriyoni v. Vriyoni, Mihail v. Marko, Luka v. Yakimo, Zorzi v. Bavli, Arslan v. Eymur şeh, and others: Let my state, or reputation, *(hal)* be recorded. I have no desire to drive him from the priesthood *(papaslik)*. (4 40–1 I Rebiᶜ II 1044)

Yakimo v. Vriyoni, Ilyas v. Hiristofi, Tomazo v. Vriyoni, zimmis, and others of Kizilbaş koy in Lefkoşa kaza claim *(iddiᶜa/tk)* before Baba Ciryako v. Savu of the village: He does not support himself. He cursed us all. Let his state, or reputation *(hal)* be asked. (4 145–3; I Şevval 1045)

On several occasions clergy alone or with others of their quarter or village passed information on to the court, ostensibly as communal leaders. After the murderers of janissary Emir ʿAli beşe were discovered, Baba Luka was among those villagers informed that no claim would be made against the village for blood money *(dem diyeti)* (4 70–1; 71–1; I Receb 1044). Baba Kostintin, Baba Vasil, and Baba Bahtodi were among the zimmis of Terbiyoti quarter of Lefkoşa who came to court to request an investigation of the fatal fall of zimmi Yakimo from the castle walls, and the priests *(babaslar)* of the Armenian quarter of Lefkoşa were among those who asked the court to investigate the condition of a dying elderly woman in their quarter (4 16–2; 4 Şevval 1043. 4 39–3; I Rebiᶜ II 1044). Baba Yorgi v. Aleksendre was among the people of Çaluce (?) village of Baf kaza who negotiated a compromise *(sulh)* in a dispute with their spahi Arslan beg (1 67–4; Muh. 1003).

Clergy were exempt from most taxes, although they would pay taxes on land they cultivated. Sometimes it was necessary to go to court to secure that privilege.

Hasan bn Kasim, spahi of Ayos (?) village of Lefkoşa: I renounce the *çift bozan* akce due from Papa Yano v. Hiritim (?) and his son Yakimo. I have no further claim. (1 273–7; I Zil-Kade 1002)

Rahib Yanaci, vekil-i şerᶜ of rahib the abbot *(gumonos filosofo)* of Belikano (?) monastery in Hirsofi nahiye says *(bk/tm):* Mariye bint Loizo gave us her three-year-old son Simiyo eight [years] ago. From then until now he has not been able to support himself *(kar u kesb)* or to mingle with people *(ihtilat)*. He became a monk *(rahib)*. They want *cizye* and *ispence* from this minor even though he does not support himself or mingle with people. I want his *cizye* and *ispence* to be canceled *(sakit)*. This is true. It is not permissible in accordance with the Sharia to demand *cizye* and *ispence* from him. (4 192–1; II Receb 1046. Cf. 1 311–4 where Papa Kipriyano v. Ferenci is called a re'aya to Ahmed aga because of the lands he cultivates. Muh. 1003.)

Zimmis as Local Officials

In a few instances zimmis held positions which placed them on the periphery of official local authority in administration. The case of Isak the Jew has already been introduced. Often a zimmi was a tax farmer *(multezim)*. So Lefkoşa muhtesib haci Huseyn bn Bilal transferred the revenues due for his salary from the wax factory *(mum hane)* to Andreye v. Pernardi for three years at 10,000 akce per year, a total of 30,000 akce for three years (1 304–3; Muh. 1003). Girniye sancagi begi Dilaver beg bn 'Abdullah commissioned *(siparis)* Sinan efendi bn Musa of the notables *(zu'ama)* to collect his 120,000 akce salary *(saliyane)* due for 1016, but the steward *(emin)* sent to collect the salary was zimmi Ferendci, who hitherto had only received 45,000 akce (3 127–1; I Ramazan 1019).

'Ali Paşa, present governor *(valiy-i vilayet)* of the island of Cyprus has Mehmed aga in his place for the investigation, who says *(ihzar/bk)* before tavern tax farmer *(meyhane multezimi)* of Lefkoşa Totori v. Ferencesko and Yorolimo (?) v. Cakuh: Tonight zimmi Yakimo went to their tavern *(meyhane)* which they possess as a tax farm *(iltizam)*. He drank wine and became unconscious *(la ya 'kil)*. He fell from the castle *(hisar)* and perished *(helak)*. Let them be asked. Denied. When proof is demanded of Mehmed, he had none. When he proposed on oath to the zimmis, they took it. (4 13–2; I Şevval 1043)

Non-Muslims commonly dealt with matters concerning wine; for example, a former imperial wine steward *(hamr emini)*, a Jew named Franko, was banished to Cyprus, perhaps unjustly (2 59–1; II Sefer 1016).

Two important offices which regularly fell to zimmis on Cyprus were those of translator and of chief architect. Two chief architects *(mi'mar başis)* were named: Zeynel bn 'Ali in 1003 and Pira v. Luka in 1044 (1 304–4; I Muharrem 1003. 323–1; II Muh. 4 23–2; III Sefer 1044).

Şa 'ban Paşa, for the medrese of Suleyman bn Selim Han, had his agent (illegible): The medrese needs repairs *(ta'mir)*. 30,000 akce is given to zimmis (?) v. Baba Nikola and Nikola v. Petro to repair it. (3 112–1; II Ramazan 1019)

Andon v. Petre, architect *(mi'mar)*, who is spahi of Kilohedere (?) vil. of Lefkoşa, acknowledges *(ik/i 't)* before Hiristofi v. Petra: When Mehmed beg died without male offspring *(evlad-i zukur)*, his fields *(tarla)* in the village were suitable for a title deed *(tapu)*, in accordance with kanun. Hiristofi has taken it for 4000 akce registration fee *(resm-i tapu)*. I confirm his right of possession. (1 39–3; II Şaban 1002. Probably to his brother).

The earliest reference to a translator *(tercuman)* is Sari in 1003; thereafter, a translator might be one of the instrumental witnesses (1 62–2; II Muh. 1003. cf 2 63–2; 3 148–3, 151–5. Sari may have been a Muslim, but the others were Greek Orthodox Christians).

Order to Mevlana Lefkoşa kadisi from governor Mustafa Paşa: Sulursin (?), who is in the translation service *(tercuman hidmeti)* in Cyprus, presented a petition *('arz-i hal)* here asking for a letter that spahis stop interfering with his collecting customary taxes *('usr)* from re'aya in accordance with his berat. See if this is so. They should not interfere. (2 63–2; II Cumadi I 1016)

Foreigners, Latins or Franks, and Foreign Merchants

Non-Muslims who had not submitted to the authority of an Islamic state were considered to be perpetually in a state of war *(harbi)*, or might be labeled infidels. Sometimes, in the interest of diplomacy or the economic benefits of trade, the Ottoman government unilaterally granted such foreigners a temporary legal status, the privileges of which were defined in capitulations *('ahid name)*. In the period 1580–1640 this class of protected people, called *muste'min*, consisted of a very small number of consuls and foreign merchants, mostly Venetian, but also French, Dutch, and English. Their privileges lapsed with the death of each successive sultan, who might interrupt or alter them at any moment. While those foreigners managed their individual communal affairs under their own consuls, their business dealings on Cyprus occasionally led to their appearance in court.[11]

The Ottoman conquerors converted most Latin churches into mosques, although they handed over several to the large Greek orthodox community and at least one ot the Armenian Gregorians. Dandini (1596) reported the presence of a Franciscan monastery at Larnaka which served Italian merchants. In Lefkoşa they had "but a small church, or rather chapel, which is well maintained, and has a priest of age and wealth for a pastor, but very ignorant." Cotovicus, when he saw the church in

Larnaka in 1598, expressed relief at the great consolation it provided travelers and pilgrims.[12] What happened in the twenty-five-year interval is not clear.

Many of the Latin nobility either adopted Islam and became spahis or first became Christian spahis but gradually were islamicized. Others interacted with the Greek Orthodox and became hellenized; some of those even penetrated the Orthodox church. Probably very few lost their lives after the establishment of provincial government in Cyprus. Only a few noble families experienced loss of status.[13]

The fate of Venetian and Latin property at the time of the conquest of Cyprus is not known. Probably Ottoman military commanders confiscated much of it as booty, particularly around Lefkoşa and Magosa, although it would have been unusual for the military to have applied a single policy uniformly over the whole island. Soon an imperial order was issued authorizing the return of property to harbis. Two cases in the sicils preserve references to harbi landowners. Both date from 1580, the oldest fragments of judicial records surviving, and both are in damaged condition. In one a man named Mehmed bn Muhalla (?) of the Magosa gediklu presented a signed memorandum *(tezkere)* of the inheritance *(beyt ul-mal-i ʿamme)* defterdari Ibrahim efendi indicating that he had bought houses *(evler)* which remain from harbi Pertamese (?) v. Rugendava (?) in Aya Yorgi quarter for 700 akce and houses *(evler)* of harbi Liracerler (?) zimmiye for 600 akce, a total of 1300 akce (1 3–3; 28 Ramazan 988. Zimmiye harbi is not defined further and does not occur often but is a strange combination). Similarly Ferhad bn ʿAbdullah sold vineyards and gardens at a village of Lefkoşa which had been the property of harbi Piro v. Paveret (?) to zimmi Naziri (?) v. Gatili (?) for 600 akce (1 11–1; II Ramazan 988. cf. 12–5; 16 Ramazan 988). It seems that in both cases the property was acquired from the harbis in an orderly fashion.

One of the main concerns of musteʾmins was protecting their property from entanglement in Ottoman judicial procedures.

Kalotiya v. Fesenco, zimmi, merchant *(tuccardan)* of Franks *(Efrenc taifesi)* of Lefkoşa, says *(tm)* before Mavridi v. Yano: The aforementioned Mavridi came here with me for trade *(ticaret)*. Then I became sick (hasta). If I die, I have no claim *(hakk)* against him for money *(akce)*, or movable goods *(emval, emtiʿa)*. I request that no one be annoyed *(rencide)*. I have no claims against anyone. (1 60–3; Muh. 1003. Cf. 60–1, where the same merchant announces that he has received in full the cloth (eight *şipka* and *çuka*) he left in emanet with Nikola v. Pay (?)).

Kalotiya v. Fesenco, zimmi, one of merchants *(tuccar)* of Franks *(Efrenc taifesi)* in Lefkoşa, says *(tm)* before Ferencesko v. Zolfino, zimmi: Ferencesko came with me for trade. Here I became sick. If I die, he owes me no money nor goods nor anything. Let no one trouble him for me. If anyone claims anything, let the court not hear it or accept it. A berat is given to Ferencesko. (1 326–2; 15 Muh. 1003)

Being both Efrenc and zimmi at once is likewise a strange combination. Apparently the foreign merchants were resident in Lefkoşa until some time after 1610 when they settled in Larnaka and Tuzla. Both of the above documents refer to merchants who have come from the outside for trade. If such merchants died, a share of their property went to the treasury *(beyt ul mal)*.

Perviz beg bn ʿAbdullah, who holds a tax farm *(iltizam)* as steward *(emin)* of inheritance on the island, acknowledges *(ik)* before zimmi Bafriço: Inez (?) bint Ladestiyo (?), widow of the late Pavlo, went to Venice. I want the shares of his estate which accrue to her and to the treasury *(miri)*. With the mediation of upright people *(muslihun tevassut)* a compromise *(sulh)* is reached for 13,000 akce. I have received it. (1 83–2; Sefer 1003)

Consuls of three governments were sometimes represented in Cyprus: Venice, Holland, and France. The name given those consuls *(balyos/balyas)* is the same given to the Venetian ambassador to the Porte. A series of cases and imperial orders in 1593–1595 (1002–1003) involve a claim for restitution of 180,000 akce in excessive charges regarding sale of over 800 kantar of cotton by the Cyprus defterdar kethudasi Mehmed to a Venetian merchant named Kordovan (?). The Venetian merchants reportedly had confused the Cyprus kantar with the heavier Egyptian *(Misr)* one and felt cheated (1 72–3; Muh. 1003. 126–1; Şevval 1001, in Konstantiniye. 126–2. 127–1; 26 Şevval 1002, in Konstantiniye. 128–1). In that case orders from the Porte, the treasury, and the imperial council, as well as a fetva, were sent to the Cyprus begler begi, the kadi, and the defterdar kethudasi in order to try to satisfy the appeal of the Venetian baylos for justice to the merchant. The assembled Muslim experts *(ehl-i vukuf)* certified that the defterdar kethudasi was right in accordance with the Sharia.

The foreigners were merchants interested in trade. On Cyprus their main interests were cotton, sugar, and local cloth, as well as provisions for ships in preparation for the return voyage to the western Mediterranean. One imperial order of early August 1594 (III Zil-Kade 1002) addressed to the begler begi and defterdar of the island of Cyprus responds to a petition from the tax farmers *(multezim)* of the sugar factories *(şeker hane)* at Piskobi, Kulaş, Kukla, Lefka, and Hirsofi and from the *baylos* of the island; certain revenues were specified part of the official income of the begler begi, who presumably insisted on selling all his sugar and cotton—at a high price—before others could sell their produce, thus causing loss both to tax farmers and to village cultivators (I 286–1).

Muste'min Yakimoto v. Mile/Moyle, the Dutch consul *(Fiyamenk balyasi)*, says *(ihzar/bm)* before Erik (?) v. Vesikaro (?), Frank merchant: He and I made some cotton transactions *(penbe mu'amelesi)*; after calculation, he owes me 571 sikke altun and 56 akce. I want it. Denied. When Yakimoto is asked for proof, Frank Pavlo v. Vile (?) and Covani v. Eziraste (?) confirm Yakimoto's testimony. It is registered that it is necessary for him to pay. (3 128–5; I Ramazan 1019)

The French consul *(Fransiz balyosi)* on the island of Cyprus, an Efrenc named Ilaka (?) says *(iddi'a/tk)* before Baba Betro v. Luka of Degirmenlik village of Lefkoşa kaza: He and I had transactions *(mu' amelat)* and trade *(ahz u 'ita)*. He owes me *(hakkum)* 36 riyali guruş. When I wanted it, he stalled *(te'allul)*. I want justice. Betro denies that: the balyos and I had transactions and trade for 193½ riyali guruş, which he owed me. I have received them. He (?) acknowledges that in the presence of Lefkoşa kadi seyyid Ya'kub efendi. (4 120–1; I Cumadi II 1045)

Although he muste'mins seem to have preferred trade with other foreigners or with Ottoman Christian subjects, the instance of the very large credit of 2222½ riyali guruş by the French merchant *(Fransiz tuccari taifesi)* Ferencesko v. Latiko (?) nam dome birinc (?) to the Cyprus begler begi Ahmed Paşa for Paris and Merzifon (?) cloth *(çuka)* has already been cited. It will be remembered that Muslim witnesses upheld Ferencesko's claim in regard to the debt; when he was asked by the representative of the deceased Paşa to take an oath that the debt had not been repaid, Ferencesko swore on the Bible (Incil) (4 60–1; I Sefer 1044).

After 1600 the growing numbers and new aggressiveness of European pirates threatened trade in the eastern Mediterranean. Indeed, the ease with which some vessels and crews passed back and forth between commercial respectability and piracy prompted a general suspicion of foreigners. One duty of the consuls was to try to make legitimate trade possible. An interesting case of this sort survives.

Present mesned nişin Çerak (?) on the island of Cyprus ʿAbdur-Rahman efendi, and Sufi zade Mahmud çelebi, Ibrahim su başi, and others of Lefkoşa say *(bm)* before musteʾmin Antoniyo, vekil and consul *(balyos)* of the Dutch *(taife-i Fiyamenk)* of the musteʾmin taifesi presently in the town of Larnaka on that island: The Dutch who are here with the kalyon Santa Kuruz want to make a trip to Tamyat (Dumyat) in their kalyon. They are at Tuzla harbor *(iskelesi)*. Let him be asked if that kalyon is trustworthy. Antoniyo replies: All of the Dutch *(Fiyamenk taifesi)* on the galleon *(kalyon)* Santa Kuruza are trusted merchants *(tuccar)*. All are known and trusted. I am guarantor *(kefil)* for the behavior *(hal)* of the galleon. (4 172–3; II Cumadi II 1046. Kefils were regularly to guarantee *mal* (money, property) and *nefs* (personal presence); *hal* is a usage I have not encountered previously. Cf. 1 280–4; 3 151–5.)

Perhaps the identification of musteʾmin and harbi in court records reflects their integration into the Ottoman system, at least from the Ottoman point of view if not from their own. The court system could handle such disputes, although the foreigners probably resented, and sometimes even misunderstood or were confused by, the procedure by which they were settled.

Wine and Wine Production

Grape cultivation and wine manufacture were two major industries in Cyprus, particularly in the coastal region between Baf and Larnaka. The Ottoman government and the Muslim community on Cyprus showed a sometimes ambivalent interest in controlling wine production and consumption, particularly by zimmis. Drinking wine by Muslims was no doubt a subject of some moral concern, although trading in it was usually permitted. Public drunkenness was a special offense, but the privacy of the home was so sacrosanct that even moral zealots would approach no closer there than to observe the entry and departure of visitors. Drinking wine in taverns with zimmis apparently was forbidden, and at least briefly during the reigns of sultans Ahmed I (1603–1619) and Murad IV (1623–1640) all wine production was categorically banned. Several Latin travelers gossiped that the people of Cyprus drank wine excessively; some said they had been told that the local Muslims drank wine surreptitiously, often in the company of Christians. Most eagerly exaggerated Muslim, Ottoman, and Greek Orthodox immorality. Cyprus wine was notoriously strong, so perhaps many foreigners, before they learned to dilute it, projected their own stupor on to the locals. Another of their stories attributes the conquest of Cyprus to Selim II's love for the local wine.

Spahi Kasim bn ʿAbdullah had an agreement with zimmis Papa Lefteri v. Kiryako, Vasil v. Ka . . . (?), and Papa Andon v. Kiryako of Paliçoz (?) village of Pendaye kaza in his timar: He collected 371/2 loads *(yuk)* of wine *(şerab)* from the winery *(şerab hane)* every year when the wine was sweet, instead of collecting the tax ʿuşr-i şira (1 184–2; 26 Cumadi I 1003). Haci ʿAbdi bn Davud of Lefkoşa sold three and a half loads *(yuk)* of wine to Sozomeno v. Istavrino of Kaymakli (?) village of Lefkoşa for one altun apiece; after the sale he sealed them (3 67–6; II Receb 1019. Cf. 168–2; II Şaban 1019). The same ʿAbdi gave Pereşkoga v. Mihail of Kaymakli village (?) one and a half loads of wine to pay a debt (3 168–1; II Şaban 1019. Cf. 168–2). Zimmiye Atosa (?) was in a dispute with Muslim Hamze over whether he had wanted two loads or six loads of wine (3 168–9; II Şaban 1019).

Totori and Yerolimo (?), zimmis of Lefkoşa, set forth a claim *(da ʿva/tk/tm)* before Yorgi v. Kostintin: He tries to sell wine in our houses. Up until now the right to sell wine has been held as a tax farm *(iltizam)*. Yorgi often sells it without permission. Yorgi denies that. When the claimants are asked for proof, two unnamed zimmi witnesses confirm their claim. (4 36–1; I Rebiʿ II 1044)

Yorolimo v. Cakuri of Lefkoşa says: I took the winery *(meyhane)* at Balik bazari at the covered market *(suk)* in Lefkoşa from the treasury *(miri)* for 45,000 akce for three years (15,000 akce/year). After I possessed it one year, the present mir miran of Cyprus Caʿfer Paşa forbade (?) dealing in wine, whether at that winery *(meyhane)* or in the quarters *(mahalle)* of Lefkoşa. . . . I paid 15,000 akce to the treasury *(miri)* for one year, and received the winery. When it was necessary in accordance with the Sharia to forbid the drinking and sale *(şurb ve beyʿ)* of wine *(hamr)* . . . (4 114–2; I Şevval 1044)

The effect of this prohibition on wine production is difficult to conjecture. Nothing should have affected the cultivation of grapes. Probably the prohibition was short-lived and had little impact beyond Lefkoşa anyway.[14] The evidence of the sicils does not suggest that Cyprus had a

serious drinking problem. Occasionally police officials apprehended local people for vice, and occasionally local people would lodge a complaint at the court. The ban itself was the whim of sultans, not a
reasoned attempt to deal with special problems.

ʿAbdul-Kadir ogli Ahmed, su başi of Lefkoşa, and Piri su başi, şehir zabiti, who
is yaya başi, says: In the city at the home of Gavraʿil two Muslims are sitting
with Mariya, wife of that Gavraʿil, and one or two other infidels are there. Let a
man be sent from the court. Hasan bn ʿAbdullah went with the Muslims from
the quarter whose names are listed below. The aforementioned Gavraʿil, another
Gavraʿil v. Lefteri, and Filibo v. Lefteri were found. Both Gavraʿils were apprehended, but the third zimmi fled. They also found Menekşa hatun sitting there.
All were summoned to court. When they were brought to court, Gavraʿil v.
Lefteri said, we came to drink wine, but Gavraʿil had already come before us
and was sitting. They sat down. I knew nothing about them. That Gavraʿil
smelled of wine. (1 222–1; Ramazan 1002)

Hiristofi v. Yorgi of Lefkoşa says *(tm)*: Yakimo, zimmi, always drinks wine
(şurb-i hamr). Yakimo says he will not drink wine *(şurb-i hamr)*. His father
Sozine is guarantor *(kefil)*. (1 328–2; Muharrem 1003)

Zimmiye Hiristine says *(bm)* before Hasan bn ʿAbdullah: Hasan always drinks
wine in our village. He infringes on the Sharia. He does annoy *(rencide)* me. (3
146–3; III Cumadi II 1019)

Haci Keyvan, ʿAbdul-Kadir boluk başi bn Ahmed, Yusuf bn Ahmed, and Huseyn
bn ʿAli, spahis of the village, and from the village Piyale bn ʿAbdullah, ʿAli beşe
bn ʿAbdullah, Marko v. Kistiniti, Yorgi v. Yakimo, Lare (?) bint Çelepo (?),
Hiristine bint Yakimo, Vero bint Zanoca (?), zimmis, and other people of the
village say *(bm)* before Hasan bn ʿAbdullah: He always drinks wine in our
village. He annoys us *(rencide)* without cause; he treats us cruelly *(zulm* and
teʿaddi) contrary to the Sharia. We do not want him in our village. Registered.
(3 146–10; III Cumadi II 1019)

Anderik v. Keşiş, Armenian of Terbiyota quarter, has claim made against him
for drinking wine *(şurb-i hamr)* in the quarter by zaʿim ul-vakt Mustafa su başi
and chief nightwatchmen *(ʿases başi)* ʿAli su başi. (3 149–3; III Cumadi II 1019)

Mehmed bn ʿAbdullah says: Kirat (?) v. Piyu (?) drank wine *(şurb-i hamr)*. It is
registered that he came to the court *(mahkeme)* drunk *(sarhoş)*. (3 161–8; III
RebiʿII 1019)

Yakimo v. Covan of Aya kuşani quarter: Zimmi Kurt drank wine at the tavern
(meyhane) with Mehmed bn ʿAbdullah. They struck me on the head and injured

me. I want them to be asked in accordance with the Sharia; I want justice done *(ihkak-i hakk)*. Denied. When proof was sought from ʿudul-i muslimin Yusuf bn Mustafa and (omitted) confirmed Yakimo; their testimony was accepted. (3 162–3; III Rebiʿ II 1019)

Yakimo v. Covan of Aya Kuşani quarter acknowledges *(ik/iʿt)* before Loizo v. Marko, (?) v. Loiz, and other people of the quarter *(ehl-i mahalle)*: Zimmi Kurd and Mehmed bn ʿAbdullah struck *(darb)* me in front of my house and injured my head. I have no claim against the people of the quarter. (3 162–4; same)

Loizo v. Nikolo, Bavlo v. Petro, Tomazo v. Yorolimo, Marto v. Eliyodi, Ragoşi (?), Zorzo v. Yorolimo, Andoni v. Nikolo, and others of Eliyodi (?) quarter say *(ihzar/td/tk)* before Yorgi v. Kostintin: He always sells wine *(hamr)* in our quarter. Most days he fights and causes trouble *(gavga ve fesad)*. We invited him to come to court *(daʿvet-i şerʿ idub)*. When we summoned him *(murafaʿa)*, he did not come. ... (?) or he should be killed *(katl)*. He has taken much of our property *(mal)*. He is always disputing *(muʿaraza ve munakaşa)*. He does not have a good reputation *(hali degildur)*. We want him to be asked and his reply recorded. Denied. When the claimants are asked for proof, Yorgi v. Aleksandri and Nikolo v. Zorzi confirm them. Recorded. (4 34–1; III Sefer 1044)

Summary

Very few Greek Orthodox Christians had full legal rights or economic opportunities in Cyprus under the authority of the Latin Catholic Lusignan dynasty, nor in the Venetian empire. As the judicial records indicate, all non-Muslims had extensive opportunities to use the court legally. Absolutely no restrictions were placed on the Orthodox majority, nor on the small Armenian or Jewish communities. Everyone had the same opportunities. There were no restricted crafts or trades. Anyone could become a farmer, butcher, silk weaver, or moneylender. Probably that came with the conquest.

Ottoman kadis were charged to apply the same standards of justice for zimmis and Muslims, although the zimmis had legal disadvantages in testifying against Muslims. Of the 2800 cases found between 1580 and 1637, 321, or 15%, involved just zimmis. Fully 953, or 34%, of the cases involved at least one zimmi. Muslims initiated cases against zimmis in 321 cases, or almost 12%, while zimmis initiated against Muslims in 211, or 8%, of the cases. (Admittedly, that does not really provide a clear-cut distinction because a very large number of all cases involve very noncontroversial matters, and also frequently cases initiated by one person may be revived at later times by other individuals.) At any rate, more than a third of all of the cases studies involved at least one zimmi.

Zimmis used the court to question other members of their families, even a brother or brother-in-law or son. They arranged marriages, settled estates, and they transferred land or houses from one community to another. They made criminal complaints against Muslims, as against other zimmis.

The kadi's register was the only official record of land and property transfer, although it would be very difficult to estimate what proportion in Cyprus were ever actually registered through the years. In both property and land transfers, the greatest proportions were intracommunal. Thus of 276 recorded property transfers 159 or 58% involved just Muslims, and 56 or 20% involved zimmis. Of 102 recorded land transfers, 59 (or 58%) involved Muslims, and 18 or 13% involved zimmis. No scruples seem to have been felt about living near peoples of other faiths, for in 30 instances Muslims sold property and in 9 instances they sold land to zimmis. As for the zimmis, in 31 instances they sold property and in 16 instances they sold land to Muslims. That means that numerous Muslims had no objection to living or working near Christians, and vice versa. Although permitted by Islamic law, preemption was very uncommon in Cyprus at that time.

Conversion to Islam was very common in Cyprus between 1580 and 1637. Several instances of individual conversions occurred but nothing was found involving small groups. Based on a perusal of the disparate evidence from the judicial records, the amount of conversion rose considerably between 1580 and 1593–1595, but by 1609–1611 the rate of conversion had begun to taper off, and by 1633–1637 it seems to have fallen a lot more.

People were supposed to convert only of their own free will, another responsibility of the kadi. Women had the same rights as men in this area. A few women converted before, or after, marrying Muslims. In a few marriages having a mixed marriage clearly interfered, although in other cases that was not so. In a few instances the Orthodox church seems to have tried to make intermarriage difficult.

Although Jews may ave been somehow restricted to Magosa under the Venetians, and they do not appear in survey of 1572, the judicial registers mention them in a village, also having a tax farm, and being in long distance trade. A small number lived in Lefkoşa, one was a thief at

Genose (Kenose) village of Hirsofi. Also, two villages of Lefka (Aya Yorgi and Aya Nikola) and two of Girniye, Koromadi and Mamili are mentioned. No indication is given about why Jews were so widely distributed in the island, or what they were doing, but we can say for sure that there were no restrictions on their movements, and they were not needed for money lending.

The Armenians are known only in regard to their quarter in Lefkoşa where they lived back to Lusignan times. Some of the Armenians had Anatolian Turkish names and must have been immigrants. Several can be identified as buying or selling houses, or lending money, usually within their own communities, although sometimes with local Muslims.

Almost nothing is known about the Maronites except that since Lusignan times their villages had declined in number, but they still had a small community connected with the Lefkoşa Maronites. The Catholics and the Maronites had in common that they both recognized the pope. Both were at least occasionally associated with villages, and the Latins with Limosa/Tuzla.

One of the most conspicuous groups of zimmis using the court were priests and monks of towns, villages, and monasteries. Many of them have faced the same problems of many Muslim ulema, that is of having to support themselves at least partially. They shared the same category of being only partially tax-exempt. In towns and villages alike, clergy seem to have no more aversions to dealing with Muslims than did other zimmis. Many owned land, and participated in trade and commerce, but clearly they were more often borrowers then lenders. A small number were even criminals. Not surprisingly, however, many others were communal leaders.

Not surprisingly a few zimmis held local office, as tax farmers *(multezim)*, as architects, or as translators *(tercuman)*.

A special group of foreigners *(harbis)* acted as consuls, and in a few cases foreign merchants. In general those people don't seem to have been very important people in Cyprus, although the extent of their documentation may be somewhat surprising, as is the way that they participated in the court. Unfortunately it is really difficult to identify various foreign merchants, or their consuls particularly since some of the people who had been important under the Venetian rule or even descendants of the French Lusignan might have felt the need to be discreet in their behavior with the new government. The fate of Venetian or Latin property is not

Table 5.1
Zimmis (Non-Muslims) at Court

sicil no.	year	total cases	total cases involving zimmis	%	zimmi vs. Muslim	Muslim vs. zimmi	zimmi vs. zimmi	z–z % of zimmis	z–z % of total	% of total cases inter-communal
	1580	130	56	43%	17	28	11	20%	8%	35%
	1593–1595	958	287	30%	60	101	126	44%	13%	17%
1A		1088	343	32%	77	129	137	40%	13%	19%
3	1609–1611	1184	415	35%	80	138	197	47%	17%	18%
4	1633–1637	528	195	37%	54	54	87	45%	16%	20%
Totals		2800	953	34%	211	321	421	44%	15%	19%

Table 5.2
Transfers of Property Ownership

sicil no.	year	Land					Property					total land & property
		z–z	z–m	m–z	m–m	total	z–z	z–m	m–z	m–m	total	
1A	1580, 1593–1595	4	3	4	29	40	28	16	16	66	126	166
3	1609–1611	1	4	3	12	20	14	8	3	39	64	84
4	1633–1637	13	9	2	18	42	14	7	11	54	86	128
Total		18	16	9	59	102	56	31	30	159	276	378

Table 5.3
Total Land and Property Transfers: 378: 102 Land + 276 Property

	land	*property*	*total*
at start zimmis owned	34 (33%)	87 (32%)	121 (32%)
at end zimmis owned	27 (26%)	86 (31%)	113 (30%)
decrease	21%	1%	7%
at start Muslims owned	68 (67%)	189 (68%)	257 (68%)
at end Muslims owned	75 (74%)	190 (69%)	265 (70%)
increase	10%	1%	3%
intercommunal transfers	25 (25%)	61 (22%)	86 (23%)

known. As the cases described indicate, at least a number of them were able to act publicly.

Cyprus remained under the Ottomans an important source of wine. In general, the greatest objections were against those who violated public scrutiny. Public drunkenness was probably often considered reprehensible. Possibly because of the very strong nature of the local wine drunkenness happened more easily than people might anticipate. Usually zimmis who produced it were taxed like businesses. Occasionally Muslims got involved. Whoever drank only within the privacy of their own homes was much better off.

NOTES

1. C. Cahen, "Dhimma," *EI²*. J. Schacht, *Introduction* . . . , pp. 130ff, 194. A. Fattal, *Le Statut des Non-musulmans en Pays d'Islam.* Beyrouth, 1958.
2. Figures for legal agents *(vekil)*, witnesses *(şuhud)*, and instrumental witnesses *(suhud ul-hal)* were all utilized for this study. They come from the judicial registers of Lefkoşa. 988–#1A, pp. 1–20; 1002–#1A, pp. 21–40; 1018–#3, pp. 1–25; 1043–#4, pp. 1–40. On Cyprus, see C. Kyrris, "Symbiotic Elements . . . ," *K.L.* 8.1976.245ff. He has important perceptions about conversion there, although perhaps he overstates his case a little. For 18th- and 19th-century conversion, see V. Bedevi, "Kıbrıs şer 'i mahkeme sicilleri üzerinde araştırmalar," First Congress . . . , Ankara, 1971. pp. 141f, with English summary, pp. 150ff. Ö. L. Barkan made a pioneering study of the role of dervishes and their organizations in the period of Ottoman expansion. "Osmanlı İmparatorluğunda bir İskân ve Kolonizasyon Metodu

olarak Vakıflar ve Temlikler: I. İstilâ devirlerinin Kolonizatör Türk Derviş-leri ve Zaviyeler," *VD* 2.1942.278–353. Vryonis has recently written an enlightening study of conversion to Islam in Anatolia, 11th to 15th century. *(Decline . . .* , pp. 351–402) Among his conclusions are (1) that in general the people follow the religion of the ruler, and (2) that the determination of sufi missionaries, and the similarity of their preaching to much of the popular belief of the Greek Orthodox Christians, led to widespread conver-sion to Islam. A further extenuating factor was the inability of the disorga-nized, impoverished, and often disoriented Orthodox church to compete with the wealth and vigor of the victorious political and socioeconomic forces of the Muslims. In a recent detailed study of the city of Trabzon based on defters H. Lowry has shown that 28.6% of the Muslims there were converts in 1553 and 22.57% in 1583. There only after more than a half-century of Ottoman rule did conversion become a very dynamic factor, whereas conversion in Cyprus had already begun to decline within that time span. According to Lowry, ". . . while the city of Trabzon was well on its way to being 'Islamicized' in 1583, with 53.62% of its residents listed as Muslims, ethnically the non-Turkish element (including the first and second generation converts) still totaled 70.35% of the total population." "Reli-gious Conversion as a Variable in the Religious Profile of Trabzon: ca. 1486–1583," chapter 6 of *Ottoman Tahrir . . .* , pp. 246f, 231f, 238. Lowry strongly endorses Vryonis' argument that the religion of the people follows the religion of the ruler but he points out that the situation in Trabzon, unlike as Vryonis has shown for elsewhere in Anatolia, the church hierarchy was not weak and unable to defend the Greek Orthodox Christians. That is, the period follows the millet reforms of Mehmed the Conqueror which greatly strengthened the Orthodox church. Vryonis, *Decline . . .* , pp. 351, 500; Lowry, *Ottoman Tahrir . . .* , pp. 243f, 241. Of course, the conquest of Cyprus comes long after those millet reforms. Lowry attributes much of the conversion in Trabzon to the extra tax burden on the Christians, which both Vryonis and Goitein have concluded, for Anatolia and for 11th–13th-century Cairo respectively, was an onerous burden for zimmis. Lowry, *Ottoman Tahrir . . .* , pp. 290ff; Vryonis, *Decline . . .* , pp. 359, 348ff. Goitein, *Mediterranean Society . . .* , v.2, pp. 380ff; "Evidence on the Mus-lim Poll Tax from Non-Muslim Sources. A Genizeh Study," *JESHO* 6.1963.278–295, esp. 294f. For legal cases illustrative of conversion in Kayseri, see Jennings, "Zimmis (Non-Muslims) . . . ," *JESHO* 21.1978.240–246.

3. Kyrris, "Symbiotic Elements . . . ," pp. 245f. A possible comparable source is J. Schiltberger, who mentions a general practice of collections for poor converts to Islam. (Schiltberger and Neumann, pp. 130–132; and Schiltber-ger and Hakluyt, pp. 74f; cited in Vryonis, *Decline . . .* , pp. 357f, who however does not cite further sources.) Exemption from the cizye/harac was an economic incentive of a different sort.

4. A large Mevlevi convent *(tekke)* was established in Lefkoşa soon after the conquest. That order had played a major role in converting Anatolian Christians to Islam. See Vryonis, *Decline* . . . , pp. 362–402, especially pp. 381–396. (Lowry supports Vryonis in this. *Ottoman Tahrir* . . . , p. 244.) Also Barkan, ". . . Kolonizatör Türk Dervişleri . . . ," *VD* 2.1942.278–353.

5. Cobham, pp. 182f; "A Voyage . . . ," in J. Pinkerton, v. 10, pp. 222–304.

6. Cotovicus in Cobham, p. 197. Lithgow in Cobham, p. 204; *The Totall Discourse* . . . , Glasgow, 1906, p. 167. Des Hayes, *Voiage de Levant* . . . Paris, 1624. p. 328. Hurtel in Cobham, p. 233; from Enlart, *L'Art Gothique* . . . , pp. 103–109.

   According to C. Kyrris great pressures to cooperate and be assimilated were placed on the Christians, particularly the Latins. He estimates that 25,000 people were forced to convert to Islam between 1570 and 1632. "L'Importance sociale . . . ," pp. 439, 499; nevertheless, many Latins also were known to feign Orthodoxy. p. 455. Elsewhere, in a study based on local Cypriot family traditions of Latin ancestry, both Muslim and Greek Orthodox, he mentions ". . . the unfixed number of Latins, i.e. Venetians, French and others, resident in Cyprus, who to save their life and/or property during and after the conquering expedition chose or had to get converted to Islam." *K.L.* 8.1978.245. For Kyrris, the crypto-Christians (Linobambakoi) were not just a few but "the vast majority" of Muslims in Cyprus. p. 271 n38. According to T. Papadopoullos the Ottoman conquest brought about "the practical elimination of the Frankish colony which formed the dominant class among the population of the island"; the survivors were "quickly assimilated." "Mass conversion" ". . . provided the source for the growth" of the Muslim community. I wonder, however, whether the "extermination and disappearance of the Frankish ruling class" was not de jure rather than de facto. . . . *Population,* 31f.

   The story of Zindanci Mahmud kapudan, supposedly a governor of Cyprus in the second half of the 17th century, gives evidence of a fine line between Islam and Christianity through which certain Muslims and Christians passed back and forth at will. As A. Tietze observed, the gulf between Christian and Muslim corsairs was not great; it was not even unusual to find a Christian captain and partially Christian crew in a galley of Tunis. Andreas Tietze, "Die Geschichte vom Kerkermeister-kapitan, ein türkischer Seeräuberroman aus dem 17. Jahrhundert," *Acta Orientalia* 19.1943.152–210, especially p. 158.

7. Cobham, pp. 74f; *Revue de Géographie* 5.1879.222f. But such services were not needed after the Ottoman conquest.

8. Many were assimilated to the Orthodox population before the end of Venetian rule. Later they lived in Karamanzade quarter in Lefkoşa. Avedis K. Sanjian, *The Armenian Communities in Syria under Ottoman Dominion.* Cambridge, 1965. pp. 162f. Early in the 18th century, according to Pocacke, there were a small number of very poor Armenians in Lefkoşa.

Cobham, p. 269, in Pinkerton, v. 10, p. 592. By the time of Mariti (1769) the Armenians apparently had become "the richest section of the inhabitants." *Travels . . . ,* p. 44.

9. Cobham, p. 182; Pinkerton, v. 10, pp. 277, 279, 293. R. Janin, "Chypre," *Dictionnaire d'Histoire et de Géographie Ecclesiatiques,* (Paris, 1953), v. 12, p. 815.

10. According to Costas Kyrris, many of the old Latin rulgin class on the island, sometimes voluntarily and other times by compulsion, adopted Islam, or possibly even Orthodoxy, and immediately passed into the ruling class. Halil Inalcik questioned Kyrris' idea about forced conversion, but acknowledged that those who converted to Islam might have entered the Ottoman ruling class as spahis. "L'Importance sociale de la conversion à l'Islam (volontaire ou non) d'une section des classes dirigeantes de Chypre pendant les premiers siècles de l'occupation turque (1570–fin du XVIIe siècle," pp. 437–462, 467 in *Actes du premier congrès international des études balkaniques et sud-est européennes.* v. 3. Sofia, 1969. The fate of the Latins who remained in Cyprus is not known in any sort of detail. To what extent they may have felt insecure and to what extent, and when, they would have referred publicly and openly to their church is unknown.

11. Later they were largely exempt from obligations to appear before courts. See H. Inalcik, "Imtiyazat," *EI².*

12. Dandini, in Cobham, pp 181f; in Pinkerton, v. 10, pp. 277, 279. Cotovicus, in Cobham, p. 191.

13. Kyrris has amassed important evidence on this subject; he asserts that those who resisted assimilation faced death or social and economic degradation, but his most convincing conclusion is that massive dissimulation by the Latins enabled those families to preserve their positions of importance. They readily took advantage of opportunities to advance themselves. "L'importance sociale . . . ," pp. 439, 453, 455f, 462, and *passim.* Cf. T. Papadopoullos, who similarly refers to "the extermination and disappearance of the Frankish ruling class and the elimination of the Latin ecclesiastical influence . . ." when the remainder of the Frankish people were "quickly assimilated." . . . *Population,* p. 32. Christian spahis were common in the Balkans at the time of the Ottoman conquest. H. Inalcik, "Ottoman Methods of Conquest," *Studia Islamica* (hereafter referred to as *S.I.*) 2.1954.103–129.

14. An Augustinian monk named J. de Verona who passed through Cyprus in 1335 sampled local wine: "If it were drunk neat the heat of the wine would burn up a man's entrails. . . . anyone who would drink it must put one glass of wine to four of water, and even so it is strong enough." Cobham, p. 18. Another pilgrim, the Westphalian priest Ludolf von Suchen, was equally impressed: ". . . commonly men mix one part of wine with nine of water. And were a man to drink a whole cask he would not be drunken, but it would burn and destroy his bowels. Yet many hold it wholesome to drink

this wine neat on an empty stomach. In all the world are no greater or better drinkers than in Cyprus" (after 1336). Cobham, p. 20f. According to Elias of Pesaro, the wine is "very strong, and must be diluted with two-thirds of water" (1563). Cobham, p. 75. Tommaso Porcacchi says of the wine: "One needed to drink but a tiny measure in a large quantity of water. I do not mean that this wine only is rich and good, but all the wines of Cyprus may vie with any country . . ." Cobham, p. 166. Seigneur de Villamont believed it was so strong that it should only be drunk in the morning. ". . . if you drink only two pegs of this in the morning you can easily pass the rest of the day without meat or drink, so remarkable is the strength and goodness of the wine. But taken in excess it burns you up at last." Cobham, p. 173. Likewise Cornelius de Bruyn, in 1674: "There are red wines and white wines, both excellent, but so strong that for ordinary use you need to put twice as much water as wine. I do not remember meeting with stronger wine." Cobham, p. 243.

SIX

Disastrous Effects of Locusts, Plague, and Malaria on the Population of the Island

A few Venetians who were seriously concerned about declining population urged easing the financial and economic burden on the island's people and indeed sought a policy of encouraging new settlement there. While some official efforts were made, emigration always exceeded immigration and the problem was never solved.[1] Restrictions were placed on emigration. Huen (1487) reported that, even though no one could legally leave the island, many people emigrated to nearby Ottoman territory to escape oppression on Cyprus.[2] Marin von Baumgarten (1508) praised the extreme fertility of the island but noticed that the cities and villages had extremely low populations "as if it was barren and a desert place."[3]

Doubtless seen as divine retribution, natural disasters—earthquakes, endemic disease (plague, and reawakened malaria), and locusts—impoverished the towns. On 25 April 1491 a very severe earthquake did great damage to Mesariye and Lefkoşa districts, while knocking down one of the two seaside walls of Baf (Paphos) and part of the castle at Limosa. Very slight damage to the island was done in a minor earthquake of 1542, but a much stronger one of 1546 struck both Lefkoşa and Magosa and damaged Aya Sofya church.

On 25 April 1567 "shocks were felt throughout Cyprus which lasted for 53 days and went on for two years; the shocks occurred at intervals of 8, 12, and 20 days or in alternate months, five or eight shocks at a time." Most affected was Limosa, and then Lefkoşa; little damage was done. On 7 and 13 October 1569 several slight shocks were felt in Magosa and Lefkoşa, but no damage was reported.

Strong earthquakes began to shake the island late in 1567, continuing through December. On 28 January "very violent shocks caused some damage at Limassol," where some people "were driven to live in the open country as the shocks increased in number and intensity." A total of 140 were recorded in one two-week period. Some damage was done, but the earthquake was not very powerful. In 1583 an earthquake threw down a house in Limosa, although possibly that refers to the earthquake of 1576–1577. (No subsequent earthquakes occurred before 1718.)

Although the earthquakes between 1491 and 1718 caused some moderate damage, the real destruction that they caused was minimal. Possibly no lives were lost. However, one must not underestimate the terrifying experience of feeling such tremors.[4]

A substantial demographic and economic decline in the towns of Cyprus began in the 14th or 15th centuries, perhaps initially related to the Black Death. Before the end of the 15th century some improvements had begun. Probably the population doubled during the Venetian century, but that growth may have been confined to rural areas, for the towns continued to experience socioeconomic setbacks. Hill has set out several estimates for the period which range between 90,000 and 250,000.[5]

The casualties associated in western sources with the Ottoman conquest are greatly exaggerated; no doubt Ottoman casualties were over 50,000, but it was very much to Ottoman advantage to spare local people not within the fortresses of Lefkoşa and Magosa; anyway, those people generally cooperated with the Ottomans. However, literally thousands of people—perhaps tens of thousands—were enslaved. A register dated 7 October 1570 (7 Cumadi I 978), within a month of the fall of Lefkoşa, lists the names and sales tax paid on 13,719 newly enslaved people from Cyprus. Although apparently no other registers survive, Magosa did not fall until August 1571, when slaves enough to fill another register must have been taken. The demographic effects of that policy were profound, for certainly all but a very few slaves were taken away from Cyprus (MMD 325; asıv 5471). Taxes were collected on 1,786,678 people.

Several estimates of the results of the first Ottoman census in Cyprus in 1571 have been published. The Ottoman historian Kara Çelebi 'Abd ul- 'Aziz efendi gives the figure of 120,000 re'aya (which in that instance must also mean zimmis).[6] The Greek Orthodox historian of Cyprus Kyprianos (late 18th century) gives a figure of only two-thirds that, namely c. 85,000 taxable persons (255,000 to 297,000 people).[7] Both Kyprianos and Kara Çelebi purport to give accounts of that first "census." Both their figures are hard to relate to the Latin estimates. Kyprianos also gives a figure of 196,986 from Coronelli's *Isolario*.[8] Some tax farmers *(multezim)* of the tax farms *(mukata'at)* of the sugar factories *(şeker haneleri)* at Piskopi, Kulaş, Kukla, Lefka, and Hirsofi, and the Venetian consul *(baylos)*, complained to the Porte that people who are oppressed by other tax farmers flee to Venice thereby impoverishing Cyprus.[9] Dandini (1596) estimated only 12,000 or 13,000 Muslims on the island, while Cotovicus (1599) estimated 6000 male Turks and 28,000 male Christians.[10]

With few exceptions foreigners presumed that the population was declining throughout the 17th century. For Calepio (1573) the island was virtually deserted.[11] De Villamont (1589), who described the detail of Ottoman tax registers which enabled the sultan to know the numbers and even names of his subjects, was astonished to find the island scantily populated, particularly given its fertility.[12] Henry de Beauvau (1604) believed that Cyprus had become very depopulated, although it had been populous at the time of the conquest.[13] Olfert Dapper reported the island depopulated from the cruel Ottoman rule.[14]

The imperial policy of compulsory population transfers during the first decade of Ottoman rule indicates the perceived need for new settlers. So do the orders prohibiting the transporting of anyone from the island without official written permission. Expressions of imperial concern for the well-being of the local people also indicate a realization that the island was underpopulated.

Locusts

The plight of the colony Cyprus was well known in Venice in the 16th century. The popular geographical book of islands of the world by Benedetto Bordone, first published in Venice in 1528, warned: "But among so much good, that there may be found nothing in this world without its bitterness, the luck of the island has one drawback . . . that a vast multitude of *cavalette* or locusts appear with the young wheat"; those locusts "hide the sun" "like a thick cloud," "and where they light they devour and consume not only the grain and grass, but even the roots below the ground, so that one might say that fire had blasted everything." To destroy them, according to Bordone, people dug out the eggs—some 30,000 bushels *(stara)*/year, and also they brought a certain water from Syria in which they soaked the eggs of the locusts.[15]

The German traveler Jodicus de Meggen, who visited Cyprus in 1542, gave a vivid description of the destruction left by the locusts. ". . . there is a plague of caterpillars, about one in three years, especially after a period of drought; these gradually get bigger until, by the month of March, they are the thickness of one's finger, having grown wings and some long legs, and resemble the locust; they fly about in the wind, in such immense numbers, that they look like a cloud; and any crops on which they may settle are completely devoured, right down to the roots, leaving no hope of blade or ear. That is why, sometimes, there is a woefully bad harvest." Consequently the Venetian government maintained the requirement that villagers be required to turn over a certain specified weight of locusts to the magistrates.[16]

In the year 1542 there was a great earthquake in Cyprus and great multitudes of locusts passed over from Syria and remained a long time. Estienne de Lusignan, who reported that, was of the former ruling family, which had been replaced by the Venetians. That Dominican friar wrote a detailed description of the island, which he completed in 1568.[17]

The English merchant John Locke landed on the island on 12 August 1553 at the port of Limosa.

This day walking to see the towne, we chanced to see in the market place, a great quantitie of a certaine vermine called in the Italian tongue Cavalette. It is as I can learne, both in shape and bignesse like a grassehopper, for I can judge but little difference. Of these many yeeres they have had such quantitie y[t] they destroy all their corne. They are so plagued with them, y[t] almost every yeere they doe well nie loose halfe their corne, whether it be the nature of the countrey, or the plague of God, that let them judge that best can define. But that there may no default belaied to their negligence for the destruction of them, they have throughout the whole land a constituted order, that every Farmor or husbandman (which are even as slaves bought and sold to their lord) shall every yeere pay according to his territorie, a measure full of the seede or egges of these forenamed Cavalette, the which they are bound to bring to the market, and present to the officer appointed for the same, the which officer taketh of them very straight measure, and writeth the names of the presenters, and putteth the sayd egges or seed, into a house appointed for the same, and having the house full, they beate them to pouder, and cast them into the sea, and by this policie they doe as much as in them lieth for the destruction of them. This vermine breedeth or ingendereth at the time of corne being ripe, and the corn beyng had away, in the clods of the same ground do the husbandmen find ye nestes, or, as I may rather terme them, cases of the egges of the same vermine. Their nests are much like to the keies of a hasel-nut tree, when they be dried, and of the same length, but somewhat bigger, which case being broken you shall see the egges lie much like unto antes egges, but somewhat lesser.[18]

Following his visit in 1569, Lusignan reported that great multitudes of birds came to the island from Syria in flocks. They cried out very loudly and made so loud a noise when more than a thousand gathered in an assembly that they resembled a small army. The Cypriots call them "locust-birds" *(oiseaux de sauterelles)* because they subsist on locusts. They are all white except for the beak and the front of their stomach, which is black, and they are slightly larger than pigeons.[19]

The Dominican Angelo Calepio of Cyprus, long superior of their convent in Nicosia, writing in 1572, indicated that Cyprus ". . . was scourged for many years with such swarms of locusts that they ate even stems of trees." That was God's punishment on the Orthodox of the island for this schism, along with an earthquake in 1556, a whirlwind, and other awful punishments thereafter.[20]

Sir George Hill: "Apart from ecclesiastical affairs, and the relations of the island with the Western Powers, the history of Cyprus for about a century after the Turkish conquest is little but a record of plague, locusts, drought, famine and earthquakes."[21] Hill, europeanophile in values, obviously wished to belittle that century, but he was much too good a historian not to appreciate the profound effects of disasters on history.

Ulrich Krafft, a German seaman who was enslaved by Muslims in the Mediterranean between 1573 and 1587, made several visits to Cyprus, beginning in 1573. His description of locusts and the locust problem in Cyprus is more precise and accurate than any before his time or indeed any before the mid-19th century. How he could provide such accurate information is a puzzle, but obviously he did not dream it. Some people in Cyprus were intimately informed about the life of locusts on the island. Only in Krafft's precision did he err.

He said that locusts are called "Zuuor" by the Turks of Cyprus. Previously, before the Turks took the island, locusts frequently were produced, but never in such great quantities and not with so much damage as in the past five or six years. According to Krafft, they live in a yearly cycle as follows: They come out of the ground between 1 and 3

March, resembling small ants. In enormous numbers they crawl on the ground until 23 April, St. George's day. On the next three days they grow wings, and from 26 April until the end of June they swarm about together and block out the sun. Those that do not have wings are carried by those locusts that do, until they grow wings of their own. They fly about from one green place to another and eat every green thing, grass, grains, and fruits, right down to the very roots. They eat trees down to the hard wood.

Every year the Ottoman governors give very strong orders that every inhabitant must collect a large sackful every week and burn it and the worms, although that does not make any considerable reduction in their numbers. As soon as the last day of June comes, it is time for the locusts to lay their eggs. They all come down to the ground and put their hind part half (a quote) a finger length into the ground, up to their wings, and lay their eggs. Then they die, their upper portion decays. The eggs remain in the ground until the following year, until the beginning of March. They grow in greater numbers than the previous year, as the new cycle begins. (Note: Many eye witnesses attest that the locusts devour everything except colococas, because it is so bitter.[22])

The conquest of Cyprus by the Ottoman empire in 1571 obviously did not affect the circumstances of the locusts. The French pilgrim Seigneur de Villamont of Brittany entered the island on 11 May 1589, nearly time for the grain harvest. According to him,

... with the many blessings which God has scattered over the island there is also one drawback, for about the time that the corn is ripe for the sickle, the earth produces such a quantity of *cavalettes* or locusts that they obscure sometimes the splendour of the sun. Wherever these pass they burn and spoil all. For this the Cypriots have no remedy, since the more they destroy the more the earth produces next year. God however raised up a means of their destruction, which happened thus. In Persia, near the city of Cuerch, there is a fountain of water, which has a wonderful property of destroying these locusts, provided it be carried in a pitcher in the open air, without passing under roof and vault: and being set on a high and exposed place certain birds follow it, and fly and cry after the men who carry it from the fountain. These birds are red and black, and fly in flocks together, like starlings. The Turks and Persians call them Mahometans. These birds no sooner came to Cyprus, but with their song and flight they destroyed the locusts which infested the island. But if the water be spilt or spoilt, these creatures disappear. Which accident fell out when the Turks took Cyprus, for one of them going up into the steeple of the Cathedral Church at Famagusta, and finding there a pitcher of this water, he, fancying that it contained some precious thing, broke it, and spilt the water: since when the Cypriots have been always tormented by the locusts. Nor have they found anyone willing to journey to Persia to fetch some of this water, for he must needs traverse the Arabian deserts. The Greek monk of Famagusta told me, however, that a Turk had engaged to go thither for six hundred ducats. So it is that there is nothing in this world, however sweet and pleasant, but is attended by some trouble and bitterness![23]

Ioannes Cotovicus, a Dutch knight of the Holy Sepulchre, who visited Cyprus between September 1598 and March 1599, described how expedient the collection of locusts and their eggs had become.

Cyprus suffers from yet another plague, that now and then a certain insect infests it. About every third year, if the seasons are dry, they grow slowly in the likeness of locusts, and in March, being now winged and as thick as a finger, with long legs, they begin to fly. At once they come down like hail from heaven, eat everything voraciously, and are driven before the wind in such huge flights that they seem dense clouds. They devour every green herb, and dying at last of hunger leave behind them a terrible stench, which infects the air and the soil and breeds a fearful plague. The natives seek out their eggs diligently, and destroy them with their nests and lurking places. Unless they did so the insects would increase in that torrid soil beyond all reckoning or belief.[24]

Locusts particularly plagued the island between 1610 and 1628, that latter year being so severe as to create famine. Cyprus archibishop Matthew Kigala wanted to bring the head of St. Michael of Synnada from Mt Athos to counter the locusts, but the monks would not give their approval.[25]

In his account of his travels written about 1645, the Orthodox patriarch of Antioch Macarius (Makarios) mentioned using the right hand of St. Michael, bishop of Sonada, against locusts. By bringing the hand to the place, the locusts are driven into the sea. They sprinkle the holy water on the fields and dispense it to the populace. Then, by the intercession of the saint, the locusts are driven into the sea.

We have been informed, that some years ago there was a great dearth in the island of Cyprus, caused by an invasion of locusts among them, which was uninterrupted for a series of seven years. They represented, therefore, their condition to the Soltan; and requested a Khatti-sherif, or imperial mandate, directing the people of the above-mentioned convent to grant them the head of the Saint. In consequence of this petition, an Aga was dispatched, from before the Soltan, with the desired mandate; and he repaired to the convent, to ask for the head. It was the custom of the house, and the established rule of old, not to suffer this holy relique to be removed from their precincts, except upon pledges. The Cypriots, therefore, lodged with them, as sureties, forty Archons, of the most noble of the island, till they had carried the head over to Cyprus, made an *Ayiasmos* and sprinkled with it their whole territory:—and, wonderful to relate! the locusts were instantly expelled from the island, and drowned in the sea: and, as votive offering, the island's people carried five thousand piastres to the convent, on returning with the head, and, having given thanks to God, departed. Thus, it is said, do all the people of Romelia, as well Moslems as Christians: for this saint, at his death, among other requests, made this one especially to Almighty God: and this is a subject delightful to be known.[26]

The present governor *(begler begisi)* a Cyprus Hasan Paşa and the kadi of Lefkoşa mevlana ʿAli, your well-wisher, sent a petition *(ʿarz)* concerning the problem faced by the slaves *(kullari)* of Zul-Fikar who were assigned to collect the head tax *(cizye)* of the infidels of the island as calculated for 1647–1648 (1057). When they began to gather, all of the holders of ziʿamets and timars appeared in person to the court and made known that in our lands locusts *(çekirge)* were spreading everywhere *(mustevli)*, that there was no grain harvest *(gilal hasil olmiyub)*, and that the village cultivators *(reʿayasi)* were dispersed or had perished. The circumstances *(hallari)* of the villagers became very difficult. We counted among ourselves many times. Every taxpaying villager has been forced to pay taxes for two or three or in some villages even four people. Fifteen hundred taxpaying villagers *(reʿ aya)* are dead or missing and cannot be counted. They made known a request to do kindness in this matter by not taking what was assessed *(tahsil)* from those who are missing (*gurihteler* içun). From what was made known earlier in this matter, the amount of the head-tax of those who are missing is 609,000 akce, of which the tax collectors have already collected 599,680. It is my exalted wish *(ʿinayet-i ricasina)* in that matter to register as missing those who are not registered *(tahrir)*. . . .

A petition *(ʿarz)* was sent to the slaves of Zul-Fikar aga, who were charged with collecting the head tax of the infidels of the island for 1647–1648 (1057) warning that, on account of scarcity *(kahtlikdan)* more than half of the villagers of the island were dispersed or had perished. More than 4,000 or 5,000 hane who pay head tax *(cizye)* are gone. While perserverance is important, 1500 taxpayers *(haneden)* are dead *(murdesi)*, and from the survivors the taxes of two or three or in some villages even four people were wrongly being collected. You should be careful to prevent this. . . .

Late in May, 1647 (1057) the slaves of Zul-Fikar aga were ordered to appear in the presence of the governor Hasan Paşa concerning the matter of collecting the head tax from the infidels for 1057 and informed that the religious class *(ʿulema)* and the pious *(suleha)* on the island and the notables *(aʿyan)* and the populace *(fukara)* and the ziʿamet-holders and the timar-holders, all of the Muslims *(muslimin)* en masse *(cemm-i gafir ve cemʿ-i kesir)* had come to the court *(meclis-i mezbure)* and made known that because of hunger *(kaht)* arising from the attack on the island of locusts *(cerad istilasindan)* most of the village taxpayers *(reᶜaya)* were dispersed or had perished, that more than 4000 thousand had perished *(murdesi)* and every single taxpayer *(hane)* gave for two or three and in some villages four others. ... The aforementioned 7500 dead or missing should not be registered ... (late May 1647; III Rebiᶜ II 1057. MMD 3660; arşiv 6268)

The Dutch Orientalist Cornelis van Bruyn, who visited the island between 19 April and 26 May (the height of the locust season) was an eyewitness to the devastations of 1683.

I saw myself in the neighbourhood of Nicosia a great quantity of these insects, and remarked that the fields they had cropped were burnt as though by fire; my horse too at every step crushed ten or twelve. Several persons assured me that from time to time certain birds, natives of Egypt and called in Arabic *Gor,* visit the island. They are not unlike ducks, but have a pointed beak. They eat the locusts and thus lessen their ravages. The same thing is said of storks.

People in Cyprus told van Bruyn much about an unusually severe plague of locusts which beset the island fifteen years earlier.

In the year 1668 throughout the island, but especially in the country around Famagusta, there was such a vast quantity of locusts that when they were on the wing they were like a dark cloud through which the sun's rays could scarcely pierce. This lasted about a month, and the Pasha ordered all the country people to bring a certain measure full of the insects to his palace at Nicosia, and afterwards he had holes dug outside the city where they were thrown, and covered with earth lest their corruption should infect the air. For ten days together the Greeks made processions and prayers to be delivered from a curse so ruinous to the land. They carried too in procession a certain picture of the Virgin Mary with the child Jesus in her arms said to be the work of S. Luka. This picture is generally kept in a convent called Chicho (Kykko, the most famous monastery on the island), to which belong some four hundred Caloyers, part of whom are sent to Muscovy and elsewhere on various duties. This convent is built on Mount Olympus, the highest mountain on the island. In times of drought the picture is brought with great ceremony out of the convent, and placed on a stage about twenty steps high, with the face turned to the quarter from which they may expect rain. Now it happened that the same ceremony had been observed on account of the locusts, and as soon as the picture had been set on the stage there appeared forthwith certain birds not unlike plovers, which swooped upon the locusts and devoured a great quantity. Moreover, the next day, when the heat of the sun forced the insects to rise from the ground, there arose a mighty land wind which swept them before it, and towards evening, when the sun had lost its power, they all fell into the sea, and were drowned. Which was made plain some time afterwards when a sea breeze drove them in heaps on the shore, and thus was the island delivered from this terrible plague.

The birds which ate the locusts, the story adds, had never been seen before, nor were ever seen again. But the Pasha had forbidden them to be killed, under pain of death.[27]

Plague

In a recent seminal study Michael W. Dols examined the impact on the Middle East—particularly the Arab part—of the Black Death and other plagues of the 14th and 15th centuries. Plague, really a disease of rats and similar rodents, passed to humans by their fleas, is endemic to the central Asian steppes, especially Mongolia, Turkestan, and Manchuria, but rooted itself so deeply in the Middle East that for centuries it remained endemic there. Frequently new plagues have found their way to the Middle East, and Cyprus, via land and sea routes from central Asia or India.[28]

After documenting the catastrophic consequences of the Black Death (1347–1348) on the population and economy of Egypt and Syria, he presents evidence of the continuing occurrence there of plagues, which kept population at low levels or reduced it even further. Dols asserts that the result was not improved living standards for the survivors, even in rural areas (the effect often presumed in Latin Europe), but rather a weakening of both government and economy by reducing tax revenues, lowering the demand for luxury goods, and gradually impoverishing the economy. For Dols the plague, rather than the hitherto supposed "oppressive rule" of the Mamluks, brought Egypt and Syria into economic decadence. Cyprus is a neighbor of Syria and Egypt, in intimate contact by trade, and for centuries a Mamluk vassal. Magosa at that time was the emporium for the long distance and local Levantine carrying trade; surely Cyprus was vulnerable to the very same problems.

Both Hill and Cobham make frequent references to the effects of plague. The body of sources most abundantly available for Cyprus— Frank merchants and pilgrims—correlate with Dols' explanation for Egypt and Syria from Arabic sources: ". . . the drastic destruction of Muslim population and the subsequent impoverishment of Muslim society by plague epidemics."[29] According to Dols, ". . . the Black Death initiated a series of plague recurrences that substantially reduced Middle Eastern population. This prolonged reduction of the population was the fundamental event in the social and economic history of Egypt and Syria during the later Middle Ages."[30]

One of the great disasters regularly striking Cyprus from the mid-13th century onward through the end of the 17th was plague. George Hill paid careful attention to such occurences. In the period before the Ottoman conquest, he mentions plague in 1268, 1349, 1362–1363, 1392–1393, 1410, 1419, 1420, 1422, 1438, 1470, 1494, 1505, and 1533. Michael Dols lists several of those and an additional one in 1460 (865 AH). Although all estimates of mortality are conjectural, the Black Death which reached Cyprus in 1348 is considered the most severe.

Based on his study of the sources, Hill says: "It was said to have carried off half to two thirds of the population. As we have already seen, the mortality caused by the plague was given in 1351 as a reason for stopping the preaching in Cyprus of the Crusade against the Truks."[31] Dols says, "The Black Death struck Cyprus in 1348 and was particularly devastating, according to Latin and Arabic sources."[32]

"In an account of the island of Cyprus during the pandemic, an Arabic chronicler testified that the Christian Cypriots 'feared that it was the end of the world.' "[33] The 15th century Cypriot chronicler Leontios Machaeras said: "And in the year 1348 God sent a great plague for our sins, and the half of the island died. . . . And in 1363 another plague came upon the children, and (the greater part of) the island was destroyed."[34] "When the Turks heard that the plague had wiped out the men of Cyprus, and the king was in France, all the Turks together fitted out twelve galleys and appointed a captain called Mahomet Reis, and came to Cyprus and landed at Pentayia and raided many people: and he carried them off prisoners and went away (to Turkey)."[35] In 1392 a third plague came, lasting to the following year, and the king ordered that many priests "carry (all) the icons (in the town) in a circuit of two miles round the city; and a procession was made from the keep, (and they went out from the bishop's palace and outside St. Paraskevi and by the Lower Gate) and so went to St. Therapon, and there they sang mass and preached." All where barefoot.[36] According to F. Amadi, the plague of 1392 was a very terrible one, but the king generously reduced the taxation of the people so that they could endure (and urged landholers to be kind).[37] Machaeras wrote: "And in the year 1410 after Christ there came another plague, which lasted more than a year."[38] D. Strambaldi adds that that plague was accompanied by locusts.[39] Another great plague lasted from 1419 to 1420, and another came in 1422.[40] "And from the beginning of June 1438 after Christ a (great) plague fell upon Lefkosia and the villages, and there were many deaths in all parts of Cyprus; and it lasted seventeen months."[41] Dols mentions one more in 1460 (865 AH).[42] In 1470 plague began again, following famine the previous year, lasting 2½ years and killing a third of the people, according to George Boustronios. "And the king took those he thought fit to Akaki. He took much care of them, and of them not one died . . . And when the plague had passed, all came back to Lefkosia."[43] In the summer and autumn of 1494, plague struck again.[44]

In the summer of 1494 plague was raging in Lefkoşa. The Italian pilgrim Pietro Casola was forbidden by the captain of his ship to visit the island's capital city. "As the captain heard that at Nicosia, one of the principal cities of Cyprus, people were dying (of the plague) he made a general exhortation to the pilgrims, and advised them not to go to that city." There were, however, some impatient Germans, who, when they heard that the captain had to stop there some time, went to see the island at their pleasure. Later on, when they reached Rhodes, word came that people were dying of plague in Limosa and elsewhere, and people nearly were prevented from disembarking there, because of fear of the plague.[45]

In 1505, according to a letter from the Venetian governor *(luogo tenente)* of Cyprus Piero Balbi, plague killed more than a quarter of the citizens of Girniye (Zerines).[46]

On 28 March 1533 the governor *(luogo tenente et Consieri)* in Lefkoşa Marco Antonio Trivixan and his council reported to Venice that the plague had entered Famagusta, coming by way of Syria, and more than 200 people had already died. A letter of 5 May from that governor informed the Venetian government that a very severe plague raged in Syria, that locusts were devastating all the grain around Famagusta, and that 800 people had died from the plague. Three days earlier, Francesco Bernardo, captain *(capitanio)* of Famagusta, had sent a dispatch advising Venice that plague continued to afflict the people, who were in great misery, reduced to living by begging. Everywhere was contaminated and of 9000 inhabitants, 2000 had fled. The rest endured in poverty, especially the women and girls; five soldiers had died. The governor and the other officials had taken refuge in a village. Through the purveyor general *(proveditor zeneral)* provisions were being turned over to the city, to comfort and console the people. 250 measures *(moza)* of wheat *(formento)* was received. Appeals for help were made in "Mesaria, Saline, Limiso, Baffo, and Nicosia."

Also the purveyor general *(proveditor zeneral)* of Cyprus Stephano Tiepolo sent letters dated 4 and 5 May from Nicosia which made known that 5500 people in Famagusta were dead, women and children, and that locusts were ravishing the countryside. On 26 May Bernardo, captain of Famagusta, in a second letter, informed the authorities that plague had continued there for 5 months and over 1072 people had been killed; many soldiers were infected, too, and locusts were devastating Mesaria and Carpasso. In a letter of 4 June Stefano Tiepolo, who was raised to the governorship, informed the Venetian government that over 1100 people had died in Famagusta, as well as about 100 soldiers. The governor and council asked for extraordinary powers to deal with an accompanying crime wave which seems to have broken out in the Famagusta area.[47] In a letter of 22 June Bernardo, the captain of Famagusta, praised the role of the governor in handling the plague, which had affected thousands of people. On the same day, the governor Tiepolo and counselors *(consieri)* Bernardin Venier and Segondo da Pexaro wrote from Nicosia that the plague had ceased in Famagusta, but that 2000 people had died form it, including 150 soldiers. The villages of Tricomo, Trapasa (Karpas?), and Pomodadamo also had been infested by plague.

The pilgrim Jodicus de Meggen (1542) reported that the island was somewhat susceptible to plagues and blights.[48]

The Jew from Pesaro who settled in Magosa as a moneylender wrote in a letter of 18 October 1563 that the people of the city were ". . . very well behaved and clean, careful to protect themselves from contagion, especially from the plague, which is common enough in the neighbouring parts of the Levant. Their precautions are very thorough, as in Italy, and no person arriving from an infected or suspected locality can enter the town before he has been detained forty days in the harbour." People there were also susceptible to ophthalmia, which lasted from the longest day of the year to the vernal equinox. It began with a fever and two or three days of violent headaches.[49]

There is much less testimony about plague in Cyprus in the second half of the century. That may have been a general Mediterranean-wide trend; evidence from Cyprus *ex silentio* supports that conjecture; never-theless, severe epidemics still occurred. One people may be simply distin-guishing descriptions of malaria from those of plague.

Braudel asserts that in the 17th century there was a "recurrence of outbreaks of plague," during which time probably no Mediterranean cities completely escaped it.[50] He further asserts that ". . . a quarter or a third of the inhabitants of a town could suddenly vanish at a time when imperfect knowledge of hygiene and medicine afforded little protection against infection." Towns were most threatened, many of them virtually emptying during the insalubrious summer plague season. Those in the eastern Mediterranean suffered most during this period. "This preva-lence of epidemics made a significant contribution to the insecurity of life in the towns . . ."[51]

An imperial order dated December 1573 (Receb 981) was sent to the governor *(begler begi)* and the chief financial officer *(defterdari)* of Cy-*prus in response to the governor's early letter in which he notified the Porte that their money to pay the salaries (ʿulufe) of the janissaries was* inadequate because so many taxpayers had died from the plague *(hayli reʿayaʿun murd olmakla)* that it became impossible to pay the janis-saries. The Porte had earlier pointed out to the governor the importance of building a castle at Baf, ordering that if more than 50,000 filori remained from the tax revenues due the treasure *(miri)*, it should be spent on that castle. "Many villages are hungry *(garas)*. However, infidel ships *(gemi)* came and freely pillaged the coasts. It will be very beneficial to build a castle at Baf. If any money remains from the expenses, it is ordered to build that castle as strong as necessary" (161/71 (19),3 #372).

The French pilgrim Seigneur de Villamont, chevalier de l'Ordre de Hierusalem, entered Cyprus on 11 May 1589. First landing at Baf (Baffo), nearly uninhabited on account of malaria, his vessel then sailed along the coast to Limosa and then Larnaka. At Larnaka he changed ship for another destination, determining to sail to Jaffa without first stopping at Tripoli (Trablus) where, he had learned, 120 people a day were dying of plague. At Larnaka, also, he learned of conditions in Magosa, "where the plague had long been raging, and its inhabitants and those of the country round were nearly all dead." Six days earlier in Magosa a

... Turk, dancing and jumping about the square said, 'Rejoice all of you and dance with me, for I announce that in half an hour I shall die on this spot, and immediately after my death the plague shall cease.' They wondered at his words, and waited to see the issue, but when the moment came for the Turk to visit the abode of Pluto his body fell stark on the square. Great was the alarm and wonder of all, which increased yet more when the plague ceased. The news was carried forthwith to the Pasha, who gave thanks to Mahomet and ordered that a grand tomb should be built for the dead man, around whose body was a great procession, the Pasha himself joining in with much devotion.

On 17 May de Villamont's ship left for Jerusalem, where he was dubbed a knight of the Holy Sepulchre. On his return, he reached Limassol on 18 September, ill with fever, and remained there until 6 October.[52]

According to the English traveler George Sandys (1615) Cyprus "is in the Sommer exceeding hot, and unhealthy; & annoyed with serpents,"[53] while the French consul at Aleppo (1623–1625), whose sphere of authority included Cyprus, stated: "Cyprus is completely abandoned on account of the plague, which has made the island deserted."[54] Plague on Cyprus is mentioned for 1624.[55] Hill mentions a serious plague of 1641 when the growing miseries of the people led to emigration to Crete, the Morea, and Corfu.[56]

One of the most severe plagues was in 1692, when some sources report that 2/3 of the population died.[57] C. von Bruyn, who visited the island that year says that the air there is unhealthy for the three or four hot months of summer. The pirate Mr. Robert (1696) mentions how the island is "subject to contagious Distempers," and accordingly that Tuzla (Salina) was abandoned in 1693; 4000 people were "cut off by the Plague" in three months.[58]

Ottoman records tell of one severe plague of the mid-17th century:

Let it be registered. The petition of the slaves *(kullarinun)* of vezir Mehmed Paşa, who is in defense of Cyprus. The religious class *(ʿulema)*, the pious *(suleha)*, the ziʿamet-holders, the timar-holders, and other notables *(aʿyan-i vilayet)* who are in Cyprus came to the Cyprus council *(divan)* and made a petition *(ʿarz)*, requesting that, since there are 15,000 head-tax paying *(hane)* infidels on that island who pay head tax *(cizye)*, but 3000 have been missing *(gurihteleri)* for three or four years, only 12,000 head-tax payers should be registered *(tahsil)*, By the decree of God, plague *(taʿun)* has been prolonged for the past year and a half; the number of deceased was excessive, and it was determined to register them again. Let it be registered *(tahrir)* as 12,000 hane.

The religious class, the pious, the ziᶜamet-holders, the timar-holders, and other notables who were situated in the island of Cyprus gathered at the Cyprus divan, and they made known the circumstances as follows: There were 15,000 infidels on that island who pay head tax, and 3000 missing. For the past three or four years, only 12,000 hane have been registered, and they cannot endure more because, by the decree of God, plague *(taᶜun)* is widespread. In the past year and a half more than half of the 12,000 head-tax payers *(hane)* have died. Very many of the villages are vacant and ruined. It is necessary to register them again. Let there be pity from the exalted sultanate for the circumstances of the poor. I order that they should be registered as 12,000. (22 September 1656/3 Zil-Hicce 1066. MMD; Arş. 9839)

Malaria

Oddly, although malaria is a very severe disease of long standing in Cyprus, Hill, Cobham, Dawkins, and many others simply ignore it. As has been mentioned earlier, certain coastal areas of Cyprus became malarial, most notably Magosa. After its pestiferous nature became known in the 14th century (or whenever it became pestiferous), it declined rapidly. Of the towns on the island, only Lefkoşa and Girniye (Kyrenia) seem free from malaria, and of course people suffering from the disease moved back and forth around the island.

Braudel has pointed out that in the 16th century the inland plains of the Mediterranean were largely depopulated because of malaria, including those on the islands of Corsica, Sardinia, and Cyprus. Malaria emerges after flooding during the rainy season. "To avert disaster their inhabitants must take precautions, build dams and big channels." Neither Venetian nor Ottoman rulers undertook such projects in Cyprus.

In Cyprus, large salt lakes near Limosa and Larnaka fed by winter rainfall and snow in the Tröodos had dimensions which fluctuated with the season. Since they were used for commercial salt gathering, one can be sure that they were spread over as wide but shallow an area as human ingenuity would allow. Those both involved relatively limited hinterlands, cut off by the mountains, but the vast swampy area and marshes in the Mesariye west of Magosa affected a much more extensive area. The eastern Mesariye is very flat, making drainage into Magosa bay extremely slow, and through there meanders the only river of any length on the island, the Pediyas. That region has small lakes and seasonal streams which also contribute to its swampy nature. Since no attempts were made to keep the mouths of streams clear, and the land was so flat, they silted up, causing inland water to build up even more.

Malaria has greater and lesser periods of virulence. According to Braudel, the late 15th century was one of particular virulence, and then there were fresh outbreaks of virulence late in the 16th century, when virtually all of the Anatolian and Syrian ports were malarial, and Iskenderun (Alexandrette), the port of Aleppo, was abandoned. Magosa, the port of Lefkoşa, faced virtually the same fate. Malaria "... is a disease that directly results from the geographical environment. Plague, carried from India and China by long-distance travellers, although greatly to be feared, is only a passing visitor to the Mediterranean. Malaria is permanently installed there." [59]

As early as 1394 the pilgrim N. Martoni found Magosa located near a marsh and, hence, "wholly destroyed." "And it is held that on account of that marsh, and the great number of courtesans, a bad air affects the men who dwell in that city." [60] Even earlier the royal family, the nobility, and the wealthy merchants had moved from there to Lefkoşa, because the latter was more healthful, according to Ludwig von Suchen (1350). [61]

The first good account of the malaria problem in Cyprus was written by Pero Tafur, the Catalan adventurer who traveled between 1435 and 1439 and sufficiently impressed the Lusignan ruler that he sent Tafur on a special embassy to the king's overlord, the Mamluk sultan in Cairo. Tafur sailed to the island from Rhodes, first reaching Baf (Paphos), which he found uninhabited because of its "bad air and water"; Magosa, then under Genoese control, was depopulated because of bad air and water also. Lefkoşa, the capital, was one of the healthiest places on the island, although the tiny port of Girniye (Cerina) actually was the healthiest of all because it was exposed to the west wind. Tafur claimed to be pleased with the young king: "Without doubt, if his country were not so unhealthy, I should have been glad to place myself at his service for a time, but it is almost impossible for a stranger to live in such a wretched country . . ." [62]

Another pilgrim, a gentleman from Padua named Count Gabriele Capodilista, in 1458 visited a village where the Venetian Corner (Cornaro) family had established model agricultural cultivation, particularly sugar cane. There they disembarked ". . . at this place Episcopia (Piskopi); the air there is very bad, and they all got ill, one of a fever, another of a flux, except M. Gabriele who remained well; but for fifteen days his chest and stomach suffered from nausea from having imbibed that foul and almost pestiferous air; and some of his companions died."[63]

When the Dominican monk from Ulm Felix Fabri visited Magosa in 1483, he found that ". . . ruin threatens the city and all that is in it. It is said that no man can stay long there on account of the corruption of the air."[64]

The German pilgrim Sebalt Rieter of Nuremberg, who visited the island in July 1480, reached Baf (Waffa), where the air was bad, and Limosa, ". . . where we lay all night on the galleys because of the bad air which is on the land of the island." That pilgrim, too, had encountered malarial seaports.[65] Hans Tucher (1479), a near-contemporary German pilgrim, found bad air in Baf.[66] A Jew traveling from Italy to Jerusalem visited Magosa for three days beginning 29 August 1495; there he found "the air is very bad and the water unwholesome."[67]

When the Italian pilgrim Canon Pietro Casola toured the extensive ruins of Limosa (1494), he was surprised to find it virtually empty. "When I asked why the Signoria did not seek to repopulate it, standing as it does on the sea, he told me that people do not care to settle there on account of the earthquakes, and also because it is a very unhealthy place. The inhabitants have in truth an unhealthy appearance. They all appear to be ill. True there are only a few of them."[68]

Attestation of the precarious condition of Magosa in the decades before Ottoman rule came from the English merchant, John Locke.

Locke (1553) wrote: "The aire of Famagusta is very unwholesome, as they say, by reason of certain marish ground adjoyning unto it. They have also a certaine yearely sicknesses raigning in the same towne, above all the rest of the Island: yet neverthelesse, they have it in other townes, but not so much. It is is certaine rednesse and paine of the eyes, the which if it bee not quickly holpen, it taketh away their sight . . . either of one eye or both . . ."[69]

In an introductory chapter on the island, the Venetian Antonio Graziani, who lived there before the Ottoman conquest, wrote: "Its Ayr, in truth, is not answerable to the goodness of its Soyl; immoderate heats rendring the whole Island unhealthy, and in some parts contagious, so that it seems as if its Malignity would ravish from the *Cypriots* the pleasure of a long enjoyment of Natures Favours; few of them arriving to great maturity of Years."[70]

The French pilgrim Seigneur de Villamont, when he reached Baf

(Paphos) on 11 May 1589, found it ". . . half ruined, so that it profits little by the beauty of its site and the frutifulness of the soil. . . . all is nearly uninhabited now on account of the unhealthy climate: so great are the vicissitudes of things!"[71]

The Dutch seaman Jan Somer of Middleburgh (1591–1592), though impressed with the fortifications and agriculture of Magosa, knew that the place had pestilential air and was very dangerous, so what was eaten should be boiled.[72] To Cotovicus certain places had unhealthy air.[73] de Stochove (1630) heard that Lefkoşa still had the best air on the island.[74] The former French ambassador Louis des Hayes (1621) reported that the heat was unpleasant, the land low lying, the water dangerous, and there were so many marshes that the air became corrupt, and a sojourn there was uncomfortable.[75]

The Dutch Orientalist C. von Bruyn (1692) learned that the air was unwholesome during the three or four hot months of the year, especially for foreigners. People have pale and sickly looks which last all their lives; some die from this, and others have violent fevers. The presence of this sickness on the island influenced von Bruyn to end his stay in Cyprus.[76] The Corsair Mr. Robert (1696) said Larnaka was "subject to contagious Distempers."[77]

Observations on the Patterns of the Population of Ottoman Cyprus, 1571–1640

The first Ottoman budget, from 1571–1572 (979–978), mentions 23,000 payers of the head tax *(cizye-i gebran)*, who were all adult male non-Muslims *(zimmis)*, married and unmarried, which with families means between 70,000 and 80,000 non-Muslims on the island. The detailed tax survey and sensus of November 1572 (10 Cumadi II 980) gives very reliable figures, but for villages and urban quarters only; tallying them all, even by districts, was not feasible at the archive, although presumably the total was close to the 23,000 figure, plus a small number exempt because of age, disability, or performance of a particular military service. Scattered in villages throughout the island were no more than twenty-five Muslim adult males, most of whom were converts to Islam, who were also registered as reʿaya. Since the bureaucracy for making official assessments had barely been established, one might conjecture that the figure 23,000 represented at least a slight undercount. Remote or mountainous areas might be undercounted. Moreover, many were slain in the sieges of Lefkoşa and especially Magosa, and since at least in those two cities large numbers were enslaved, and since numerous Latins fled the island, one might expect the population to be far below normal.

The non-Muslim population probably grew steadily for more than three decades, nearly reaching 31,000 taxpaying adult males (interchangeably called *nefer* and *hane*, even in official documents): 30,100 in 1604 (1013), 30,120 in 1606 (1015), and 30,569 in 1607 (1016), representing a peak of between 93,000 and 110,000 non-Muslims. Undoubtedly the island's population growth somehow was intimately linked with the Mediterranean-wide population growth of the 16th century, but it also must have depended on the establishment of law, order, and justice.

Other Mediterranean population began to decrease late in the 16th or early 17th century, depending on the place. In Cyprus, by 1612 (1021) the number of payers of head tax *(cizye)* had fallen to 26,840, representing between 80,000 and 95,000 non-Muslims. Within another decade their numbers had fallen to 22,500 adult male non-Muslim taxpayers (67,500 to 79,000 people in 1624 (1034)), and by 1626 (1036) this had fallen to 20,000. Either it remained at that level, or the need to reduce it further was ignored. Although in some other Ottoman provinces fiscal surveys provide more precise population figures, those in Cyprus usually seem to have intended only rough approximations.

In any case, a decade later in 1636 (1046) thousands of re'aya were said to have fled or died on account of excessive taxation and oppression on the part of the governor. At that time the number of head-tax payers was reduced to 17,000 (between 51,000 and 60,000). With better rule, despite the severe plague, locusts, and famine of 1641, their numbers rose to about 18,000 in 1643 (1053)—54,000 to 63,000 people. A series of disasters necessitated a new assessment of 1647 (1057), which found that over 1500 re'aya had perished or become dispersed because of a new wave of locusts, reducing the head-tax paying population to about 17,848 (between 54,000 and 63,000). Already having fallen to 15,000 in 1655, a serious plague of some tenacity killed approximately 3000 head-tax payers, leaving only 12,000 alive (between 36,000 and 42,000 non-Muslims) in 1656.

In 1572, when virtually the only Muslims in Cyprus were the conquering Ottoman army, the one place in the island with any claim to being an urban center, according to the fiscal surveys, was Magosa, which had 1741 registered adult males, of whom all but 113 were taxpayers. A total of 27% of the taxpayers were unmarried—mostly young men—while the remainder were married men with families *(hane)*. If one estimates the population on the basis of the total number of adult males, it ranged between 5300 to 6100; based on the number of families one might conjecture between 6000 and 6600.

The capital, Lefkoşa, was a run-down place of 235 males, of whom 94% (221) were married with families. Calculating on the basis of the number of taxpayers, the population ranged between 700 and 825; on the basis of families it was between 1100 and 1225. At that time the northern port and fortress Girniye had 198 adult male taxpayers, of whom a quarter (49) were unmarried. Calculating from the number of taxpayers, one gets a population between 600 and 700; from families one gets 735 and 800. Tuzla (Larnaka) had only 63 adult male taxpayers, of whom 94% (59) were married *(hane);* its population was between 200 and 225, or between 300 and 325. The southern port Limosa had a mere 177 adult males, virtually all married (164, 93%); its population in 1572 probably ranged either between 550 and 625 or between 820 and 900. The southwestern port Baf had 274 adult male taxpayers registered, of whom 13% (35) were unmarried; Baf population was between 825 and 1000 or from 1200 to 1300.

Villages for which districts were named, even without any histories as towns, often were larger in population. Mountainous Gilan, for example, had 523 adult male taxpayers, of whom 77% (404) were married with families. Karpas, on the notheastern peninsula, had 399 taxpayers, of whom 74% (297) were families. Lefka, on the other hand, only had 159 taxpayers, of whom 81% (128 or 129) were families, Pano Evdim had only 140 (89% with families—123), and Morfo merely 87 adult male taxpayers (93% or 81 with families). Such places were not distinguished from other villages in the tax surveys, and while some were large, many others were quite modest in size. Only infrequently were they the largest villages in their districts.

By 1606 a substantial Muslim minority had appeared in Cyprus, from banishment and conversion, although of what proportion there is no useful Ottoman evidence. Surely the Muslim population was not negligible, and it was, as it always remained, somewhat disproportionately concentrated in the towns. There is, unfortunately, no way of determining in a satisfactory way the religio-ethnic mix of these places. Presumably, by that time at least a majority of the inhabitants of Lefkoşa and Magosa were Muslims, but of other places even that is problematic. Some villages may have had absolutely no Muslim, while others had a handful of Muslims and a few had Muslims exclusively. The official registers giving population after the 1572 survey are concerned with determining only the number of adult male non-Muslims who were liable to pay the head tax *(cizye)*.

In 1606 the population of Ottoman Cyprus neared its zenith (at least until the middle of the 19th century). The island still had virtually nothing approximating urban life, even if one fancies the Muslim population of Lefkoşa and Magosa to have been double that of the non-Muslims. Certain villages still had more payers of the head tax *(cizye)* than any "town" except Magosa. Of the towns, only Magosa had a population in excess of 2000 non-Muslims. Although the number of non-Muslims had dropped 58% since 1572, there remained 730 adult male taxpayers: between 2200 and 2600 people.

At that time, the only other "town" with more than 1000 non-Muslims was Baf, where 349 taxpaying adult males (between 1050 and 1225 non-Muslims) lived, an increase of 27% over the first survey. The non-Muslim population grew a scant 12% to 263 taxpaying adult males (only 800 or 900 in number!), but the non-Muslim population of Limosa dropped 20%, to 141 taxpaying adult males *(hane)*, between 425 and 500 people. As in 1572, some of the largest villages were the places after which the districts are named. Adult male non-Muslim taxpayers in Gilan increased 3% to 541, a community in the neighborhood of 1600 to 1900. Lefka dropped 14%, to 136. The non-Muslim population of Karpas, on the other hand, plummeted 27% to 291 adult males, Morfo 25% to 65, and Pano Evdim 46% to 26.

The largest districts in 1606 (1015) were Lefka with 2816 non-Muslim adult males in 87 villages (between 8450 and 9900 non-Muslims) and Mesariye with 2851 (between 8500 and 10,000), also in 87 villages. Next followed Lefkoşa with 2636 non-Muslim adult males in 110 villages and Baf with 2616 in 78 villages. Their non-Muslim populations must have ranged between 7800 and 9300. Much the smallest district in number of non-Muslims was Morfo, with 969 taxpaying adult males (between 2900 and 3400 people) in 38 villages. Kukla had only 32 villages with 1120 non-Muslim taxpayers (3350 to 3900) (MMD 1702, arçiv. no. 5094).

The following year in 1607 (1016) an increase from 30,120 (or 30,169) non-Muslim payers of the head tax to 30,569 was noted, most of that growth occurring inexplicably in Magosa district, where 321 new non-Muslim taxpayers were added, although apparently eliminated before 1623. While several districts increased in numbers between 1606 and 1607, between 1607 and 1611 every single district except Morfo, the smallest, declined. In the five years between 1606 and 1611, the non-Muslim population in Lefkoşa district declined by 5%, in Magosa by 6%, in Karpas by 11%, in Lefka by 12%, in Piskopi by 13%, and in Hirsofi by 25%.

In the two decades between 1606 and 1623 Magosa remained the "town" with by far the largest number of non-Muslims. Nevertheless, their numbers declined 7% to 676 non-Muslim taxpayers (between 2000 and 2400 in numbers). Lefkoşa grew steadily, becoming their second largest concentration, its population growing 57% to 414 head-tax payers (between 1250 and 1450 people). Although non-Muslim taxpayers in Baf fell 20% (to 279—850 to 950 people), Limosa grew rapidly by 70% to 244 (750 to 1250 people). Of villages, the non-Muslim population in Karpas remained steady at 291 taxpayers, while Morfo increased slightly to 76. However, Gilan lost one-third of its numbers (down to 362 non-Muslim taxpayers—1050 to 1250 people), Hirsofi declined 28% to 71, Kukla 17% to 88, and Pano Evdim 13% to 65.

All the towns declined between 1623 and 1643 except Lefkoşa which became the one with by far the greatest number of non-Muslims. There their numbers grew by 37% in the two decades, to 649 head-tax payers. At that point the people lived in 10 quarters, the largest of which was Terbiyodi (the Armenian one), with 220 taxpayers. One quarter had seven adult male Suryani Maronites, another nine Armenians (and 182 additional Armenians dispersed in rural areas *(haymana)*, although attached to Lefkoşa). Between 1606 and 1643 the non-Muslims there increased by almost 150%, by over 175% compared with 1572.

The non-Muslim population of Magosa, which remained second largest in towns, declined by 53% after 1623, to 321 head-tax payers (950 to 1100 people), nearly a third of whom (103) were unmarried. Since 1606 the non-Muslim population declined by 56%, by 80% since 1572. Although after 1612 the population of Baf dropped by 32% to 191 head-tax payers (45% since 1606), it rose in rank to third among towns. Baf had eight non-Muslim quarters, the largest of which was Aya Cindiye (?) with 43 head-tax payers; the town had between 575 and 675 non-Muslims in 1643. The next two places had virtually the same non-Muslim populations: Limosa with 152 head-tax payers, Tuzla with 140. In the former place 16% (25) were unmarried, 25% (35) in the latter. Despite a sharp drop in numbers after 1623, Limosa still had 8% more non-Muslims than in 1606; non-Muslims lived in four quarters, the largest of which was Katelogi, where presumably 74 Latin head-tax payers lived. Limosa and Tuzla both had between 450 and 550 non-Muslims. Although they declined 43% between 1623 and 1643, they still occupied three quarters; Tuzla's largest quarter was Aya Yani with 53 payers of head tax.

The decline in the villages after which districts were named was even more severe than that of the towns. Gilan fell to 155 head-tax payers in 1643, a decline of 57% since 1612, 71% since 1606. Hirsofi fell by two-thirds between 1623 and 1643, to a mere 23 head-tax payers; that means a decline of 77% from 1606, or 93% from 1572, more than any other place considered. Kukla fell by 22% after 1623, by 35% after 1606, to 69 payers of head tax. At 41 head-tax payers, Lefka had fallen by 70% since 1606, by 74% since 1572. The fortress of Girniye fell 44% between 1612 and 1643, to 100 head-tax payers (16 unmarried), a decline of 49% since 1572. The non-Muslim head-tax payers in the village of Karpas declined 48% between 1623 and 1643, 62% below 1572, to 150. With 108 head-tax payers (25 unmarried) in 1643, those in Piskopi had fallen 58% in three decades, 78% is seven. Non-Muslim head-tax payers in Pano Evdim fell to 26, 60% below 1623, 81% below 1572.

In 1643 (1053) only 5 of the 16 districts still had more than 1000 non-Muslim taxpayers. By far the largest district was Lefkoşa, which had actually grown 23% since 1606, to 3248 payers of the head-tax; it numbered between 9700 and 11,400 non-Muslims. Next followed Baf (1714), Mesariye (1629), and Lefka (1557), bunched together in a group, with between 4700 and 6000 non-Muslims. Although Baf's population declined 35%, it rose in rank from 4th to 2nd. Lefka plunged 45%, as it fell from 2nd to 5th, while Mesariye fell 43%, from 1st to 3rd. Much the smallest district was Kukla, with 524 taxpaying non-Muslims— probably merely between 1600 and 1800 people. Then followed Magosa with 606 (between 1800 and 2100), a 49% drop, and Morfo with 684 (between 2000 and 2400), which dropped 29%.

The head tax *(cizye)* is a tax required of non-Muslim subjects of Islamic states. The tax only applies to free, adult males who are of age (i.e., have reached puberty, never later than 15 lunar years in the Hanefi law supported by the Ottomans) and capable of supporting themselves. Thus the sick, the disabled, the elderly, and the very poor, as well as slaves, are exempt from this tax. Keeping lists of adult non-Muslims was required. People entered in those registers are not to be considered families *(hane)*, for each of whom demographically there might be five or five and a half individuals; rather they are to be considered simply as adult males *(nefer)*, for each of whom one might anticipate three or three and a half individuals. Ottoman bureaucrats mixed the terms *nefer* and *hane* in confusing ways, but it must be understood that, in the context of discussing people bound to the head tax in Cyprus, the sources always mean non-Muslim adult males. In detailed *tahrirs* like that of 1572 all free adult males are listed by name and residence, and those tax-exempt are explicitly identified as blind, or elderly, or very infrequently as cannoneers or architects in fortresses. Head tax registers, however, simply report those zimmis (non-Muslims) who are bound to pay that tax. Probably, at that time, in a place like Cyprus, even counting slaves no more than 5% of the non-Muslim men were exempt from the head tax.

Up till this time Ottoman archival sources have not provided anyone with any insight into the non-Muslim population. The Venetian churchman Cotovicus (1598) includes a good deal of authentic-sounding observations and data in his account. His assertion that the island, "according to the statements worthy of credit," at that time had 28,000 non-Muslims is remarkably close to the 27,500 head-tax payers Ottoman sources mention for 1604. If we assume that he simply misunderstood the meaning of the category (since he shows little understanding of Ottoman practices), and that at that time the island had 28,000 non-Muslim adult males, then perhaps we can also accept as authentic his figure of 6000 adult male Muslims. That would suggest at that time the Muslim population of Cyprus constituted 18% of the population of the island, interestingly almost exactly the proportion in recent years. By 1598 the policy of population transfers from Anatolia had ended, but much evidence of further conversion to Islam among local Cypriots has been presented. Probably frequent conversion to Islam among local Cypriots continued for the next two decades thereafter slowing down considerably.[78]

Table 6.1
The Non-Muslim Population of Cyprus, According
to Ottoman Archival Records

979	1571	23,000 hane
980	1572	23,000 hane
1012	1604	27,500
1013	1604	30,071 nefer (also 30,100)
1015	1606	30,120 hane (also 30,069)
1016	1607	30,569
1017	1608	29,616 nefer (?) (also 30,717)
1021	1612	26,840 hane
1026	1617	26,500
1027	1618	25,450
1030	1621	25,000
1032	1623	22,500 hane
1034	1624	22,500 hane
1036	1626	20,000 hane
1038	1628	20,000 hane
1040	1630	20,000 hane
1041	1631	20,000 hane
1046	1636	16,500 hane
1051	1641	17,000 hane [1]
1053	1643	18,050 nefer (also 17,848)
1057	1647	17,848 nefer
1065	1655	15,000 hane
1066	1656	12,000 hane

1. Includes 500 presumed for Kukla, for which figures are missing

There is much authenticity in Cyprianos' discussion of the post-Ottoman period, particularly in regard to initial attempts to rule well, but the local government's finally becoming blatantly oppressive, and along with locusts, plague, and famine forcing large-scale emigration. If the figure of 25,000 re'aya that he mentions for 1640 really refers to the tax-paying population and not just non-Muslims, it probably refers to a detailed new census and fiscal survey reportedly ordered for 1641 (nothing survives except a detailed head-tax register).[79] It is conceivable that in 1641 the island had about 25,000 adult males, of whom 17,000 were non-Muslims and 8000 Muslims. That would mean the population of Cyprus had become 32% Muslim, although because of their greater concentration in towns and in accessible flat areas, undercount of the

Table 6.2
The Non-Muslim Population of the Districts of Cyprus, According to
Ottoman Archival Records

	1013 (1604)	1015 (1606)	1016 (1607)	1020 (1611)	1033 (1623)	1052 (1643)	1053 (1643)
Lefkoşa	2636	2636	2702	2499	2495 hane	2850	3248
Tuzle (Tuzla)	1846	1846	1957	1741	1721 (or 1741)	1248	1359
Pendaye	1586	1586	1578	1490	1440 (or 1490)	796	845
Girniye	1595	1595	1592	1512	1514	920	975
Lefka	2816	2816	2782	2468	2467	1451	1557
Morfo (Omorfa)	965	969	997	1031	1031	631 (Amorfe)	684
Mesariye	2851	2851	2868	2684	2672 (or 2683)	1546	1629
Karpas	2012	2024	2007	1805	1805	838	894
Limosa	2435	2435	2435	2076	missing	939	985
Gilan	1744	1745	1739	1569	missing	726	806
Kukla		1120	1140	866	missing	?	524
Baf	2616	2616	2616	2120	missing	1538	1714
Evdim	1583	1582	1628	1411	missing	527	587
Magosa	1196	1196	1517	1117	missing	528	606
Piskopi	1346	1346	1338	1167	missing	624	694
Hirsofi	1716	1706	1673	1275	missing	842	943

Muslims would have been much less likely. It is not very satisfactory to
base important points like this on single pieces of evidence, sometimes
tenuous. Otherwise, however, nothing can be said of the numbers of
Muslims.

Summary

Venice, concerned about the island's declining population, long worked
to encourage new settlement. Doubtless seen usually as divine retribution, natural disasters—earthquakes, endemic diseases (plague and malaria), and locusts—improverished the people. A considerable demographic decline took place in the 14th and 15th centuries, probably
initially related to the Black Death; but during the Venetian century

Table 6.3
Non-Muslim Population of Selected Towns and Villages, According to Ottoman Archival Records

	1016 (1606)	1021 (1612)	1033 (1623)	1053 (1643)	980 (1572)
Lefkoşa	263	303	414	649 (with 178 muc.)	235 (221 hane)
Tuzla	247	66 or (Larnaka)	69	140 (with 35 muc.)	63 (59 hane)
Magosa	730	676	676	321 (with 103 muc.)	1741 (1193 hane)
Baf	349	279	279	191 (with 41 muc.)	274 (236 hane)
Limosa	141	124	244	152 (with 41 muc.)	177 (164 hane)
Gilan	541	362	362	155 (with 25 muc.)	523 (404 hane)
Hirsofi	98	71	71	23	340 (111 hane)
Kukla	106	88	88	69 (with 16 muc.)	
Pano Evdim (Evdim)	75	65	65	26 (with 6 muc.)	140 (123 hane)
Karpas	291	291	291	150	399 (297 hane)
Lefka	136			41 (with 7 muc.)	159 (129 or 128 hane)
Girniye	65	177		100 (with 16 muc.)	198 (147 hane)
Morfo		76	76		87 (81 hane)
Piskopi	255	255	61	108 (with 25 muc.)	482 (428 hane)
Kitriya (Lefkoşa)	65	61		54	81 (72 hane)
Kato Lefkare	86 (Tuzla)	80		69 (with 18 muc.)	259

Kormakidi (Girniye)	188			54 (with 5 muc.)	(224 or 217 hane)
Vasiliya	85	120	120	50 (with 2 muc.)	44 (42 hane)
Tembriya (Lefka)	95	114	114	61	134 (115 or 112 hane)
Akaci (Morfo)	62	72	72	63 (with 7 muc.)	150 (130) (Pendaye)
Peristerona	141	152	152	110	
Lefkoniko (Mesariye)	170	160		83 (with 6 muc.)	178 (143 or 2 hane)
Yenagre	74	71	71		144 (113 hane)
Tirikomi (Karpas)	154	149	139 (Tridomi)	118 (with 17 muc.)	200 (155 or 154 hane)
Manelogi (Limosa)	63	53	53		
Kato Foka (Gilan)	87	79	79		108 (Limosa) (84 or 85 hane)
Filuse (Kukla)	60	56	56	49 (with 6 muc.)	
Daliye (Baf)	70	66	66		130 Dalye (112 hane)
Malye (Evdim)	99	91 (Maliye)	91		130 (113 hane)
Aya Sergi	107	105	105	51 (with 14 muc.)	105 (86 hane)
Derine	55	52	52	40 (with 7 muc.)	
Malye (Piskopi)	50				130 (113 hane) (Evdim)

population doubled, although mostly in the villages. The Ottoman attempts to impose compulsory population transfers in the first decade of Ottoman rule indicates that they, too, believed the island needed more people.

The best way to deal with the locust problem was to dig up and destroy the eggs, the turning in of which was actually required of the villages by the Venetian government. Apparently the Ottoman government was even more effective in dealing with locusts, for it gave very strong orders that everyone was to collect and burn a sackful a week when they were in season. While some people dealt with the locusts in a rational fashion, others sought to assuage evil spirits.

Towns were the most threatened by plague, many being virtually unihabitable during summer seasons. Plague regularly struck in Cyprus as it made its way through the Mediterranean world, meandering its way around.

Malaria, too, was a disease of the towns of the island. Very little is known about its appearance or spread, but townspeople took great cares to avoid it. It really contributed to general decline, too, although most villages were much less affected. Malaria seems to have periods of greater and lesser virulence. It was most deadly in Magosa, Limosa, and Larnaka.

The number of non-Muslims on the island seem to have grown steadily, at least through the first decades of Ottoman rule, from 23,000 zimmi taxpayers to 30,000 or 31,000, although the lack of the normal precision which one might expect to find in Ottoman documents makes one quite wary. It might be possible to pin these great fluctuations into actual changing social and economic circumstances. Immediately after the Ottoman conquest, the towns all had strikingly low populations. Only the court records give any indication of the presence of Muslims there, for the only population survey was taken immediately after the conquest.

APPENDIX

Order *(hukm)* to Cyprus governor *(begler begisi)* and kadi *(kadisine):* The taxpayers of the island of Cyprus *(Kibris re'ayasi)* presented a petition *('arz-i hal)* to my exalted presence *(rikab-i humayunum).* Formerly they were 20,000 payers of head tax (i.e., adult male non-Muslims, here called *hane* but more

Defters. Ankara, Tapu ve Kadastro Dairesi, Kuyud-i kadime arşivi.
Cyprus: 10 Cumadi II 980 (Nov. 1572).

Istanbul, Başbakanlık arşivi. Maliyeden Müdevver Kataloğu.		
kat.nu.	*arş.nu.*	
1702	5094	1015 (1606). cizye defter-i icmal.
1996	5084	1021 (1612). cizye icmal defteri.
2516	14634	1032–1041 (1623–1631). cizye.
3653	279	1051–1053 (1642–1644). cizye defteri.
2557	16112	1033 (1623). cizye.
3805	8428	1053 (1643). cizye defteri.
3701	17716	1052 (1643). zimmi tahrir defteri.
	9839	1066 (1656).
3660	6268	1057 (1647). muhasebe defteri.
3296	2772	1046–1049 (1636–1639). ahkam defteri, p. 2.
3703	16543	1052 (1643). zimmi tahrir defteri.
1569	20093	1013 (1604). muhasebe defteri, p. 8, 10.
2437	524	1030 (1621). muhasebe defteri, p. 25.
2475	12842	1031–1037 (1622–1628). varidat/mesarif defteri, p. 40.
2229	12782	1026–1027 (1617–1618). varidat/mesarif defteri,/ p. 5, 42.
2971	3922	1040 (1630–1631). muhasebe, p. 62, 110.
3020	16114	1041 (1632). varidat/mesarif defteri, p. 15, 18.
324	5168	980 (1572). muhasebe defteri, p. 7.
1801	4399	1017 (1608). irad ve masraf muvacib defteri, p. 16?

A *sicil* of I Cumadi II 1046 mentions collecting certain expenses from 14,351 *hane* on the island, but that is not explicitly said to constitute all non-Muslim taxpayers (4 173-1). An imperial order requires collecting cizye from 30,717 *nefer* zimmis in 1017 (2 52-1; undated).

properly *nefer*), but on account of the abundance of taxes *(kesret-i tekalif)* and the weight of oppression *(siklet-i te'addiden)* a few thousand taxpayers *(re'aya)* fled and abandoned the country *(terk-i diyar)*, Although only 16,500 head-tax payers *(hane)* remain in their places, those who are charged with collecting the head tax *(haraççiler)* say that 20,000 hane is written in the new register *(mucedded defterde)*. The collectors of the head tax are oppressive to the 16,500 head-tax payers *(hane)* concerning the 3500 missing *(gurihte)* ones. They collect 720 akce from every head-tax payer *(hane)*, a total of 116,000 guruş. 80,000 guruş they send to the Porte, and they spend *(harç ve sarf)* 30,000 guruş in that province for salaries *(saliyane)* and other important expenses; the remainder belongs to the collectors of head-tax. . . .

They made an announcement of the circumstances:

Thus, if there is no compassion *(merhamet)*, and if our taxes *(tekalif)* and head tax *(haraçimuz)* is not reduced, we will not be able to endure any longer. It is certain that all of us will become dispersed or will perish *(perakende ve perişan)*. . . . In accordance with the register *(defter)* I order that head tax should be taken only from 16,500 head-tax payers *(hane)*, and no more than 560 akce apiece should be collected. Every year 60,000 guruş should be sent to my Porte, 30,000 guruş for the salaries *(saliyane)* specified in Cyprus, and 2000 guruş for the collectors of the head tax. Not one akce more should be taken. . . . 16 June 1635 (12 Muharrem 1046). (MMD 3296; arşiv 2772, p. 2)

NOTES

1. Hill, v. 3, pp. 640n, 729n. Although Venice refused to allow emigration to Cyprus from other Venetian territories, dissatisfied Greek Orthodox from the Morea were encouraged to migrate and the government agreed to help finance the transportation to Cyprus of "mercenaries" from Italy.
2. Cobham, pp. 51f.
3. Cobham, p. 55; *Travels* . . . , p. 441; *Peregrinatio* . . . , p. 139. *Peregrinatio.* . . . and *Travels.* . . . are variants of Baumgarten.
4. Cyprus has a "reputation as one of the most seismatic parts of the Eastern Mediterranean. . . ." Even there, however, no earthquakes in the 16th or 17th century appears to have had devastating effects anywhere on the island, never mind causing loss of life. In comparison with the effects of locusts, plague, or malaria, earthquakes apparently are of minimal consequence. N. N. Ambraseys, "The Seismic History of Cyprus," *Revue de l'Union Internationale de Secours* 3.1965.25–48. See also pages 25, 30ff, 38f. Cf. "Value of Historical Records of Earthquakes," *Nature* 232.1971.375–379. Cf. Hill, v. 2, pp. 19n, 157n, 177n; v. 3, pp. 818–821, 645f.
5. Hill, v. 3, p. 787. Cf. M. W. Dols, *The Black Death in the Middle East*, pp. vii, 4, 302, and *passim*. The earlier estimates are consistently lower than the later ones, and although Hill is too cautious to suggest anything more than "some" population increase, in fact the 106,000 estimate of a deputation to Venice, the 110,000 estimated by the Lieutenant, and the 90,000 estimated by the Syndic (1490, 1504, 1504) preceded estimates of 180,000 for 1562 by Savorgnan and 200,000 in 1570 by A. Graziani. Although admittedly imprecise, the sources presented by Hill support Braudel's contention that doubling of population was Mediterranean-wide in the 1480–1580 period. The 250,000 reported by Accidas from figures supplied by the Archbishop of Cyprus had the purpose of convincing the Duke of Savoy to participate in a military adventure and so may be dismissed along with the 400,000 Cypriots mentioned by the grand vezir in a letter to Charles IX announcing the conquest of Cyprus. Hill, v. 3, pp. 778f.

   In his recent study of Ephesus Clive Foss has identified malaria as one of the factors in the complete decay of Ottoman Ephesus. "With the decline of prosperity, the swamps produced by the silting were no longer drained and gave rise to malaria, which further reduced the population." *Ephesus after Antiquity: A Late Antique, Byzantine and Turkish City.* Cambridge, 1979. p. 168. Cf. pp. 175, 178. Although Foss acknowledges the general paucity of sources for that period, he believed that occurred because silt was allowed to build up when the harbor fell out of use. Certainly that was not the case for Magosa. While malaria was becoming firmly entrenched, the island's Venetian masters took extraordinary measures to encourage Magosa's development. In any case, the development of malaria there (and probably at Baf, Limosa, and Larnaka) antedated Venetian rule in Cyprus, or even the beginning of Ottoman rule in Ephesus (1425). In Magosa malaria developed late in the Lusignan period when the city may have experienced its busiest trade and greatest prosperity ever, not decline. Possibly the reasons for the development of malaria were not strictly local phenomena. Possibly malaria in the eastern Mediterranean had entered a period of growing virulence.

6. *Ruzat ul-abrar*, p. 450, cited by G. Hill, v. 3, p. 788n. If it means adult male zimmis who pay taxes, that might mean 360,000–420,000 people.

7. Hill, v. 3, p. 788n. Cobham, p. 345.

8. 1696. v. 2, p. 292, from Hill, p. 787n.

9. 1 286–1; emr-i şerif of III Zil-Kade 1002 (August 1594).

10. Fr. Jerom Dandini, *A Voyage to Mount Libanus . . . ,* in John Pinkerton, *A General Collection of the Best and Most Interesting Voyages and Travels . . .* London, 1811. v. 10, pp. 279. Cobham, p. 182. According to C. Niebuhr (1766) 80,000 Greek Orthodox paid harac. *Reisebeschreibung . . . ,* v. 3, p. 26.

11. Cobham, p. 158.

12. Cobham, p. 173.

13. *Relation Journaliere . . .* 1608, p. 116; 1619, p. 89. Cobham, p. 209.

14. *Naukeurige Beschryving . . . ,* pp. 25f. C. Niebuhr (1766) was, if anything, even more negative about the impact on population of Ottoman rule, indicating that many Christians either converted to Islam or emigrated to escape harac. Carsten Niebuhr, *Reisebeschreibung nach Arabien und andern umliegenden Landern.* v. 3, p. 26. Hamburg, 1837.

15. *Isolario*, f. LXV, LXVI. Venetia, 1534. Quoting Cobham, p. 62.

16. Mogabgab, *Supplementary Excerpts . . . ,* v. 3, p. 152; cf. Hill, v. 3, p. 819n. Relics were sometimes used to drive off the insects. Jodicus's description is pretty accurate except for the fact that there is no three-year cycle of locusts and drought by itself is not stimulus to their breeding. Cf. L. F. H. Merton, a warm, moist February is best; high, well-distributed rainfall may increase numbers. *Studies in the Ecology of the Moroccan Locust* (Dociostaurus maroccanus *Thunberg*) *in Cyprus. Anti-Locust Bulletin* 34. London, 1959. p. 110.

17. *Description de Toute l'Isle de Cypre . . . ,* f. 211. Paris, 1580 (reprinted Famagouste, 1968). Presumably the locusts from Syria would have been desert locusts, although the Moroccan species also occurs in Syria. Of course Lusignan's claims about their coming from Syria cannot be presumed accu-

206 Disastrous Effects of Locusts, Plague, and Malaria

rate, although he was well informed about local events. In any case, if the
locusts reaching the island were from anywhere other than possibly southern Anatolia, they would probably be the highly mobile desert locusts. Very
likely there was an upsurge in desert locusts for a few years, enabling some
to move far beyond their normal range.

On the periodicity of desert locusts, Z. Waloff points out that there have
been no major swarms in Cyprus since 1915 (writing in 1966). "All major
plagues on which adequate historical data is available have lasted for several
consecutive years, and have been characterized by numerous reports of both
swarms and gregarious hopper infestations." Desert locusts have a flying
speed of about 12 mph and what she characterizes as "considerable flying
endurance." Desert locusts often traverse "thousands of kilometeres before
they encounter conditions in which they can endure and breed." *The Upsurges and Recessions*, pp. 22, 15f.

18. Richard Hakluyt, *The Principal Navigations Voyages Traffiques & Discoveries of the English Nation*. v. 5, pp. 85f. Glasgow, 1903. Cobham, pp. 68f.
The date 12 August is too late in the year to find swarming locusts in
Cyprus. Presumably Locke went to the marketplace and observed the locust
eggs which people brought to meet their tax obligations. Possibly a few of
the specimens survived alive.

If Moroccan locusts were not endemic to Cyprus prior to the mid-16th
century, they must have been by then. Most years the farmers of Cyprus lost
almost half their grain crop (which was the staple in the diet and hence
almost universally cultivated, even in villages where orchards or vineyards
predominated); many years they lost all their grain. People did not stand
back passively and watch the locusts act destructively; and the colonial
Venetian government made a concerted effort against them, by closely
overseeing the collection and destruction of their eggs.

Beating the locust eggs into powder before throwing them into the sea
was essential, for otherwise most of them would survive, thrown up on to
the shore by passing storms. Near coastal areas the pulverized eggs might
be thrown into the sea, but in many places that would not be possible.

19. *Description de Toute l'Isle . . .*, f. 212. Cf. Hill, v. 3, p. 1147. The hope of
somehow attracting sufficient birds to consume enough swarming locusts to
reduce their numbers is an old one. That, indeed, was the underlying hope
from the locust water in Persia. Although doubtless many birds greatly
enjoyed having a surfeit of locusts, there is no hard evidence of swarms of
locusts ever having been decimated by birds.

Cf. a 1915 *Report on the Great Invasion of Locusts in Egypt in 1915*
and the measures adopted to deal with it published by the Egyptian Ministry
of Agriculture. "Most birds eat the young very readily. The most energetic
at this work, however, were:—(1) A small bird called *Ombah* by the
Bedouins. This little bird, about as large as an average house sparrow,
seemed to live practically entirely on the nymph. (the crested lark) (2) The
Anas. (the stork) "This bird was very energetic, but unfortunately was

rather rare. It is a large bird, with the wing-spread of a kite, white, with black wing-tips. Long legs." p. 64. Cairo, 1916. That might be the bird described by Lusignan.

Z. Waloff says that small swarms or groups might be eliminated by birds such as kites, kestrels, vultures, and storks in east Africa. One thousand locusts were found in the alimentary canal of a marabou stork, 300 in a white stork; hence 100 white storks might "have a disruptive effect which could help break up small swarms." ". . . when locust breeding was both heavy and widespread the available predatory birds could not control an infestation, but . . . small bands resulting from scattered layings were completely eliminated." *The Upsurges and Recessions . . .* , pp. 72f. Cf. C. Ashal and Peggy E. Ellis, *Studies on Numbers and Mortality of Field Populations of the Desert Locust* (Schistocerca gregaria *Forskal*). *Anti-Locust Bulletin 8.* London, 1962. pp. 50ff.

20. Cobham, p. 143. A Latin ruling class had ruled Greek Orthodox Cyprus since the 3rd Crusade. The aristocracy and the ruling class, of French or Italian origin, long worked unsuccessfully to lead Cypriots to acceptance of the Papacy.

21. v. 4, p. 67.

22. Hans Ulrich Krafft, *Reisen und Gefangenschaft.* ed. K. D. Haszler. *Bibliothek des Litterarischen Vereins in Stuttgart* 61.1861.296f. Oberhummer, p. 339. The policies of the Ottoman governors resemble those of their Venetian predecessors, except perhaps in ordering the daily collection of eggs and warms they were showing more zeal than had ever been shown before.

It seems plausible that the first years of Ottoman rule could have been distinguished by unusual swarms of locusts, since such periods can occur at any time—there is no regular periodicity. That statement is identified with the year 1577. If Moroccan locusts were becoming endemic to the island in the mid-16th century, that would explain much about the authenticity of Krafft's reports.

Krafft described the yearly cycle perfectly, except for assigning to specific days phenomena which occur over a period of weeks, the actual days ultimately depending on the weather. L. F. H. Merton, *Studies in the Ecology . . . , passim.* J. P. Dempster, *The Population Dynamics of the Moroccan Locust* (Dociostaurus maroccannus *Thunberg*) *in Cyprus. Anti-Locust Bulletin 27.* London, 1957. *passim.* Dempster, *Observations on the Moroccan Locust . . . , Anti-Locust Bulletin 10, passim.* The statement that their numbers increase every year is a superstition.

Either Krafft had some special informant or that information was "common knowledge" to some people.

23. Cobham, p. 177. Oberhummer, p. 338. The belief that however many are destroyed, more will reappear the following year is not a surprising one, considering the capacity of the locusts to reproduce themselves. Indeed the Moroccan locusts in Cyprus lay their eggs in places and ways that might

influence others to agree. The particularly favored egg-laying areas are on "islands" of uncultivated barren spots on the flat, intensively cultivated central plain. "Those 'islands' of undisturbed soil, with short grass cover, appeared to be particularly suitable for the breeding of the locust, which occurred mostly in concentrations." B. P. Uvarov, "Cyprus Locust Research Scheme," p. 1 in Dempster, *Observations on the Moroccan Locust* (Dociostaurus Maroccanus *Thunberg) in Cyprus, 1950. Anti-Locust Bulletin 10.* London, 1951. According to L. F. H. Merton, eggs are laid on "irregular patches of bare soil, usually 1–4 feet across." "The breeding areas . . . are in contact with, or surrounded by, arable land . . ." *Studies in the Ecology of the Moroccan Locust . . .* , pp. 9f, 11, 26ff.

De Villamont believes that the locusts are not consumed by the birds but are destroyed by their song and flight. Possibly that is part of the account of his monk-informant from Magosa (Famagusta), but is seems more likely that he somehow misunderstood what he was told and distorted it.

24. Ioanne Cootwijk, *Itinerarium Hierosolymitanum.* Antverbiae, 1619. p. 112. Quoting Cobham, p. 201. Oberhummer, p. 339. The wind is very important in the movements of Moroccan locusts. If the wind is strong, they simply do not move. Otherwise they fly with it. If it leads them to the sea, they are destroyed, of course.

The stench of millions of dead locusts was all too evident to those who visited the island in August or September like Cotovicus.

25. Hill, v. 4, p. 67.

26. *Travels of Macarius.* ed. F. C. Belfour. London, 1836. v. 2, p. 349. Cf. Machaeras, *Recital concerning . . .* , v. 2, pp. 348f. In Aleppo, to combat locusts, Muslims, Christians, and Jews "combine in supplication" using icons or holy water and "even share the same procession." F. W. Hasluck, *Christianity and Islam under the Sultans.* Oxford, 1929. v. 1, pp. 66n. Cf. Hill, v. 4, pp. 68, 353.

27. *Reizen van Cornelis de Bruyn Door de vermaerdste Deelen van Klein Asia . . .* Delft, 1698. Quoting Cobham, pp. 241f. Oberhummer, p. 339.

De Bruyn arrived at just the right time to see the locust hoppers grow into adults and reach their full growth. L. F. H. Merton, *Studies in the Ecology* of the Moroccan Locusts . . . , pp. 38, 111f. Little rain would fall in the season when adult locusts were swarming, so if the insects were thick enough to cloud the sky, the sky was bright and clear. Rounding up locust or catching locust hoppers is a relatively easy task, but collecting large quantities of adults, as the governor ordered in 1668, was a formidable task despite their ubiquity.

Apparently de Bruyn never saw the birds in action. Both incidents in regard to which he mentions birds, however, concern their eating locusts. Possibly that was just his "scientific" explanation. For storks and other birds, see Z. Waloff, *The Upsurges and Recessions . . .* , pp. 72f and *Report on the Great Invasion . . . in 1915*, p. 64.

28. *The Black Death in the Middle East.* Princeton, 1977. pp. 68ff, 42f. For the

history of earlier plagues in the region, see pp. 13–34. See also E. Ashtor, *A Social and Economic History of the Near East in the Middle Ages*. Berkeley and Los Angeles, 1976. pp. 87, 91f, 170f, 219, 238, 277f, 290, 301ff.

29. *The Black Death* . . . , p. vii.
30. *The Black Death* . . . , p. 4. "Later, there was a revival of trade because of the resurgence of the international spice trade in the middle of the fifteenth century, but population and agricultural productivity continued to decline due to successive epidemics of plague, famines, foreign campaigns, and domestic insecurity." p. 185.
31. v. 2, p. 307. He does point out J. C. Russell's warning that the death toll from that plague was probably not over 20%.
32. *The Black Death* . . . , pp. 58f. Cf. p. 192.
33. *The Black Death* . . . , p. 290.
34. *Recital concerning* . . . , v. 1, p. 61. That plague began in March. p. 119.
35. *Recital concerning* . . . , v. 1, p. 121. Hill, v. 2, p. 323.
36. *Recital concerning* . . . , p. 611. Hill, v. 2, pp. 441, 446. Dols, *The Black Death* . . . , p. 308. That lasted until 1393.
37. *Chronique d'Amadi*. ed. R. de Mas Latrie. Paris, 1891. p. 495. Cf. D. Strambaldi, *Chronique* . . . ed. R. de Mas Latrie. Paris, 1893. pp. 260f.
38. *Recital concerning* . . . , p. 623. Hill, v. 2, p. 464. Dols, *The Black Death* . . . , p. 309.
39. *Chronique* . . . , p. 265.
40. Machaeras, *Recital concerning* . . . , v. 1, p. 627. Hill, v. 2, p. 465.
41. Machaeras, *Recital concerning* . . . , v. 1, p. 683. Dols. *The Black Death* . . . , p. 311. Oberhummer says 17 years.
42. *The Black Death* . . . , p. 311.
43. *The Chronicle of George Boustronios, 1456–1489*. tr. R. M. Dawkins. Melbourne, 1964. p. 31, 92, 94.
44. Hill, v. 3, pp. 820f; Oberhummer, pp. 240–243.
45. *Canon Pietro Casola's* . . . , 293, 305; Mogabgab, v. 1, pp. 41f, 47.
46. Marino Sanuto, *I Diarii*. ed. G. Berchet. Venezia, 1881. v. 6, p. 212. Letter of 13 August 1505. Hill misread that as half the population of Lefkosha. v. 3, p. 821.
47. Sanuto, *I Diarii*. ed. G. Berchet, N. Barozzi, and M. Allegri. Venezia, 1903. v. 58, pp. 187, 251f, 589, 682, 720, 733f. Hill, v. 3, p. 821.
48. Mogabgab, v. 3, p. 152.
49. Cobham, p. 73; *R. de G.* (1879), p. 222.
50. Braudef, *Mediterranean* . . . , v. 1, pp. 259, 289, 332, 334.
51. On the subject of plagues in Cyprus, see Oberhummer, pp. 240ff. On the more general subject see also W. H. McNeill, *Plagues and Peoples*. Oxford, 1977.
52. Cobham, pp. 170f, 175f, 178.
53. *Travels*. London, 1615. p. 221.
54. Gedoyn "Le Turc", *Journal et Correspondance de Gedoyn "Le Turc" Consul de France a Alep (1623–1625)*. ed. A. Boppe. Paris, 1909. p. 186.

55. Hill, v. 4, pp. 68f, from Ricaut, *Present State of the Greek and Armenian Church*, 1679, p. 91.
56. v. 4, pp. 68f.
57. Hill, v. 4, p. 67n.
58. *Mr. Robert's Adventures and Sufferings amongst the Corsairs of the Levant* . . . , p. 173 in William Damier, *A Collection of Voyages*. London, 1729. v. 4.
59. Braudel, v. 1, p. 44, 62ff. On malaria in Cyprus, see also Oberhummer, pp. 237ff and Leonard J. Bruce-Chwatt and Julian de Zulueta, *The Rise and Fall of Malaria in Europe. A Historico-epidemiological Study*. New York, 1980. pp. 54–60. They attempt to link the spread of malaria with deforestation, and they conceive of a long-term growth in the severity of the disease. Cf. pp. 17–27 and *passim*. Cf. J. de Zulueta, "Malaria and Mediterranean History," *Parassitologia* 15.1973.1–15, esp. p. 9. According to F. F. Cartwright the 17th century was a period when malaria was unusually widespread in Europe. *Disease and History*. New York, 1972. p. 142. Braudel suggests the possibility that colder, wetter weather in the Mediterranean starting just before 1600 may be responsible for frequent flooding and the spread of swamps, and consequently of malaria. v. 1, pp. 270f.
60. Cobham, p. 22; *R. O. L.*, pp. 628f.
61. Cobham, p. 20; Stuttgart, pp. 32f; de Mas Latrie, v. 2, pp. 213f.
62. *Travels and Adventures* . . . , pp. 64f, 103, 105; Cobham, pp. 31ff.
63. Cobham, p. 35; *l'Itinerario di* . . . , pp. 178f.
64. Cobham, p. 45; Stuttgart, v. 3, p. 236.
65. Mogabgab, v. 1, p. 35; Stuttgart, v. 168, p. 51.
66. *Reise in das gelobte Land*. Augburg, 1486. (no pagination). So did N. le Huen (1487). Cobham, p. 51.
67. Mogabgab, v. 3, p. 134.
68. *Canon Pietro Casola's* . . . , p. 215; Mogabgab, v. 1, p. 41.
69. Cobham, p. 71; Hakluyt, v. 5, p. 96. Cyprus is somewhat liable to plagues and blights, according to another pilgrim, Jodicus de Meggen. Mogabgab, v. 3. p. 152.
70. *The History of the War of Cyprus*. tr. Robert Midgley. London, 1697. p. 5.
71. Cobham, p. 171.
72. *Beschrijvinge van een Zee* . . . , p. 11.
73. Cobham, p. 201; Antverbiae, p. 113.
74. Cobham, pp. 216f.
75. *Voiage de Levant* . . . , pp. 326f.
76. *Reizen* . . . , p. 378.
77. *Adventures and Sufferings* . . . , p. 173.
78. *Itinerarium Hierosolymitanum*, p. 109f. Cobham, pp. 197f; Cotovicus surely did not want to overestiamte the number of Muslims on the island.
79. Cobham, p. 350. On the population of Ottoman Cyprus, see H. Inalcik, "Kıbrıs'ta Türk Idaresi altında Nüfus," pp. 27–58; Hill, v. 4, pp. 17ff, 31ff, 42, 46; T. Papadopoullos, *Social and Historical Data* . . . , *passim*. The

Venetian nobleman Ambrosio Bembo, who visited Cyprus for 16 days in 1671, says, "The kingdom is almost entirely destroyed and with few inhabitants. The majority of these are Greeks, about twenty-thousand, while the Turks are about six-thousand." That is consistent with the earlier findings. Michael D. Willis, "A New Document of Cypriote History. The Journal of Ambrosio Bembo," *Anatgiosis ek ton Kiriakon Spogdon* 1978.35–46, esp. p. 38.

SEVEN

Forced Population Transfers and the Banishment of Undesirables

Forced population transfers were an important part of Ottoman social and economic policy, particularly from the time of Mehmed the Conqueror. Much of the Muslim Turkish population of Rumeli resulted from the compulsory transferal of thousands of nomadic Yuruk families from western Anatolia, a policy which long antedated Mehmed. The early growth of Istanbul was spurred by policies requiring widespread migrations of families, especially from central Anatolia and the Black Sea littoral. Losses of population through willing and unwilling migration of Orthodox Christians from Trabzon to Istanbul, as well as the disproportion of Christians over Muslims in that city, influenced the Ottoman government to move its Muslim families from the districts of Tokat, Amasya, Çorum, and Boz OK in the area between the bend in the Kizilirmak river and the Black Sea mountain range.[1]

The policy of banishment to Cyprus, then, was just another aspect of such population policies. The low population of the island had so concerned Venice that substantial energy had been devoted to encouraging immigration there. Sometimes the Ottomans had grandiose dreams of making Magosa (Famagusta) and Lefkoşa (Nicosia) as brilliantly wealthy as they had been in the 14th century; they envisioned a province which included not just the island but also the adjacent littoral of southern Anatolia to the north as well as Tripoli to the east. They imagined Muslim townspeople, villagers, and nomads from Anatolia as settlers, and even Jews from Safed.

The policies of forced population transfers to Istanbul and to Rumeli were brilliantly successful. Instanbul quickly became splendidly wealthy, not a little because of the skills and diversity of the immigrants; the final proof, of course, is the rapid growth of that city. Rumeli gained a substantial nomadic and agricultural Turkish Muslim population which not only formed the nucleus of large "colonies" of immigrants whose interests usually lay closer to those of the ruling class than to the Christian subjects, but also fulfilled the more basic requisite of repopulating empty countryside. Perhaps to some extent the Straits barred the return of the dissatisfied, but then Cyprus inexplicably failed to hold so many of those banished there even though its closest ports were about 100 kilometers from the closest Anatolian ports. Rumeli provided ample grazing land and arable fields for those banished there, while residence in the new capital entitled one to a privileged tax status with unparalleled economic opportunities. Cyprus has a much hotter climate than the home lands of virtually all the migrants; pasture land is scarce and dry farming is difficult. Perhaps the agricultural land available there was not as attractive as that in Anatolia, where most of the migrants came from. Of course, if Anatolia was overpopulated, for most migrants the move should have been a blessing. Perhaps the migrants were not treated as well as in Istanbul and Rumeli, but the documents do not indicate that, and anyway the whole project was organized and overseen by the same central government that had succeeded in Istanbul, Rumeli and Trabzon. Perhaps if a large proportion of those moved to Cyprus were poor, unskilled, or even criminals, they may have made life unpleasant for more desirable immigrants and families.

One wonders how widespread was Cyprus' reputation in recent centuries of being an unhealthy place, an obstacle that neither Rumeli nor Istanbul had to face in the 15th or 16th centuries. Whatever the reasons, the Ottoman policy of compulsory population transfers to Cyprus was at best moderately successful. Undoubtedly a number of the immigrants from Anatolia did remain in Cyprus with their families, where they were settled in towns and villages throughout the island. As always, a lot more imperial attention needed to be given to those who resisted than to those who obeyed. What proportion of the immigrants were satisfied is a mystery. Of course, some had come voluntarily to start with. The one Cyprus census came too early to provide any evidence of their actual places of settlement on the island. Indeed, evidence concerning their residence is almost totally lacking.[2]

Latin emigration from Cyprus was not infrequent in the decades before the Ottoman conquest in 1571, but it reached its greatest intensity in the decade after the Ottoman conquest. Some Greek Orthodox also emigrated to Venice and elsewhere, particularly intellectuals, although in general they applauded the overthrow of the Venetians.[3] If the numbers were never too great, the mercantile and intellectual skills lost may have been serious.

Conversely, certain Cypriots in Venice petitioned the Ottoman government for permission to return to their homes, and not only were granted permission but also promised help in expediting their move.[4]

The problem of the underpopulation of Cyprus in the Venetian period has been well documented by Sir George Hill, who was sensitive to the importance of population. Special efforts aimed to encourage disenfranchised Latins all over the Levant, in the face of Ottoman advances, to take up residence on the island. The Venetian government contemplated means of attracting settlers there from its own territories and certain other parts of Italy. Some combination of disease (both plague and malaria), locusts, periodic earthquakes, widespread piracy, and an exploitative colonial economic system caused the problem. Cyprus did benefit from the virtually Mediterranean-wide population growth of the first three-quarters of the 16th century, but not enough. The Ottoman conquest cost many lives.

The best evidence of Ottoman concern about building up the population of Cyprus (presumably to make it flourish, for I consider a lower priority the idea that the Ottomans wanted to change the religious and ethnic balance) lies in the voluminous imperial correspondence emanating from the Porte, first to begin the necessary preparations and then to ensure that the orders were carried out fairly. When the Porte initiated the policy of banishing criminals to Cyprus, then of course the amount of correspondence had to be even greater for it can take as much paperwork to banish one person as a hundred. Suffice it to say that the transfer of people to Cyprus was a very important aspect of Ottoman internal policy in the period between 1570 and 1590.

The first Ottoman Muslim to establish themselves in Cyprus undoubtedly were soldiers. After the conquest, 1000 janissaries and a very small force of 2779 connoneers and various unmarried volunteers were left to garrison the island's five castles. Perhaps some already had wives at that time, and undoubtedly others took Christian Cypriot women as wives or concubines, although again we do not know in what numbers. Furthermore, the district of Canik was required to provide Muslim Turkish brides for some unmarried Ottoman soldiers. Unfortunately, only the orders to local authorities in Canik survive. No evidence is provided of why Canik was chosen, or how local people reacted, or how many if any brides were provided.

In June 1571 (late in Muharrem of 979) three orders on this subject were sent to Canik district-governor Memiş begi regarding providing unmarried Muslim women for unmarried victorious Ottoman soldiers resident in Cyprus. Memiş begi was reminded that at an earlier time unmarried girls *(bakire kizi)* from his territories had been requested for the janissaries *(kul taifesi)* in Cyprus: The Porte orders *(emr)* young girls *(kizlarinuz)*, however many are unmarried, for the janissaries *(kul taifesi)* in Cyprus. It seems that some kadis were hurrying to marry these unmarried women to poor men *(fukara)* (probably in order to protect the local women from banishment) with the consequence that the women received only very small dowries *(nikah akcesi, ʿakar)*. Everywhere deputy kadis *(naibler)* were required to register their names in detailed registers. The Porte was quite alarmed that kadis would usurp their dowries.

Doubtless, transporting numbers of unmarried girls to Cyprus safely was a matter of grave concern. Memiş begi was also put in charge of girls banished from Surkut (?) and Huseyn Abad kazas in Zul-Kadriye province. He was instructed to take them into custody, register them, imprison them, and send them to Cyprus for their dowry. He was further instructed to make certain that none of the girls disappeared *(gaybet)* on the way. They were to be sent in the custody of reliable people (p. 12; selh Muharrem 979. p. 13, selh Muh. 979. p. 13, 25 Muh. 979).[5]

The Porte consistently took the position that no members of the military class banished to Cyprus should get military salaries again, and that no banished reʿaya should be admitted to the military class. The frequency with which those commands had to be issued suggests, however, that local pressures to admit such people were often intense. Some reʿaya must have gotten mixed in with the army of conquest, at least with the irregular forces. Members of the military class who were banished usually were only temporarily out of favor and often expected to have regular salaries soon (just as virtually all dismissed kadis or spahis did). When the names of such people were discovered registered, they were to be removed immediately (118/58 (12); 8 Şaban 985. 123/88

(43); undated. 140/57 (8); 22 (?) (98?)5. 160/88 (61); 986?. 160/88 (64); 7 Sefer (98?) 5. 161/71 (13); 8 Şaban 985. 7 Sefer (98?) 5. 20 Muharrem 986).

A fundamental aspect of the process of settlement in Cyprus was that every Ottoman re'aya was fully entitled to go there to receive free land. Banishment was not punitive. Indeed it was the duty of local officials to encourage emigration. Not surprisingly, however, local officials and military, whose income was more or less dependent on the number of economically active people in their vicinity, sometimes strongly discouraged emigration of re'aya. Nevertheless, it was the firm policy of the Porte that any interference with emigration constituted a serious offense.

Order to district governors *(sancak begleri)* and kadis in Anatoli and Karaman provinces. Present Cyprus governor emir ul-umera Ca'fer sent a letter and made known that when some people *(ba'z kimesne)* in your spheres of rule *(taht-i hukumetunde)* wanted to rise up of their own free will *(rizasile kalkub)* and pass to Cyprus, some spahis and others prevented *(mani')* them saying, 'You are not banished' *(surgun degilsin)*. Now the prohibition *(men'yok)* against their passing of their own will to the island of Cyprus is wrong. I order that you should not let any spahi or other person interfere *(dahl ve te'arruz)* with anyone who of his own will wants to pass to that island from your spheres of rule. You should write the names of any who interfere *(mani')*, contrary to my order, and make them known. If a spahi does that, let his timar be taken; if other people do, let them be punished. (p. 11; 24 (?) 983)

Although the general orders regarding the banishment of people to Cyprus are addressed to provincial governors and district administrators, in fact the actual administration was primarily the duty of local kadis, who either supervised or even personally directed the actual implementation of those orders. Former Antaliya and Kizil Kaya kadis supervised *(mubaşiret)* in accordance with the orders which arrived for banishing re'aya to Cyprus (138/88 (2); 9 Zil-Kade 981). The Ic Il district governor was ordered to inquire about the reputations *(ahval)* of certain evildoers from the local *(toprak)* kadis (p. 2; selh Zil-Hicce ?)). The Palu kadi reported the details of banishing re'aya from certain villages in his district which, although in Karaman province somehow were administratively dependent on Hudavendigar district (p. 11; 16 Zil-Hicce 981). Those same local kadis *(toprak kadileri)* oversaw the sale at fair market prices of the movable and immovable property of banished re'aya (138/88 *(6);* 10 Cumadi II 983). When some people in Egridur and Antaliya districts extorted bribes from other people who did not want to be banished but then banished them anyway, the local kadis had to investigate to prevent recurrence of that abuse (145/60; 9 Zil-Kade 981. p. 11; 9 Zil-Kade 981).

As the documents indicate, local kadis supervised, and in some cases actually directed, the process of banishment from the province to the port of embarkation for Cyprus. The kadi possessed record books which listed the names of all the adult males in the province, town by town, village by village, nomad pasture by nomad pasture. Each kadi was responsible, then, to ensure that one-tenth of all those registered should be notified of their impending banishment. In the case of Cyprus, the banished were to include a cross section of the whole community; certainly from among the heads of urban quarters, villages, and tribes, as well as other local notables, he could collect that information rather easily.

Although the poor and landless might be expected to volunteer for banishment, probably few other people would. It is well known that many people in Turkey today feel very close ties to their native districts *(memleket)*, often leaving there only with great reluctance; even the economically most active segments of the society, who may live for decades away from those districts, usually try to make periodic visits there and continue to consider themselves as being "from" that place. Presumably residents of Anatolia in the 16the century felt the same sort of ties to their native districts. Banishment meant leaving relatives, neighbors, and community, as well as unique local commercial or agricultural conditions, and going to an entirely new place where one's economic skills might no longer be sufficient. Small wonder how strong the resentment and bitterness felt by those who were banished. No wonder so many resisted, or later escaped to return home.

Lists of those banished were compiled in triplicate by the local kadis, who forwarded one copy to the Porte, and sent the other copy to the governor of Cyprus *(begler begi)*, whose agents met the banished at the port of Silifke, signed documents that the individuals had entered their charge, and then placed them on boats for Cyprus, where they would again be registered and assigned new homes. Those who accepted banishment, as well as those who volunteered for it, made their way at their own pace, with their families and movable property, to Silifke. They did not need supervision, although sometimes they needed protection from brigands.

The kadi's job was not done even after people from his district reached Cyprus. He had to retain copies of the list of banished people to ensure that none of them returned illegally. Should they do so, they would have to be sent with police supervision to Silifke, involving more paper work, as would those who refused to go on their own.

By 24 September 1572 (13 Cumadi I 980), 15 months after the policy of settling only first class re'aya on the island of Cyprus had been initiated, that policy was changed to make possible the inclusion of less desirable elements of Anatolian society. Apparently the failure of the policy of population transfers as originally conceived, because re'aya did not want it and because Ottoman officials did not support it, had necessitated lowering the minimal threshold of acceptability.[6] The order is addressed to the kadis of all but easternmost Anatolia (Anadolu, Karaman, Rum, and Zulkadriye) regarding a letter the Porte had received from Sinan, the second governor *(begler begi)* of Cyprus. Sinan informed the Porte that many regions of the island were suitable for cultivation but had been devastated during the conquest. Vineyards, gardens, and sugar cane flourished there; grains grew so profusely that a single measure of seed produced 50 or 60 measures of grain. Therefore, Cyprus could quickly regain its former prosperity if people occupied the towns and villages.[7]

Sinan further added that Cyprus enjoyed a most moderate climate and that security was guaranteed by the presence of a suitable number of soldiers garrisoned in the fortresses. No one needed fear; complete security was established. Consequently, it became necessary for new settlers to colonize Cyprus and to restore its prosperity.

The Porte ordered, therefore, that one household of 10 from all the villages and all the towns in those provinces should be deported to Cyprus, with an adequate escort, before winter. Moreover, the migrants were to be excused for two years from the tithe and all other taxes. They were to bring their tools, beasts of burden, and farming implements.

They will be chosen from among the people. Those who have unfertile lands and rocky soil will be selected first. Next will be brigands and other evildoers, those whose names are not listed on the most recent provincial census (and their sons), recent emigrants from other places, and subjects who do not own their own farm land but rent. That also includes those who for a long time have claimed full ownership of pastures, vineyards, gardens, or plains and whose litigation has not yet been settled; villagers who, after having abandoned their villages, have established themselves in cities and towns; and those unemployed in towns, villages, and cities who live as vagrants. Finally some craftsmen and artisans were required: shoemakers *(papuççu)*, makers of coarse shoes *(başmakçi)*, tailors *(derzi)*, hatmakers *(takyeci)*, weavers *(kembaci)*, spinners of goat hair *(mutaf)*, wool-carders *(hallaç)*, silk manufacturers *(kazaz)*, cooks *(aşçi)*, cooks of sheep's heads *(başçi)*, candlemakers *(mumcu)*, packsaddle makers *(semerci)*, blacksmiths *(nalbant)*, grocers *(bakkal)*, tanners *(debbag)*, blacksmiths *(demirci)*, carpenters *(dulger)*, stonemasons *(taşçi)*, goldsmiths or silversmiths *(kuyumcu)*, coppersmiths *(kazanci)*, etc.

You must requisition one hearth in 10, particularly villagers known for their crimes and malevolence, those who are not registered in the cadastral registers and who have neither households nor position but take land by lease; usurers; villagers who at court contest among themselves the ownership of land. People who meet those conditions and who possess land or other movable property should have it sold to the highest bidder at a price equal to cost price. You shall give them the proceeds of the sale and then send them, with only the briefest delay, to Silifke, where they will embark for Cyprus.

You must also secure one in 10 of the aforementioned artisans and laborers; they must be vigorous and capable of working. You should direct them, too, to Cyprus via Silifke. You must be sure that none of the artisans or villagers stay back in their towns and villages. You must take measures to ensure that all the land and immovable property of the emigrants is sold at a very just price, without causing loss or damage. You must record in a register whether the emigrants are cultivators or artisans, as well as their names, descriptions, and the names of their villages or places of origin. You must also calculate the total number of beasts of burden of the cultivators and tools of the artisans. You must make a register with three copies, one for my Porte, one for the governor of Cyprus, and one to remain at your courts. Those whose names are on this list who do not go voluntarily will be found and deported.

The overseers *(mubaşir)* assigned should take special care to ensure that all that is done properly; they should not threaten to deport to Cyprus anyone who does not give them presents of money. The overseers must give the kadis certificates attesting that they have not accepted money from anyone. When the registers are being drawn up, they must include the names of all the towns or villages of origin of those deemed fit for emigration, and also the names and descriptions of their guarantors (kefil). You should be vigilant. You should take every precaution to ensure that no unnecessary constraints are exercised on those wealthy who need not be transfered to Cyprus.

You should encourage emigration and make known that according to my orders two years' exemption from taxes will be granted those who settle in Cyprus. If anyone registered in the register who is directed towards Cyprus with his livestock escapes to a strange country, contrary to my sacred orders, he shall be executed there where he is discovered.

You who are kadis of my provinces, if one of the emigrants comes to find refuge in your district, imprison him immediately and make that known to my Porte so that justice may quickly be done. Send to Silifke immediately those designated to be deported in a way that they are immediately able to pass to the other shore where the governor of Cyprus will settle them in the places that he judges most favorable. A copy of the register should go to the governor of Cyprus, and a copy of the discharge should be sent to my Porte.

You should carry out my noble orders with great diligence. If anyone wishes to hinder the departure of those assigned to be deported, if others are deported in their places, contrary to my orders, and those complaints reach my Porte, I will punish them in an exemplary fashion. You should put a stop to all intervention on their part; if they persist in their evil designs you should send their names and ranks to me.[8]

In organizing population transfers the Porte seems to have been caught between a desire to ensure high quality emigrants and a competing desire to give preference to the poor and weak. The latter impulse was humanitarian, the former reflected the intensity of imperial desires to build a flourishing Cyprus. Initially the Porte required emigrants who were highly capable, but soon compromises were required. Chronic litigants, usurers, newcomers to districts, and people who had avoided being registered in the tax rolls became eligible, and soon even criminals. If migration to Cyprus had been at all an attractive prospect, so many compromises on moral standards would not have been needed.[9]

One of the most attractive incentives held out to immigrants was the period of tax exemption. (Presumably that exemption would not have included the cizye, or head tax, of non-Muslims, but then few if any non-Muslims do appear among the banished.) Initially the Porte promised tax exemption for three years, but subsequently, and undoubtedly retroactively, that period was reduced to two years. Why the change occurred is not indicated, but the counsel of those who wanted to build Cyprus into a prosperous and populous region was preempted by short sighted officials wanting quick profits.

The earliest orders to the governor of Cyprus, to the Nigde district governor, and to the kadis of Konya, Larende, Kaysariye, and Nigde, mandate that every immigrant to Cyprus should be exempt from all traditional and extraordinary taxes *(hukuk, rusum,* and *tekalif)* for three years (141/57 (last page); undated. p. 15, undated). Then an order to the governor and defterdar of Cyprus dated 11 July 1575 (2 Rebiᶜ II 983) informed them that taxes *(hukuk ve rusumlari)* should not be taken for two years from all those who practice agriculture *(zira'at ve hiraset);* people were exempt *(mu'af)* for two years, but after that those taxes were to be collected in accordance with the Sharia, kanun, and the record books *(defter)* (116/66 (8); 2 Rebi' II 983).

The three Ottoman historians who have done pioneering work on the economic history of the empire in the 16th century, Barkan, Inalcik, and Akdağ, all agree, at least loosely, with Braudel's assessment about population growth and overpopulation in the Ottoman empire. Each presumes overpopulation in Anatolia, reaching a dangerous stage in the second half of the 16th century when lawlessness and brigandage (and immorality, for Akdağ) swept the countryside, leaving villagers increasingly unable to support themselves. Overcrowded cultivators occupied marginal and even poor lands, and many migrated to cities where they formed a restless, unemployed class. (Personally, I think that Anatolia, like Cyprus, was generally underpopulated and could have benefited from continued population growth at that time.)

Barkan and Inalcik hold that population transfers to Cyprus were designed to help alleviate the land shortage in Anatolia. If that were so, one might expect people lining up waiting at Silifke to go to Cyprus. Of course, not all the landless and poor would have been so economically motivated, but surely free transportation, free land, and two or three year's exemption from taxes would have provided a strong incentive to thousands of landless, hungry people, if they really were there. Likewise, if the Anatolian countryside was overpopulated, local officials and timar holders would have encouraged the superfluous to leave, but those in charge of the population transfers complained that they got no help and indeed protested that officials and timar holders protected and sheltered locals whom they did not want to go. Meanwhile, throughout the whole period the population of Cyprus remained dismally low.

To what extent the orders of banishment could be carried out is a serious question which unfortunately cannot be answered satisfactorily. Barkan knew all the details, but the materials are too fragmentary for him or anyone else to suggest what proportion of the banished are mentioned in the records; since the Porte changed orders several times, sometimes mentioning other places like Haleb (Aleppo), we are left confused about imperial goals. That, however, is not completely inappropriate, for the Porte had no consistent goals. 10% of the population

of Aleppo would have been a large number, but since Konya and Kayseri, the other large cities in the area from which people were banished,
were exempt, perhaps only Aleppo province was intended.

A register of 1572 lists 1689 families ready for transferal to Cyprus
from the following districts: Aksaray, 225; Beyşehir, 262; Seydişehir,
202; Endugi, 145; Develihisar, 197; Urgup, 64; Koçhisar, 88; Nigde,
172; Bor, 69; Ilgin, 48; Ishakli, 87; Akşehir, 130.[10] At least by 1574,
however, some people were so desperate to escape deportation that they
would pay 100 altin for a substitute.[11]

Eight adult males were banished from the small town of Beg şehri in
Karaman province. Of that number, half volunteered. Each, a Muslim,
had to produce two guarantors (kefil) who pledged that if the banished
one did not leave, they would go in his place (52/39; undated).

Among nomadic tribes men banished to Cyprus were At çeken and
other Yuruks from Karaman, Ak şehir, and Koç Hisar areas of Karaman
province, but most especially from the district of Ic Il along the Mediterranean littoral who were transferred to the province of Cyprus.[12]

An order of 6 May 1572 to the governor, kadi, and defterdar of
Cyprus urges that no harm should be done to the re ʿaya of the newly
conquered island, that they should be treated with justice, in accordance
with the Sharia, so that the island may "revert to its former prosperous
state. . . . Those responsible for scattering the re ʿaya through oppressing
them and imposing too heavy taxes on them, shall be chastized."[13] On
19 Cumadi II 979 (9 October 1571) an order was sent to the new
governor Sinan Paşa to order a tax survey (tahrir). That would form the
basis for provincial organization and taxation. (The required taxes would
be based on an average of the revenue of the past three years.)

Barkan has estimated that 30% of those banished had volunteered or
cooperated voluntarily. That made the use of force very necessary.[14]
Barkan has also estimated that 7% of the heads of families (hane)
banished to Cyprus were criminals of one kind or another.[15]

A neglected factor in analyzing the data is mortality. If many of the
banished died in Cyprus, particularly without leaving record, Ottoman
registers would have been seriously thrown off. Officials would then
tend to underestimate the numbers actually banished. Of course, deaths
of re ʿaya were supposed to be registered. In any case, in 1575 the
Venetian B. Sagredo reported that the Ottomans were always sending

new families to live in Cyprus because most of them died in the great heat.[16]

Two questions arise in regard to possible connections of Jews with Cyprus. One involves the role of Joseph Nasi in the conquest of the island and its possible use as a place of settlement for Marrano Jews. The other concerns population transfers of Jews from Safed to Cyprus after the Ottoman conquest.

Nasi's life is surrounded by a mass of myths. In a recent study P. Grunebaum-Ballin has rather deftly shown that the supposed great influence of Nasi over Selim II is largely fanciful, that there is no evidence that the two ever discussed matters of state policy, and that there is no evidence that Nasi had more interest in Cyprus than anywhere else in the empire.[17] Although Jews in the Latin Christian parts of the Mediterranean world may have acutely needed a refuge, and although many places in the empire were used to meet that need, it was against Ottoman policy to concentrate immigrants so as to make a decisive demographic impact on a single place, and even more important, high-ranking Ottomans simply never conceived of Cyprus as a Jewish refuge.

The Ottoman government issued orders for the transferal of 1000 Jewish families from Safed in 1576 and 1577, soon after the conquest of Cyprus. Preceding that, however, was an order of August 1573 responding to a petition by members of the Jewish community in Safed about "several Jewish thieves and scoundrels" who commit "corrupt deeds . . . and are receivers of stolen goods." The Porte replied: ". . . send these men who are not upright and law-abiding, but rather receivers of stolen goods, thieves and scoundrels whose corrupt deeds have been discovered, immoral and villainous, guarded by appropriate men, together with a copy of the register concerning them, to Cyprus."[18] Then in October 1576 an order was issued for the expulsion of "1000 wealthy Jews, together with their families and possessions, from Safed and its environs to Famagusta, in Cyprus . . ." In August 1577 orders were issued for the expulsion of another 500 families, to be settled on the same island. However, the following year, before either group had actually been sent, the Jews of Safed got those orders "canceled" because of possible economic effects on the district. "If it is decided to deport them to Cyprus, the Public Revenue will lose the above mentioned amount of money and the town of Safed will be on the verge of ruin."[19]

The Porte decided not to deport them at that time. In 1579 100 Jewish families entered Magosa on their way from Salonika to Safed and were detained to be settled there, to which the Porte at least initially consented.[20]

The logic for transferring Jewish settlers to Cyprus from Safed was consistent with the current Ottoman scheme. Safed is contiguous to the Mediterranean like Tirablus and Aleppo. Cyprus had first been conceived as a grand province including other points on the mainland to the east and north. The Safed region itself, however, was also short of population. More important, high-ranking officials in Damascus and Aleppo who profited from its prosperity doubtless brought to bear in Istanbul all the influence that they could muster to preserve the status quo.

Although Jewish settlers from Safed province were part of the original plan for settlement, none actually reached Cyprus. The notion that making Cyprus into a Jewish colony was ever seriously considered by the Porte seems extremely unlikely. Equally unlikely is the idea of Kyrris and Papadopoullos that Greek Orthodox and Armenian Gregorian Christians from Anatolia were the primary target of the official orders for banishment from Anatolia. To some extent the confusion rises from unfamiliarity with the old use of re ʿaya to include all the taxpaying populace, Muslim and Christian. In any case, wherever the names of banished individuals are given, Christians (zimmis) are conspicuously lacking. Why the Ottomans chose to banish so few Christians is unknown, for at earlier times thousands had been transfered to Istanbul.

Another part of the misunderstanding comes from the notion of Kyrris and Papadopoullos that banishment was punitive, and so more likely to be imposed on Christian subjects. In fact, the banishment (surgun) first imposed on Ottoman Cyprus had absolutely no implications of moral impropriety. Perhaps if choosing between two possible surgun, a kadi might permit the morally better one to stay in his local community. However, surgun by itself had absolutely no moral implications. If an order said "evildoers," then "evildoers" could be sent; if an order just said "people," then absolutely no moral connotations were involved. Indeed, the original orders for banishment to Cyprus, as to Rumeli, to Trabzon, and to Istanbul, presumed that the banished would move to better circumstances than they had at that time.

Although some evidence exists of banishing non-Muslims to Cyprus, such banishment was virtually unknown. Zimmi Nikilo of (?) kaza was banished to Cyprus for acting contrary to the Sharia; Nikilo was to be transfered there via the Rhodes district governor (162/60 (1); undated. Another zimmi was banished to Rhodes. 120/55 (8); 15 Sefer 987). The Cyprus kadi sent an inquiry to the Porte regarding the status of a zimmi named Nikola (?) of that kaza who was banished to Cyprus by an imperial order *(emr-i şerif)*. The court ultimately had to determine his status (p. 13; 19 Sefer 990). "Some offences *(ba 'z kabahati)* appeared in zimmi Nikofor, who was seeking the patriarchate *(patriklik)*; then he was ordered released, and now a second order has been sent out to that effect" (160/89 (41); 13 Sefer 994). In any case, no record books *(defter)* detail their settlement into particular villages on Cyprus, or even collectively as residents of Cyprus villages.[21]

Keeping the banished in Cyprus once they got there was a deep Ottoman concern. Reluctant emigrants showed remarkable vigor in finding means of escape. Some used force, others bribery. Even 100 kilometers of Mediterranean did not make a very effective barrier.

Orders were sent to the governors of Cyprus and Karaman concerning a letter form the former complaining that some of those banished *(surgun taifesinden)* had seized piers *(iskeleler)* and escaped back to the other side *(beru yaka)* in ships. The Porte ordered that such boats, along with their owners, should be seized (116/66 (10); 21 Cumadi I 983). High-ranking officers of the 'Ala' iye district governors were to be sent to Cyprus to prevent such flights (138/88 (12); 13 Muharrem 983). The Ic Il district governor was under strict orders to return to Cyprus everyone who escaped from there (146/40 (2); selh Zil-Hicce 983 (?). p. 2; selh Zil-Hicce (?)).

The Porte regularly exhorted the governor of Cyprus to prevent escape: It must not be possible *(mumkun)* for anyone to go to the other side *(ote yaka)* without permission *(icazetsuz)* . . . If anyone flees *(firar)*, it is from your carelessness in defense *(muhafazada)* (164/75 (23); 29 Şevval 986 (?)). The governor was warned repeatedly that it was not permissible for anyone who was banished to Cyprus to pass back to Anatolia *(beru yaka)*, contrary to that order; harbor agents *(iskele eminleri)* had to be forced to act firmly and carefully (124/65 (7); 24 Muharrem 985). All of the banished, according to one account, were fleeing to their homelands *(vatanlarina)* by ships *(gemiler)* which came close to the shore everywhere; again the governor was exorted to take every precaution and to be sure to register in full everyone who reached Cyprus (161/71 (16); 8 Şevval 988) Cf. 161/71 (20); 25 Zil-Hicce 981 (?)).

Order to Cyprus begler begi. You sent a letter that some of those who are banished to Cyprus maintain connections (*alakalari*) with their native regions (*vatan-i asillar*). They have property (*mulk*) which they did not sell. Some even live in those cities, although they are not supposed to go there for any reasons other than trade. They went to the mainland (*ote yaka*) for trade in many ships (*gemi*), putting up guarantors (*kefiller*) for their return. I order that you should make permanently settled (*temekkun*) in castles (*kal 'elerde*) those who want to make trade (*ticaret*) like that. You should not give permission to anyone who was banished to pass back to the mainland (*beru yaka*). (138/88 (10); 10 Muharrem 981–12 May 1573)

An order to the governor of Cyprus presents the magnitude of the problem: Since the conquest of Cyprus (Kibris *fetih*), there have been 12,000 families (*hane*) banished (*surgun*). You made a petition (*'arz*) saying that there are now 800 adult males (*nefer*) registered in the new register (*defter-i cedid*), and at present only half of them remain in Cyprus. Of course, the Porte gave the strongest orders to record the names and villages of all those who had been banished, as well as those who have already escaped and are missing (*gaybda idenler*), and to send them to the Porte (163/70 (17); undated).[22]

Sometimes the banished protested to the Porte that the services which they performed in their native districts were so important or useful that they should not be banished. Re 'aya from 'Ayntab district, for example, complained (*şikayet*) to the Porte that they are useful (*yarar*) and protect the district (*hifz ve hiraset*) (124/65 (1); 18 Muharrem 985). They also struck the court summoner (*muhzir*) with a sword and injured him when he tried to induce them to come to court. Another time five men were exempt from being banished to Cyprus when they became lieutenants (*kethuda*) of the governor of Yemen province (25 Cumadi II (?) 988). Objections to orders for banishment were handled just the same as all other personal appeals for justice and imperial intervention.

Many people in the districts of Egridur and Antaliye apparently were willing to pay substantial sums of money to escape banishment (145/60 (?); 9 Zil-Kade 981). The Nigde district governor and the kadis of Konya, Larende, Kayseriye, and Nigde complained to the Porte that local people did not wish (*murad*) by their own choice (*ihtiyar ile*) to live on the island of Cyprus. The Porte exhorted them to compel to migrate those who had not yet settled in and to remind the banished of its advantages (p. 17; undated). Cyprus governors continually had to send letters to the Porte to request imperial help. Local people had not wished to go to Cyprus from Konya, Larende, Nigde, and Kaysariye districts (141/57 (last page); undated). The Porte complained that some of those people banished to Cyprus had kept connections *('alakalari)* with their native regions *(vatn-i asillar)*. Some held property *(mulk)* which they did not sell. Some actually lived again in their native cities, although they were legally forbidden to go back there for any reasons other than trade (138/89 (10); 10 Muharrem 981).

Resistance to banishment was considerable at every stage. Those banished complained and prevaricated, and some simply refused to go. They fled their homes, or they failed to appear at the ports of embarkation. Sometimes the officials who supervised the migrations discovered that people whose names were registered on the official lists never appeared at the ports of embarkation; sometimes hardly anyone from a certain district appeared. Other people disappeared after reporting to the local supervisers at the ports of embarkation, either at sea or before the transport vessels ever left port. Still others escaped after reaching Cyprus, presumably by buying transportation back to the mainland legally or even illegally from sailors. Although harbor officials in Cyprus had strict instructions not to let anyone without special authorization leave the island, forged documents, bribery, or good luck permitted numerous unhappy migrants to return to the mainland; unscrupulous seamen also contributed to the problem. Some who escaped from Cyprus were apprehended in transit by harbor officials on the mainland, although probably that was a small proportion of those who fled the island.

The banished probably behaved so boldly because penalties for refusal to comply were nonexistent. The security of their persons, families, and property were guaranteed. The penalty for refusing to comply at any stage of the banishment merely meant subjection to the process again. A man who fled his town or village to escape banishment to Cyprus, if apprehended, was subjected to the same conditions of banishment as those who had complied immediately. A man who escaped from Cyprus and returned to his home, if apprehended, was simply banished to Cyprus like everyone else. No corporal punishment was administered, nor criminal charges brought, nor even fines levied. Compulsory population transfers of innocent individuals violates the Sharia; Ottoman officials charged with handling the process were exhorted to all possible delicacy and gentleness. Officials were warned to protect the banished, their families, and their property at every stage of the process, from beginning to end; those who failed in that charge faced corporal punishment, or even dismissal from office. Generally speaking, then, recalcitrant migrants had little to lose if they tried to escape banishment.

What proportion of the migrants resisted is no better known than the number of migrants.

The Ottoman purpose in banishing so many undesirables to Cyprus is unfathomable, even remembering its low population. Of course, as a large island fairly remote from the mainland and quite remote from other islands, the Ottoman government may have considered Cyprus a safe, secure place to send criminals. Walled fortresses like Magosa or Girniye could hold even the most dangerous convicted criminals, but very few were confined there. Doubtless most simply settled into villages and towns; nevertheless, they were forcibly separated from friends, allies, or relatives around their homes.

Although a few of the convicts may have been petty criminals, most were not. Their arrival must have scandalized Cypriot society, for merely forcibly transfering them to Cyprus was not likely to reform them. Probably most continued the same illegal or unsavory activities in Cyprus. That threat must have reduced the attractiveness of the island to more desirable immigrants, whether they came voluntarily or not, and must have dissuaded many potential immigrants from moving there.

The documents provide no information about where the criminals settled, whether or not they came with families, or how long they remained there. The settlement of convicted criminals in Cyprus was antithetical to the ideals expressed about restoring prosperity and implementing justice there.

Members of the religious class in Maraş and Mimariye (?) accused Kalender of oppression and illicit acts *(zulm ve te 'addi)*, conviction of which could lead to his banishment to Cyprus if 15 years had not passed. (117/30 (10); 8 Sefer 985)

Sefer bn Seydi 'Ali, Yusuf bn Ilyas, and Sefer bn 'Osman were ordered banished because they were brigands and evildoers *(ehl-i fesad ve haramzade)*. (120/55 (6); 15 Sefer (?) 987)

Brigands *(eşkiya)* in Hamid district *(sancagi)* were banished after attacking Muslims. (124/65 (17); 996)

In Elmalu, Ramazan, who was not good *(kendu halinde)*, committed oppression *(rencide)*. (137/69 (21); undated)

Evildoers *(ehl-i fesad)* in Atana raped the wives of two spahis, killing one and kidnapping the other; they were to be banished to Cyprus. (137/69 (42); undated)

Çakir did evil in Menteşe and also owed the Saru Han district governor 50,000 akce; he was banished with his family *(ehl ve ʿayal)*. (138/88 (5); 19 Şevval 983)

Another evildoer *(ehl-i fesad)* was banished from Rhodes to Cyprus. (158/99 (4); 29 Rebi ʿII 995)

Haci Seydi of Mud did evil and performed acts of brigandage *(şirret, şaka);* he is dishonest *(tecvir, teblis)* also, and may be banished if convicted. (160/89 (33); III Cumadi II 996)

Men called Şah Kuli ogullari, ʿAla ed-din, Gazi, Ebu Bekr, Suhrab, and Seyfeddin, fought *(kavga ve cenkleri)* with the men of Hakari district-governor Zeyneb and so are banished to Cyprus. (160/89 (57); 5 Receb 985)

Melaş ʿarablari who did evil *(fesad)* in Konya, Larende, and Nigde were ordered banished to Cyprus with their families and all their property. (164/75 (10); 26 Cumadi II 980 (?))

Delvine Ahmed of Mud was banished for wickedness and rebellion *(şirret ve şekavet)*. (164/75 (16); 29 Sefer?)

According to the Ic Il begi most of the people banished locally were evil *(telhis, eşer)* (p. 2; selh Zil-Hicce (?)). In Selanik certain people who extorted money and oppressed *(zulm ve teʿaddi)* the reʿaya were banished (p. 4; 1 Şevval 981).

Order to Karaman governor *(begler begi)* and to Turgud and Diyakuk (?) kadis. Pir Ahmed came to my Porte and said: A man named Ahmed did not obey *(itaʿat)* the Sharia, and he made oppression *(fesad)*. He was banished to Cyprus. You should sell his property *(rizk ve emlak)* and hand him over for Cyprus. He may take 15,000 akce. He should be imprisoned *(habs)* in order to be banished *(surgun)* to Cyprus. He did evil *fesad ve şenaʿat)*. Now it was heard that he is missing *(gaybet)*. I order that you should investigate *(teftiş)* and see if this is so. If 15 years have not passed, and if that is true . . . you should banish him to Cyprus. (p. 10; undated)

Order to Palu kadi: You sent a letter saying, When you are supervising the banishment of brigands and evildoers *(eşkiya, ehl-i fesad)* in accordance with my order to the island of Cyprus from Karaman, a few villages which are in Palu kaza in Karaman but which nevertheless are dependent on Hudavendigar district *(sancagi)*, prevaricated (?) *(te ʿallul)*. They did not banish brigands *(eşkiya)* and evildoers *(ehl-i fesad)*. They must do so . . . (p. 11; 16 Zil-Hicce 981)

Order to Lala Antaliya kadi: Mevlana Mehmed Muhiyeddin, who is inspector *(mufettiş)* of tax farms *(mukata ʿat)*, sent a letter to my Porte saying: All the Muslims of that judicial district *(kaza)* came to court *(meclis-i şer ʿe)*. They made known that Kara Hizir ogullari of that kaza are evildoers and brigands *(ehl-i fesad ve şakileri)* who fled *(firar)* when banished to Cyprus. They took the wife of a spahi named ʿOsman by force . . . He perverted *(izlal)* the black slave *(ʿarab kuli)* of Hasan and sold him to another person. He robbed the house and goods of a man named Hamze . . . He joined with religious students *(suhte)* who are brigands and killed many Muslims . . . (p. 12; undated)

Order to Anatoli governor and to Enguri district governor and Murteza Abad kadi: You sent a letter to my Porte about a brigand *(şaki)* named Kalender ogli of Yassi (?) viran village of that kaza, who wandered with *(gezub)* 70 or 80 brigands *(eşkiya)* . . . It was ordered that he be sent to Cyprus . . . When he was invited *(da ʿvet)* to the Sharia, he came to the court *(mahkeme)* with 70 or 80 brigands and cursed the Sharia *(şer ʿ-i şerife şetm)-i galiz idub)*, shot an arrow, and drew his sword *(kilic geçub)*; he did evil *(fesad)* . . . If that is so he should be banished to Cyprus . . . (p. 19; 27 Cumadi I 1001)

Turgud, Haci Bayram, Ramazan, Musa, and 50 or 60 other Ak Keçilu Yuruk of Kutahya kaza stormed a hamam occupied by women and carried them away by force, only being stopped from the merriment, accompanied to fife and drums, by the intervention of an imperial courier named Derviş çavuş who happened to be passing by. Finally all the tribesmen and their families were ordered sent to Silifke so that they might be banished to Cyprus.[23]

An imperial order to the district governor *(begi)* of Ic Il refers to a letter received from the governor of Karaman province about a man named Ramazan from the Koselu clan *(cema ʿatden)* of the Boz Togan tribe *(tayifesinden)* which lives in Ic Il district who had become a notorious brigand but managed to escape earlier summons to court by claiming to be under the sphere of authority of different districts. He and 40 or 50 others with him were to be apprehended and banished to Cyprus with their households immediately.[24]

Another group prominent among those banished to Cyprus for criminal activities were the *suhte (softa)*, revolting higher-level religious students who between 1575 and 1600 were a very destabilizing element in Anatolian society. Traditionally higher-religious students spent their summers in rural areas and small towns where they performed simple religious functions for people who otherwise had no access to such services, in return for which they were provided with food, shelter, and perhaps "pocket-money" as they wandered. When that class fell upon hard times because of the penetration of the slave class into the higher levels of bureaucracy and the burgeoning numbers of students competing for a small number of positions, groups of these suhte began forcibly extorting higher payments from villagers and even engaged in outright robbery. Roaming in small to medium-sized bands many became predators.[25] Ultimately, by the number and nature of the crimes they commited, no one can distinguish them from any other brigands and cutthroats.

Şemseddin and Kara Sunduk of the suhte community *(taifesi)* were banished to Cyprus for doing evil *(fesad ve şena' at)* and pillaging property in Menteşe district *(sancagi)* (116/66 (22); 4 Rebi' I 983). Brigands *(eşkiya)* and suhtes *(suhte taifesi)* in Hamid district attacked Muslims and were ordered banished to Cyprus (124/65 (17); 996). When Tarsus kadi 'Abdul-Hayy reported to the Porte that the people of that city *(Tarsus ahalisi)* had come to court to complain that many suhte had gone to the homes of people and made extortions *(recide)* and were not free from evil doing *(fesad)*, an order was sent to the kadi that all those who went around as suhte should be expelled *(men' ve def' olub)* from that kaza (160/89 (80); undated).

Order to Alanya district governor and kadisi: You sent a letter. While serving *(hidmet)* in defense of Cyprus, 200 or 300 brigands appeared as suhte in Alanya district *(sancak)*. They did much oppression *(te' addi)* to the Muslims. They took 50 or 60 beardless boys *(emredd oglan)*. They took a tax called *saliyane* from villagers. When the villagers asked for an investigation, it was learned that they took 500,000 akce (five *yuk* akce) from the Muslims. They made rebellion *(ihtilal)* contrary to the Sharia. If they are not brought to justice and banished *(surgun)* to Cyprus, there will be no possibility of stopping those evildoers *(ehl-i fesad)*. It is ordered, therefore, that they are banished to Cyprus immediately. (164/75 (12); 21 Zil-Hicce 981?)

Another order complains of brigands *(ehl-l fesad ve şakileri)* who fled Cyprus after being banished there, who raped and robbed, and who then joined up with suhtes who were evildoers *(eşkiyadan olan ehl-i fesad suhtelere karişub)* and killed many Muslims (p. 12; undated).

The suhte obviously would make very undesirable residents of Cyprus.

Among groups frequently banished to Cyprus were Shia Kizilbaş, who were punished in anticipation that they might cooperate with the Safavid empire or simply because they were heretics. In the 1570s Cyprus became the place to which they were most frequently banished.[26] Although some orthodox Muslims in Cyprus may have considered such exiles even more objectionable neighbors than bandits, thugs, or thieves, Shia exiles, unless perhaps seditious, should have made good settlers and honest neighbors.

A person named Kara Baş was banished to Cyprus, where he was to be brought in the custody of Mustafa çavuş. (118/58 (12); 8 Şaban 985)

Ottoman officials are very conspicuous among the banished. That category ranges from the lowest ranks in the state to the level of kadis and provincial governors. Their offences range from the petty to the heinous. Some are minor, probably connected with being temporarily in or out of favor, or with the rise and fall of their protectors. Although the orders regarding the banishment of such individuals do not say so, it seems that many would have been released within a couple of years.

The out-of-office banished group in general seems not very reprehensible. Some were probably relatively reliable officials who had exceeded the scope of their office a little, either having acted corruptly or perhaps having refused to act corruptly. Many of them would make good neighbors, although others were every bit as reprehensible as the worst desperados banished there.

Such banishment typically involved single individuals, although occasionally two or three might be involved. One exceptional case involved eight soldiers (ʿasker) whom the Trablos Şam kadi had identified as rebellious and as highway robbers on account of whom the populace was becoming dispersed (perakende). The Porte approved their banishment to Cyprus (p. 6; 8 ? 995). The Porte urged the banishment of some 200 volunteers (gonullu), along with their leader (baş ve bug) and weapons (yat ve yaraklari) to Cyprus from Diyar Bekr province. (140/57 (5); c. 25 Muharrem 978). If the smaller group were out and out criminals, the latter do not seem to have been particularly reprehensible.

Cezayr governor (begler begi) ʿAli, son of former Tunus kadi (hakim) mevlana Ahmed, was sent to Cyprus in 1585(?) (993) and imprisoned in Magosa castle (kal ʿesi), where he died (137/69 (28); 993?). Six men (Hasan, ʿAlaeddin, Gazi, Ebu Bekr, Suhrab, and Seyfeddin) of the Van governor, called Şah Kuli ogullari (probably Kizilbaş), were ordered banished to Cyprus after their battle *(gavga, cenk)* with Hakkari begi Zeyneb; they were to receive salaries of 10/akce day (123/89 (27); 6 Receb 986). The overseer *(nazir)* of another provincial governor was banished to Cyprus for oppression (117/30 (12); 23 Muharrem 985).

Istanbul su başi Ahmed çavuş was banished to Cyprus, as was a man named Tat ogli in Tarsus kaza who wandered with the su başi, oppressing *(rencide)* the people *(te ʿaddi, tecavuz)* and being rebellious *(ihtilal)* (124/65 (1); 23 Muharrem 985. p. 20; 23 Sefer (?) 993). From Amasya district za ʿim Divane Ahmed was to be escorted to Cyprus by Hizir çavuş for his evildoing *(şirret ve şekavet)* (120/55 (5); 5 Zil-Kade 983).

Order to Cyprus begler begi: Iskender çavuş, besides oppressing *(zulm ve te ʿaddi)* the poor contrary to the Sharia, made treachery *(ihanet)* against the Homs kadi, and he struck those in service of the court *(mahkeme)*. He struck that kadi with a sword while he was praying *(nemaz kilurken)* . . . By petition *(ʿarz)* of Mekkeʾ-i mukerrime kadi mevlana Seyfullah, Şemseddin is ordered banished to Cyprus . . . (160/89 (48); 20 Sefer 994)

The district governor of Rhodes (Rodos begi) was ordered to deliver Behram çavuş to be handed over to the Cyprus provincial governor, to whom he should be useful (161/71 (52); 19 Cumadi I 986). A brigand named Veli çavuş, who had a 10,000 akce timar in Kavak nahiye of Canik, was an evildoer *(ehl-i fesad)* banished to Cyprus (161/71 (57); undated. Also 160/89; undated). Janissary Mustafa was banished from Larende to Cyprus because he was an evildoer *(fesad)* (137/69 (1); 27 Rebiʿ II 996). When Sinan of the sons of spahis *(sipahi ogullari)* became a brigand *(şaki)*, he made oppression *(fesad ve şena ʿet)*, wounding Yunus and Yusuf with arrows and killing Hizir. The Porte ordered Elbasan district governor and Dirac kadi that, if Hizir died, Sinan should be sent to Cyprus (118/58 (12); 6 Şaban 985. Cf. 123/89 (18). 154/63 (LPG). 122/98 (44). 162/60 (14). p. 20).

A few members of the religious class, too, were banished to Cyprus, although usually only when they had committed very serious offenses. When they were implicated in illegal activities with people of other positions, even the military, usually only the member of the religious class would be banished.

Dismissed Larende kadi ʿAbdul-Kerim and other brigands *(eşkiya)* attacked eight janissaries with weapons of war and fighting *(alat-i harb u kital)* and robbed them. After they were convicted of that, the kadi was banished to Cyprus and the brigands were to be brought to justice (122/98 41); 21 Cumadi I 997). Later, however, reconciliation *(sulh)* was made at a court in Istanbul and then it was ordered that ʿAbdul-Kerim and his family *(ehl u ʿayal)* be released *(itlak)* from Cyprus (160/89 (21); undated 979? 160/89 (78); undated (985?)). When Çeki, the former college teacher *(muderris)* of Taşlik in Valorna (?), was found to be a malicious person and a brigand *(şirret ve şekavet)*, the Geliboli kadi was ordered to banish him to Cyprus (116/66 (7); 28 Şaban 983. 116/66 (11); 17 Cumadi I 983.) Two years later the preacher *(hatib)* of the mosque *(camiʿ -i şerif)* at Mustafa Paşa bridge *(koprusi)*, also in the district of the Gelibolu kadi, was ordered banished to Rhodes because he was an evildoer and a brigand *(şirr ve şaki)* (123/89 (33); 27 Rebiʿ II 985).

Order to Temeşvar begler begi and kadi: You, governor *(mir miran)*, sent a letter with the notables *(a ʿyan-i vilayet)* about the illegal actions *(hilaf-i şerʿ hususlari)* of Kurd ʿAbdul-Kadir, imam, who was dismissed because he placed the Koran in a pocket below a belt *(kuşakdan aşaga ceybinde)*, drank liquor *(şurb-i ʿarak)* during Ramazan, and raped the families of Muslims *(ahal-i muslimine fiʿ l-i şeniʿ)*. We do not want him. When his reputation *(ahval)* was asked, and it appeared that he was not suitable for the office of imam *(imamete ʿadem-i liyaketi)*, and it was petitioned that he was greedy *(bula)* and dissimulative *(ketm)* with the property of pious foundations, I ordered that this should be investigated and, if substantiated, he should be banished to Cyprus. (p. 19; 9 Receb 1001)

Sometimes officials were banished for collecting excessive taxes from reʿ aya. Boyaci ogli Mehmed oppressed *(zulm ve teʿ addi)* the poor and took head tax *(cizye)* from reʿ aya on imperial lands *(havass-i humayun reʿ aya)* in ʿAlaʾ iye (138/89 (10); 4 Muharrem 981). In Istiniya (?) in Kostendil Mustafa, too, collected more taxes than he was supposed to, for which he was banished (p. 18; 13 Şevval 980).

Summary

Since the time of Mehmed II the Conqueror forced population transfers had been an important part of Ottoman social and economic policy, using most often Turkish Muslims, but also other Muslims, and even Christians and Jews to advance the various aims of the state. The government really was desirous of making the island of Cyprus flourish.

Unfortunately the surviving documents do not make it all clear why such a large proportion of the banished did not want to be settled in Cyprus, but that was the only place known where the policy failed.

At that very time the movements of Latins from the island had reached their peak, and we also know of departures of Greek Orthodox. Serious losses may have occurred to the mercantile class in particular. Other migrant Cypriots returned to their homeland soon after the Ottomans took over. However, the small population growth which did occur was connected with determined Venetian and Ottoman policies, and the Mediterranean-wide doubling of population in the 16th century.

As usual, most aspects connected with compulsory migrations were supervised by local kadi everywhere. Lists were sent to them to oversee any problems which might arise. Often they directed many other matters connected with the transfers, too.

Banishment meant leaving relatives, neighbors, and community, as well as the local commercial and agricultural conditions which one lived in often requiring very different skills and crops. Living in Cyprus would have provided many great challenges; to do well in such a new environment required considerable mettle. A tenth of the people were requested, which would have enabled sizable communities of the towns and villages to remain together, in Cyprus, but even that was inadequate in encouraging volunteers. Two years' exemption from taxes, as well as bringing their own plows and other tools, were other official incentives.

If the policy of executing those trying to resist or to avoid the orders had ever actually been carried out, the results might have turned out differently. However, that is the only mention that I have found of execution, and no indication of its having been carried out was found at all. The way that the Porte steadily reduced its initial high standards is certainly the best indication that they were having difficulties implementing that policy. And the reason for that largely was because of unanticipated popular resistence. Conflicts developed within the Ottoman administration between those who wanted to encourage the greatest number of good people to help alleviate Cyprus' underpopulation, and those who wanted to derive the greatest tax benefits possible (partly because of a chronic shortage of revenues which seems to have developed in Istanbul).

Part of the problem is that the other well-known cases of forced population transfers, to southeastern Europe by nomads, to Istanbul (for

Christians and Muslims), and to Trabzon (for Muslims) worked partly because many of the people involved were more eager to go to those places. The Porte had never encountered a situation where so many of the people involved did not want to go to those places.

Because of the resistence, refusing to go to Cyprus, and returning surreptitously by sea, forced the local officials to inspect vessels, and harbors, and also the places in Cyprus where people were expected to be.

Resistance to banishment was strong at every stage: Some prevaricated, or even refused to go, some fled, and others failed to appear at the ports of embarkation; still others escaped after reaching Cyprus, whether legally or illegally finding ships back to Anatolia. Those who objected to settling in Cyprus seem in fact to have had little to lose, for in most cases the only punishment was being sent back to Cyprus.

The officials involved were ordered to protect the lives, families, and property at every stage. Among those banished for their evil actions were suhte, nomads, bandits, brigands, and Kizilbaş.

Some scholars have misunderstood the real goal of the government. The original purpose was to build up the population of Cyprus by compulsorily transferring competent people who had families and would become taxpayers, and sending Muslims there rather than Christians, for the population of Cyprus was almost totally Christians. It was believed that a Muslim population would be likely to be loyal to the Ottoman state.

NOTES

1. Ömer Lüfti Barkan, "Les déportations comme méthode de peuplement et de colonisation dans l'empire Ottoman," *Revue de la Faculté des Sciences Économiques de l'Université d'Istanbul* 11.1949–1950.67–131. Barkan's other pioneering studies on this subject include "Osmanli Imparatorluğunda bir Iskân ve kolonizasyon metodu olarak sürgünler," *İ.Ü. Iktisat Facültesi Mecumuası* II 1949–1950. 523–569, and "Osmanlı İmparatorluğunda bir İskan ve Kolonizasyon metodu olarak Vakıflar ve Temlikler: I. İstila devirlerinin Kolonizatör Türk Dervişleri ve Zaviyeler," *V.D.* 2.1942.279–386. Cf. H. Inalcik, "Ottoman Methods of Conquest," *Studia Islamica* 2.1954.122–128. Cf. H. W. Lowry, "The Ottoman *Tahrir Defters* as a Source for Urban Demographic History. The Case Study of Trabzon (c. 1486–1583). UCLA Ph.D. dissertation, 1977. pp. 96ff, 217ff, 238f. Trab-

zon Şehrinin Islamlaşma ve Türkleşmesi, 1461–1583. Istanbul, 1981. pp. 55ff, 123ff, 135f. See also H. Inalcik, "Istanbul," *EI²*. "The Policy of Mehmed II toward the Greek Population of Istanbul and the Byzantine Buildings of the City," *Dumbarton Oaks Papers* 23–24.1969–1970.229–249. M.T. Gökbilgin, *Rumeli'de Yürükler, Tatarlar ve Evlad-i Fatihan.* Istanbul, 1957.

2. Barkan guesses that 30% of the banished went of their own volition. He further guesses that 7% of the heads of families had committed crimes, whether major or minor. "Les déportations . . . ," p. 98. Since the later registers enumerate only non-Muslims, one cannot know where the people were religiously intermixed and where not.

3. Much of the evidence for that has been collected by Costas Kyriss, "Symbiotic Elements in the History of the Two Communities of Cyprus," *K. L.* 8. 1976.243f. Also "Cypriote Scholars in Venice in the 16th and 17th centuries . . . ," *passim.* Cf. the account of B. Sagredo (1575) in de Mas Latrie, *Histoire . . . ,* v. 3, p. 560.

4. Başbakanlik Arşivi Mühimme Defteri *nu.* 14, *hüküm* 15. *nu.* 17, *hüküm* 16. Cengiz Orhonlu, "The Ottoman Turks Settle in Cyprus (1570–1580)," pp. 92, 99f.

5. Istanbul Başbakanlık Arşivi Maliyeden Müdevver Defterler, nu. 5168, s. 10. nu. 7168, s. 247. Cf. Cengiz Orhonlu, "The Ottoman Turks Settle . . . , pp. 92, 100. The janissary "slaves," of course, were mostly not of Turkish origin.

The erroneous figure of an army of 20,000 being encouraged to settle is no longer used by Alasya in the second edition. H. Fikret Alasya, *Kıbrıs Tarihi ve Kıbrıs'da Türk Eserleri.* ikinci baski. Ankara, 1977. Hill, v. 4, p. 20.

6. Barkan published the text in a French translation in 1949. At that time, not only was it the only order treating Cyprus sürgün (population transfers) thoroughly, it was also the earliest known document dealing with any Ottoman sürgün, so Barkan took it to be typical. "Les déportations comme méthode de peuplement et de colonisation . . . ," p. 89, text pp. 91–95, followed by commentary.

7. Oddly no mention is made of what to the Ottomans would have been the most highly prized export of Cyprus—sugar. The Ottomans already had abundant cotton.

8. Ö. L. Barkan, "Les déportations . . . ," pp. 90f. "The Price Revolution in the Sixteenth Century," *IJMES* 6.1975.3–28, esp. 24–28. M. Akdağ, *Celâli İsyanları . . . ,* p. 6 and *passim.* "Osmanlı İmparatorluğunun Kuruluş ve İnkişafi devrinde Türkiye'nin İktisadi Vaziyeti," *Belleten* 19.1950.319–411. "İktisadi darlığın cemiyet bünyesindeki tesirleri," *Belletin* 14.1950.379–386. H. Inalcik, *The Ottoman Empire,* pp. 46f. See also M. Cezar, . . . *Levendler.* Istanbul, 1965, pp. 82, 212.

9. Kyrris and Papadopoullos presume that the deportations were punitive in character. Kyrris, "Symbiotic Elements," p. 244. T. Papadopoullos, *Social*

and Historical . . . , pp. 20f, 22, 24ff. In the 18th century Cyprus, particularly Magosa, became a place of banishment for "sensitive" prisoners, but that was a new development. Although in a few selected instances the deportations were punitive, in the general the goal was solely to build up the population of Cyprus.

10. Orhonlu, "The Ottoman Turks . . . ," p. 94 p. 102; Barkan, "Les déportations . . . ," pp. 556ff, from Başbakanlık Arşivi, Kamil Kepeci tasnifi, mevkufat defteri no. 2551., 120 sahife.

11. Maliyeden müdevver defterler, nu. 22089, s. 2; Orhonlu, "The Ottoman Turks . . . ," pp. 96, 103.

12. Faruk Sümer, *Oğuzlar (Türkmenler)*. Ankara, 1967. pp. 177, 179. An important part of today's Turkish Cypriots trace their origin to Ic Il Yuruks.

13. H. Inalcik, "Ottoman Policy and Administration in Cyprus after the Conquest," p. 63, p. 61, from A. Refik, *Edebiyat Fakültesi Mecmuası* 5.1926.71 (document 47).

14. Barkan, "Les déportations . . . ," p. 98. T. Papadopoullos, *Social and Historical* . . . , pp. 25f. from A. Refik, *Edebiyat Fakültesi Mecmuası* 5.1926, no. 32.

15. Barkan, "Les déportations. . . ," p. 98. Papadopoullos wrongly calls this 70%. *Social and Historical* . . . , p. 26.

16. de Mas Latrie, *Histoire* . . . , v. 3, p. 560. Hill, v. 4, p. 19n.

17. *Joseph Naci duc de Naxos*, pp. 134ff, 138f, 142, 150f. A Galanté and C. Roth have urged the view that Joseph Nasi rivaled Sokollu Mehmed Paşa in influence over Selim II, who supposedly was indebted to Nasi both financially and for Cyprus wine he provided. Roth attributed the Ottoman attack on Cyprus to Nasi's hatred for Venice and suggested that he may have wanted to open Cyprus for the settlement of Jewish refugees and even hoped to become governor of the island. A. Galanté, *Don Joseph Nassi. Duc de Naxos* . . . , *passim*. C. Roth, *The House of Nasi. The Duke of Naxos*, pp. 17ff, 22f, 41f, 46f, 50f, 140ff, 145, 154. P. Grunebaum-Ballin patiently refutes the whole basis of that viewpoint.

18. U. Heyd, "Turkish Documents Concerning the Jews of Safed in the Sixteenth Century," p. 112 in M. Ma'oz., ed., *Studies on Palestine during the Ottoman Period*, Jerusalem, 1975.

19. U. Heyd, "Turkish Documents . . . , pp. 112f. C. Roth, *The House* . . . , pp. 98ff.

20. U. Heyd, "Turkish Documents . . . ," p. 115.

21. Kyrris and Papadopoullos both hold that largely Christians were banished. C. Kyrris, "Symbiotic Elements . . . ," pp. 243f. T. Papadopoullos, *Social and Historical* . . . , pp. 24f. The exemption from banishment afforded the family of the great architect Sinan and their village Agirnas in Kayseri district is taken by Kyrris, Papadopoullos, and even Hill (v. 4, pp. 18f and n) as further evidence of punitive banishment of Christians. The document constitutes one of very few pieces of evidence, and it was issued as a special favor in advance, *not* as a reaction to orders of banishment to Agirnas

villagers. Since early in the 16th century western and central Anatolia had a Christian minority (Greek Orthodox and Armenian Gregorian) of only 7½%, few of them would have remained had they borne the brunt of the banishment policy. Indeed, at least in Karaman province, their numbers increased rapidly through the 16th century.

General exemptions were given to the two large urban centers in Karaman province, Konya and Kayseri. That policy is consistent with general Ottoman policy favoring such places.

22. Orhonlu, "The Ottoman Turks Settle . . .," pp. 97, 103, 7 January 1581.
Orhonlu refers to this document from the *Mühimme defteri*, nu. 43, s. 134, *hüküm* 241 but wrongly gives 8000 adult males rather than 800 *(sekiz yüz nefer)*. If this document is to be dated 10 years after the Ottoman invasion of the island, and the figures are reasonably accurate, the banishment was a disastrous failure, far worse than I can conceive. If Orhonlu amended the figure in the text as obviously wrong, I can sympathize with that feeling, but surely there is absolutely no evidence anywhere to suggest that *yüz* was wrongly written in place of *bin* by the scribe; one might as easily posit a missing initial *bin* or *alti bin*. However, I cannot accept the idea, without additional documentary evidence, that less than 7% of those ordered banished actually ever reached Cyprus—of whom only half remained. (However, I do feel comfortable with the idea that a good half of those banished may have escaped back home.) Perhaps this document is the basis for Barkan's assertion that 7% of the banished heads of families had committed crimes.
Had the banishment policy failed so overwhelmingly, it seems doubtful that the imperial bureaucracy would have even bothered to suggest that the governor might attempt to make a complete list of all those who were still in Cyprus.

23. Ahmet Refik, *Anadolu'da Türk Aşiretleri (996–1200)*. Istanbul, 1930. pp. 15f, #29; 26 Sefer 980.

24. A. Refik, *Türk Aşiretleri . . .*, pp. 26f, #50. 26 ca 984.

25. M. Akdağ, *Celali İsyanları . . .*, pp. 85–108 and *passim* esp. 87ff, 104f.

26. Ö. L. Barkan, ". . . sürgünler," 228f. Bekir Kütükoğlu, *Osmanlı-İran Siyasi Münasebetleri*. v. 1, 1578–1590. Istanbul, 1962. p. 9. Usually Kizilbaş who had relations with the Safavids were banished to Cyprus with their families and isolated. C. M. Imber, "The Persecution of the Ottoman Shi'ites according to the mühimme defterleri, 1565–1585," *Der Islam* 56.1979.pp. 250–272.

EIGHT

Slaves and Slavery

Slavery was an important institution in the Mediterranean world. In long distance trade few goods could have rivaled slaves in volume or profitability.[1] In Cyprus colonial powers like Genoa and particularly Venice established extensive slave plantations for sugar cultivation starting as early as the second half of the 14th century. Places on the south coast of the island like Piskopi, Kolossi, and Kouklia became centers of sugar production. Sometimes colonists imported slaves for those purposes. Ruthless use of slaves, in combination with advanced techniques of irrigation and mills, produced better, cheaper sugar. When slave plantations in Madeira and the Canaries began to produce even cheaper sugar, the colonial plantations in Cyprus switched to cotton. In the eastern Mediterranean slavery continued to thrive throughout the 16th century, even if it was more important in the New World and South Asia.[2]

The Ottoman conquest brought profound consequences in the nature and extent of slavery in Cyprus. According to the testimony of widespread sources, Venetian and otherwise, the status of the parici, who made up over 80% of the island's population, was virtually that of slaves. The Ottoman conquest instantly freed virtually that entire class, and if remnants survived for a decade or more, those too disappeared. Agricultural slavery virtually disappeared.

The Ottomans, in the process of conquest, enslaved thousands of Venetian soldiers. Many of them were immediately sold to slave markets in Syria and Anatolia, which reportedly became flooded temporarily; others may have remained in Cyprus with their new masters. So the revolutionary change is that a huge "slave" class, almost exclusively Greek Orthodox in faith, became free village landholders while a large part of the former Latin ruling class was at least temporarily reduced to slavery. The latter, of course, were only a small proportion of the population; they served in towns and cities, presumably as household servants, for under Ottoman rule neither agricultural nor industrial slavery ever took root on the island.

Cyprus in the 16th and 17th centuries did not resemble the Mediterranean society of half a millenium earlier so well described by S. D. Goitein in which slaves played important roles in trade and commerce, frequently acting in cooperation with their owners, and sometimes traveling alone over the entire Mediterranean world.[3] Such relations were not unknown either, however. Belal, black slave *(zengi l-asl gulam)* of the merchant haci ʿOmer, sold a musket *(tufenk)* to janissary Arslan beşe bn Hasan (4 11–1; III Ramazan 1043). Huseyn and his slave *(kul)* bought 180 keyl of wheat from Suleyman beg bn ʿAli beg of Lefkoşa (4 173–2; II Cumadi II 1046). Haci Yusuf of Lefkoşa owed his slave *(ʿabd-i memluk)* Ridvan 7000 akce (3 133–3; after 28 Rebiʿ II 1019).

Some founders of pious foundations *(evkaf)* ordained that their freed slaves and their descendants should serve as administrators *(mutevelli)* of their foundations. When Suleyman su başi, administrator of the foundation of the late Mustafa Paşa, died, the Paşa's freed slave *(i ʿtak)* Sarikci Caʿfer beg replaced him (1 225–1; III Ramazan 1002). Bevvab Hamze, a freed slave of the late Mustafa Paşa, replaced another freed slave, Piyale, as administrator of that foundation (2 48–1; I Şevval 1016). When Kasim was removed because of his treachery from the office of administrator of the foundation of the late Ahmed Paşa, from among the Paşa's freed slaves Murad bn ʿAbdullah was appointed (1 27–3; III Receb 1002).

Za ʿim Perviz beg, present superviser of the public treasury *(beyt ul-mal ʿamme ve hasse emin)*, states *(tm)* before ʿOmer kethuda, lieutenant *(kethuda)* of the late Mehmed beg who died while Baf sancak begi: His female slave *(cariyesi)* and treasurer *(hazinedar)* Rahime bint ʿAbdullah, who came to Lefkoşa, brought four loads *(yuk)* of jewels, goods, and money. The *kassam-i ʿasker* (who fixed shares of inheritance of soldiers), and Hasan beg, who was agent (in *mubaşiret)* for the founder of the foundation, had letters registered and sent to me. Then he demanded her and the money that she took from the treasury *(miri)*. That 'Omer came to the female slave. Then defter kethuda Mustafa took her and all the goods by force. (1 38–5; Şaban 1002)

Perviz beg bn 'Addullah again states *(tm)* before 'Omer kethuda: You took 15,000 filori worth of the property of the deceased. Why have you not turned it over to the treasury *(miri)?* I want an answer before the court. 'Omer kethuda replies: God forbid that I took it. His treasurer *(hazinedar)*, the female slave Rahime bint 'Abdullah, knows where it is. Ask her. (1 38–6; Şaban 1002)

The above Perviz beg states *(tm)* before the above-mentioned 'Omer kethuda: 15,000 altun was brought to Lefkoşa by a slave named Rahime, but she did not give it to the Paşa's administrative officer *(musellim)* Mustafa kethuda. I have a claim against her, but she has fled. 'Omer replies: Yes, we brought it to Rahime. Now defter kethudasi Mustafa has fled with her. (1 38–7; I Şaban 1002)

Judging from the court records an overwhelming proportion of both slave owners and slaves were Muslims. Virtually no non-Muslims (zimmis) appear to have held slaves, and virtually no zimmis were slaves. Possibly Orthodox Christian traditions did not permit holding slaves, but there was no reason that Muslims could not own such slaves.

Undoubtedly slaves in Cyprus constituted only a very small proportion of the population. Probably females worked as household servants and looked after children, in some cases also serving as concubines. Besides those few males in the military class who were slaves of the imperial government, a few male slaves must have worked in trades and crafts, but the evidence for that is slight; they too served primarily as household servants.[4] There are enough similarities between Cyprus and the well-documented case of Cairo to conjecture that slaves there generally were treated with respect and affection, almost like members of the family, but there really is too little evidence about Cyprus itself to demonstrate that convincingly.

Emancipating slaves is a good work extolled both in the Koran and in the Sharia. Emancipation was proper at any time, but it was most common at the death of the slave holder.[5]

Kadin Paşa bint Mehmed, wife of the late merchant *(tacir)* Musli of Lefkoşa, says the 18-year-old black *(Habeşi l-asl)* slave *(kul)* of the deceased is free *(mutlak)*. Let him be like all Muslims. (1 234–1, 2; Şevval 1002)

Petro v. Hiristofi, Greek Orthodox *(Rum ul-asl)* zimmi, says: Previously I was freed for serving well. I was given this receipt *(tezkire)*. Let no one interfere. (1 265–2; II Zil-Kade 1002)

Baf begi Mustafa beg has as agent *(vekil)* for the matter Ridvan beg bn ʿAbdul-Mennan who states *(tm)* before slave *(gulam)* Hovat (?) v. Nikola of Croat origin *(Hirvadi l-asl)* of the Latin Christian community *(Nasara taifesi)*, who is 35 years old: Hovat (?) worked for six years in Lefkoşa. Now he is freed, after having done his service *(hidmet)*. He has a document from the court *(huccet)*. (1 279–3; II Zil-Kade 1002)

Za ʿim ʿAli çelebi bn Musa says before his black *(Habeşi l-asl)* slave *(ʿabd-i memluk)* Turmuş bn ʿAbdullah: I have freed him (i ʿtak). (1 327–2; 15 Muharrem 1003).

Racil Halil çelebi bn Hizir su başi, of the imperial infantry commanders *(dergah-i ali yaya başis)*, acknowledges *(ik/it)* before black slave girl *(ʿarab cariyesi)* Mercane bint ʿAbdullah: I inherited her *(intikal)* from my late father. I free her. (2 27–2; 14 Şevval 1016)

Haci Yusuf bn ʿAbdullah of Lefkoşa acknowledges *(ik/it)* before blue-eyed, blondish Hungarian *(Macari l-asl)* slave *(ʿabd-i memluki)* Ridvan bn ʿAbdullah: He is my slave; he is my property. I free him. Let him be like all free people. (3 139–6; after 28 Rebiʿ II 1019)

Yasemin bint ʿAbdullah of Lefkoşa has as agent *(vekil)*, according to the testimony of two witnesses, Mustafa oda başi bn ʿAbdullah, who acknowledges *(ik/it)*: The person who appointed me agent *(vekil)*, of her own free will, frees this tall, fair eyebrowed *(açik kaşlu)* Russian female slave *(cariye)* Gulistan bint ʿAbdullah. (4 6–2; III Şaban 1043)

Derviş Kadri bn Ugurli of Lefkoşa acknowledges *(ik/it)* before blond eyebrowed, blondish Russian slave *(ʿabd-i memluki)* Yusuf bn ʿAbdullah: I have freed him. (4 23–4; I Rebiʿ I 1044)

Mevlana Hasan efendi bn ʿAbdul-Fettah of Lefkoşa frees his blondish Russian female slave of medium height Satime bint ʿAbdullah. (4 66–2; III Sefer 1044)

Kumari zade Ibrahim beg bn Nasuh, presently superviser of the imperial treasury in Cyprus *(beyt ul-mal ʿamme ve hassa emin)*, acknowledges *(ik/it)* before tall *(uzun boylu)* Circassin *(Çerkesi l-asl)* slave *(ʿabdi-i memluki)* Dilaver bn ʿAbdullah: I free my slave Dilaver. (4 195–1; III Receb 1046)

Sometimes circumstances forced a former slave to demonstrate to the court that he really had been emancipated.[6]

Mercan bn ʿAbdullah, slave *(kul)* of Suleyman su başi, states *(tm)* before Lalezar bint ʿAbdullah, guardian *(vasiye muhtar)* of the orphans of the late Suleyman: Suleyman freed me while he was alive. Now Lalezar has made me a slave again. Let this be investigated. Lalezar denies that Mercan had been freed. When proof was wanted, from upright Muslims *(ʿudul-i Muslimin)* Pervane kethuda, Mustafa bn ʿAbdullah, ʿAli Başa bn Bali, Ahmed bn Nasuh, and Huseyn bn ʿAbdullah confirm that Mercan truly had been freed. (1 40–1; II Şaban 1002)

Mustafa Kethuda, administrative officer *(musellim)* of governor *(mir miran)* Ramazan Paşa, has Haydar aga, who appears before Cemal bn Mahmud: Cemal said, I am not a slave, I am the son of an ʿArab. I am from Suleymaniye quarter in Damascus *(Şam)*. I served with Tanner's *(tebbaklar)* şeyh haci Mehmed. My mother's name is Fatma, my uncle's name is Mehmed, and my father's name is Mehmed. When the court met again *(ʿakd-i meclis)*, Cemal said: No, I am a Georgian *(Gurci)* from Simav. My father was Mekyo (?), my mother Burhan, and my name is Bolad. Cemal is returned to his owner. (1 50–1; III Şaban 1002)

Cennet bint Caʿfer states *(bm)* before Ahmed oda başi bn ʿAbdi: I am the daughter *(sulbiye kizi)* of Caʿfer of Seydi Şehr town; my mother's name *(validem)* was Sati. Formerly when I went to Aleppo *(Haleb)* with my husband *(zevc)* ʿAcem ʿAli, brigands *(eşkiya)* came upon us, killed my husband, and brought me to Silifke. Then ʿAli Paşa came and took me to Cezire, where he sold me to the above-mentioned Ahmed. I have witnesses that I am free born *(hurre l-asl)*. Let them be asked. Ahmed denies that. When Cennet is asked for proof, Hamamci Mehmed dede bn Hasan and Ahmed bn Gulabi confirm her: She was born in Kara Hisar village of Seydi Şehri. Her husband was Mercan, slave *(ʿabd-i memluk)* of a merchant *(tacir)* named Çaylak Sefer. (3 89–1; III Sefer 1019)

Meryem bint Mubarek, unmarried girl of Ata (?) village of Silifke kaza on the mainland (Ote Yaka) states *(tk)* before Huseyn bn haci Ilyas: I am free born *(hurre l-asl)*. My father's name was Mubarek. My mother was a freed slave *(mutlak)* named Dondi. Her brother (?) ʿAli took me by force and sold me to Huseyn saying I was a slave girl. Mustafa bn haci Ramazan, who is here, bought me. Now I want my freedom. Huseyn says he has no evidence that Meryem is free born. (3 162–6; III Rebiʿ II 1019)

Huseyn bn haci Ilyas of Silifke on the mainland (Ote Yaka), now of Girniye, acknowledges *(ik/it)* before Meryem bint Mubarek, an unmarried girl *(bakire)*: Meryem is a slave girl *(cariye)*. I bought her from ʿAli of Ata (?) village. Now I have learned that she is of free birth. In place of 3600 akce that I paid for her, I have received 1200 akce for Meryem and drop my claim. I have no further claim against her. If any are raised, they should not be heard. (3 129–4; 28 Rebi' II 1019)

As with any other purchase, the buyer of slaves could specify special terms regarding the condition of the slaves and then return the purchase to the seller if the condition was not met. Several cases occurred regarding female slaves *(cariye)* who failed to meet the specifications and consequently were returned. That may indicate that such purchases were not normally inspected in public. Anyway, all the cases found at Lefkoşa involved female slaves.

Racil Mehmed bn Huseyn of Lefkoşa says: I bought a female slave *(cariye)* named Faide from Ibrahim bn Mustafa for 6000 akce. But there is an old defect *(marazi kadim)* in her foot *(ayak)*. Let this be referred to court. Place her for safe keeping *(emanet)* with Ahmed bn Nurullah. (1 253–3; III Şevval 1002)

Then Mehmed stated that there was an old wound *(marazi kadim)* on the black female slave *('arab cariye)* Faide when I bought her. Ibrahim countered that the defect had been there when he bought her. (1 253–4; III Şevval 1002)

Finally, following the mediation of upright people, Ibrahim returned 1000 akce of the purchase price and their dispute was settled. (1 253–5; III Şevval 1002)

Bekr çavuş of Lefkoşa makes a claim against 'Abdi bn Mahmud of Lefkoşa: I bought a female slave from 'Abdi. She was defective. I want to return her. 'Abdi says: When I sold the female slave, she was well *(sag salim)*. Registered. (3 7–2; 29 Zil-Hicce 1018)

Ahmed bn Mustafa states *(bm)* before Mehmed bn Ibrahim: I bought a female slave on condition that she have no defects *(bila 'ayyib)*; now she has become defective *(ma 'yuba)*. (3 63–7; I Receb 1019)

Mehmed bn 'Ali states *(bm)* before Mustafa beşe bn 'Ali: Tonight I bought this foreign black *('acemi 'arab)* female slave on condition that she have no defects *(bila 'ayb)*. However, she is injured *(mecruh)* on her neck. (3 73–4; II Receb 1019)

Of 44 slaves whose origin I could discover exactly half were black *(siyah, 'arab, habeşi zengi)*. The next largest group were Russian *(Rus, including one Moskovi)* with nine, followed by Circassian *(Çerkez, Çerkes)* and Hungarian *(Macar)* with four each.[7] None were of Greek Orthodox Cypriot origin. 57% (25) of the slaves were male. Although 12 out of 22 black slaves and 4 out of 9 Russian slaves were female, a disproportion of other slaves were male. A total of 42 of those 44 slaves were

Muslims (only the Greek Orthodox and the Croatian slaves were non-Muslims). Virtually all the much larger number of slaves mentioned in the court records whose origins are not given were also Muslims. The regular influx of foreign slaves contributed to the continuing racial intermixture of Cyprus, which has been a notable melting pot since antiquity. Probably the assimilation of slaves into the society would not have been as rapid as that of free people, but free Muslim males had female slaves whom they used as concubines. Slaves too must have intermarried, and gradually many of those may have been emancipated. Probably the Russians, Circassians, and Georgians were fairer than the local norm, while the blacks would have had skin of a much darker color than the normal range found in Cyprus then, whatever that was. The introduction of slaves like that must, over a long period of time, have had a considerable impact on local hue of skin and physiognomies.

Summary

Slavery was an important institution in the Mediterranean world. In Cyprus under Latin domination (Lusignans, then Venice) agricultural slavery was introduced as a way of enhance colonial revenues. A few outsiders, mostly black, may have been acquired outside the island, but the vast majority of the agricultural slaves were almost certainly Greek Orthodox Cypriots. There is little evidence of how freeing those agricultural slaves took place. When it occurred, little if any slave agriculture continued.

In the process of the Ottoman conquest, thousands and thousands of Venetian soldiers were captured, and carried away from Cyprus, to be sold as slaves.

Few slaves in Cyprus seems to have engaged in artisanal work or in other aspects of trade and commerce. Most were involved in household tasks. Almost all seem to have been Muslims, and owned by Muslims; none of the local Greek Orthodox Christians seem to have owned slaves. Most slaves worked as household servants. A few men of the military class were slaves of the imperial government. Emancipating slaves were always considered a very pious action.

Of 44 slaves mentioned in the sicils, half were black; the next largest group, with nine, were Russians.

NOTES

1. Braudel, *The Mediterranean* . . . , pp. 754f. W. Heyd, *Histoire du Commerce du Levant au Moyen Âge.* tr. Furcy Raynaud. Amsterdam, 1959 (Leipzig, 1885–1886). v. 2, pp. 555–563. H. Inalcik, "Servile Labor in the Ottoman Empire," pp. 25–52 in Abraham Ascher, Tibor Halasi-Kun, and Bela Kiraly, eds., *The Mutual Effects of the Islamic and Judeo-Christian Worlds, the Eastern European Patterns.* New York, 1979.

2. W. McNeill, *Venice* . . . , pp. 54, 76. Braudel, *The Mediterranean* . . . , pp. 154f. W. Heyd, *Histoire* . . . , v. 2, pp. 689f. J. Heers, *Gênes* . . . , pp. 391f, 487, 494f.

3. See S. D. Goitein, *A Mediterranean Society* . . . , v. 1, pp. 130–147, "Slaves and Slave Girls." R. Brunschvig, "Abd," *EI²*. Halil Inalcik found that slavery predominated in the thriving silk industry of Bursa, although few other industries operated that way. "Servile Labor . . . ," pp. 27ff. Little evidence for such activities in Cyprus was found. Cf. R. Jennings, "Black Slaves and Free Blacks in Ottoman Cyprus, 1590–1640," *JESHO* 30.1988.286–302. Moreover, in the Cairo of the 18th century described by A. Raymond that phenomenon was hardly evident.

4. Cf. Goitein, v. 1, pp. 131ff, 147.

5. Goitein, v. 1, pp. 144f, 175f. R. Brunschvig, "Abd," *EI²*. H. Inalcik, "Servile Labor . . . ," pp. 34f.

6. Goitein, v. 1, pp. 136f. H. Inalcik, "Servile Labor . . .," *passim.*

7. Also identified were two Wallachian *(Eflak),* and one each of Georgian *(Gurci),* Greek Orthodox *(Rum),* and Croatian *(Hirvad).* J. Heers lists the origin, age, and price of 29 female slaves bought in Chios between 1449 and 1467. *Gênes* . . . , table XIX. W. Heyd gives the relative selling prices of slaves of different origins in Cairo at a slightly earlier time. v. 2, pp. 558f. H. Inalcik gives the prices of several slaves in Bursa during the second half of the 15th century. "Servile Labor . . . ," pp. 43f.

NINE

The Cities and Towns

The Cities and Towns

Ever since Hellenistic times Cyprus has been noted for its highly developed urban life. Because of natural problems like disease and insects, and because of general social and economic problems facing the island, drastic declines both in the population and in the quality of urban life had occurred by the beginning of Venetian rule. Probably sometime after the Lusignans had ruled for over a century problems began to appear which unsettled life in the cities and towns of Cyprus. How the size of cities and the quality of urban life under the Lusignans compares with these under the Romans is not at all certain, but it is indisputable that urban life declined starting late in the 14th century and that very few positive developments can be perceived between then and the 1650s, our end.

Traditionally, from antiquity, Cyprus has had six towns, or "cities": Lefkoşa, Magosa, Girniye, Larnaka, Limosa, and Baf. All but the first are seaports, so much of their role in ancient and medieval history has been connected with the way they served that function. The port towns are dispersed almost equidistantly from each other, except that the long western third of the island from Girniye to Baf lacks any good ports. The sole inland location is Lefkoşa, which usually has been the capital. So centrally located is Lefkoşa that it can be served about as well by ports in Larnaka, Magosa, or Girniye.

All of the towns depended on the existence of walled fortresses, at least since the Latin crusading Lusignan family established itself as ruler over the largely Orthodox island after the Third Crusade. Fortified towns protected the Lusignans from both external and domestic enemies. The Venetian empire took this system over almost intact. Whatever town and "urban life" means in Ottoman Cyprus is little different from what it meant in Venetian Cyprus. These places are towns or cities in the administrative parlance of the governments. For the Venetian empire, Lefkoşa and Magosa were important centers of a powerful empire; Larnaka and Lefkoşa played similar roles in Ottoman Cyprus.

Towns

Larnaka. Of the five or six towns only Larnaka and its port Tuzla (Salines) were not noticeably poorer and smaller after a century of Venetian rule. The ruined condition of the port was observed by Fra Suriano (1484), N. le Huen (1488), J. le Saige (1518), D. Possot (1533), and G. Affagart (1534).[1] Partly because of efficient Venetian management of the local salt industry and partly because it was replacing Magosa as the port of call on Syrian voyages, the village became transformed into the "busiest port on the island."[2] Martin von Baumgarten (1508) extolled the salt as the best found anywhere, being exported to Syria, Greece, and Italy.[3] Le Saige (1518) and John Locke (1553) also praised the quality of the salt and marveled at the ease with which it was gathered.[4] By 1529 Larnaka was considered "fairly large and populous," and although it lacked a strong tower it was growing daily because of its convenient harbor; Locke (1553) called it "a pretie Village."[5] Jodicus de Meggen (1542) found an immense quantity of salt produced, giving great profits to Venice.[6]

Limosa (Limassol). The decline of Limosa dates back to the early 14th century when constant earthquakes and floods from the mountains laid the once-fair city to waste.[7] By the end of that century it had been destroyed by the Genoese and became mostly uninhabited; they attacked it again in 1407. Mamluks attacked for three successive years (1424–1426), twice taking the castle and sacking the town.[8] In 1459 the Latin bishop resigned his post because piratical devastations had left the site quite deserted. In 1482 Joos van Ghistele described the place as a village of only thirty or forty houses; in that same year Paul Walther found only a single church stood there, along "with a few hovels."[9] Felix Fabri (1483) described a barren port which nevertheless had a good harbor and excellent wines, and Fra Suriano (1484) reported the place "in ruins" and "entirely destroyed by earthquakes."[10] Even at that time the air was believed so unhealthful that Latin merchants and pilgrims slept on their ships.[11] After the earthquake of 1491 Pietro Casola (1494) found all the churches but one in ruins and no good houses anywhere. The few people appeared ill. Because of the earthquakes and malaria, no one could be induced to settle there. Venice had plans to rebuild and fortify the place but never carried them out.[12] Nevertheless, an immense amount of sugar and carobs were shipped to Venice, and production of cotton and melons was also substantial. Excellent water could be found there.[13] The salt lake temporarily reverted to fishery because the return on salt was so small. Finally in 1539 Turkish pirates nearly destroyed Limosa.[14] When Locke (1553) saw the place as his ship took on wine and carobs, he observed the tiny market place and the "grasshoppers" which destroyed about half the year's grain crop.[15] Calepio (1573) reported another earthquake of 1556.[16] Limosa was no town at all.

Baf. If Baf had less misfortune than other towns during the Venetian century, the reason is simply that an earthquake of 1222 so completely destroyed the town and its castle that people virtually abandoned it. Even the harbor dried up. According to Ludolf von Suchen (1350) the place had experienced frequent earthquakes.[17] Martoni (1394) reported that nearby villages had been destroyed by the Turks and were left deserted.[18] Tafur (1435) found the place very unhealthy and quite uninhabited.[19] Devastations accompanied the Venetian-Genoese struggles and the Mamluk attacks, but serious damage was avoided when it surrendered to the Genoese in 1460. Still Baf remained a miserable place; only ships in distress used the harbor.[20] Capodilista (1458), Fabri (1483), Suriano (1484), and le Huen (1480) all point out its miserable ruined condition.[21] Huen and Sebalt (1480) knew the insalubriousness of the place, although the former points out that the soil is good and fertile.[22] Martin von Baumgarten (1508) alluded to desolation and ruin on account of earthquakes and bad air.[23] Affagart (1534) reported, accordingly, that no one lived there.[24] Nevertheless, sugar and cotton cultivation were important.[25]

The Venetians decided to abandon the two castles for economy and because they were considered useless; indeed, one had collapsed in an earthquake of 1491. Although they still existed in 1529, they were useless for defense, the town was "all ruined" with few inhabitants, and the harbor was used only by some small ships. Since there were no other harbors in the southwest of the island, Baf never died out entirely. A Venetian report of about 1540 identifies the population as around 2000.[26] However, the climate was considered so dangerous that those who were able moved inland, up to Ktima. The fort near the sea was built by the Venetians on a Lusignan tower which was later repaired by the Ottomans.[27]

Girniye (Kyrenia). Although Girniye was a town of no consequence, its fortifications were noteworthy. The town walls were not very formidable, but the citadel, until finally surrendered through treachery, had resisted a Genoese siege late in the 14th century as well as a four-year siege by Mamluks and a faction of Lusignans starting in 1460. Tafur (1435) saw it as a small but strong castle with a good harbor which could be closed by a chain; in addition it was the healthiest part of the island. To Piri Reis it had the only harbor and fortress in the north. Jodicus de Meggen (1542) too considered the fortress very strong. Soon the fortifications would need improvements to withstand cannons, but the Venetians either could hardly afford the necessary changes or were behaving with typical frugality. Peter Sanudo reportedly asserted that Girniye was the key to mastery of the island, although its position actually is quite isolated.[28] One population estimate for about 1540 was 950 people including the garrison; a slightly later one was 600.[29] Apparently the fortifications were almost torn down in 1570 when it was feared that they would be unable to withstand an Ottoman assault.[30]

Lefkoşa (Nicosia). Early in the Lusignan period Lefkoşa had already become an important commercial and administrative place. So in 1211 the pilgrim von Oldenburg observed its newly built fortifications. "It has inhabitants without number, all very rich, whose houses in their interior adornment and painting closely resemble the houses of Antioch."[31] Even when Magosa temporarily emerged as the premier city of the island,

Lefkoşa on its fine open extensive plain still appeared a great city to Ludolf von Suchen (1350). In fact, because of its healthy climate, it had become the residence of the king, bishops, prelates, nobles, barons, and knights, who in Cyprus are the richest in the world; merchants of every nation were to be found there.[32] Martoni (1394) called the city larger than Aversa, with many fine houses, gardens, and orchards which made the place appear sparsely inhabited. The gardens led him to compare the place with Alisia.[33] By the visit of Tafur (1435) Lefkoşa was again the preeminent city: "This is the greatest and most healthy city of the kingdom where the kings and all the lords of the realm always live."[34]

Soon after it fell to Venice it was extolled by the pilgrims Fabri (1483) and Suriano (1484). The former called Lefkoşa "a great city . . . surrounded by fertile and pleasant hills" where are found "merchants from every part of the world, Christians and infidels," where everything was cheap, and where dyes and perfumes of the island and the Orient were sold.[35] Although nearly destroyed by an earthquake in 1480, including palaces, houses, and churches, the town was "twice as big a Perugia."[36]

Although le Saige (1518) considered the city still very large, he could "see that at some former time it was a grand thing;" it had two large castles but the houses were mostly of adobe.[37] Jodicus de Meggen (1542) and John Locke (1553) noted the importance of the place although their impressions were mixed. The former mentions "quite a large town" with lots of ruins within the walls and inadequate fortifications.[38] The latter was impressed by the extensive gardens with date palms and pomegranates. Although all the nobility on the island lived there, the unpaved streets made him think the place rural despite the presence of many good buildings.[39] Fürer von Haimendorf (c. 1566) observed that many of the nobles "are greatly given to amusements, especially hunting and hawking . . .," to games and banquets of "great cost and splendour." They kept their vassals (*parici*) like slaves.[40] Calepio (1573) considered the city to have been a great prize: "As they themselves owned, they enriched themselves to such an extent that never since the sack of Constantinople had they won so vast a treasure, as well of things sacred, as those of common use."[41] Lusignan (1573) held a similar view: "In this city lived all the nobility of Cyprus, Barons, Knights and Feudatories . . ."[42] Graziani called it "the most wealthy and important place of all the Country."[43]

Although Lefkoşa suffered less from disease and natural calamity than the other towns, during the 15th century its economy was weakened and its society unsettled. The Lusignan capital of the 14th century had walls four, seven, or nine miles in circuit, a huge area even though full of gardens.[44] The consequences of rioting over the Genoese-Venetian rivalry in the late 14th and early 15th centuries were not so serious as elsewhere, and the Genoese never occupied the city. Although the Mamluk armies occupied Lefkoşa for a few days in 1426 (from where 2000 people reportedly were carried off to Egypt), the destruction may not have been too great since the Lusignans fled the city without resistance, leaving those citizens who chose not to flee to submit in as pleasant a way as possible.[45] By the beginning of the 15th century Lefkoşa had become the major trading emporium in the eastern Mediterranean. Probably its prestige declined steadily after that until Aleppo unsurped its position sometime after the Ottoman conquest in 1517. Reliable estimates of the population place it in the range of 15,000 to 20,000 people in the 16th century.

Reports of the early 16th century describe the shrunken city: Peter Mesenge in 1507 reported the city only one-fourth inhabited, but with walls in excellent repair. In 1529 Minio found the walls old and weak, although the city was not undistinguished by fine dwellings and gardens. The wealthy had no independent incomes but engaged in trade or farmed estates.[46] A dispute raged over whether Lefkoşa or Magosa was more fit to be capital of the territory: those who supported Lefkoşa pointed to its central location, plentiful good water, and pure air; opponents criticized the unpaved streets, dusty and dirty. In 1567 Venice began an economic and military reentrenchment in the capital. The walled area was reduced to a round, modern defensive fortification three miles in circuit, with low thick walls and a deep moat, and all the buildings and walls outside the fortified area were leveled, including reportedly some eighty churches.[47]

Magosa (Famagusta). In the 14th century Magosa was one of the largest, wealthiest, and most prosperous cities in the entire Mediterranean world. John Mandeville (after 1322) called it "one of the principal havens of the sea that is in the world; and there arrive Christian men and Saracens, and men of all nations."[48] An anonymous Englishman (1344–1345) found it "a paradise of delight" with beautiful buildings and churches, high walls and a deep moat, and irrigated plantations and gardens.

"There reside in it merchants of Venice, Genoa, Catalonia and Saracens from the soldan's dominions, dwelling in palaces which are called 'Loggias,' living in the style of counts and barons; they have abundance of gold and silver. All the precious things of the world may be found in their hands."[49] Ludolf von Suchen (1350) called Magosa "a concourse of merchants and pilgrims ... It is the richest of all cities, and her citizens are the richest of men ... I dare not speak of their precious stones and golden tissues and other riches, for it were a thing unheard of and incredible. In this city dwell many wealthy courtesans, of whom some possess more than 100,000 florins. I dare not speak of their riches."[50] The pilgrim Martoni (1394) extolled it too: "The city of Famagusta is large, as large, I reckon, as the city of Capua, and has fine squares and houses very much like those of Capua, but a greater part, almost a third, is uninhabited, and the houses are destroyed, and this has been done since the date of the Genoese lordship. The said city has finer walls than I have seen in any town, high with broad alleys round them, and many and high towers all round." The fine harbor was protected from every wind, and a great amount of camlet was made there. Formerly Magosa was large and prosperous with 2000 hearths, but now it is "wholly destroyed, so that there is not one sound house, and not one person lives there." The unhealthiness was commonly blamed on a nearby swamp. "And it is held that on account of that marsh, and the great number of courtesans, a bad air effects the men who dwell in that city."[51]

The fate of Magosa was tragic. The "richest of all cities" whose citizens were "the richest of men" became a "hotbed of rioting" and violence between Venetians, Genoese, and their supporters. The city then had to endure a vengeful 91-year occupation starting in 1373 when a Genoese naval force took Magosa through trickery. To that occupation falls much of the blame for Magosa's decline. The monopoly established by the Genoese drove other foreign merchants to Larnaka where the Lusignans offered some concessions. Of course the frequent attempts by kings of Cyprus to recover the city further accelerated the destruction and further undermined trade. Sieges of 1404–1406 and 1407–1410 failed, and the city was surrendered to the Mamluks in 1425 to avoid pillage. As early as 1441 attempts were made to secure the migration of some Armenians in Syria and Anatolia.[52] By the 15th century Magosa had lost much of its brilliance. A report by the Venetian Loredan in

1476 called Magosa "the key and heart of Cyprus," which was becoming deserted and so the rest of the island was going to ruin as a consequence. Venetian plans to settle a few noble families there came to naught, as did considerations of settling Christian refugees from Scutari (Uskudar), Morea, and Corfu. In 1489 Venice offered free transportation and cash benefits (three ducats) to any inhabitants of Corfu and Morea who would move to Magosa. At the same time people banished from Cyprus for homicide were still to be permitted to live in Magosa. Indeed, people banished from other Venetian territories were to be allowed to settle there, and ultimately Magosa was used as a place of banishment. At the end of the century serious consideration was being given to transferring the capital to Magosa in order to revive it.[53] Even a 10-year tax exemption from corvee and a 25-year exemption from salt tax were approved. These seem to be acts of desperation. People knew Magosa's unhealthiness, which Hill considers "largely responsible" for the decay.

Apparently no one would settle there. According to Pero Tafur (1435) Magosa was depopulated because of bad air and bad water around a nearby lake.[54] Felix Fabri (1483) indicated that, despite the good harbor, the place had lost its fame: "Our brethren have a convent there, but it is almost a wreck, for ruin threatens the city and all that is in it. It is said that no man can stay there on account of the corruption of the air." Once Magosa had "a crowd of all nations and tongues. But day by day all these things are vanishing."[55] According to Locke (1553), an English merchant, and Elias of Pesaro (1563), sickness resulting in blindness was rampant among those who lived in the marshy area.[56] Consequently, although the harbor was excellent, the fortifications formidable, and food cheap and abundant, the town failed.[57] Elias praised the bread as the best he had ever eaten anywhere and enumerated other quality crops. The houses were fine and well built, the roads well kept up . . ." and fountains of running water are found at every street corner." The townspeople were very clean and particularly careful to protect themselves from the plague, which is common elsewhere in the Levant.[58] Between the period 1510 and 1560 Venetian estimates of the population ranged between 6000 and 8000.[59] Piri Reis knew it as the only large harbor on the island, with a beautiful castle. Fürer von Haimendorf (1566) admired the fortifications and harbor of the town, which was not very large; he noted the use of oxen and wheels to draw water.[60] Lusignan also mentioned the water wheels.[61] The water supply never failed there. The port, however, had become choked up because the Signory "takes no care of it."[62]

Towns and Villages Which Bear the Same Names as Districts, According to the Ottoman Census and Tax Survey

Lefkoşa. So thorough was the destruction of Lefkoşa in 1570 that in November 1572 when a survey of population and property in the once-resplendent city was taken only 235 adult males lived there. Of that number 11 (5%) were unmarried *(mucerred)*, one blind *(aʿma)*, too elderly to pay taxes *(pir-i fani)*, and one (Piyero (?) Nikola) was canno-neer *(topci)* of the men of the castle. No priests of any kind were evident. The population probably ranged between 1100 and 1200.

The two smallest of the seven surviving quarters of Lefkoşa were occupied by members of religio-ethnic minorities: Armenians and Jacob-ites, who together constituted some 11% of the surviving population. Possibly there were 90 to 95 (18 *hane*, 1 *mucerred*) of the former, 30 to 35 (7 *hane*, 1 *mucerred*) of the latter. They all lived in separate quarters, the quarter of the Armenians *(Ermeniyan)* and the quarter of the Maron-ites *(Yakupi)*. At least in their names the Armenians were completely hellenized, using names like Nikola Zorzi, Hiristofi Toma, Yani Andon, and Loizo Istavriye. Not one Turkish name appeared. The remaining 89% of the populace then presumably were Orthodox Christians. The five quarters they occupied sheltered between 22 and 82 families *(hane)*. Nearly 37% of all the inhabitants (and 42% of the Orthodox) lived in Tripyone (?) quarter.

The total revenues coming from the town amounted to only 147,000 akce annually, of which a mere 5% came from head tax *(cizye)*. (An alternative accounting gives 155,390 akce including an additional 8390 akce from the tax farm of the annual dues paid to timar holders *(ispence)* and unpredictable income *(bad-i heva)* of the Gypsies *(Kibtiyan)* of the entire island, few if any of whom really resided in the walled city of Lefkoşa.) Commerce and industry were of small consequence. A total of 10% (15,000 akce) of the revenues came from wineries *(meyhane)*, and 1% apiece (1500 akce) from a dye factory *(boya hane)* and places for processing heads *(ser)* and tripe *(şikem)*. Another 15% came from the tax farm of market dues *(bac-i bazar)*, the ihtisab, and taxes from the sale of sheep, cattle, and horses *(bac bay-i agnam u kav u esb)*, and the market tax on slaves *(esara)* within the town. Another 2% of the revenues (2500 akce) came from the tax on gardens *(resm-i bustan)* outside the walled city. The three largest sources of revenues from Lefkoşa were: (1) the tax farm of the gates of the walled city *(ebvab-i kal ʿe)* 35,000 akce (24%); (2) unpredictable income, blood money *(dem)*, offences *(cinayet)*, and marriage tax *(resm-i ʿarusane)* of the men of the castles and the re ʿaya, and the wine tax *(baç-i hamr)*, 34,000 akce (23%); and (3) the tax farm of the public treasury *(beyt ul-mal)*, lost property *(mal-i gayb ve mal-i mefkud)*, runaway slaves *(yave ve kaçkun ve murdegan-i ʿabd-i abik)*, 27,500 akce (19%). Obviously the Ottoman conquest of Lefkoşa, besides decimating the population, had at least temporarily bereft the place of its economic significance.

Girniye (Kyrenia). Because of the surrender of the town's small fortress, the Ottoman army had no need to remain long in the vicinity of Girniye. The port was of very small consequence, so Ottoman forces did not land in that area. Since the town had relatively few Latins, the populace was probably affected less than other towns. In 1572 three quarters of Orthodox Christians lived outside the citadel walls *(varoş)*, for that reportedly was forbidden to them. Another indication of relative continuity is that each quarter had its own priest: Baba Filipo Bernardo, Baba Piyero Enadam (?), and Baba Maniko (v.) Baba Zako. Girniye had a total of 198 adult males, and its quarters ranged between 60 and 76. Besides 147 married taxpaying males *(hane)*, the town had 49 unmarried adult males *(mucerred)*, 1 blind, and 1 cannoneer. Also included was one kethuda'-i Girniye Parlat (?), who lived in Aya Yorgi quarter. Probably the town had between 735 and 810 inhabitants.

Largely as a consequence of the minimal destruction which Girniye saw during the Ottoman conquest, it paid over 50% more taxes than Lefkoşa. Clearly the predominate urban function of Girniye was as a port. A total of 59,000 akce of the 90,500 akce annually paid in taxes by the townspeople went for a single tax, identified as the tax farm of the pier *(iskele)* and the harbor customary dues *(hakk-i liman)* and the customary anchorage dues *(resm-i lenker)*. Another 4000 came from revenues of fishing from enclosures of nets fixed on poles used for catching fish *(talyan-i mahi)*. Thus 69% of all revenues came from Girniye's position on the sea: 65% from the harbor and 4% from fishing. Another 3% (2500 akce) came from the urban function of the tax farm of the market place *(bac-i bazar)*, ihtisab, butcher shops *(kassabhane)* and processing sheep heads *(ser hane)*. Nearly 2% of the revenues came from water for arable lands around the Platane stream *(maᶜ -i mezra ᶜa)*. The remaining 26% (23,500 akce) in revenues came from the two sequences identified as "unpredictable incomes" and "the public treasury."

Hirsofi (Khyrsokhou). Except for its designation as a town *(nefs)*, Hirsofi was indistinguishable from villages. There 141 adult males, including 111 with families *(hane)*, 14 unmarried *(mucerred)*, and 1 widow *(bive)* occupied two quarters, Kiyutole (?) and Ayo Nikola. Villagers produced 225 kantar of cotton annually, worth 67,500 akce; that amounted to 28% of the total produce. Over half of the town's produce was derived from grain. 6000 keyl of wheat worth 72,000 akce, and constituting 30% of all agricultural produce were cultivated, as well as 4725 keyl of barley (worth 33,350 akce, 14% of all produce). In addition, 940 keyl of lentils worth (11,700 akce, 5% of all produce) and 625 keyl of broad beans (worth 6,250 akce, 3%) were grown. Other crops in much smaller amounts were produced, including olives, sisam, and flax. A total of 8150 akce worth of other fruits and vegetables were produced (3% of production) and 4500 akce worth of fish were caught. Since the people of Hirsofi paid 47,955 akce in taxes annually, their total agricultural produce probably was worth around 220,000 akce.

Baf (Paphos). Because of its location, Baf probably experienced little destruction from the Ottoman conquest. Nevertheless, the town paid only 56,059 akce in taxes annually despite a population of 1100 or 1200, virtually the same as Lefkoşa. The registered taxpayers in the town included somewhere between 236 and 247 married adult males *(muzevvec,* instead of the usual *hane)*, between 31 and 35 unmarried adult males *(mucerred)*, and 3 blind. Possibly the notation unmarried was omitted from some names which thus may be considered married; only the names of 68 married men are listed in Asomato quarter even though the scribe indicates 78. Baf had five quarters in 1572, ranging from Pano Domati (?) with 33 adult males to Asomato with 90. Each quarter had a priest, and Pano Domati (?) indeed had four.

The people of Baf paid 34% of all their taxes (19,300 akce) for a tax farm connected with the customs of the pier *(gumruk-i iskele)*, weighing grain *(kabban-i dakik)*, selling sheep *(baç bay-i agnam)*, the customary anchorage dues *(resm-i lenker)*, and the selling of slaves *(pencik-i esara)*. No other tax rivaled that one. Of all the taxes 7% went for market dues *(bac-i bazar)*, ihtisab, and wine dues (3900 akce). Another 750 akce went for dyehouses *(boya hane)*. Three percent were paid by revenues from the saltworks *(memleha)* of the district (1950 akce) and another 3% (1375 akce) from fishing *(mahi)*. Agricultural taxes included 4500 akce (i.e., 8%) for customary taxes on acorns *(resm-i bellut)*, indicating an acorn crop worth some 22,500 akce. Eleven percent of tax revenues (30,000 akce) came from 2500 keyl of wheat and 7% (19,500 akce) from 3250 keyl of barley. Other grains were produced in very small amounts. A total of 1350 akce (3% of the taxes) came from the customary tax on fruits and vegetables *(resm-i meyve u bosatin)* and 900 akce for pigs. Eleven percent of taxes went for the series of taxes labeled the tax farm of the public treasury and another 7% for that labeled unpredictable income.

Pano (Upper) and Kato (Lower) Evdim (Evdimon). Although these two villages passed their name to the district of Evdim *(nahiye)*, in fact they are listed as villages rather than towns. Their tax obligations indicate no connection with district administration nor any other kinds of urban functions. The lower village was a large and very prosperous one with a diversified economy, while the upper village was of medium size and probably below average in its wealth.

Pano Evdim village had 140 adult male residents, of whom 14 were unmarried and 2 blind. Perhaps its population was 600 or 650. The villagers paid 49,583 akce in taxes annually (or 40,583 akce according to another entry); undoubtedly they produced crops worth over 220,000 akce. The leading crops were cotton and grains, which amounted, respectively, to 39% and over 36% of total produce. A total of 320 kantar of cotton was produced, worth 96,000 akce, and 5500 keyl of wheat and 3250 of barley were cultivated, worth 66,000 akce and 19,500 akce respectively. Another 8% of agricultural taxes came from carobs; 535 kantar worth 18,725 akce were produced. In addition, 3% (1500 akce) of taxes came from wineries *(meyhane)*, with produce worth 7500 akce, and 2% (957 akce) from 435 kantar of olives, which were worth 4785 akce.

Kato Evdim on the other hand, had only 250 to 300 villagers; they paid taxes of 4650 akce on agricultural production that may have been worth 14,000 akce. The register noted 61 adult males, of whom 5 were unmarried. The leading crop in Kato Evdim was carobs, which accounted for 15% of village taxes, wheat, which accounted for 14%, and barley, 8%. Villagers produced 100 kanatar of carobs annually, worth 3500 akce, alone with 270 keyl of wheat worth 3240 akce and 310 keyl of barley worth 1860 akce.

Limosa (Limassol). In 1572 Limosa was a very small town with 177 adult males, including 13 unmarried *(mucerred)*. Probably it had between 800 and 850 people, divided into three quarters. One of those is named quarter of the Catholics (?) *(Katelogi),* so presumably at least its 63 married and 6 unmarried adult males belonged to the Church of Rome. Possibly others in Ayanbe (? Atyabe?) or Ayo Mama quarters were also Catholic, although most likely just the nearly 40% of the population in the quarter of Catholics were.

However modest its size, Limosa really did serve important functions as an urban port. Nearly two-thirds of the taxes paid by the townspeople dealt with such functions. A total of 63% (27,000 akce) of the 42,957 akce in taxes paid locally went for the tax farm of the customs of the pier *(gumruk-i iskele)* and the weighing of flour *(kabban-i dakik).* Another 3% (1400 akce) went for the bazaar dues *(bac-i bazar)* and ihtisab. Some 15% of taxes went for grains, including 10% for wheat and 4% for barley. Villagers produced 1875 keyl of wheat, worth 22,500 akce annually, and 1950 keyl of barley worth 8700 akce, as well as numerous fruits and vegetables in very small quantities.

Larnaka, dependent on Tuzla. Although designated as town *(nefs)* rather than village, in every other way Larnaka exactly resembled the villages. With 63 adult males, 3 of whom were unmarried *(mucerred)* (and 1 of whom had a defective memory *(nasiye)*), the town had between 290 and 320 people.

Larnaka was simply a grain-growing village, where a disproportionate amount of barley was produced. About half, 51%, of all taxes came from grain cultivation, and 2070 akce of the 5934 akce in agricultural taxes came from barley, as Larnaka produced 1725 keyl worth 10,350 akce. Another 385 keyl of wheat was produced, worth 4620 akce. This meant 35% of the revenues came from barley, 16% from wheat, and 5% from flax, of which 750 bunches *(demet)* worth 1500 akce was produced. In all the townspeople produced less than 17,500 akce worth of agricultural crops.

No population figures appeared for Tuzla, but revenues of 100,000 akce came annually from the tax farm of the saltworks *(memleha)* and 12,500 akce came from the customs duty of the pier *(gumruk-i iskele)*, weighing flour *(kabban-i dakik)*, customary taxes of the bazaars *(bac-i bazar)*, and ihtisab.

Pano (Upper) and Kato (Lower) Lefkare. Although a Mazoto village existed it clearly was a place of small consequence, for it only had about 40 people (5 married adult males). If any village in Mazoto district *(nahiye)* had any administrative significance, that would be Lefkare.

Pano Lefkare village had 35 or 36 unmarried adult males out of a total of 259 adult males, meaning a population between 1225 and 1275. Villagers were divided into some six quarters, half of which had priests. The largest quarter, Istavro Kateloko, comprising 20% of the village population, presumably was occupied by Latin Christians.

To the extent that taxation represents wealth, Pano Lefkare was not an unusually wealthy village, although it did produce at least small quantities of a great number of crops. Of the taxes of the villagers 43% (12,800 akce) came from wine. They produced 1600 keyl worth 64,000 akce. A further 10% of revenues came from olives; of them the villagers produced 1300 keyl, worth 14,300 akce. Another 12% of revenues came from grains, of which 9% was from wheat. The villagers produced 1100 keyl of that, worth 13,200 akce, and 650 keyl of barley worth 3900 akce. Total village taxes were close to 30,000 akce annually (not the 18,613 erroneously recorded), meaning agricultural production must have been worth over 100,000 akce. The village even had a tannery *(debbag hane)* which paid taxes of 150 akce.

Kato Lefkare village had 91 adult males (including 4 unmarried), making a total population between 450 and 475. The village had two quarters, one of which had a priest. Villagers paid taxes of 11,292 akce on their agricultural produce, of which 42% came from wine, 8% from olives, and 7% from wheat. The villagers produced 600 keyl of wine worth 24,000 akce, 40 keyl of olives worth 4400 akce, and 350 keyl of wheat worth 4200 akce. Kato Lefkare was apparently slightly richer than Pano Lefkare.

Pendaye. Pendaye was one of the wealthiest villages on the island of Cyprus, but despite bearing the same name as a district, it was clearly registered as a village and had no urban or commercial significance. Forty-three adult males lived in the village, of whom eight were unmarried and three widowers *(bive)*. That means the village had a population of between 1600 and 2000. Almost three quarters of village revenues came from grains, including 72% wheat, 10% barley, and almost 1% lentils. Villagers produced 4500 keyl of wheat annually, worth 54,000 akce, 1250 keyl of barley, worth 7500 akce, and 45 keyl of lentils worth 585 akce. Another 3% of the revenues came from 20 keyl of olives worth 2200 akce. Villagers paid 15,102 akce in taxes on agricultural produce worth some 67,500 akce.

Karpas. The village of Karpas was one of the wealthier villages in Cyprus in 1572, and one of the largest ones. Like most other villages from which districts took their names, the place served no urban functions at all. Having 102 unmarried adult males and 297 married ones, the village probably had a population of between 1475 and 1500.

Karpas was strongly a grain-growing village, more than two-thirds of its agricultural tax revenues coming from such crops, including 37% from wheat, 19% from barley, and 11% from lentils. Karpas produced 12,750 keyl of wheat worth 153,000 akce, 13,000 keyl barley worth 78,000 akce, and 3500 keyl of lentils worth 45,500 akce. In addition, 5% of the tax revenues came from sheep tax and 1% (1200 akce) from wineries. Karpas also produced an array of goods in smaller quantities. In all it may have produced agricultural goods worth 330,000 akce. (In one place 80,000 akce is used for the total taxes, in another 47,886 akce; the latter seems to be only a slight undercount.)

Magosa. Interestingly, while Lefkoşa seems to have been utterly destroyed in the conquest, the fall of Magosa in 1571 does not seem to have had consequences quite so devastating. Although the population of Lefkoşa in the 1560s must have been at least double that of Magosa, in November 1572 Magosa had five or even six times as many inhabitants. Although Lefkoşa had been the economic heart of the island in the

1560s, with Magosa reduced to naval and port services so that even Limosa was beginning to challenge it, Magosa in November 1572 was able to pay nearly three times as much in taxes as Lefkoşa. Whatever its circumstance, Magosa was the only place on the island with any claim to being a commercial center. Apparently accounts of its destruction have been exaggerated. Nor can population transfers account for the circumstances, for no indication is given that any were from other places, and clearly none were Muslims.

Magosa had 20 quarters, the largest of which were Ayo Yani Gopoz (?) with 143 adult males (including 34 unmarried, 4 widows (bive), 1 disabled (ma'luc), 1 old man, 1 imperial architect (benna'-i hass), 1 aquaduct worker (su yolci), and 1 priest. Second largest was Aya Nikola with 120 adult males, including 31 unmarried and 11 widows. Eight other quarters had at least 100 adult males, the smallest quarters were Ayo Ana with 38 adult males (including 10 unmarried and 3 widows), Ayo Anton with 47 (11 unmarried, 3 widows), and Ayo Mama with 49 (12 unmarried, 2 widows).

Magosa had between 1621 and 1628 taxpaying adult males in 1572. A total of 1621 people are listed as paying ispence but 1628 names are entered in the register. Of the 1628 names listed, 1193 were married and 435 unmarried. An additional 113 are listed as tax-exempt adult males, including 15 blind, 89 widows, 1 disabled (ma'luc), 1 elderly, 1 water channel superviser (su yolci), 1 imperial architect, 1 paralyzed (kuturum), and 3 cannoneers (topci-i kal'e) (?). Magosa had a population between 5950 and 6300, which probably was little changed from the 1560s.

Among the population were six married and one unmarried male Jews who lived not in a single quarter but dispersed. They had names like Şimail Abraham, Abraham David, and Musa Abraham.

Residents of Magosa paid 418,250 akce in taxes annually, of which 60,000 went to the governor of the subprovince (mir liva-i Magosa) and the remainder to the imperial government (the padişah). Magosa was quite a commercial city, influenced primarily by its position as a port but also in an important way as an important commercial center. A total of 18,000 akce came from fishing with ropes and nets (talyan-i mahi), 4% of the total revenues. Another 6750 akce (2%) came from title deeds for slaves (pencik-i esara), the customary harbor dues (hakk-i liman), and the customary dues for anchorage (resm-i lenger). In addition, 4500 akce (1%) came from taxes on dye houses *(boya hane)*, and another 500 akce from tanneries. The sum of 4500 akce came from customs on sheep, cattle, and places for processing heads and tripe, and butcher shops *(baç bay-i agnam u kav u ḫaşhane u şikem hane)*. A total of 25,500 akce (6%) of the revenues came from the tax farm of ihtisab and the customs on slaves *(baç bazar-i esara ve baç-i esir)*, and 47% of all the revenues—195,000 akce—annually came from the tax farms of the customs duties of the harbor *(gumruk-i iskele)* of the walled city of Magosa, weighing flour *(kabban-i dakkik)*, and the custom of the gates of the city walls *(baç-i ebvab-i kalʿe)*. Another 18% (75,000 akce) came from the windfall series which included customary tax on wine *(baç-i hamr)* and revenues from wineries *(mahsul-i meyhane)*.

Gypsies *(cemaʿet-i taife-i Kibtiyan-i perakende der cezire-i Kıbrıs)*

In 1572 207 adult males scattered across on the island of Cyprus were classified as Gypsies (Kibtiyan). Each Gypsy paid 30 akce as his main agricultural tax *(ispence)*; besides 6210 akce ispence, the Gypsies paid another 2180 akce for unpredictable income, blood money, and so on, adding a total of 8390 akce annually to the revenues for the sultan from Lefkoşa.

Thirteen of those adult male Gypsies are identified as Muslims, the largest single group of Muslims in the whole tax survey. Nine of them are identified as converts to Islam, so possibly they lived in Cyprus before the Ottoman conquest, although equally possibly they may have accompanied the new conquerors in hope of booty. Since they have typical Muslim names like Mehmed bn ʿAbdullah, Yunus bn ʿAbdullah, Huseyn bn ʿAbdullah, and Ahmed bn ʿAli, it is impossible to guess their ethnic or linguistic origin. Moreover, since they are identified only as adult males *(nefer)*, their total numbers may be anywhere from 13 to 65 or 70. Apparently in 1572 their taxation remained as it had been prior to their accepting Islam, hardly an inducement to conversion.

Among the non-Muslim Gypsies one counts 194 adult males *(nefer)*, of whom some 30 were unmarried, meaning a total of about 850 people. Like the Armenians of Lefkoşa, the island's non-Muslim Gypsies were probably quite hellenized. Most of them had typical Greek Cypriot names like Yorgi Kiryako, Mihail Yani, Filipo Andon, Kiryako Zako, and Mihail Ergiro. No hint is given of their ethnic, religious, or linguistic origins, either.

Magosa after 1571

Surely the Ottoman conquerors regarded Magosa with enthusiasm, but to them also fell the burden of its defense. They could not easily forget the cost in lives and money of subduing the place. If it were lost to enemy hands it might be recovered only with the greatest difficulty, and indeed be used to terrorize them. The Ottomans competently rebuilt and restored the damaged fortifications. Although occasionally attempts were made to seize Magosa, they were never serious threats. Certain traditions report a panic in Magosa in February 1572, when a few ships appeared offshore. Supposedly the walls were in ruin and the Ottomans feared that the ships were the vanguard of a Latin fleet, so they put on Cypriot dress, fled to Lefkoşa, or made terms with the Cypriots, but this smacks of Latin Christian optimism projected in the enthusiasm after the Ottoman defeat at Lepanto.[63] In 1590 Cypriot Mark Memmo of Baf proposed the conquest of Magosa with a single merchantship, 200 Italians, 50 Cypriots, and bribery.[64] On may 24, 1607 a small Tuscan fleet of eight galleys and nine galleons appeared at Magosa and failed in an attempt to seize it, withdrawing with heavy casualties.[65] Thereafter although plotting remained frequent, no more real attempts followed.

Magosa remained an enigma. The Ottomans neglected to utilize the advantages of the position in either commercial or naval strategy. By excluding foreign merchants, by locating the governor in Lefkoşa, and by letting the foreign merchants and their consuls collect in Larnaka, they seriously weakened the position of Magosa. Ships occasionally stopped there to collect cheap supplies for their westward journeys, but hardly anyone else visited Magosa. Greek Orthodox Christians had been allowed to remain there, or indeed to move into the walled city after the conquest; they continued to use their cathedral, St. George's, and the nearby chapel of St. Simeon until 1573–1574 when suddenly they were forced to sell their property and to move outside the walls.[66] Within a decade or two after the conquest, when the Ottomans had lost the impetus of being on the offensive in the Mediterranean, they simply sat back in defense. Piracy against Ottoman shipping in the eastern Mediterranean again became rampant. While the fortress was not threatened, the Ottomans never utilized the potential of Magosa to collect a fleet and strike those pirates who passed nearby, as they had in Algiers, for example.

Palerne (1581) regarded Magosa as one of the most beautiful harbors in the world, although neglected by the Ottomans. The fortress was very small, but it was one of the strongest and most beautiful he had ever seen (guarded by 50 Turks, 50 janissaries, and 50 others). Christians were not allowed to live within the walled city, and the main churches had become mosques.[67] According to Calepio (1573) Magosa was in ruins and defenseless; it had suffered from a whirlwind in 1566 and eight or 10 earthquakes in 1569. When the townspeople had surrendered they supposed that their property would be guaranteed, but many of them were driven out by the conquerors; they were allowed the right of preemption if Turks wanted to sell. The Greek Orthodox got possession of their cathedral and the church of St. Simeon, as well as houses not possessed by the Turks, and the Latins could only live as Orthodox there, so they were compelled to dissemble.[68] Zvallart (1586) discovered that Tuzla (Salines) was the new port for exports because the Ottomans rarely allowed foreigners to Magosa lest they seize the fortress.[69] De Villamont (1589) heard that nearly all the inhabitants had died from the plague raging there. He reported that the pasha usually lived there an account of the "fine harbor and incomparable fortress."[70] Thévenot (1590) challenged the reports of Ottoman brutality and massacres: "And still you see the Greeks and others live in entire liberty."[71] But he was aware of the great Ottoman losses in the siege. In the same year Somer found the area prolific in sugar, olive oil, and cotton, but with such pestilential air that the capital had to be moved to Lefkoşa. Still, the town was as great in area *(wesen)* as Amsterdam, although not so populous. The town for him was a beautiful one, inhabited by both Turks and Greeks.[72] Magosa then was the only real harbor on the island.[73] Ten Christian refugees from a 1597 revolt in Magosa were picked up on Castel Rosso (Meis ada); the revolt supposedly had failed because the rebels lacked leadership.[74] The English merchant John Sanderson (1598) considered Magosa "a very strong citie and port for their gallies."[75] Cotovicus (1599) called the harbor "remarkable and most safe"; the town was "fairly spacious and populous," although the walls were neglected and had breeches.[76] The clockmaker Thomas Dallam (1600) thought Magosa "a grate and large towne."[77] For Henry de Beauvau (1604), although its harbor was too small for some vessels, it and Rhodes were the best fortresses in the empire, and Magosa was one of Cyprus' capitals.[78] Pedro Teixeira (1605) also identifies Magosa as one of two capitals, both shadows of their former selves.[79] Lithgow (1610) considered Rhodes and Magosa the strongest fortresses in the empire. He mentioned an unsuccessful attack by Ferdinand, duke of Florence with five galleys in 1607.[80] Sandys (1610) also mentioned the Florentine attack on that "very strong citie."[81] Des Hayes (1621) gave a good description of the city and harbor, with a map. The town, he said, was pretty large and well built, with a small narrow harbor and straight roads, uncommonly handsome, in fact. Christians were not allowed to live there.[82]

De Bruyn (1683) had a bad experience in Magosa. He was not allowed to enter the walled city or even approach the outer walls. He reports on silk and mulberries in local villages and also on locusts.[83] Olfert Dapper (1688), however, was able to describe the port and harbor in some detail. He was very impressed by the walls. He considered the town pretty large and well built, with very straight roads, although the harbor was small and narrow. Christians could not live in the town. The region produced the best of cotton.[84] For Van der Nijenburg the Magosa area had the worst air on the island and was extremely unhealthy; the town was small, most of the residents being Turkish soldiers, although in the suburbs there were houses with gardens.[85] Richard Pococke (1738) considered the place sparsely inhabited with very little trade although extremely cheap provisions.[86]

Larnaka and Tuzla after 1570

Larnaka and Tuzla (Salines) seem to have been burned in the process of Ottoman conquest.[87] When Leonhart Rauwolff and his business associates landed there in 1573 to get water and to ask about friends working for a German firm, they were met by three armed, mounted Turks and an Italian interpreter who interrogated them about their business purposes and about conditions in Europe. Later they found the market area was still in ruins from 1570 but the saltworks were flourishing.[88] London merchant Laurence Aldersey (1581) described Tuzla as "a ruinated citie" with only seventeen inhabitants.[89] Jean Zvallart (1586), chevalier du Sainct Sepulchre, found Tuzla (Salines) the port for exporting sugar, cotton, and other goods because the Ottomans rarely admitted foreigners to Magosa. In fact the place really did not have a port like Limosa or Tripoli in Syria for a beach prevented approaching land.[90] When de Villamont arrived in 1589 he found that the church of St. Lazarus had been bought for 3000 aspers (e.g., about 31 gold crowns) just two months earlier and was again being used by both Latin and Greek rites; another church had been converted to a mosque.[91] There was plentiful salt production, and abundant wheat.[92] De Villamont mentioned signaling the kadi to get permission to land; Cotovicus (1599) visited and offered the "customary gifts" to the "emir." According to Cotovicus, salt production had declined under the Ottomans because of their neglect. Larnaka had small huts where visitors could stay, and also a small Latin chapel of the Minorites, whose work he extolled, adding that every Venetian vessel paid them a ducat. There was also a small Greek chapel.[93]

Because, whether through pious intention or benign neglect, the Ottomans timidly limited the use of Magosa to military and naval concerns, Larnaka and its port Tuzla (Salines/Scala) managed to avoid total decay. Larnaka was further blessed by the unwillingness of the Porte to have consuls and foreign merchants resident in Magosa, while they themselves refused to reside in Lefkoşa, far from the sea and easily under the thumb of the governor *(beglerbegi)*. Of course, life expectancy must have been short, with malaria rampant around the salt lake and swamps.

John Sanderson passed two months in Larnaka in 1598 waiting for a ship to be loaded with salt.[94] According to Henry de Beauvau (1604), Tuzla had become the main port for exporting the cotton and other produce of the island; copper and Karaman carpets were also exported from there, where the French consul resided.[95] The small fort being erected in 1605 when Pedro Teixeira passed there, for fear of the Spanish or Maltese, was of no great significance, but doubtless enabled the garrison to hold out until help could be mustered in Lefkoşa and Magosa; P. della Valle (1625) described it as small and of little importance.[96] Larnaka, according to Teixeira, had about 300 houses of mud and stone, poor and small, with terraced roofs. The port was good and safe, but large ships had to anchor half a league offshore in 12 to 15 fanthoms of sea.[97] Louis des Hayes Courmenin (1621) mentions Salines as a large town near the sea with a tower and some cannon commanding the shore where trade in cotton, wine, and carobs was carried on. Tuzla had become the leading port on the island.[98]

The port was the principal and most frequented landing place in

Cyprus, surrounded by a large bay, according to P. della Valle (1625). Tuzla is a "small roadstead with a small fort, square, with a platform and a few pieces of artillery." Most of the Franks lived at Larnaka, including the Venetian merchants and consul. The place was "half destroyed" because of the neglect of the Ottomans.[99] Christian corsairs approached there to take on water or dispose of prizes, but they waited at a distance at first to see whether a white flag or a red one was flying.[100] C. de Bruyn pointed out that all the European merchants (mostly French) lived there. Although the village was of low quality, the salt pits were flourishing and new salt was gathered every day.[101] Dapper (1688) also reported the presence of merchants and consuls, and that all trade was handled there; he viewed the salt pans half a mile away and reported on a great decline in salt production and sugar cultivation under the Ottomans.[102] Mr. Robert (1696) held that disease made the main port dangerous.[103] Two early 18th-century travellers, van der Nijenberg (1720) and Pococke (1738), also emphasized the unhealthy location. For the former it had the worst air in Cyprus because of the salt pans and swamps.[104] Nevertheless Larnaka remained the chief port of the island until the 20th century.

Teixeira mentioned consulates of Venice, England, France, and Flanders.[105] At the conquest the Ottomans had seized the Latin church of St. Lazarus, but in 1589 they sold it to the Greek Orthodox for the nominal sum of 3000 aspers (c. 25 Italian ducats). The Latins were allowed in courtesy to use the church for two annual processions. In 1593 the Friars Minor were allowed to build a convent, although they were not allowed to construct a church before 1596; in 1605 the Venetian merchants had a small chapel with a Franciscan friar, later probably replaced by Capuchins.[106]

Limosa after 1570

De Villamont carefully observed the Limosa region in his visit of 1589. The "village" was located on a beautiful plain of olive, fig, and carob trees; the thinly populated plain was planted with wheat and barley. An earthquake five years earlier had destroyed many houses, which had been rebuilt in a slovenly fashion; they were of earth covered with rushes and fascines, with low doors to prevent Turks from entering them on horseback. The wine was strong and cheap but "corrosive." The Turks wore roses, violets, and other flowers on their turbans and frequented the baths daily.[107] As de Villamont's vessel had to send to the kadi for permission to enter, so did that of Cotovicus. A mosque and public bath are mentioned, and a small Greek church. The Ottomans had a small fortress in the middle of the village, with a cannon and some janissaries to protect against pirates. Cotton was produced in great quantity; other crops included grapes, shrubs, garden produce, figs, olives, carob trees, melons, pumpkins, gourds, and fine bananas. Most of the people were Greeks, who were usually engaged in commerce or agriculture, while a few Jews were involved in trade and "the Turks are sunk in sloth."[108] Dandini (1596) had reported that there was no church for his retinue to worship in, but presumably he would not have counted an Orthodox church.[109] Henry de Beauvau (1604) observed the small fortress and pointed out the good quality of the surrounding land, where cotton and other crops were grown.[110] Des Hayes described the place, like Larnaka, as a large town with a tower and a cannon, where cotton, wine, and carobs were cultivated and exported.[111] To della Valle (1625) the town was "fairly large and populous."[112] Olfert Dapper (1688) pointed to the good cotton, as well as to wine, carobs, oranges, and lemons. The janissary garrison in the castle was still necessary to guard against pirates. The Greeks and Jews, who mostly were merchants, lived in the same quarter and the Turks in another; the Turks had a small mosque and the Orthodox a church.[113] The vineyards of the small place were praised by R. Pococke (1738), as was the cheap food. By that time the Orthodox had two churches and the Muslims a dervish convent.[114] Both Pococke and Tollot (1731) emphasize the continuing need to be on defense against pirates.[115]

Baf (Paphos) after 1570

When Zvallart visited the well-watered villages in Baf in 1586, grain, cotton, sugar, and good water were abundant.[116] O. Dapper (1688) also praised the good cotton.[117] De Villamont (1589), Cotovicus (1599), Henry de Beauvau (1608), de Bruyn (1683), and Pococke (1738) all attest to the town's ruined condition and small population.[118]

Girniye (Kyrenia) after 1570

Girniye continued to be an important fortress. Since it had surrendered, no repairs were needed. The few visitors who got to Girniye in the early

Ottoman period describe it as the most prosperous, healthiest, and best-fortified place on the island.[119] For example, Porcacchi (1576) called it the coolest and healthiest place on the island and extolled the wonderful fertility of the nearby Lapta (Lapithos) region.[120] Cotovicus (1599) called the fortress impregnable and reported that the place had many inhabitants.[121] Sandys (1610) called the fortress very strong.[122] Stochove (1631) found the town pretty ruined, but the small harbor all right for small vessels; most of the people were Greek Orthodox, and the Turks all spent the night in the castle.[123] A memorandum of 1668 presented to the Duke of Savoy by Peter Senni of Pisa relates that Girniye could easily be conquered.[124] Hurtel (1670) was unimpressed with the dwellings, mostly inhabited by Greek Orthodox, but de Bruyn thought the fortress pretty strong.[125] O. Dapper (1688) found the small market town pleasant, with the castle very strong and inaccessible; the site was the healthiest on the island. He also learned of trade from Karaman and Payas.[126] R. Pococke (1738) mentioned that trade, and the presence of a church and five or six Christian families.[127]

Lefkoşa after 1570

The destruction of the conquest of Lefkoşa is dwelled upon by Calepio (1573), who was there, Graziani (1571?), and Lusignan (1573). According to those accounts wholesale massacre and enslavement took place, no one being spared.[128] The earliest visitor after the conquest was Zvallart, (1586), who say little except that there were churches of many nations and monasteries of many orders to be found there.[129] Dandini, who spent several days there on his way to the Maronite patriarchate as a papal legate, called the city "large and fair," with at least 30,000 inhabitants, of whom 4000 or 5000 were Turks. The city had a small Latin church with an old priest and also a Maronite church in poor condition. The Greeks there very much hated the Latins, insulting them, boxing their ears, and punching their noses.[130] De Beauvau (1604) found the place well fortified.[131] For Teixeira (1605) Lefkoşa was merely one of two capitals, and a shadow of its former self.[132] Lithgow, while observing that most of its greatness was gone, called Lefkoşa a "strong handsome city," and the principal one on the island.

Gedoyn (c. 1623) called it a rich and beautiful city; he and de Beauvau both agreed that the Ottoman governor and the French vice consul resided there.[133] Sandys (1610) described the formidable circular walls and the residence there of all the French factors. "The buildings are low, flat rooft, the entrances little, for the most part ascended by staires for the more difficult entry." Once Lefkoşa was "not yeelding in beauty (before defaced by the Turke) unto the principall cities of Italy."[134] For Stochove (1630) Lefkoşa is "a most delightful place" with the best air in Cyprus, and the residence of the French consul. "The city is rich in gardens chiefly of date palms: the number of crows is incredible, the trees are black with them;" the Turks would not kill them nor countenance others' disturbing them. The gates of the fine but then-neglected fortifications closed at sunset. The houses were Venetian; some were large and of fine cut stone, but the streets were narrow.[135] Sebastian Manrique (1643) was ambivalent on the subject. On the one hand he describes his arrival at ". . . what had in days gone by been the lovely and famous town of Nicosia. But nowadays, although it retains the same name, most of its greatness has disappeared, save ruins and traces of what once was." Still it had a "strong handsome City wall."[136]

Several Europeans visited Lefkoşa late in the 17th century. For Van der Nijenburg (1684? Heyman 1720) Lefkoşa was a "pretty handsome" place even though the fortifications had been neglected.[137] Dapper described the fertile, well-watered plain of Mesaoria, with four Greek churches, two Latin (one Italian, the other French), and one Armenian, and the best cotton anywhere.[138] Hurtel saw the town as "pretty large" on a "vast plain" with beautiful gardens, wide and handsome streets, and houses (reportedly Venetian in origin) of good cut stone.[139] For de Bruyn (1683) the town and its houses were pretty mediocre and not well cared for. Although he could not enter St. Sophia mosque he was allowed to look at the outside. The Greeks had their own quarter and occupied almost half the town. Very good silk stuff and dimities were made there.[140] The pirate Robert had heard that the city was very populous and well fortified.[141] Pococke (1738) goes in detail about the fine quality cotton stuffs, dimities, and half satins produced in abundance there.[142] Pococke, Sonnini (century, referred to in LeSaige), Corancez (pre-1816), Clarke (1812), and the Archduke Louis Salvator (1881) praise the abundance and quality of the town's water supply.[143]

Summary

All of Cyprus's traditional cities, Lefkoşa, the capital, Magosa, Girniye, Larnaka, Limosa, and Baf were in relative decline starting at least from the early 16th century, under Venetian rule. All except the centrally located capital benefited from being ports, although often with dismal facilities. the most important factor in their viability was the degree to which they were, or could be, fortified. The Lusignans, like the Crusaders, depended on fortresses for protection from hostile locals.

Lefkoşa, with its great wealth, had a relatively healthy location in the interior, and was a major trading emporium until it lost out to Aleppo. Its once very formidable fortifications, based on very high walls were inadequate because of the increasingly powerful cannons of the 16th century, and so city walls were reduced to three miles of very thick but low walls, additionally protected by a deep moat. The great emporium and manufacturing center of Magosa suffered terribly from malaria by the 16th century, so that it seemed to get worse daily. It had an excellent harbor surrounded by very formidable walls, along with a more-than-adequate water supply.

The destruction of Lefkoşa by the Ottomans was of very high magnitude. Immediately after the conquest a survey was taken which found only 235 adult male taxpayers remaining. Within the walls a small number of Armenians and Maronites survived, each with their own church, but over 90% of the survivors were Greek Orthodox. Commerce and industry were of small consequence, mostly wineries, a dye house, places for processing animal heads, and tripe. Obviously the Ottoman conquest had not only decimated the people, but also bereft the place of its real economic significance.

Girniye, on the other hand, had surrendered; probably it suffered few adverse consequences, and continued to operate as a port, paying customs and anchorage taxes, for net fishing, and a market place. Although Baf, because of its location, probably experienced little destruction during the conquest, it had a very small population, and paid very little in taxes, much of which was connected with agriculture; only minor revenues came from its customs duties and market dues, although it did have a dye house, and fishing facilities.

Limosa, although it only had 177 adult males according to the survey of 1572, did seem to function as an urban port. Nearly two-thirds of the taxes involved the customs of the pier and weighing flour; also enumerated were bazaar dues and a muhtasib. Larnaka, dependent on Tuzla, with 63 adult males was not easily distinguishable from a village in the taxes it paid. No population is given for Tuzla, although it paid 100,000 akce annually from the tax farm of the salt works, and another 12,500 akce from combined customs, weighing flour and market taxes.

Lefkoşa apparently was utterly destroyed when it was conquered. At the time of the survey of 1572 Magosa's population was at least double that of the provincial capital, despite the fact that Lefkoşa had become the economic heart of the island by the 1560s. Magosa apparently paid three times what Lefkoşa paid; it had 20 quarters, for its 1621 or 1628 taxpayers, which probably meant a little changed population after the Ottoman conquest. It was important for its port, but also as a commercial center, with fishing, harbor dues, dye houses, tanneries, butcher shops, and flour mills, and wineries. After 1572, Magosa was then turned into some sort of fortress, from which even the local Greek Orthodox were excluded, and all of its long distance trade was ended, so it was reduced to being almost useless strategically, and militarily, despite the advantageous location and fortification.

After 1570 Larnaka and Tuzla, despite the fact that they really did not have a good harbor, were the only places where the Ottomans would allow any foreign merchants, for they were forbidden in Magosa. Foreign merchants and consuls were very strongly encouraged to live in Tuzla; so it soon became the leading port on the island. Limosa became almost totally a place given over to agriculture, and was only infrequently visited by foreigners.

As for Baf, many sources attest to its small population and ruined condition as late as the early 18th century. Girniye continued to have an important fortress, and remained very fertile, and one of the healthiest places on the island. The handful of Muslims there resided within the fortress.

Despite the very great destruction which Lefkoşa underwent at the time of the conquest in 1572, at least by c. 1600 it seems to have become restored, and to be again the principal urban center on the island, with its large Greek Orthodox population, its smaller Muslim population, and tiny Armenian, Maronite, and Latin communities. The walls were well preserved, and foreign merchants were at least occasionally to be found there. Eventually much of the commerce and industry must have been restored, too.

NOTES

1. Suriano, *Il Trattato* . . . , p. 242; Cobham, pp. 49, 52; once a city, now a village, *Voyage* . . . , pp. 57, 136; ruined port near Larnaka, Cobham, pp. 64, 65.

2. Hill, v. 2, pp. 17, 473. v. 3, pp. 813, 863. W. Heyd, *Histoire* . . . , v. 2, p. 426. de Mas Latrie, v. 3, p. 489.

3. Cobham, p. 54; *Travels* . . . , p. 440; *Peregrinatio* . . . , p. 137.

4. *Voyage* . . . , p. 60; Cobham, pp. 60, 69; Hakluyt, v. 5, pp. 93f. Cf. Zeebout (1481), p. 224; Pietro Casola (1494); Mogabgab, v. 1, pp. 44f; Newett, p. 293, and Jean Palerne (1581) who was with a ship that purchased salt, *Peregrinations*, p. 327.

5. Hill, v. 2, p. 17. v. 3, pp. 813f, 863. Estimates of Venetian revenues from the salt range between 100,000 and 800,000 ducats annually, Hill favoring about 300,000. Cobham, p. 71; Hakluyt, v. 5, pp. 96f.

6. Mogabgab, v. 3, p. 142.

7. Hill, v. 2, pp. 306n, 16. Loredano reported 2000 deaths in 1330. Mogabgab, v. 1, p. 40; Newett, p. 383. Ludolf von Suchen (1350), in Cobham, p. 19; Stuttgart, pp. 31f; de Mas Latrie, v. 2, pp. 212f.

8. Hill, v. 2, pp. 16, 458, 470, 473, 477. O. d'Anglure (1395), in Cobham, p. 28; Paris, 1878, p. 81, #290; de Mas Latrie, v. 2, p. 430. Khalil, son of ez-Zaheri, mentions an immense booty. Mogabgab, v. 3, pp. 70ff; de Mas Latrie, v. 2, pp. 506–514. Enguerrand de Montsrelet's chronicle, in Mogabgab, v. 2, pp. 60, 64.

9. Hill, v. 2, p. 16. Mogabgab, v. 1, p. 38; *Itinerarium* . . . , v. 192, pp. 95f.

10. Cobham, pp. 37, 45f; Stuttgart, v. 1, p. 43 v. 3, pp. 240f. *Il Trattato*, pp. 241f; Cobham, p. 48f. Cf. Santo Brasca, *Viaggio* . . . (1480), p. 63, #46.

11. Sebalt (1480), in Mogabgab, v. 1, p. 35; Stuttgart, v. 168, p. 51.

12. Hill, v. 2, p. 16. v. 3, pp. 814, 835f, 863. Mogabgab, v. 1, pp. 40f; Newett (Casola), pp. 214f. Piri Reis knew of a ruined castle. *Kitab'i Bahriyye*, v. 2, pp. 280f.

13. Mogabgab, v. 1, pp. 41, 46. Newett (Casola), pp. 214ff, 295f.

14. Jodicus de Meggen (1542), in Mogabgab, v. 3, p. 141. Cf. John Locke (1553), in Cobham, p. 68; Hakluyt, v. 5, pp. 99f.

15. Cobham, pp. 68, 72; Hakluyt, v. 5, pp. 99f.

16. Cobham, p. 143. Not in the version of Calepio published by de Lusignan, *Description* . . . , p. 211. W. Heyd, *Histoire* . . . , v. 2, p. 426. de Mas Latrie, v. 3, p. 488.

17. Hill, v. 2, p. 18. Cobham, p. 18; Stuttgart, p. 30; de Mas Latrie, v. 2, p. 211.
18. Cobham, p. 28; *R.O.L.*, p. 637.
19. Cobham, p. 33; Tafur (Letts), pp. 68, 103.
20. Hill, v. 2, pp. 18, 390f. v. 3, p. 565.
21. Cobham, p. 35; *Viaggi*, v. 4, p. 177, #36; de Mas Latrie, v. 3, p. 76. Cobham, p. 45; Stuttgart, v. 3, p. 240. *Il Trattato*, p. 242; Cobham, pp. 48ff, 51.
22. Cobham, p. 51. Mogabgab, v. 1, p. 35; Stuttgart, v. 168, pp. 51f.
23. Cobham, p. 55; *Travels . . .*, p. 400; *Peregrinatio . . .*, p. 138.
24. Cobham, p. 67, 244.
25. Cobham, p. 67, 243. Cf. A. Zeebout (1481), *L'voyage . . .*, p. 295.
26. Hill, v. 3, p. 787n; de Mas Latrie, V. 3, p. 534.
27. Hill, v. 2, pp. 18ff. v. 3, p. 862. Palerne (1581), p. 337.
28. Hill, v. 2, pp. 405f, 409, 434. v. 3, pp. 562, 565, 850, 955. Cf. Tafur in Cobham, p. 34; Letts, p. 105; Jodicus, in Mogabgab, v. 3, p. 146.
29. Hill, v. 3, p. 787; de Mas Latrie, v. 3, p. 534, "Memoirs of François Attar," and "Memoirs of the Count of Tripoli." Piri Reis, *Kitab'i Bahriyye*, v. 2, p. 431.
30. Hill, v. 3, p. 955.
31. Cobham, p. 14. Cf. Jacobus de Verona (1335), in Cobham, p. 17; *R.O.L.*, pp. 176f.
32. Cobham, p. 20; Stuttgart, p. 33; de Mas Latrie, v. 2, pp. 214f.
33. Cobham, p. 26; *R.O.L.*, pp. 634f.
34. Cobham, p. 32; Letts, p. 64. *Andanças é Viajes . . .*, pt. 1, p. 67. Cf. O. d'Anglure (1395), "a very goodly city, and fair and great," in Cobham, p. 29; Paris, 1898, p. 84, #299; de Mas Latrie, v. 2, p. 431. Nompar II (1418), "a great city," Cobham, p. 30.
35. Cobham, pp. 41ff; Stuttgart, v. 3, p. 230.
36. Suriano, *Il Trattato*, pp. 219n, 242; Cobham, pp. 48f.
37. *Voyage . . .*, pp. 137ff; Cobham, pp. 58f. Cf. Martin von Baumgarten (1508), in Cobham, p. 55; *Travels . . .*, p. 441; *Peregrinatio . . .*, p. 139.
38. Mogabgab, v. 3, p. 143.
39. Cobham, p. 71; Hakluyt, v. 5, p. 97.
40. Cobham, p. 78f; *Reis-Beschreibung . . .*, pp. 302f.
41. Cobham, pp. 140f; Lusignan, *Description . . .*, p. 262.
42. Cobham, p. 120; Lusignan, *Chorograffia*. 1573.
43. Graziani, pp. 12f.
44. Hill, v. 2, p. 13.
45. Hill, v. 2, pp. 400, 461, 483.
46. Hill, v. 3, pp. 808ff.
47. Hill, v. 3, pp. 808–813.
48. Cobham, p. 21; Mandeville (Letts), pp. 19, 242; Mandeville (Seymour), pp. 22–23. Mandeville's travels may be dated to the second quarter of the 14th century. See Letts, pp. xvii–xxvii.

49. Mogabgab, v. 2, pp. 56ff; Anonymous Englishman (Golubovich), v. 4, pp. 431, 437f.
50. Cobham, pp. 19f; Stuttgart, pp. 32f; de Mas Latrie, v. 2, pp. 213f.
51. Cobham, pp. 22ff; *R.O.L.*, pp. 628f, 631f.
52. Hill, v. 2, pp. 14ff, 288, 290, 292f, 312, 316, 382f, 394, 412ff, 424f, 434, 458ff, 471. v. 3, pp. 503f, 506f.
53. Hill, v. 3, pp. 727ff, 732, 806ff.
54. Cobham, p. 31; Letts, p. 64;
55. Cobham, p. 45; Stuttgart, v. 3, p. 236. Cf. Pietro Casola (1494), in Mogabgab, v. 1, pp. 41f; Newett, p. 215. Anonymous Jew (1495), in Mogabgab, v. 3, p. 134.
56. Cobham, p. 71; Hakluyt, v. 5, p. 96. Cobham, p. 73f; *R. de G.* (1879), p. 222.
57. Suriano (1484), *Il Trattato,* p. 242; Cobham, p. 49. Anonymous Jew (1495), in Mogabgab, v. 3, p. 134. Martin von Baumgarten (1508), in Cobham, p. 55; *Travels . . . ,* p. 441; *Peregrinatio . . . ,* p. 139. Le Saige (1518), who praises the produce in the surrounding area. *Voyage . . . ,* p. 135; Cobham, p. 57. Affagart (1534), in Cobham, p. 66; *Relation Journaliere . . . ,* pp. 298f. Locke (1553), the cheapest prices in Cyprus. Cobham, pp. 70f; Hakluyt, v. 5, p. 96. Jodicus de Meggen (1542), in Mogabgab, v. 3, p. 45.
58. Cobham, p. 73; *R. de G.* (1879) pp. 221f. They used quarantines of up to 40 days.
59. Hill, v. 3, p. 787n. Cf. de Mas Latrie, v. 3, p. 534.
60. Cobham, p. 77; *Reis-Beschreibung . . . ,* pp. 298f. *Kitab'i Bahriyye,* v. 2, p. 283.
61. Cobham, pp. 121f.
62. Cobham, pp. 121f. W. Heyd, *Histoire . . . ,* v. 2, pp. 425f. "Réponse du doge Augustin Barbarigo à une supplique des habitants de Famagouste . . . ," de Mas Latrie, v. 3, pp. 485–492.
63. Hill, v. 4, p. 38.
64. Hill, v. 4, pp. 42f.
65. Hill, v. 4, pp. 48ff.
66. Hill, v. 4, pp. 21, 308f.
67. *Peregrinations,* pp. 332f, 344f.
68. Cobham, pp. 143f, 160ff; Lusignan, *Description . . . ,* pp. 288f.
69. Anvers, pp. 165ff; Roma, pp. 90ff. Anvers and Roma are variants of Zvallart.
70. Cobham, p. 175.
71. Cobham, pp. 178, 180.
72. *Beschrijvinge . . . ,* p. 11.
73. Dandini (1596). Cobham, p. 183; Pinkerton, v. 10, p. 280. Cf. Porcacchio (1576), in Cobham, p. 164; *L'Isole . . . ,* 1572 ed., p. 21; 1620 ed., p. 146.
74. A. Teneti, *Piracy and . . . ,* pp. 40f.
75. *Travels . . . ,* p. 63.

76. Cobham, p. 195; Ioanne Cootwijk, *Itinerarium Hierosolymitanum*. Antverpiae, 1619. pp. 102f.
77. *Early Voyage* . . . , p. 28.
78. Cobham, pp. 85, 90; *Relation Journaliere* . . . , 1619, pp. 83, 89, map on 92.
79. *The Travels* . . . , pp. 135f. Cf. Stochove (1631), who chose not to enter the place because of rumors about the malevolence of the pasha. Cobham, p. 217.
80. Cobham, pp. 203, 204; *The Totall Discourse* . . . , pp. 160, 164, 168.
81. Cobham, p. 206; *Travels,* p. 219.
82. *Voiage* . . . , pp. 328ff, with a good map of the harbor.
83. Cobham, pp. 236, 241; *Reizen* . . . , pp. 365ff, 374.
84. *Naukeurige Beschriyving* . . . , pp. 28, 30, 52.
85. Cobham, pp. 246, 248.
86. Cobham, p. 255; Pinkerton, v. 10, pp. 577ff.
87. Hill, v. 3, p. 960.
88. Dannenfeldt, *Leonhard Rauwolf* . . . , pp. 40ff.
89. Hakluyt, v. 5, p. 213.
90. Anvers, p. 165; Roma, pp. 92f.
91. Cobham, p. 176. Cf. Martin von Baumgarten (1508), in Cobham, p. 54; *Travels* . . . , p. 440; *Peregrinatio* . . . , p. 137.
92. Cobham, p. 175.
93. Cobham, pp. 190ff. Laurence Aldersey (1581), in Hakluyt, v. 5, p. 213.
94. *Travels of* . . . , p. 16.
95. Cobham, p. 209; 1608 ed., p. 114; Nancy, 1619, p. 90.
96. Hill, v. 4, pp. 47, 52n; *The Travels* . . . , p. 136. Hill, v. 4, p. 52n; Cobham, pp. 211f; *Viaggi,* 1843 ed., p. 881; *Viaggi,* 1667, pt. 3, p. 440.
97. *The Travels* . . . , pp. 135f.
98. *Voiage* . . . , pp. 330f.
99. Cobham, pp. 210ff; *Viaggi,* 1843 ed., pp. 880f; *Viaggi,* 1667, v. 4, pp. 536ff.
100. Earle, *Corsairs of* . . . , p. 144.
101. Cobham, p. 240; *Reizen* . . . , pp. 373f. Cf. Chevalier d'Arveux, *Memoires,* p. 483.
102. *Naukeurige Beschryving* . . . , pp. 23, 33, 35.
103. *Adventures and Sufferings* . . . , pp. 172f.
104. Cobham, pp. 244, 246. Cobham, p. 252; Pinkerton, v. 10, p. 576.
105. There is no independent confirmation of an English consulate (actually a vice consulate under Aleppo) until 1626 or a regular consul until 1636 Nor is there evidence of a French consulate before 1673. Hill, v. 4, pp. 63f. Possibly the Dutch were first. A. H. de Groot, *The Ottoman Empire* . . . , pp. 90, 216f.
106. Hill, v. 4, p. 360.
107. Cobham, pp. 171f, 178. Jean Palerne (1581) reported the purchase of cotton, pitch, and carobs there. *Peregrinations,* pp. 327f.

108. Cotovicus (1599), in Cobham, pp. 188f; Antverpiae, p. 95.
109. Cobham, p. 181; Pinkerton, v. 10, p. 277.
110. Cobham, p. 209; 1608 ed., p. 114; *Relation Journaliere* . . . , 1619, p. 90.
111. *Voiage* . . . , pp. 330f.
112. Cobham, p. 214; *Viaggi*, 1843 ed., pp. 890ff; *Viaggi*, 1667, v. 4, pp. 544f. The Venetian consul resided there.
113. *Naukeurige Beschryving* . . . , pp. 45f, 52. Cf. de Bruyn (1683), in Cobham, p. 243; *Reizen* . . . , p. 379.
114. Cobham, pp. 251ff; Pinkerton, v. 10, p. 575.
115. *Nouveau Voyage* . . . , pp. 218ff.
116. Zvallart Anvers, pp. 161f; (Roma), pp. 90f.
117. *Naukeurige Beschryving* . . . , p. 52.
118. Cobham, p. 171. Cobham, p. 193; Antverpiae, pp. 100f, 106. Cobham, p. 209; *Relation Journaliere* . . . , 1608, p. 115; 1619, p. 86. Cobham, p. 241; *Reizen* . . . , p. 374. Cobham, p. 265; Pinkerton, v. 10, p. 587.
119. Even Nompar II (1418) had called Girniye the strongest fortress on the island. Cobham, p. 30.
120. Cobham, p. 175; *L'Isole* . . . , 1572 ed., p. 21; 1620 ed., pp. 147f.
121. Cobham, pp. 193f; Antverbiae, p. 107.
122. Cobham, p. 207; *Travels* . . . , p. 220.
123. Cobham, pp. 215ff.
124. de Mas Latrie, v. 3, pp. 578–580.
125. Cobham, p. 232. Cobham, p. 241; *Reizen* . . . , pp. 369ff.
126. *Naukeurige Beschryving* . . . , p. 42.
127. Cobham, p. 261; Pinkerton, v. 10, pp. 583f.
128. Cobham, pp. 125ff, 148; Lusignan, *Description* . . . , pp. 237ff, 269ff. Graziani, pp. 111, 74ff. Cobham, pp. 120ff. A register of the taxes paid on slaves taken from Cyprus lists, by name and price, 13,719 people enslaved. Since that register is dated 7 October 1570 (7 Cumadi I 978), within a month of the fall of Lefkoşa, presumably most of the enslaved came from there. The demographic effects of such a policy must have been profound, for presumably all but a few were carried elsewhere; indeed, many were sold at Galata in Istanbul. (The official income from the sale of just that group of slaves was 1,786,678 akce.) Magosa fell only the following August; slaves from there presumably filled a different, but much smaller, register, for the Ottoman conquest did not reduce its population very much (MMD 325; archiv 5471, muhasebe defter 978/1570).
129. Anvers, pp. 173ff. Not in Roma version.
130. Cobham, pp. 181f; Pinkerton, v. 10, pp. 277ff.
131. Cobham, p. 209; *Relation Journaliere* . . . , 1608, pp. 117f; 1619, pp. 88f, with map of city.
132. *The Travels* . . . , pp. 135f.
133. Lithgow, *The Totall Discourse* . . . , pp. 163ff; Cobham, p. 202. Gedoyn, *Journal* . . . , p. 157. In 1606 (1015) 15 of the 263 cizye-payers were Armenians and 5 Maronites; both had their own quarters.

134. Cobham, p. 207; *Travels*, p. 220.
135. Cobham, pp. 216f.
136. *Travels* . . . , v. 2, pp. 384ff. French consul at Larnaka.
137. Cobham, p. 248.
138. *Naukeurige Beschryving* . . . , pp. 31f, 52.
139. Cobham, pp. 232f. French consul at Larnaka.
140. Cobham, p. 239; *Reizen* . . . , pp. 371f.
141. *Adventures and Sufferings* . . . , p. 172.
142. Cobham pp. 260, 268; Pinkerton, v. 10, pp. 581, 592.
143. Cobham, p. 260; Pinkerton, v. 10, p. 581; *Voyage* . . . , pp. 103f; *Itinér-aire* . . . , p. 232; *Levkosia* . . . , p. 2.

TEN

Loans and Credit

The impact of Ottoman rule, particularly the legal system, on credit and money lending in Cyprus is all too evident if one considers the letter written in 1563 from Magosa by the Jew Elias of Pesaro to a brother or friend in Italy inviting him to come there.

People who want to borrow money come here. This money-lending business is really remarkable. One lends to no one except on a thoroughly sound security. No trust or credit. If the pledge is of gold or silver the interest is twenty per centum: if of wool, thread or silk twenty-five per centum. . . . As soon as the Christians see a fresh Jew arrive to stay here they ask him if he wants to lend money. If he says yes, they are kindly towards him, and he need not fear that the other Jews will look askance at him as though he were poaching on their preserves. The country is big enough to feed them all.

Some loans reached 50,000 ducats. Sometimes, with brokers' fees ". . . the borrower pays as much as forty per centum interest: but nobody cares."[1] Ottoman rule must have revolutionized the business of credit and money lending in Cyprus.

Credit was a common feature of the socioeconomic order of Lefkoşa and indeed of Cyprus during the period 1571–1640.[2] People freely lent and borrowed what usually were small to moderate sums. In the absence of banks, lending even from a very small surplus was quite normal. Creditors and debtors were not two rigidly separated classes; presumably many men were both at once, and many more would be both at least once in their lives. The rich and powerful borrowed as well as lent, and so did townspeople and villagers. In 1580/1593–1595 19% of all judicial cases involved matters of loans and credit; in 1609–1611 the proportion was 22% and in 1633–1637 20%. If 20% of all the judicial cases examined (591 of 2975) involved various forms of credit and debts, then some 1200 to 1500 people must have been involved.

Lefkoşa was the center of local business and commerce on the island. Regular daily business activities, in the absence of savings and lending institutions, benefited from and, indeed, required the use of large or small cash surpluses which people temporarily had in hand. The documents show that moneylenders were no small class or clique; rather, anyone who temporarily acquired a little surplus money, if only through inheritance, might be expected to put out part of it in credit. A shoemaker or butcher might extend credit to his customer, a military officer to another military officer, a resident of an urban quarter or village to other residents there. The court system guaranteed repayment, and moderate profits of 20% interest were legal. That interest rate, the one sometimes mentioned in judicial registers, ought to have been high enough to ensure a plentiful supply of credit on the market, other than in times of severe inflation or flagrant debasement of coinage.

The court recordes show clearly that both giving and receiving credit —under the formal sanction of a court representing the sacred law of Islam—were considered respectable behavior. Among the many creditors and debtors are found the names of people of the highest classes of society: leading ulema, military officers, and merchants, as well as craftsmen, villagers, and even women. Many donors of evkaf prescribed lending their capital for interest,[3] and estates of minors were used similarly by guardians. Probably dealing in credit maintained respectability because of the absence of chronic poverty among the borrowers.

The court records use the term *karz* for a formal loan, usually in the form *karz-i hasen,* a good or just loan, or less often *karz-i şer*ᶜ, a loan in accordance with the Sharia. The usury *(riba)* categorically forbidden in the Koran was obviously considered in 16th and 17th century Ottoman interpretations to refer to excessive or unjust profits rather than to all interest. Consequently, credit and money lending were not at all the province of undesirables and social outcasts, whether some small unsavory group of Muslims or some "immoral" infidels, but were practiced by hundreds of upright Muslims. The interest rate charged was considered fair by a consensus of all the contemporary legal and political institutions. The rarity of bankruptcy may be considered a test of its fairness.[4]

Interest on debts is rarely mentioned in the sicils, although presumably that was the main inducement to giving credit. It was not a subject that the courts wished to be secretive about; indeed, credit for interest was widely given through much of the Ottoman empire in the 16th and 17th centuries. The usual rate of interest was 20% per annum, although before about 1600 15% or even 10% were the rule.[5] Some Cyprus vakfiye stipulated the lending of foundation money at 10% interest, as does at least one judicial case.

Suleyman beg bn ʿAbdullah acknowledges *(ik)* in the presence of ʿAbdur-Rezak halife, *nazir* (overseer of the guardian) for the children *(sagiran)* Suleyman and Saliha of the late Meryem bint ʿAbdullah: I received 2656 akce with interest *(akceʾ-i murabaha)* from ʿAbdur-Rezak, from the money of the orphans, at 10% interest *(onda on bir hesabi uzere)*. I acknowledge by debt. (2 113–2; 4 Sefer 1017)[6]

Haci Huseyn bn ʿAbdullah, vasi for minor son Mehmed of the late haci Huseyn of Lefkoşa acknowledges *(ik/iʿt)* in the presence of Kurd çelebi bn haci ʿAli: I sold Kurd 100 head of goats and sheep which the orphan inherited from his mother Hadice, for 105 akce apiece. Then I lent him 5500 akce of that money at 20% interest *(onin on iki hesabi uzere muʿamele)*. (3 11–3; 10 Şevval 1018)

Haci Derviş beşe bn Mustafa of Lefkoşa sets forth a claim *(d/tk)* in the presence of haci Yusuf ota başi, vasi before the Sharia for the minor children *(evlad-i sigar)* of the late Huseyn boluk başi of Lefkoşa who died in Cairo *(Misr-i Kahire)*: I gave the deceased 20 riyali guruş in principal *(asl-i mal)* at 20% interest (10 for 12) for one year. I had not received the 20 riyali guruş and the 4 riyali guruş (interest) before he left. When he died in Egypt *(Misr)*, I was still owed 24 guruş. Let the aforementioned loan be inquired about. I want that from his property *(mal)*. When Derviş is asked for proof, Ibrahim ota başi bn Emrullah and Huseyn beşe bn ʿAbdun-Nasir confirm him. When an oath is proposed by the vasi that Derviş had not received the money, Derviş took it. Then he was paid the 24 riyali guruş in full. (4 111–1; II Muh. 1045)

ʿAli, called Çelenk, of Karaman on the mainland (Ote Yaka) acknowledges *(ik/tk)* in the presence of Gavrayel v. Zor (?), Marko v. Zozi, Yorgi, and Solimo of Lefkoşa: When they were in a state of wealth *(kudretleri (?) hali)* on the mainland, I gave then 238 riyali guruş to go to Cyprus. Now when the term *(vaʿde)* has expired, 42 riyali guruş is added, making a total of 280 riyali guruş. They acknowledge this debt. (4 190–3; II Receb 1046)[7]

ʿAyni bint ʿAbdullah of Merdibanli çeşme quarter says: I took 3000 akce at 20% (10 for 12) interest from Ibrahim beg, administrator (mutevelli) of the mosque (mescid) of the quarter, saying I will pay 3600 akce at the end of a year. (4 234–2; 18 Ramazan 1045. Another case refers to 7000 akce being due from the 4800 originally owed from the purchase of 220 vakiye of soap *(sabun)*, but the term is not given, unfortunately. 3 94–3; I Şevval 1019)

Unless hard pressed debtors threw themselves upon the mercy of the court to negotiate a reasonable delay in payment, the claims of unpaid creditors must have reduced them to misery.[8] However, only two cases of bankruptcy were found, so that may not have been a problem.

A copy of the certificate of bankruptcy of zimmi (Christian) Lefter is published: Lefter v. Covan owes janissary Mehmed bn ʿAbdullah of Lefkoşa 1000 akce from a loan *(karz)*. After it happened that a claim was made against him and evidence presented *(istishad-i şerʿi)*, in the presence of janissary, from the upright Muslims *(ʿudul-i Muslimin)* Huseyn (?) bn Ahmed and Mehmed bn Hasan who were present at the court *(haziran)* testified saying: That zimmi is poor *(fakir)*; he is supported by the charity of the charitable *(muhayyirun sadakatindan)*. He is not capable of any other liability *(mesʾuliyet)*. It is in every way most beneficial *(enfaʿ)* to release him from imprisonment *(habs)* in order to make it possible for him to support himself *(kar u kesb)* and to pay the debt *(eda)*. When they gave evidence testifying in that way, it was ordered to release *(itlak)* Lefter from imprisonment and that he was bankrupt/insolvent *(iflas)*. (1 192–3; I Cumadi II 1003)

Ahturi v. Ziya of Degirmenlik village of Lefkoşa states: I owed a debt *(deynum)* to Ibrahim bn Ridvan of that village. I was imprisoned for the 50 previous days and was released *(itlak)* when I gave up all my property *(mal)*. Since I had nothing, I was not able to pay *(iktidarum olmadugina)*. Consequently they released me from jail *(habs)*, but since I was also indebted to a few other people, they said he is not free from malice. I asked that people present at the assembly *(meclis)* be asked about my good reputation and act accordingly. I do not want to be imprisoned again. When the Muslims whose names are listed below came and investigated his reputation *(hal)*, they said: He has released all his property except his clothes *(libas)*. He has no other possessions at all. He is truly insolvent (bankrupt? *iflas*). That is recorded. (4 24–1; I Rebiʿi 1044)

Although a few individuals became considerable debtors, even in those instances either they or their heirs settled the debts easily and routinely. So ʿAbdi çavuş owed 4000 akce to Hizir su başi, another 4000 to Ulak (?) Ahmed of the Cyprus janissaries, 2000 akce in Dowry *(mehr)* to his wife Hatuniye, 3000 akce to the foundation *(evkaf)* of Sefer Paşa,

20 keyl barley to Isma'il beşe, 2400 akce to another woman, 300 akce to bezazistan kethudasi Mehmed, 1000 akce to his janissary captain *(boluk Başi)*, 900 akce to the kadi for a baggage horse *(bargir)*, and 2000 akce to his mother-in-law (1 145−4,5,6; 146−2,3,4,5,6,7,8,9; II Rebi' I 1003). The 13, 958 akce debts of the late Mevlana Musliheddin efendi included 6300 akce to the vakf of 'Abdi çavuş, 384 akce to janissary Huseyn, 54 to the Lefka kadi, 1620 to Kasim çavuş, 2000 to janissary 'Ali beşe, and 3600 to Hasan kethuda (1 222−2; II Şaban 1001). When zimmi Karçire v. Zazo borrowed 25,200 akce for 30 days from racil yasakci Memi beşe bn 'Abdullah, he still owed 10,000 akce to the multezim of his village in Mesariye kaza (1 308−8; 3 Muh. 1003. 310−2; III Zil-Hicce 1002). The late 'Ali bn Kasim left debts of 19,450 akce to nine different individuals including two women and four military officers; the smallest debts were 240, 240, and 360 akce, the largest 12,000 akce to Hamze aga and 3000 akce to a woman (3 130−6; 28 Rebi'II 1018). Zimmi Çakoleki (?) v. Zorzi of Koremeno (?) village of Lefka nahiye reduced his 10 debts amounting to 27,110 akce to a mere 9000 akce; formerly he had owed 11,400 akce to racil Receb beşe of Lefkoşa, 4300 akce to Mustafa Hoca, 2000 akce to Halil boluk başi, 4000 akce to Ahmed beşe, and so on (4 182−2; I Receb 1046).

The debts of the late Halil Paşa zade Ahmed Paşa, who died while governor *(mir miran)* of Cyprus, were extraordinary not only for their size but even more so for the diversity of economic interests that the late governor had pursued. Bear in mind that his estate handled his debts with no problems. The Paşa owed his man Isma'il tayi 13,280 akce for 166 vakiye coffee *(findik kahvesi)*. He owed Mahmud çelebi 50,000 akce for sable furs. He had owed his aga Aslan aga bn Mehmed 79,524 akce from a loan *(karz)* plus 9920 akce for 124 vakiye coffee, a total of 89,444 akce, although later he had managed to repay some 20,000 akce. However, Ahmed Paşa owed still another 2550 riyali guruş to Arslan aga, who had borrowed from Cyprus cizyedar Mustafa aga. He owed mumci haci Ramazna of Lefkoşa 2200 akce for beeswax. He owed 2713 akce for olive oil *(revgan-i zeyt)*, onions, raisins, and grape juice *(şire)* to bakkal haci Habib beşe, racil, and 800 akce for fines *(cerime)* ·and fugitive slaves *(abik)* to kavvaf haci Ru's bn Isma'il. In addition Ahmed Paşa had a debt of 2222½ riyali guruş for Paris and Moroccan *(Moralkun)* broadcloth *(çuka)* to a French merchant named Firancesko v. Lanko (?). He owed 8380 akce for sheep and goats to kassab Şahdi of

Lefkoşa and 1000 akce to haci Yusuf of Lefkoşa for gum labdanum *(aksam ul-ban).* The Paşa had only repaid 10,500 akce of the 16,676 that he owed racil Nebi beşe from the purchase of olive oil *(revgan-i zeyt).* He owed haci Hizir su başi bn Karaman hoca of Lefkoşa 9000 akce, 6000 for ʿistani (?) and 3000 for 150 vakiye honey *(ʿasl).* Moreover, he owed his chief tailor *(terzi başi)* zimmi Musa 36 riyali guruş for six cloth pillows/cushions *(yasdik kumaş,)* and he owed money from loans *(karz)* to two of his own seaman *(gemi yoldaşlari),* 100 riyali guruş to Ibrahim and 21,840 akce to ʿAli kapudan.

The late Ahmed Paşa also owed 11,160 akce for bread *(etmek)* to etmekci Loizo, a zimmi (Christian) of Lefkoşa, and 11,150 akce to Zimmiye female broker *(dellale)*[9] Maro bint Karide (?) of Lefkoşa for silk shirts *(harir gomlek),* sugar *(şeker),* and handkerchiefs *(makrama).* Of the 9109 akce owed zimmi Viryoni (?) of Lefkoşa for 13 whole pieces *(top)* of Cyprus cloth *(kumaş)* from the loom, weighing 3036 dirhem, he had paid only 4000 akce. Similarly he owed Arslan kethuda of Beşiktaş of Galata 8560 akce for 107 vakiye coffee and more for cloth of Rumeli. He still owed 12,800 akce of the 22,800 due Hasan çelebi bn Mehmed of his court *(divan)* for 228 vakiye coffee; and he owed his man Ibrahim bn ʿAli 8560 akce for 107 vakiye coffee *(fındik kahvesi).* Finally, he still owed 500 of his debt of 4000 riyali guruş to Mustafa aga, collector of cizye on the island *(cizyedar)* (4 19–2, 3, 21–1, 2, 58–3, 59–2, 3, 60–1, 2, 62–1, 2, 63–1, 2, 64–1, 2, 66–1, 67–3, 68–1, 85–2). The debts of Halil Paşa zade Ahmed Paşa provide a cross section of the local economy. He owed payment on three very large cash loans. He left five separate debts for coffee, some extremely large. Coffee in transit through Cyprus from the Yemen to the capital must have been a profitable item of trade, and the island itself had several coffee houses.[10] Another five debts involved various kinds of cloth which were made on the island or traded there in local and international trade, while others were for sugar, beeswax and honey, olive oil, grape and garden products, sheep and goats, and grain, all important products of the local economy. Only the sable fur, the coffee, probably the gum labadanum, and some of the cloth products were strictly goods of trade; the rest were important local produce. If Ahmed Paşa was involved in purchasing large quantities of bread over a period of time, he may have attempted to control the price of bread, the staple of every diet on the island, but possibly that debt came simply from supplying his large household. Of course much bread and other food was consumed thus. Undoubtedly it was easy for a provincial governor with a high salary and many retainers to borrow extensively from local people. Many of Ahmed Paşa's debts were to his own dependents, like Ismaʿil tayi, Arslan aga, cizyedar Mustafa aga, his chief tailor Musa, his naval officers Ibrahim and ʿAli kapudan, Hasan çelebi of the Cyprus council *(divan)*, and his man Ibrahim. Maybe giving credit under such circumstances was not entirely voluntary, but the profits probably were good.

The men mentioned more than once as creditors do not rival the most conspicuous debtors in the volume of their lending but nevertheless some examples are worth considering. Zimmi Behine v. Petro (?) of Lefkoşa is a creditor mentioned in 1580 (988), 1593 (1002), and 1609 (1018). He had given two loads *(yuk)* of wine *(hamr)* to Ciryako v. Yorgi of Kazuniye (?) village of Pendaya kaza for a two-month period *(vaʿde)* and eight altun to janissary Mehmed bn ʿAbdullah for an eight-month period. Behine sold Ergiro v. Yako of Nisu village of Lefkoşa three kantar of carded cotton *(mahluc penbe)* for 73 kirmizi filori which had to be paid. He lent Ferenci v. Zeyno 39½ altun for making bread *(ekmekcilik)*, the latter's wife being guarantor *(kefil-bil-mal)*. Tomazi v. Zendil of Dikimo village of Girniye kaza, who had borrowed 73 kirmizi filori for a period of 180 days, then paid his debt to Behine with three Cyprus kantar of carded cotton *(mahluc penbe)*. Sixteen years later Filibo v. Pernardi owed Behine 20 kirmizi guruş and Armenian Parsun (?) v. Mircan owed him nine guruş. The evidence suggests that Behine was probably not a large scale lender but a merchant who over three decades repeatedly made medium-sized loans (1 6–3; I Ramazan 988. 9–7; 14 Ramazan 988. 242–1; I Şevval 1002. 248–4, II Şevval 1002. 253–1; III Şevval 1002. 3 5–6; 29 Zil-Hicce 1018. 17–4; 27 Şevval 1018).

Another persistent giver of credit was janissary Mehmed beşe bn ʿAbdullah, at that time yasakci at the Lefkoşa court. He lent 1200 (akce?) to the priest Papa Nikola. he also lent 2500 akce *(karz-i hasen)* for 20 days to zimmis Peydro v. Luyi and Marko v. Zano of Agya (?) village of Baf kaza for them to pay their head tax *(harac)*. Mehmed lent 27,296 akce for a one-month period *(vaʿde)* to Nikola v. Veledati of Lefkoşa. Besides lending 420 akce (or seven altun) to Kostendin v. Zorci and Ohturi v. Yakimo, he gave a loan *(karz-i hasen)* of 25,200 akce to Karcire v. Zazo of Lefkoşa for 30 days (1 58–1; I Ramazan 1002. 94– 4; I Rebiʿ I 1003. 157–3; 19 Rebiʿ II 1003. 273–3; I Zil-Kade 1002.

288–1; III Zil-Kade 1002. 308–8; 3 Muh. 1003). Mehmed's specialty was straight short-term loans. He was wealthy enough to provide some very large loans while still dealing with minor ones.

Helvaci Mehmed bn ʿAli of Lefkoşa had several debts due him from matters connected with his trade from a young man *(emred)* named Ahmed bn Mahmud. First Ahmed owed five guruş for some goods *(mal)*. Next he acknowledged a debt of 15 guruş from a personal loan *(karz-i hasen)*. Helvaci Mehmed then received nine guruş for some business concerning sugar *(şeker işi)*. When Mehmed claimed that Ahmed owed him 43 guruş for 120 vakiye of helva, Ahmed claimed to have paid three guruş. Immediately thereafter it was determined that only seven guruş remained for Ahmed to pay Mehmed (3 21–1,2,3,4,5: I Zil-Kade 1018). Mehmed's credit was of a moderate scale, and presumably it all was ancillary to his work in his own shop. He was no wealthy merchant.

Cyprus collector of cizye *(cizyedar)* Mustafa aga was owed 2550 riyali guruş from a loan *(istikraz)* to Arslan aga which finally was paid after six months; Arslan aga still owed him another 500 riyali guruş from a 4000-akce loan (4 22–2, 23–1; III Sefer 1004. 85–2; I Şaban 1044). Racil Receb beşe of Lefkoşa made a 33-guruş loan *(karz-i şerʿ)* to racil Mehmed Beşe bn ʿAbdullah as well as one for 11,400 akce to Çakoleki v. Zorzi of Koremeno (?) village of Lefka nahiye (4 35–3; I Rebiʿ II 1044. 182–2; I Receb 1046). When former Lefka kadi Musliheddin efendi died, his brother ʿAli efendi made a claim that Mahmud bn ʿAbdur-Rahman still owed 2000 of the 7000 akce he had borrowed from the deceased; 274 akce owed the late Musliheddin by Luyi v. Papa Yano was paid by Solimo v. Nikola who was guarantor *(kefil)*, and then Solimo claimed the money from Luyi (1 237–4; II Ramazan 1002. 267–6; II Zil-Kade 1002). In fact, few people gave credit to more than one person. Although many men had enough resources to make an occasional loan, apparently few had resources adequate for lending to more than one person at a time.[11] Some of the credit was on a very large scale, but much was on a small scale.

There are substantial numbers of local zimmis, local Muslim merchants and artisans, and local ulema among the creditors and debtors, although the military achieve a certain predominance. A third of all the instances of credit involved men who can be identified as members of the military class. Their credit matters were handled by the court like any others. The military were half again more likely to be creditors as debtors. Thus, 16% (94 cases) of all credit examined was by members of the military class to civilians, while only 10% (60) was given to military by civilians. Since both parties were military in an additional 7% (42) of all instances of credit, 23% of all credit originated with members of the military class and they received 17%. Like everyone else the military were often involved with modest or even petty amounts of credit, but it seems a fair presumption that they were involved with bigger than average credit even if one excludes the huge sums that a few pashas dealt in.

Most of the military class involved with credit can be divided into two distinct groups, janissaries (including all those called *beşe, cavuş, racil, oda başi,* and *boluk başi*) and spahis (those called *beg* and *cundi*). In dealing with other members of the military class, both corps gave and received credit in about equal proportions. Twice as many janissaries as spahis (118 to 57) were involved in credit. Members of both corps gave more credit to civilians than they received, the janissaries by twice as much (64 to 32), the spahis by one and a half times (22 to 15). The men of those two traditional corps provided a continuous source of local credit and capital.

Another easily recognizable group of creditors and debtors are non-Muslims (zimmis). Credit from zimmis to other zimmis accounted for 16% (96 to 591) of all instances of credit registered in the sicils (court record books). (Within the three sicils the proportion fluctuated erratically, perhaps meaninglessly, from 14% to 21% to 10%). Since 54% of all credit remained entirely within the Muslim community, 70% of all credit was given along sectarian lines. The remaining 30% was intercommunal. As the table indicates, intercommunal credit in Ottoman Cyprus grew steadily from 23% of all credit in 1593–1595 to 31% in 1609–1611 and 38% in 1633–1637. (Oddly, 33% was the figure in the small sample of 1580).

In intercommunal credit the creditors overwhelmingly were Muslims, the borrowers Christians. During the period 1593–1595 instances of credit from Muslims to zimmis were more than 12 times as frequent as from zimmis to Muslims (37 to 3), while in the small sample from 1580 such credit was 4.5 times as frequent (9 to 2); by 1609–1611 that figure had fallen to 2.8 times as frequent (59 to 21), but in 1633–1637 it still remained 2.4 times as frequent (29 to 12). Of all known instances of credit in 1580/1593–1595 22% was given from Muslims to zimmis and only 2% from zimmis to Muslims. Of all credit given in 1609–1611, 23% was given by Muslims to zimmis, while that given by zimmis to Muslims had reached 8% of all credit. By 1633–1637 intercommunal credit of Muslim origin had increased to 27% of all cases while that of zimmi origin had increased to 11%. As the proportion of intercommunal credit slowly increased between 1593 and 1637, the proportion given by zimmis grew very slightly. Although the proportion of intercommunal credit of zimmi origin experienced a significant growth, Muslim creditors remained predominant. In all there were 135 instances of credit from Muslims to zimmis compared with only 38 instances from zimmis to Muslims. Of all credit registered, 77% (457 cases) originated with Muslims and 22% (134 cases) with zimmis. The Muslim community of Cyprus was overwhelmingly the source of credit on Cyprus; doubtless the zimmis were considerably in debt.[12]

Ameliorating the circumstances of the zimmis was the prevalence in Cyprus of a kind of credit which really was a commercial partnership (commenda) in which one party put up the money while the other party pledged to fulfill certain services among which might be to engage in trade or commerce.[13] Zimmis with economic, mercantile, or commercial skills participated in that sort of partnership not unfavorable to the borrower. Of course Muslims carried out those roles, too. But one may imagine that since the Muslim community, or part of it, had a virtual monopoly on the sources of wealth in the new provincial administration (including all the bureaucrats and military); many who had no mercantile or commercial skills or interests, at first anyway, would eagerly provide capital in a commenda partnership for a local zimmi or Muslim with such experience and skills.

Zimmiye Filozide, mother and *vasi* (guardian) before the Sharia of the minor daughter Hiristine of the late Filori of Istefani (?) village of Baf nahiye, acknowledges and states *(ik/tk)* before racil Huseyn çelebi of the Cyprus janissaries: He gave my late husband Filori money by means of a commenda *(mudaraba)* for sustenance *(zindelik haline)*. With both his own money and the aforementioned money my husband bought coarse leather *(gon)*, a shirt (*gonlek = gomlek,* or *gunluk* = frankin-cense, myrrh?), and other goods of commerce *(mataᶜ)* which Huseyn took. After Huseyn makes claims of his own, a compromise *(sulh)* is made for 3000 akce, which the woman receives in full before the court. (4 145–1; III Ramazan 1045)

Veli ota başi bn Suleyman of Lefkoşa makes a claim *(d/tk)* against haci Yusuf ota başi, guardian *(vasi)* for the children *(evlad-i sigar)* of the late Hasan boluk basi who died in Cairo *(Misr Kahire):* When the deceased went to Egypt I gave him a loan *(mudaraba)* of 50 riyal guruş. I want it from his effects. Yusuf denies this. When Veli is asked for proof, upright Muslims *(udul-i muslimin)* Yusuf beg bn Musa and Mehmed aga confirm his claim. (4 115–2; II Muh. 1045)

Mustafa bn ʿAbdullah of Dalya (?) village acknowledges *(ik)* before Cuneyd v. Kiryako: I gave him 51 filori for cotton *(penbe)* in *(mudaraba).* He still owes me 16½ filori. (1 6–6; I Ramazan 988)

Until 1611 (1018) between 15% and 20% of the civilian male Muslim creditors and debtors whose full names are used were identifiable as converts to Islam. Presumably those were Orthodox or Latin Christians of Cyprus converted to Islam. That group lent money with exactly the frequency that they borrowed. In 1593–1595 11 of the 72 civilian Muslim male creditors (15%) whose full names are given were converts, as were 12 of 68 of the debtors (18%); in 1609–1611 15 of the 80 such creditors (19%) were converts and 11 of 71 debtors (15%). The total for the two volumes was 26 of 153 creditors (17%) and 23 of 139 debtors (17%), indicating that the behavior of the Muslim converts was remarkably like that of the group as a whole. By 1633–1637, when conversion had slowed considerably, that group had disappeared completely; none are identifiable among the civilian creditors and debtors, because conversion had slowed down so much.

Women, frequently property holders, played a not-insubstantial role in the Cyprus community both as creditors and as debtors. the concise reports in the sicils often prevent distinguishing whether the woman is indeed the original creditor or lender, whether she has inherited a claim or liability, or whether the claim involves property that originally was part of her dowry and so cannot be considered outstanding credit even if a man owes it to her. Women frequently arranged estate settlements, either for themselves or as guardians for minor children. They collected debts due to the estate and paid its outstanding debts. It is unfortunate that more cannot be learned about the role of women in those settlements. It may be useful to look in detail at a few such cases.

The debts of the janissary officer ʿAbdi çavuş have already been referred to. They included a 2000-akce debt to his wife Hatuniye for dowry *(mehr),* 2400 akce to the wife of Monla Piri (?), and 2000 akce to his mother-in-law *(kayin anasi)* (1 146–1,5,9; II Rebiʿ I 1003).

Hadice bint ʿAbdullah of Lefkoşa has a vekil for the matter Yusuf çavuş bn ʿAbdullah who sets forth a claim *(t.m.)* in the presence of Sakina bint Mustafa of Lefkoşa: When I wanted to collect Sakina's 13,711-akce debt to the woman who appointed me her agent *(my muvekkile)*, a settlement *(sulh)* for 10,711 akce was made with the mediation of upright people. There are no further claims. (1 163–1; III Rebi' II 1003)

Demirlu bn Ayvan says in the presence of Receb bn Hasan, racil: My daughter was his servant *(hidmetkar)*; he owes her money. Receb says he paid her three altun. Demirlu denies that. When an oath is proposed to Demirlu that the money was not paid, he takes it. (1 239–6; I Şevval 1002)

Hadice bint Murad of Lefkoşa sets forth a claim *(t.d.)* against Ibrahim çavuş bn Veli: I have been without maintenance *(nafaka)* from my husband 'Abdus-Selam for two years. Ibrahim çavuş owes my husband money. Let maintenance for the amount of his debt be paid to me from his house *(menzil)* in Lefka. Ibrahim admits that the debt exists. However, he says before leaving here her husband said, if I do not return within six months, let my wife Hadice be divorced from me three times. It is now more than two years since he left. If this is so then I need not give her one akce. Hadice denies this. When Ibrahim is asked for proof, from the upright Muslims *('udul-i Muslimin)* Şa'ban çavuş and Receb bn 'Abdullah confirm him in regard both to the condition of divorce and to the absence for two years. After *tezkiye* and *ta'dil*, their testimony is accepted. (1 155–2; II Rebi' II 1003)

Ayla bint Suleyman of Lefkoşa acknowledges *(ik)* in the presence of Habib bn Ebul-Hayr of Lefkoşa: Habib owed me 100 guruş. Now he has paid me in full. (2 4–5; III Zil-Hicce 1018)

'Ayni bint Yunus of Lefkoşa sets forth a claim *(td)* in the presence of Mehmed beg: He owes 2000 akce to Saliha, the orphan of the late Mehmed. Mehmed says he has paid this in full. Registered. (3 7–4; Muh. 1019)

Elif bint 'Abdi of Lefkoşa has as legal agent *(vekil)* for the matter 'Ali bn Fazli who states in the presence of Murad bn (sic) Elyod (?), Armenian: Elif, who made me her agent *(muvekkile)*, gave 34 guruş, to Armenian Kara Goz. Murad was guarantor of the money *(kefil bil-mal)*, and I have received the amount in full from him. I have no further claim. (3 29–3; II Zil-Kade 1018)

Fatma bint Ahmed of Lefkoşa has as agent her husband Itili (?) bn Ahmed: She wants 600 akce from Cum'alu bn Ahmed. He claims he has paid, but he has no proof, so his is ordered to pay. (3 63–6; I Receb 1019)

Mehmed bn haci Ahmed acknowledges *(ik/it)* in the presence of his sister Raziye: I took a 3000-akce loan *(karz-i şer'i)* from her. Now I owe her that much. (3 152–2; II Rebi' II 1019)

Receb, appointed guardian *(vasi)* before the Sharia for his minor brothers, the orphans of the late Mustafa beg of Degirmenlik village of Lefkoşa, sets forth a claim *(d/tk)* in the presence of Musa, grown son of the late Fatma bint Himmet of Catoz village of Lefkoşa. Musa's late mother owed my late father 5000 akce. I want it from her estate. With the mediation of upright people *(muslihun)* sulh is made for 2000 akce. (4 134–1; III Receb 1045)

Hanim bint Mehmed of Lefkoşa sets forth a claim *(d/tk)* in the presence of racil Ahmed beşe: He owes me 4000 akce. When I asked for it, he delayed *(te'allul)*. then he struck me *(darb)*. I want justice done *(ihkak-i hakk)*. Ahmed denies that. When Hanim has no proof, Ahmed takes an oath that he did not strike her. (4 179–3; I Receb 1046)

Summary

Until the Ottoman conquest, credit and moneylending seems to have been very much under the control of a small group of Jews. As the only source of credit, they were eagerly welcomed by businessmen and other people needing cash. Under the Ottomans, that system changed drastically, for under the Sharia, lending money at a fair interest rate was in no way reprehensible. Suddenly one finds people of all faiths involved in lending money for interest. Especially in the absence of banks, this was very important for the community. People often lent money out of their surpluses. Among the people giving or receiving credit were numerous janissaries and spahis, especially the former.

In the sicils the same people in business are often noted as both lenders and borrowers to meet their changing circumstances. All sorts of townsmen, and villagers too, were deeply involved. In a normal year about one-fifth of all cases involved credit of some sort. Leading members of the local communities were actively giving credit, usually at a rate of 20%. Even some pious foundations participated in this.

Sometimes people in bankruptcy benefitted from the mercy of others. Hard-pressed debters often could depend on the generosity of the local kadis. The court records give no evidence of very poor debtors, or very wealthy creditors. And most all of the cases involve relatively minor amounts of credit. Although many men had enough resources to make an occasional loan, most loans were on a small scale, as were most of the debts.

The proportion of intercommunal credit rose steadily between 1593

Table 10.1
Cases of Loans and Other Credit

Lefkoşa	Year	Muslim to Muslim	%	Muslim to zimmi	%	zimmi to Muslim	%	zimmi to zimmi	%	Total	
	1580	19	58%	9	27%	2	6%	3	9%	33	
	1593–1595	108	62%	37	21%	3	2%	27	15%	175	
1A	1607–1609	127	61%	46	22%	5	2%	30	14%	208	(=19% of 1088)
2	1609–1611	13		1		0		0		14	(= 8% of 175)
3	1609–1611	126	48%	59	23%	21	8%	55	21%	261	(=22% of 1184)
4	1633–1637	56	52%	29	27%	12	11%	11	10%	108	(=20% of 528)
Total		322	54%	135	23%	38	6%	96	16%	591	(=20% of 2975)

and 1637. Often it is difficult to distinguish between credit and inheritance. Of all credit 54% was Muslim to Muslim, and 16% was zimmi to zimmi. Another 23% was Muslim to zimmi, while only 6% was zimmi to Muslim. The zimmis were falling in debt, relatively.

Under the Ottomans, a large number of people became involved in lending their surplus capital, although normally those amounts were minor. People who found themselves short of cash, or in debt, could borrow small amounts without having to get deeply in debt.

Lefkoşa was the economic and commercial center of Ottoman Cyprus, especially in the first century of Ottoman rule, or at least the court records indicate that, when one considers the many people who used the court from outside the capital. A number of respectable people served in provincial offices, including provincial governors and kadis, which suggests that there was no stigma against either lending or borrowing, as long as one acted in a fair way. Engaging in business activities, including lending and borrowing, were both praiseworthy activities, even when dealing with people of other religions. As long as the rate of interest was considered fair in accordance with the Sharia, it was acceptable.

Not infrequently women are mentioned in the judicial registers as lenders and borrowers, especially the former although the question of where the women got their money is often obscured by inheritance settlements. Widowed and divorced women frequently acted on behalf of their minor children.

NOTES

1. Cobham, p. 74; *R. de G.* 5.1979.223.
2. On interest and profit incentive, see Ö. L. Barkan, pp. 30–46, *Edirne Askeri Kassamına ait Tereke Defterleri (1545–1659)* in *Belgeler. Türk Tarih Belgeleri Dergisi.* 3.1966. Cf. pp. xxx–xxxviii. Ö. L. Barkan and E. H. Ayverdi, *Istanbul Vakıfları Tahrir Defteri 953 (1546) Tarihli.* H. Inalcik, "Capital Formation in the Ottoman Empire," *Journal of Economic History* 29.1969.90, 101, 126, 130, 134. R. Jennings, "Loans and Credit . . ." On the restrictions of the traditional Sharia, see *Hedaya,* pp. 289–293; d'Ohsson, v. 6, pp. 102ff. André Raymond, *Artisans et Commerçants au Caire au XVIIIe siècle.* pp. 280ff.
3. On the matter of vakfs lending money for interest, see Jon E. Mandaville, "Usurious Piety: The Cash Waqf Controversy in The Ottoman Empire," *IJMES* 10.1979.289–308. Cf. Barkan and Ayverdi, pp. xxxvff; Inalcik, "Capital Formation . . . ," p. 134.

4. On exploitative interest, see Ö. L. Barkan and Ayverdi, p. xxxvii. See also H. Inalcik, "Capital Formation . . . ," p. 139, regarding exploitative interest charged by the military in the period 1596–1610. The evidence of Lefkoşa judicial records does not permit such a conclusion, despite their importance as lenders. See also M. Akdağ, *Celâli Isyanları* . . . , pp. 37ff; M. Cezar, *Levendler,* pp.62f. For 17th- and 18th-century Cairo see A. Raymond, *Artisans et Commerçants* . . . , pp. 281f.

5. At that time legal interest rates commonly ranged between 10% and 20% per year. Besides specific examples cited in the works mentioned above, N. Steensgaard mentions money lent by Armenian merchants to Dutch merchants in Isfahan in 1637–1638 at 20% interest. Generally, when the lender and borrower stayed in the same town, the interest was 3/4% per month; otherwise it might be more. *Carracks, Caravans and Companies: The Structural Crisis in the European-Asian Trade in the Early 17th century.* pp. 376, 392, 26. The Venetian Mariti, a careful observer of Cyprus, wrote in 1769 that 12% had long been the local interest rate there. According to Mariti, the local Muslims engaged in money lending but always disguised the interest by combining it with the principal in all legal documents. *Travels* . . . , p. 124. Cf. A. Raymond, *Artisans et Commerçants* . . . , pp. 280ff. Normally the rate of interest in Cairo in the 17th and 18th centuries was 12%. At about that time M. d'Ohsson wrote that a 12% rate and that sort of concealment were general in the empire as a whole. Concealment was not practiced in Lefkoşa between 1580 and 1640, however.

6. *Murabaha,* of course, is the Koranic *riba* which is forbidden, an unusual choice of words. A fetva cited in a case of II Şaban 1043 incidentally refers to *riba* as an acceptable form of interest. 4 5–1.

7. In that case the rate of interest might be estimated to be about 18% per annum, but the term is not specified.

8. On imprisonment for debt, see d'Ohsson, v. 6, pp. 104ff.

9. S. D. Goitein, *A Mediterranean Society,* v. 3, p. 330. A. Raymond, *Artisans et Commerçants* . . . , pp. 274ff.

10. Increasingly through the 17th century coffee became a major good of trade in the eastern Mediterranean. A. Raymond, *Artisans et Commerçants* . . . , pp. 175ff and "café" in index for detailed information about the coffee trade.

11. Of course a complete set of sicils, rather than the fragments that survive from the period, would make identifying multiple lenders and debtors easier.

12. Unfortunately it has not been possible to speak precisely of the changing proportions of Muslims and Christians in Cyprus, or even in Lefkoşa where the court operated.

13. A. Udovitch, *Partnership and Profit in Medieval Islam.* Princeton, 1970. pp. 170–248. Goitein, v.1, pp. 169–179. v.3, p. 294. J. Mandaville, "Usurious Piety . . . ," pp. 294f. Ö. N. Bilmen, v. 7, pp. 101–122 *(müzarabe).*

ELEVEN

The Economy as Seen through Western Sources

Cyprus has often been renowned for its agriculture, industry, and commerce. The Arab Muslim geographer al-Muqaddasi (985) believed that Cyprus was ". . . full of populous cities and offers the Muslims many advantages in their trade thither, by reason of great quantities of merchandise, stuffs and goods, which are produced there."[1] Geoffrey de Vinsauf, in his chronicle of the 3rd Crusade, asserted that all the wealth of Croesus was to be found there.[2] John Mandeville (after 1322) observed that pilgrims always stopped in Cyprus "to buy things that they need for their living."[3] and Ludolf von Suchen (1350) reported Cyprus ". . . an island most noble and fertile, most famous and rich, surpassing all the islands of the sea, and teeming with all good things . . . It is productive beyond all other lands."[4] Referring to the years 1359–1360 the Cypriot chronicler Leontios Makhairas wrote: "And the riches which they had are beyond my power to describe for the merchant ships of the Christians which came from the west did not venture to do their business anywhere else but in Cyprus; (and all the trade of Syria was done in Cyprus)."[5]

Anthoine Regnault (1449) described the salt industry at Larnaka. Salt congealing over the water was simply removed; "The said Salines furnish all the countries in the Levant—even Italy, Calabria, Apulia and Romania—with salt; and it is esteemed the fairest in Christendom."[6] Le Saige (1518) praises the quality and expresses surprise how it comes "of itself" without labor from "a great frozen marsh" four leagues around.[7] Pietro Casola (1494) considered the salt free because it was acquired with so little effort. Seamen simply cut whatever quantity they wished and loaded that on their vessels; by the next morning a new supply was ready.[8] Locke (1553) indicated that the salt was a tight Venetian monopoly; he was impressed at how the salt accumulated without the use of a still.[9] No ship could leave for Venice without salt from Tuzla in its hold.[10] Cyprus salt was a major source of Venetian revenues.

The wine of Cyprus was drunk cautiously by the Latins. Regnault calls the wines good and potent, despite a smell of pitch.[11] The wine was very strong but good if mixed with lots of water.[12] According to the popular historian Porcacchi (1576) the wines of Cyprus were "very luscious and handsome"; ". . . all the wines of Cyprus may vie with those of any country, and they are appreciated accordingly in Venice and Rome, wherever indeed they reach."[13] Perhaps the best grapes and wine were to be found in Piskopi.

In sugar production too Piskopi was prolific. Estates there belonged to the Corner (or Cornaro) family.[14] Pietro Casola (1494) viewed the great sugar plantation of the Venetian patrician Don Federico Corner in Piskopi, where they made so much sugar that it seemed enough for the whole world. Coarse and fine sugar were manufactured in huge cauldrons by over 400 workers. Supposedly the best sugar went to Venice.[15] By the mid-16th century sugar production had declined considerably. According to Porcacchi (1576) sugar formerly was one of the chief products "but the culture of the cane was abandoned for that of cotton as being more profitable."[16]

An account of Cyprus by Aeneas Sylvius (1509) mentions huge squashes, abundant wine and oil, much grain and sugar cane, and particularly cloth of goats' hair, called camlet. The island exported much and imported little but had an unhealthy climate.[17] Paul Walther (1482) praised the "sweet and good waters" of the island, very cheap lamb, and abundant wine, wheat, oil, milk, honey, wax, pomegranates, carob, cassia, flax, and cottonwool, as well as salt, metals, and timber. For Walther the island was "exceedingly fertile but very hot."[18] Pietro Casola (1494) singled out the sugar, cotton, and carob trees: "I like everything on the island except for the reisonous taste of the wine."[19] Piskopi had impressed Capodilista (1458), not only for its sugar plantations, but for its lovely and well-watered gardens of oranges, citrons, carobs, and bananas.[20] While all the towns but Lefkoşa and Magosa appeared ruined to Suriano (1484), in the countryside there was plenty of sugar, good cotton, plenty of cheese, laudanum, honey, wool, the finest camlets known, and samite; meat was of poor quality, though abundant and cheap. When there were no locusts the grain harvest was adequate for four years. However, the "inhabitants are few and lazy."[21] Martin von Baumgarten (1508) contrasted the fruitfulness of the land with the exploitation of the cultivators. Grain, silkworms, silks, oil, sugar, and wine were abundant, and the countryside was most beautiful. "Yet not withstanding this fruitfulness and pleasantness, neither its cities nor villages are much frequented, but as if it was barren and a desert place it is inhabited by a few people that live in cottages." "Besides all the inhabitants of Cyprus are slaves to the Venetians . . ." They pay one-third of all their income in taxes, work for the state two days a week, and pay other taxes "with which the poor common people are so flayed and pillaged that they hardly have wherewithal to keep soul and body together."[22] Piri Reis knew the extraordinary island as very green, with lots of running water and sugar refineries. For Bordone (1528) Cyprus was the "most noble island, which yields to none other in merit, where wine, oil, wheat, barley, sugar and cotton greatly abound and there is just one 'drawback,' that locusts appear at the time of young wheat."[23]

For D. Possot (1533) Cyprus was "hot, rich and fertile in produce, and cheap, with the best wines possible . . ." "There is good wheat, whereof is made bread which is sweet and wonderfully good." Although the meat was bad tasting, and there was pestilence every summer, sugar, cinnamon, silk, and mulberry trees were abundant. "In Cyprus the water of the springs is such that if a man drink of it as much as he will it never does him harm."[24] Affagart (1534), however, feared to eat food there because of the "tainted and poisonous air."[25] Jodicus de Meggen (1542) left a valuable account of how the water is used, for the sugar and cotton need "assiduous irrigation" in the summer and the people ". . . spare no expense to achieve it." There were ". . . very deep and wide wells from which plentiful springs of water are drawn up and poured into the dry fields by means of chains of earthenware jars driven round by wheels operated by a draft horse." "The Cypriot race is addicted to good living and sensual gratification . . ."[26] To J. Palerne (1581) the abundance of grains and vineyards was impressive, and the cotton was the best in the Levant. Though mountainous the place was very fertile, indeed being called the little France by the "Persians and Romans."[27] According to Graziani (c. 1571) a third of the grain harvest is more than enough for the local people, prodigious quantities of fruits are produced, and the land is very fertile, though often short of water. Other products included olives, honey, wax, saffron, flax, and medicinal herbs and drugs. "The Gentry lived in as great splendor as Princes . . ." and the lower classes hated them because they treated them badly. Therefore because of their own desperation, the people supported the Turks in the war. The air is very unhealthy, so few Cypriots lived to an old age.[28] The popular account of Porcacchi (1576) enumerates the agricultural production of the mid-16th century: large black raisins, wheat and barley "in abundance," and all kinds of vegetables, including cauliflowers, cabbages, colocasia, and oranges, lemons, and citrons "of such a quantity as few other countries can surpass." Also saffron, sesame, coriander, sumach, lentisc seed, honey (from hives, sugar, and carobs), and many more. Cotton was the staple, replacing sugar. ". . . I will shortly say that Cyprus certainly deserves to be ranked with those lands that produce in most abundant measure all that is necessary for man's use. And if the inhabitants were more industrious, or less sluggards, especially in the way of increasing their water supply, their fields would be even more fertile still; but so great is the profit which a very little labour wins for them from cotton and wool, that other produce is generally neglected."[29]

Although both Zvallart (1586) and Somer (1590) believed that a decline had taken place in the economy and population of the island, exactly when that decline began is by no means clear to them. According to Zvallart some traces of the former great cities and wealth remained.[30] Somer thought that population had declined sharply from a time when there were supposedly 15 towns and 850 villages, for currently people were living on fruits, beans, and carobs while paying 20 gulden/year annual head tax.[31] According to de Villamont (1589), the wines, wheat, barley, cattle, salt, oil, sugar, cheese, flax, fine wool, sheep (with 25-pound tails), capers, pomegranates, sweet and bitter oranges, dates, cucumbers, melons, fruits, and particularly cotton of Cyprus were all excellent, although locusts often ruined harvests. Around Limosa people caught falcons and sold them to the pasha. De Villamont observed sugar cane being crushed by wheels turned by water and the liquid being boiled to make sugar. The local oranges were twice the size of those in Italy. He was told that people concealed the existence of mines from the Ottoman authorities, and that the taxation system did not allow for increase or decrease in the amount of taxes paid as population changed.[32] Dandini (1596) praised the fruit of the mountains and the plains, "which renders the country fertile and plentiful."

This isle abounds in wheat as well as wine, and other excellent viands, and supplieth other countries; the sun and soil render the wines very strong and agreeable, but after they are put into pitched vessels, they receive such a gust as is not pleasing to those that are not accustomed thereto, nevertheless all agree they are good for the stomach. You will find there all manner of pulse in abundance; barley, dates, mulberries, oranges, lemons, citrons, and all other fruits, except cherries, chestnuts and sorb-apples. There is no want of sugar, saffron, coriander, sesamun [sesame], lintel-feed [linseed], honey, and sometimes manna; the Egyptian bean [the carob], the herb whose ashes serves to make sous, and that with which they wash camblets and other cloths. There may be had rhubarb, turpentine, and scamony, and other things that are valuable.

"Besides, there is so great a quantity of cotton, that the inhabitants not only cloath themselves, and make all sorts of cloths therewith, but they furnish also Italy, and other parts; it is that which makes their principal revenues." Salt, capers, and fat-tailed sheep with good-quality mutton are also important. "Finally, we may say, that this isle aboundeth with all delicacies: before they became subject to the Turks, they lived splendidly, and in freedom, but sensual."[33] Georg Rauwolff, brother of Leonart, died in 1573 while loading cotton in the heat in Magosa after having drunk too much heavy wine; the best bay-salt was still found at Tuzla (Salina) at that time.[34]

Cotovicus (1598) too praised the fertility of the island. Well-watered grain, cotton, and sugar fields were found in Cithera (Kythrea) and Couclia (Kouklia). Lapheto (Lapithos or Latta) had the most fruitful soil on the island, producing cotton, sugar, lemons, and oranges. "It abounds in silk, cotton, flax, wool, grain, oil, honey, cheese, and wine of excellent quality." (Formerly the Venetians took 50,000 scudi from salt and that much again from other commerce.) Raisins and sugar were abundant. "One could hardly exaggerate the richness of the soil . . . ," which is very well irrigated. "On this matter they spare neither money nor labour, for when the rivers or torrents fail they have deep and wide wells from which, by means of large wheels driven by horses, they draw up in earthen vessels abundance of water for the use of their fields." Minerals, spices, herbs, and vegetables are enumerated in detail. Although famous for its agriculture and other wealth, "towns and villages lie desolate and forgotten . . ." and much of the island is now "uncultivated, neglected and deserted."[35] The English merchant John Sanderson (1598) passed two or three months in Cyprus while his ship was being loaded with salt at Larnaka; he knew about the marketing of Cyprus wool in Aleppo.[36] The English clockmaker Thomas Dallam (1600) said, "This Iland is the moste pleasante of any that hetherto I did ever see."[37] The Levant Company chaplin William Biddulph (1600–1608?) described Cyprus as "a famous and fruitfull Island" with much "cotton-wooll growing," "exceeding good wine," and "the best dimetey" anywhere.[38] Henry de Beauvau (1604) reported that the Porte received 300,000 crowns/year from the island, which is a fifth of the revenues. "It is very fertile in all kinds of grain, olive trees, grapes, lemons, carobs, capers, salt and other necessary products." But the island was very underpopulated.[39] In 1605 Teixeira's vessel took on a load of cotton. Some 5000 bags/year of cotton were exported, as well as 3000 bags of very fine wool, some silk and sugar, much excellent wine, some cheese, and other produce. ". . . it is fertile, and its produce all of excellent quality, but none of great amount, nor at all equal to what was yielded to the Venetians." "The trade was great in former days, but has much fallen off since the Turkish conquest."[40] For Lithgow (1610): "It yieldeth infinite canes of Sugar, Cotton wooll, Oile, Honey, Cornes, Turpentine, Allom, Verdegreece, Grograms, store of Metals and Salt; besides all other sorts of fruit and commodities in abundance." "Scarcity of water" and "scorching heate" were the two greatest problems, and "unspeakable is the calamitie of that poore afflicted Christian people under the terror of these Infidels . . ."[41] Sandys (1610) too details the rich produce of the island: ". . . the staple commodities are cotton wooles (the best of the Orient), chamolets, salt and sope ashes."[42] According to des Hayes (1621) the most fertile part of the island was the north, where the oranges were of very high quality. The whole island can produce a great abundance, but it is marshy, swampy, and unhealthful. The Turks have ruined it, now everyone lives on carobs.[43] Della Valle (1625) too believed that the Christians neglected the mines and the Turks could not operate them. 10,000 piastres in revenues came from the salt flats. "The Turks are too negligent to clean and clear it properly, and every day it gets smaller, and will eventually be filled up.[44]

De Bruyn (1683) found very good wines, the strongest he had ever tasted, which he mixed with two parts water. People were few but agriculture was good; wheat was very good; cotton had completely replaced the former sugar cultivation; mulberry trees and silkworms were abundant, but the air was extremely unwholesome for three or four months of the year. However, "a man may Travel as securely all over the island as he may do in his own House."[45] A catalog of Cyprus products in Van der Nijenburg (1684?) singles out wool, a quarter of which was exported at very low prices, cheese of goat's milk "in great request all over the Levant," and flowered silks and cotton "little inferior to those of the Indies", which were the main trade.[46] According to Dapper (1688) the once-populous and wealthy villages were now depopulated under the cruel Turkish rule. The best cotton was grown at Lefkoşa and Magosa, although much also came from Baf and Limosa; the cotton was the best in the whole Levant. Still the fertile Mesarye had abundant grain crops.[47]

Venetians were eager to demonstrate that revenues accruing to the government declined abruptly under the Ottomans. For example, according to the supposed testimony of two Cypriot gentlemen he recently had encountered Bernard Sagredo asserted that in 1575 the Ottomans derived a revenue of 140,000 ducats from the island; the gentlemen asserted that the island had fallen into a miserable state under Ottoman rule. Many inhabitants had abandoned their homes and fled, and more were leaving daily. The Ottomans had had to rely on settlers they brought from their own territories, and because of the great heat, few of those survived long; there were 1000 cavalry and 8000 footsoldiers to defend the whole island. In 1585 Sagredo reported from similar sources that revenues from the island had declined from 940,000 ducats under the Venetians to 208,000 ducats under the Ottomans. In particular revenues from the saltworks of Larnaka had plummeted from 300,000 ducats to 8000. The revenues of 60 villages in Girniye (Kyrenia, Cerines) district declined from 30,000 ducats to 8000, those of 120 villages of Mesariye (Mesaoria) fell from 70,000 to 18,000, those of 124 villages of the Vicomte (Lefkoşa) fell from 70,000 ducats to 22,000, those of 22 villages of Larnaka (Salines), from 25,000 ducats to 4000, and those of 119 villages of Limosa from 70,000 ducats to 24,000.[48] In 1566 the total revenues of the Signory had been 546,000 ducats, of which only 184,331 ducats were needed to meet the expenses of the military and civil institutions of the island; the excess of 361,669 ducats fell to the Signory. (Ottoman revenues came from the saltworks, a tithe on grains, vineyards, and animals, and the *harac (kharaj)* which is a sequin or a ducat for every inhabitant of the island from 15 to 60.) Since the Ottomans spent 276,000 ducats on the island now, they had a loss of 68,000 ducats there every year. Perhaps the Venetians wanted to boast about the efficacy of their administration and even about the island's wealth. Indeed Sagredo raised the possibility of convincing the Porte to lease the island for Venice to exploit in return for a large annual payment.[49] Nevertheless, even if some revenues were lost through decline in population, villagers must have been delighted by the lower taxes under the Ottomans.

According to modern historians, Cyprus had been immensely profitable to the Venetians. Large-scale sugar production began in Cyprus from about 1368, with irrigation, imported slave labor, and improvements in processing; ". . . full-blown plantation agriculture increased the supply of sugar from Cyprus and, to a lesser extent, from Crete." The Corner family became the richest in Venice. "Massive capital investment in sugar mills, irrigation systems, and slaves paid off handsomely, for there was a vigorous demand for sugar in Europe and the Near East, and Corner's large-scale methods produced a cheaper as well as a better product."[50] Cyprus became increasingly important for the Venetian economy. Both the number of vessels and volume of trade with Syria and Cyprus far exceeded those headed for the Atlantic or for Constantinople and the Black Sea.[51]

There is a local shift in trade center from Syria to Cyprus for in 1558 to 1560 there were almost no clearances for Syria, whereas in 1450 Cyprus had been of secondary importance. Apparently cotton, which in the fifteenth century furnished the bulk of the cargo of the ships from Syria, was in the sixteenth century produced in Cyprus, whose sugar plantations, famous in the fifteenth century, had meanwhile been ruined by the competition of the new Portuguese possessions in the West. While, however, Cyprus furnished the bulk of the freight in the sixteenth century, Venetians were still active in Syria and some part of the ship cargoes may have come directly or indirectly from the mainland.[52]

Early in the 15th century Genoese cotton exports from Cyprus and the west coast of Anatolia competed with those of Venice from Syria and Palestine; by late in that century Venice had won control of that trade.[53] Under Venice cotton production in Cyprus increased three-fold, and huge profits accrued to its merchants and nobility, rescuing the economy of the island "just at the time when Portuguese sugar was driving down the price".[54] Much of the wheat of Venice also came from Cyprus; much of the revenues of Venice came from the salt of Cyprus, and wine also was a very important commercial product.[55]

Cyprus' population never recovered from the blow of the Black Death in the mid-14th century and the re-emergence of malaria in the mid-15th century. Considerable immigration contributed to what probably was rapid growth on the island, especially in the late 13th and early 14th centuries. Thereafter, and especially during the 400 years of Venetian and Ottoman rule, Cyprus is a conspicuous exception to Braudel's idea that all the islands "exported their people."[56] As he himself points out, Cyprus had a very small population even in 1570.[57] No better evidence of that underpopulation is to be found than the official and unofficial attempts of first Venice and then the Ottoman empire to build up the local population. Nevertheless, except for the brief period when the Ottomans organized compulsory migrations *(surgun)* from adjacent Anatolian regions, immigration was rare. Clearly, more than anything else the problem was disease. The late 15th century apparently was a period of growing virulence of malaria; besides the virtual abandonment of Magosa and Baf, there was the temporary abandonment and tiny population at Iskenderun/Alexandrette, best port of Aleppo, and the general dread with which Europeans regarded the Levant littoral. The Ottoman system was not capable of organizing and maintaining the kind of elaborate drainage systems requiring long years of forced labor such as Venice, Medici Florence, and Rome accomplished. There simply were no grounds for legally requiring such service, and even if an occasional official might arbitrarily require it, in the long run such illegal behavior could not prevail. Neither could the Ottomans successfully force villagers or townspeople, especially Muslims, to live at unhealthy sites or to drain swamps.[58]

Venetian, Genoese, and other Italian landowners organized efficient plantation systems in Cyprus. As Braudel has pointed out, such monocrop cultures of cotton, sugar, and vines often became responsible for famine. When one crop failed, or when the market for a crop failed, then the poor cultivators suffered.[59] Wholesale failures of that crop impoverished cultivators who otherwise would have been cultivating a variety of crops, including most of their own food.[60] The Venetian and Genoese aristocracy on Cyprus profited immensely, living in luxury while exploiting the local people. They forced serfs to cultivate whatever they wanted. Although they enriched both themselves and Venice, they were singularly unpopular in Cyprus. "So the Turkish conquest unleashed a social revolution."[61] The Ottoman system simply was not organized to permit such exploitation. Law and society were not elitist. Coercion of the poor and weak was despised. Legal rights and obligations applied to everyone. Ottoman law did not permit landowners to force villagers to cultivate what they wanted, when they wanted, or how they wanted. The taxes that spahis could collect were limited by law. Although there were restrictions on villagers leaving timar lands uncultivated, the penalties were slight, particularly when inflation was severe. So if indeed cotton, sugar, and salt production did decline after the Ottoman conquest, then as Braudel says: "But this does not necessarily mean the decline of Cyprus. There is no evidence that Turkish rule led to a fall in living standards for the inhabitants of the Island."[62] An exploitative class was eliminated, wealth was better distributed, and the villagers were liberated from an onerous serfdom. (Only later did the Ottoman system there become corrupt, or ineffective, leaving the villagers vulnerable to a new exploitation.)

The problems of maintaining adequate food supplies for the populace are another set which have particularly interested Braudel. He maintains that the problem of how to live within local resources is common to all islands, and so that Corfu, Crete, and Cyprus were "constantly threatened by famine" in the second half of the 16th century.[63] Elsewhere he states that the Mediterranean world was "always on the verge of famine."[64] Ottoman Cyprus, however, seems to have been blest with a comfortable living standard. All of the evidence points to a very small number of imports compared with the rich abundance of foods locally produced and consumed.[65] Europeans found prices low and fruits, vegetables, and meat widely available. However, Cyprus is in some ways "exceptional," for although only one-twentieth of the land on the island was cultivated, "the wheat yield was 6 to 1, barley 8 to 1."[66]

Another chronic problem was defense against piracy. Muslim pirates terrorized the island under Venetian rule, and Christian pirates filled their void after the Ottoman conquest. Defense against them was no easy matter. Defensive bastions were built at places lacking them, like Larnaka and Baf and Limosa, but everywhere the suburbs lay exposed, and none of the rest of the coast line could be defended securely. On the one hand, pirates plundered with impunity; on the other hand, they appeared by prearranged signal to rendezvous and sell their loot. On Cyprus, at least, the raids seem to have been confined to the coastal littoral; such adventures did not advance much inland even though the flat central plateau may have appeared vulnerable.

Summary

The island of Cyprus was noted for its fertility, its diverse agricultural, commercial, and industrial skills, much of which was exploited through monopolies which had been established under Venetian rule especially. The island's production of salt, wine, and sugar were renowned. Also very important were cotton, raisins, and carobs. Many contemporary observers point to the exploitation of Cypriots who were not part of the ruling class.

Venetians wanted to show that they had exploited the resources of the island better than the Ottomans had. Perhaps the Ottomans were naive, for they never really considered being exploitative. Usually they were more concerned with creating a situation where the people were able to flourish because they lived under a more just rule. It was only infrequently an Ottoman policy to require village cultivators to engage in any kind of forced labor, or require that commercial crops be cultivated intensively, even if done before the conquest.

According to many modern historians, Cyprus had been immensely profitable to the Venetians, with full-blown plantation agriculture, once in sugar, and later cotton, enriching many Venetians, especially the Corner family. Even most of their wheat started to come from Cyprus. Requiring fixed services was not normally Ottoman policy. Likewise, the Ottomans could not force people, particularly Muslims, to live in places which were believed to be unhealthy. Ottoman law permitted people to cultivate what they wanted. An exploitative class was eliminated, and wealth was much better distributed. At least some were blessed with a comfortable living standard.

Cyprus never recovered from the continuing blows to its population of the Black Death and malaria. Neither Venetians nor Ottomans were able to bring about any significant migration to the island, even though it certainly was in their best interest to do so. Cyprus suffered all of the disadvantages of underpopulation. Neither Venetians nor Ottomans were capable of draining swamps or creating other conditions beneficial to population growth, despite all the talk expended on that subject.

NOTES

1. Cobham, p. 5. *Description of Syria* . . . , tr. G. Le Strange, p. 82, in Palestine Pilgrims' Text Society, v. 3. London, 1896.
2. Mogabgab, v. 1, p. 15.
3. Cobham, p. 21; Letts, p. 21.
4. Cobham, p. 18; Stuttgart, v. 25, pp. 29f; de Mas Latrie, v. 2, pp. 210f.
5. *Recital* . . . , v. 1, p. 81.
6. Mogabgab, v. 3, p. 160. Martin von Baumgarten (1508) called it the best salt anywhere. Cobham, p. 54; *Travels*, p. 440; *Peregrinatio* . . . , p. 137. Noribergae, 1594.
7. Cobham, p. 60; *Voyage* . . . , pp. 143f. Cf. Jodicus de Meggen (1542), in Mogabgab, v. 3, p. 147. John Sanderson, *The Travels* . . . , p. 238.
8. Mogabgab, v. 1, p. 45; Newett, p. 293f. According to J. Palerne (1581) and Graziani the value of the salt to Venice had been 300,000 crowns or ducats a year. *Peregrinations*, pp. 330f. Graziani, p. 4.
9. Cobham, p. 69; Hakluyt, v. 5, pp. 93f.
10. Fürer von Haimendorf, *Reis-Beschreibung* . . . (1566), pp. 297f.
11. Mogabgab, v. 3, p. 160. Cf. Jacobus de Verona (1335), in Cobham, p. 18. von Baumgarten (1508), in Cobham, p. 55; *Travels*, p. 441; *Peregrinatio* . . . , p. 139. Cf. Jodicus de Meggen (1542), in Mogabgab, v. 3, p. 148.
12. Fürer von Haimendorf, *Reis-Beschreibung* . . . (1566), p. 306. Graziani (c. 1571), p. 4. J. Palerne (1581), *Peregrinations*, p. 329f.
13. Cobham, p. 166; *L'Isole* . . . , p. 21, Venetia, 1572; p. 148, Padova, 1620.
14. Gabriele Capodilista (1458), in Cobham, p. 35; *Itinerario*, p. 178; de Mas Latrie, v. 3, pp. 76f.
15. Mogabgab, v. 1, p. 42; Newett, pp. 212, 216. Cf. Jodicus de Meggen (1542): The sugar of Couclia is taller than a man, and the canes are thicker than three fingers. Mogabgab, v. 3, pp. 147, 155f.
16. Cobham, p.166; *L'Isole* . . . , pp. 21f, Venetia, 1572; pp. 146–149, Padova, 1620.
17. Mogabgab, v. 2, p. 78; *Cosmographia*, p. 78.
18. Mogabgab, v. 1, p. 38; *Itinerarium* . . . , v. 192, p. 93.
19. Mogabgab, v. 1, p. 42; Newett, p. 216.
20. Cobham, p. 35; *Itinerario*, p. 178; de Mas Latrie, v. 3, p. 76.
21. Cobham, p. 49; *Il Trattato* . . . , p. 242.
22. Cobham, p. 55; *Travels*, p. 441; *Peregrinatio*, p. 139.
23. Cobham, p. 61; *Libro di* . . . , p. LXVII. *Kitab'i Bahriyye*, v. 2, p. 278.
24. Cobham, pp. 63f.

25. Cobham, p. 67; *Relation* . . . , pp. 39f, 243f.
26. Mogabgab, v. 1, pp. 147f, 152, 155f.
27. *Peregrinations*, pp. 328ff.
28. Graziani, pp. 22f, 73.
29. He mentions the *parici*, who are "a kind of slaves bound for life to their masters." Cobham, pp. 164, 166f; *L'Isole* . . . , p. 21f. Venetia, 1572; pp. 147–150, Padova, p. 1620.
30. Anvers, p. 160.
31. *Beschrijvinge* . . . , pp. 10f.
32. Cobham, pp. 173f, 176f.
33. Cobham, p. 183; Pinkerton, v. 10, pp. 280f.
34. Dannenfeldt, pp. 40f.
35. Cobham, pp. 193f, 199ff.
36. *The Travels* . . . , pp. 16, 130.
37. "The Diary . . . ," p. 28.
38. *The Travels* . . . , p. 35.
39. Cobham, p. 209; *Relation* . . . , 1608, pp. 115f; 1619, pp.88f.
40. *The Travels* . . . , pp. 134f.
41. Cobham, pp. 202f; *The Totall Discourse* . . . , pp. 164ff.
42. Cobham, p. 208; *Travels*, p. 221. For soap, see also Earle, p. 199.
43. *Voiage* . . . , pp. 326ff.
44. Cobham, pp. 212ff; *Viaggi*, 1843, v. 2, pp. 885ff; v. 4, p. 536, Venetia, 1667. Ottoman law and tradition did not permit the sort of forced labor that flourished under the Lusignans and Venetians, so at that time people only needed to cultivate as they wanted.
45. Cobham, pp. 241ff; *Reizen* . . . , pp. 367, 373, 377f.
46. Cobham, pp. 247f, 250, 240f. He reports the English consul's lending money for 20% interest, or 30% against their future harvests.
47. *Naukeurige Beschryving* . . . , pp. 23, 25f, 51f, 92. By the 18th century Cyprus' economic importance was largely as a point of transit. Food and other provisions were abundant there and could be procured extremely cheaply, so it remained an important stop for European vessels. In addition, illegally, grain, cotton, wool, and madder could be procured there, as well as what Pococke considered the only good cheese in the Levant. Taxes were not exorbitant, and people could live in plenty, but the oppression of the musellims was such that many people left for Cilicia. Richard Pococke (1738), in Cobham, pp. 255, 260, 267; Pinkerton, v. 10, pp. 590ff. Alexander Drummond (1750), in Cobham, pp. 281f; *Travels* . . . , pp. 155ff, 146ff. London, 1754. C. S. Sonnini, *Voyage* . . . , pp. 60ff, 76ff. Paris, 1801. E. Clarke, *Travels* . . . , pp. 312f, 315f, 340. L. Corancez, *Itinéraire* . . . , p. 239. Van der Nijenberg, in Cobham, pp. 247f. *Mr. Robert's Adventures and Sufferings* . . . (1696) p. 172. The long-term population trends are discussed in ch. 6. Disease and locusts were the main causes, of course, but even in the 17th century after few Europeans were willing to give Muslims credit for much of anything.

48. de Mas Latrie, v. 3, pp. 560ff. Doubtless the debasement of coinage and the inflation affect such estimates.
49. de Mas Latrie, v. 3, p. 563. Revenues called "seigneurs propriétaires" amounted to 394,000 ducats and "seigneurie" was 546,000 ducats.
50. McNeill, *Venice . . .* , pp. 76, 54.
51. Lane, "Venetian Shipping . . . ," p. 24.
52. Lane, "Venetian Shipping . . . ," pp. 17, 38. Cf. McNeill, *Venice . . .* , p. 76.
53. Lane, *Venice. A Maritime Republic*, p. 298. "Even after Cyprus was lost to the Turks in 1571, its cotton was still for some decades marketed through Venice."
54. Lane, *Venice. A Maritime Republic*, pp. 297f. Cf. McNeill, *Venice . . .* , p. 76: "Cotton was a second new plantation crop of increasing importance; it later escaped the plantation production pattern and became a major peasant-produced cash crop in Syria, Anatolia, and the southeastern Balkans."
55. Lane, *Venice, A Maritime Republic*, pp. 305, 324. McNeill, *Venice . . .* , p. 52.
56. *The Mediterranean . . .* , v. 1, p. 158.
57. *The Mediterranean . . .* , v. 1, p. 156.
58. In fact, Venetian attempts to organize drainage in Cyprus met with only minimal success, and even the drainage efforts in Italy were of limited success. *The Mediterranean . . .* , v. 1, pp. 67–82.
59. *The Mediterranean . . .* , v. 1, pp. 154f.
60. *The Mediterranean . . .* , v. 1, pp. 155f.
61. *The Mediterranean . . .* , v. 1, p. 156.
62. *The Mediterranean . . .* , v. 1, p. 156.
63. *The Mediterranean . . .* , v. 1, p. 152.
64. *The Mediterranean . . .* , v. 1, p. 244.
65. Cf. Richard Pococke (1738), in Cobham, pp. 252, 266f, 268f; Pinkerton, v. 10, pp. 575, 590f, 592, and *passim*. According to Sieur de Mont, "Provisions are so incredibly cheap, that, as the French consul assur'd me, the greatest Lover of his Belly cannot . . . spend Forty Piasters a Year in Eating and Drinking." *A New Voyage to the Levant. . . .* 3rd ed. London, 1702. pp. 199f.
66. Braudel, *The Mediterranean . . .* , v. 1, p. 426. Braudel's observation that islands are isolated worlds between poles of archaism and innovation (pp. 147, 150) seems particularly apt in regard to Cyprus. Under the Lusignans Cyprus was located on important trade, military, political, and pilgrim routes and became a marvelous center of innovation. Regular contacts with Venice, Genoa, Constantinople, Cairo, and the Levant assured that. Ottoman rule, in turn, brought with it archaism and isolation, partly because of changes in trade routes and in goods of trade as the empire became increasingly an exporter of agricultural goods and an importer of manufactured goods, and partly as a result of Ottoman policies. Island villagers probably were little affected by such changes, profound as they may be on townspeople.

TWELVE

The Economy as Seen through
Ottoman Sources

The agricultural produce of Cyprus was rich and varied in the century
after the Ottoman conquest. That variety impressed and often surprised
merchants and other travelers who visited the island. Either out of
curiosity or to inform merchants and other countrymen, some listed the
crops in detail. So inexpensive were foods and supplies that by the mid-
17th century European ships regularly provisioned there for their return
voyages to the western Mediterranean. Incidental cases in the judicial
records, and even more important the few complete or partial lists of the
maximum legal market prices *(narh)* of agricultural goods show the
nature of agricultural produce. At the markets is Lefkoşa a rich variety
of local fruits, vegetables, dairy products, and meats was available year
round; so too were numerous imported goods. Despite the immeasurable
impact of the irregularity of winter and rainfall and the regularity of
locusts and malarial mosquitoes, the island of Cyprus produced in abundance foods needed for a healthful diet.

Urban Revenues, Order in the Marketplace, and the Muhtesib

Three imperial orders of 23 Sefer 979 (17 July 1571), after the fall of the
island except Magosa, require that the governor of the province of
Cyprus look after *(nazar)* all of the imperial wealth of the island. In
particular the governor should protect all that wealth *(emval-i miri)* and
oversee the preparation of detailed *(mufassal)* and summary *(icmal)*

registers of the island and of the mainland sancak of Ic Il (KB 161/71 (12)/m.d.).

Some of the most important revenues from urban Lefkoşa accrued to the muhtesib. The largest of these was that of the tanners factory *(debbag hane = tabak hane)* which in 1607 (1016) was given to haci Piyale and Yasef of Lefkoşa as a tax farm *(iltizam)* for 35,000 akce/year (2 43–3, 71–2; I Zil-Kade 1016). Another important urban revenue was the factory of the dyers *(boya hane)*. That amounted only to 10 filori in 1607 (1016), even with that of Girniye joined to Lefkoşa (2 9–2; I Receb 1016).

El-fakir Mehmed, el-muhtesib bi-Lefkoşa, 25 Rebiᶜ II 1016. Since the conquest of Cyprus the dye factory of Girniye has been joined to that of Lefkoşa *(nefs-i Lefkoşa)*. I gave the Girniye dye factory to another person, but Huseyn presented a receipt *(temessuk)* showing that Girniye dye factory has always been joined to Lefkoşa, so he again possesses it (2 16–1). Boyaci Mehmed çorbaci, know that: Formerly the dye factory *(boya hane)* was a tax farm *(iktaᶜ)* for 20,000 akce/year, held by you. Then kapi kuli serdari Veli çelebi raised the payment by 5000 akce to 25,000 akce, which was accepted. Finally you offered 1000 akce more to the treasury *(miri)*, or 26,000 akce/year. That has been accepted. Take possession of the dye factory for 26,000 akce/year. (4 217–1; 7 Rebiᶜ I 1045)

Another job of the muhtesib was supervising the weights and measures of the merchants in Lefkoşa. In September–October 1594 muhtesib haci Huseyn apprehended bread baker *(etmekci)* Solimo v. Luyi for selling bread *(ekmek)* 25 dirhem too light *(eksik)* and bazarci Seydi kadi for selling sweet pomegranate *(tatlu enar)* 75 dirhems too light (1 311–5, 316–3; Muharrem 1003). In March, 1610 muhtesib Saᶜban found Ibrahim's soap *(sabun)* which was sold as weighing 50 tarak actually weighed 28, and Yusuf sold cotton that was of deficient weight (3 3–6; III Zil-Hicce 1018. 6–1; 29 Zil-Hicce 1018) Cf. 11–6; 16 Şevval 1018). Likewise Şaᶜban apprehended Huseyn bn Hasan for selling watermelons *(karpuz)* above the official price (3 61–5; III Cumadi II 1019). Sometimes the charge might be made by a private citizen, as when Ishak bn ᶜOsman of Magosa claimed that Fethullah bn Huseyn sold him something underweight (3 34–6; after II Zil-Kade 1018).

The testimony of a muhtesib usually was presumed correct. It might have been difficult to refute his claim.

Nuᶜman bn ᶜAbdullah of Lefkoşa, who is muhtesib, makes claim and states *(daᶜva/tk)* before Ibrahim of the grocers *(zumreʾ -i bakkalan)* of that marketplace *(suk):* While the maximal fixed price *(narh)* for a vakiye of roasted chick-peas *(leblebi)* was fixed at the court as eight akce, Ibrahim sold a vakiye for 15. Let him be asked. I want justice. Ibrahim acknowledges: In truth, I gave Nu'man chick-peas *(leblebi)* for 15 akce/vakiye when the official price was eight akce, but the muhtesib was hostile *(garaz)* to me. He separated out *(ifraz)* some of the aforementioned chick-peas (i.e., he surreptiously removed some of the chick-peas before weighing them). Fifteen akce was right. When an oath was proposed to Nu'man, he took an oath that he did not separate out any and that he did not make deception *(hile).* (4 109–3; 1 Muh. 1045)

Some of the cases involved fairly sophisticated trickery, such as one involving imported French and Venetian satin.

In the presence of present governor *(mir miran)* of Cyprus 'Ali Paşa, at the Sharia court racil Kara Mehmed beşe of Degirmenlik village of Lefkoşa kaza, of the janissaries of that island, makes a claim and states *(iddi'a/tk)* before racil Ibrahim beşe of the janissaries: formerly court was held before the governor in the presence of the notables and merchants *('ayan-i vilayet ve eşraf-i memleket ve tuccar ta' ifesi)* and trustworthy people. For every sort of cloth *(akmişe ve çuka)* an official price *(narh)* was given according to what it could bear *('ala vech ut-tahammul).* When I wished to buy enough European satin *(Firenci atlas)* to make a garment *(tonluk)* for Huseyn at the official price *(narh),* although the official price for French satin was 25 riyali guruş, Ibrahim took 28 riyali guruş for Venetian *(Venedik)* satin, which is a different satin. I want justice *(ihkak-i hakk).* Ibrahim acknowledges that. The aforementioned people testify that Mehmed bought the aforementioned satin from Ibrahim for Huseyn for 28 riyali guruş. For every cubit *(zira')* Ibrahim took an extra 100 akce. He did injury *(zaruret).* It is registered. (4 142–3; III Ramazan 1045)

Prices

Prices occur in two forms: (1) actual market prices and (2) legally fixed official maximal prices. (When the system was functioning effectively, the two coincided.) Inadequate data prevents a definitive study of prices in Cyprus. Any generalizations must be attempted with great caution. There is virtually no information about seasonal effects on food prices. There is too little data to coordinate prices with the even sparser data on good or bad harvests or with disasters like plagues and the swarming of locusts. Presumably official policy in the province aimed to hold prices as stable as possible, although in a time of debasement of coinage and inflation that would be an elusive goal.

Grain and Bread

The legally fixed price *(narh)* of bread, the single most important food, varied erratically, although there is too little evidence to document that fluctuation adequately. The price in 1636 (1046) was 33% to 43% higher than in 1593 (1002). One akce bought 300 to 350 dirhems of bread *(etmek-i somun, pan)* in 1593 (1002) but only 275 dirhems in 1594 (1003). Although an akce again bought 300 dirhems in 1607 (1016), it could by only 200 dirhems of bread in 1636 (1046).[1] Other bread products, like *Firenk etmegi, çorek, borek, kahi, beksemed, kirde, simid, tabe boregi, nohud etmegi,* and *halka^c-i beyaz,* were available for sale, but all were more expensive than plain bread. In 1593 (1002) when one akce bought 300 to 350 dirhems of plain bread, it bought only 250 to 300 dirhems of fancy Firenk etmegi.[2] Çorek[3] (at 170 dirhems for one akce) was twice the price of plain bread. Kirde[4] was even more expensive (130 dirhems for one akce), while kahi[5] (80 dirhems), simid[6] (80 dirhems), and borek[7] (60 dirhems) were five or six times as costly as plain bread. In 1607 (1016) when plain bread *(pan)* was 300 dirhem for one akce, 100 dirhems of hubz,[8] 80 dirhems of hubz çakilli,[9] 40 dirhems of halka' -i beyaz,[10] and 25 dirhems of tabe boregi[11] all sold for one akce. (References to those bread products occur too infrequently to permit tracing price trends.) A considerable array of bread products were sold in the markets of Lefkoşa.

In 1593 (1002) official prices for a kile of wheat ranged between 21⅓ akce and 50 akce, although the latter perhaps was the latest and is consistent with a doubling of prices by the following year. In 1593 the prices 24 and 25 akce/kile each occurred twice, 26 akce and 30 at least once. In 1594 (1003) official prices of 60 akce and 50 akce/kile were noted at the imperial market *(suk-i sultaniye)*. In 1609 (1018) the price was 50% to 100% higher than in 1594; prices of 90 akce, 1 altun (=118 akce) and 2 guruş (=156 akce) occurred. Slightly lower prices of 70 akce and 80 akce were found in 1633 (1043). Possibly the price reached 182 akce/kile in 1636 (1046) (although possibly I misread the 182). Clearly the price of wheat behaved erratically, an evidence of the great variations in the volume of annual production.

Clearly the price of barley, too, was mercurial. (Barley commonly sold for about half the price of wheat in Anatolia and Cyprus during the period under study.) For example, in 1593 (1002) official prices of 8,

10, and 24 akce/kile, as well as .14 altun, were noted in the judicial records; the following year prices of 28 and 30 akce/kile occurred at the imperial market *(suk-i sultaniye)*. In 1609 (1018), obviously a dear year, the price reached 60 akce/kile. Another sharp rise occurred between 1633 (1043) and 1634 (1044) when the official price of barley soared from 30 akce/keyl to 72 and 80 akce. Perhaps it is safe to say the "range" of barley prices increased about three-fold. This eccentricity in prices, reflecting variations in harvests, is well known in contemporary Cyprus and the Middle East, where one year out of four or five may have very reduced rainfall.

The legally fixed price of bread *(narh)* rose in sequence with the market price of wheat. The fixed price of wheat, 50 or 60 akce/kile in 1594 (1003), had risen between 33% and 40% to 70 or 80 akce in 1633 (1043). In 1609 (1018) the selling price ranged between 1 (=78 akce) and 2 guruş or altun (=118 akce) per kile. The price of barley, which was 28 or 30 akce in 1593 (1003), was exactly the same in 1633 (1043). Apparently the price of barley was stable, a boon for the poorer people, and even the price of wheat had increased moderately. Indeed, between 1593 (1002) and 1636 (1046) inflation more than canceled out the absolute value of any increase. Nevertheless, grains were the most important crops, overwhelmingly so on the flat central plateau. If grain prices did not rise, villagers as consumers might have had less to spend for those goods which increased substantially in price. Since grains were the most important crops on Cyprus, and bread was the most important food, the Porte tried to regulate closely their prices. Policy favored the consumer over the producer: the price of grains was held low on the principle that bread really was the staff of life. The socioeconomic and political consequences of doing otherwise were potentially dangerous. Therefore, grain prices in the Ottoman empire were lower than in the lands to the west. In order to keep grain supplies plentiful and to hold prices down Ottoman policy often forbade all exports of grain.[12] That caused severe distress in places like Venice which hitherto had gotten the bulk of their supply in the eastern Mediterranean and Aegean. Both Ottoman subjects and foreigners sometimes circumvented official Ottoman policy by bribing customs officers or by engaging in clandestine commerce with local merchants or farmers in isolated areas. Officially, however, the government operated exclusively at the fixed prices. Local officials implemented those prices in the markets and bazaars of Lefkoşa during the period 1580–1640, so the prices of grain and breads were kept inexpensive.

Perviz beg of Lefkoşa states *(tm):* For this year 1592 (1002) on the island of Cyprus what shall the official fixed price *(narh cari)* be on wheat *(bugday)* and barley *(arpa)* at the imperial market *(suk-i sultaniye)?* Let it be asked, and registered in the sicil. Experts *(ehl-i vukuf)* say, For 1592 (1002) wheat shall buy and sell for 60 akce/kile and barley for 30 akce. (1 168–3; selh Rebi˚ II 1002) Ibrahim çavuş bn Veli, for the governor *(mir miran)*, states *(tm):* The governor has ordered *(tenbih)* saying he has appointed someone to see that barley is sold at the official fixed price *(narh car)*, because he has had to pay more. It should be sold at that price at every storehouse *(mahzen)* and at the imperial market *(suk-i sultani)*. A supervisor *(mubaşir)* will be appointed, and from the Muslims ˚Abdur-Rahman kethuda' -i boluk-i yeniçeriyan, Hasan kethuda' -i boluk-i yeniçeriyan, Piri kethuda' -i boluk-i yeniçeriyan, Hizir bn Himmet, and others of the people *(cemm-i gafir* and *cem˚ -i kesir)* are ordered to carry out the order. (1 82–4; Sefer 1003)

The cause of writing is this: There is a possibility *(ihtimal)* that the grain *(zahire)* which is in the Lefkoşa storage place *(anbar)* will rot *(çurumek)*. Let the new harvest be stored *(der anbar)*. Distribute *(tevzi˚)* the old grain for the poor *(fukara)* by means of credit *(karz)* to the bread bakers *(etmekciler)*. Previously when this memorandum *(tezkere)* was commissioned *(sipariş)* for Huseyn çelebi, 760 keyl of barley *(şa˚ ir)* and 145 keyl of wheat *(bugday)* in that granary were taken out. This memorandum *(tezkire)* was written and given to him. (2 38–2; III Zil-Kade 1016, Haleb)[13]

In Cyprus grains and bread were also the most common goods of commerce. Some bakers and merchants traded on a small scale, others on a large one. Mustafa çavuş bn ˚Abdullah sold Zorza v. Istepaven (?) 190 kile of wheat and 462 kile of barley for 9000 akce (1 44–2; III Şaban 1002). Husam efendi of Mesariye claimed that Ohan (?) v. Emir şah owed him for 164 kile of wheat (2 2–4; III Zil-Hicce 1018). Ahmed sold ˚Ali beşe 42 kile of barley for 6 altun (1 241–8; I Şevval 1002). ˚Ali bn Mehmed sold Suleyman bn Selim 36 kile of wheat at 30 akce apiece (1 242–3; I Şevval 1002). The late ˚Abdul-Latif had sold Papa Luka 107 kile of barley (1 294–4; III Zil-Hicce 1002). The late Kupe giyim Yusuf bn ˚Abdullah sold 1000 akce worth of wheat to Lefter v. Covan (1 303–5; Zil-Hicce 1002). Keyvan boluk başi bn ˚Abdullah sold Armenian Bedr v. Tanri virdi four kile of wheat for 90 akce apiece (3 33–1; II Zil-Kade 1018). Janissary Yusuf beşe bn Mehmed sold 20 kile of wheat to Piro v. Gasparo for two guruş each (3 13–1; 18 Şevval 1018).

Mehmed çelebi bn ʿAli beg of Lefkoşa states *(bm)* before Fatma bint Suleyman, wife and guardian *(vasi)* for the minor children of the late Hamze aga, who has as legal agent *(vekil)* ʿAbdur-Rahim çelebi bn Mehmed: I gave the deceased 5 kile of wheat for 1 altun each, 10 kile of barley for 60 akce apiece, and 4 kile of common vetch *(burçak)* for 1 guruş apiece. Nineteen guruş is owed me. I want it. Fatma denies that. Çemsid oda başi bn ʿAbdullah and ʿAli bn ʿAbdullah confirm Mehmed. (3 165–1; 13 Şaban 1019)

Ahmed bn ʿAbdullah states *(tm)* before Ahmed bn Ahmed: I gave Ahmed 19½ kile of wheat for 26 akce apiece. Ahmed says it was 18½ kile for 24 akce apiece. The former acknowledges that. (1 270–2; II Zil-Kade 1002)

Bakers were valued members of the society. Possibly they were in short supply. Several instances occurred of local communities' offering credit or cash bonuses to a baker who would serve them.

Solimo v. Pavli and his mother (?) bint Filori of Aya Kuşa quarter of Lefkoşa acknowledge *(ik)* before Paskali v. Bernarto, Zano v. Karçere, and others: My father Pavli took 12 altun in capital *(sermaye)* from the people of the village from bread baking *(ekmekcilik)*. I will be guarantor for the property *(kefil bil-mal)*. The people of the quarter accept. (1 246–4; II Şevval 1002)

Above Solimo and (?) of the aforementioned place say: Besides the 12 altun already mentioned, a 300 akce loan *(karz-i hasen)* was taken from Paskali, Zano, and the others of the quarter. Registered. (1 246–5; same)

Andreye v. Luka of Aya Luka quarter, Andon v. (?), Luçiyo v. (?) make a claim *(daʿ va)* against (?) v. Covan: He was appointed *(taʿ yin)* baker *(etmekci)* to make bread in our quarter. We gave him 16 altun in capital *(sermaye)*. Now he is not doing that and we want the money back. He acknowledges that. (1 249–9; II Şevval 1002)

Zimmis of Aya Luka quarter say: Previously we gave 1200 akce as capital *(sermaye)* to ekmekci Lefter. He fled. Now we give 1800 akce capital to Ziya v. Zanetoye to make bread *(ekmek)*. He accepts. (1 259–2; I Zil-Kade 1002)

People of Aya Luka quarter say *(bm)* before Yasef (?) v. Kara Goz: We gave him 3000 akce to make bread *(etmek)* in our quarter for three years starting 28 July 1610 (7 Cumadi I 1019). At the end of three years the money becomes his for his service. No one should interfere. He acknowledges that. (3 133–8; 28 Rebiʿ II 1019)

Zimmi breadbaker *(etmekci)* Loizo of Lefkoşa claimed that the late Ahmed Paşa, who died while governor of Cyprus, had owed him 11,160 akce for bread *(etmek)*, which obviously represented a huge quantity. Loizo's oath was accepted as proof of his claim (4 64–1; II Sefer 1044).

ʿAvs bn Musa and haci Mehmed bn haci Mehmed of Lefkoşa had an agreement to buy together for their bakeries. (1 74–2; Muharrem 1003)

The breadbakers of the city *(şehir habbazlar)* have made Tuesday *(selase)* a non-work day *(ta ʿtil dutub)*. It is registered that they are ordered not to sell stale *(bayat)* bread. (3 11–5; 16 Şevval 1018)[14]

Farm Animals and Meat

Except for live sheep and goats, the prices of farm animals (oxen, mules, donkeys, cattle, and horses) were quite stable, as were the prices of freshly slaughtered meats. The market prices of sheep *(koyun)* and goats *(keçi/keci)* rose from 25 to 30 akce apiece in 1593–1594 (1002–1003) to slightly over 100 akce in 1609 (1018), and in 1636 (1046) the market price was still 100 akce. Donkeys *(merkeb, har)*, on the other hand, which sold for 330 akce and 400 akce in 1593 (1002) and 300 akce in 1594 (1003), sold for a slightly lower average of 200 to 300 akce in 1609 (1018), but in 1633 (1043) the price again was 400 akce. Five oxen *(okuz)* were sold for 1000 akce each in 1593–1594 (1002–1003), the same price as one in 1636 (1046); in the interval prices of 800 and 840 akce occurred for what may have been inferior animals. Cattle *(inek)* had little prestige. They sold for less than donkeys (180 akce, 275 akce, 300 akce). No pigs were mentioned. By far the most costly stock animal was the mule *(katir)*. In 1593 (1002), one mule was sold for 2520 akce and another for 2220 akce, while two others from an estate were estimated to be 2000 akce apiece in value. In 1607 (1016) one sold for only 800 akce, undoubtedly of lower quality. In 1609 (1018) a mule sold for 2000 akce, and in 1633 (1043) and 1634 (1044) two sold for 20 guruş (about 110 akce) and 15 guruş (about 120 akce) respectively. In 1593–1594 (1002–1003) six horses were sold, all but one for far less than the cost of mules: a colt *(tay)* for 1000 akce, two mares *(kisrag)* for 1520 akce and 300 akce respectively, and three stallions *(at)* for 1200, 1500, and 2000 akce. Although the price of horses vacillated greatly, apparently in Cyprus the horse was not the prestige animal, as might have been expected; only one reached the value of the cheaper mules.[15]

The official fixed prices of freshly slaughtered meats actually declined slightly between 1607 (1016) and 1635 (1045). A vakiye of lamb *(lahm-i kuzi, kebab-i koyun)* declined from eight akce in 1593 (1002) and 1607 (1016) to six and seven akce in 1634–1635 (1044–1047) — seven akce without the head *(başsiz/kuzi)*. Goat meat *(lahm-i keçi, kebab-i keçi)* declined from six akce/vakiye to five akce. Preserved sun-cured or smoked meats *(pasdirma* and *sucuk)* remained at virtually the same prices throughout the period, even when there were some variations in the products. Some pasdirma and sucuk could be bought for 18 akce/vakiye in 1594 (1003) and 1607 (1016); sucuk could be bought for as little as 12 akce, while that of an estate was valued at 10 akce/vakiye. In 1635–1636 (1045–1046), imported pasdirma was 24 akce and sucuk 12 akce.[16]

Dairy Products

The official fixed price *(narh)* of dairy products remained very stable. In 1593–1594 (1002–1003) the price of both an earthenware pot *(çanak)* of yogurt *(yogurd)* and an earthenware jug *(çomlek, deşti)* ranged between two and three akce; in 1607 (1016) the range was between two and four akce; in 1633 (1043) an earthenware pot of yogurt was three akce and in 1636 (1046) two akce. Neither did the price of cheese increase. Although various cheeses were sold, the official list does not always specify which were meant. In 1594 (1003) cheese *(peynir/beynir)* sold for 12 akce/vakiye while Karaman cheese (either a cheese imported from Karaman immediately to the north, or a type of cheese typical of Karaman that was produced in Cyprus) sold for 14 akce/vakiye. In 1609 (1018) cheese made in skin *(tulum peynir)* sold first for 12 akce/vakiye and then 16 akce while regular cheese *(baş peynir)* was only 8. Cheese was still 12 akce/vakiye in 1636 (1046). Butter generally ran at slightly more than twice the price of cheese. The official price of butter *(sade yagi, tere yagi)* declined from 30 akce/vakiye in 1593 (1002) to 28 akce in 1594 (1003) to 26 akce in 1609 (1018) before rising to 32 akce in 1636 (1046). In 1593 (1002) a large quantity of butter sold for 23 akce/vakiye while the estimated value of that of an estate was 30 akce/vakiye.

Fruits and Vegetables

Cyprus, particularly the southern coastal region, produced bountiful grapes, the cheapest of which were very inexpensive. Between 1594 and

1635 the range of fixed prices was quite steady. In 1594 (1003) fancier grapes ranged from 8 akce/vakiye for Balbek grapes *(uzum-i Balbek, from the Lebanese mountains)* to 12 to 14 akce/vakiye for grapes from Syria *(uzum-i Şam),* although black grapes *(siyah)* sold for only 4 akce/vakiye and a vakiye of fresh local grapes *(yas uzum)* for as little as 1 akce. Estimated values of grapes belonging to an estate settled in 1593 (1002) included 3 akce/vakiye for black grapes *(kara uzum),* 6 akce for a small seedless (?) grape *(kişniş = kişmiş?)* and red grapes *(kizil),* and 10 akce/vakiye for grapes of an unspecified type. When fresh grapes were 3 or 4 akce/vakiye in 1607 (1016), a vakiye of black grapes was 8 akce and one of red grapes was 13 or 16 akce. In 1635 (1045) the price of black grapes remained at 8 akce/vakiye and the red ones were 12, while local raisins were available for 5 akce/vakiye.

Another abundant and inexpensive fruit was figs. Fresh figs *(incir,* or *taze incir)* sold for 1 or 2 akce/vakiye in 1593 (1002), while Galata figs *(incir-i Galata)* sold for only 3 akce. By 1607 (1016) the price of the latter had risen to 8 akce/vakiye, although other figs were still 2 or 3 akce. In 1633 (1043) figs were 6 akce/vakiye; in 1635 (1045) fresh figs *(sulu inciri)* were 6 akce but all others were 4 akce.

One akce, which bought 200 dirhems of apples *(elma)* in 1594 (1003), bought 300 dirhem in 1635 (1045); in 1607 (1016) they had sold for 3 akce/vakiye. Even slightly cheaper than apples were pomegranates. In 1593 (1002) sweet pomegranates *(enar tatlu* or *leziz)* sold for 1 or 2 akce/vakiye or 500 dirhems for 1 akce, while the sour ones *(enar ekşi* or *turş)* sold for 500 or 600 dirhems for 1 akce or 3 akce/vakiye. The following year sweet pomegranates were 2 akce/vakiye or 400 dirhem for 1 akce, while the sour sold 500 dirhem for 1 akce or 1 akce/vakiye. In 1607 (1016) 450 dirhems of sweet pomegranates sold for 1 akce as did 300 dirhems of sour pomegranates.

In 1594 (1003), 1607 (1016), and 1635 (1045) the official price of roasted chick-peas *(leblebi)* was 8 or 10 akce/vakiye, although in 1635 the price reached as high as 12 akce; in 1593 the estimated value of roasted chick-peas of an estate was 6 akce/vakiye and about 8 akce/vakiye. Onions *(sogan, basal),* 1 akce/vakiye in 1593 (1002), were 300 dirhems for 1 akce in 1594 (1003), 300 dirhems for 1 akce or 2 akce/vakiye in 1607 (1016), and 10 akce/vakiye in 1635 (1045), a very severe increase. Grape *pekmez (pekmez-i uzum,* grape juice boiled to a sugary solid or heavy syrup) sold for 10 or 12 akce/vakiye in 1607 (1016) and

8 akce in 1635 (1045), while carob *pekmez (pekmez-i harnob,* carob juice boiled to a heavy syrup) sold for 5 and 6 akce in 1607 (1016) and 5 akce in 1635 (1045). Rice, apparently always imported from Egypt, was one of the most expensive goods available. The price of 50 akce/kile is mentioned in 1593 (1002). Rice from Rashid *(pirinc-i Reşid)* (Rosetta) sold for 40 to 45 akce/kile in 1594 (1003), while that from Dimyat *(pirinc-i Dimyat)* (Damietta) sold for 45 to 50 akce. In 1607 (1016) the price of rice ranged between 50 and 80 akce, but in 1636 (1046) the official price returned to 50 akce.

Olive trees predominated in much of the Cyprus landscape, particularly in dry and hilly areas. The official fixed price of olive oil *(zeyt yagi, revgan-i zeyt)* increased substantially from 10 to 12 akce/vakiye in 1594 (1003) to between 16 and 28 akce in 1607 (1016). By 1634 (1044) the price had reached 18 to 20 akce; in 1635 (1045) it stayed at 20 akce/vakiye. In 40 years the price had doubled. Market prices of olive oil in 1609 (1018) and 1634 (1044) ranged between 22½ akce and 28 akce, and an instance of 28 akce/lidre *(lodra)* occurred in 1609 (1018), when Marko v. Kostinti of Aya Demri village of Lefkoşa bought 74 lidre of olive oil from Ferencesko v. (?) and Ferenci v. Ahturi for 2070 akce (3 28–2, 3; II Zil-Kade 1018).

The official price of honey *('asl, bal)* rose sharply between 1594 (1003) and 1607 (1016), before it began to decline a little. Twelve akce/vakiye in 1594 (1003), it was set variously at 20 akce, 27 akce, and 30 akce in 1607 (1016). However, the price set for 1635 (1045) was only 20 akce/vakiye, and the following year that fell to 16 akce. Sales of honey for 15 akce/vakiye in 1633 and 20 akce/vakiye in 1634 (1044) were recorded.

Sugar

As certain contemporary travelers indicate, the Ottomans experienced disappointments and losses in the cultivation and preparation of sugar, an imperial monopoly intended exclusively for the palace larders. An order of 29 June 1575, for example, required the Cyprus begler begi (provincial governor) and *defterdar* (chief financial officer) to send all the sugar present there *(mevcud)* to the Porte immediately, as if unaware how much sugar there was or should have been. A pair of orders dated 6 April 1577 to the Cyprus begler begi and the Rodos begi (district governor) require the former to dispatch all the sugar he has on ships *(gemiler)* to Rhodes in chests *(sunduklar)*, where the district governor would accept the sugar, give his receipt, and forward the sugar to the Porte. Less than a decade later the situation had become desperate. True, an order of 29 September 1586 to the Cyprus defterdar and to the kadis of Lefkoşa and Gulnar (?) revealed that a Jew *(Yahudi)* named Şa ʿban wanted to raise the tax farm *(iltizam)* of the sugar factories *(mukata ʿa -i şeker hane)* from 6000 filori to 16,000 filori/year.

However, two letters addressed jointly to the Cyprus begler begi and defterdar on 14 March 1588 show the sad condition into which the sugar industry had fallen. One points out that since the conquest of the island those two officials had been assigned to ensure that all sugar was prepared *(tedarik)* with care and delivered to the imperial pantries *(kilar)*. Although sugar had not come properly for a few years *(bir kaç seneden beru)*, in 1586 not one kantar had entered the pantries and in 1583 only 68 kantar had reached there. The beglerbegi and the defterdar then were exhorted not to be deceitful *(gadr ve bahane)* and to send 500 kantar of sugar without fail, as in other years. In the second order the Porte spells out its indignation in detail:

When I heard that the sugar factories *(şeker haneleri)* on that island are ruined *(harab)* and that they were barren *(ʿuryan)* because water *(su)* was not in places as it used to be *(ʿadet-i kadime uzre)* and that sugar did not come at all because of neglect *(ihmal)*, I ordered that you are responsible in that matter. Now do not be negligent *(gaflet)*. You should see to it personally. Do not trust anyone. Henceforth you should give complete attention to the sugar and sugar factories, and you should make the water flow *(icra)* as it used to. It was ordered that you should make repairs fully and that the sugar should be sent in full. I order that you should have all the sugar factories looked after *(gordurdub)* and you should make known in full what the reason was for that sugar not coming to my imperial domain *(hassaʾ -i humayunum içun)*. You should write the truth as it happened and present it *(ʿarz)*. (164/75 (29) #673,674. 123/89 (29) #281, 282. 160/89 (37) #487, (39) #484. 122/98 (46) #34, (55) #487. 162/60 (4) #234. 117/30 (12) #20)

In 1593 (1002) the procedure which led to injustice both to tax farmers *(multezims)* and to cultivators in the selling of cotton tax farms *(mukata ʿat)* was also practiced with sugar (1 286–1; III Zil-K. 1002. Cf. 226–1). In 1609 (1018) Mehmed bn ʿAli and ʿAli bn Mahmud dealt with nine guruş worth of sugar (3 23–3; I Zil-K. 1018). In 1610 (1019) ʿOmer çavuş was cultivating at the Kukla sugar factory *(şeker hane)* with the consent of the superviser of tax farmer *(emin)*, although possibly he was cultivating cotton (3 38–4; III Cumadi I 1019). In 1634 (1044) zimmiye broker *(delale)* Maro sold some sugar to Ahmed Paşa (4 64–2; II Sefer 1044).[17]

Saltpeter

Among the first concerns of the Ottoman government after the conquest of Cyprus was to locate the supply of saltpeter known to be there and to begin mining it. Saltpeter, essential to the manufacture of gunpowder, had long been scarce. By late 1571 an inspector of saltpeter *(guhercile naziri)* 'Ali çavuş had reached Cyprus with orders to begin producing saltpeter with the labor of sons of spahis *(sipahi zadeler)* from Ic Il province, who were obligated to carry out that service. When the latter failed to carry out their duties, the inspector complained. New orders then were sent to both Cyprus and Karaman governors. On 19 March 1572 one such order went to the Cyprus begler begi and defterdar reminding them that when the Porte had heard of the saltpeter on the island it had ordered them to go with experts *(ehl-i vukuf)* and useful people who know *(bilur yarar kimesneler)* the nature *(ahval)* of gunpowder to the saltpeter mines *(guhecile ma˓ denleri)* and to look over the situation. If in truth saltpeter was found and if it was possible *(mumkun)* to mine it, then it should be produced. Those orders obviously were not carried out with the anticipated diligence, for an imperial order of November, 1573 to the Cyprus governor and defterdar makes very emphatic the disappointment of the Porte. Although it was well known that before the conquest a sufficient amount *(kefayet)* of saltpeter had been prepared on Cyprus, people gave up *(feraget)* producing that and so an inadequate amount of gunpowder was available. Therefore, the Porte immediately sent experts *(ustad)* to ensure the preparation of a sufficient amount of gunpowder for the island (138/89 (20) #254. 118/ 58 (37) #1026. 161/71 (19) #371).[18]

Salt

Hasan çavuş, supervisor *(mubaşir)* of loading salt *(tuz)* at Limosa pier *(limon iskelesi)* reported to Yakimo Mavri (di), zimmi captain *(re˒ is)*, the loading of salt *(tuz)* on 32 ships *(gemi)*; Yakimo acknowledged accepting 1500 Istanbul kile in freight *(navlun)* (1 93–1; I Rebi' I 1003). Between 1590 (999) and 1592 (1001) the village of Çete (?=Kiti?) of Tuzla district *(nahiye)* paid 60,000 akce/year from salt for the salary of the Baf begi (1 294–3; Zil-Hicce 1002. Cf. 1 114–1; 18 Ramazan 1002. 116–1; III Zil-Kade 1002). For 1608 (1017) some villagers in Mesariye district were required to pay four akce/nefer salt tax *(resm-i milh)*, among other taxes (2 52–1; 14 Şevval 1016). In 1635 (1045) former beyt ul-mal 'amme ve hassa emini Kumari Zade Ibrahim beg bn Nasuh was supervisor *(nazir)* for collecting the revenues of villages the revenues of which accrue to the Porte *(havass-i humayun)*, namely Bali Ketri, Pano Horuş, Kato Horuş, and Trahoni. Among the taxes he collected wee those on salt. In that position Ibrahim beg received 10 ta' yin (rations?) of salt *(milh)* from the notables *('ayan)* of Lefkoşa. He was to pay them 150,000 akce within 30 days (4 122–2; I Receb 1045. 221–2; Lefkoşa, II Rebi' II 1045). In 1594 (1003) the official fixed price of one vakiye of salt was 2/3 'osmani. In 1607 (1016) prices of five akce and 12 akce/vakiye were recorded.[19]

Soap

Cyprus produced its own soap, but the highest quality soap was imported from the Levant. So in 1594 (1003) the official fixed price of soap *(sabun)* made in Cyprus *(Kibris sabuni)* was 10 akce/vakiye, while Beyrut (?) sabuni sold for 12 akce/vakiye and that of Trablus *(sabun-i Trablus)* (Tripoli) sold for 14 to 16 akce.In 1607 (1016) soap of a type not specifically designated sold for between 24 and 34 akce. A product simply called soap sold about 22 akce/vakiye in 1609 (1019); soap from Trablus sold for between 20 and 28 akce/vakiye, that from Jerusalem *(sabun-i Kudus)* for between 30 and 40 akce. In 1636 (1046) the fixed price of soap, not further identified, was listed as 24 akce/vakiye. The price of soap rose sharply, doubling between 1594 (1003) and 1607 (1016); although by 1636 (1046) the price had declined some, soap was still far costlier than 40 years earlier.[20]

Wood

A document of the late 16th c. indicates that lumbering continued in Cyprus as an occupation.[21] The Cyprus governor wrote a letter to the kadi of Lefkoşa.

ʿAli Paşa's letter *(mektub)* to Lefkoşa kadi: Know that, in accordance with custom, wood *(odun)* is needed here from villages in mountainous districts *(dag semti)*. We send çavuş kethuda Hasan aga to get the wood and send it here. Purchase it at the current official fixed price *(narh ruzi)* when it arrives. Take whatever the amount is, as in the past, and send it right away. (1 161–2; III Rebiʿ II 1003)

In 1607–1608 (1016) the head *(şeyh)* of the woodcutters *(tahtaciler)* was a janissary convert to Islam, Mehmed beşe bn ʿAbdullah; like other craftsmen, the woodcutters had a set of official fixed prices that they maintained (2 1–2,3; 1016).

At the time of the establishment of Ottoman provincial rule in Cyprus, however, it was presumed that there was no timber. An order of 7 May 1572 to the Cyprus begler begi and to the kadis in Tarsus sancak, for example, pointed out the need for boards *(taht)* for gun stocks *(kundaklik)* to supply the local arsenal *(tophane muhimmati)*, as well as for masts *(direk)*, palisaded mast tops *(kulek)*, and railings *(parmaklik)*. Since adequate wood was not available in Cyprus, it had to be transported there from Tarsus. Three orders of 1573–1574 to the Cyprus begler begi, the Cyprus defterdari, and the Izmir begi detail the need for lumber *(kereste)* for masts *(direkler)*, spars *(serenler)*, and other lumber *(kereste)* necessary for the imperial galleys and transport ships *(kadirgalar, kalyete, at gemileri)* in Cyprus. Although they were old and needed new boards *(taht)*, there was no lumber *(kereste)* in that place. Since there was lumber in Izmir sancagi, the Izmir begi had to have that cut for wages by day laborers *(akce ile rencber taifesine kesdurub)*. Then the Cyprus defterdar had to pay the Izmir begi for the lumber after it arrived and was inventoried and inspected *(yokliyub)* (161/71 (21) #253,254; (22) #252).

Cotton

Trade in cotton exceeded that of all other noncomestibles, both by volume and in cash value. Cotton was sold in three units of weight: the lidre *(lodra)*, the sack *(çuval)*, and the *kantar*. In 1580 (988) Papa Yani v. Vasil and Ergiro v. Pavli sold 2½ kantar of cotton to ʿOmer bn Ibrahim for six years, each worth 14 filori (1 15–5; II Ramazan 988). In 1592 (1001) the official fixed price for one Cyprus kantar of cotton was 800 akce. Loizo sold Gavraʾ il 117 lidre of cotton for 18 altun (about

.15 altun/lidre) in 1593 (1002) (1 226–3; II Ramazan 1002). In 1594 (1003) Baf sancagi begi Mustafa beg was owed 22,950 akce in revenues from cotton in Lefkoşa for his salary *(saliyane)*; 21 kantar and 86 lidre were received, each kantar valued at 1050 akce (1 163–2; III Rebiᶜ II 1003. 163–3; I Cumadi I 1003. 166–1; selh Rebiᶜ II 1003). A sale in excess of the official 800 akce/kantar to the Venetian merchant Kordovan (?) was also noted (1 126–1,2; Şevval 1001, Konstantiniye). In 1610 (1019) Mehmed çelebi bn ᶜAli sold Mustafa beg bn ᶜAli two sacks *(çuval)* of cotton for three years for 10,000 akce, that is 5000 akce/sack (3 47–6; I Cumadi II 1019). Yakimo v. Pavla bought 20 sacks of cotton from Istavriye v. Fesenco for 25 altun, about 1.2 altun/sack (3 84–1; 9 Şevval 1019). Filibo v. Bernardi of (?) village of Lefkoşa bought 25 lidre of cotton from Ziya (?) v. Simiyoni (?) for 900 akce, that is 36 akce each (3 101–5; 9 Şevval 1019). Komi v. Agosti of Kato Deftera village gave Hasan çavuş bn Kasim one kantar of cotton for 1920 akce (4 187–1; II Receb 1046).[22]

Occasionally the cotton was identified as having seeds *(çiyyidlu/ceyyidili = çigit)*, although usually no such designation was given. Nikola v. Liyo bought 67 lidre of raw cotton *(ciyyid)* at 18 akce/lidre and 57 lidre at 20 akce/lidre from Piyero v. Gasparo, having it delivered by his man Loizo v. Mihail, called Menteş zade (3 9–2; 13 Şevval 1018. Cf. 12–3; 18 Şevval 1018. 13–2). The young man *(emredd)* Huseyn bn Veli of Makoka (?) village in Mesariye kaza inherited, among other things, 3½ vakiye cotton with seeds (3 21–6; 2 Zil-Kade 1018).

The form in which cotton *(penbe)* was most commonly sold was carded *(mahluc)*.[23]

In 1593 (1002) a kantar of carded cotton sold for about 25 kirmizi filori, twice the price of uncarded cotton. Ergiro v. Yako of Nisu village of Lefkoşa sold three kantar of carded cotton to Behine v. Petro for 73 kirmizi filori, and then Tomazi v. (?) of Dikomo village of Girniye kaza sold Behine another three kantar for the same price; Mustafa bn ᶜAbdullah bought a kantar for 25 kirmizi filori from Petro v. Nikola (1 242–1; I Şevval 1002. 253–1; III Şevval 1002. 244–1; I Şevval 1002). The following year Luka v. Elistodiro (?) of Lefkoşa sold 105 lidre of carded cotton to Zenito v. Ganber (?) for a price identified as 42 kirmizi altun or 5040 akce. That means, 48 akce or .4 altun/lidre (1 156–2; 15 Rebiᶜ II 1003). In 1609 (1018) Kamer bint Piri, the widow of the late Pir ᶜAli beg and guardian *(vasi)* of his orphans, made a claim for two kantar of carded cotton for which her late husband had paid 9000 akce in advance (that is, 4500 akce/kantar) (3 24–7; I Zil-Kade 1018). Zimmi Nikola also paid in advance for 10 lidre of carded cotton. Since he paid four kirmizi altun, that means the price per lidre was .4 altun (3 28–5; II Zil-Kade 1018). In 1610 (1019) Bali çavuş sold 50 lidre of carded cotton to Nikola v. Vasil of Temriye village of Lefka kaza for 25 altun, a price of ½ altun per lidre (3 171–1; II Şaban 1019).

Frequent interrelationships between Muslims and non-Muslims characterized the cotton business, particularly carded cotton. Of a small sample of 15 cases involving carded cotton seven were mixed communally; in two instances zimmis sold to Muslims and in five instances vice versa. ʿOmer bn Ibrahim bought 2½ kantar of cotton at 14 filori/kantar from Papa Yani v. Vasil and Ergiro v. Pavli (1 15–5; II Ramazan 988). A transaction of 1594 (1003) involved 104½ kantar of carded cotton sold for 15,000 akce to the late zimmi merchant *(tacir)* Kordovan by zaʿim Halil aga bn ʿAbdul-Mennan (1 189–3; 20 Cumadi 1003). Halil aga in turn owed former aga of the harbor Memi aga 36 filori for 4½ kantar of carded cotton (1 190–2; 20 Cumadi II 1003). Ergiro v. Yako (?) of Nisu village of Lefkoşa sold Behine v. Piro three kantar of carded cotton for 73 kirmizi filori (1 242–1; I Şevval 1002. Cf. 253–1). Mustafa bn ʿAbdullah of Lefkoşa bought a kantar of carded cotton from Petro v. Nikola of Lapta (Laputa) village of Girniye kaza for 25 kirmizi filori. (1 244–1; I Şevval 1002). Hasan çavuş of the council (divan-i Kibris) çavuşes sold Zazo v. Zozi of Pano (?) village 45 filori worth of carded cotton (3 145–2; III Cumadi II 1019). Istavrito v. Miçelli (?) of Dimiyo (?) village of Lefkoşa sold carded cotton to the late Hamze aga for 30 altun which is still outstanding (3 164–4); 13 Şaban 1019).[24]

Cotton processing and marketing was widespread, involving all elements of the community, civilian and military, Muslim, Christian, and foreign. Some transactions involved sums as large as any found in the records, while others involved only small amount of cotton.[25] The revenues *(mahsul)* accruing of Baf district governor *(sancagi begi)* Mustafa beg from the tax farm *(mukataʿa)* of Lefkoşa in 1593 (1002) amounted to 22,950 akce. That came from 21 kantar and 86 lidre of cotton, each kantar worth 1050 akce. (1 163–2; III Rebiʿ II 1003. 163–3; I Cumadi I 1003. 166–1; I Cumadi I 1003). Mustafa çavuş and beyt ul-mal emini Perviz beg sold to muteferrika Mustafa beg bn Paşa ogli 70 kantar of cotton which came to them as the revenue of an estate *(çiftlik)* (1 163–

328 *The Economy through Ottoman Sources*

4; I Cumadi I 1003). Ramazan bn Hamze acknowledged his debt of 20 vakiye of cotton to Hamze bn Husrev (1 246–3; II Şevval 1002). Davud beg bn ʿOmer of Mesariye kaza sent 424 lidre of cotton to Yerolimo v. Filipo of Tuzla (3 11–7; 16 Şevval 1018). Seyyid Mehmed bn seyyid ʿOsman owed topcilar boluk başi Hamze boluk başi 150 lidre of cotton from his estate *(çiftlik)* (3 28–8; II Zil-Kade 1018). Marko v. Ciryako of (?) village of Mesariye kaza owed Nikolo v. Ciryako one sack *(çuval)* of cotton, and Yakimo v. Pavlo was owed 20 sacks by Istavriye v. Fesenco (3 72–9; II Receb 1019. 3 84–1; III Receb). Foreigner (musteʾmin) Yakimoto was owed 571 altun and 56 akce for his dealing in cotton (3 128–5; II Şevval 1019). Haci Eymur v. Ahmed gave (?) v. Guge (?) 600 akce worth of cotton *(kutn)* (3 163–13; III Rebiʿ II 1019).

Yusuf beşe bn Mehmed, janissary of Inaktine (?) village of Mesariye kaza makes a claim *(daʿva)* against Piro v. Gasparo: I sold Piro 13 donum of planted cotton *(ekilmuş penbe)* at (?) for 200 guruş. He paid 24 guruş; 176 guruş remained unpaid. I want it. Denied by Piro, who says, I paid it all in cotton. (3 12–4; 18 Şevval 1018).

Karçere v. Nikolo makes a claim *(t.d.)* against Kosdindi v. Filipo: I gave him 16 lidre of cotton seeds *(penbe çekirdegi)* at 10 akce apiece. Kosdindi acknowledges that. (3 33–10; II Zil-Kade 1018)

Because of the large revenues to be gained, the government exercised closer control over cotton (and sugar to a lesser extent) than other agricultural cultivation. When abuses occurred, the Porte expressed genuine concern for the weak and helpless.

Imperial order *(emr-i şerif)* arrived for emir ul-umera Cyprus governor *(cezireʾ-i Kibris begler begisi)* and Cyprus defterdar: When my imperial order *(emr-i şerif)* arrives, know that: The tax farmers *(multezim)* of the tax farms *(mukataʿat)* of the sugar factories *(şeker hane)* at Piskobi, Kulaş, and Kukla and the farmers of tax farms of Lefkoşa and Hirsofi in Cyprus and the baylos on the island sent a petition *(ʿarz-i hal)* to my Porte: The aforementioned tax farms used to be given for ready cash *(nakdiye)*. That condition *(şart)* for giving sugar and cotton causes suffering *(iztirab)* to the tax farmers. Now every year the governor and defterdar are not able to sell cotton *(hasil-i penbe)* at the official fixed price *(narh cari)*. They make trade *(ticaret)* and distribute it for their own benefit, so they exceed the official price and do great harm to the poor and weak. For a few years those who are oppressed *(paymal)* have been fleeing to Venice, causing loss to the treasury *(miri)*. For the tranquility of the poor, the tax farmers should sell cotton according to the official fixed price and loss should not be caused to the tax farms. I order that: When my imperial order *(hukm-i şerif)* and Cyprus deputy

(Kibris kethudasi) Mustafa kethuda arrive, carry out my order. If it is best for the re‘aya, do what is best for the re‘aya. Be careful not to cause loss of revenue *(mal)*, and do not do harm to the re‘aya. Ask the doorkeepers *(kapuci)*, stewards *(emin)*, and collectors of tax-farm revenues *(‘amil)* about the matter. Take down the names of any who interfere. (1 286–1; III Zil-Kade 1002)

Petition *(‘arz)* of Piskobi kadi ‘Ali efendi. Day laborers *(irgad taifesi)* in service of Piskobi and Pulaş came to my court *(kaza)* and made a complaint of oppression *(tezallum):* When we perform the service of planting *(fidana hidmet)* and when we work the cotton *(penbeye hidmet)* in cotton time, they do not give us enough for our services to supply the necessities of life *(kefaf-i nefs)*, and they give no grain *(tereke)* for subsistence *(nafaka)*. Our families are starving with hunger *(ac ve zelil)*. If we miss one day they treat us with oppression. Let our condition *(ahval)* be known . . . (1 226–1; undated 1002).

Wool and Woolen Cloth

Unlike cotton, wool was not at all an article of commerce.[26] Possibly the cotton cloth industry was de-centralized, with separate cultivators, carders, and weavers, while wool may have been spun and turned into cloth within households of sheep raisers. At any rate, in Lefkoşa fine and coarse wool cloth was frequently bought and sold, but no evidence was found of commerce in raw wool.

The wool cloth traded most frequently was a good quality one, a broadcloth called çuka *(çuha)*. Although no useful information about prices is given, some of the transactions involved large sums of money.

Keyvan bn ‘Abdullah acknowledges *(ik)* in the presence of Emine bint ‘Abdullah, who as guardian *(vasi)* of the orphans of the late janissary Mehmed has as agent *(vekil)* haci Ca‘fer: The late Mehmed owed me 4800 akce and 960 akce for woolen cloth *(çuka)*. Emine admits that and is given one year to pay. (1 332–4; 1002)

Yakimo v. Ferencesko claimed that, at the order of Luka v. Zorzi, he gave ‘Ali beg a measure of woolen cloth *(çuka)* adequate for making a veil *(peçelik)*. (3 43–4; 3 Cumadi II 1019)

Zimmi ‘Abdullah (?) v. Ilyas claimed to have given Esma‘Ali beşe woolen cloth *(çuka)* worth 15,000 akce (3 77–6; III Receb 1019). Istofi (?) v. Ferencesko was owed 1600 akce for woolen cloth by another zimmi (3 163–13; III Rebi‘ II 1019).

Maro bint (bn, sic) Loizo, widow and executrix *(zeve³-i metruke)* of the late Yorolimo v. Ferencesko, and guardian *(vasi)* for his children stated *(bm)* before Hiristofi v. Ferencesko: Hiristofi owed the deceased 3000 akce for woolen cloth *(çuka)* and *kumaş.* (3 105–1; 4 Ramazan 1019)

Maro bint Loizo, widow and executrix *(zevce³-i metrukesi)* of the late Yorolimo v. Ferencesko, and guardian *(vasi)* for his children stated *(ihzar/bm)* before ʿOmer beşe bn ʿAli: ʿOmer had bought 10 cubits *(ziraʿ)* of purple woolen cloth *(mor çuka)* from the deceased for 200 akce apiece. He owes the money. ʿOmer denies that but has no proof. Maro takes an oath that the debt exists. (3 164–4; 13 Şaban 1019)

Yayci Mehmed aga of Lefkoşa acknowledges *(ik/iʿt)* before Melamoto v. Dolfino: He owes me 31,000 akce for woolen cloth. He paid 10 guruş less than the official fixed price *(narh cari)* for each kantar. (3 150–4; III Cumadi II 1019. Cf. 151–1)

Ferencesko v. Laniko (?) of the French merchants *(Fransiz tuccari taʾifesi)* made a claim *(daʿva/tk)* against Arslan kethuda, guardian *(vasi)* before the Sharia for the minor son Mehmed beg of the late Ahmed Paşa who died while governor *(mir miran)* of Cyprus . . . : He still owes me 2222½ riyali guruş from Paris and Merzifon (?) woolen cloth *(çuka).* Let the guardian be asked. Arslan kethuda denies that. When Ferencesko is asked for proof, upright Muslims (ʿudul-i Muslimin) Yusuf su başi bn ʿAbdul-Mennan and Ridvan kethuda bn ʿAbdul-Vehhab confirm him: It happened in our presence. When an oath on the Bible *(Incil)* was proposed to the claimant, he took it. (4 60–1; Sefer 1044)

Arslan kethuda of Besiktaş in Galata bought cloth from Rumeli for 80 akce/vakiye from Ibrahim bn ʿAli . . . (4 67–2; III Sefer 1044)

Seyyid Ahmed çelebi bn Receb of Lefkoşa made a claim *(daʿva/tk)* against Kumari zade Ibrahim beg bn Ismaʿil, present inheritance supervisor *(beyt ul-mal ʿamme ve hassa emini):* Ibrahim owes me *(hakkum)* 200 riyali guruş from a loan *(karz).* Of that I have received 169½ riyali guruş worth of cloth *(çuka)* and cash. I am still owed 31½ riyali guruş; he delays *(teʿallul).* Ibrahim claims he paid in full, but he also has no proof. When Ahmed is asked to take an oath, he does. (4 113–1; II Muharrem 1045)

Coarse woolen cloth *(ʿaba)* was marketed in bolts *(top),* as when Ahmed beşe bn ʿOsman gave Suleyman beg bn ʿAbdullah 25 top coarse white woolen cloth *(beyaz ʿaba)* (3 73–5; III Receb 1019).

Caʿfer bn ʿAbdullah of Lefkoşa states *(tm)* in the presence of seyyid Mehmed bn Mustafa: I gave him 140 top of white coarse woolen cloth for 45 sikke filori altun. I want the money for the cloth *(kumaş).* (3 126–7; II Şevval 1019)

Vriyoni of Lefkoşa makes a claim *(daʿva/tk)* against Arslan kethuda, guardian *(vasi)* for the minor son of the late Ahmed Paşa: I sold the Paşa 13 rolls (?) of Cyprus cloth *(Kibrisi kumaş)* for 3036 dirhem or 9108 akce. I received 4000 akce; 5108 akce is still due me. I want it from his effects . . . (4 66–1; III Sefer 1044)

Katib Ibrahim çelebi bn haci Hasan of Lefkoşa makes a claim *(daʿva/tk)* against Mustafa bn Yusuf, heir of the late Ermenaki zade Hasan çelebi: This Mehmed bn Ahmed of the people of the covered market *(bezasten ahalisi)* has owed me 120 akce of cloth *(kumaş bahasi)* for one and a half years. When we wished to go to the mainland *(Ote Yaka)* this debt was transferred *(devir)* to the late Hasan çelebi . . . (4 165–2; I Rebiʿ II 1046)

Coffee

First introduced to Istanbul around 1550 from Egypt or Syria, coffee won great favor there, in fashionable circles as well as popular ones. Coffee caught on fast. Coffee houses spread not only all over the capital but also in provinces like Cyprus, often in the possession of foundations. The earliest surviving references to coffee in the Lefkoşa sicils concern trade in coffee, first between Mehmed bn Ahmed and Huseyn bn ʿAbdullah, and then, for 10 vakiye coffee, between Hasan and Usta Piri of (?) village (3 76–2; III Receb 1019. 106–2; 4 Ramazan 1019). By the 1630s coffee had become one of the key goods of trade.[27]

Ibrahim oda başi bn Emrullah of Lefkoşa claimed that, along with other goods, he had sold Yusuf beg bn ʿAbdullah of Girniye 3000 vakiye of coffee at 80 akce eight years earlier and still had not collected the 240,000 akce due him (4 5–1; II Şaban 1043). When Ahmed Paşa died while still provincial governor *(mir miran)* in Cyprus, he left a debt of 13,280 akce to his man Ismaʿil tayi for 166 vakiye of coffee (at 80 akce/ vakiye) (4 19–2; III Sefer 1044). Among Ahmed Paşa's debts to his aga Arslan aga bn Mehmed was 9920 akce for 124 vakiye of coffee (at 80 akce) (4 21–1; III Sefer 1044). When a vakiye of cloth *(çuha)* in Rumeli was 80 akce, and a vakiye of coffee was 80 akce, Arslan kethuda of Besiktaş in Galata gave Ibrahim bn ʿAli 107 vakiye of coffee beans *(findik kahvesi)* for 107 vakiye cloth (4 67–2; III Sefer 1044). Hasan çelebi bn Mehmed sold 228 vakiye of coffee to the late Ahmed Paşa when the price was 100 akce each; Hasan çelebi, scribe of the paşa's council *(divan katibi)*, had received 10,000 akce of the 22,800 akce due him and claimed the rest (4 67–3; III Sefer 1044). Another of Ahmed Paşa's men, Ibrahim bn ʿAli, had sold the Paşa 107 vakiye of coffee beans for 8560 akce when the price had been 80 akce/vakiye (4 68–1; III Sefer 1044). In 1633 and 1634 the free market price of a vakiye of coffee was almost always 80 akce; alternately, 1 akce bought 300 dirhem of coffee in 1645 (1045).

The existence of several coffee houses *(hahve hane)* is known through documents concerning the establishment of pious foundations *(vakfiye)* and judicial cases involving their rental for foundations. A coffee house in the walled town of Magosa was among property dedicated as vakf by Caʿfer Paşa in 1601 (1010) (16/116, p. 310–311, #152; I Receb 1010). Coffee houses were among the property in Lefkoşa made vakf by that same Caʿfer Paşa (2 20–3; I Ramazan 1016). A coffee house of the vakf of Suleyman beg rented for four akce/day or 120 akce/month, the revenues going to the Mevlevi Tekke (2 76–1; 1 Rebiʿ I 1017). Another vakf coffee house in the marketplace *(çarsu)* of Lefkoşa, was rented for 15 akce/day to kahveci Derviş ʿAli bn Mehmed (3 47–5; I Cumadi II 1019). Coffee houses probably were becoming much frequented in the first decades of the 17th century. Demand for coffee in Cyprus had become considerable by the 1630s.

Urban Rentals

Renting commercial facilities was an important business in Lefkoşa. The most expensive of these were *hamams* (public baths), *hans* (large commercial buildings), and candle factories *(mum hane)*, which rented for anywhere between 4,000 akce/year and 28,200 akce/year. Most were the property of pious foundations. A han belonging to that of the late Sultan Selim Han (called Büyük Han) rented with its eight rooms, 12 shoe stores *(kavvaf)*, coffee house, and borek oven for 28,200 akce/year for three years to Perviz, who agreed to pay 2,300 akce/month (1 280–4; I Zil-Kade 1002). In 1607 the old Han *(han-i ʿatik)* was rented, with shops and coffee houses, for 21,000 akce by the foundation of the late Caʿfer Paşa, to Yaʿkub oda başi (2 20–3; 1 Ramazan 1016). Buyuk hamam of the late Mustafa Paşa rented for 17,000 akce in 1593 but that was raised to 20,000 for the following year (1 292–1; I Zil-Hicce 1002. 85–1; Sefer 1003). In that same period the rent of the Kucuk hamam of the late Mustafa Paşa declined from 14,000 akce/year to 12,000 (1 244–

7; II Şevval 1002. 245–2; same. 85–4; Sefer 1003). Korkud efendi rented his Kucuk hamam to Mehmed Dede bn Hasan for 11,000 akce/year (1 306–1; III Zil-Hicce 1002). The Hamam-i Cedid of the foundation of the late Mustafa Paşa, which had been rented to haci Bayram for 4000 akce/year, was raised 500 akce/year for three years, to be paid monthly (2 21–2; III Şaban 1016).

Sometimes rents fluctuated sharply. Property owners had to reduce rents when demand decreased, although in good times they might increase them considerably. Sometimes even the possession of a written lease by the rentee could not prevent the administrators from awarding the property to the highest bidder. In the case of foundation property the term sold *(furuht)* was sometimes used almost interchangeably with rent *(icare)* to describe the right to use the property for a specific length of time in exchange for regular payments.

Present Lefkoşa muhtesib haci Huseyn bn Belal states *(tm)* before Andreye v. Bernardi: I gave Andreye my candle factory *(mum hane)* for three years starting in 1594—for 10,000 akce/year, a total of 30,000 akce. Andreye accepts that. (1 304–3; Muh. 1003)

Haci Huseyn, present muhtesib of Lefkoşa, states *(tm)* before Bernardi v. Yakimo: I sold *(furuht)* Andreye v. Bernardi the candle factory *(mum hane)* in the city for 10,000 akce/year for three years. Now Bernardi has offered two akce/year more, a total of 36,000 akce for three years. Will Andreye accept this? No, Andreye renounces his claim, so it is sold to Bernardi, who accepts it. (1 312–3; 1 Muh. 1003)

Shop *(dukkan)* made vakf for Aya Sofya cami^c by the late Sultan Selim, next to the shops of Filipo and of Loizo, was rented by zimmi Paskali. The former administrator *(mutevelli)* Hidayetullah çelebi sold it *(furuht)* to Saleb ogli for 1200 akce; now Paskali pays 10 akce/month more rent *(icare)* to the vakf. He has a title deed *(temessuk)*. (2 42–4; 1 Receb 1011)

Maro bint Nikolo of Aya Andoni quarter sets forth a claim *(t.d.)* against Kato (?) v. Yakumi of Degirmenlik village: Formerly my guardian *(vasi)* rented *(icare)* my mill *(degirmenlik)* to him for 24,000 akce for three years. Every six months he should pay 4000 akce rent. He delays paying *(te^{c}allul)*. Kato (?) acknowledges that. (4 244–5; III Receb 1044)

Numerous shops, including some private property, were rented to merchants and artisans of Lefkoşa on a per diem basis. Mehmed bn Mehmed rented a bread shop *(ekmek dukkan)* at the bazaar *(çarşu)* for three akce/day, while haci ʿAli rented a storehouse for sheep heads and trotters, or an eating house *(baş hane)* in the castle for six akce/day and Ibrahim bn Memi rented a barbershop *(berber)* (1 84–4; Sefer 1003. 144–2; 1 Receb 1003. 239–3; I Şevval 1002).

Hidayet çelebi, present administrator *(mutevelli)* of the foundation of the late Sultan Selim Han, acknowledges *(ik/kiʿt)* before sagir (deaf) ʿAli, butcher *(kassab):* The butcher shop of the foundation in Lefkoşa is rented for 10 years at one akce/day to ʿAli. ʿAli accepts that. (1 323–1; III Cumadi I 995)

Among other rental shops identified with specific trades were a weaver's shop of the foundation of the mosque *(mescid)* of the late Mahmud çelebi in Nobet hane quarter which was rented for six months to Usta bn Veli for 25 akce/month and a tailor's shop rented by hayyat ʿAli bn ʿAbdullah of Lefkoşa to Murad v. Eymur beşe.

Tailor ʿAli bn ʿAbdullah of Lefkoşa makes a claim *(daʿva/tk) against Murad v. Eymur beşe:* A shop *(dukkan)* at Bezistan gate in Lefkoşa was rented to Murad for eight akce/month. Murad has agreed to give 22 akce more, a total of 30 akce/month, for a period of 10 years. It has been in his possession *(tasarruf)* for 14 months. Murad must pay 30 akce/month for that time. Murad denies that claim. When ʿAli has no proof, an oath is proposed to Murad and he takes it. (4 131–2; III Receb 1045; 3 155–6; II Rebiʿ II 1019)

Long Distance Trade

Merchants from Cyprus traveled regularly in Anatoli and Karaman provinces, to Aleppo (via Trabulus or Iskenderun), and to Egypt (at Iskenderiya, Dumyat, and particularly Cairo).[28] Likewise merchants from those places reached Cyprus. Trade with Istanbul, Salonika, and even Venice was not unusual. The merchants were both Muslims and Christians; many were janissaries. Disputes over trade brought them to the court at Lefkoşa, as did settling estates of deceased trading partners. Such cases give a glimpse of the nature of that trade in the eastern Mediterranean.

Yakimo, zimmi of Lefkoşa, sets forth a claim *(td)* against haci ʿAli bn ʿAbdullah, merchant of Aleppo (Haleb *tacir*): Formerly I took 48 vakiye of incense *(buhur)* from ʿAli at 100 akce/vakiye and loaded it in bags *(keyse)* on donkeys *(har)*. After I received it, I opened every bag. Someone had taken a little out of the bags. I want it returned in accordance with the Sharia. ʿAli acknowledges *(ik):* When Yakimo bought them he looked in one bag, not in the rest. Experts *(ehl-i vukuf)*, when they receive word of the deficiency *(kemlik)* of incense, say that all of it must be returned. (1 170–3; II Cumadi I 1003)

Haci Halil bn 'Ali came to court. After he made a claim *(da'va)* and testimony was asked for, from the upright Muslims *('udul-i Muslimun)* Mustafa bn Şu'eyb, Mehmed bn 'Abdullah, Mehmed bn 'Avs, and Musa bn Nebi testify: Formerly 'Isa bn Mehmed of Hoca Mahmud quarter near Imla' ed-din's houses *(evler)* in Larende, where he is now, took a loan *(karz-i hasan)* of 55 filori from the claimant haci Halil. Then he went to Egypt (Misr) for trade *(ticaret içun)*. At that time he owed money. After ascertaining the antecedents and character *(ta'dil, tezkiye)* of the witnesses, their testimony is accepted. 'Isa has no letter of credit *(havale)* to present. After Halil took an oath *(yemin billah)*, that was ordered and registered in the record book *(sicil)*. Then a copy *(suret)* mas made to present to the present Larende kadi and to others there. (1 231–3; I Şevval 1002)

Bayram bn [sic] Ishak of the Jewish community *(yahudi zumresi)* in Lefkoşa makes a claim *(da'va)* against Yasef bn [sic] Ibrahim, who came from Venice *(Venedik)* with goods of trade *(meta')*: Formerly I gave him some money *(nice akce)* and sent him in trade. Let him be asked. Why did he use my money? Yasef admits having taken the money and capital *(sermaye)*: I brought 120 vakiye of tin *(kalay)*, 1 barrel of tin plate *(teneke)*, 1 barrel of brass *(sari teneke)*, and 420 knives *(çift bicak)*. Now they are in Kucuk Han, bought with the money he gave me. All are his, but he owed me 1500 akce for my service. I have made a claim *(da'va)* against him. (1 293–3; I Zil-Hicce 1002)

Luka re'is v. Marko [states] before Hasan beşe bn Ilyas: We agreed (?) that I would bring a shipload *(navlun)* from Selanik to Cyprus for 100 filori. [The amount of] 3250 akce was paid in cash *(nakd)* and now he has paid 1 kantar of grapes. (3 154–6; II Rebi' II 1019)

Luka v. Marko, captain *(re'is)*, states *(bm)* before Hasan beşe bn Ilyas: At the city *(kasaba)* of Selanik Hasan gave me a load *(navlun)* to bring to Cyprus for 100 sikke. Of that he paid 3250 akce in cash *(nakd)* and 1 kantar of black grapes. He owes me the rest. Hasan denies that: In truth I came from Selanik to Cyprus by the ship *(gemi)* of the captain *(re'is)*, but I paid him everything I owe him. Luka has no proof. When Hasan was asked for an oath that he did not owe anything, he took it. (3 155–1; same)

Kumari zade Ibrahim beg bn Nasuh, presently superviser of inheritance *(beyt ul-mal 'amme ve hasse emini)* in Cyprus, makes a claim and states *(iddi'a/tk)* before Ahmed oda başi bn Gazi of Lefkoşa, with Şa'ban aga in the office of agent *(mubaşiret)* for the provincial council *(divan-i Kibris)*: Sohte Yusuf, who died in Anatoli, came here 10 years ago in trade *(ticaret tarikile)*. He placed a white slave *(gulam)* and 600 riyali guruş in trust *(emanet)* with the aforementioned Ahmed ota başi. Since Yusuf has no heirs *(varis)*, the 600 riyali guruş and the slave belong to the state treasury *(miri)*. Ahmed denies that. When Ibrahim has no adequate proof, Ahmed is allowed to take an oath. (4 93–1; I Ramazan 1044)

Haci Derviş beşe bn Mustafa of Lefkoşa sets forth a claim and states *(daʿva/tk)* before haci Yusuf ota başi, guardian *(vasi)* before the Sharia of the minor children *(evlad-i sigar)* of the late Hasan boluk başi of Lefkoşa who died in Cairo (Misr-i Kahire): I gave the deceased 20 riyali guruş in principal *(asl-i mal)* at 20% interest (10 for 12) for one year. I had not received the 20 riyali guruş or the 4 riyali guruş before he left. When he died in Egypt I was owed 24 guruş. Let the aforementioned loan *(karz)* be inquired about. I want it from his property *(mal)*. When Derviş is asked for proof, upright Muslims *(ʿudul-i muslimun)* Ibrahim ota başi bn Emrullah and Huseyn beşe bn ʿAbdul-Nasir (?) confirm him. When an oath is proposed that he did not receive it, Derviş takes it. He receives the 24 riyali guruş in full. (4 111–1; II Muh. 1045)

Veli ota başi bn Suleyman of Lefkoşa sets forth a claim and states *(daʿva/tk)* before haci Yusuf ota başi, guardian *(vasi)* for the minor children *(evlad-i sigar)* of the late Hasan boluk başi who died formerly in Cairo: When the deceased went to Egypt, I gave him 50 riyali guruş in a commenda *(mudarebe)*. I want it from his effects. Yusuf denies that. When Veli is asked for proof, upright Muslims Yusuf beg bn Musa and Mehmed aga confirm Veli. (4 115–3; II Muh. 1045)

Racil haci Ibrahim beşe of the Cyprus janissaries *(cezireʾ-i Kibris yeniçerileri)* makes a claim and states *(iddiʿa/tk)* before present beyt ul-mal ʿamme ve hassa emini seyyid Mehmed çelebi bn seyyid Ahmed: haci Mustafa of the merchants *(tuccar taifesi)* via Jerusalem (Kuds-i şerif) formerly sent me 10 sacks *(çuval)* of soap *(sabun)* from Dimyat (Damietta). While the 10 sacks of soap were placed with the seal *(muhr)* of haci Veli of Magosa castle, Mehmed seized *(ahz ve kabz)* them contrary to the Sharia. I want the Sharia carried out. Mehmed denies that: haci Mustafa died 10 months ago in Dimyat, according to ʿudul-i muslimin haci Mehmed bn Ibrahim and Ahmed tayi bn Mustafa. The soap was seized because the deceased had no heir, on account of testimony before mevlana Suleyman efendi related to present Tuzla kadi Ahmed efendi by the above witnesses; it was seized for the state treasury *(miri)*. The document *(huccet)*, dated mid-January 1636 (II Şaban 1045), signed by mevlana Suleyman efendi, was presented. Ibrahim was prevented *(menʿ)* from making his claim. (4 144–2; III Ram. 1045)

Ancelo v. Gavrayel of the merchants *(tuccar taʾifesi)* in Lefkoşa makes a claim and states *(daʿva/tk)* before Yerolimo (?), (?), Mihayel, Nikolo, and Ziya: At a pier *(iskele)* called (?) in the emporium of Dimyat (bender Dimyat) one and a half months ago I appointed this Melemado (?) v. Ferencesko, who is present here, as my agent *(vekil)* to bring 23 coarse water buffalo skins *(camus goni)* to the vessel *(sunbak)* of this Nikolo re'is and then to my father Gavrayel who lives in Limosa. I made this Melemado (?) v. Ferencesko my agent. The ship *(sunbak)* was brought to Magosa pier *(iskelesi)* in Cyprus. This Kumari zade Ibrahim beg bn Nasuh, presently beyt ul-mal ʿamme ve hassa emini, presumed *(zuʿum)* that I had died and he took the 23 water buffalo skins from the possession of the ship *(gemi)*. He sold them to Ahmed aga. The others reply: We bought our 21 hides *(gun)* from the aforementioned Ahmed aga. We had no information about Ancelo owning them. When Ancelo is asked for proof, upright Muslims Receb beşe bn Mustafa and infidel *(kefere)* (?) v. (?) confirm him. Their testimony is accepted. Ibrahim is ordered to give the 21 hides to Ancelo. (4 161–1; I Muh. 1046)

Zimmi Ziya of Lefkoşa makes a claim and states *(iddiʿa/tk)* before Zorzi, zimmi: Formerly I made a trip *(sefer)* to Istanbul with Zorzi. We made a partnership *(iştirak)* dividing equally *(ʿala s-seviye)* and bought two towels (napkins?) *(peşkir)* for 60 riyali guruş. In Istanbul, apart from our principal *(asl-i mal)*, he received 60 riyali guruş profit *(faʾide)*. I want my 30 guruş profit *(faʾidesi)*. Zorzi denies that. When Ziya is asked for proof, he has none. When an oath is proposed to Zorzi, he takes the oath by God who sent down the Gospel *(Incil)* by Jesus (ʿIsa). Ziya is prevented *(menʿ)* from making a claim *(daʿva)*. (4 180–2; I Cumadi I 1046)

From the merchants *(tuccar taʾfesi)* of the emporium *(bender)* of Iskenderiye haci Mehmed bn haci Suleyman makes a claim and states *(iddiʿa/tk)* before Baba Yasef v. Yorgi of the poor and destitute *(nam gureban)*, brother of the late Habib (?) re'is of (?) village of Trablus kaza: Formerly I placed 1200 head of Cyprus (hellum?) cheese *(baş Kibris beyniri)* on the ship *(gemi)* of the deceased Habib (?) at Limosa pier (Limon *iskelesi*). While at sea *(ruy-i derya)*, an infidel ship *(kuffar gemi)* was encountered. They made Umit Mehmed and me prisoner *(esir)*. Yasef took my 1200 head of cheese. I want it. Let the Sharia be carried out *(icray-i şerʿ)*. Yasef denies that. When Mehmed is asked for proof, he has none. When an oath is proposed to Yasef, he takes it. (4 181–2; I Cumadi I 1046)

ʿAli, called Çelenk, of Karaman on the other shore (Ote Yaka) acknowledges and states *(ik/tk)* before Gavrayel v. Zor, Marko v. Zozi, Yorgi, and Selimo of Lefkoşa: When they were in a bad situation *(kudretleri hali)* on the other shore (Ote Yaka), I gave them 238 riyali guruş to go to Cyprus. Now, with time *(vaʿde)* 42 riyali guruş is added, making a total of 280 riyali guruş. They acknowledge that. (4 190–3; II Receb 1046)

The Ottoman government imposed many sanctions on trade with foreigners, both in goods of trade and in who legitimate trading partners were. The restrictions were proclaimed in imperial orders issued regularly, sometimes in response to reports from frustrated officials.

On 19 Şevval 980 (23 February 1573) an order had been sent to the governor and chief financial officer of Cyprus reminding them that neither grain *(tereke)* nor cotton *(penbe)* may be sold to foreigners. However, carobs *(habob)*, wine *(hamr)*, salt *(tuz)*, olives *(zeytun)*, and olive oil *(revgan-i zeyt)* from the harvests of the island *(mahsul)* may be sold, but only to infidels *(kefere)* who come in French ships *(Firance gemiler)*, as in the past. If it is not sold to them, it is not to be sold to anyone. It is not permissible to sell them to the abode of war *(dar ul-harb)*. Sugar *(şeker)*, ginger *(zencebil)*, and hemp *(kendir)* should be loaded on ships at the naval arsenal *(tersane)*. Formerly they were sent to Fineke harbor, but since many ships raid there now it is not safe (broken). (164/75 (6) #300)

Two days later an imperial order of 21 Şevval (25 February) addressed to the district governor of Aydin *(Aydin begi)* berated him because a large galley *(barça)* had come to the pier of Cyprus and picked up forbidden goods by claiming to have in their possession an imperial order which they did not show. The ship was seized with leather *(sahtiyan)*, beeswax *(bal mumi)*, cotton *(penbe)*, and other goods which are forbidden to sell to the Latin world *(Firengistan)*. Apprehended with the ship's illicit goods were Mustafa, Muharrem, ʿOsman, and Huseyn, who claimed that they wished to establish relations with the foreigners in order to rescue *(helas)* Muslim prisoners *(esirler)* there. (158/99 (13) p. 114, #275)

According to a letter received by the Porte from former Tuzla kadi mevlana Mustafa, the financial officer *(cabi)* of the tax farm *(mukataʿa)* of the late Sultan Selim han foundation in that district *(kaza)*, Nurallah ogli Ibrahim, had entered into a conspiracy with a zimmi captain *(reis)* named (?) Palavi (?) ogli to smuggle forbidden goods and sell them to the infidel. The captain came with his 35 cubit *(ziraʿ)* ship *(gemi)* to various places in the kadi's sphere of authority. He secured foodstuffs *(zahair)* including wheat *(bugday)*, beeswax *(bal mumi)*, cotton thread *(rişteʾ-i penbe)*, almonds *(badam)*, fish *(balamud, or the fruits of a tree used for tanning)*, and gallnuts *(mazo)*. For nine years this went on (78/34 (33) KVK#1238).

Local Trade

Within Cyprus a vigorous local trade existed. The small size of the island permitted townspeople and villagers to visit the bazaars and markets of Lefkoşa even if the road system was not very well developed. Small caravans of camels and donkeys passed back and forth frequently. No place on the island is more than 75 miles from Lefkoşa, and the grain-growing heartland of the island is a rather flat plain extending from Magosa (Famagusta) bay to Morfo (Morphou) bay, bounded by the high Trodos to the south and the Kyrenia range to the north. In addition, the testimony of travelers, some of them admittedly in the late 17th and 18th centuries, bears witness to small mercantile communities at Magosa, Larnaka, Limosa, and Girniye where local agricultural produce was distributed. Villagers brought the surplus of their produce to those places to trade. Numerous legal cases illustrate the nature of the relationship of the villagers and towns, particularly Lefkoşa, although few details of the actual commerce are given.

Ramazan bn Hasan of the muleteers *(mugari)* states *(bm)* in the presence of Arslan bn Ibrahim: He agreed to bringing rice *(pirinc)* from Tuzla pier *(iskelesi)* to Lefkoşa for 3½ akce/kile. Now he delays *(te'allul)* in paying me. Arslan says: I offered 2½ akce/kile. When proof is asked for, there is none. When Arslan is asked to take an oath that he accepted 2½ akce, he does. (3 161–5; III Rebiᶜ II 1019)

Davud beg bn 'Omer of Mesariye kaza sets forth a claim *(td)* against Yerolimo v. Filipo of Tuzla: Two years ago I sent Yerolimo 424 lidre cotton *(penbe)*. I have no idea what happened to it. Yerolimo denies having received it. Registered. (3 11–7; 16 Şevval 1018)

Suleyman çavuş of the council of Cyprus *(divan-i Kibris)* and Nasuh bn Yunus state *(bm)* before Ilyas bn Ahmed: We bought 50 donkey loads of carobs *(harnob)* in partnership *(iştirak)* in Ote Yaka (on the other side, i.e., Karaman). We sent it to Ilyas for security. He sold it. Ilyas denies that. When an oath is proposed to Ilyas, he takes it. (3 153–1; II Rebiᶜ II 1019)

Covana bint Fezenco (?), zimmiye of Miliye (?) village of Karpaz kaza states *(bm)* in the presence of 'Abdun-Nebi bn Musa and Hasan bn Çelab virdi of the village: Twenty days ago they bought plums *(erik)* in partnership *(iştişrak)* with my husband Ciryako v. Yorgi. They went together to sell them in the Lefkoşa area *(canib)*. They have returned. Why has my husband Ciryako not come? I want it asked in accordance with the Sharia and registered. When 'Abdun-Nebi and Hasan were asked, they said: In truth we bought plums in partnership with the aforementioned Ciryako, loaded them on a donkey *(merkeb)*, and went together to the Lefkoşa area. When we came to (?) village of Lefkoşa kaza, Ciryako gave the donkey to us for safe keeping *(emanet)*. He lay down and rested by a bridge near that village. What happened to him since then we do not know. (3 158–3; III Rebiᶜ II 1019)

Rahib Baba Eksendi, abbot *(gemonos = igumenos)* of the monastery *(manasteri)* of Aya Mama in Morfo nahiye acknowledges *(ik/i^ct)* before present Tuzla kadi mevlana haci Ahmed efendi: Ahmed and I had a dispute *(niza^c)* over business and trade *(mu^camelat ve ahz ve i^cta)*. Formerly a settlement *(sulh)* was made for 18,000 akce, but when he did not give that *(bedel-i sulh)*, I went to the Porte *(asitane³-i se^cadete)*. When I brought up *(ilka)* the aforementioned matter, I was given an imperial order *(emr-i şerif)*, and I received a letter *(mektub)* and order *(emr)* and again I made a claim *(da^cva)*. Then a settlement *(sulh)* was again made, for 30 keyl barley *(arpa)* and 20 keyl wheat *(bugday)*. I have now received in full from Ahmed the aforementioned 30 keyl barley and 20 keyl wheat in accordance with the settlement and I have no further claim. (4 92–2; I Ramazan 1044)

Summary

The agricultural produce of Cyprus in the century after the Ottoman conquest was rich and varied, and not only that, but prices were so low that European ships regularly stopped there on return voyages for cheap foods. The official price lists indicate clearly the variety and the low prices: local fruits and vegetables, dairy products, meats, as well as breads, and other grains, which provided for a potentially healthful diet.

The *muhtesib* played an important role overseeing marketplaces, and preventing illegal business practices, as well as supervising weights and measures. Often he seems to have brought people to the kadi's court to be tried.

Although important lists of maximum fixed prices have been found, they are too few to give more than broad hints.

Barley was not as highly esteemed as wheat or at least it always sold for half the price of wheat. A limited number of varieties of bread products were known in Cyprus, in addition to bread itself. Unfortunately too little evidence survives to give any general understanding of fluctuating prices. The very important figures that Raymond collected for Cairo provide a model for comparison, whenever people are able to find adequate prices elsewhere. The eccentricity of prices in Cyprus reflect variations in harvests, where one year in four or five may have a reduced rainfall. They were often the most important goods of trade. Muslim and non-Muslim bread bakers were both very widespread in Cyprus.

Sheep, goats, donkeys, oxen, cattle, and horses all had their roles in the local economies, certainly, although little is known about it; but even less is known with certainty about how frequently sheep and goats were used, or what they were used for. One can say little beyond consuming meat was by no means unknown. Likewise nothing can be said about the role or importance in the diet of yogurt, cheese, or butter.

Probably the most important fruit was grapes, which could be used fresh, dried, as sugar syrup, and wine, and at least in small quantities could be cultivated over much of the island, in various styles, and even some came from abroad. Figs, which could be consumed fresh or dried, were widespread, as were apples and pomegranates. Chickpeas, rice, carobs, onions, and olives were also widespread; they were consumed dried and also made into an oil. In the 16th and 17th centuries many local varieties seem to have been preserved.

By the time of the conquest sugar factories probably were declining in importance as part of the annual produce assigned to the government; apparently people found other sources. Although saltpetre, used for gunpowder, was a well-known attraction for the Ottomans in conquering, making it must have been very unpleasant, or difficult, because for a while anyway, it was not produced. Very little is known about the fate of the once-important salt production of Tuzla and Limosa, although in that case Ottomans had many other possible sources. Some could affort to import fancier soaps. The island was lucky that it had enough timber or scrub wood to satisfy the need of cooking and warmth; ships had to be repaired across the Straits in Tarsus. Merchants came from Anatoli and Karaman provinces in Anatolia, Aleppo, and Iskenderiya.

At least based on number of cases, cotton exceeded all other non-comestibles, both in volume and cash value. It was sold with seed, or without, and carded. It was very important for both Christians and Muslims. Wool and woolen cloth also were widespread, and coffee was almost as important. Cotton and wool seem to have been produced entirely by local people, but coffee was always imported. Demands for coffee was increasing in the 1630s.

The main rental properties in Lefkoşa were baths, *hans,* and candle factories in that order.

Sometimes rents fluctuated sharply. Merchants from Dumyat, and especially Cairo, frequently had business in Cyprus; Istanbul, Salonika and Venice were close behind in the importance of their trade. Merchants might be either Muslims or Christians. Within Cyprus itself a vigorous local trade existed. The small size of the island enabled lots of people to utilize the bazaars and markets of Lefkoşa. Villagers brought the surplus of their often-varied production. Also, there were small communities of merchants in Magosa, Larnaka, Limosa, and Girniye, because of the central location of the provincial capital. Camels and donkeys were vital to trade.

NOTES

1. André Raymond has shown clearly how between 1620 and 1800 the price of wheat fluctuated greatly from year to year (pp. 54ff, table 5 following p. 68). The eccentric variations of annual rainfall in the Middle East make such fluctuation common. The Ottoman government carefully regulated the collection and distribution of wheat, so that when the year's grain production fell drastically in one region, it could be supplemented by grain from another. Cf. L. Güçer, *XVI–XVII asırlarda Osmanlı İmparatorluğunda Hububat Meselesi ve Hububattan Alınan Vergiler*. Istanbul, 1964. pp. 7ff. Possibly in Cyprus officials held the fixed price relatively stable. Possibly the paucity of evidence just prevents such variations from showing up.

2. European style, or Frankish, bread.
3. A round, sweetened cake.
4. A kind of round cake.
5. A three-cornered pastry puff.
6. A ring-shaped roll of bread.
7. Flaky pastry with thin layers of filling.
8. Bread (?)
9. Bread baked on hot pebbles.
10. Ring-shaped plain biscuit.
11. *Borek* made on a flat, iron plate.
12. In the huge Ottoman empire every year some regions had unusually bad harvests while others had unusually good ones. According to L. Güçer, the Ottomans began managing the sale and distribution of grain because of the frequent problems of grain scarcity, not only in large cities but also particularly in areas where drought, locusts, or other natural disasters had struck. That practice became an important element of Ottoman economic policy. L. Güçer, *Hububat Meselesi . . .*, pp. 38f. Also Le commerce intérieur des céréales dans l'Empire Ottoman pendant la seconde moitié du XVIème siècle," *Revue de la Faculté des Sciences Économiques de l'Université d'Istanbul* 11.1949–1950.166,168,169f. In 1555 for the first time the Ottoman empire forbade the export of grain to foreigners, on account of internal needs; according to M. Aymard, that policy was then frequently implemented until the end of the century, when the problem ceased. *Venise,*

Raguse et le Commerce du Blé pendant la seconde moitié du XVIe siècle.
Paris, 1966. pp. 124–140, esp. pp. 125, 139. His map for 1550 notes
Cyprus as an important source of grain for Venice. pp. 40f. Cf. Hill, v. 3,
pp. 815f. The eastern Mediterranean had a sizeable grain surplus. According
to Braudel Ottoman territories had "plenty of grain to sell" to Italy "in
good years"; the price of grain was two or three times as high there. pp.
583ff, 591ff, 1090. Cyprus, for example, supplied Venice. Once it had
supplied both Venice and Genoa. J. Heers, *Gênes au XVe siècle.* Paris,
1961. pp. 342, 373. F. C. Lane, *Venice. A Maritime Republic.* Baltimore,
1973. pp. 305f. On the problem of smuggled grain illegally sold to Europe,
see also Mustafa Akdağ, "Osmanlı İmparatorluğunun Kuruluş ve Inkişafi
devrinde Türkiye'nin İstisadî Vaziyeti," *Belletin* 14.1950.389ff; U. Heyd,
Ottoman Documents on Palestine 1552–1615, Oxford, 1960, pp. 128ff,
82f; P. Earle, *Corsairs of Malta and Barbary,* Annapolis, 1970, p. 144. See
also S. J. Shaw, *Ottoman Empire . . . ,* v. 1, p. 172. Braudel, pp. 583ff,
592f, 875ff. Inalcik, "Capital Formation in the Ottoman Empire," *Journal
of Economic History* 29.1969.119f; "Impact of the *Annales* School on
Ottoman Studies and New Findings," *Review* 1.1978.69–96.

13. For grain, see also 1 8–6, 30–1, 62–2, 3, 5, 303–5, 308–7, 311–1,2, 318–
3; 2 55–1; 3 13–1, 21–6, 48–5, 51–5, 51–9, 73–3, 151–7; 4 92–2, 230–
1,2, 231–1, 233–1. *Kile* and *keyl* are variant forms of the same unit of
weight.

14. For bread see also 1 84–4, 248–4, 259–3, 280–4, 311–5; 3 86–5, 161–7.

15. In 1625 (1035) a vakf was estimated to own the following animals:

500 sheep worth	25 akce piece
8 donkeys	800
17 buffalo *(kara sigir)*	1000
4 mares	1200 akce

According to Braudel, a great many mules were found in Cyprus from the
1550s, leading to a drop in the number of horses. Mules carried heavy loads
over bad roads. pp. 284f.

16. The price of meat in Bursa was fairly stable between 1616 and 1633. If a
gradual decline in meat consumption in the Mediterranean world was un-
derway, Cyprus was immune. Pasdirma was highly prized. Braudel, pp.
350f, 459, 518. In the forms *sucuk dudi* and *cevzi sucuk* sweetmeats is
meant.

17. In the Venetian period a monoculture of sugar plantation is based on slave
labor (sometimes imported) spread over the more accessible regions of
Cyprus. Until cheaper sources of sugar appeared in the Atlantic, Cyprus
supplied Venice and Genoa. Braudel, pp. 154f, 1082. W. McNeill, *Venice . . . ,* pp. 54, 76. J. Heers, *Gênes . . . ,* p. 342. W. Heyd, v. 2, pp. 680–
693.

Early in the 17th century the amount of sugar to be turned over to the
Porte from Egypt ranged in value between a low of 32,600 paras and a high

of 191,539 paras. Between 1572 and 1586 800 kantar of sugar (=28,000 Istanbul okke or vakiye) was required annually by the Porte; then that was raised to 1400 kantar (=42,600 okke). Shaw, *Financial and Administrative Organization* . . . , pp. 176f, 273f. Cf. Raymond, p. 62.

18. Similar orders were also sent concerning Palestine in 1571. U. Heyd, *Ottoman Documents* . . . , pp. 129, 137f. Saltpeter was a central part of English trade in the eastern Mediterranean. Braudel, pp. 622f.

19. On the great importance of Cyprus salt to Venice in the 16th century, as to Genoa in the 15th, see Braudel, pp. 312, 1082f. Cf. W. McNeill, *Venice* . . . , p. 52. J. Heers, *Gênes* . . . , pp. 342, 376f. Indirect taxes from that salt provided a major source of Venetian revenues. F. Lane, *Venice* . . . , p. 324.

20. The price of soap in Cairo in 1621 was 1660 para/kantar. Raymond, p. 63. Prices between 1682 and 1799 also are given. On 18th-century soap trade from Syria and especially Palestine, see pp. 190, 477f. See also pp. 173, 337f, 478f.

21. Timber was scarce in the Mediterranean world, although the Taurus mountains in southern Anatolia had extensive forests. Cf. Braudel, pp. 238f.

22. In 1687 cotton sold for 278 para/kantar in Cairo. Raymond, pp. 63ff.

23. Cf. 3 171–5; 6–1, 24–7, 171–1. 2 8, 97–3. 4 178–3, 200–2. Cf. 3 2–8, 6–1, 24–7, 171–1, 5. 4 178–3, 200–2.

24. For other cotton see 1 240–2, 246–3, 75–2. 3 38–4, 48–4, 101–5, 103–1, 104–6.

25. For centuries cotton had been a major export of Cyprus. J. Heers, *Gênes* . . . , pp. 157, 342, 392f. F. W. Lane, *Venice* . . . , p. 298. W. Heyd, v. 2, pp. 611–614. By the 16th century cotton plantations had replaced sugar plantations there, and they provided large quantities for Venice. Most of that was raw cotton rather than cloth. Braudel, pp. 155f, 287, 300, 312, 613. W. McNeill, *Venice* . . . , p. 176. F. W. Lane, "Venetian Shipping during the Commercial Revolution," pp. 37f in B. Pullan, ed. *Crisis and Change in the Venetian Economy* . . . London, 1968. For decades after the fall of Cyprus in 1571 Cypriot cotton continued to be marketed through Venice. F. W. Lane, *Venice* . . . , p. 298.

26. In the 14th and 15th centuries, at least, Cyprus produced fine woollen cloth. J. Heers, *Gênes* . . . , p. 377. W. Heyd, v. 2, pp. 10f.

27. Raymond, pp. 69–72, 131–133, and graphique 6. See also C. van Arendonk, "Kahwa," *EI²*. Braudel, p. 762. For coffee houses in Palestine, see U. Heyd, *Ottoman Documents* . . . , pp. 152, 160ff.

28. "The *raison d'être* of long distance trade is that it connects, sometimes with difficulty, regions where goods can be bought cheaply with others where they can be sold for high prices," Braudel, pp. 441ff. Cf. ". . . I am inclined to think that Mediterranean trade had reached a large volume by the end of the century. How could piracy, which is reported to have been a profitable occupation, otherwise have prospered(?)" pp. 292, 286f.

THIRTEEN

The Sea: Navies, Trade, Smuggling, and Piracy (Linking Cyprus to the Mediterranean World)

Cyprus has an ideal location for a naval base, for long distance trade, for smuggling, and for piracy. Had the Ottomans chosen to do so, they could have made either Lefkoşa or Magosa the kind of international trading emporium that Aleppo was fast becoming in the 1570s, and that Izmir became in the mid-17th century. Indeed, Lusignan Cyprus had played that sort of role in the eastern Mediterranean; only the exclusionary policies of the Mamluks and then particularly the Ottomans hindered Venice from that. When the Ottomans came to dominate every inch of the eastern Mediterranean and Aegean littorals, they obviously could have chosen to revive Cyprus. Indeed, an important group of Ottoman policymakers intended to return Cyprus to that very role. Only other and perhaps conflicting Ottoman trade policies, the acumen of the people of Aleppo, the rapid spread of piracy in the 1580s, and the entry into the Mediterranean of the sailing ship, with heavy cannon, prevented that from happening.

Making either Lefkoşa or Magosa into the great Levantine entrepôt was no impossible scheme. The Lusignans had made Magosa serve that role splendidly. When disease and temporary Genoese occupation of the port made change advantageous, Lefkoşa won the role of entrepôt. No port between Rhodes and Lebanon had the advantages that Magosa had even for sailing ships. Aleppo was well over twice the distance from the sea as Lefkoşa, required passage over rough mountainous terrain, and, despite Iskenderun, Lazikiye, and Trablus lacked the facilities of a good port.

The profits that the Venetians had exacted from Cyprus were prover-
bial: Sokollu Mehmed Paşa was right if he compared its loss to cutting
off an arm of Venice. Of course, since Venetian Cyprus had very powerful Muslim neighbors, colonial Venice did not dare use the island as a
naval base for full-fledged crusades all over the Levant, as some Lusignan rulers had. Even under Venetian rule, however, it provided an ideal
haven for Latin pirates, who harassed Muslim commerce from the Mamluk and Ottoman empires. Although the true "mix" of reasons for the
Ottoman occupation in 1570–1571 may be elusive, there can be no
doubt that regular use of the island by pirates had long aggravated the
Ottomans.[1]

Halil Inalcik has wisely written: "The conquest of Cyprus in 1570–
71 was the last great Ottoman military success . . . This victory, achieved
by the cooperation of the army and the fleet, was the greatest feat of
Ottoman arms . . ." In that same sentence, however, he asserts that their
very victory led to a decisive anti-Ottoman alliance in Europe: "but the
creation of a Christian alliance during the course of the campaign was a
realization of the Ottomans' greatest fears."[2] There Inalcik perhaps can
be faulted, for that fleeting alliance of Venice, Habsburgs, and Papacy,
which produced nothing except a victory at Lepanto, can only very
loosely be considered a "Christian alliance." True, the Habsburgs controlled the most extensive empire west of the Ottomans, but on their
many fronts with the Habsburgs that empire had for decades been on
the defensive, if not in outright retreat. The rising Ottoman state had
stripped Venice of all its colonies outside the Adriatic sea except Crete.
The Papacy was no longer a formidable military power; it had lost so
much of its moral authority that it could hardly persuade any monarch
to undertake a crusade, even though Pius V (1566–1572), Gregory XIII
(1572–1585), Sixtux V (1585–1590), and Clement VIII (1592–1605)
were virulently anti-Ottoman popes who preached Christian crusades.[3]
Indeed "Latin" Europe was divided by the reformation. However re-
spectfully they might have entertained papal ambassadors, no other
European states seem likely to have joined an anti-Ottoman alliance.
Indeed, France, England, and some German territories more likely would
have joined with the Ottomans than against them.[4]

After the conquest of Syria and Egypt in 1516–1517, the Ottoman
fleet remained unchallenged in the Aegean and in the eastern Mediterranean. Since the late 1520s the Ottoman fleet had frequently made spring

expeditions, not just into the Ionian and Adriatic seas, but beyond the straits of Messina, into the Tyrrhenian sea, and into the western Mediterranean. Ottoman galleys, along with their associates from North Africa, pillaged the coasts of Sicily and the Italian mainland, reaching even as far as the littoral of France, an Ottoman protégé, and Habsburg Spain. According to Guilmartin, Ottoman and western galleys were about the same quality but the Ottoman ones were slightly better, particularly in sailing efficiency.[5]

True, the Latin victory at Lepanto was an overwhelming one, but clearly it was an anomaly. Losing a great battle, however decisively, to a brave and competent adversary cannot be of momentous consequence unless somehow followed up. Within the year the reconstructed Ottoman navy burst into the central Mediterranean, sailing around the coast of the Morea and into the Ionian sea, virtually to Lepanto, with a force which exactly matched the one it had been sending regularly—but under new leadership, Kiliç, ʿAli Paşa. If it did not precisely match the fleet of 1571, there is no way of knowing, for no Latin alliance again dared to challenge Ottoman galleys.[6]

Temporary desperation had influenced both Habsburg and Venetian participation in the alliance. Neither trusted the other in 1571, nor in 1572 or 1573. The Venetians were so vulnerable to the Ottomans because not only did Venice depend on trade with the Levant, particularly in luxury goods, for most of the wealth that pervaded is aristocracy, but also Venice depended on wheat and other grain of the Levant to feed its populace. By that time the Ottomans had come to control virtually every dot of real estate on the Mediterranean littoral, from north of Ragusa nearly to Fiume in the upper Adriatic to west of Algiers. There was no way that Venice could challenge that tight Ottoman hold. Even in alliance with the Habsburgs and the Papacy it seems unlikely that at that time Venice could have secured, through any kind of show of force, the goods of trade it needed. Venice desperately needed the Ottoman empire.[7]

The Ottomans, on the other hand, possibly needed "a" Venice, but they certainly did not need Venice. Venetian merchants may have had special mercantile and maritime skills. So too, however, did the people of Marseilles, who had been admitted to the Ottoman realms as trading partners since 1517. Likewise the Ragusan merchants had the requisite skills. Marrano Jews from Spain had excelled at that trade in the middle of the 16th century. In the 1580s English merchants, and in 1612 Dutch merchants were admitted under special terms at times when the Ottoman government judged them of possible utility to the empire. Terms of trade, including customs duties, were manipulated to serve the economic and diplomatic interests of the Sublime Porte.

Ottoman power and ambition were undiminished by the loss at Lepanto in 1571. That single, isolated victory of the Habsburgs did little to interrupt the momentum of Ottoman success against them, continuing in Tunis in 1574, and soon thereafter in Morocco, until relieved by a truce which the Ottomans bestowed on them in 1580. As they had for decades before, they continued to carry the battle to their enemies. Venice, in order to return to their good graces, agreed to pay extensive reparations (100,000 ducats). The Ottomans lost thousands of skilled seamen and marines, as well as most of their galleys. In the sieges of Lefkoşa and especially Magosa Ottoman forces took very heavy casualties. Rapid 16th-century advances in fortification and artillery cost the Ottomans heavily, for those benefited defenders while slowing down conquerors. Such casualties were, for the Ottomans, the sorest consequence of the battle of Lepanto.[8]

Some local circumstances combined with the external influence of the development of Aleppo to stifle the plan to make Cyprus a behemoth. Ottoman officials were reluctant to join to Cyprus the contiguous Mediterranean littoral. The Levantine littoral from Meis island and Finike on the west to Trablus and Beyrut on the east could have made Cyprus one of the wealthiest of provinces, whose governors would have been among the mightiest of Ottoman warriors, but that would have encroached on Aleppo's development. Had Magosa been made the capital of the province, rather than Lefkoşa, then circumstances might have forced the governors to consider the sea more. If the Ottomans had tried to use Magosa commercially and as an offensive naval base, rather than just protecting it, then they would have been forced to improve sanitary conditions and to provide clean water. Residents of Magosa would have been healthier, and foreign merchants might once again have been encouraged to settle there. Larnaka (Tuzla) had little possibility of becoming an important port or commercial center, but Magosa had great possibilities even for fleets of ships. The presence of Ottoman and foreign merchants would have stimulated the production of luxury goods.

While it is true that much of the value of Cyprus for the Latins had been as a safe offshore island, long distance trade in the Levant remained quite important to Ottomans as well as Europeans, even after 1571. Iskenderiye was so defenseless as to be vulnerable even to a single bold ship. While Magosa had first-class fortifications already constructed, Iskenderiye was a tiny place with no fortifications, and if anything it was even more vulnerable to malaria, plague, and other virulent diseases than Magosa. Not even English or Dutch ships could threaten Magosa, although getting goods there from the Syrian coast was fraught with difficulty.

The introduction of the Atlantic ship, replete with its powerful cannon, into the eastern Mediterranean was far more grievous for the Ottoman navy than any loss of men and materials during the galley wars could have been. No one ever built and operated galleys more effectively than the Ottomans. Disaster eventually came to the Ottoman navy in the Mediterranean only because it continued so long to rely on galleys; the fates experienced by other countries using galleys in the Mediterranean were even more terrible than that of the Ottomans.

The slowness of the local Mediterranean states, and particularly the Ottomans, to copy the sailing ships introduced into the Mediterranean by English and Dutch merchants (and pirates) undercut the naval preeminence of the northeastern Mediterranean world. Not only did the sailing ships outrun galleys in many instances, but they also carried heavier cannon and so outshot them. Since, in addition, the Atlantic ships usually carried heavier loads of cargo, they were in every way advantageous.[9] From 1595 English ships dominated not just the long distance trade of the Levant but also the local carrying trade. Soon a strong Dutch presence also was felt. Goods which once had been carried on Venetian and Ottoman commercial vessels then preferred English ships, which additionally provided security from the pirates. Indeed many sailing ships seem to have been used indiscriminately as merchant ships and for piracy as opportunities appeared.

In the 1550s and 1560s Ottoman galleys fearlessly penetrated every quarter of the Mediterranean. By the 1590s the navy had fallen on the defensive, unsure, for example, of even being able to protect the coasts of Cyprus. From sending out hundreds of galleys of the highest quality, crewed by disciplined and fearless oarsmen and marines, the Ottoman navy of the Mediterranean was reduced to merely dozens of mediocre galleys, sometimes with timid commanders and unreliable crews. Not just Cyprus was affected by that, of course. Commerce over the entire Levant was affected. Foreign ships of Atlantic origin took up virtually all the burden of transportation to the Latin Mediterranean and beyond. While Egypt and particularly Syria had alternate land routes within the Ottoman empire that they could exploit for trade, Cyprus had no such possibilities. Without regular connections with Antalya, Silifke, Ayaş, Iskenderun, Trablus, Beyrut, Damietta, and Alexandria, Cyprus lost many of the advantages of being part of a large empire. Although some limited trade with the south coast of Anatolia and with the Syrian coast continued, the economic and commercial situation of Cyprus must be considered grave. Increasingly Ottoman merchants, like Venetian ones, began to depend for security on English ships, even for short distance hauling in the eastern Mediterranean.

Already plagued by disease and locusts, Cyprus lost any hope of entering the mainstream of Levant commerce. In effect, it became a "backwater," where local people probably had increasingly to produce more and more of what they consumed and, given the population decline, find only a small demand for artisanal crafts and trade. Since the soil of Cyprus was so rich and the climate so productive, foods were of good quality and their prices strikingly cheap, at least in the view of foreign merchants and travelers. By late in the 17th century many European ships stopped there to take on provisions for their return across the Mediterranean.[10]

Smuggling

In the 16th century the Ottoman empire succeeded in controlling exports to benefit its own political and economic needs. Only merchants from certain countries were permitted to operate in Ottoman territories, and only certain goods could be traded with them. Moreover, the Ottomans applied such policies when and how they wanted, leaving Venice, France, later England and Holland, among others, little choice but to acquiesce.

In the 16th century, the trade of the Atlantic world was growing rapidly. Although completely new trade routes were developing around southern Africa to the Indian ocean, and across the Atlantic ocean to the New World, markets both for domestic Levantine goods and for goods from South and East Asia and Persia, carried to Levant ports, were growing. Despite the opening of new routes never before used by Atlantic Europe, the old routes on which Cyprus had long been a key point continued to be important, even though the entrepôts of Cyprus were almost completely replaced by Aleppo, with its ports Iskenderun and Trablus.

Cyprus ceased, then, to provide large quantities of artisanal goods or imported silks and spices in the luxury trade, although silk, wool, and particularly cotton cloth production never completely lost their attraction. It did continue to produce comestibles, particularly fine wheat and barley. Since it was Ottoman policy to hold food prices under strict control at a level well below prices in Italy, and since Cyprus remained a place of remarkable fertility, except when locusts or drought intervened, those policies encouraged smugglers in the eastern Mediterranean to perfect their skills.

It was impossible to police the entire Aegean and eastern Mediterranean against smugglers. The coastline was so long, with many isolated places. There were countless islands. Cyprus itself had remote bays and promontories where smugglers could operate safely and effectively. Cypriot cultivators frequently sold their crops illegally to both domestic and foreign smugglers, or sometimes they sold to middle men. In any case, smuggling was particularly profitable for those who could carry grain to Venice or elsewhere in the northwest Mediterranean.

As Braudel has pointed out, the piracy rampant in the Mediterranean did not end trade altogether. Rather the continuing existence of that brisk trade encouraged pirates, who preyed on it.[11] Some smuggling was destructive to local cultivation, but more commonly producers willingly sold their own produce, either to smugglers along the coast or to middle men. The middle men and smugglers both might be Ottoman subjects or foreigners, Christians or Muslims.

Of course, many smugglers must have been ruthless pirates, while many others probably combined acts of smuggling with acts of piracy when they found themselves strong enough to do so. Surely village cultivators could not complain to authorities when the smugglers used violence against them. In general, however, that smuggling must have produced a very attractive supplement to normal farm incomes, buying their grain at twice the legal price in Cyprus—or even more—for smuggling to foreign markets.

Since Cyprus lay on such important shipping lanes, pirates naturally were very active in the area. Especially between Cyprus and Rhodes, but also west of Rhodes to Crete and north of Rhodes to Chios, were the areas in which pirates were most active. Many modern historians have noted that, as did seamen, merchants, and travelers of that time.[12] The Venetian Dandini (1596) particularly mentioned English pirates.[13] P. Teixeira (1605) noticed a fear of pirates after passing Rhodes, although, when pirates finally beset his ship, they were bought off with talk and pistachios. Teixeira also pointed out that the governor of Cyprus was building a strong but not very large fortress at Larnaka against pirates.[14] The English traveler George Sandys (1615) reported the alarm to ship passengers that the imminence of pirates aroused.[15] The ship of the gentleman-traveler de Stochove (1631) was pursued by pirates at the end of its overnight voyage from Anatolia to Girniye.[16] That situation had not changed by midcentury, when J. de Thévenot (1656) reported conditions at least that bad.[17] de Bruyn (1683) was delayed on the island of Rhodes and then at Limosa by warnings of pirates at Baf, and finally experienced anguish in the gulf of Antalya when a Greek ship was mistaken for a pirate one.[18] At least by the time of R. Pococke's detailed and accurate account of 1738 land near the sea was uncultivated because of those pirates.[19]

Although for various reasons, some valid but others fraudulent, some scholars have treated the situation of trade after the Ottoman conquest with a certain superciliousness, the state of that trade was certainly not dismal. According to F. C. Lane, for example, Venetian ships continued to trade with Cyprus, the "bulk of the cargo" being in cotton.[20] G. Hill points out in some detail how trade with the northwest Mediterranean soon resumed, despite the position of Roman Catholics in Cyprus at that time. Hill refers particularly to the salt trade and to the establishment on the island of foreign consular officials from Venice, England, France, and Holland by 1605.[21] According to D. Jenness, "soon after the expulsion of the Venetians, ships of many nations began to put in" to Baf, Limosa, and Larnaka, "vying" for the island's commerce; the commerce in salt and cotton with Venice and Holland resumed, the carob trade flourished, and the Ottomans "vigorously" encouraged silk production.[22] The Greek historian A. E. Vacalopoulos found that by the 17th century Lefkoşa had become an important center of commerce, with its silk, cotton, salt, wine, and olive oil production and merchants from England, France, and Holland.[23] Even the French historian P. Masson, who believed the island was ruined in 1630 because of inadequate food, noted important 17th-century French trade in sugar, cotton, wheat, wine, olive oil, turpentine, safran, and beans, as well as silk.[24]

The most important sources for that trade are contemporaries like Dandini (1596), papal agent to the Maronites, who found Italian merchants at Larnaka and reported a flourishing Cypriot cotton cloth industry which not only clothed the local people but was widely sold in Italy and elsewhere.[25] John Sanderson (1598), who spent two or three months with a ship loading salt in Larnaka, mentioned the availability of Cyprus wool in Aleppo.[26] G. Sandys (1615) found the island "abounding with all things necessary for life," and particularly the best raw cotton in the eastern Mediterranean, as well as prolific in oil, grain, wine, and raisins.[27] When the Portuguese merchant Pedro Teixeira (1605) visited Larnaka two Venetian vessels and one Dutch ship were in the harbor loading cotton. Besides exporting much salt to Venice, he reported that the island exported 5000 bags of cotton (at about 20 Castillian arrobas), 3000 bags of "very fine wool," silk, much wine, cheeses, and other things.[28] According to Richard Pococke (1738), a particularly thorough source, ". . . it is a surprizing thing to see Cyprus maintain its own people in such great plenty, and export so many things abroad." Pococke singles out the wheat sold to the Latin Mediterranean, cotton (to Holland, England, Venice, and Livorno, wool (to Italy and France), cotton cloth, and raw silk (sold to London).[29]

The Ubiquity of Piracy

Until the advent of sailing ships in the hands of English and Dutch pirates, the main pirates in the Levant after the Ottoman conquest of Cyprus were from Malta and Livorno. Particularly after 1574 they entered the Levant seas.[30] By that time galleys from Italy could make a round trip to Rhodes and Cyprus and back in 29 days.[31] Even then there was "no clear distinction" between "piracy and commerce," and "religious motivation" further clouded the problem.[32] Under cover of their own artillery, galleys could "give an effective cover to a landing party either in the assault or withdrawal phase of a raid. The key point here was that a galley could be maneuvered with precision right up against the shoreline to bring its guns to bear."[33] "Small-scale raiding operations could be launched from improvised bases in bays and along beaches." Then the raiders needed places to dispose of their booty.[34]

Pirates swarmed in the seas around Cyprus, or sometimes so it seems. In April 1571 the district governor (Rodos *begi*) was ordered to capture and punish infidel galleys *(kadirgalar)* which came to Cyprus (118/58 (8) #47; 24 Zil-Kade (?) 978). An order of 15 December 1571 points out to the district governor of Iskenderun (Iskenderiye *begi*) that he had been sent 20 galleys *(kadirga)* to bring to justice the infidel ships *(kuffar gemileri)* around Cyprus (118/58 (27); 27 Receb 979). In August (?) 1573 the governor of Cyprus was ordered not to be negligent of the tricks of the infiden pirates *(kuffar korsanlari)*, but to operate with the spahis which the district governors *(begler)* of Tarsus, Ic II, Sis, and ʿAlaiye were bringing (164/75 (29) #672; 11 Rebiʿ II (?) 981). Baf district governor Mustafa beg, who was ordered to transport gunpowder *(barut)* from Trablus Şam to Istanbul, had to delay carrying out his orders because of "fear of the infidels" *(kuffar havf)* on the high seas (160/89 (76) #277; undated). Another Baf district governor *(sancagi begi)* was ordered to bring supplies *(muhimmat)* for an imperial campaign from the Black sea *(Kara deniz)* to the Mediterranean *(Ak deniz)* so that pirate ships *(korsan gemileri)* should not harm Muslim pilgrims (92/53 KASK 6/1-45 #67; undated). In July 1591 Magosa district governor was warned to prepare himself because pirate ships *(korsan gemileri)* had reached the region of Cyprus (121/57 (28) #265; before 23 Ramazan 999).

On 13 September 1575 the Porte responded to a letter of inquiry from the Cyprus governor *(begler begisi)*, who had quizzed the Porte about what to do with a badly ruined galley which had reached Tuzla (Larnaka). That was the ship *(gemi)* of commander *(kapudan)* ʿAla ed-din of the imperial arsenal, which had been moored at Abukir harbor when

criminals *(mucrimler)* attacked it and drove it to Limosa in Cyprus, where they took on water; finally they were driven upon land near Tuzla. All the crew perished, and all the weapons and goods and some oars were lost. It needs repair. Cutting sufficient wood *(agac)* in Anatolia to repair the galley is ordered. The wood must be brought to Payas, from where it may be shipped to Tuzla so that the ship can be repaired. (116–66 (4) #642; 7 Cumadi II 983)[35]

Building and Repairing Castles

One of the best defenses against pirate raids was castles. The three walled cities have been discussed elsewhere. While the walls of Lefkoşa and Magosa needed considerable and expensive repair to the damage which the Ottomans had inflicted during the sieges, Girniye surrendered, so its walls were untouched. Some urgency was felt about fortifying Baf, although that process was delayed because local revenues were expected to pay for the construction. In November 1573 an imperial order dealing with that problem was sent to the governor *(begler begi)* and chief financial officer *(defterdar)* of Cyprus. It seems that formerly it was ordered to build Baf castle, partly from local funds. Then, however, many re*ʿaya* died from the plague, leaving too little money to pay for the construction. Consequently infidel ships *(gemiler)* were pillaging that area *(garet ve hesaret)*. The Porte reminded the governor and financial officer of the importance of building a castle there and urged doing so as soon as they had enough money (161/71 KB (19) #372; 8 Receb 981. Cf. 137/69 (29); undated, for repairs of other necessary walls). According to Cotovicus (c. 1598) a small fort had been built in the middle of Limosa (Limassol) to protect it "from the raids of pirates."[36] According to van der Nijenberg (1684) Tuzla (Salina) had a small "ravelin" with eight cannon for use against the pirates.[37]

Nature of Piratical Operations

Some pirates were in very intimate relationship with local people of the areas which they frequented, and so could make profits from occasionally pillaging and occasionally trading. On the other hand, it must have been exceedingly difficult to distinguish local fortifications erected for protection from other constructions erected to facilitate smuggling.

An imperial order of 23 October 1570 to the Delvine district governor *(begi)* made that problem very clear:

Now some people in Delvine district *(sancagi)* built stables *(mandralar)* and towers *(kuleler)* in places near the coast *(yaliye karib)*. It was made known that by means of them they make commerce *(muʿamele)* with infidels and they sell grain by sea to the infidels. I order that places near the coast like that, whether towers or stables, should be knocked over *(defʿve refʿ)*. After that, no one should be permitted to build stables and towers near the coast *(yalilere)*. You should write down the names of any who do what is forbidden *(memnuʿ)*; make known their salaries *(dirlikler)* and banish them to Cyprus. (roll #20, p. 126, #275; 23 Cumadi I 978)

An imperial order to the governor *(begler begisi)* of Cyprus regarding a letter to the Porte by Mehmed, commander of the Baf volunteers *(gonuller agasi)*, concerned a rebellion *(fesad ve şenaᶜat)* of infidel *(kafir)* Pero Pavlo and some of his followers.

He was a maker of intrigue *(fitne)*. He caused loss to Frank captain *(Firenk kapudan)* Filibo. Pero Pavlo met secretly *(hafyeten)* with a Venetian *(Venediklu)*. He should be taken into custody and executed. (154/63 KPG 6/4–217 #308; 5 Ramazan 979 (21 January 1572))

On 27 June 1573 the Porte dispatched a letter to the kadi of Manavgat, in response to a letter that kadi had sent previously.

Infidel ships *(kuffar-i haksar gemileri)* come into harbors *(limanlar)* called Eski Antaliya and Kugla, which are by the sea in that district *(kaza)*. They pillage and plunder the flocks and other property of reᶜaya, and they take prisoners *(esirler)*. They are not free of oppression. The people *(ahalisi)* and spahis should come in turn to protect the harbors *(limanlari)*. Now that district *(liva)* is joined to Cyprus. This year the infidels have done harm and destruction beyond limit to the Muslims. They have enslaved many people . . . (roll #5, p. 96, #198; 27 Sefer 981)

On 15 July 1575 an imperial order was dispatched to the governor of Cyprus in response to a letter received from Veli, Ic Il district governor *(sancagi begi)*.

Three infidel *(kafir)* ships *(gemiler)* appeared opposite ᶜAlaiye in the middle of the night. After they took one cargo *(rencber)* ship *(gemi)*, they came to Baliyaz (?) off Silindi district *(kaza)* dependent on Ic Il district. Orders were issued to the local people to beware. Still the infidels encountered a couple of farmers *(ekinciler)*. They struck blows, killing two Muslims, and a few infidels were wounded. Then another battle was fought, and again two Muslims died and some more infidels were wounded. The infidel ship has not been prevented from appearing. They seize garden produce *(bostan)* and cotton *(penbe)* from the produce peddlars *(rencber taifesi)*. There is great fear along the coast *(yali)*. The infidel ship has watered in 10 or 15 places on the coast of Ic Il . . . What is the cause of their not being brought to justice? . . . (116/66 (12) #285; 6 Rebiᶜ II 983)

The Porte sent a response to a letter requesting help from Ic Il subgovernor and the Silifke kadi.

When Ak Liman in your district *(liva)* was unprotected, two infidel galleys *(kadirgalari)* came to that harbor, seized two cargo ships *(rencber gemi)*, and chased a few ships *(gemiler)* aground. They pillaged Kuri Taş village near the sea *(sahil-i deryada)* and captured 23 men *(nefer adam)*. I order that you should go immediately with 30 spahis to defend that harbor *(liman)*. You should protect that region *(memleket ve vilayet)* from infidels and other brigands. Those (spahis) should not be sent in defense of Cyprus. (138/89 (11) #613; undated)

In those years the adjacent south Anatolian coast was the sphere of the governor of Cyprus. The governor complained in a letter to the Porte that the previous year when the spahis were on campaign infidel ships *(gemiler)* had caused losses to merchant ships *(tuccar gemilerine)* at the pier *(iskele)* of a place called Selendi in Ic Il district *(sancagi)*, the pier of Karaman province *(vilayet)*.

The governor was ordered to protect that place. He was to assign timars of 2000 akce, 2500 akce, or 3000 akce to 60 spahis in that district *(liva)*. Night and day those spahis should work to protect everyone. (160/89 (24) #572; undated)

In December 1590 the Porte sent the Ic Il district governor *(begi)* a response to his letter complaining about infidel ships *(gemiler)*

which capture re'aya along the coast *(yali)* and seize Muslims passing to the island of Cyprus and enslave them . . . Where are the spahis of that district *(liva)* who are supposed to defend and protect those areas, as in the past(?) (137/69 (40) #77; before 16 Muharrem 999)

Lefkoşa kadi mevlana Zeyn ul-'Abidin wrote a letter to the Porte about the grave insecurity which much of Cyprus lived in, prompting replies addressed to the governor *(begler begisi)* and to all the kadis on the island. Spahis and other notables of that island *('ayan-i vilayet)* had come to court *(meclis-i şer'e)*.

Infidel ships *(harbi kuffar gemileri)* came upon our villages, to the harbors *(liman)*, and to other places on the shores of Cyprus, causing great loss. They plundered the property *(emval ve erzaklari)* and flocks *(tavarlari)* of the re'aya, and they carried off and enslaved re'aya. The lands of Islam *(memalik-i Islamiye)* are not free from attack. They join with infidels who wish to bring destruction to the island and the state. Many martyrs *(şehid)* are made and many slaves taken. I order that . . . you should bring order . . . (159/57 (10); undated)

Organization of Defensive Systems

Although such efforts obviously found only limited success, the imperial government worked to organize a defensive system that would effectively resist the surprise incursions of pirates. Defensive efforts usually had to be made with small numbers of ships.

An imperial order was sent to Magosa district governor Şa'ban in response to a message delivered to the Porte by a man of present Cyprus governor *(begler begi)* Ca'fer. The Porte pointed out the necessity of bringing order *(hifz ve hiraset)* to the sea *(derya)*

... There are a total of four ships in your possession, counting your own galley *(kadirga)*. You are appointed leader and ordered to bring order to the island of Cyprus and its shores *(sevahil)*. I order that as in the past the aforementioned ships *(gemileri)* should be loaded with implements of war *(edevat-i harb)*. You must deal with the pirate ships *(korsan gemileri)*. (154/63 KPG 6/4–234 #107; undated)

The sort of problem was also discussed in an imperial order written to the governor of Cyprus in response to a letter from that same Şa'ban, who then was also commander of the fleet of the island *(kapudan-i cezire'-i Kibris)*.

The governor was urged, whenever all the sea around Cyrpu is not free of *(hali)* pirate galleys *(levend ve korsan kadirgalari)*, to bring security *(hifz ve hiraset)* to the lands *(memleket)*. Be on the sea *(derya)* in summer and winter. (162/60 (5) #348; undated)

In March 1574 an order was sent to Ic Il district governor in response to his own letter to the Porte about providing men from the castles *(hisar erlerin)* dependent on Ic Il. While the Porte recognized the strategic importance of places like Akce Kal'e, it still had to order sending to Istanbul certain of the weapons from those palaces (161/71 (26) #38; 16 Zil-Kade 981).

Tarsus district governor sent a letter to the Porte informing it that certain weapons taken from Ic Il for use by Tarsus spahis were never registered *(mukayyed)* (161/71 (27) #768; 17 Zil-Kade 983 (17 February 1576).

In response to a letter received from the governor of Cyprus Ahmed regarding the deposition *(takrir)* of the imperial fleet, an order dated September 1579 was sent from the Porte to the Rhodes district governor urging him not to neglect *(gaflet)* the infidels.

You should carefully search out infidel ships *(gemilerin)* and those in alliance with them *(yekdil ve yekcihet)* ... You should always be aware of the infidels ... (137/69 (2): 20 Receb 987)

Ahmed bn Ca'fer beg of the sons of spahis *(sipahi oglanlari)*, and timar holders *(erbab-i timar)* Gazanfer, Mehmed bn Karaca, and *(illegible)* were banished to Cyprus, but during an 'infidel scare' *(kuffar havfi)* they were confined to Rhodes castle. Now, in August (?) 1588, according to an imperial order addressed to

Rhodes district governor Receb Paşa, they must be sent to Cyprus. (122/98 (44) #512; 10 Ramazan (?) 1588)

An order of 1591 to the Rhodes district governor that pirate ships *(korsan gemileri)* had again come and that with the district governors of Sigla (?), Mytilene (Midillu), and Magosa he is charged with defense . . . They should gather at Rhodes and go in defense of the sea . . . (roll #5, #185, undated (999?)

Although the "Jailer-Captain" is a work of fiction from the last quarter of the 17th century, some half-century after the terminus of this study, it reflects faithfully the problems of piracy which Cyprus endured. The scene is the pirate-infested eastern Mediterranean, alive with pirate ships of diverse origins who often preyed on each other, seizing one another's prizes, or enslaving crews. One pirate ship from Tunis fell upon a Christian vessel from Cyprus carrying a cargo of hides, vinegar, wool, and cotton but refrained from plundering it when its captain provided intelligence of an impending circumcision party in a village just inland from Magosa, where 15 or 20 high officials and rich agas were sure to appear. At that time the vessel had a crew of 53 Muslims and only 17 Christians, although clearly some Muslims were only superficially converts to Islam who feigned to be Christians if it suited their circumstances. Obviously many Cypriot villagers and even townspeople, especially those near the sea, were vulnerable, for it has been demonstrated how many lived in great insecurity at least from the 1590s to the 1730s.

During all that time opportunities existed for profiting through illegal dealings with pirates. Most booty only had value if it could be sold; the sooner it could be disposed of, the more quickly the pirates could strike again. The ability to sell plunder quickly and close at hand made it possible for pirates to flourish.

Since many of the pirates would not rob, murder, or plunder the homes of co-religionists, all but the most devout believers who fell into the hands of enthusiasts of other faiths would have been sorely tempted to pass themselves off as members of any appropriate faith. No doubt recent converts to Islam could do that with particular facility. That is a message of the "Jailer-Captain." Pirates of a particular faith might also be expected to treat with amelioration, or even to emancipate, crews of co-religionists whose vessels they subdued, just as they might enslave others. As the story indicates, the line between Muslim and Christian pirates was also often a fine one.[38]

Revolts and Uprisings

Evidence about local revolts in Cyprus in the period up to 1640 is sparse. Numerous claims of incidents may simply reflect widespread opinion that the Porte ruled by oppression and consequently must have incited revolts. Both locals with particular grievances and foreigners who occasionally wished to induce the rulers of their countries to intervene stressed popular readiness for revolt. The tactic adopted was to emphasize the wealth of Cyprus, the high proportion of Christians among the populace, and the small expenses necessary for success.

Of course Venice had the best claim to Cyprus of any European state. No one had to remind Venetians how profitable owning the island had proved. Whatever the vicissitudes of Ottoman power between 1571 and 1640, Venice's fortune was even more uncertain. By and large, Venice, which still had a profitable relationship with the Ottoman empire, had reason to believe that as time passed it was even less likely to recapture Cyprus than in 1573. However rapidly Venice's Levant trade may have withered from the 1620s on, it still boosted the Venetian economy. Indeed the only "serious" talk of Venetian dreams involved "renting" the island from the Ottoman empire for an annual fee which was larger than the empire was able to secure in taxes, because of Venice's supposed superior administrative skills.

One potential meddler in Cyprus affairs was the Medici state of Tuscany. The Medici dukes dreamed of becoming kings, and one way of achieving that would be to secure Cyprus and resurrect the Lusignan title. Although the rulers of Tuscany made considerable profits from the Levant by making Livorno a free port and by establishing there a pseudo-chivalric order, mostly of foreigners, which preyed on Muslim shipping, decades of quiet intrigue came to no avail. Certainly Tuscany lacked the resources to take on the Ottoman empire, even in cooperation with the crafty Druze emir Fahreddin, who from his base in the Lebanese mountains twice made himself autonomous of Ottoman power. (Other schemes of the Medici included seizing Jerusalem and much of Syria with the help of Fahreddin, who would then become independent of the Ottomans.)

The third state involved with revolts in Cyprus was the duchy of Savoy, which had dreams of grandeur similar to those of the Medici. Savoy, too, had claims to the Lusignan title "king of Cyprus" and aspired to that rank, but in the period 1571–1640 Savoy was far less likely even than the Medici to threaten the Ottoman empire in any way.

Venetians seem to have taken some sort of pleasure from claiming that Cyprus was much more wealthy under their rule than under Ottoman rule and that Ottoman rule was oppressive, leaving the people of the island, who had in general welcomed the beginning of Ottoman rule, in despair. Tuscany and Savoy also sought information about Cyprus; they heard that while the Muslim population was miniscule, the Christian populace would in a moment rise up and fight the Ottomans by themselves if only they had weapons. Part of the appeal made to the ambitious north central Mediterranean states, with quite limited resources, was that they would not have to carry the full burden themselves.

Evidence about their adventures is sparse, which probably indicates that they were of little substance, rarely rising above the level of being vague hopes. Similarly it suggests that between 1571 and 1640 revolt in Cyprus was never, or hardly ever, imminent. Probably nearly all of what is considered "revolt" was in fact local criminal activity.

Savoy and Ottoman Cyprus

In around 1600 Charles Emmanuel I, duke of Savoy (1580–1630), began to demonstrate an interest in advancing his family's century-old claim to Cyprus, an interest which persisted as long as he lived. The Lusignan queen Charlotte inherited the throne from her father John II (1432–1458) and assumed the rule immediately. Her husband Louis was from the ruling family of Savoy, which gave her some support after the Mamluk army had established by force as king her illegitimate brother James II (1406–1473). Charlotte refused to surrender the title, and in 1462 made a formal agreement with the duke of Savoy that the title would pass to his family if she died without heirs. In 1485 she formally relinquished her title to the kingdom of Cyprus, which she had only ruled for two years. The ruling family of Savoy was very eager to win the title of king; in 1488 grand duke Charles I unsuccessfully sought Mamluk recognition for his line.[39] As Hill has pointed out, even the settlement over Cyprus between Venice and the Ottoman empire on 7 March 1573 did not mean the cessation of scheming by those who fancied that they had rights to the Kingdom of Cyprus, or of efforts on the part of the Christian subjects of the Sultan to induce them to undertake expeditions against the island. Such efforts met with most sympathy from the Dukes of Savoy, who continued to cherish hopes of 'recovering' the Kingdom for something like a century after it was lost. Charles Emmanuel I seems at first to have entertained the design of submitting himself as a tributary to the Porte, and holding the island as the Sultan's vassal.[40]

The rulers of Savoy badly wanted a royal title.

Negotiations took place between agents of Charles Emmanuel I and the Orthodox archbishop of Cyprus about the duke's intervening by sending a force of 3000 or 4000 men. Then the local Christians were to rise up, massacre all the Turks, and welcome the duke as their ruler. Such negotiations continued all through 1601 when, for unknown reasons, they ceased.[41] Perhaps inadvertently, the first agent, Francis Accidas, became acquainted with the Orthodox patriarch of Jerusalem. The locals sorely underestimated the numbers of Muslims, and probably also the supposed readiness of the Greek Orthodox people to rebel. In 1583 a Cypriot in exile had advised the duke of Savoy to claim the right to be invested by the sultan with a fief, and the duke seems to have been credulous enough at least to have sent a special ambassador to the Porte.[42] In 1608 the duke of Savoy received further letters about the ripeness of the situation in Cyprus. This time he supposedly had contracts with the first recorded dragoman of Cyprus, Piero Guneme. According to Hill the duke ". . . by 1608 had spent more than 30,000 scudi in making gifts to such people, and defraying their expenses."[43] Similar letters reached the duke in October 1609 and April 1611.[44] In 1632 duke Victor Amedeus I of Savoy received a letter of appeal from the abbot of a monastery in Macedonia who claimed to be a nephew of the archbishop of Cyprus. That letter beseeched the duke to rescue Cypriots from Ottoman oppression with 25 warships, 25,000 men, and arms for 10,000 peasants. Again no actions followed, but the following year duke Victor Amedeus I proclaimed himself king of Cyprus, an act doubtless unnoticed by the Ottomans, although it infuriated Venice, which broke off diplomatic relations for 30 years.[45]

Tuscany and Ottoman Cyprus

Two important events of the 16th century prior to the Ottoman conquest of Cyprus helped determine the role that Tuscany played in the eastern Mediterranean: opening Livorno as a free port and founding the knights of St. Stephen. Livorno grew into a large city with a thriving sea trade, largely replacing Venice because it was opened to the English and Dutch ships which dominated more and more of the trade of the eastern Mediterranean starting in the 1580s, although that aspect of its development was almost exclusively in the hands of foreigners. The knights of St. Stephen, founded by Cosimo di Medici, were formally authorized to seize the ships and goods of any states which were not Roman Catholic. They were an international, multinational organization like the knights of St. John of Malta except that they were not so well disciplined. Operating out of Livorno, they considered themselves crusaders.[46]

According to R. C. Anderson changes came about in the nature of naval warfare. "Whatever the reasons, the naval history of the Eastern Mediterranean shrinks for some time to a mere chronicle of raids by the Turks on southern Italy and of isolated exploits by the rival Knights of St. Stephen and St. John." Indeed, in 1574 the grand duke of Tuscany gave up his official fleet, doubtless as too costly for him, but sold some of his galleys to the knights of St. Stephen.[47] In 1575 the four Tuscan galleys in the Levant barely escaped the Ottoman fleet. In 1577 they cruised with the four galleys from Malta and "made a good profit from their captures."[48] By 1584 those four Tuscan galleys, still profitably cruising the eastern Mediterranean, had been joined by five galleys from Malta.[49]

On 2 February 1576 an imperial order was sent to the district governor of Rhodes (Rodos *begi*) informing him of destruction that the duke of Tuscany *(Filorvine dukasi)* did with four ships *(gemiler)*.

They are evil-doing pirates *(ehl-i fesad korsan-i kafir)*. He sends them to the land of Islam. They are not free from evil-doing *(fitne ve fesad)*. Last year they took ships *(gemiler)* in the districts of Egypt and Trablos . . . You should bring them to justice . . . (120/55 (5) #550; 2 Zil-Kade 983)

The first major endeavor of the knights of St. Stephen was a surprise night attack on the island of Chios in May 1599 by five galleys with about 300 men who at first seized the harbor, which then was retaken quickly by its Ottoman guard, who drove off the attackers with very heavy losses.[50] Interest in raiding held firm, and when a raid on Cyprus in May 1597 provided information that Christian slaves in Magosa had recently revolted, no doubt Cyprus began to appear ripe for attack.[51]

In 1602 Ferdinand I (1587–1609) of Tuscany purchased his first two sailing ships *(berton)*, the same year that Malta purchased its first one. By 1604 his fleet included several such ships. "As a matter of fact, the Grand Duke of Tuscany was equally ready to extend his patronage to almost any adventurer who proposed to act against the Turks."[52] In 1603 the grand duke of Tuscany, eager to advance himself economically and militarily in the Mediterranean, had established contact with an ambitious erstwhile Ottoman governor who was acting with increasing autonomy and expanding his authority in Syria.[53] In 1604 six galleys were sent not just to win booty but also to aid the rebels. Ottoman vigilance prevented an intended landing in the gulf of Antalya, but after they cruised around Cyprus and past Iskenderun (Alexandretta), they took some small prizes before returning home.[54]

In 1605 a Venetian named Raphael Cacciamari recommended to Ferdinand that he immediately occupy the Holy Land, and take the title king of Jerusalem. The project commenced in 1607, when a small Tuscan fleet embarked for Cyprus.[55]

Meanwhile, in May 1606 their squadron intercepted the "Alexandria caravan" off the south coast of Anatolia, taking much booty and 1000 prisoners. On 31 May they attacked Anamur castle, and on 16 June they took a caramursal near the castle of Finika.[56] Cyprus became a major interest of Tuscany, which not only had growing connections with Fahreddin the Druze emir but also with 'Ali Canbulad, who had established himself in the districts of Aleppo, 'Azaz, and Kilis, to the north of Fahreddin's territories. While the seven Tuscan ships sailed elsewhere in the Levant in the summer of 1606, the six galleys struck that part of the Anatolian coast which was part of Cyprus province.[57]

In 1607 ". . . Charles Emmanuel's rival, Ferdinand I (1587–1609), Grand Duke of Tuscany, conceived a plan for a grand expedition to the Levant, which would include in its objects the conquest of Cyprus. From Cyprus, if he conquered it, as a base he would be able to establish himself as ruler of Syria, where he had already entered into an alliance with Jambulad and the Emir of the Druses, Fahr ed-Din, who were in open revolt against the Sultan." With eight galleys and nine (or 10) galleons and a mixed army of 2200 soldiers, the Tuscan force under the Marquess Francis del Monte arrived at Magosa on 24 May expecting that 6000 Greek Orthodox Cypriots would revolt. According to Hill, the forces were "insufficient for his purposes," and the fortifications had been "improved." "The garrison had been reinforced by 400 Janissaries, and excellent order had been taken to keep the Greeks and other Christians quiet."[58] Moreover, the moment the Porte learned of the agreement, it crushed 'Ali Canbulad. Tuscany was powerless to interfere.[59]

Ferdinand I, who requested a special investigative report from a well-known Norman corsair, was informed that his commanders had not performed well. A new attempt was recommended, in winter when nights were longer, but involving only 1700 soldiers and 800 sailors.[60] Also in 1607 Tuscan agents had tried to negotiate with Fahreddin an agreement that, if he aided them in conquering Damascus and Jerusalem, they would help him against his enemies.[61] By the time that report had come out the Tuscan expedition of 1608 had already sailed for the Levant under William de Bauregard with eight vessels. After visiting Tyre and Sidon, Fahreddin's ports, they came across an Ottoman convoy from Alexandria near Cape Kelidonya (Khelidonia) at the western edge of the gulf of Antalya, just beyond the frontier of Cyprus province. On 21 October 1608 they captured two large vessels and several smaller ones, of 42 Ottoman vessels, along with 700 prisoners and two million ducats.[62]

The year 1607 was a bad year for grand duke Ferdinand's erstwhile allies in Syria. Janbulad's forces were crushed on 24 October 1607. Fahreddin's territories were reduced to Beirut, Sidon, and Kisrawan. Cosimo II (1609–1621) immediately renewed his alliance with Fahreddin, but he dropped the plan to attack Cyprus.[63] Apparently the new grand duke refused to believe further reports of the difficult conditions and readiness for revolt, for no further attempts were made to interest rulers of Tuscany for almost 20 years.[64] Raids to the east continued at least until 1610, when Beauregard and four galleons wintered in the Levant; the following spring he encountered an Ottoman fleet of 21 galleys and one galeass, losing heavily in the exchange. He reached Livorno in April 1611 with only 215 captives, having himself lost 400 killed or wounded. That was ". . . the last expedition of Tuscan sailing ships for some years."[65] At the same time, according to Guarnieri, another Tuscan force, under Guadagni, reached Sidon and reconfirmed in the name of the grand duke of Tuscany the treaty of commerce and alliance with emir Fahreddin. Subsequently that squadron raided along the south Anatolian coast, disembarking men who pillaged vigorously and exterminated many Turks. They also made an important action against the fortress of Girniye (Cerine) in Cyprus. Even the appearance of an Ottoman fleet with 43 galleys *(galere)* and three galeass did not discourage the knights, although they did return to Livorno in spring 1611.[66]

Nevertheless, expeditions of galleys to the Levant did not cease. The same J. Inghirami who led the 1605 expedition, and indeed was commander of the Tuscan galleys between 1602 and 1623, commanded an expedition to the Levant in 1613. His six galleys, which he temporarily joined with four Maltese galleys, made an unsuccessful attempt to land near the island of Samos (Sisam). Then Inghirami separated his force when he "heard that a large sum of money from the tribute of Cyprus was at Agha Liman on the mainland north of that island." Although he took the place on the night of 17 May, along with two Ottoman galleys, the losses were heavy and the booty "disappointingly small."[67] Thereafter Tuscany was not interested in Cyprus.

Interest in the Levant continued, however, particularly the commercial relationships which had been established with Fahreddin. Tuscany was unable to give Fahreddin any protection. Finally, an attack by Ottoman land and sea forces forced the Druze emir to flee for his life. Fahreddin passed five years in exile, mostly in Florence, where he unsuccessfully plotted his return supported by Latin Christian armies—all to no avail. He only returned to Lebanon in 1618, after he successfully persuaded Ottoman officials to allow him to take the provinces of Nablus and 'Ajlun. So no longer did he get Latin Christians involved with Cyprus.[68] Interest in Cyprus did not die out completely, for in 1628 a local Cypriot named Maximilian Tronchi urged grand duke Ferdinand II that 10,000 Christians and 8000 Turks and renegades were ready to revolt, that the island had no fortifications of consequence ready, and that 10,000 men, 20 ships *(navi)*, and 6 galleys could, with arms for the Christians, subdue the island.[69] For whatever it is worth, however, for the first time in many years (because they had been busily involved in the central and western Mediterranean and North Africa) six Tuscan galleys toured the Levant, although with no successes.[70] Probably that expedition was not unconnected with the letter of Tronchi.

Popular Revolt or Brigandage?

George Hill carefully chronicled every so-called uprising concerning which he discovered even the weakest evidence, but still treated them with a touch of sanguinity.

> The history of the abortive revolt was to repeat itself many times; a series of appeals by the Cypriotes to the western Powers, with optimistic but unconvincing calculations of the degree of support which would be forthcoming from the Christian population in the case of an invasion; and, consequently, unwillingness of those Powers to involve themselves in speculative undertakings, or, if they did so, to equip them efficiently.[71]

Kyrris, on the other hand, thinks the revolts have higher, even symbolic meanings. He considers them numerous: "As for the uprisings, which occurred frequently, almost every decade between 1572 and about 1670, they were organized by both and carried out by the Christian armed forces of the island—mainly Greek, but also including some remnants of Albanians, Armenians, Italians and Maronites, especially those settled on the north coast and mountain range . . ." "The basic characteristics of that transitory age were a fluidity in ethnic, religious and administrative concepts and institutions and an oscillation between Christianity and Islam, collaboration and revolt against the Ottoman regime in 'secret' contact with Western states. . . . So an element of symbiosis between the remnants of the still Christian old ruling classes and the conqueror was converted into an element of friction which in fact involved the moslemized section of the former."[72]

Kyrris feels that the more stalwart elements of the society demonstrated their vitality by revolting and by plotting with European foreigners. "As for the revolts and uprisings which occurred in the first hundred years of Ottoman rule they were instigated by a section of the muslimized and non-muslimized old ruling classes playing a double game and by some western powers, and in fact reflected an interesting struggle within the ranks of the mixed ruling classes of the island."[73]

Since not everyone could stand the pressures of the new situation, those unable to resist converted to Islam and became crypto-Christians, mostly Armenians, Maronites, and Albanians in the northern mountain range and along the north coast, particularly at Tellyria, Kambyli, Ayia Marina Skillouras, Platani, and Kornokepos. "But their consciousness

remained 'Cypriote', rooted in the spirit of coexistence . . .", so no conflicts occurred between the Muslim and non-Muslim local population.[74]

To me, the internal situation seems to have been rather quiet. Although popular feeling may sometimes have supported insurrection,
there is precious little evidence of any successes. Indeed, in a period
characterized by insurrection in the contiguous areas of Anatolia and
Syria, when first religious students, then demobilized soldiers, and finally
thousands of villagers revolted en masse and when thousands more
participated in "a great flight" to Istanbul and Ottoman Europe, Cyprus
seems almost a model of decorum, although the people still faced destruction from the incursions of pirates.

One of the more puzzling revolts took place in 1578. Venetian agents,
according to Hill, instigated a number of disgruntled janissaries to join
in a revolt with the Greek Orthodox Christians. Governor *(begler begi)*
'Arab Ahmed Paşa was killed by his own soldiers, whom he reportedly
had brutalized and neglected to pay.[75] Later janissaries killed the newly
dispatched governor as well. Finally, although the janissaries mixed in
with the Christians, raised flags of Spain, Venice, and the pope, and
notified the governor of Crete, their appeals received no response and
the revolt collapsed.[76] Unfortunately little is known of that revolt. 'Arab
Ahmed Paşa was district governor of Rhodes at the time of the conquest
of Cyprus; after Lepanto when Kilic 'Ali Paşa was transferred from
Algiers to command of the fleet, 'Arab Ahmed took the governorship of
Algiers.[77]

Another cause of revolts, according to Kyrris, was the devşirme levy.
He says: ". . . the threat of imposing the *devshirmé* or tithe in young
boys made life desperate for the *reayas*." He refers to devşirme levies in
1570, 1580, 1606, 1609, 1611, etc., which were very unpopular.[78] It is
difficult to find authentic sources for this, since no devşirme levies at any
time are mentioned in Cyprus in standard studies.[79] Moreover, by the
1580s use of the devşirme had been dramatically reduced by introducing
first sons of janissaries and then free Muslims into the corps. Hill alludes
to the threat of the devşirme levy but not to its actual use.[80] Since no one
has found any Ottoman archival references to such a levy, its existence
is highly unlikely.

Kyrris also mentions revolts by "Greco-Albanian captains" like Petros
Renessis in 1590, Jeronymos Erelessa in 1613, and Petros Aventanios in

1606–1613, which all were abortive because western states did not provide arms and supplies.[81]

The supposed alarm in Magosa when a few ships appeared in 1572 and were feared to be the vanguard of a Christian fleet, which influenced the Ottoman garrison to make terms with the local people, then put on Cypriot clothes, and flee to Lefkoşa, for which Kyprianos is the only source, seems rather unlikely.[82]

Although the fleet of Habsburg Sicily was not ordinarily of consequence to Cyprus, for about a decade it made summer cruises to the Levant. In 1616 occurred what Anderson calls "the first regular fleet action between galleys and sailing ships." Six ships from Sicily with 191 guns passed by the north side of Cyprus, searched in vain for prey at Baf and Limassol, but found 10 merchantmen anchored at Larnaka and took six of them. Five Ottoman pirate ships (corsairs) took refuge in Magosa harbor. The ships then returned to near Cape Kelidonya, where they encountered the Ottoman fleet of 55 galleys with some 250 or 300 (presumably smaller) guns. In the three-day fight which ensued, the Sicilian ships experienced heavy casualties, although they lost no ships; 10 Ottoman galleys were badly damaged and perhaps 20 disabled.[83]

It is difficult to decide how much credence to give these claims, for seeking outside assistance is a perfectly normal way to try to change any situation which one does not want. The complaint of three people from Baf might epitomize the complaints of the entire island. However, it might also reflect only the feelings of three people with grudges and so tell nothing at all about local circumstances. The people who sent letters to Savoy or Tuscany, or Spain or Venice have their own self-interest which they are looking after. If they really sought outside intervention, probably they would minimize the size and capability of the Ottoman military forces, and even the size of the Muslim populace, while exaggerating the numbers and military prowess of the Christians and others who had grievances.

When Dandini, a Venetian, visited Cyprus in 1596, he was on an intelligence-gathering operation for the Papacy, which still supported crusades. Probably the central purpose of his embassy was to establish contacts with the Maronites and their patriarch; he even met with Maronites in Lefkoşa. He returned with a report that there were only 12,000 or 13,000 "Turks" on the island, and most were converts who had converted to preserve family property and social influence, "... so that it seems an easy matter to recover this isle from under the tyranny of the Turks, and re-establish it in the Christian faith, for the renegadoes could no sooner see the Christian soldiers, but they would throw off their turban, and put on hats instead, and turn their arms against the Turks."[84] Dandini, however, did not know Greek or Turkish and so found himself at a real disadvantage in trying to understand local circumstances. Since he represented the islamophobe Papacy, his visit had to be concealed. While he was doubtless a pious and wise man, he was at the mercy of his guides to explain whatever he saw. It would be surprising if the element of the local population most favorably disposed to an anti-Ottoman Latin Christian crusade did not seek him out and influence his perceptions. No doubt Dandini had the ability and determination to prepare an accurate account of conditions in Cyprus if he were given information in a clear and unbiased way.

Of course all observers had their limitations.

Venice and Ottoman Cyprus

An imperial order of 18 January 1572 to the governor of Cyprus required the execution of an infidel named Propavlo and his followers for their secret dealings with Venice. Whether or not this can be "scheming by those who fancied that they had rights to the Kingdom of Cyprus ...," however, is questionable. Although both Hill and Kyrris suppose that this involves a plot "for restoring the island to Venice ...", those men probably belong more in the class of brigands than rebels.[85]

A letter dated 21 January 1572 immediately followed which gives much more detailed information. Since the order was written only six months after the surrender of Magosa, and it involved a reply to an official letter from the head of the volunteers *(gonulluler agasi)* of Baf, a rugged mountainous province where enemy soldiers could safely have taken refuge, it hardly seems likely that any kind of revolt was going on. Pero Pavlu and some other infidels dependent on him did make a rebellion *(fesad ve şena'at)* and caused harm to captain *(kapudan)* Filibo and to other wandering Latins *(gezer Firenkler)*. Indeed it seems that they made a secret contract *(mu'amelesi hifzen; 'akd-i bey'; 'akden mu'amelesi)* with some Venetians which interfered with the livelihoods *(kar ve kes-*

blerinde) of some re'aya. The Porte wanted increased precautions *(ziyade ihtiyat)* taken about the livelihoods of re'aya.

Although a sizable Venetian minority lived in Cyprus at the time of the Ottoman conquest, in the first years of Ottoman rule when their position was ambiguous, when security of both life and property was in doubt, many left Cyprus. Likewise, many Cypriots left the island. C. Kyrris observed: "It is well known that a considerable number of Cypriotes emigrated to Venice or Venetian territory or elsewhere in Europe previous to, during, and following the Ottoman conquest of Cyprus (1570–71)."[86] Eventually they were assimilated into Venetian culture, although they did "maintain close connections" with Cyprus. According to Kyrris, "many" were in professions: law, medicine, teaching, theology, copying, art, the priesthood; others were in banking and shipping.[87]

The Knights of St. John of Malta and Cyprus

The knights of St. John were, by mid-16th century, an ancient order. Founded in Jerusalem prior to 1080 as a hospice for pilgrims, the order won prestige during the crusades, first as a hospital and then ultimately for fighting. When it was chartered as an independent order by the papacy in 1113, it was charged to care for the poor and sick. Gradually it became involved in military activities, especially after 1206. Headquartered first in Jerusalem, then in Acre until its fall in 1291, and then in Limosa, Cyprus, their conquest of Rhodes at the beginning of the 14th century offered the possibility of autonomy.[88] Until 1522, when they surrendered to besieging Ottomans on terms of being allowed to evacuate the island with their weapons, the knights acted as pirates against Muslim shipping in the Levant—something they did with great success because of Rhodes' excellent harbor and even more because of its position astride major sea-lanes.

In about 1531 the knights of St. John established themselves in Malta, where they took up the same calling that they had followed at Rhodes. Even at the end of the 16th century they still were recruited exclusively from nobility and still took vows of chastity and obedience. Most of the recruits were from France, and economically and politically the order depended increasingly on France, which sometimes embarrassed France in its relationship with the Ottoman empire.[89]

The grand master issued "privateering commissions to individual knights." Such corsair ships sailed "under the flag of the order subject to an impost of nine per cent of the booty captured." Apparently "noble birth" was the only requirement, for they do not seem to have behaved any less reprehensibly than the other Mediterranean pirates. Neither Muslim lives nor property were safe from their relentless plundering. According to P. Cassar, "piracy attracted the most restless and turbulent characters among the knights who, under the pretext of defending the Christian faith, ranged the Mediterranean to pillage and plunder."[90] John F. Guilmartin viewed the order with deep skepticism: "Were the Knights of St. John of Rhodes and Malta crusaders, or pirates? A good case can be made for either. The same sort of consideration applies to the ghazi seafarers of North Africa . . ."[91] According to P. Earle, ". . . particularly in the early seventeenth century they behaved very like corsairs, if not pirates, in their rampages through the seas of the Levant."[92]

While the Ottoman navy disdained the use of sailing ships, Malta developed a particularly effective tactic of using a galley and a ship in coordination. The ships, which were fitted out for five years at a time, could attack summer and winter. The ships of Malta permitted smaller crews than those of Barbary; they were of heavier construction because of their extra dependence on gunnery and artillery, although their speed was correspondingly diminished. Despite their advantage in firepower, the ships could not equal galleys with oars for velocity in a quick chase, nor enter shallow water. When a ship and a galley worked together, the galley might tow a becalmed sailing ship. Except for the inability of the galleys to function during the stormy winter, that was an effective plan.[93]

Muslims and Muslim property were their only legitimate prey, so often they used French and other European ships for security. Also use might be made of Greek Orthodox vessels to conceal Muslim property. Greek shipping was harassed by the knights of Malta, and sometimes Greeks would act in deceit about transporting Muslims and Muslim cargo; sometimes Muslims would pretend to be Greek Orthodox. In any case, legal appeals might be made to Malta or to Rome, although the chance was a long one.[94]

Pirates from Malta cruised into the Levant seas almost every summer, and wintering there was not uncommon for the ships. As R. C. Anderson said of 1588, "The galleys of Malta went on their usual raids in the Levant . . ." His by no means definitive tabulation of the actions by

Maltese vessels in the Levant include 1587 (5 galleys), 1589 (3 galleys), 1596, 1599 (5 galleys), 1601 (5 galleys, and that was the year they bought their first sailing ship), 1604 (3 ships), 1609 (ships), 1611 (5 galleys), 1612 (galleys), 1615 (5 galleys and 6 ships, indicated as their regular force "disturbing the Levant"), 1616 (3 galleys), 1617 (5 galleys), 1618 (3 ships, 2 galleys), 1621, 1624 (3 galleys), 1626 (6 galleys), 1630 (4 galleys), and 1634 (6 galleys).[95] As Guilmartin saw it, "The perpetual wars of the Knights of St. John on Muslim shipping and coasts (and almost anything else if times were lean) played a central part in the struggle between Habsburg and Ottoman at sea."[96]

Presumably such forces passed around Cyprus almost every year, even if sometimes they did not penetrate Cypriot waters. Often in the earlier decades they looked for the Alexandria caravan. Of course, through most of that period even larger forces from Istanbul and North Africa were causing similar distress in Italy. Sometimes Maltese vessels acted for part or all of a season in conjunction with other small naval forces from Sicily, the western coast of Italy, or Spain, but most agglomerations probably were formed in the central area of the Mediterranean, where Ottoman vessels were most feared.[97]

Summary

Magosa really had an excellent location as a naval base, for long distance trade, smuggling, and piracy. When the Ottoman government did not make much effort to turn it into a naval base, hard discussions must have occurred. Ultimately Magosa was virtually ignored as a port.

Because Venice had become so vulnerable to the Ottomans, despite the brief interlude which led to the Ottoman defeat at the battle of Lepanto, it is very difficult to conceive of any effective anti-Ottoman alliance in Latin Europe. The old Ottoman policy of encouraging long distance trade within all its realms had always been beneficial. The problems arising from dealing with the pirates and the failure to develop a fleet of sailing ships were the greatest obstacles that the Ottomans faced in the Levant, and especially in Cyprus. Ottoman vessels were less used for local commerce.

Smuggling enriched many different kinds of people, allowing them to make enormous profits. Trade continued to boom, which made possible the depredations. The main centers of piracy against the Ottomans were

Malta and Livorno. They had to find ways to dispose of the booty. Sometimes local people showed no hesitation in buying their booty, especially when attractively priced. Sometimes people involved were reticent, or even reluctant converts. Still others were interested in doing anything which would benefit themselves. Some pirates deftly stayed on good terms with certain local people, with whom they always traded. Whether city people or villagers, many developed lasting enterprises.

Frequently in Latin Europe, especially on the Italian peninsula, it was believed that, because of an imagined cupidity, or laziness, that Ottoman security was extremely lackadaisical, and so that provinces like Cyprus were easy prey. Venice was always eager to have Cyprus back. Partly connected with their desires to become kings, and partly because of other policies, dukes of Tuscany and dukes of Savoy manipulated ineptly to have Cyprus under their control. Any ideas of Savoy's getting Cyprus through generous payments, or even bribes, seems farfetched. Perhaps being totally blocked on all other fronts led to such a farfetched scheme. Perhaps partisans of Savoy worked for such a scheme, but absolutely nothing was ever achieved.

By the bold steps of making Livorno a free port and by establishing a new crusading order, the knights of St. Stephen, the Medici of Tuscany had certainly enhanced their position in the Levant. Soon Tuscany was too poor to support a regular navy of its own, but pirates from the Atlantic world found ample opportunities to enrich themselves there. Often alone, but also together with the knights of Malta, first using galleys, but then operating in conjunction with sailing ships, they advanced Tuscan interests, and even got some booty in their "holy wars." Efforts to cooperate with Druze leader Fahreddin were most hopeful, from the Tuscan point of view, but Fahreddin was not powerful enough to resist concerted Ottoman efforts. At least they got enough booty to make the scheme profitable; easy prey in the wide Levant seas encouraged them.

One of the most difficult tasks for a historian is to judge to what extent people reported as ready for revolt actually were. Usually such people turn out not to be really oppressed, unhappy, or ready to revolt. To what extent were large numbers of people taking every opportunity they could find to oppose local government officials? Even the very important revolt involving provincial governor ʿArab Ahmed Paşa is too little known to make any proper judgments. It is difficult to guess what part of the population might have joined such revolts.

Some Venetians of Cyprus, along with their dependents, returned to Venice, or to different Venetian possessions, where some at least were successful in trades and crafts, or more learned professions, while preserving certain of their old contacts with the island. The knights of St. John of Malta and the knights of St. Stephen, although legitimately entitled to interfere only with Muslim property, frequently acted beyond the limits of their charges. They often enriched themselves and others as well, especially against Orthodox Christians. Temporary desperation along with papal imprecations had influenced the Habsburgs and Venetians into an uneasy alliance. The Ottomans had shrewdly encouraged protégés, such as France, with Marseilles, Marrano Jews, Ragusa, England, or the Dutch, who benefitted from Ottoman protection.

Not just ship, but ship with cannon were the problem. Ottoman merchants increasingly had troubles, and frequently relied on foreign ships for security.

While Cyprus lost its preeminent role in the luxury trade of silks and spices under the Ottomans, trade in other cloths, especially the locally manufactured cotton cloth continued to be an esteemed part of trade and commerce. Cottons, especially cloth, wool and wool cloth, silk and silk cloth, olives, olive oil, grapes, wine, raisins, carobs, and salt continued to be important local products after the Ottoman conquest. Wheat and barley remained highly esteemed.

Much attention was devoted not only to repairing old fortresses like Magosa, Lefkoşa, and Girniye, but new ones were established in Baf, Limosa, and Tuzla. They were part of the policies designed toward resisting pirates. Many, but by no means all, people would spare the lives of co-religionists; but a large body of the people readily embraced Islam or Christianity if it would save their lives, or often only their property.

Although the Ottomans may have disdained sailing ships in some ways, they always gave great importance to artillery, including naval artillery. The artillery of their galleys was always the match of that of other galleys. The problem grew as sailing ships increased the size of their artillery.

NOTES

1. Ottoman chronicles mention piracy as a reason for the attack on Cyprus. Among those of high quality and closest proximity to the events is Ibrahim Peçevi (1574–1649), who asserts that there was no way to maintain peace with the Venetians in 1570 (978) because brigands from Cyprus always were attacking Ottoman ships, travelers, merchants, and pilgrims going to Egypt. *Tarih.* Istanbul, 1283. v. 1, pp. 486f. That view is followed by Katib Çelebi (1609–1658) in his naval history, who mentions the interference of pirates *(bu cezire eşkiyasindan),* particularly from Mesine (Messina) and Malta. *Tuhfet ul-Kibar fi Esfar l-Bihar.* Istanbul, 1329. p. 95. According to Muneccim Başi (Derviş Ahmed efendi) (d. 1702) there was no way to keep the agreement that Sultan Suleyman had about Cyprus because infidel ships violated it by attacking and plundering Ottoman ships. *Sahaif ul-Ahbar.* tr. Nedim beg. Istanbul, 1280. v. 3, p. 523. The chronicler Selaniki (d. 1599), a contemporary of the conquest, takes the line that the invasion of Cyprus was prompted directly by local plundering of the property of Selim, while still a prince, when a vessel bearing property of his was forced to take refuge there from a storm. *Tarih.* Istanbul, 1281. p. 100.

Apparently the devastation was not all one-sided, however, for in his book of the sea (1521) in which he gives a detailed description of the Mediterranean littoral, Ottoman admiral Piri Reis describes the island as a very wealthy place of 7000 villages, which have now been reduced to 4000 because ships of the padişah have begun to reach there. *Bahrije,* Berlin, 1926. v. 1, p. 769.

2. *Ottoman Empire,* p. 41.

3. L. von Pastor, *The History of the Popes,* v. 18, pp. 63f, 258f, 353f, 368, 441. v. 19, pp. 323, 326. v. 22, pp. 145f, 148. (Some believed that Sixtus might lead a crusade in person.) On several occasions there were diplomatic efforts aimed at involving the Safavid empire. See also v. 25, pp. 363, 365f.

4. L. von Pastor, v. 18, p. 13. Spain opposed alliances against the Ottomans in 1566, fearing they would antagonize France and the German Protestants, while making conditions in the Low Countries more difficult.

5. John F. Guilmartin, *Gunpowder and Galleys. Changing Technology and Mediterranean Warfare at Sea in the Sixteenth Century.* Oxford, 1974. pp. 206f.

6. I. H. Danişmend, *Izahlı Osmanlı Tarihi Kronolojisi.* Istanbul, 1948. v.2, p. 414. There was also a cruise in 1573. See A. Hess, "The Battle of Lepanto and its place in Mediterranean history," *Past and Present* 57.1972.53–73. According to Hess the Ottoman strategic position in the Mediterranean improved between 1569 and 1571 despite the loss at Lepanto. p. 62. Cf. A. Hess, *The Forgotten Frontier. A History of the Sixteenth-Century Ibero-African Frontier.* Chicago, 1978. pp. 90f, 92f. Cf. Ibrahim Peçevi, v. 1, pp. 449f. Although Ottoman chroniclers differ greatly about the number of

Ottoman vessels at the battle of Lepanto in 1571, they all stress the fact that the Ottoman fleet replaced all its losses and sailed out on time the following spring with a fleet that the enemy were unwilling to confront. It is true that Ibrahim Peçevi maintains that the Ottoman fleet also was unwilling to confront the enemy on account of what happened the previous year. The history of the Rumanian Demitri Cantemir, based on Ottoman sources, asserts, however, that Kilic 'Ali Paşa vigorously attacked the enemy fleet until nightfall necessitated their separation. Selaniki, *Tarih*, pp. 104–107. Peçevi, *Tarih*, v.1, pp. 499f. Katib Çelebi, *Tuhfet ul-Kibar* ..., pp. 95f. Muneccim Başi, *Sahaif ul-Ahbar*, v. 3, pp. 528–530. Demetrius Cantemir, *The History of the Growth and Decay of the Ottoman Empire.* tr. N. Tindal. London, 1734. pt. 1, pp. 223–226.

7. Ottoman trading policy shifted Venetian trade from Syria to Cyprus. In 1450 Mamluk Syria was the main point of Venetian trade, Cyprus "of secondary importance." During 1558–1560, however, after Syria was almost half a century under Ottoman rule, Venetian vessels made "almost no clearances" for Syria; nearly all then went to Cyprus. F. C. Lane, "Venetian Shipping during the Commercial Revolution," in *Venice and History. The Collected Papers of Frederic C. Lane.* Baltimore, 1966. pp. 37f. According to Lane, Venetian trade beyond the Adriatic "probably" was the greatest ever in the mid-16th century. On the Papacy's view of Venice's special interests in the Levant, see L. von Pastor, *The History of the Popes*, v. 19, pp. 332, 344. Cf. v. 22, pp. 148, 273f, where it is suggested that Venice may up to a certain degree even support the Porte in claims against Christendom. Clement VIII, however, wanted Venice secretly to betray the Ottomans. Cf. J. F. Guilmartin, *Gunpowder and Galleys* ..., p. 21. "To Venice protracted war with the Ottoman Empire meant certain economic ruin which could hardly be balanced by strategic and territorial gains."

8. Hess suggests that, if Cyprus had fallen more easily, they might have shifted more to the western Mediterranean. A. Hess, "The Moriscos: An Ottoman Fifth Column in Sixteenth-Century Spain," *AHR* 74.1968.16 n. 60. Guilmartin stresses the importance to the Ottomans of the heavy losses they experienced in the conquest of Cyprus and the battle of Lepanto, particularly the "traditionally trained manpower." That, he argues, caused the "end of the golden age of Ottoman power at sea." *Gunpowder and Galleys* ..., pp. 251f. The spread of heavy bronze artillery also required changes in fortifications, of both of which Venice had become master by the 1530s. *Gunpowder and Galleys* ..., pp. 253, 260. Costs of cannon soared, and sieges became much more difficult. Elsewhere Guilmartin reveals that the improvements in artillery toward the mid-16th century increased the firepower of galleys but, since larger vessels were needed, their speed and maneuverability were reduced. *Gunpowder and Galleys* ..., p. 221. By 1600 the "great fleets of war galleys were in decline and their ports were beginning to decay." *Gunpowder and Galleys* ..., p. 1. G. Hill's detailed description and analysis of Venetian application of the new principles of

artillery and fortification at Lefkoşa and Magosa is excellent. v. 3, pp. 844–849 (Lefkoşa), pp. 850–886, 990–993, 1135f (Magosa).

9. According to Tenenti, English and Dutch ships *(bertoni)* were especially formidable against Mediterranean galleys because of the 20 or 30 cannon which they carried when engaged in piracy. Their high sides made it difficult to consider ramming and boarding them, the typical Mediterranean galley tactics. Indeed, their high sides actually concealed whether the ship was devoted to commerce or heavily armed for fighting, until a galley was already within the range of its artillery. For a number of reasons the Venetians did not build sailing ships, so by 1615 Venice was "very frequently forced to rely on foreign ships, even for Levantine trade." Alberto Tenenti, *Piracy and the Decline of Venice 1580–1615.* tr. J. & B. Pullan, Berkeley and Los Angeles, 1967. p. 55. Nevertheless, by the end of the 16th century nearly all Mediterranean pirates had adopted sailing ships. pp. 53ff, 64ff, 128ff, and *passim.* Guilmartin particularly emphasizes the impact of the "heavy and powerful" cannons. *Gunpowder and Galleys . . . ,* p. 39. Heavier artillery, however, required heavier galleys, which were more expensive to build, and more marines and rowers. p. 266. The galleys still had the advantages, however, of precision in movement and ability to come close to the shore. pp. 81, 97.

10. Richard Pococke, *A Description of the East* (1738), in John Pinkerton, *A General Collection of the Best and Most Interesting Voyages and Travels . . . ,* London, 1811. v. 10, p. 592; also in C. D. Cobham, *Excerpta Cypria,* p. 268. Van der Nijenburg (early 18th century), in Cobham, p. 247, says: "This renders everything cheap here, so that vessels frequently put into Cyprus to take in provisions for their voyage." Cf. Mr. Robert, *Adventures and Sufferings amongst the Corsairs of the Levant* (1696), in William Damier, *A Collection of Voyages.* London, 1729. v. 4, p. 172.

11. Braudel says: ". . . when there were no merchant vessels, there were no pirates." Prosperity in the Mediterranean continued at least until 1648. "One is bound to conclude that piracy cannot have had the disastrous results described or suggested by the chorus of contemporary accounts and complaints, since this prosperity endured despite the increased threat from corsairs. There was in fact a close connection between trade and piracy: when the former prospered, privateering paid off correspondingly." *The Mediterranean . . . ,* p. 883. It ". . . required a market for its spoils." p. 870. Mediterranean piracy increased after 1580, asserts Braudel. p.873. For him piracy is ". . . simply another form of agression, preying on men, ships, towns, villages, flocks; it meant eating the food of others in order to remain strong." p. 869. For Tenenti one of the great strengths of the English and Dutch sailing ships after they entered the Mediterranean between 1575 and 1580 lay in their combining trade and piracy: ". . . their originality lay in their merchantmen being as fully equipped for war as for trade." They also were "more ruthless and dangerous than any others." *Piracy and the Decline of Venice . . . ,* pp. xvi, 61, 83. Tenenti, too, points to an increase in

piracy in the Mediterranean; he feels it proliferated in the first two decades of the 17th century pp. 43f, 52. Venice at that time was the least able of any of the naval powers to resist piracy. pp. 107ff. For Guilmartin piracy was "the central fact of her existence." *Gunpowder and Galleys* . . . , pp. 82f.

12. See R. C. Anderson, *Naval Wars in the Levant, 1559–1853.* Liverpool, 1952. pp. 65f, 79, 86, 122ff. A. Tenenti, *Piracy and the Decline* . . . , pp. 29, 34, 40f, 48. Peter Earle, *Corsairs of Malta and Barbary.* Annapolis, 1970. pp. 144, 149, 162, 138. Earle points out that even under Ottoman rule Christian pirates often found refuge in Cyprus. Cf. Andreas Tietze, "Die Geschichte vom Kerkermeister-Kapitan, ein Türkischer Seeräuberroman aus dem 17. Jahrhundert," *Acta Orientalia* 19.1943.152–210. P. Masson, *Histoire du Commerce Français dans le Levant au XVIIe siècle.* Paris, 1896. p. 394, regarding the 17th century. Cf. F. Braudel, *The Mediterranean* . . . , pp. 149, 153. "The Levant was easily the most rewarding hunting-ground for Christian privateers." A "steady stream" took "rich prizes" on the Rhodes-Alexandria route. v. 2, p. 875. The 15th-century chronicler Makhairas observed that the Mamluk empire endured similar piratical depredations from Cyprus. *Recital concerning the Sweet Land* . . . , v. 1, pp. 629ff.

13. Fr. Jerom Dandini, *A Voyage to Mount Libanus; wherein is an account of the Customs and Manners, &c. of the Turks. Also, a Description of Candia, Nicosia, Tripoli, Alexandretta, &c.* (originally in Italian), in John Pinkerton, *A General Collection of the Best and Most Interesting Voyages and Travels* . . . London, 1811. v. 10, p. 301. The Dutch traveler J. Somer (1591), however, reported being troubled there by "Turkish" pirates. *Beschrijvinge* . . . Amsterdam, 1649. p. 7.

14. Pedro Teixeira, *The Travels of Pedro Teixeira.* tr. W. Sinclair. London, 1902 (Hakluyt). pp. 136, 139f.

15. *Travels.* London, 1615. pp. 92, 209.

16. In Cobham, *Excerpta Cypria* . . . , p. 215.

17. Jean de Thévenot, *Reisen in Europa, Asia und Africa* . . . Franckfurt am Mayn, 1693. pp. 52, 65, 161, 309f, 313f.

18. *Reizen van Cornelis de Bruyn Door de vermaerdste Deelen van Klein Asia, De Eylanden Scio, Rhodus, Cyprus* . . . Delft, 1698. pp. 377f.

19. Pococke reported that pirates infested the Karpas peninsula and made "constant depredations." *A Description of the East* . . . , v. 10, pp. 580f, 592; Cobham, *Excerpta Cypria* . . . , pp. 257, 269. The French traveler Tollot (1731–1732) reported that at Limosa two fires customarily were burned as people watched for pirates. Nevertheless, two Maltese ships had recently appeared there, landed 25 or 30 men, and carried off three ships full of wheat and other merchandise. Le Sieur (Jean Baptiste) Tollot, *Nouveau Voyage fait au Levantes années, 1731 & 1732.* Paris, 1742. pp. 218ff. Of course, it should not be thought that piracy was new to the Ottoman period, for it was frequently widespread prior to 1571. M. L. De Mas Latrie, *Histoire de l'Ile de Chypre.* Paris, 1852–55 (Famagouste, 1970) v. 2, p.

506. M. Margaret Newett, *Canon Pietro Casola's Pilgrimage to Jerusalem in the Year 1494*. Manchester, 1907. pp. 55, 212f, 216–219. S. N. Fisher, *The Foreign Relations of Turkey, 1481–1512*. Urbana, 1948. p. 54. Joseph Hacohen, *The Veil of Tears*. tr. Harry May. The Hague, 1971. pp. 110f. A. Hess, "The Moriscos . . . ," p. 15. I. H. Uzunçaşılı, "Kıbrıs Fethi ile Lepant (İnebahtı) Muharebesi sırasında Türk Devletile Venedik ve Müttefiklerinin Faaliyetine Dair Bazı hazinei evrak kayıtları," *Türkiyat Mecmuası* 3.1935.259f. S. J. Shaw, *History of the Ottoman Empire . . .* , v. 1, pp. 177f. G. Hill, v. 3, pp. 834f for Latin Christians, and p. 884 for Muslims, especially from Rhodes. A half-century before the Ottomans added Cyprus to their empire they had detailed and accurate information about all its harbors, watering spots, and fortifications, just as they did of their own coasts. Such maps and atlases could be used in naval warfare, for piracy, or even to counter enemy pirates. Piri Reis, *Kitab'i Bahriyye*. ed. Y. Senemoğlu. Istanbul, 1973.

20. "Venetian Shipping . . . ," p. 38.

21. *The History . . .* , v. 4, pp. 61ff.

22. Diamond Jenness, *The Economics of Cyprus. A Survey to 1914*. Montreal, 1962. pp. 59, 56, 76f, 89, 193.

23. *The Greek Nation, 1453–1669. The Cultural and Economic Background of Modern Greek Society*. New Brunswick, 1976. p. 273.

24. *Histoire du Commerce Français . . .* , pp. 393ff.

25. *A Voyage to Mount Libanus . . .* , pp. 277, 281.

26. *The Travels of John Sanderson in the Levant 1584–1602*. ed. Sir William Foster. London, 1931. p. 16, 130. On the salt see also J. Palerne (1581), who also mentions pitch, sugar, and carobs. *Peregrinations*. Lyon, 1606. pp. 327, 330. Somer also mentions carobs and fruits. *Beschrijvinge . . .* , pp. 10f.

27. *Travels*, p. 221. Olfert Dapper also regarded Cyprus cotton as the best in the Levant. *Naukeurige Beschryving der Eilanden in de Archipel der Middelantsche Zee*. Amsterdam, 1688. p. 92.

28. *The Travels of . . .* , pp. 132, 134f, 137. J. Zuallardo (1586) calls Larnaka the new export port. *Il devotissimo viaggio . . .* , Roma, 1587. pp. 90f. De Bruyn (1683) considers that place the residence of European merchants, most of who were French. *Reizen . . .* , p. 373.

29. *A Description of the East . . .* , v. 10, p. 592. Compare the early 18th-century observation of Van der Nijenburg, who asserted that Cyprus produced one-third more than it consumed. Cobham, *Excerpta Cypria . . .* , p. 247.

30. Braudel, *The Mediterranean . . .* , v. 2, pp. 875, 877.

31. Braudel, *The Mediterranean . . .* , v. 2, p. 877.

32. J. F. Guilmartin, *Gunpowder and Galleys . . .* , p. 23.

33. Guilmartin, *Gunpowder and Galleys . . .* , p. 81.

34. Guilmartin, *Gunpowder and Galleys . . .* , p. 97.

35. For examples of general piracy, see also 137/69 (43) #185; undated. 137/69 (LL) #119; 3 Sefer (?) 983 (14 May 1575). 120/55 (5) #550; 2 Zil-Kade

983 (2 February 1576). Roll #19, #336; 23 Ramazan 999 (July 1591). Fear at sea around Cyprus did not end in 1640, of course. For a striking parallel involving Knights of Malta, see Andreas Tietze, "Die Geschichte vom Kerkermeister-Kapitan, ein Türkischer Seeräuberroman aus dem 17. Jahrhundert," *Acta Orientalia* 19.1943.152–210.

36. Cobham, *Excerpta Cypria* . . . , p. 189; Antverbiae, pp. 95f. O. Dapper, *Naukeurige Beschryving* . . . , p. 45.

37. Cobham, *Excerpta Cypria* . . . , p. 244.

38. A. Tietze, "Die Geschichte vom Kerkermeister-Kapitan . . ." According to Tietze the story was written between 1673 and 1695. It is ". . . ein legendiges und treues Bild des türkischen Seefahrer und Seeräuberlebens im 17. Jahrhundert." The author is well informed about trade by sea and knows the conditions of the Mediterranean and North Africa; and it was not unusual for the captain and part of the crew of a galleon from Tunis to be Christian.

39. Hill, v. 3, pp. 548–586, 587, 611f, 614f.

40. Hill, v. 4, p. 37.

41. See Hill, v. 4, pp. 44–47. Kyrris, "The Role of the Greeks . . . ," pp. 156, 164, who mentions that two converts of 1570, Memo and Mustafa, would revert to Orthodoxy.

42. Hill, v. 4, pp. 41f; text in de Mas Latrie, v. 3, pp. 566ff, 570ff, 574ff.

43. Kyrris, "The Role of the Greeks . . . ," p. 164. "Cypriote Scholars in Venice . . ." p. 74. Hill, v. 3, pp. 41, 53f.

44. Hill, v. 4, p. 54; text in de Mas Latrie, v. 3, p. 576.

45. Hill, v. 4, pp. 56f. de Mas Latrie, v. 3, pp. 576f.

46. Cf. A. Tenenti, *Piracy* . . . , pp. xiii, 58, 85. See also pp. 17, 34f, 37f, 40ff, 53, 57, 93. In 1562 Cosimo I (1537–1574) had founded the order; throughout his reign he encouraged the development of Livorno. Francesco I (1574–1587) opened the port to pirates. See also F. Braudel, *The Mediterranean* . . . , v. 1, pp. 46, 122, 139; v. 2, pp. 870, 1148. After 1574 Tuscan galleys to the east increased. p. 877. Gino Guarnieri, *I Cavalieri di Santo Stefano nella storia Marina Italiana (1562–1859)*. 3rd ed. Pisa, 1960.

47. *Naval Wars* . . . , pp. 57f. G. Guarnieri, *I Cavalieri* . . . , *passim*.

48. R. C. Anderson, *Naval Wars* . . . , p. 58.

49. Anderson, *Naval Wars* . . . , p. 60. G. Guarnieri, *I Cavalieri* . . . , p. 117. Francesco Medici (1574–1587) tried to negotiate simultaneously with Portugal and the Ottoman empire in order to win control of at least one spice route. Braudel, *Mediterranean* . . . , v. 1, p. 570.

50. Philip Argenti, *The Expedition of the Florentines to Chios (1599) described in contemporary diplomatic reports and military dispatches*. (London), 1934. pp. x–xxii. G. Guarnieri, *I Cavalieri* . . . , pp. 129f. Anderson, *Naval Wars* . . . , pp. 65f. Interestingly, the advisers and instigators had oversimplified the situation and minimized possible opposition.

51. Tenenti, *Piracy* . . . , pp. 40f. They also heard of a revolt which supposedly occurred in June 1591. p. 165n.

52. Anderson, *Naval Wars* . . . , pp. 68f.
53. G. Guarnieri, *I Cavalieri* . . . , p. 123. K. Salibi, "Fakhr al-din," *EI*². Adel Ismail, *Histoire du Liban du XVIIe siècle à nos jours.* v. 1. *Le Liban au Temps de Fakhr-ed-din II (1590–1633).* Paris, 1955. pp. 48, 77 for commercial privileges and activities.
54. Anderson, *Naval Wars* . . . , p. 70. P. P. Carali, *Fakhr ad-din II principe del Libano e la Corte di Toscana 1605–1635.*
55. Ismail, *Histoire du Liban* . . . ; P. Carali, *Fakhr ad-din II principe del Libano e la Corte di Toscana* . . . Roma, 1938. v. 2, pp. 181f.
56. G. Guarnieri, *I Cavalieri* . . . , p. 137.
57. K. Salibi, "Fakhr al-din." R. C. Anderson, *Naval Wars* . . . , p. 71.
58. G. Hill, *A History* . . . , v. 4, pp. 48f. The explosives failed to open the gate and the scaling ladders were far too short. A Venetian source stated that the duke wished to conquer the island, claim the title king, and then either sell Cyprus to Venice or cede it to Spain for certain favors. An English source conjectured that he was flattered by his earlier successes, wanted a royal title, wanted to monopolize the cotton trade, or wanted to establish his knights of San Stefano there. Hill, v. 4, pp. 48f. R. C. Anderson, *Naval Wars* . . . , pp. 72f. An Armenian chronicler of limited credibility, Krikor of Taranagh, reported that the local Armenians, armed by the Ottomans, helped put down a Greek Orthodox revolt in 1606. Avedis K. Sanjian, *The Armenian Communities in Syria under Ottoman Dominion.* Cambridge, 1965. p. 163. Cf. Hill, v. 4, p. 50n. The Englishman William Lithgow, who spent a long period of time in Cyprus, wrote in the 1614 edition of his travels that Ferdinand had sent five galleons and 5000 soldiers. When the navy entered the wrong bay and were becalmed and discovered, Greek Orthodox Cypriots helped defend Magosa. He said that 400 Greek Orthodox of Baf did revolt but were massacred. *The Totall Discourse* . . . , p. 168. Hill, *A History* . . . , v. 4, p. 50. According to G. Guarnieri in *I Cavalieri* . . . , Don Antoni di Medici commanded the well-armed squadron of eight galleys *(galera)* and nine ships *(bertoni)* sent to conquer, while Conte Alfonso Montecuccoli commanded the landing force. Since the Ottomans had been informed in advance of the entire plan, they resisted and launched a counteroffensive. Nevertheless the *cavalieri* fought bravely and courageously. pp. 138f. Cf. G. Mariti (pub. 1769), *Travels in the Island of Cyprus.* ed. C. D. Cobham.
59. A. Ismail, *Histoire du Liban* . . . , p. 77; Carali, v. 2, pp. 168, 171.
60. G. Hill, *A History* . . . , v. 4, p. 50. G. Mariti, *Travels* . . . , p. 147.
61. K. Salibi, "Fakhr al-din."
62. G. Hill, *A History* . . . , pp. 50f. G. Mariti, *Travels* . . . , p. 148. G. Guarnieri refers to a magnificent victory. *I Cavalieri* . . . , pp. 139f. R. C. Anderson, *Naval Wars* . . . , p. 73. Anderson said de Bauregard had eight sailing ships; Hill and Guarnieri mention two galleons and six galleys.
63. G. Hill, *A History* . . . , v. 4, p. 51. K. Salibi, "Fakhr al-din."
64. G. Hill, *A History* . . . , v. 4, pp. 51f.

65. R. C. Anderson, *Naval Wars* . . . , pp. 76f. According to Guarnieri, the vessels had taken on water both in Cyprus and near Iskenderun (Alexandretta). *I Cavalieri* . . . , pp. 154f.
66. G. Guarnieri, *I Cavalieri* . . . , pp. 155ff, 159f. He reports the capture of 12 vessels, and the taking of 150 prisoners while killing 700 Turks.
67. R. C. Anderson, *Naval Wars* . . . , pp. 78f, 110f. Salvatore Bono, *I corsari barbareschi*. Torino, 1964. pp. 128–131. Guarnieri, on the other hand, says Inghirami returned in 1614 with 243 prisoners, after having freed 237 Christians. *I Cavalieri* . . . , pp. 137f, 124ff, 164.
68. K. Salibi, "Fakhr al-din." A. Ismail, *Histoire du Liban* . . . , pp. 54ff.
69. G. Hill, *A History* . . . , v. 4, pp. 51nf. G. Mariti, *Travels* . . . , pp. 148f.
70. R. C. Anderson, *Naval Wars* . . . , p. 113.
71. Hill, v. 4, p. 40.
72. "Symbiotic," p. 254.
73. "Symbiotic," p. 249.
74. "Symbiotic," pp. 255, 257.
75. Hill, v. 4, p. 39. Kyrris, "Symbiotic . . . ," p. 252.
76. He was a black slave, the protégé of grand vezir Sokollu Mehmed Paşa. Hill, v. 4, p. 39. *Calendar of State Papers*, Foreign, 22 June 1578 no. 32; 19 July 1578 no. 95. J. von Hammer, *Geschichte des Osmanischen Reiches*, Pest, 1829, v. 4, p. 45, from Ali and S. Gerlach, *Tagebuch*, p. 480. See Hill, v. 3, p. 963n for ʿArab Ahmed Paşa.
77. I. H. Danişmend, *Osmanlı Tarihi* . . . , v. 2, p. 397. Charles-André Julien, *History of North Africa. Tunisia, Algeria, Morocco*. tr. J. Petrie; ed. C. C. Stewart. London, 1970. p. 301. Algiers begler begi, 1571–1574. Peçevi lists him among well-known governors *(mir miran)* of Selim II, attributing his murder by the janissaries *(Kıbrıs kullari)* to vile fate. *Tarih* . . . , p. 446.
78. "Symbiotic," pp. 252, 255.
79. E.g., I. H. Uzunçarşılı, *Osmanlı Devleti teşkilatından Kapukulu Ocakları*, 2 v. Ankara, 1943, and B. D. Papoulia, *Ursprung and Wesen der 'Knabenlese' im osmanischen Reich*. München, 1963.
80. v. 4, p. 2.
81. "Symbiotic . . . ," p. 254.
82. Kyprianos, in Cobham, pp. 349. Hill, v. 4, p. 38. Hill also mentions the revolt of a Vittorio Zebeto, who killed a few Turks and fled. v. 4, pp. 54f.
83. Anderson, *Naval Wars* . . . , pp. 86ff.
84. J. Dandini, *A Voyage to Mount Libanus* . . . , p. 279. C. Kyrris, "The Role of the Greeks . . . ," p. 165.
85. Hill, v. 4, p. 38. Hill gives the date 7 February, but the Islamic date 2 Ramazan is indeed 18 January. Kyrris, "Symbiotic . . . ," p. 252.
86. ʿThe Cypriote Family of Soderini and other Cypriotes in Venice (XVI–XVII Centuries)," *Neo-Hellenika* 1.1970.58.
87. "Cypriote Family . . . ," p. 59. France was almost always the ally of the Ottoman empire and so rarely was involved in plotting against it. After 1631, however, Richelieu actively encouraged the pope to try to arrange a

crusade which would involve Tuscany, Savoy, and the Austrian Habsburgs. A. Ismail, *Histoire du Liban . . .* , pp. 94f.

88. Jonathan Riley-Smith, *The Knights of St. John in Jerusalem and Cyprus c. 1050–1310.* London, 1967. pp. 37, 38f, 40f, 43ff, 53, 198–226.

89. P. Earle, *Corsairs . . .* , pp. 100ff. Paul Cassar, "The Maltese Corsairs and the Order of St. John of Jerusalem," *Catholic Historical Review* 46.1960.141. He says Malta was given as a fief in 1530.

90. Paul Cassar, "The Maltese Corsairs . . . ," pp. 141, 151.

91. *Gunpowder and Galleys . . .* , p. 23.

92. *Corsairs . . .* , p. 106.

93. P. Earle, *Corsairs . . .* , pp. 133, 136. According to Guilmartin, English and French pirates began to use oared galleys in the new world because they could approach shore so easily with them, and then Spain transported galleys of its own there to protect its commerce and possessions. *Gunpowder and Galleys . . .* , pp. 81ff.

94. P. Earle, *Corsairs . . .* , pp. 112ff. Cf. P. Cassar, "The Maltese Corsairs . . . ," "All Christian vessels, except those sailing without the license of their government, were immune from assault by Maltese pirates . . ."; violators might be excommunicated. Likewise the property of Jews was to be respected. Although the case of Greek Orthodox Christians was complicated by their sailing under the "Turkish flag," their property was technically inviolable. Interestingly, English maritime commerce was considered "fair game" because they supplied the Barbary states with arms and goods. pp. 144ff. Braudel says that Spanish, Tuscan, and Maltese pirates "scoured" "merchant vessels" and seized "any merchandise belonging to Jews . . ." They also plundered property of Christians. *The Mediterranean . . .* , v. 1, pp. 641ff. Cf. v. 2, pp. 878, 880.

95. *Naval Wars . . .* , pp. 61, 62, 64, 65, 66ff, 69f, 75, 77, 78, 83, 85, 106, 110, 111f, 113, 114.

96. *Gunpowder and Galleys . . .* , p. 82. Braudel wrote that after 1574 Maltese pirates "virtually abandoned the Barbary coast to make expeditions into the eastern seas." *The Mediterranean . . .* , v. 2, p. 877.

97. Cf. R. C. Anderson, *Naval Wars . . .* , P. Earle, *Corsairs . . .* , John B. Wolf, *The Barbary Coast. Algeria under the Turks 1580–1830.* New York, 1979.

Conclusions

By the time that an extensive fragment of court records is available, within 25 years of the conquest (1593–1595), large numbers of women from Lefkoşa and the surrounding villages were active participants at the court. On the basis of the small fragment from 1580, probably that was true even then. The protection of Islamic law, particularly from their traditional protectors the kadis, was available to all women, even the Greek Orthodox majority for whom it was probably often not mandatory. Islam places great emphasis on personal and family morality. Islamic legists strove to make the law permeate the lives of all. Undoubtedly the Ottoman conquest revolutionized the position of women at least as much as it did the lower level of village serfs under Venetian rule.

Almost a quarter of nearly 3000 cases involved at least one woman. 65% of the time those women handled the matters themselves, in person at court, without legal agents. They could make serious charges of any kind against any man, and they were fully obligated to defend themselves in court against serious charges made against them. Women frequently served as guardians of minor children. They acted as legal agents, usually for other women but sometimes for men. Intermarriage of Muslim men and Greek Orthodox women was not uncommon, but never Christian men and Muslim women. Polygamy was almost unknown.

Women in Lefkoşa, and Cyprus, became important property holders. Twenty-two percent (84 of 378) land and property transfers involved women. They sold four times as much as they bought, because they accumulated through inheritance and dowries. As Islamic inheritance and marriage rules became more entrenched, and perhaps as women became more used to kadis, their share of involvement increased from 14% in 1593–1595 to 26% in 1609–1611 to 30% in 1633–1637.

As the society and economy of Cyprus developed under the influence of Ottoman institutions, the position of women was enhanced. The traditional system was oriented to providing women with a reasonable level of support, whether married, widowed, or divorced. Dowries had to be paid to women when they married, although the amounts varied greatly. Divorce was not uncommon, particularly in a form at the request of the wife (or by mutual agreement). Frequently women had to seek the support of the kadi to protect their property from men, but the court seems to have provided firm support or maintenance allowances necessary for their livelihoods, to secure their personal property, and to complain of physical violence of one kind or another.

Pious foundations are among the most important of Islamic institutions. They represent irrevocable donations in perpetuity for pious purposes which benefit the community. That included the building or maintenance of mosques, salaries of functionaries, or even regularly reading parts of the Koran for the soul of the deceased donor. The foundation had to have an administrator who was capable of carrying out the stipulations of the donor, even if they were complex, although it was permissible to stipulate that administrators of the foundations had to be chosen from among the descendants of the donor. Every aspect was under the close surveillance of the kadi of Lefkoşa.

Donations could be of land, buildings, or cash. Land, which was easiest to maintain, was rented to the highest bidder for short periods of time. Buildings such as shops, houses, or mills were rented to the highest bidder; they were less permanent than land, needing maintenance. Cash in Cyprus was lent for 10% to 20% annual interest, depending on the stipulations of the donor (which were vulnerable to the debasements of coinage that sultans were carrying out late in the 16th century and early in the 17th). Normally pious foundations were exclusively Islamic institutions, but sometimes, for reasons which are not specified, certain ones dedicated to and run by local Cypriot Christians were approved.

The courts seem to have determined that preserving the goals of the donor was even more important than slavish adherence to exact terms and conditions. When a house or mill was in ruins it was rented for a long time at a low rent on promise that the renter would then restore it. If the location of a rental house became undesirable, that house might be sold for another house or building which could then be rented more satisfactorily. Pragmatism and flexibility won out.

As with other Ottoman courts, the law enforced in the court of Lefkoşa was the Sharia, the sacred law of Islam. Even Christians and Jews used that court for important personal and business matters. The proceedings of the court were always explicitly noted as being in accordance with the Sharia. When people made claims about violations of their personal rights, they insisted that the Sharia be carried out. They criticized others acting contrary to the Sharia. The imperial government ordered that the kadis should not do anything contrary to the Sharia.

Neither ignorance nor inexperience were supposed to interfere in implementing justice, so everyone involved was encouraged to come in person. Legal agents were not a professional class, and when they were used it was in the absence of the person they were representing. Kadis were conceived to have a special obligation to protect widows and orphans. They were also protectors of women and non-Muslims. Kadis received the complaints made against tax collectors, military officers, and even other kadis, and they judged the veracity of written records, whether imperial, provincial, or private. Likewise they determined the relevance for real cases of the hypothetical opinions of muftis.

Zimmis had the same rights as Muslims in property ownership, making or refuting complaints, and taking oaths. Their most serious disability was that the testimony of two zimmi eyewitnesses against Muslims did not constitute sure proof, as it did with Muslims. Women had the same rights as men in property ownership, in making complaints, refuting complaints, and taking oaths. Their main disability was in limitations of their ability to serve as eyewitnesses against men, in inheritance, where they usually inherited half of what men did, and in marriage, where women have no right to divorce. Compromise, or reconciliations, was greatly esteemed in those cases where the right and wrong were not absolutely clear.

Based on the evidence studied, police power was not used arbitrarily in Lefkoşa and Cyprus. Voluntary compliance with summons was expected. If market inspectors, nightwatchmen, and chiefs of police acted effectively, they also were subject to the law of the state. In general, the privacy and sanctity of the home were highly esteemed, and police were most concerned with public violations, particularly in the area of moral law.

Both of the traditional Ottoman military corps, the janissaries and the spahis, continued to play important and useful roles in Cyprus. No longer an elite infantry corps restricted to the capital, between 800 and 1000 janissaries were stationed on Cyprus, a major budgetary expense. In Lefkoşa many acted as merchants and artisans, owned buildings, and lent money frequently. The spahi cavalrymen continued to be paid through the timar system, whereby the revenues of villages were assigned to them. Spahis who accumulated wealth did so as landholders rather than as artisans and merchants. Villagers could complain in court about their abuses, and spahis had to summon the recalcitrant to court. A large but diminishing proportion of both corps in Cyprus consisted of converts to Islam.

Recent studies have shown that many members of the Latin nobility of Cyprus found ways to preserve their family status. Many became Ottoman spahis, either by converting to Islam immediately, or by remaining as Christians for a brief time, becoming spahis nevertheless, and gradually become islamized. Alternately, they might pass as Orthodox and immediately find ways to attain high positions within that community. Few Latins lost their lives, contrary to earlier notions.

Priests and monks regularly used the courts, sometimes for religious matters, but most often for their business dealings, since most of them had to be self-supporting as Muslim imams, muezzins, and kadis were. Grape cultivation and wine production, which the Christians consumed and used in their liturgy, continued unimpeded, especially in the mountainous region of Baf, Limosa, and Larnaka districts.

Foreigners *(harbis)*, whether Latins or Franks were surprisingly integrated into the social and economic order and the legal system, despite the fact that virtually all other writings on the subject maintain that the class of foreign merchants and consuls operated exclusively within extraterritorial spheres. Having foreigners called "harbis" use the court in person and disposing of property is almost unique, but it probably indicates that the pressures which have previously been imagined for Latins to find security in a new legal identity in fact were not at all insurmountable. The practice found in Cyprus indicates that some foreign merchants and others of different nationalities did readily submit to the authority of an Ottoman court and obey its decisions.

Conversion to Islam has been one of the most controversial subjects in the study of this period. From a tabulation of the names of Muslims using the court at those three times, 34% were converts in 1593–1595, 24% in 1609–1611, and only 12% in 1633–1637, indicating that conversion had become exceedingly rapid within two decades after the Ottoman conquest, it had slowed down by at least a third within another 15 years, and by 1633–1637 the rate was two-thirds below that of 1593–1595. Certain foreigners reported that the conversion was not sincerely felt by masses of the converts, and that given the chance they would gladly return to Christianity. Conversion had to be registered at the court to make it legitimate, and to change the tax status of the converts officially, who then had more legal rights and were exempt from the head tax. Only a few scattered incidents of individual conversion, sometimes connected with marriage, have been found in the Lefkoşa court records, but at some point there must have been massive conversion that was not recorded or else there would be no way to explain the huge proportion of converts at large in the 1590s.

The Ottoman kadis of Lefkoşa were obligated to apply the same standard of justice for Muslims and for zimmis, and zimmis do not seem to have felt any qualms about consulting the kadis. Over a third (34%) of all of the cases studied involved at least one zimmi, and possibly that proportion had been increasing slowly. Close integration of Muslims and Christians in the social and economic order is evidenced by the fact that 56% of the cases involving zimmis were intercommunal. No markets or professions were reserved for specific groups, but rather all were open to anyone. Zimmis made complaints at court against the abuses of Muslims in the same way that Muslims complained about injustices done by zimmis. People of each religion sold land and even shops or houses to those of the other religion. Rather than consulting outside mediators, monks, or the Christian clergy, 44% of the cases involving zimmis involved other Christians as well, so they must have had some sort of confidence in the kadis and their courts.

Since we have no idea about the population of Lefkoşa, because there is no sound evidence showing the numbers of the Muslims, it is not possible to compare the proportion of Muslim and Christian users of the court with their proportion of the total population. Probably Christian zimmis made up 75% to 80% of the population of Cyprus, but since the number of Christians in Lefkoşa was so small and yet it remained a vigorous center of the island, Muslims probably made up well more than half (60%?, 70%). That is an unsettling factor in trying to compare the proportions of members of the different faiths in Lefkoşa.

Neither the Muslim population of Lefkoşa nor of the island contains any factions or segments into which it can be subdivided. The zimmis do have other elements to consider. In Lefkoşa, Armenian Christians, Maronite Christians, Latin Christians, and Jews probably made up at least 10% of the city's population, in that order of importance, although possibly the Latins were able to remain a large faction under the Ottoman rule. When considering the island as a whole, probably the Maronites were largest because of the existence of many of their villages; probably the Armenians and particularly the Jews had very little numerical strength outside of the capital; hardest to speculate is the numbers and residences of Latins, for much of the same reason as in the capital.

The usual Ottoman sources for detailed population registration in the 16th and early 17th century are sorely lacking for Cyprus, except for the one taken just after the process of conquest had been completed, when there were merely a handful of Muslims outside of the conquering armies. After that none of the later registers give information about the numbers or locations of Muslims. To make matters even worse, the figures that are given for non-Muslims, which usually concern payers of the head tax, lack the kind of precision and accuracy that one has come to expect from registers, often being rounded off to whole hundreds, or even thousands. Since Islam, through immigration and conversion, was very unequally spread throughout the island, one cannot conjecture that growth or decline of Christians in particular districts actually is paralleled by similar results among Muslims. Moreover, since widespread conversion to Islam was occurring at very different times and rates in towns and villages within those districts, there is no connection between the changing patterns of growth and decline of the Christians with those of the Muslims.

Lefkoşa and Magosa, especially the former, endured a terrible depopulating as a result of their tenacious resistance to the besieging Ottoman armies, leading to death, or to widespread enslavement. If the figures for the non-Muslims can be accepted as accurate, we may conjecture that the population grew by about 20% between 1572 and 1604, that it peaked at about 25% greater than in 1572 for about five years shortly after that, and then steadily dropped so that in 1612 it was less than in 1604. Declining slowly, in 1621 it still stood about 10% greater than in 1572. By 1623 it had dropped slightly below the level of 1572; by 1626 it had fallen to almost 15% below 1572 but stayed at that level until at least 1641. It grew a little between 1641 and 1647, but then by 1655 it had fallen by more than a third. The figure for 1656 was set at 25% below 1655, which means nearly 50% below 1572 and 1623. Beset by severe problems, the towns and districts showed erratic fluctuations in their numbers of Christian populace.

Although occasionally responding with healthful periods of growth, the populace of the island suffered intermittent demographic tragedies throughout the 16th century and the first half of the 17th century. No one can sort out the impacts of plague, malaria, and locusts, for they are so closely interrelated. Each, in its time, could make people more vulnerable to the others by weakening or sickening them. Sporadic oppressive rule under the Ottomans may occasionally have had dire effects on Cypriots, as Venetian rule frequently had, but such probably was the exception rather than the rule. Certainly there is no evidence that standards of public health or resistance to locusts changed after 1572, and between 1570 and 1650 the Venetians did not develop better ways to deal with those problems. Migration could not solve those problems. The immense loss of life resulting from the incursions of locusts, plague, and malaria required frequent recounts of the surviving population so as to reduce the numbers of taxpayers. From year to year tragedy threatened, bringing uncertainty to everyone.

Locusts darkened the skies. Governments required villagers to gather and turn into the local officials specified weights of locusts. Farmers regularly lost half or more of their grain because in most seasons locusts are just at the right stage of maturation for eating grain when it becomes ready for harvest. Hans Ulrich Krafft, a German seaman enslaved in the Mediterranean, who visited Cyprus several times between 1573 and 1587, gives a very precise description of their life cycle and breeding habits, adding that every Ottoman governor gave orders that each week every inhabitant must collect a sackful and burn it.

Plague, a disease of rats passed to humans by their fleas, rooted itself in the Middle East for centuries, leading to drastic reductions in numbers and then the impoverishment of society. From the mid-13th century to the end of the 17th plague struck at Cyprus with disastrous regularity. Almost any where on the island could be reached by plague, and it became endemic in several. Efforts were made to isolate victims and prevent their movements, and Magosa harbor often had travelers waiting for 40 days.

Earliest reports of malaria come at the very end of the 14th century, particularly at Magosa. Lefkoşa and Girniye were largely free of malaria, but Baf suffered sometimes. The dreaded centers of malaria were Magosa, Larnaka, and Limosa, the latter two in close proximity to salt lakes, and the former in an extremely marshy area.

As to population transfers, at first a cross section of the community was ordered. Volunteers were called for to occupy free land in Cyprus, where they would be exempt from taxes for three years, and Cyprus would be made a large, wealthy province including extensive lands in coastal Anatolia and Syria, and high quality migrants were to be recruited. Few people seemed inclined to go, and so more force was used. The policies followed by the Ottoman government suggest that probably not all elements in the government approved of the scheme. Numerous districts briefly assigned to Cyprus were reassigned to former places, the tax-free period was reduced to two years, and people who were suspected of being immoral or dishonest and then even criminals were banished to Cyprus.

Although the Ottomans had used forced population transfers very effectively in many places, for Cyprus that policy was a dreadful failure, a fact that has not often been appreciated. Unforeseen problems were encountered. Repeatedly the local officials had to deal with people who had escaped deportation by bribery or trickery or who fled from Cyprus after their arrival there. The hotter, more arid climate and unhealthy reputation of the island probably both were important factors working against the cooperation of those who received orders to move with their families. Orders to banish hundreds of criminals, when they became known, must also have contributed to the unpopularity of the place. Finally, there is evidence that many of the cooperative migrants died en route to Cyprus, or soon after they arrived.

Almost all of the intended forced migrants were Anatolian Muslims. Whether or not southern and western Anatolia were actually overpopulated is a moot point (certainly Christians constituted a tenuous minority there), but clearly Cyprus was seriously underpopulated. Rather than build up Cyprus with more Orthodox Greeks, the Ottomans would have benefitted more by introducing Muslim Turks into religiously homogeneous areas, as they had in the Balkans and in Trabzon. Likewise they would not have wanted to make the island exclusively Jewish. In any case, Joseph Nasi had had no special access to the sultan, and so could not have enticed the sultan to conquer Cyprus, and no Jewish migrants reached there. Virtually no Christians are listed among those transferred to Cyprus. Although one set of orders permitted executing people who refused to be moved, virtually all the orders talk about finding those who do not cooperate with the authorities and making sure that they arrive and stay there. Usually those who resisted faced no worse fate than being delivered to Cyprus. The moderation of that punishment certainly would not have discouraged recalcitrant people.

Slavery was a very important Ottoman institution. Many slaveholders adopted the practice of patronizing their slaves. Sometimes they did so by bestowing prestigious positions on them like administrators of pious foundations, but often they would emancipate the slaves, immediately or conditionally for a later time. Sometimes even when emancipated they preserved great loyalty for the families of their former owners. One of the important benefits from the Ottoman conquest of Cyprus was the emancipation of the large proportion of Venetian serfs who were practically slaves. Within a short time, virtually all of the agricultural slavery in Cyprus was ended, turning people into village cultivators whose status was at least equal to the more favored classes in the Venetian system.

It has frequently been asserted that Ottoman rule brought with it an immediate end to urban life in Cyprus, or at least severely reduced it to a low level. Contemporary observers and archival sources reveal, in fact, that the first seven decades of Ottoman rule brought little if any decline to urban life. Pilgrims, merchants, and other travelers give descriptions of the towns under Venice that remarkably parallel those under early Ottoman rule. True, the status of Magosa did change abruptly, and for the worse, under Ottoman rule when the Ottomans initiated the policy of changing it from its former role as an international port, but in that case the Ottomans implemented a policy which had been started even before Venetian rule began, of moving commerce out of Magosa because of health problems. Indeed Larnaka, which is closer than Magosa to Lefkoşa, had already found new users late under Venetian rule.

Little by little the Ottomans developed a policy which led to closing Magosa to foreign merchants and then even to local Christians. Precisely why they carried out this policy is very obscure but may be connected with the great cost in lives and money which went into taking that place. As sailing ships with heavy cannon, especially in English and Dutch ownership, took the initiative in the Mediterranean from the galley-using Mediterranean empires, the Ottomans seem to have been content to neutralize Magosa. Disease remained a crucial factor in all the towns, although Girniye and Lefkoşa had marginally better environments.

The Ottomans wisely and effectively managed the harbors of Cyprus. Magosa was extensively repaired and carefully maintained, but needed little in improvements. It remained a fine naval fortress. The other strong coastal fortress was Girniye, which had surrendered and so was left intact. A small new fortress was built in Baf, previously defenseless. Fortifications were also repaired and strengthened at Limosa, at least enough to provide more security from pirate attacks. Larnaka had its fortifications completely rebuilt by the Ottomans and became the leading commercial port on the island, and after a time, the residence of most foreign consuls and many foreign merchants. Larnaka greatly benefitted from Ottoman rule.

No substantial evidence was found about the religious or ethnic composition of the towns, but they all had large numbers of Christians and Muslims (the latter probably having a slightly disproportionate edge in towns, in comparison with villages). Tiny numbers of Armenian and Maronite Christians as well as unknown numbers of Latins and Muslims and Christian Gypsies lived in Lefkoşa. Latins were also involved in the trade of Larnaka. If other towns were not necessarily just Orthodox and Muslim, nothing is known about them.

Credit was a very important part of the economy of Lefkoşa and the rest of Cyprus, as is mirrored in the fact that 20% of all of the court cases studied involved it. Under the Venetians, credit was somewhat scarce and loans were regularly given at excessive rates. Under the protection of the Ottoman court, credit was regularly offered by and to a broad spectrum of people, not just merchants. Moderate profits of up to 20% per annum were legal. Small loans were most frequent, but occasionally merchants, members of the military, or of the religious class might give or receive very large loans.

It has often been wrongly imagined that Muslims do not give loans for interest, and that Christians predominate in business and commerce with Muslims, but the official Ottoman court had a kadi who was responsible for enforcing the Sharia, the religious law of Islam, and all of its actions were scrutinized as being in accordance with the Sharia. Some Islamic objections concern not "interest" but rather "excessive" interest. Money lending does not appear to have been the activity of a narrow group of very wealthy men. Borrowing does not seem to have involved desperately poor men, very few people got hopelessly into debt, and bankruptcy was quite unusual. As for the intercommunal credit, of 173 instances discovered, 135 were offered by Muslims to Christians whereas there only occurred 38 instances of Christians giving credit to Muslims.

Cyprus was a land renowned for its fertility and for both the diversity and wealth of its harvests because of its very favorable environment. Cyprus was immensely profitable to the Venetian empire, which introduced full-scale plantation agriculture in certain favorable places, first in sugar, and later in cotton. Ottoman rule brought quick relief to the cultivators from much of the oppression of the plantation system. As Braudel has pointed out, not only did the Ottomans unleash a social revolution in rural Cyprus but they did so without causing any decline in local living standards. Ottoman law and society were not elitist, but fairly egalitarian. Agriculturalists largely could grow the crops that they chose, under methods that they chose.

Ottoman policy favored the consumer, by encouraging low prices and by fixing prices that could be afforded. Maximum prices were set for foods, services, and crafts in conjunction with the vendors, under the supervision of the courts. Inspectors oversaw the markets and bazaars in Lefkoşa, to ensure fair business practices and prices. Considerable diversity existed, even though wheat and barley probably were the most important foods everywhere. A rich variety of fruits and vegetables were produced, especially grapes and olives. Sugar and coffee were very popular. Commercial crops like cotton, flax, and carobs were produced in many villages and extensive cotton and wool cloth industries flourished. A wide array of rental facilities served the people of Lefkoşa. Within Cyprus, most villagers had nearby towns or markets that were easily accessible, with their camels, mules, and donkeys, and certain townsmen went out to villages. Cypriot merchants frequently sailed to nearby ports in Anatolia, Syria, and Egypt, and merchants from all of those places could reach Cyprus easily by boats.

Cyprus had an ideal location for a naval base, for long distance trade, for smuggling, and for piracy. Lefkoşa could easily have been turned into an international trading emporium. The port of Magosa stood almost unique in the entire Levant. Cyprus truly enriched the Venetians, especially after it became their colony. It was not nearly as important for the Ottoman empire, for the Ottomans by that time controlled all of the land trade routes, and could have continued to bypass that island if necessary. Since the Levant trade contributed so much to the wealth of the Venetian empire, and since the Ottomans had come to control the entire Levant, and since the Ottoman empire was much more powerful, Venice depended absolutely on its good will. While the Venetians might provide a very good trading partner, in the late 16th and early 17th centuries the Ottomans might just as well have, and did, choose Marseilles, Ragusa, Marrano Jews, and English or Dutch Protestants; any enemy of the Habsburgs would do.

The conquest of Cyprus in 1570–1571 was the last and greatest Ottoman victory. Ottomans were on the offensive at every frontier, against Habsburgs, Venetians, and the Papacy in the Latin west. Important 16th-century advances in fortifications benefitted defenders, making sieges like those of Lefkoşa and Magosa frightfully costly in men and money. Nevertheless, the Ottomans were still unchallengeable at sea in galley warfare. However soundly their fleet may have been defeated at Lepanto, that did not affect Ottoman momentum in the Mediterranean. Cyprus was not threatened; Ottoman fleets did not suddenly lose their technical superiority; there was no change in the balance of power; and it did not lead to any advances on the Latin side. All of the galley-using states of the Mediterranean continued to use them. Venice paid huge reparations. The battle of Lepanto drained the Ottomans of wealth, vessels, and seamen, but only in a limited way.

Much more important to the Ottomans and to the balance of power in the Mediterranean was the new sailing ship. Only that led to drastic changes. Sailing ships of the English, very large, and armed with heavy, powerful cannon, and with their very great carrying capacities started having drastic effects in the region from the 1570s. By the 1590s the Ottomans were on the defensive; their fleet had declined in both quality and quantity. By 1595, English ships took over not just long distance but even domestic local carrying trade. Communications with Cyprus were endangered. Increasingly the islanders fell outside the mainstream of Levant commerce. Slowness of local Mediterranean states, particularly the Ottomans, to adopt ships undercut their preeminence, although that did not cost them any territories. Apparently the ship was not preferable in every way, however. The Habsburgs of Spain had a great fleet of sailing ships that they used in the Atlantic, but they persisted with galleys in the Mediterranean. Likewise, since Ottoman vassals in Algiers, Tunis, and Tripoli mastered the sailing ship at a very early time, and the Ottomans had hitherto been at the cutting edge in technical advances, so they must have consciously chosen to stay exclusively with galleys (which they even used in the Indian Ocean).

The 16th century was marked by great advances in world trade for both Venetians and Ottomans. Both practiced restrictive policies in Cyprus. Because of its fertility and the intelligent methods of cultivation, prices were quite low. The Venetians strictly imposed monopolies. The Ottomans also made restrictions on external trade, although only in a few goods. Ample trade in cotton, silk, salt, wine, olive oil, carobs, and grains all flourished. Besides Ottoman subjects, Venetians, English, French, and Dutch traded there. The Ottoman state implemented a system of low prices favoring the consumers.

So piracy and smuggling thrived. Smugglers, both Ottoman and foreign, could easily find isolated places to land in Cyprus, buy goods at local prices, and then a month or two later sell them for two, four, or 10 times as much in Latin or Protestant Europe. With the growth of piracy and smuggling, the best method was to build defensive fortifications. The Ottomans did that with aplomb, to resist surprise incursions of pirates. Since certain pirates and smugglers would not plunder or kill their co-religionists, some people were tempted to pass themselves off as the same faith as the pirates. The line between Christian and Muslim pirates sometimes was very thin.

Evidence of local revolts or uprisings before 1640 or 1650 is sparse. The Medici family, who wanted to be kings, worked to expand their power and influence in the Levant by establishing a free port at Livorno and by creating the order of St. Stephen to develop a fleet. None of their activities actually threatened the Ottomans or won and wealth for Tuscany, although if they had coordinated campaigns with the Druze emir

Fahreddin at the height of his power in Syria, they might have struck threatening blows against the Ottomans.

The duchy of Savoy also tried to claim the Lugsignan title of king, but despite all of their machinations, they did not strike a single solid blow against the Ottomans or for Cyprus. The Knights of St. John of Malta gave privateering commissions to individual knights, mostly of the noble class, from France. They were especially effective on Ottoman shorelines when they combined ships and galleys. Their annual cruises to Levant seas benefitted the Habsburgs.

Enemies of the Ottomans of all sorts speculated how Cyprus might be particularly open to revolt because of its great wealth, the high proportion of Christians, and the low cost of a revolt. In fact there is surprisingly little evidence of revolts in Cyprus at that time. Compared with the religious students, demobilized soldiers, and marauding villagers of Anatolia or Syria under Fahreddin and other rebels, Cyprus seems a bed of tranquility. Almost all of the so-called revolts seem to be known through single sources. Painfully little is known of the revolt against governor ʿArab Ahmed Paşa and his successor. Protests against devşirme levies never taken are perplexing. Venice did not really hope to regain Cyprus, despite secret talks. Some of the Venetian minority there did leave Cyprus for Venice after 1571. Venice, however, was falling behind faster than the Ottomans were.

Many foreigners had great difficulties understanding what was going on or what government policies were. Hardly any knew Turkish, although some had personal dealings with Muslims. Many did not know Greek either. Some were honest and sincere, others blindly prejudiced or ignorant or inexperienced. Even honest and sincere people can err.

In general, fairly good relations between Greek Orthodox and Muslims occurred. Of course that should not be considered surprising since observers of the 19th century have generally pointed to fairly positive relationships there. The existence of numerous crypto-Christians is easy to document from that time period. Possibly that community was established right from the very beginning in Cyprus, as some scholars have argued, and then continued as communities right down to modern times. However the evidence available for that is only partly convincing. It seems to me at least as likely, or slightly more likely, that the appearance of most of the crypto-Christians must be dated to later time periods, under different circumstances.

Part of the continuity that the Ottoman government provided allowed Cyprus to remain a central part of the Mediterranean world. In general, the same crops continued to be produced, and in the same places, only the system of landholding and cultivation changed, with the overthrow of serfdom. Cypriots continued to cultivate goods which had a strong demand outside of their island and to prepare artisanal products which also remained in demand. Merchants from Cyprus continued to seek their fortunes elsewhere in the Levant, and particularly the Levant trade. Merchants from Ottoman territories and the western Mediterranean continued to visit Cyprus, although the entry and thriving of merchants from Atlantic Europe did, of course, bring some striking changes.

Transition from Venetian to Ottoman rule in Cyprus was in general rapid and smooth. The provincial government was quickly fashioned into an effective institution. The new Ottoman government did not act heedless of concern for its new subjects but quickly established a different system of law and order and justice which better considered the long-term benefits of the people. Often that government acted effectively by making decisions which helped people through their troubles. Whether or not they were aware, practical benefits would accrue to the state through a flourishing treasury if circumstances were created which provided people with security so that they could thrive. Probably the Ottoman empire was much more favorably concerned about the well-being of the populace of Cyprus than its predecessor, the Venetian empire, or, for that matter the Lusignan family which Venice had overthrown.

Select Bibliography

Archival Sources

Ottoman judicial registers *(Şer' i mahkeme sicilleri)* from Lefkoşa are preserved in Lefkoşa at the Etnografya Müzesi and the Evkaf Dairesi.

Microfilm documents are in the Kıbrıs Türk Milli Arşivi in Girne. Although the archive holds virtually no original documents before the 19th century, the founder and director of the archive, Mustafa Haşim Altan, built the archive after having spent months on trips to Turkey, collecting materials on microfilm. Not only did he receive the full cooperation of archivists in Istanbul and Ankara, but he was also allowed to search on his own through uncataloged materials. He sought any document which had even the slightest relevance to Cyprus. Since Altan is a skilled Ottomanist and Arabist, and in recent years he has made similar trips to other libraries in Austria and Germany, virtually everything known can be found in a single place, Girne. This is a unique archive for anyone interested in Cyprus.

Aigen, Wolffgang. *Sieben Jahre in Aleppo (1656–1663).* ed. A. Tietze. Wien, 1980. Beihefte 10, Wiener Zeitschrift fur die Kunde des Morgenlandes.

'Ali, Mustafa. *Counsel for Sultans of 1581.* ed. A. Tietze. pt. 1. Wien, 1979.

———. *Mustafa 'Ali's Description of Cairo of 1599.* v. 120. Wien, 1975.

Amadi, F. *Chronique d'Amadi.* ed. R. de Mas Latrie. Paris, 1891.

Anglure, O. d'. *Le Saint Voyage de Jherusalem du Seigneur d'Anglure.* v. 52. ed. F. Bonnardot & A. Longnon. Paris, 1858. Anciens Textes Français. Le Saint Voyage de Jherusalem. (1360–1413).

——— (Oger, seigneur d'Anglure). pp. 430f in de Mas Latrie, v. 2. (Cyprus only).

———. *The Holy Jerusalem Voyage of Ogier VIII, Seigneur d'Anglure.* ed. & tr. R. A. Browne. Gainesville, 1975.

Anonymous Englishman (1344–1345). *Itinerarium ciuisdam Anglici Terram Sanctam et alia loca sancta visiantis* (1344–45). text, pp. 435–460, intro, pp.

427–434 in v.4 of P. G. Golubovich, Biblioteca Bio-Bibliografica della Terra Santa e dell'Oriente Francescano. Firenze, 1923. ser. 1 v. 4. On Cyprus, in Mogabgab, v. 2.

Arveux, Chevalier Laurent d., envoye extraordinaire du Roy, a la Porte, Consul d'Alep, d'Alger. Memoires. v.5, Paris, 1735, pp. 482–493.

Aysan, Emin. Kıbrıs Seferi (1570–1571). Ankara, 1971. Türk Silahli Küvvetleri Tarihi. IIIncü cilt, 3ncu kisim eki.

Barkan, Ö. L. *XV. ve XVI inci asırlarda Osmanlı Imparatorluğunda Zirai Ekonominin Hukuki ve Mali Esasları.* c. 1, Kanunlar. Istanbul, 1943.

Baumgarten, Martin von. *Martin á Bavmgarten in Braitenbach Peregrinatio in Aegyptum, Arabiam Palaestinam & Syriam.* Noribergae, 1594.

Beauvau, Henry de baron. *Relation Journaliere du Voyage du Levant.* Nancy 1619.

Belon, Pierre. *Les observations de plusieurs singularitez trouvées en Grece et autres pays.* Paris, 1555.

Biddulph, William. *The Travels of Certaine Englishmen into Africa, Asia, Troy, Bythinia, Thracia, and to the Black Sea . . .* London, 1609.

Bordone/Bordoni, Benedetto. *Libro di B. B. Nel qual si ragiona de Tutte l'Isole del mondo . . . Vinegia, 1528.* LXVI–LXVII.

———. *Isolario.* Venetia, 1534.

Boustronios, George. *The Chronicle of G. B. 1456–1489.* tr. R. M. Dawkins. Melbourne, 1964.

Bruyn, Cornelis de. *Reizen van Cornelis de Bruyn Door de vermaerdste Deelen van Klein Asia, De Eylanden Scio, Rhodus, Cyprus . . . Delft,* 1698.

Canaye, Philippe. *Le Voyage du Levant de Philippe du Fresne-Canaye. (1573.)* Paris, 1897.

Capodilista, Gabriele. *l'Itinerario di G. C. (1458.)* pp. 159–237 in I Cento Viaggi. v.4 Milano, 1966. Other one plate 33 p. 240 Famagosta, 34, Saline-dine color. ms. of Grunemberg, Gatha. Le Comte Gabriel Capodilista, gentil-homme de Padoue, on Cyprus, pp.76f inde Mas Latrie, v. 3.

Casola, Pietro. *Canon Pietro Casola's Pilgrimage to Jerusalem in the year 1494.* by M. Margaret Newett. Manchester, 1907.

Charriere, E. *Negociations de la France dans le Levant . . .* 4 v. Paris, 1848, 1850, 1853, 1860.

Chesnau, Jean. *Le Voyage du Monsieur d'Aramon, Ambassadeur pour le roy en Levant. (1547.)* ed. C. Schefer. Paris, 1887.

A Chronicle of the Carmelites in Persia and the Papal Mission of the XVIIth and the XVIIIth centuries. 2 v. London, 1939.

Clarke, Edward D. Travels in various Countries of Europe, Asia, and Africa. 3v. London, 1812, 1814, 1816. v. 2, pp. 307–358.

Cobham, C. D. *Excerpta Cypria.* Materials for a History of Cyprus. Cambridge, 1908.

Corancez, Louis A. Itinéraire d'une partie peu connue d l'Asie Mineure. Paris, 1816.

Cotovicus, Johannes (Ioanne Cootwijk). *Itinerarium Hierosolymitanum et Syriacum.* Antverpiae, 1619.

Dallam, Master Thomas. *Early Voyages and Travels in the Levant* I. *The Diary of Master Thomas Dallam 1599–1600.* London, 1893.

Damier, William (ed.). *A Collection of Voyages.* 4 v. London, 1729.

Dandini, Fr. Jerom. *A Voyage to Mount Libanus; wherein in an account of the Customs and Manners, &c. of the Turks.* Also, *A Description of Candia, Nicosia, Tripoli, Alexandretta, &c.* (1596, written originally in Italian), in John Pinkerton. *A General Collection of the Best and Most Interesting Voyages and Travels in all parts of the world.* v. 10, London, 1811. pp. 222–304.

Dapper, Olfert. *Naukeurige Beschryving der Eilanden inde Archipel der Middelantsche Zee.* Amsterdam, 1688.

des Hayes Courmenin, Louis. *Voiage de Levant fait par le commandement du Roy en l'année 1621.* Paris, 1624.

Drummond, Alexander. *Travels through different Cities.* London, 1754.

Elias of Pesaro. "Voyage éthnographique de Venise à Chypre." (1563.) ed. & tr. from Hebrew by Moise Schwab. *Revue de Geographie* 4.1879.206–228. Also in Cobham.

Fabri, Felix (Felix Faber). *Fratris Felicis Fabri: Evagatorium in Terrae Sanctae, Arabiae et Egypti Peregrinationem.* 3 v. ed. C. D. Hassler. Stuttgardiae, 1843, 1849. v. 2, 3, 4 in Bibliothek des Literarischen Vereins in Stuttgart. cf. of H. F. M. Prescott, *Friar Felix at Large, A Fifteenth-century Pilgrimage to the Holy Land.* New Haven, 1950. Almost complete translation of all but trip to Egypt & return to Germany by Aubrey Stewart. *The Wanderings of Felix Fabri,* in Palestine Pilgrims' Text Society, v. 7–10. London, 1887–1897/New York, 1971.

Gedoyn "Le Turc." *Journal et Correspondance de Gedoyn "Le Turc" Consul de France a Alep (1623–1625).* ed. A. Boppe. Paris, 1909.

Graziani, Antonio. *The History of the War of Cyprus.* (c. 1571.) tr. Robert Midgley. London, 1697.

Guarnieri, Gino. *I Cavalieri di Santo Stefano nella storia della Marina Italiana (1562–1859).* 3rd ed. Pisa, 1960.

Hacohen, Joseph (and anonymous continuator from c. 1575). *The Veil of Tears (Emek Habacha).* tr. Harry May. The Hague, 1971.

Hakluyt, Richard. *The Principal Navigations, Voyages, Traffiques & Discoveries of the English Nation . . .* Glasgow, 1903. extra ser. v. 1–12.

Harff, Arnold von, knight. *The Pilgrimage of A. v. H., knight from Cologne, through Italy, Syria, Egypt, Arabia, Ethiopia, Nubia, Palestine, Turkey, France and Spain, which he accomplished in the years 1496 to 1499.* ser. 2 v. 94. tr. Malcolm Letts. London, 1946.

Heyd, Uriel. *Ottoman Documents on Palestine 1552–1615.* Oxford, 1960.

Katib Çelebi (Haji Khalifeh). *The History of the Maritime Wars of the Turks.* tr. James Mitchell. London, 1831.

Katib Çelebi, *Tuhfet ul-Kibar fi esfar el-bihar*. Istanbul, 1329.

———. *Fezleke*. Istanbul, 1297.

Koçi Bey. *Risalesi*. tr. Zuhuri Danışman. Istanbul, 1972.

Krafft, Hans Ulrich. *Reisen und Gefangenschaft*. ed. K.D. Haszler. Bibliothek des Litterarischen Vereins in Stuttgart. v. 61 in 1861.

le Saige, Jacques. *Voyage de Jacques le Saige de Douai a Rome, Notre-Dame-De-Lorette, Venise, Jerusalem et Autres Saints Lieux*. (1518.) ed. H. R. Duthilloeul. Douai, 1851.

Lezze da Donado. *Historia Turchesca (1300–1514)*. ed. I. Ursu. Bucureşti, 1910.

Lithgow, William. *The Totall Discourse of the Rare Adventures & Painefull Peregrinations of long Nineteene Yeares Travayles from Scotland to the most famous Kingdomes in Europe, Asia and Affrica*. (1610.) Glasgow, 1906.

Locke, John (Lok). *The Voyage of M. John Locke to Jerusalem*, pp. 76–105, in *Hakluyt's Voyages*. (1553.) extra ser. v. 5.

Ludolf von Suchen (or Suchem). *Ludolphi, rectoris ecclesiae parochialis in Suchem: De Itinere Terre Sanctae*. ed. Ferdinand Deycks. Stuttgart, 1851. v. 25 in Bibliothek des Litterarischen Vereins in Stuttgart.

———. *Extraits du voyage en Terre-Sainte de Ludolphe, curé de l'église de Suchen en Westphalie, relatifs a l'ile de Chypre*. (1350.) pp. 210–217 in v. 2 of *de Mas Latrie*. Pretty complete translation by Aubrey Stewart, *Description of the Holy Land* in v. 12 Palestine Pilgrims' Text Society, London, 1895. (New York, 1971.)

Lusignan, Estienne de. Description de toute l'Isle de Cypre. Paris, 1580 (reprinted Famagouste, 1968). (Do not use the Italian original; use the expanded French version.)

Macarius, patriarch of Antioch. *Travels of Macarius*. ed. F. C. Belfour. 2v. London, 1836.

Makhairas (Machaeras), Leontios. *Recital concerning the Sweet Land of Cyprus entitled 'Chronicle.'* 2 v. ed. & tr. R. M. Dawkins. Oxford, 1932.

Mandeville, John. *Mandeville's Travels. Texts and Translations*. (after 1322.) 2 v. London, 1953. ed. Malcolm Letts ser. 2 v. 101, 102. *The Bodley Version of Mandaville's Travels* (and Latin text). ed. M. C. Seymour. Oxford, 1963.

Manrique, Sebastian. *Travels of Fray S. M. 1629–1643*. v. II ser. 2 v. 61. London, 1927.

al-Marginani. *The Hedaya or Guide: a Commentary on the Mussulman Laws*. tr. Charles Hamilton. Lahore, 1963.

Mariti, Giovanni. *Travels in the Island of Cyprus*. (1769.) ed. C. D. Cobham. Cambridge, 1909.

Martoni, Nicolas (Nicolai de Marthono). *Relation du Pélerinage à Jerusalem de Nicolas de Martoni notaire Italien (1394–1395)*, pp. 566–669 in v. 3, *Revue de l'Orient Latin* 3.1895. ed. L. Legrand. (Nicolai de Marthono, notarii: *Liber Peregrinationis ad Loca Sancta*.)

Mogabgab, Theophilus A. H. *Supplementary Excerpts on Cyprus or further materials for a history of Cyprus*. 3 v. Nicosia, 1941, 1943, 1945.

Muneccim başi Derviş Ahmed efendi. *Sahaif ul-Ahbar.* tr. Şaʿir Nedim efendi. Istanbul, 1285.

Newett, M. Margaret. *See* Casola, Pietro

Niebuhr, Carsten. *Reisebeschreibung nach Arabien und andern umliegenden Landern.* (1766.) v. 3. Hamburg, 1837.

Noe, Fra dell' Ord. D. S. Francesco. *Viaggio da Venezia al Sepolcro, et al Monte Sinai* . . . Lucca, (1700).

Novare, Philippe de. *Memoirs 1218–1243.* v. 10 ed. Charles Kohler. Paris, 1913.

Palerne, John. Peregrinations du S. J. P. Lyon, 1606.

Peçevi, Ibrahim. *Peçevi Tarihi.* ed. Murat Uraz. 2 v. Istanbul, 1968.

———. *Tarih-i Peçevi.* (1283.) 2 v. Istanbul, 1866.

Pietro della Valle. *Viaggi* . . . 4 v. (v. 4, about 1625.) Venezia, 1667.

———. *The Travels of Sig. P. D. V., a noble Roman* . . . London, 1665.

———. *Viaggi* . . . 2 v. Brighton, 1843.

Pinkerton, John. *A General Collection of the Best and Most Interesting Voyages and Travels in all parts of the world.* (1738.) 17 v. London, 1808–1811.

Piri Reis. *Bahrije: das türkische Segelhandbuch für das Mitellandische Meer vom Jahre 1521.* ed. & tr. Paul Kahle. Berlin, 1926.

———. *Kitabi Bahriye.* Istanbul, 1935.

———. *Kitab'i Bahriyye.* ed. Y. Senemoğlu 2 v. Istanbul, 1973.

Pococke, Richard. *A Description of the East, &c.,* in v. 10 of John Pinkerton, *A General Collection of the Best and Most Interesting Voyages and Travels in all parts of the world.* (1738.) London, 1811. v. 10 pp. 406–770.

Porcacchi, (Porcacchio) di Castiglione, Thomaso. *L'Isole Piu Famose del Mondo.* Venetia, 1572. (Four pages on Cyprus, with map.)

———. *L'Isole piu famose del Mondo.* Padova, 1620. (Greatly expanded, but still stops in 1575!)

Rauwolff, Leonart. *Aigentliche Beschreibung der Raiss inn die Morgenlaender.* Graz, 1971.

Report of the Great Invasion of Locusts in Egypt in 1815. Cairo, 1916.

Robert, Mr. Y. *Mr. Robert's Adventures and Sufferings amongst the Corsairs of the Levant: His Description of the Archipelago Islands, etc.* (in 1696) in William Damier, *A Collection of Voyages,* v. 4. London, 1729.

Sanderson, John. *The Travels of John Sanderson in the Levant 1584–1602.* ed. Sir William Foster. London, 1931.

Sandys, George. *Travels.* London, 1615.

Santo, Brasca. *Viaggio,* in Terrasanta. pp. 43–158 in *I CentoViaggi.* (1480.) Milano, 1966.

Sanuto, Marino. *I Diarii.* v. 6 ed. G. Berchet Venezia, 1881. v. 58 ed. G. Berchet, N. Barozzi, and M. Allegri. Venezia, 1903.

Sebalt. Röhricht, Reinhold & Meisner, H. (ed.). *Das Reisebuch der Familie Rieter.* (1480.) in v. 168 of Bibliothek des Litterarischen Vereins in Stuttgart. Tübingen, 1884.

Selaniki. *Tarih-i Selaniki.* Istanbul, 1281.

Sestini, Domenico. *Viaggio da Constantinopoli.* Yverdun, 1786.

Somer of Middleburgh, Jan. *Beschrijvinge van een Zee ende Landt Reyse, Naer de Levante als Italien, Candien, Cypres.* Amsterdam, 1649.

Sonnini, C. S. *Voyage en Grèce et en Turquie fait par ordre de Louis XVI, et avec l'autorisation de la cour ottomane.* 2 v. Paris, 1801. v. 1, pp. 55–109.

Strambaldi, D. *Chronique d'Strambaldi,* ed. R. de Mas Latrie. Paris, 1893.

Suriano, Frate Francesco. *Il Trattato di Terra Santa e dell'Oriente.* (1484.) ed. P. Girolamo Golubovich. Milano, 1900.

Sylvius, Aeneas. (Pius II): *Cosmographia* (1484.) n.p., 1509.

Tafur, Pero. *Travels and Adventures, 1435–1439.* tr. & ed. Malcolm Letts. New York & London, 1926.

Teixeira, Pedro. *The Travels of P. T. London, 1902 (Hakluyt).* tr. William Sinclair. *travels 1600–1601;* book, 1609. ser. 2 v. 9.

Thévenot, Jean de. *Reisen in Europa, Asia und Africa . . . Franckfurt am Mayn, 1693.*

Tietze, Andreas. *"Die Geschichte vom Kerkermeister-Kapitän, ein Türkischer Seeräuberroman aus dem 17. Jahrhundert," Acta Orientalia* 19.1943.152–210. Makale-i zindanci Mahmud Kapudan berayi feth u zafer-i keşt -i maltiz-i la⁶ in-i duzeh-mekin.

Tollot, Le Sieur (Jean Baptiste). *Nouveau Voyage fait au Levantes années, 1731 & 1732.* Paris, 1742.

Tucher, Hans, *Reise in das gelobte Land.* Augburg, 1486.

Tünçer, Hadiye. *Osmanlı İmparatorluğunda Toprak Hukuku, Arazi Kanunları ve Kanun Açıklamaları.* Ankara, 1962.

Verona, Jacobus de. *Le Pélerinage du moine Augustin Jacques de Vérone (1335),* pp. 155–302 in v. 3, *Revue de l'Orient Latin* (1895). ed. R. Röhricht.

Walther, Paul (Fratris Pauli Waltheri). *Itinerarium in Terram Sanctam et ad Sanctam Catharinam.* ed. M. Sollweck. 1482 Tübingen, 1892. Bibliothek des Literarischen Vereins in Stuttgart.

Zeebout, Ambrosius. *chaplain Voyage.* Ghent, 1557.

Zvallart, Jean, chevalier du Sanct Sepulchre. *Le tres devot voyage de Jerusalem, etc.* Anvers, 1661 (in 1608).

Modern Sources

Akdağ, Mustafa. *Celâli Isyanları (1550–1603).* Ankara, 1963.

———. Türkiye'nin İktisadi ve İçtimai Tarihi. 2 v. İstanbul, 1974.

———. "Osmanlı İmparatorluğunun Kuruluş ve İnkişafi devrinde Türkiye'nin İktisadi Vazıyetı," *Belleten* 14.1950.319–411.

Alastos, Doros. *Cyprus in History — A Survey of 5,000 Years.* London, 1955.

Alasya, H. Fikret. *Kıbrıs Tarihi ve Kıbrıs'da Türk Eserleri.* ikinci baski. Ankara, 1977.

Altan, Mustafa Haşim. *Kıbrısın Fethi.* Lefkoşa, 1974.

Altan, M. H., J. McHenry, & R. Jennings. Archival Materials and Research

Facilities in the Cyprus Turkish Federated State: Ottoman Empire, British Empire, Cyprus Republic", IJMES 8.1977.29–42.

Ambraseys, N. N. "The Seismatic History of Cyprus," *Revue de l'Union Internationale de Secours* 3.1965.25–48.

———. "Value of Historical Records of Earthquakes," *Nature* 232.1971.375–379.

Anderson, R. C. *Naval Wars in the Levant, 1559–1853.* Liverpool, 1952.

Ankori, Zvi. "From Zudecha to Yahudi Mahallesi: The Jewish Quarter of Candia in the Seventeenth Century" (A Chapter in the History of Cretan Jewry under Muslim Rule). In Salo Wittnayer Baron Jubilee Volume. Jerusalem, 1974, v. 1, pp. 63–127.

Argenti, Philip P. *Chios Vincta or The Occupation of Chios by the Turks (1566) & their Administration of the Island (1566–1912).* Cambridge, 1941.

———. *The Expedition of the Florentines to Chios (1599) described in contemporary diplomatic reports and military dispatches.* (London) 1934.

———. *The Occupation of Chios by the Genoese 1346–1566.* Cambridge, 1958.

Ashal, C. and Ellis, Peggy E. "Studies on Numbers and Mortality of Field Populations of the Desert Locust (Schistocerca gregaria Forskal)." *Anti-Locust Bulletin* 8. London, 1962.

Ashtor, E. *A Social and Economic History of the Near East in the Middle Ages.* Berkeley and Los Angeles, 1976.

Aslanapa, Oktay. *Kıbrısda Türk Eserleri.* Lefkoşa, 1978.

Aymard, Maurice. *Venise, Raguse et le Commerce du Blé pendant la seconde moitie du XVIe siècle.* Paris, 1966.

Barkan, Ö. L. "Les déportations comme méthode de peuplement et de colonisation dans l'empire Ottoman," *Revue de la Faculté des Sciences Economiques de l'Université d'Istanbul* 11.1949–1950.67–131.

———. "Osmanlı Imparatorluğunda bir Iskân ve Kolonizasyon Metodu olarak Vakıflar ve Temlikler" I. "Istilâ devirlerinin Kolonizatör Türk Dervişleri ve Zavıyeler," pp. 278–353. II. "Vakıfların bir iskân ve kolonizasyon metodu olarak kullanılmasında diğer şekiller," pp. 354–386. *Vakıflar Dergisi* 2.1942.

———. "Osmanlı Imparatorluğunda bir Iskân ve Kolonizasyon metodu olarak Vakıflar ve Temlikler," *VD* 2.1942.279–386. "Les fondations pieuses comme méthode de peuplement et de colonisation," *VD* 2.1942.59–65.

———. "Osmanli Imparatorluğunda bir Iskân ve Kolonizasyon metodu olarak sürgünler," *I.Ü.* Iktisat Fakültesi Mecumuası. 11.1949–1950.523–569.

———. "Social and Economic Aspects of Vakifs in the Ottoman Empire," Gabriel Baer (ed.) International Seminar on the Muslim Waqf. Jerusalem, 24–28 June 1979.

Barkan, Ö. L. and Ayverdi, E. H. *Istanbul Vakıfları Tahrir Defteri 953 (1546)* Tarihli. Istanbul, 1970.

Baynes, N. H. and Moss, H. St. L. B. (eds.) *Byzantium. An Introduction to Eastern Roman Civilization.* Oxford, 1962.

Bedevi, Vergi H. "Kıbrıs Şeri Mahkeme Sicilleri Üzerinde Araştırmalar" Milletlerarasi Birinci Kibris Tetkikleri Kongresi (14–19 Nisan 1969). Türk Heyeti Tebligleri. (The First International Congress of Cypriot Studies.) Ankara, 1971, pp. 139–148.

———. "Tarih Boyunca Kıbrıs-Anadolu Ilişkilerine Genel bir Bakış. Lefkoşa, 1978.

Benzoni, Gino. (ed.) Il Mediterraneo nella seconda metà del '500 alla luce di Lepanto. Firenze, 1974.

Berki, Ali Himmet. "Hukuki ve Içtimaî Bakımdan Vakıf," VD 5.1962.9–13.

Bilmen, Ö. N. Hukuki İslamiyye ve Istılahatı Fıkhıyye Kamusu. 8 v. Istanbul, 1967–1970.

Blouet, Brian. The Story of Malta. London, 1972 (1967).

Boase, T. S. R. (ed.) The Cilician Kingdom of Armenia. New York, 1978.

———. "Ecclesiastical Art," in A History of the Crusades, K. M. Setton (ed.) v. IV: The Arts and Architecture of the Crusader States, Madison, 1977, pp. 165–196.

Bono, Salvatore. I corsari barbareschi. Torino, 1964.

Braudel, Fernand. The Mediterranean and the Mediterranean World in the Age of Philip II. tr. Sian Reynolds. New York, 1976.

Bruce-Chwatt, Leonard J. and de Zulueta, Julian. The Rise and Fall of Malaria in Europe. A Historico-epidemiological Study. New York, 1980.

Buckler, Georgina. "Women in Byzantine Law about 1100 A.D.," Byzantion 11.1936.391–416.

Çağdaş, Cevdet. Kıbrısta Türk Devri Eserleri. Lefkoşa, 1965.

Cahen, Claude. "Dhimma," EI. 2nd edition.

Carali, P. Paolo. Fakhr ad-din II principe del Libano e La Corte di Toscana 1605–1635. 2 v. Roma, 1936, 1938.

Carayon (S. J.), August. Relations Inédites des Missions de la Compagnie de Jésus à Constantinople et dans le Levant au XVIIe siècle. Poitiers & Paris, 1864.

Cassar, Paul. "The Maltese Corsairs and the Order of St. John of Jerusalem," Catholic Historical Review. 46.1960.137–156.

Cezar, Mustafa. Osmanlı Tarihinde Levendler. Istanbul, 1965.

Cohen, Amnon and Lewis, Bernard. Population and Revenue in the Towns of Palestine in the Sixteenth Century. Princeton, 1978.

Cook, M. A. Population Pressure in Rural Anatolia 1450–1600. London, 1972.

Çuhadaroğlu, Fikret and Oğuz, Filiz. "Kıbrıs'ta Türk Eserleri/Turkish Historical Monuments in Cyprus," Rölöve ve Restorasyon Dergisi 2.1975.1–76.

Danişmend, Ismail Hami. Izahlı Osmanlı Tarihi Kronolojisi. v. 1: 1258–1512. Istanbul, 1947. v. 2: 1513–1573. Istanbul, 1948. v. 3: 1574–1703. Istanbul, 1950.

Dannenfeldt, Karl H. Leonhard Rauwolf: Sixteenth-Century Physician, Botanist, and Traveler. Cambridge, 1968.

Darkot, B. "Kıbrıs," I. A.

Delatte, Armand. Les Portulans Grecs. Paris, 1947.

Dempster, J. P. "Observations on the Moroccan Locust (Dociostaurus maroccanus Thunberg) in Cyprus, 1950." *Anti-Locust Bulletin* 10. London, 1951.

———. "The Population Dynamics of the Moroccan Locust (Dociostaurus maroccanus Thunberg) in Cyprus." *Anti-Locust Bulletin* 27. London, 1957.

Dixon, C. W. *Smallpox*. London, 1962.

D'Ohsson, I. Mouradgea. *Tableau général de l'Empire Othoman*. 7. Paris, 1787–1824.

Dols, Michael W., *The Black Death in the Middle East*. Princeton, 1977.

Duckworth, H. T. F. *The Church of Cyprus*. London, 1900.

Düzdağ, M. E. *Şeyhülislam Ebussuud Efendi Fetvaları Işığında 16. Asır Türk Hayatı*. Istanbul, 1972.

Earle, Peter. *Corsairs of Malta and Barbary*. Annapolis, 1970.

Enlart, C. L'Art *Gothique et la Renaissance en Chypre*. Paris, 1899.

Faroqhi, Suraiya. "Rural Society in Anatolia and the Balkans during the Sixteenth Century," II. *Turcica* 11.1979.103–153.

———. "The Tekke of Hacci Bektaş: Social Position and Economic Activities," *IJMES* 7.1976.183–208.

———. "Vakif Administration in 16th Century Konya. The Zaviye of Sadreddin-i Konvei," *JESHO* 17.1974.145–172.

Fattal A. *Le Statut des Non-Musulmans en Pays d'Islam*. Beyrouth, 1958.

Fisher, Sydney Nettleton. *The Foreign Relations of Turkey, 1481–1512*. Urbana, 1948.

Foss, Clive. *Ephesus after Antiquity: A Late Antique, Byzantine and Turkish City*. Cambridge, 1979.

Galanté, Abraham. *Documents officiels Turcs concernant les Juifs de Turquie. Recueil de 114 Lois, Règlements, Firmans, Bérats, Ordres et Décisions de Tribunaux*. Stamboul, 1931.

———. "Don Joseph Nassi. Duc de Naxos d'après de nouveaux documents," Conférence faite à la Société 'Béné-Bérith' le Samedi 15 Fevrier 1913. Constantinople, (undated).

Gerber, Haim. "The Waqf Institution in 17th century Anatolian Bursa," International Seminar on the Muslim Waqf. Jerusalem, 24–28 June 1979.

Goitein, S. D. *A Mediterranean Society: The Jewish Communities of the Arab World as Portrayed in the Documents of the Cairo Geniza*. 5 v. Berkeley, 1967–1988.

Gökbılgın, M. Tayyib. *Rumeli'de Yürükler, Tatarlar ve Evlad-i Fatihan*. Istanbul, 1957.

Gölpınarlı, Abdülbaki. "Mevlevilik," *IA*.

Göyünç, Nejat. "Türk hizmetine giren bazi Kıbrıs müdafileri," Milletlerarasi Birinci Kıbrıs Tetkikleri Kongresi, pp. 105–107.

Groot, A. H. de. "Kubrus," *EI*. 2nd edition.

———. *The Ottoman Empire and the Dutch Republic. A History of the Earliest Diplomatic Relations 1610–1630*. Leiden/Istanbul, 1978.

Grunebaum-Ballin, Paul. *Joseph Naci duc de Naxos*. Etudes Juives no. 13. Paris & La Haye, 1968.

Güçer, Lutfi. "Le commerce intérieur des céréales dans l'Empire Ottoman pendant la seconde moitie du XVIème siècle," *Revue de la Faculté des Sciences Économiques de l'Université d'Istanbul* 11.1949–1950.163–188.

———. *XVI–XVII asırlarda Osmanlı Imparatorluğunda Hububat Meselesi ve Hububattan Alınan Vergiler*. Istanbul, 1964.

———. "XV–XVII asırlarda Osmanlı Imparatorluğunda Tuz İnhisari ve Tuzlarin İşletme Nizamı," *ISIFM* 23.1962–1963.81–143.

Guilmartin John F., Jr., *Gunpowder and Galleys. Changing Technology and Mediterranean Warfare at Sea in the Sixteenth Century*. Oxford, 1974.

Gunnis, Rupert. *Historic Cyprus. A Guide to Its Towns and Villages, Monasteries and Castles*. London, 1973 (1936).

Hackett, J. *A History of the Orthodox Church of Cyprus from the Coming of the Apostles Paul and Barnabas to the Commencement of the British Occupation (A.D. 45–A.D. 1878) together with some account of the Latin and other churches existing in the island*. London, 1901.

Hammer, Joseph von. *Geschichte des Osmanischen Reiches*. 10 v. Pest, 1827–1835.

Hasluck, F. H. *Christianity and Islam under the Sulltans*. 2 v. Oxford, 1929.

Heers, Jacques. *Gênes au XVe siècle. Activité économique et problèmes sociales*. Paris, 1961.

Hess, Andrew C. "The Battle of Lepanto and Its place in Mediterranean History," *Past and Present* 57.1972.53–73.

———. *The Forgotten Frontier. A History of the Sixteenth-Century Ibero-African Frontier*. Chicago, 1978.

———. "The Evolution of the Ottoman Seaborne Empire in the Age of Oceanic Discoveries, 1453–1525," *AHR* 75.1970.1892–1919.

———. "The Moriscos: An Ottoman Fifth Column in Sixteenth-Century Spain," *AHR* 74.1968.1–25.

———. "The Ottoman Conquest of Egypt (1517) and the Beginning of the Sixteenth-Century World War," *IJMES* 4.1973.55–76.

———. "Piri Reis and the Ottoman Response to the Voyages of Discovery," *Terrae Incognitae* 6.1974.19–37.

Heyd, U. V. L. Ménage (ed.) *Studies in Old Ottoman Criminal Law*. Oxford, 1973.

———. "Turkish Documents Concerning the Jews of Safed in the Sixteenth Century," in Moshe Ma'oz (ed.) *Studies on Palestine During the Ottoman Period*. Jerusalem, 1975, pp. 111–118.

Heyd, W. Historie du Commerce du Levant au Moyen Âge. tr. Furcy Raynaud. 2 v. Amsterdam, 1959 (Leipzig, 1885–1886).

Hill, Sir George. *A History of Cyprus*. v. 1: *to conquest of Richard Lion Heart*. v. 2: *Frankish Period, 1192–1432*. v. 3: *Frankish Period, 1432–1571*. v. 4: *The Ottoman Province. The British Colony 1571–1948*. Sir Harry Luke (ed.). Cambridge, 1940–1952.

Hoexter, M. "Waqf al-Haramayn and the Turkish Government in Algiers," International Seminar on Social and Economic Aspects of the Muslim Waqf.

Hughes, Quentin. *Fortress. Architecture and Military History in Malta.* London, 1969.

Hütteroth, Wolf-Dieter & Abdulfattah, Kamal. *Historical Geography of Palestine, Transjordan and Southern Syria in the Late 16th Century.* Erlanger Geographische Arbeiten, no. 5. Erlangen, 1977.

———. *Palastina und Transjordanien in 16. Jahrhundert. Wirtschaftsstrutur landlicher Siedlungen nach osmanischen Steuerregistern.* Beihefte zum Tubinger Atlas des Vorderen Orients. Reihe B., no. 33. Wiesbaden, 1978.

Imber, C. M. "The Persecution of the Ottoman Shi'ites according to the mühimme defterleri, 1565–1585," *Der Islam* 56.1979, p. 250–272.

Inalcik, H. "Capital Formation in the Ottoman Empire," *Journal of Economic History.* 29.1969.97–140.

———. "The Impact of the *Annales* School on Ottoman Studies and New Findings," *Review* 1.1978.69–96.

———. "Introduction to Ottoman Metrology," *Turcica* 15.1983.311–348.

———. "Istanbul," *EI.* 2nd edition.

———. "Kıbrıs fethinin tarihi manası," in Cevat Gürsoy, H. Inalcik, E. Kuran, and H. F. Alasya (eds.) *Kıbrıs ve Türkler.* Ankara, 1964, pp. 21–26.

———. "Kıbrıs'ta Türk Idaresi altında nüfus," in Cevat Gürsoy, H. Inalcik, E. Kuran, and H. F. Alasya (eds.) *Kıbrıs ve Türkler.* Ankara, 1964, pp. 27–58.

———. "Lepanto in the Ottoman Documents," in Gino Benzoni (ed.) *Il Mediterraneo nella seconda metà del '500 alla luce di Lepanto.* Firenze, 1974, pp. 185–192.

———. "The Main Problems Concerning the History of Cyprus," *Cultura Turcica* 1.1964.44–51.

———. "Military and Fiscal Transformation in the Ottoman Empire, 1600–1700," *Archivum Ottomanicum* 6.1980.283–337.

———. "Notes on N. Beldiceanu's Translation of the *Kanunname,* fonds turc ancien 39, Bibliotheque Nationale, Paris," *Der Islam* 43.1967.139–157.

———. "The Ottoman Decline and its Effect upon the *reaya,*" pp. 338–354 in H. Birnbaum & S. Vryonis. *Aspects of the Balkans.* The Hague, 1972.

———. *The Ottoman Empire: The ClassicalAge 1300–1600.* London, 1973.

———. "Ottoman Methods of Conquest," *Studia Islamica* 2.1954.103–129.

———. "Ottoman Policy and Administration in Cyprus after the Conquest," in Proceedings of the First International Congress of Cypriot Studies. Ankara, 1971, pp. 59–77.

———. "The Policy of Mehmed II toward the Greek Population of Istanbul and the Byzantine Buildings of the City," *Dumbarton Oaks Papers* 23–24. 1969–1970.229–249.

———. Review of Uriel Heyd in V. L. Ménage (ed.) Studies in Old Ottoman Criminal Law. *BSOAS* 37.1974.696–698.

———. "Rice Cultivation and the Çeltik-Re'aya System in the Ottoman Empire," *Turcica* 14.1982.69–141.

Inalcik, H. "Servile Labor in the Ottoman Empire," in Abraham Ascher, Tibor Halasi-Kun, Bela Kiraly (eds.) *The Mutual Effects of the Islamic and Judeo-Christian Worlds: the Eastern European Patterns.* New York 1979, pp. 25–52.

International Seminar on the Social and Economic Aspects of the Muslim Waqf. Jerusalem, 24–28 June 1979.

Ismail, Adel. *Histoire du Liban du XVIIe siècle à nos jours.* v. 1: *Le Liban au temps de Fakhr-ed-din II (1590–1633).* Paris, 1955.

Janin, R. "Chypre," *Dictionnaire d'Histoire et de Géographie Ecclésiastiques.* Paris, 1912-.

Jeffery, George. *A Description of the Historic Monuments of Cyprus.* Nicosia, 1918.

Jenkins, R. J. H. "Cyprus between Byzantium and Islam, A.D. 688–965," in G. E. Mylonas & D. Raymond (eds.) Studies Presented to David Moore Robinson. St.Louis, 1953, vol. 2, pp. 1006–1014.

––––––. "Social Life in the Byzantine Empire," *Cambridge Medieval History.* Cambridge, 1967, v. 4, pt. 2, pp. 79–104.

Jenness, Diamond. *The Economics of Cyprus. A Survey to 1914.* Montreal, 1962.

Jennings, R. "Black Slaves and Free Blacks in Ottoman Cyprus, 1590–1640," *JESHO* 30.1988.286–302.

––––––. "The Development of *Evkaf* (Pious Foundations) in a New Ottoman Province: Cyprus, 1571–1640," International Seminar on the Muslim Waqf. Jerusalem, 24–28 June 1979.

––––––. "The Legal Position of Women in Kayseri, a Large Ottoman City, 1590–1630," *IJWS* 3.1980.559–582.

––––––. "The Locust Problem in Cyprus," *Bulletin of the School of Oriental and African Studies* 51.1988.279–313.

––––––. "Loans and Credit in Early 17th Century Ottoman Judicial Records — The Sharia Court of Anatolian Kayseri," *JESHO* 16.1973.168–216.

––––––. "Pilgrims View the Women of the Island of Venus," *Balkan Studies* 30.1989.213–220.

––––––. "The Population, Taxation, and Wealth in the Cities and Villages of Cyprus, According to the Detailed Population Survey (Defter-i Mufassal of 1572," Raiyyet Rusumu, Essays Presented to Halil Inalcik on his Seventieth Birthday. *Journal of Turkish Studies* 10.1986.175–189.

––––––. "Women in Early 17th Century Ottoman Judicial Records — The Sharia Court of Anatolian Kayseri," *JESHO* 18.1975.53–114.

––––––. "Urban Population in Anatolia in the Sixteenth Century: A Study of Kayseri, Karaman, Amasya, Trabzon, and Erzurum," *IJMES* 7.1976.21–57.

––––––. "Zimmis (Non-Muslims) in Early 17th Century Ottoman Judicial Records — the Sharia Court of Anatolian Kayseri," *JESHO* 21.1978.225–293.

Julien, Charles-André. *History of North Africa. Tunisia, Algeria, Morocco.* tr. J. Petrie, C. C. Stewart (ed.). London, 1970.

Kahane, Henry and Renée and Tietze, Andreas. *The Lingua Franca in the Levant. Turkish Nautical Terms of Italian and Greek Origin.* Urbana, 1958.

Khachikian, Lvon. "Le registre d'un marchand Arménien en Perse, en Inde et au Tibet (1682–1693)," *Annales. Economies, Societies, et Civilisations.* 22.2.1967.231–278.

Konyalı, I. H. *Abideleri ve Kitabeleri ile Karaman Tarihi.* Istanbul, 1967.

———. *Abideleri ve Kitabeleri ile Konya Tarihi.* Konya, 1964.

Köprülü, Fuad. "Vakıf müessessesinin hukuki mahiyeti ve tarih tekamülü, *VD* 1.1938.1–6.

Kramers, J. H. "Mustafa Pasha Lala," *EI.* 1st edition.

Kunt, I. M. "Kulların Kulları," Boğaziçi Üniversitesi Dergisi 3.1975.27–42.

Kunter, Halim Baki. "Türk Vakıflari ve Vakfiyeleri üzerine mücmel bir etüd," *VD* 1.1938.103–129.

Kütükoğlu, Bekir. "Mustafa Paşa," *IA.*

———. *Osmanli-Iran Siyasi Münasebetleri.* v. I: 1578–1590. Istanbul, 1962.

Kypriologikon, Diethnes. *Synedrion.* Nicosia, 1969. (Lefkosia, 1973.)

Kyrris, Costa P. "The Cypriote Family of Soderini and Other Cypriotes in Venice (XVI–XVII Centuries)," *Neo-Hellenika* 1.1970.50–77.

———. "Cypriote Scholars in Venice in the 16th and 17th Centuries," in J. Irmscher & M. Mineemi (eds.) *Über Beziehungen des Griechentums zum Ausland in der Neueren Zeit.* Berlin, 1968, pp. 183–272.

———. "L'Importance sociale de la conversion à l'Islam (volontaire ou non) d'une section des classes dirigeantes de Chypre pendant les premiers siècles de l'occupation turque (1570–fin du XVIIe siècle)," in *Actes du premier congrès international des études balkaniques et sud-est européennes.* v. 3: *Histoire.* Sofia, 26 Août–1 Septembre 1966. Sofia, 1969, pp. 437–462.

———. "The Jewish Community and the Rise and Fall of Some Urban Agglomerations in Cyprus under Ottoman Rule," *Kypriakai Spoudai.* (Hetaireia Kypriakon Spoudon) Nicosia. 30.1966.175–181.

———. "The Role of the Greeks in the Ottoman Administration of Cyprus," 155–179.

———. "Symbiotic Elements in the History of the Two Communities of Cyprus," *Kypriakos Logos* 8.1976.243–282.

Laiou-Thomadakis, Angeliki E. *Peasant Society in the Late Byzantine Empire. A Social and Demographic Study.* Princeton, 1977.

———. "Observations on the Life and Ideology of Byzantine Women," *Byzantinische Forschungen* 9.1985.59–102. Internationale Zeitschrift für Byzantinistik.

Lamansky, Vladimir. *Secrets d'état de Venise. Documents, extraits, notices et études servant à eclaircir les rapports de la Seigneurie avec les Grecs, les Slaves et la Porte Ottomane à la fin du XVe et au XVIe siècles.* 2 v. New York, 1968 (Saint-Petersbourg, 1884).

Lane, Frederic C. "The Mediterranean Spice Trade: its Revival in the Sixteenth Century," in B. Pullan (ed.) *Venice and History. The Collected Papers of*

Frederic C. Lane. Baltimore, 1966, pp. 47–58. From *AHR* 45.1940.581–590.

———. "Venetian Shipping during the Commercial Revolution," in *Venice and History. The Collected Papers of Frederic C. Lane.* Baltimore, 1966, pp. 3–24. From *AHR* 38.1933.219–239.

Lesure, Michael. "Notes et documents sur les relations veneto-ottomanes, 1570–1573" I, *Turcica* 4.1972.134–164; II, *Turcica* 8.1.1976.117–156.

Lewis, Bernard. "A Karaite Itinerary through Turkey in 1641–2," *VD* 3.1956.315–325.

———. *Notes and Documents from the Turkish Archives. A Contribution to the History of the Jews in the Ottoman Empire.* Jerusalem, 1952.

Lewis, Norman N. "Malaria, Irrigation, and Soil Erosion in Central Syria," *Geographical Review* 39.1949.278–290.

Linant de Bellefonds, Yvon. *Traité de droit musulman comparé.* 3 v. Paris, 1965–1973.

Lowry, Heath W. *Trabzon şehrinin Islamlaşma ve Türkleşmesi, 1461–1583.* Istanbul, 1981.

———. The Ottoman *Tahrir Defters* as a Source for Demographic History: the Case Study of Trabzon (c. 1486–1583). U.C.L.A. Ph.D. dissertation. 1977.

Luke, Sir Harry. *Cyprus under the Turks, 1571–1878. A record based on the Archives of the English Consulate in Cyprus under the Levant Company and after.* London, 1921.

———. "The Kingdom of Cyprus, 1291–1369," & "The Kingdom of Cyprus, 1369–1489," in K. M. Setton. A History of the Crusades, v. III, Harry W. Hazard (ed.) *The Fourteenth and Fifteenth Centuries.* Madison, 1975, pp. 340–360 & 361–395.

Mandaville, Jon E. "Usurious Piety: The Cash Waqf Controversy in the Ottoman Empire," *IJMES* 10.1979.289–308.

Mantran, Robert. "L''Echo de la Bataille de Lépante à Constantinople," in Gino Benzoni (ed.) *Il Mediterraneo nella seconda metà del '500 alla luce di Lepanto.* Firenze, 1974, pp. 243–256.

Marcus, Abraham. "Piety and Profit: The Waqf in the Society and Economy of 18th Century Aleppo," International Seminar on the Muslim Waqf. Jerusalem, 24–28 June 1979.

Mas Latrie, M. L. de. *Histoire de l'Île de Chypre sous le règne des princes de la Maison de Lusignan.* v. 2. Paris, *1852 (1970).* v. 3. *1855 (1970).*

Masson, Paul. *Histoire du Commerce Français dans le Levant au XVIIe siècle.* Paris, 1896.

Mazzaoui, Maureen Fennell. *The Italian Cotton Industry in the Later Middle Ages 1100–1600.* Cambridge, 1981.

McGowan, Bruce. *Economic Life in Ottoman Empire. Taxation, trade and the struggle for land, 1600–1800.* Cambridge, 1981.

McNeill, William H. *Plagues and Peoples.* Oxford, 1977.

———. *Venice. The Hinge of Europe 1081–1798.* Chicago, 1974.

Megaw, A. H. S. "Military Architecture," in *A History of the Crusades,* K. M.

Setton (ed.) v. IV: *The Arts and Architecture of the Crusader States*, Madison, 1977, pp. 196–207.

Merton, L. F. H. "Studies in the Ecology of the Moroccan Locust (Dociostaurus maroccanus Thunberg) in Cyprus," *Anti-Locust Bulletin* 34. London, 1959.

Miller, William. *The Latins in the Levant. A History of Frankish Greece (1204–1566)*. London, 1908.

Mitchell, William A. "The Lice Earthquake," *Disasters, the International Journal of Disasater Studies and Practices* 2.1978.265.

Musset, P. Henri. *Histoire du Christianisme specialement en Orient*. v. II. Jerusalem, 1948.

Mutafčieva, V. "Problèmes fondamentaux de l'étude du Vakf en tant que partie de la structure sociale et économique des Balkans sous la domination Ottoman (XVe–XIXe siecles)," International Seminar on the Muslim Waqf. Jerusalem, 24–28 June 1979.

Oberhummer, Eugen. *Die Insel Cypern eine Landeskunde auf historischer Grundlage*. München, 1903.

O'Fahey, R. "Endowment, Privilege and Estate in the Central and Eastern Sudan," International Seminar on the Muslim Waqf. Jerusalem, 24–28 June 1979.

Ohl, Ingo. *Die Levante und Indien in der Verkehrspolitik Venedigs der Englander und der Hollander 1580–1623*. Kiel, 1972.

Ohnefalsch-Richter, Magda H. *Griechische Sitten und Gebrauche auf Cypern*. Berlin, 1913.

Ongan, Halit. "Ankara Şer'iye Mahkemesi Sicillerinde Kayıtlı Vafiyeler," *VD* 5.1962.213–222.

Orhonlu, Cengiz. "The Ottoman Turks Settle in Cyprus (1570–1580)," in the *Proceedings of the first International Congress of Cypriot Studies*. Ankara, 1971, pp. 91–103.

———. *Telhisler (1597–1607)*. Istanbul, 1970.

———. *Osmanlı Imparatorluğunun Güney Siyaseti. Habeş Eyaleti*. Istanbul, 1974.

Öney, Gönül. "Büyük Han (The Great Inn) and Kumarcilar Hani (The Gambler's Inn) at Nicosia," First International Congress of Cypriot Studies. Ankara, 1971, pp. 277–282.

Papadopoullos, Theodore H. *The History of the Greek Church and People under Turkish Domination*. Brussels, 1952.

———. *Social and Historical Data on Population (1570–1881)*. Nicosia, 1965.

Pastor, Ludwig von. *The History of the Popes*. tr. R. F. Kerr, v. 18–24. tr. E. Graf, v. 25–29. London, 1929–1938.

Pullan, Brian (ed.) *Crisis and Change in the Venetian Economy in the Sixteenth and Seventeenth Centuries*. London, 1968.

Rapp, Richard T. *Industry and Economic Decline in Seventeenth-Century Venice*. Cambridge, 1976.

Raymond, André. *Artisans et Commerçants au Caire au XVIIIe Siècle*. 2 v. Damas, 1973, 1974.

Refik, Ahmed. *Anadolu'da Türk Aşiretleri (996–1200)*. Istanbul, 1930.

Richard, Jean. "Une économie coloniale? Chypre et ses resources agricoles au Moyen-Âge," *Byzantinische Forschungen, Internationale Zeitschrift fur Byzantinistik* 5.1977.331–352.

Riley-Smith, Jonathan. *The Knights of St. John in Jerusalem and Cyprus c. 1050–1310*. London, 1967.

Roded, Ruth. "The Waqf in Ottoman Aleppo," International Seminar on the Muslim Waqf. Jerusalem, 24–28 June 1979.

Rostovtzeff, Mikhail. *The Social & Economic History of the Hellenistic World*. 3 v. Oxford, 1953 (1941).

Roth, Cecil. *The House of Nasi. The Duke of Naxos*. Philadelphia, 1948.

Sahillioğlu, Halil. "Osmanlı Idaresinde Kıbrıs'ın Ilk Yili Bütçesi," *Belgeler* 4.1967.1–33.

Salibi, Kamal. "Fakhr al-din," *EI*. 2nd edition.

Salvator, Archduke Louis. *Levkosia die hauptstadt von Cypern*. Prag, 1873.

Sanjian, Avedis K. *The Armenian Communities in Syria under Ottoman Dominion*. Cambridge, 1965.

Schacht, Joseph. *An Introduction to Islamic Law*. Oxford, 1964.

Shaw, Stanford J. *The Budget of Ottoman Egypt, 1005–1006/1596–1597*. Mouton, 1968.

———.*The Financial and Administrative Organization and Development of Ottoman Egypt 1517–1798*. Princeton, 1962.

———. *History of the Ottoman Empire and Modern Turkey*. v. 1. Empire of the Gazis. Cambridge, 1976.

Steensgaard, Niels. *Carracks, Caravans and Companies: The Structural Crisis in the European-Asian Trade in the Early 17th Century*. Kobenhavn, 1973.

———. "Consuls and Nations in the Levant from 1570 to 1650," *Scandinavian Economic History Review* 15.1967.13–55.

Stern, S. M. *Documents from Islamic Chanceries*. Cambridge, 1965.

Stripling, G. W. F. *The Ottoman Turks and the Arabs 1511–1574*. Urbana, 1942.

Stylianou, Andreas & Judith A. *The History of the Cartography of Cyprus*. Cyprus Research Center VIII. Nicosia, 1980.

Sümer, Faruk. *Oğuzlar (Türkmenler)*. Ankara, 1967.

Tenenti, Alberto. *Piracy and the Decline of Venice, 1580–1615*. tr. from *Venezia e i corsari, 1580–1615* (Bari, 1961) by Janet and Brian Pullan. Berkeley & Los Angeles, 1967.

Thiriet, Freddy. *La Romanie Vénitienne au Moyen Âge. Le développement et l'exploitation du domaine colonial vénitien (XIIe–XVe siècles)*. Paris, 1959.

Tietze, A. "The Poet as Critique of Society. A 16th century Ottoman Poem," *Turcica* 9.1977.120–160.

Uvarov, B. P. "The Cyprus Locust Research Scheme," in Observations on the Moroccan Locust in Cyprus, 1950." *Anti-Locust Bulletin* 18. London, 1951.

Uzunçarşılı, I. H. "Kıbrıs Fethi ile Lepant (Inebahti) Muharebesi sırasında Türk

Devletile Venedik ve Müttefiklerinin Faaliyetine Dair bazı hazinei evrak kayıtları," *Türkiyat Mecmuasi* 3.1935.257–292.

———. *Osmanlı Devletinin Merkez ve Bahriye Teşkilati.* Ankara, 1948.

Vacalopoulos, Apostolos E. *The Greek Nation, 1453–1669. The Cultural and
Economic Background of Modern Greek Society.* New Brunswick, 1976.

Vryonis, Speros, Jr. "The Byzantine Legacy and Ottoman Forms," *Dumbarton
Oaks Papers* 23/24.1969–1970.251–308.

———. *Decline of Medieval Hellenism in Asia Minor and the Process of Islamization from the Eleventh through the Fifteenth Century.* Berkeley & Los
Angeles, 1971.

———. "Nomadization and Islamization in Asia Minor," *Dumbarton Oaks
Papers* 29.1975.41–71.

Wake, C. H. H. "The Changing Patterns of Europe's Pepper and Spice Imports,
ca. 1500–1700," *The Journal of European Economic History* 8.1979.361–
403.

Waloff, Z. "The Upsurges and Recessions of the Desert Locust Plague: An
Historical Survey." *Anti-Locust Memoir* 8. London, 1966.

Ware, Timothy. Eustratios Argenti. *A Study of the Greek Church Under Turkish
Rule.* Oxford, 1964.

Willis, Michael D. "A New Document of Cypriote History: The Journal of
Ambrosio Bembo," *Anatyposis ek ton Kiriakon Spoudon* 1978.35–46.

Wolf, John B. *The Barbary Coast. Algiers Under the Turks 1580–1830.* New
York, 1979.

Yazici, T., Margoliouth, D. S. & Jong, F. de. "Mawlawiyya," *EI.* 2nd edition.

Yediyildiz, B. "La Portée Economique des Vaqfs Turcs au XVIIe siècles," International Seminar on Social and Economic Aspects of the Muslim Waqf.

Zulueta, J. de. "Malaria and Mediterranean History," *Parassitologia* 15.1973.1–
15.

Index of Original Sources

419

General Index

About the Author

Ronald C. Jennings is Professor of History at the University of Illinois, Urbana. He taught for two years at the Maarif Kolej in Samsun, Turkey, where he developed his interests in Cyprus and Turkey.